THE EARTH AND ITS PEOPLES

A GLOBAL HISTORY

SECOND EDITION

VOLUME II

Since 1500

Richard W. Bulliet
Columbia University

Pamela Kyle Crossley
Dartmouth College

Daniel R. Headrick
Roosevelt University

Steven W. Hirsch
Tufts University

Lyman L. Johnson
University of North Carolina–Charlotte

David Northrup
Boston College

Houghton Mifflin Company   Boston   New York

Editor-in-chief for history and political science: Jean L. Woy
Sponsoring editor: Nancy Blaine
Senior development editor: Jennifer E. Sutherland
Associate editor: Julie Dunn
Editorial associate: Gillie Jones
Senior project editor: Carol Newman
Senior designer: Henry Rachlin
Senior production/design coordinator: Jill Haber
Senior manufacturing coordinator: Marie Barnes
Senior marketing manager: Sandra McGuire

Cover design: Anthony L. Saizon
Cover image: *The Workplace.* 19th century Japanese print. David David Gallery/Superstock.

Part opener credits
Pt. 4, p. 321: Bibiliothèque nationale de France; Pt. 5, p. 441 Library of Congress; Pt. 6, p. 569: © Hulton-Deutsch/Corbis; Pt. 7, p. 697: © Corbis; Pt. 8, p. 827: © Corbis.

Chapter opener credits
Ch. 17, p. 417: G. Dagli Orti; Ch. 18, p. 444: The Metropolitan Museum of Art, Rogers Fund, 1919. (19.164). Photograph © 1998 The Metropolitan Museum of Art; Ch. 19, p. 471: Archivo General de la Nacion, Buenos Aires; Ch. 20, p. 496: From William Clark, *Ten Views in the Islands of Antigua*, 1823. British Library; Ch. 21, p. 521 : University Library, Istanbul/The Art Archive Limited; Ch. 22, p. 545: Novosti; Ch. 23, p. 572: Bibliothèque nationale de France/The Bridgeman Art Library, London and New York; Ch. 24, p. 598: Elton Collection, Ironbridge Gorge Museum Trust; Ch. 25, p. 620 : *Estracion de Orizaba, 1877.* From Casimiro Castro, *Album del Ferro-Carril Mexicano: Coleccion de Vista Pintadas* (Victor Debray and Company, 1877); Ch. 26, p. 647: Eyre and Hobbs House Art Gallery; Ch. 27, p. 673: Courtesy, Rizzoli; Ch. 28, p. 700: The Metropolitan Museum of Art, gift of Lincoln Kirstein, 1959 (JP 3346). Photograph by Otto E. Nelson. Photograph © 1986 The Metropolitan Museum of Art; Ch. 29, p. 725: Bildarchiv Preussischer Kulturbesitz ; Ch. 30, p. 751: Paul Nash (1889-1946) *The Menin Road,1919.* Imperial War Museum/The Art Archive Limited; Ch. 31, p. 779: AKG London; Ch. 32, p. 805: Popperfoto/Archive Photos; Ch. 33, p. 830: David King Collection; Ch. 34, p. 854: Paul Chesley/Tony Stone Images; Ch. 35, p. 881: Liaison.

Printed in the U.S.A.

Library of Congress Catalog Card Number: 00-132429

ISBN: 0-618-00078-X

1 2 3 4 5 6 7 8 9-VH-04 03 02 01 00

Brief Contents

CONTENTS

PART SIX

REVOLUTIONS RESHAPE THE WORLD,
1750–1870
569

PART SEVEN

GLOBAL DOMINANCE AND DIVERSITY,
1850–1945
697

PART EIGHT

THE PERILS AND PROMISES OF A GLOBAL COMMUNITY, 1945–2000

827

MAPS

Environment and Technology

Society and Culture

PREFACE

History is not easy. We met ten years ago in a conference room at Houghton Mifflin: six professional historians seated around a table hammering out our ideas on what a global history textbook at the start of a new millennium should be. Together we brought to the project a high level of knowledge about Africa, the Americas, Asia, Europe, the Middle East. We argued; we made up over dinner; we debated some more.

But there was no short cut. We were determined to write the best history we could. That meant testing ideas aloud; considering alternatives put forward by smart, articulate colleagues; and bargaining over what to include and what, with regret, to pass over. We believe the result was worth the sweat.

So began the Preface to the first edition of this book. Then came the wait for responses and a fresh wave of satisfaction as teachers and students from a wide variety of institutions reported positive results from the classroom. Unalloyed praise, however, was too much to hope for from a first edition. Users of the book spotted many possibilities for improvement, and these became our mandate for preparing the second edition.

Our overall goal remains the same: to produce a textbook that not only speaks for the past but speaks to today's student and today's teacher. Students and instructors alike should take away from this text a broad vision of human societies beginning as sparse and disconnected communities reacting creatively to local circumstances; experiencing ever more intensive stages of contact, interpenetration, and cultural expansion and amalgamation; and arriving at a twenty-first century world in which people increasingly visualize a single global community.

Along this trajectory, different parts of the world have moved or paused at different points in time, and each has followed its own path. Domestication of plants and animals in the Western Hemisphere developed independently of the analogous process in the Eastern Hemisphere, as did the growth of empires. Similarly, industrialization of western Europe and North America preceded by a century or two industrialization elsewhere. Yet the world all came together in the late twentieth century, a paradoxical period of global political and economic forces confronting intensified reassertions of particular national and cultural identities. People who speak today of an emerging global community are answered by others who insist on their own distinctive identities.

Process, not progress, is the keynote of this book: a steady process of change over time, at first differently experienced in various regions but eventually entangling peoples from all parts of the globe. Students should come away from this book with a sense that the problems and promises of their world are rooted in a past in which peoples of every sort, in every part of the world, confronted problems of a similar character and coped with them as best they could. We believe our efforts will help students see where their world has come from and learn thereby something useful for their own lives.

CENTRAL THEME

We subtitled *The Earth and Its Peoples* "A Global History" because the book explores the common challenges and experiences that unite the human past. Although the dispersal of early humans to every livable environment resulted in myriad different economic, social, political, and cultural systems, all societies displayed analogous patterns in meeting their needs and exploiting their environments. Our challenge was to select the particular data and episodes that would best illuminate these global patterns of human experience.

To meet this challenge, we adopted a central theme to serve as the spinal cord of our history. That theme is "technology and environment," the commonplace bases of all human societies at all times and a theme that grants no special favor to any cultural group even as it embraces subjects of the broadest topical, chronological, and geographical range.

It is vital for students to understand that technology, in the broad sense of experience-based knowledge of the physical world, underlies all human activity. Writing is a technology, but so is oral transmission from generation to generation of lore about medicinal or poisonous plants. The magnetic compass is a navigational technology, but so is Polynesian mariners' hard-won knowledge of winds, currents, and tides that made possible the settlement of the Pacific islands.

All technological development has come about in

interaction with environments, both physical and human, and has, in turn, affected those environments. The story of how humanity has changed the face of the globe is an integral part of our central theme.

Yet technology and the environment do not by themselves explain or underlie all important episodes of human change and experience. Discussions of politics, culture, and society constantly interweave with our central theme to reveal additional historical patterns. Most notable among these is the interplay of dominance—whether political, economic, social, religious, or gender—with human variety. When narrating the histories of empires, for example, we describe a range of human experiences within and beyond the imperial frontiers without assuming that the imperial institutions are a more fit topic for discussion than the economic and social organization of pastoral nomads or the life patterns of peasant women.

CHANGES IN THE SECOND EDITION

Our overriding concerns in conceiving the second edition were updating the scholarship, better unifying the presentation, and addressing issues raised by instructors and students who had used the first edition. The most obvious change is the adoption of a full-color format, which not only brightens the page but makes maps clearer and more effective. The opening pages of each part of the text were similarly reconceived to give students a geographic and chronological overview of what is to come. The timelines and world maps that now accompany the part-opening essays are designed to focus student's attention on broad themes and historical benchmarks. Consolidated timelines within each chapter enable students to see at a glance the sorts of comparisons being made in the text.

Guides to the pronunciation of uncommon words and foreign terms, previously at the back of the book, now appear at the bottom of each page. Key terms are boldfaced in the text, listed at the end of each chapter, and defined in the Glossary at the end of the book. In addition, focus questions at the end of the vignette opening each chapter call attention to the main themes of the chapter. We believe that these unobtrusive changes will improve students' understanding of the main narrative and make it easier for them to grasp the main points of each chapter, as well as to review for examinations.

We sifted through a mass of helpful suggestions on how to revise and reorganize the content itself. Along with hundreds of minor revisions and clarifications, we effected a number of major changes:

- To facilitate comparison among different regions of the globe, we moved discussion of the earliest periods of Western Hemisphere history from Chapter 12 to Chapter 4.
- We greatly increased the coverage of Russian history, including entirely new sections in Chapter 10 (Chapter 9 of the first edition) and Chapter 22.
- Intellectual history gained increased attention with expanded coverage of Confucianism and Legalism in China; scholasticism, the Renaissance, and the Enlightenment in Europe; and twentieth-century modernism.
- Chapters 9 and 10 in the first edition were reversed, so the discussion of the rise of Islam now precedes that of Christian Europe.
- Coverage of the Industrial Revolution was revised to take in a broader geographical purview.
- The organization of twentieth-century history (Chapters 30–35) was completely reconceived to strengthen the chronological narrative.
- Suggested Reading lists were updated with recent scholarship.

The full-color format favored substantial changes in the illustration program, and many of the feature essays also were changed. Topics for the eleven new "Environment and Technology" essays include water engineering in Rome and China, Inca roads, Vasco da Gama's fleet, biomedical technologies, and global warming. The primary-source document feature of the first edition has been renamed "Society and Culture" to emphasize its complementarity with "Environment and Technology." Topics for the thirteen essays new to this edition include the Babylonian New Year's festival, the status of women in Indian literature, everyday law in Ming China, Charles Babbage, Ada Lovelace, and the "Analytical Engine," self-government in Africa, and "Silent Spring."

ORGANIZATION

The *Earth and Its Peoples* uses eight broad chronological divisions to define its conceptual scheme of global historical development. In **Part One: The Emergence of Human Communities, to 500 B.C.E.,** we examine important patterns of human communal organization. Early human communities were small, and most parts of the world were populated sparsely, if at all. As the human species spread worldwide, it encountered and responded to enormously diverse environmental conditions. Humans' responses gave rise to many technologies, ranging from implements for meeting daily needs—such as acquiring and handling foods, fabricating clothing and shelter, and utilizing the natural forces of fire, wind, and animal power—to the compilation of exhaustive lore about plants, animals, the climate, and the heavens.

Part Two: The Formation of New Cultural Communities, 1000 B.C.E.–400 C.E., introduces the concept of a "cultural community," in the sense of a coherent pattern of activities and symbols pertaining to a specific human community. Although all human communities develop distinctive cultures, including those discussed in Part One, historical development in this stage of global history prolonged and magnified the impact of some cultures more than others. In the geographically contiguous African-Eurasian landmass, as well as in Mesoamerica and the Andean region of the Western Hemisphere, the cultures that proved to have the most enduring influence traced their roots to the second and first millennia B.C.E.

Part Three: Growth and Interaction of Cultural Communities, 300 B.C.E.–1200 C.E., deals with early episodes of technological, social, and cultural exchange and interaction on a continental scale both within and beyond the framework of imperial expansion. These are so different from earlier interactions arising from more limited conquests or extensions of political boundaries that they constitute a distinct era in world history—an era that set the world on the path of increasing global interaction and interdependence that it has been following ever since.

In **Part Four: Interregional Patterns of Culture and Contact, 1200–1550,** we take a look at the world during the three and a half centuries that saw both intensified cultural and commercial contact and increasingly confident self-definition of cultural communities in Europe, Asia, and Africa. The Mongol conquest of a vast empire extending from the Pacific Ocean to eastern Europe greatly stimulated trade and interaction. In the West, strengthened European kingdoms began maritime expansion in the Atlantic, forging direct ties with sub-Saharan Africa and beginning the conquest of the civilizations of the Western Hemisphere.

Part Five: The Globe Encompassed, 1500–1750, treats a period dominated by the global effects of European expansion and continued economic growth. European ships took over, expanded, and extended the maritime trade of the Indian Ocean, coastal Africa, and the Asian rim of the Pacific Ocean. This maritime commercial enterprise had its counterpart in European colonial empires in the Americas and a new Atlantic trading system. The contrasting capacities and fortunes of traditional land empires and new maritime empires, along with the exchange of domestic plants and animals between the hemispheres, underline the technological and environmental dimensions of this first era of complete global interaction.

In **Part Six: Revolutions Reshape the World, 1750–1870,** the word *revolution* is used in several senses: in the political sense of governmental overthrow, as in France and the Americas; in the metaphorical sense of radical transformative change, as in the Industrial Revolution; and in the broadest sense of a perception of a profound change in circumstances and world-view. Technology and environment lie at the core of these developments. With the rapid ascendancy of the Western belief that science and technology could overcome all challenges—environmental or otherwise—technology became not only an instrument of transformation but also an instrument of domination, to the point of threatening the integrity and autonomy of cultural traditions in non-industrial lands.

Part Seven: Global Dominance and Diversity, 1850–1945, examines the development of a world arena in which people conceived of events on a global scale. Imperialism, world war, international economic connections, and world-encompassing ideological tendencies, such as nationalism and socialism, present the picture of a globe becoming increasingly interconnected. European dominance took on a worldwide dimension, seeming at times to threaten the diversity of human cultural experience with permanent subordination to European values and philosophies, while at other times triggering strong political or cultural resistance.

For **Part Eight: The Perils and Promises of a Global Community, 1945–2000,** we divide the last half of the twentieth century into three time periods: 1945–1975, 1975–1991, and 1991–2000. The challenges of the Cold War and post-colonial nation building dominated the period as a whole and involved global economic, technological, and political forces that became increasingly important factors in all aspects of human life. Technology plays a central role in this part, because of its integral role in the growth of a global community and because its many benefits in improving the quality of life seem clouded by real and potential negative impacts on the environment.

FORMATS

To accommodate different academic calendars and approaches to the course, *The Earth and Its Peoples* is issued in three formats. There is a one-volume hardcover version containing all 35 chapters, along with a two-volume paperback edition: Volume I: *To 1550* (Chapters 1–17), and Volume II: *Since 1500* (Chapters 17–35). For readers at institutions with the quarter system, we offer a three-volume paperback version: Volume A: *To 1200* (Chapters 1–12); Volume B: *From 1200 to 1870* (Chapters 12–27); and Volume C: *Since 1750* (Chapters 23–35).

A new introduction to Volume II has been written for this edition to recapitulate themes contained in Volume I and lay a groundwork for students studying only the period since 1500.

SUPPLEMENTS

We have assembled with care an array of text supplements to aid students in learning and instructors in teaching. These supplements, including *@history* web site, *GeoQuest: World CD-ROM*, a *Study Guide*, an *Instructor's Resource Manual, Test Items, Computerized Test Items,* and *Map Transparencies,* provide a tightly integrated program of teaching and learning.

Houghton Mifflin's *@history* web site provides a wealth of text-based materials for students and instructors. For students, this site offers primary sources, text-specific self-tests, and gateways to relevant history sites. In addition, *History WIRED: Web Intensive Research Exercises and Documents,* prepared by Jonathan Lee of San Antonio College, offers text-specific links to visual and written sources on the World Wide Web, along with exercises to enhance learning. Additional resources are provided for instructors, including historical maps suitable for classroom presentation or assignments.

A New CD-ROM, *GeoQuest: World,* features thirty interactive maps that illuminate world history events from the days of the Persian Empire to the present. Each map is accompanied by exercises with answers and essay questions. The four different types of interactivity allow students to move at their own pace through each section. Four demo maps can be viewed on the Houghton Mifflin *@history* web site.

The *Study Guide,* authored by Michele G. Scott James of MiraCosta College, contains learning objectives, chapter outlines (with space for students' notes on particular sections), key-term identifications, multiple-choice questions, short-answer and essay questions, and map exercises. Included too are distinctive "comparison charts" to help students organize the range of information about different cultures and events discussed in each chapter. The *Study Guide* is published in two volumes, to correspond to Volumes I and II of the textbook: Volume I contains Chapters 1–17; Volume II, Chapters 17–35.

The *Instructor's Resource Manual,* prepared by Harold M. Tanner of the University of North Texas, provides useful teaching strategies for the global history course and tips for getting the most out of the textbook. Each chapter contains instructional objectives, a detailed chapter outline, lecture topics with pertinent suggested readings, discussion questions, paper topic suggestions, and audio-visual resources. The revised preface contains new information on journal writing, as well as contact information for organizations, multimedia distributors, and journals.

Each chapter of the *Test Items,* revised by Jane Scimeca of Brookdale Community College, offers 20 to 25 key-term identifications, 5 to 10 essay questions with answer guidelines, 35 to 40 multiple-choice questions, and 3 to 5 history and geography exercises. We also provide a computerized version of the *Test Items,* to enable instructors to alter, replace, or add questions. Each entry in the *Computerized Test Items* is numbered according to the printed test items to ease the creation of customized tests.

In addition, a set of *Transparencies* of all the maps in the textbook is available on adoption.

ACKNOWLEDGMENTS

In preparing the second edition, we benefited from the critical readings of many colleagues. Our sincere thanks go in particular to the following instructors: Henry Abramson, Florida Atlantic University; Paul V. Adams, Shippensburg University/University of San Carlos; Maria S. Arbelaez, University of Nebraska at Omaha; William J. Astore, United States Air Force Academy; Fritz Blackwell, Washington State University; Thomas Borstelmann, Cornell University; Byron Cannon, University of Utah; David A. Chappell, University of Hawaii; Nancy Clark, California Polytechnic State University at San Luis Obispo; Lee Congdon, James Madison University; James Coolsen, Shippensburg University; Bruce Cruikshank, Hastings College; Linda T. Darling, University of Arizona; Susan Deans-Smith, University of Texas at Austin; Gregory C. Ference, Salisbury State University; Alan Fisher, Michigan State University; Donald M. Fisher, Niagara County Community College; Cathy A. Frierson, University of New Hampshire; Rosanna Gatens, Belmont University; Lorne E. Glaim, Pacific Union College; Matthew S. Gordon, Miami University; Steve Gosch, University of Wisconsin at Eau Claire; Kolleen M. Guy, University of Texas at San Antonio; James R. Hansen, Auburn University; Randolph C. Head, University of California at Riverside; David Hertzel, Southwestern Oklahoma State University; Richard J. Hoffman, San Francisco State University; Catherine M. Jones, North Georgia College and State University; Joy Kammerling, Eastern Illinois University; Carol A. Keller, San Antonio College; Jonathan Lee, San Antonio College; Miriam R. Levin, Case Western Reserve University; Richard Lewis, St. Cloud State University; James E. Lindsay, Colorado State University; Charles W. McClellan, Radford University; Andrea McElderry, University of Louisville; Stephen L. McFarland, Auburn University; Gregory McMahon, University of New Hampshire; Mark McLeod, University of Delaware; Stephen S. Michot, Mississippi County Community College; Shawn W. Miller, Brigham Young University; Kalala Joseph Ngalamulume, Central Washington University; Patricia O'Neill, Central Oregon Community College; Chandrika Paul, Shippensburg University; John R. Pavia, Ithaca College; Thomas Earl Porter, North Carolina A&T State University; Jean H. Quataert, SUNY at Binghamton; William Reddy, Duke University; Thomas Reeves, Roxbury Community College; Dennis Reinhartz, University of Texas at Arlington; Richard Rice, University of Tennessee at Chattanooga; Jane Scimeca, Brookdale Community College; Alyssa Goldstein Sepinwall, California State University at San Marcos; Deborah Shackleton, United States Air Force Academy; Anita Shelton, Eastern Illinois University; David R. Smith, California State Polytechnic University at Pomona; Mary Frances Smith, Ohio University; George E. Snow, Shippensburg University; Charlotte D. Staelin, Washington College; Paul D. Steeves, Stetson University; Yi Sun, University of San Diego; Willard Sunderland, University of Cincinnati; Thaddeus Sunseri, Colorado State University; Sara W. Tucker, Washburn University; John M. VanderLippe, SUNY at New Paltz; Mary A. Watrous-Schlesinger, Washington State University; Eric Van Young, University of California at San Diego; and Alex Zukas, National University, San Diego.

We also want to extend our collective thanks to Lynda Schaffer for her early conceptual contributions as well as to the history departments of Shippensburg University, the United States Air Force Academy, and the State University of New York at New Paltz for arranging reviewer conferences that provided crucial feedback for our revision of the book. Individually, Richard W. Bulliet thanks Jack Garraty and Isser Woloch for first involving him in world history; Pamela Kyle Crossley wishes to thank Gene Garthwaite, Charles Wood, and David Morgan; Steven W. Hirsch extends his gratitude to Dennis Trout and Peter L. D. Reid; Lyman L. Johnson extends his to Kenneth J. Andrien, Richard Boyer, Grant D. Hones, William M. Ringle, Hendrik Kraay, Daniel Dupre, and Steven W. Usselman; and David Northrup thanks Allen Howard and Prasanan Parthasarathi. Lyman Johnson also thanks the members of the Department of History of North Carolina A&T University for their many helpful and pertinent suggestions.

The three people who kept us on course in preparing the second edition deserve our special thanks: Jean L. Woy, Editor-in-Chief for History and Political Science; Nancy Blaine, Sponsoring Editor; and Jennifer E. Sutherland, Senior Development Editor. In carrying out our task, we got to know and value the work of several new staff at Houghton Mifflin: Carol Newman, Senior Project Editor; Julie Dunn, Associate Editor; Gillie Jones, Editorial Associate; Jennifer O'Neill, Editorial Assistant; and Henry Rachlin, Senior Designer. We also had the pleasure of working again with several people who helped so much with the first edition, including Charlotte Miller, Map Editor; Carole Frolich, Photo Researcher; Anthony L. Saizon, Design Director; Jill Haber, Senior Production/Design Coordinator; and Marie Barnes, Senior Manufacturing Coordinator.

We thank also the many students whose questions and concerns, expressed directly or through their instructors, shaped much of this revision. We continue to welcome all our readers' suggestions, queries, and criticisms. Please contact us at our respective institutions or at this e-mail address: college. hmco. com/history.

ABOUT THE AUTHORS

Richard W. Bulliet   Professor of Middle Eastern History at Columbia University and Director of its Middle East Institute, Richard W. Bulliet received his Ph.D. from Harvard University. He has written scholarly works on a number of topics: the social history of medieval Iran (*The Patricians of Nishapur*), the historical competition between pack camels and wheeled transport (*The Camel and the Wheel*), the process of conversion to Islam (*Conversion to Islam in the Medieval Period*), and the overall course of Islamic social history (*Islam: The View from the Edge*). He is the editor of the *Columbia History of the Twentieth Century*. He has published four novels, co-edited *The Encyclopedia of the Modern Middle East,* and hosted an educational television series on the Middle East. He was awarded a fellowship by the John Simon Guggenheim Memorial Foundation.

Pamela Kyle Crossley   Pamela Kyle Crossley received her Ph.D. in Modern Chinese History from Yale University. She is Professor of History, Rosenwald Research Professor in the Arts and Sciences, and Chair of Asian and Middle Eastern Studies at Dartmouth College. Her books include *A Translucent Mirror: History and Identity in Qing Imperial Ideology, The Manchus,* and *Orphan Warriors: Three Manchu Generations and the End of the Qing World.* Her research, which concentrates on the cultural history of China, Inner Asia, and Central Asia, has most recently been supported by the John Simon Guggenheim Memorial Foundation and the National Endowment for the Humanities.

Daniel R. Headrick   Daniel R. Headrick received his Ph.D. in History from Princeton University. Professor of History and Social Science at Roosevelt University in Chicago, he is the author of several books on the history of technology, imperialism, and international relations, including *The Tools of Empire: Technology and European Imperialism in the Nineteenth Century, The Tentacles of Progress: Technology Transfer in the Age of Imperialism, The Invisible Weapon: Telecommunications and International Politics,* and *When Information Came of Age: Technologies of Knowledge in the Age of Reason and Revolution, 1700–1850.* His articles have appeared in the *Journal of World History* and the *Journal of Modern History,* and he has been awarded fellowships by the National Endowment for the Humanities, the John Simon Guggenheim Memorial Foundation, and the Alfred P. Sloan Foundation.

Steven W. Hirsch   Steven W. Hirsch holds a Ph.D. in Classics from Stanford University and is currently Associate Professor of Classics and History at Tufts University. He has received grants from the National Endowment for the Humanities and the Massachusetts Foundation for Humanities and Public Policy. His research and publications include *The Friendship of the Barbarians: Xenophon and the Persian Empire,* as well as articles and reviews in the *Classical Journal,* the *American Journal of Philology,* and the *Journal of Interdisciplinary History.*

Lyman L. Johnson   Professor of History at the University of North Carolina at Charlotte, Lyman L. Johnson earned his Ph.D. in Latin American History from the University of Connecticut. A two-time Senior Fulbright-Hays Lecturer, he also has received fellowships from the Tinker Foundation, the Social Science Research Council, the National Endowment for the Humanities, and the American Philosophical Society. His recent books include *The Faces of Honor* (with Sonya Lipsett-Rivera), *The Problem of Order in Changing Societies, Essays on the Price History of Eighteenth-Century Latin America* (with Enrique Tandeter), and *Colonial Latin America* (with Mark A. Burkholder). He also has published in journals, including the *Hispanic American Historical Review,* the *Journal of Latin American Studies,* the *International Review of Social History, Social History,* and *Desarrollo Económico.* He recently served as president of the Conference on Latin American History.

David Northrup   Professor of History at Boston College, David Northrup earned his Ph.D. in African and European History from the University of California at Los Angeles. He has published scholarly volumes on precolonial Nigeria, on precolonial and colonial Congo, on the Atlantic slave trade, and on Asian, African, and Pacific Islander indentured labor in the nineteenth century. His recent work appeared in the *Oxford History of the British Empire, Revue française d'histoire d'outremer, Slavery and Abolition,* and the *Journal of World History.* He currently serves on the Executive Council of the World History Association and has received research support from the Fulbright-Hays Commission, the National Endowment for the Humanities, and the Social Science Research Council.

NOTE ON SPELLING AND USAGE

Where necessary for clarity, dates are followed by the letters C.E. or B.C.E. The abbreviation C.E. stands for "Common Era" and is equivalent to A.D. (*anno Domini*, Latin for "in the year of the Lord"). The abbreviation B.C.E stands for "before the Common Era" and means the same as B.C. ("before Christ"). In keeping with our goal of approaching world history without special concentration on one culture or another, we chose these neutral abbreviations as appropriate to our enterprise. Because many readers will be more familiar with English than with metric measurements, however, units of measure are generally given in the English system, with metric equivalents following in parentheses.

In general, Chinese has been romanized according to the *pinyin* method. Exceptions include proper names well established in English (e.g., Canton, Chiang Kai-shek) and a few English words borrowed from Chinese (e.g., kowtow). Spellings of Arabic, Ottoman Turkish, Persian, Mongolian, Manchu, Japanese, and Korean names and terms avoid special diacritical marks for letters that are pronounced only slightly differently in English. An apostrophe is used to indicate when two Chinese syllables are pronounced separately (e.g., Chang'an).

For words transliterated from languages that use the Arabic script—Arabic, Ottoman Turkish, Perisan, Urdu—the apostrophe indicating separately pronounced syllables may represent either of two special consonants, the *hamza* or the *ain*. Because most English-speakers do not hear the distinction between these two, they have not been distinguished in transliteration and are not indicated when they occur at the beginning or end of a word. As with Chinese, some words and commonly used place-names from these languages are given familiar English spellings (e.g., Quran instead of Qur'an, Cairo instead of al-Qahira). Arabic romanization has normally been used for terms relating to Islam, even where the context justifies slightly different Turkish or Persian forms, again for ease of comprehension.

There is an ongoing debate about how best to render Amerindian words in English. It has been common for authors writing in English to follow Mexican usage for Nahuatl and Yucatec Maya words and place-names. In this style, for example, the capital of the Aztec state is spelled Tenochtitlán, and the important late Maya city-state is spelled Chichén Itzá. Although these forms are still common even in the specialist literature, we have chosen to follow the scholarship that sees these accents as unnecessary. The exceptions are modern place-names, such as Mérida and Yucatán, which are accented. A similar problem exists for the spelling of Quechua and Aymara words from the Andean region of South America. Although there is significant disagreement among scholars, we follow the emerging consensus and use the spellings khipu (not quipu), Tiwanaku (not Tiahuanaco), and Wari (not Huari). However, we keep Inca (not Inka) and Cuzco (not Cusco), since these spellings are expected by most of our potential readers and we hope to avoid confusion.

II

INTRODUCTION

THE WORLD BEFORE 1500

Antiquity: Humans, Cultures, and Conquests, to 400 C.E. •
Growth and Interaction, 400–1200 • **Interregional Conquests
and Exchanges, 1200–1500**
ENVIRONMENT AND TECHNOLOGY: **World Population Changes**

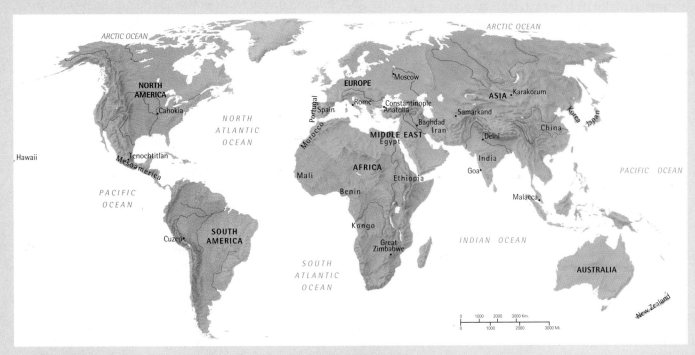

The World, 1200–1500

istory occurs in a continuous stream. Because new events are the products of their past, each historical period is intimately linked to what preceded it. As a Roman historian put it, "History doesn't make leaps." Nevertheless, modern historians find it useful to divide the past into eras or ages to make sense of the sweep of history. The longest historical eras are antiquity, the Middle Ages, and modern times. Volume II of *The Earth and Its Peoples* is devoted to the third of these—modern world history, the five centuries since about 1500.

World historians largely agree that the intensity of interaction around the world during the modern period distinguishes it from all earlier times. European maritime exploration opened up or intensified these contacts. The modern era is also characterized by the steady expansion of European political, economic, and cultural leadership in every part of the world.

How and when different parts of the world felt the impact of the West varied. By 1500 parts of the Americas were already reeling under the impact of their first contacts with Europeans, but in most other parts of the world the West did not make a big difference until the century after 1750 or even later. Thus, while in hindsight the theme of Western ascendancy seems to be a defining force of modern history, for the people of Asia, Africa, and elsewhere the modern era was a time in which the internal patterns of historical change only gradually became altered by the growing influence of Westerners and by their own reactions to these influences.

In order to explain how the modern era came into being, the first chapter of Volume II of *The Earth and Its Peoples* (Chapter 17) begins in about 1450. To help the reader understand the broader sweep of history, this Introduction provides an overview of earlier eras. The Introduction reviews three periods of decreasing temporal length. The first is the very long period from human origins until the end of ancient history in about 400 C.E. Next comes the early medieval period down to about 1200; and, finally, the three hundred years immediately preceding 1500. Because the centuries after 1200 were most important for shaping the transition to the modern era, they receive the most detailed treatment.

ANTIQUITY: HUMANS, CULTURES, AND CONQUESTS, TO 400 C.E.

All historical periods were shaped by natural environment and human technology (whether simple tools, techniques, or complex machines). The paramount role played by environmental forces is apparent when historians seek to explain how human beings—and thus history—began. Like all other living creatures, early humans were products of biological adjustments to changing environments. Over millions of years, our ancestors in eastern and southern Africa evolved biologically to enhance their chances for survival. The evolution of an upright posture enabled early people to walk and run on two legs, thereby freeing their hands for tool making. The evolution of larger brains gave them the capacity to learn and understand all sorts of new things and devise techniques for putting them to use. Finally, evolutionary changes in the throat gave humans the capacity for speech, which, as language developed, had the dual effect of making complex social relations easier and fostering the development of intellectual culture.

With these physical traits in place, humans were able to develop in a direction taken by no other creature. Instead of relying on the glacially slow process of biological evolution to adapt their bodies to new environments, our ancestors used their minds to devise technologies for transforming nature to suit their needs. By the standards of today, these early technologies may seem crude—stone tools for cutting and chopping, clothing made from plants and animal skins, shelters in caves and huts—but they were sufficient to enable humans to survive environmental changes in their homelands. They also enabled bands of humans to migrate to new environments in every part of the world. Through trial and error Stone Age people learned what could safely be eaten in new environments. Other primates acted primarily by instinct; humans acted according to the dictates of culture. The capacity to create and change material and intellectual culture marked the beginning of human history.

World Population Changes

During the millennia before 1500, human population expanded in three momentous surges. Historians associate the first with the spread of early humans from their African homeland to all of the inhabitable continents after about 50,000 B.C.E. The second, associated with the spread of agriculture around the world, saw the 5 million people, scattered thinly across the planet in 5000 B.C.E., grow to 50 million in 1000 B.C.E. and then double to 100 million over the next five hundred years. During these two surges, the parts of the world most favorable to humankind changed. Before 50,000 years ago two of every three persons lived in Africa. By about 800 B.C.E. two of every three in an enormously larger population lived in Asia, most in China and India.

Perhaps because the advantage of bringing new lands under cultivation had reached the limits of technology, during the millennium after 500 B.C.E. population stagnated. Then it underwent its third surge in the early medieval era, rising to over 350 million in 1200. Scholars do not fully understand the

reasons for the medieval population surge, but some believe it may reflect favorable climate, appropriate agricultural technology, and political stability in East Asia and Europe, where the greatest increases took place. The population of the Americas may also have increased significantly during this period.

The factors that halted this population growth for the next two centuries are better known. In China a population that numbered over 100 million in 1200 declined by a third or more during the next century as a result of the warfare, disease, and disruption of agriculture during Mongol conquest and rule. In Europe population continued to grow after 1200, reaching a peak of around 80 million in the early 1300s. Such densities were straining the environment when the plague known as the Black Death (whose spread was the product of flourishing commercial contacts) swept away a quarter of the population. However, when the plague ended and warfare diminished, Eurasia's population rebounded to about 360 million in 1500.

Figure I.1   World Population Growth, 10,000 B.C.E.–1000 B.C.E.
Source: Data from Colin McEvedy and Richard Jones, *Atlas of World Population History* (New York: Penguin Books, 1978)

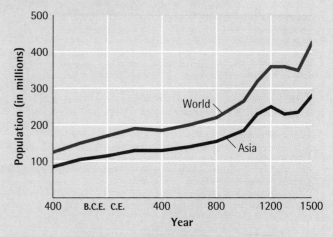

Figure I.2   World Population Growth, 400 B.C.E.–1500 C.E.
Source: Data from Colin McEvedy and Richard Jones, *Atlas of World Population History* (New York: Penguin Books, 1978)

Agricultural Civilizations

Beginning about 10,000 years ago, the transition from food gathering to food production marked a major turning point in history. Human communities in many different parts of the world learned to alter the natural food supply.

Some people promoted the growth of foods they liked by scattering seeds on good soils and restricting the growth of competing plants. In time some people became full-time farmers. Other communities tamed wild animals whose meat, milk, fur, and hides they desired, and they controlled their breeding to produce animals with the

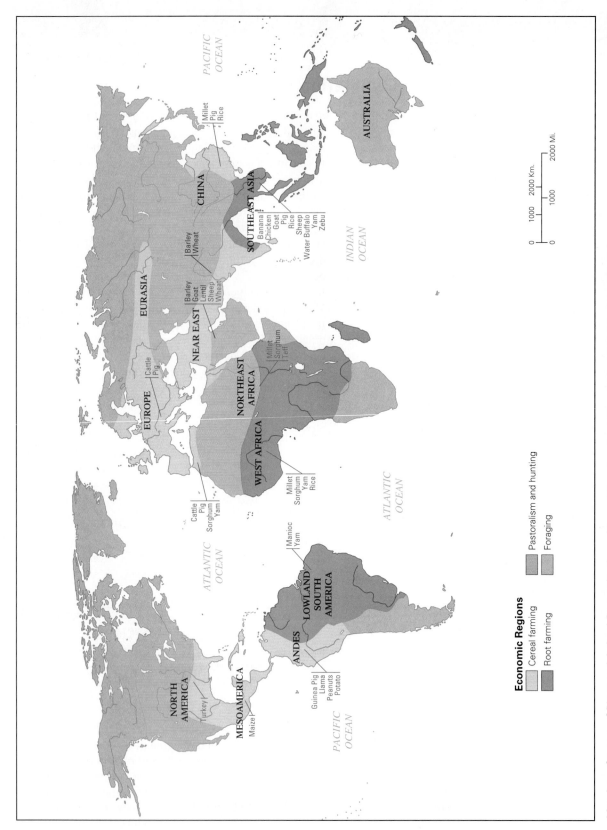

Map I.1 Centers of Plant and Animal Domestication Many different parts of the world made original contributions to domestication during the Agricultural Revolutions that began about 10,000 years ago. Later interactions helped spread these domesticated animals and plants to new locations. In lands less suitable for crop cultivation, pastoralism and hunting predominated.

most desired characteristics. Promoted by a warmer world climate, these agricultural revolutions slowly spread from the Middle East around the Mediterranean. People in South and East Asia, Africa, and the Americas domesticated other wild plants and animals for their use. Just as humans had ceased to rely on evolution to enable them to adjust to new surroundings, so too they had bypassed evolution in bringing new species of plants and animals into existence (see Map I.1).

The agricultural revolutions greatly enhanced people's chances for survival in two ways. One was a rapid increase in population fostered by the ability to grow and store more food (see Environment and Technology: World Population Changes). A second change was taking place in the composition of human communities. The earliest communities consisted of small bands of biologically related people and their spouses from other bands. However, more complex societies made their first appearances as more and more unrelated people concentrated in lush river valleys, whose soils, temperatures, and rainfall suited them for farming.

In the Fertile Crescent of the Middle East, Egypt, India, and China the existence of a regular food surplus enabled a few people to develop highly specialized talents and tools that were not tied to food production. Some specialized in fighting—to defend crops from raiders and to expand their lands. Some talented warriors became rulers of large areas and headed government with specialized administrators. Specialists constructed elaborate irrigation systems, monumental palaces, and temples. Others made special metal tools and weapons, first of bronze, then of iron. Because of the value of their talents these specialists acquired privileges. It was grandest to be a king, queen, or head priest. For the average person, life was harder in complex societies than in parts of the world where such specialization had not yet occurred.

Culture and Civilization

Complex and populous agricultural societies developed specialists who dealt with abstract and unseen forces. This development was not entirely new. For tens of thousands of years before the first settled societies, humans had used their minds to think about the meaning of life. The remains of elaborate burials and sites of worship suggest that some early societies had clear beliefs in an afterlife and in spiritual forces that controlled their lives. Many cultures believed the sun, moon, and nature had supernatural powers.

Another form of intellectual activity was the collection of technical knowledge about the environment. Cultural communities learned what plants were best for

Scene from the Egyptian Book of the Dead, ca. 1300 B.C.E.
The Book of the Dead provided Egyptians with the instructions they needed to complete this arduous journey and gain a blessed existence in the afterlife. (Courtesy of the Trustees of the British Museum)

food, clothing, or building materials and passed this knowledge along to later generations. Most specialized was the knowledge of how to make medicines and poisons. Assigning names for all these facilitated the transmission of this knowledge. In the absence of written records, very little specific information about these early treasuries of knowledge exists, but the elaborate and beautiful paintings in caves dating to tens of thousands of years before the emergence of early agricultural societies provide the clearest evidence of the cultural sophistication of early humans.

Cultural change surged as settled agricultural communities became more specialized. Temple priests devised elaborate rituals and texts for state religions and studied the heavens for signs of the progress of the seasons or for more mystical meanings. In Mesopotamia, Egypt, and elsewhere a new class of scribes wrote down laws, bodies of knowledge, and records in special codes. Writing gave rise to recorded literature and records that might be sent unchanged over long distances or even lost for millennia only to be discovered and deciphered in recent times, giving future generations specific records of what went before. Thoughtful people recorded the myths and legends passed down orally from earlier days, systematizing them and often adapting them to new social conditions.

Empires and Regional Cultures

In time governments weakened or fell victim to conquest. Egypt, for example, fell to the Assyrians from Mesopotamia, then to Nubians from up the Nile. Some conquerors created vast new empires. Late in the fourth century B.C.E., Alexander the Great brought everything from the eastern Mediterranean to India and Egypt under his sway, spreading Greek culture and language. After the collapse of Alexander's empire in the third century B.C.E., the first of a series of Indian empires arose. In the second and first centuries B.C.E., Latin-speakers spread their rule, language, and culture throughout the Roman Empire, which encompassed the Mediterranean and reached across the Alps into Gaul (France) and Britain. At much the same time, the Han consolidated control over the densely populated lands of China, and successive rulers extended the sway of imperial China over much of East Asia. In the isolated continents of the Americas, advanced agricultural societies were also building larger states in late antiquity.

Essential to empire formation was the significant enhancement of old technologies and the development of new ones. In many parts of the world iron replaced bronze as the preferred metal for tools and weapons. In the Middle East and China soldiers on horseback played important military roles. In most places there were advances in the fighting techniques and in defensive strategies and fortifications.

Empires encouraged the growth of cities to serve as administrative, economic, and cultural centers. Temples, palaces, monuments, markets, and public amenities advertised the glory of these imperial centers. Large states regularly mobilized large pools of labor for massive construction projects. By late antiquity, a few cities had populations in the hundreds of thousands—Alexandria in Egypt, Rome in Italy, Chang'an in China, Palaliputra in India—though such large numbers strained cities' capacities to supply food and water and dispose of waste. Such architectural monuments established "classical" styles that affected wide areas even after the empires were gone.

Other imperial building projects were more practical. The Roman and Chinese governments built thousands of miles of paved roads for moving troops and communication; long barrier walls and strings of forts defended frontier areas from invasion. Trade often flourished on these political frontiers, and good roads further encouraged trade. Improvements in shipping also encouraged the movement of goods over long distances. Much long-distance trade in antiquity was in luxury goods for the privileged classes in urban civilizations. The search for exotic items tied remote parts of the world together and gave rise to new specialists both within the urban civilizations and in less stratified parts of the world. Gold, animal pelts, and exotic feathers from inner Africa reached Egypt. Phoenician mariners marketed lumber, papyrus (for paper), wine, and fish around the Mediterranean Sea. Other merchants carried silk from China across arid Central Asia to the Middle East and lands to the west. The advent of coinage in the first millennium B.C.E. stimulated local and regional economies.

The routes that carried goods also helped spread religions, inventions, and ideas. The Zoroastrian religion of the Persians became one of the great ethical creeds of antiquity. The diaspora of Jews from Palestine after their northern kingdom was destroyed by the Assyrian Empire in the eighth century B.C.E. and the activities of Jewish traders also helped spread monotheistic beliefs. The beliefs and culture of the Greeks and Romans spread throughout their empires. Similarly, Indian traders introduced Hinduism to Southeast Asia.

GROWTH AND INTERACTION, 400–1200

During the Early Middle Ages expanding political and commercial links drew regions closer together. In addition, the growth of interregional trade and the spread of new world religions helped unite and redefine the boundaries of cultural regions, though divisions within religions undercut some of this cultural unity. All of these factors were interrelated, but let's begin with the one that left the most enduring impression on the course of history: the spread of world religions.

World Religions

The first religious tradition to experience widespread growth in this period was Buddhism, which spread from the Indian homeland where it had arisen around 500 B.C.E. One direction of growth was eastward into Southeast Asia. By 400 C.E. there were particular strongholds of the faith on the large islands of Ceylon and Java, whose kings supported the growth of schools and monasteries and constructed temple complexes. Traders also carried Buddhism to China and from there to Korea, Japan, and Tibet. In some places Buddhism's growing strength led to political reactions. In

China the Tang emperors reduced the influence of the monasteries in 840 by taking away their tax exemption and by promoting traditional Confucian values. A similar effort by the Tibetan royal family to curtail Buddhism failed, and Buddhist monks established their political dominance in mountainous Tibet. In India, however, Buddhism gradually lost support during this period and by 1200 had practically disappeared from the land of its origin.

Meanwhile, people in western Eurasia were embracing two newer religious systems. In the fourth century, Christianity became the official religion of the Roman Empire, adding new followers all around the Mediterranean to this once persecuted faith. But when the western half of the empire collapsed under the onslaught of "barbarian" invasions in the late fifth century, the Latin Church had to shoulder alone the tasks of converting these peoples to Christianity and preserving the intellectual, political, and cultural heritage of Roman antiquity. In its religious mission the Latin Church was quite successful. One by one Frankish, German, English, Irish, Hungarian, and other leaders were converted, and their subjects gradually followed suit. Preserving other Roman achievements was more difficult. The church continued to use the Latin language and Roman law, and Christian monasteries preserved manuscripts of many ancient works. But the trading economy and urban life that had been the heart blood of ancient Rome became only a memory in most of the Latin West.

In the eastern Mediterranean, Byzantine Roman emperors continued to rule, and the Greek-speaking Christian church continued to enjoy political protection. Greek monks were also active Christian missionaries among the Slavic peoples of eastern Europe. The conversion of the Russian rulers in the tenth century was a notable achievement. However, by the middle of the next century, cultural, linguistic, and theological differences led to a deep rift between Greek and Russian Christians in the east and Latin Christians in the west.

Meanwhile, prophetic religion founded by Muhammad in the seventh century was spreading like a whirlwind out of its Arabian homeland. With great fervor Arab armies introduced Islam and an accompanying state system into the Middle East, across North Africa, and into the Iberian Peninsula. Over time most Middle Eastern and African Christians and members of other religions chose to adopt the new faith. Muslim merchants helped spread the faith along trade routes into sub-Saharan Africa and across southern Asia. Like Christianity, Islam eventually split along cultural, theological, and political lines as it expanded. Beginning in 1095, Latin Christians launched military Crusades

Armored Knights in Battle   This painting made around 1135 shows the armament of knights at the time of the Crusades. Chain mail, a helmet, and a shield carried on the left side are the rider's primary defenses.   (Pierpont Morgan Library/Art Resource, NY)

against Muslim dominance of Christian holy places in Palestine. In later Crusades, political and commercial ends became more important than religious goals, and the boundaries between Christianity and Islam changed little.

Commercial and Political Contacts

In many other parts of the world empires played a fundamental role in defining and unifying cultural areas. Under the Tang and Song dynasties (618–1279) China continued to have stability and exhibited periods of remarkable economic growth and technological creativity. Ghana, the first notable empire in sub-Saharan Africa, emerged to control one end of the trans-Saharan trade. In the isolated continents of the Americas a series of cultural complexes formed in the Andes, among the Maya of the Yucatán, along the Mississippi, and in the arid North American southwest. But despite efforts by Christian northern Europeans to create a loosely centralized "Holy Roman Empire," a very decentralized political system prevailed in most of western Europe. In Japan development was moving in a similar direction.

Political and religious expansion helped stimulate regional and long-distance trade. The challenge of moving growing quantities of goods over long distances produced some important innovations in land and sea travel. Two of the most important land-based, long-distance routes in this period depended on pack animals, especially the camel. One was the Silk Road, a caravan route across Central Asia. On the other trade route, between sub-Saharan Africa and North Africa, camels carried goods across the Sahara, the world's largest desert.

The Silk Road took its name from the silk textiles that were carried from eastern China to the Mediterranean Sea. In return, the Chinese received horses and other goods from the West. In existence since about 250 B.C.E., this series of roads nearly 6,000-miles (9,000-kilometers) in length passed through arid lands whose pastoral populations provided guides, food, and fresh camels (specially bred for caravan work).

After 900 C.E. the Silk Road declined for a time. By coincidence, the trans-Saharan caravan routes were growing more important during the period from 700 to 1200. Here, too, horses were an important trade purchased by African rulers to the south in return for gold, slaves, and other goods. The pastoralists who controlled the Saharan oases became essential guides for the camel caravans.

Since ancient times sea travel had been important in moving goods over relatively short distances, usually within sight of land, as around the Mediterranean Sea, the Red Sea, the Persian Gulf, and among the islands of the East Indies. During this period the water links around and through the Indian Ocean were increasing enough to make it an alternative to moving goods from China to the Middle East. Shipments went from port to port and were exchanged many times. Special ships known as dhows made use of the seasonal shifts in the winds across the Indian Ocean to plan their voyages in each direction. These centuries also saw remarkable maritime voyages in the Pacific (see Chapter 17).

INTERREGIONAL CONQUESTS AND EXCHANGES, 1200–1500

Between 1200 and 1500, cultural and commercial contacts grew rapidly across wide expanses of Eurasia, Africa, the Americas, and the Indian Ocean. In part, the increased contacts were the product of an unprecedented era of empire building around the world. The Mongols conquered a vast empire spanning Eurasia from the Pacific to eastern Europe. Muslim peoples created new empires in India, the Middle East, and sub-Saharan Africa. Amerindian empires united extensive regions of the Americas. Most of Europe continued to lack political unity, but unusually powerful European kingdoms were expanding their frontiers.

Empires stimulated commercial exchanges. The Mongol conquests revived the Silk Road across Central Asia, while a complex maritime network centered on the Indian Ocean stretched around southern Eurasia from the South China Sea to the North Atlantic, with overland connections in all directions (see Map I.2). Trade in the Americas and Africa also expanded. In the fifteenth century, Portuguese and Spanish explorers began an expansion southward along the Atlantic coast of Africa that by 1500 had opened a new all-water route to the riches of the Indian Ocean and set the stage for transoceanic routes that for the first time were to span the globe.

Mongol, Muslim, and European expansion promoted the spread of technologies. Printing, compasses, crossbows, gunpowder, and firearms—all East Asian inventions—found broader applications and new uses in western Eurasia. Both the Ottomans and the kingdoms of western Europe made extensive use of gunpowder technologies. However, the highly competitive and increasingly literate peoples of the Latin West surpassed all others of this period in their use of technologies that they borrowed from elsewhere or devised themselves. Europeans mined and refined more metals, produced more books, built more kinds of ships, and made more weapons than did people in any other comparable place on earth.

Why was so much change taking place all at once? Historians attribute many of the changes in South and Central Asia directly or indirectly to the empire building of the Mongols. But other changes took place far from that area. The role of simple coincidence, of course,

Map I.2   Old World Connections   Long-distance land and sea routes fostered cultural as well as commercial exchanges

should never be overlooked in history. And some historians believe that larger environmental factors were also at work—changes in climate that promoted population growth, trade, and empire building (see Environment and Technology: World Population Changes).

Mongols and Turks

The earliest and largest of the new empires was the work of the Mongols of northeastern Asia. Using their extraordinary command of horses and refinements in traditional forms of military and social organization, Mongols and allied groups united under Genghis Khan overran northern China in the early thirteenth century and spread their control westward across Central Asia to eastern Europe. By the later part of the century, the Mongol Empire stretched from Korea to Poland. It was ruled initially in four separate khanates: one in Russia, one in Iran, one in Central Asia, and one in China.

By ensuring traders protection from robbers and excessive tolls, the Mongol Empire revitalized the Silk Road. Never before had there been such a volume of commercial exchanges between eastern and western Eurasia. Easier travel also helped Islam and Buddhism spread to new parts of Central Asia.

The strains of holding such vast territories together caused the Mongol Empire to disintegrate over the course of the fourteenth and early fifteenth centuries. The Ming rulers of China overthrew Mongol rule in 1368 and began an expansionist foreign policy to reestablish China's predominance and prestige. Their armies repeatedly invaded Mongolia, reestablished dominion over Korea, and occupied northern Vietnam (Annam). One by one the other khanates collapsed.

The Mongols left a formidable legacy, but it was not Mongolian. Instead, Mongol rulers tended to adopt and promote the political systems, agricultural practices, and local customs of the peoples they ruled. Their encouragement of local languages helped later literary movements to flower. The political influence of the administrations the Mongols established in China, Iran, and Russia lingered even after locals had overthrown their rule, creating the basis for new national regimes.

At about the same time as the early Mongol expansion, Turkic war leaders from what is now Afghanistan

Mongolian Pony This resting pony wears a head collar, as specified by Ghenghis's law. (National Palace Museum, Taipei, Republic of China)

were surging through the Khyber Pass and established a Muslim empire centered at Delhi. In short order, they overwhelmed the several Hindu states of north and central India and established a large empire ruled from the city of Delhi. The subsequent migration of large numbers of Muslims into India and the prestige and power of the Muslim ruling class brought India into the Islamic world. After their conquests in the Middle East, Mongols had recruited other Turkic-speaking Muslims from Central Asia to serve as their agents. In the decades after 1250, a large Turkic community in Anatolia (now Turkey) known as Ottomans took advantage of the weakness of the Byzantine Empire to extend their base in Anatolia. They then crossed into the Balkan Peninsula of southeastern Europe.

In the late 1300s, the Central Asian conqueror Timur (Tamerlane) shattered the Delhi Sultanate and stopped the expansion of the Ottoman Empire. The conquest and pillage of Timur's armies left the Delhi Sultanate a shadow of its former self, but the Ottoman Turks were able to reconstitute their empire in the fifteenth century. Ottoman conquerors swept deep into southeastern Europe (taking Constantinople, the last surviving remnant of the Byzantine Empire, in 1453) and southward into the Middle East, establishing a stable presence that was to endure into the twentieth century.

Indian Ocean Exchanges

In the wake of the Mongol Empire's collapse, the Indian Ocean assumed greater importance in the movement of goods across Eurasia. Alliances among Muslim merchants of many nationalities made these routes the world's richest trading area. Merchant dhows sailed among the trading ports, carrying cotton textiles, leather goods, grains, pepper, jewelry, carpets, horses, ivory, and many other goods. Chinese silk and porcelain and Indonesian spices entered from the east, meeting Middle Eastern and European goods from the west. It is important to note that Muslim merchant networks were almost completely independent of the giant Muslim land empires.

As a consequence of the Islamic world's political and commercial expansion, the number of adherents to the Muslim faith also grew. By 1500 Islam had replaced Buddhism as the second most important faith in India and was on its way to displacing Hinduism and Buddhism in Southeast Asia. The faith was also spreading in the Balkans. Meanwhile, raids by Arab pastoralists undermined ancient Christian states along Africa's upper Nile, leaving Ethiopia as the only Christian-ruled state in Africa. In the trading cities below the Sahara and along the Indian Ocean coast where Islam had established itself well before 1200, the strength and sophistication of Islamic religious practice was growing.

Mediterranean Exchanges

The Mediterranean Sea, which since antiquity had been a focus of commerce and cultural exchange for the peoples of Europe, the Middle East, and Africa, saw increased activity in the later Middle Ages. Part of the Mediterranean's importance derived from its trading links to the Indian Ocean by land and water routes. Another area that contributed to expanded trade was northern Africa. Camel caravans brought great quantities of gold and large numbers of slaves to the Mediterranean from the lands below the Sahara. This trade facilitated the growth of the powerful empire of Mali, which controlled some of the main gold-producing regions of West Africa. The rulers of Mali became rich and Muslim. Their wars and those of other states produced the captives that were sold north. In the fourteenth century the disruption of supplies of slaves from the eastern Mediterranean led to more slaves being purchased in southern Europe.

Another part of the expansion of Mediterranean trade was tied to the revival of western Europe. In 1204 the Italian city-state of Venice had shown its determination to be a dominant player in the eastern Mediterranean by attacking the Greek city of Constantinople and ensuring access to the Black Sea. Trade routes from the Mediterranean spread northward to the Netherlands and connected by sea to the British Isles, the Baltic Sea, and the Atlantic. The growth of trade in Europe accompanied a revival of urban life and culture. Both the cities and the countryside saw increased use of energy, minerals, and technologies from printing to gunpowder. Despite a high level of warfare among European states and devastating population losses in the fourteenth century (see Environment and Technology: World Population Changes), much of Europe was exhibiting cultural and economic vitality that was to have great consequences for the entire world in the centuries that followed.

The Aztecs and Inca

In the continents of the Western Hemisphere, American peoples were also creating important empires in the period from 1200 to 1500, although they had more limited resources with which to do so. For thousands of years their cultures had developed in isolation from the rest of humanity and thus had been unable to borrow any plants, animals, or technologies. Amerindian conquests were made without the aid of riding animals like the Mongols' horses, without the iron weapons all Old World empire builders had been using for many centuries, and without the new gunpowder weaponry that some Eurasians were employing in their conquests in this period.

In the wake of the collapse of the Toltec Empire, a martial people known as the Aztecs pushed southward into the rich agricultural lands of central Mexico. At first the Aztecs placed themselves at the service of strong indigenous residents, but after 1300 they began to build their own empire. Relying on their military skills, members of the Aztec warrior elite were able to conquer territories and reduce peasants to their service. The growth of a servile class at the bottom of society was paralleled by the growth of a powerful ruling class housed in well-constructed two-story dwellings in the Aztec capital cities. The servile laborers supplied the food needs of the growing cities and were impressed into building

The Mesoamerican Ball Game Among the Maya the game was associated with a creation myth and thus had deep religious meaning. There is evidence that some players were sacrificed. (Dallas Art Museum/Justin Kerr)

elaborate canals and land reclamation projects. Underpinning the power of the Aztec rulers were religious rituals that emphasized human sacrifice, mostly captives of the armies. By 1500 the Aztecs ruled a densely populated empire of subject and allied peoples.

Meanwhile, in the Andean highlands of western South America another powerful Amerindian empire was forming. Like central Mexico this region already had a rich agricultural base and a dense population when, in the fifteenth century, the Inca began using military skills to expand from a chiefdom into an empire. The Inca rulers, like the Aztecs, built impressive cities, promoted irrigation projects, and relied on religious rituals to bolster their authority. Tribute in goods and labor from their subject peoples supported their projects, and a network of mountain roads tied together the pieces of an empire that stretched for more than 3,000 miles (nearly 5,000 kilometers) north to south.

Both empires were cultural and commercial centers as well as political ones. In the Aztec Empire, well-armed private merchants controlled a long-distance trade in luxuries for the elites, including gold, jewels, feathered garments, and animal skins. There was also a network of local markets, large and small, that supplied the needs of more ordinary folks. State direction featured more prominently in Inca-ruled areas and promoted a vast exchange of specialized goods and a huge variety of foodstuffs grown at different altitudes.

■ Suggested Reading

A fuller treatment of all these topics can be found in the first volume of *The Earth and Its Peoples*. Richard Bulliet provides a brief overview of world history both before and after 1500 in "Themes, Conquerors, and Commerce," in Heidi Roupp, ed., *World History: A Resource Book* (1997).

For summaries of the latest scholarship on some select topics see these pamphlets in the American Historical Association's series "Essays in Global and Comparative History": Stanley M. Burstein, *The Hellenistic Period in World History* (1996); Richard M. Eaton, *Islamic History as World History* (1990); John E. Kicza, *The Peoples and Civilizations of the Americas Before Contact* (1998); Xinru Liu, *The Silk Road: Overland Trade and Cultural Interactions in Eurasia* (1998); Sarah Shaver Hughes and Brady Hughes, *Women in Ancient Civilizations* (1998); Jonathan S. Walters, *Finding Buddhists in Global History* (1998); Peter B. Golden, *Nomads and Sedentary Societies in Medieval Eurasia* (1998); and Janet Lippman Abu-Lughod, *The World System in the Thirteenth Century: Dead-End or Precursor?* (1993). Sarah Hughes and Brady Hughes have also edited a useful work correcting the dominance of patriarchal themes: *Women in World History*, vol. 1 (1995).

17

THE MARITIME REVOLUTION,
to 1550

Global Maritime Expansion Before 1450 • Iberian Expansion, 1400–1550 •
Encounters with Europe, 1450–1550
ENVIRONMENT AND TECHNOLOGY: Vasco da Gama's Fleet
SOCIETY AND CULTURE: European Male Sexual Dominance Overseas

Columbus Prepares to Cross the Atlantic, 1492   This later representation shows Columbus
with the ships, soldiers, priests, and seamen that were part of Spain's enterprise.

*I*n 1511 the young Ferdinand Magellan sailed from Europe around the southern tip of Africa and eastward across the Indian Ocean as a member of the first Portuguese expedition to explore the East Indies (maritime Southeast Asia). Eight years later, this time in the service of Spain, he headed an expedition that sought to demonstrate the feasibility of reaching the East Indies by sailing westward from Europe. By the middle of 1521 Magellan's expedition had achieved its goal by sailing across the Atlantic, rounding the southern tip of South America, and crossing the Pacific Ocean—but at a high price.

One of the five ships that had set out from Spain in 1519 was wrecked on a reef, and the captain of another deserted and sailed back to Spain. The passage across the vast Pacific took much longer than anticipated, resulting in the deaths of dozens of sailors due to starvation and disease. In the Philippines, Magellan himself was killed on April 27, 1521, while aiding a local king who had promised to become a Christian. Magellan's successor met the same fate a few days later.

To consolidate their dwindling resources, the expedition's survivors burned the least seaworthy of their remaining three ships and transferred the men and supplies from that ship to the smaller *Victoria*, which continued westward across the Indian Ocean, around Africa, and back to Europe. Magellan's flagship, the *Trinidad*, tried unsuccessfully to recross the Pacific to Central America. The *Victoria*'s return to Spain on September 8, 1522, was a crowning example of Europeans' new ability and determination to make themselves masters of the oceans. A century of daring and dangerous voyages backed by the Portuguese crown had opened new routes through the South Atlantic to Africa, Brazil, and the rich trade of the Indian Ocean. Rival voyages sponsored by Spain since 1492 had opened new contacts with the American continents. Now the unexpectedly broad Pacific Ocean had been crossed as well. A maritime revolution was under way that would change the course of history.

That new maritime skill marked the end of an era in which the flow of historical influences tended to move from east to west. Before 1500, most overland and maritime expansion had come from Asia, as had the most useful technologies and the most influential systems of belief. Asia also had been home to the most powerful states and the richest trading networks. The Iberians set out on their voyages of exploration to reach Eastern markets, and their success began a new era in which the West gradually became the world's center of power, wealth, and innovation.

The maritime revolution created many new contacts, alliances, and conflicts. Some ended tragically for individuals like Magellan. Some were disastrous for entire populations: Amerindians, for instance, suffered conquest, colonization, and a rapid decline in numbers. Sometimes the results were mixed: Asians and Africans found both risks and opportunities in their new relations with the visitors from Europe.

As you read this chapter, ask yourself the following questions:

- Why did Portugal and Spain undertake voyages of exploration?
- Why do the voyages of Magellan and other Iberians mark a turning point in world history?
- What were the consequences for the different peoples of the world of the new contacts resulting from these voyages?

GLOBAL MARITIME EXPANSION BEFORE 1450

*S*ince ancient times travel across the salt waters of the world's seas and oceans had been one of the great challenges to people's technological ingenuity. Ships had to be sturdy enough to survive heavy winds and waves, and pilots had to learn how to cross featureless expanses of water to their destination. In time ships, sails, and navigational techniques perfected in the more protected seas were tried on the vast, open oceans.

However complex the solutions and dangerous the voyages, the rewards of sea travel made it all worthwhile. For ships could move goods and people more quickly and cheaply than any form of overland travel then possible. Because of its challenges and rewards, sea travel attracted adventurers. To cross the unknown waters, find new lands, and open up new trade or settlements was an

CHRONOLOGY

	Pacific Ocean	Atlantic Ocean	Indian Ocean
Pre 1400	**400–1300** Polynesian settlement of Pacific islands	**770–1200** Viking voyages **1300s** Settlement of Madeira, Azores, Canaries **Early 1300s** Mali voyages	
1400 to 1500		**1418–1460** Voyages of Henry the Navigator **1440s** Slaves from West Africa **1482** Portuguese at Gold Coast and Kongo **1486** Portuguese at Benin **1488** Bartolomeu Dias reaches Indian Ocean **1492** Columbus reaches Caribbean **1493** Columbus returns to Caribbean (second voyage) **1498** Columbus reaches mainland of South America (third voyage) **1492–1500** Spanish conquer Hispaniola	**1405–1433** Voyages of Zheng He **1497–1498** Vasco da Gama reaches India
1500 to 1550	 **1519–1522** Magellan expedition	**1500** Cabral reaches Brazil **1513** Ponce de León explores Florida **1519–1520** Cortés conquers Aztec Empire **1531–1533** Pizarro conquers Inca Empire	**1505** Portuguese bombard Swahili Coast cities **1510** Portuguese take Goa **1511** Portuguese take Malacca **1515** Portuguese take Hormuz **1535** Portuguese take Diu **1538** Portuguese defeat Ottoman fleet **1539** Portuguese aid Ethiopia

exciting prospect. For these reasons some men on every continent had long turned their attention to the sea.

By 1450 much had been accomplished and much remained undone. Daring mariners had discovered and settled most of the islands of the Pacific, the Atlantic, and the Indian Oceans. The greatest success was the trading system that united the peoples around the Indian Ocean. But no individual had yet crossed the Pacific in either direction. Even the narrower Atlantic was a barrier that kept the peoples of the Americas, Europe, and Africa in ignorance of each other's existence. The inhabitants of Australia were likewise completely cut off from contact with the rest of humanity. All this was about to change.

The Pacific Ocean

The vast distances Polynesian peoples voyaged out of sight of land across the Pacific Ocean are one of the most impressive feats in maritime history before 1450 (see Map 17.1). Though they left no written records, it is now clear that over several thousand years intrepid mariners from the Malay° Peninsula of Southeast Asia explored and settled the island chains of the East Indies and moved onto New Guinea and the smaller islands of Melanesia°. Beginning some time before the

---

Malay (May-LAY) **Melanesia** (mel-uh-NEE-zhuh)

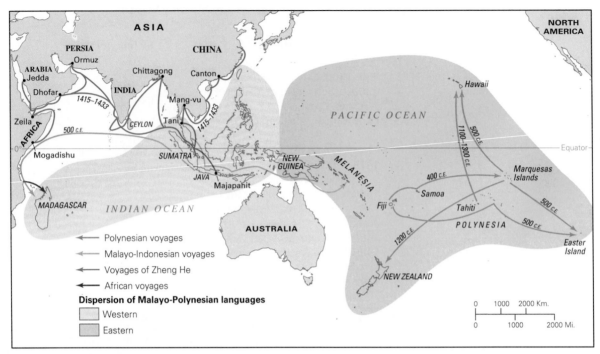

Map 17.1   Exploration and Settlement in the Indian and Pacific Oceans Before 1500   Over many centuries mariners originating in Southeast Asia gradually colonized the islands of the Pacific and Indian Oceans. The Chinese voyages led by Zheng He in the fifteenth century were lavish official expeditions.

Common Era (C.E.), a new wave of expansion from the area of Fiji brought the first humans to the islands of the central Pacific known as Polynesia. The easternmost of the Marquesas° Islands were reached about 400 C.E.; Easter Island, 2,200 miles (3,540 kilometers) off the coast of South America, was settled a century later. From the Marquesas Polynesian sailors sailed to the Hawaiian Islands as early as 500 C.E. They settled New Zealand about 1200. Then between 1100 and 1300, new voyages northward from Tahiti to Hawaii brought more Polynesian settlers across the more than 2,000 nautical miles (4,000 kilometers) to Hawaii.

Until recent decades some historians argued that Polynesians could have reached the eastern Pacific islands only by accident because they lacked navigational devices to plot their way. Others wondered how Polynesians could have overcome the difficulties, illustrated by Magellan's flagship, *Trinidad*, of sailing eastward across the Pacific. In 1947 one energetic amateur historian of the sea, Thor Heyerdahl°, argued that Easter Island and Hawaii were actually settled from the Americas. He

sought to prove his theory by sailing his balsawood raft *Kon Tiki* westward from Peru.

Although some Amerindian voyagers did use ocean currents to travel northward from Peru to Mexico between 300 and 900 C.E., there is now considerable evidence that the settlement of the islands of the eastern Pacific was the result of planned expansion by Polynesian mariners. The first piece of evidence is the fact that the languages of these islanders are all closely related to the languages of the western Pacific and ultimately to those of Malaya. The second is the finding that accidental voyages could not have brought sufficient numbers of men and women for founding a new colony along with all the plants and domesticated animals that were basic to other Polynesian islands.

In 1976 a Polynesian crew led by Ben Finney used traditional navigational methods to sail an ocean canoe from Hawaii south to Tahiti. The *Hokulea* was a 62-foot-long (19-meter-long) double canoe patterned after old oceangoing canoes that sometimes were as long as 120 feet (37 meters). Not only did the *Hokulea* prove seaworthy, but, powered by an inverted triangular sail and steered by paddles (not by a rudder), it was able to sail across the winds at a sharp enough angle to make the dif-

---

Marquesas (mar-KAY-suhs)   **Heyerdahl** (HIGH-uhr-dahl)

Polynesian Canoes   Pacific Ocean mariners sailing canoes such as these, shown in an eighteenth-century painting, made epic voyages of exploration and settlement. A large platform connects two canoes at the left, providing more room for the members of the expedition, and a sail supplements the paddlers. ("Tereoboo, King of Owyhee, bringing presents to Captain Cook," D. L. Ref. p. xx 2f. 35. Courtesy, The Dixon Library, State Library of New South Wales)

ficult voyage, just as ancient mariners must have done. Perhaps even more remarkable, the *Hokulea*'s crew was able to navigate to their destination using only their observation of the currents, stars, and evidence of land.

The Indian Ocean

While Polynesian mariners were settling Pacific islands, other Malayo-Indonesians were sailing westward across the Indian Ocean and colonizing the large island of Madagascar off the southeastern coast of Africa. These voyages continued through the fifteenth century. To this day the inhabitants of Madagascar speak Malayo-Polynesian languages. However, part of the island's population is descended from Africans who had crossed the 600 miles (1,000 kilometers) from the mainland to Madagascar, most likely in the centuries just before 1500.

Other peoples had been using the Indian Ocean for trade since ancient times. The landmasses of Southeast Asia and eastern Africa that enclose the Indian Ocean's sides, and the Indian subcontinent that juts into its middle, provided coasts that seafarers might safely follow

and coves for protection. Moreover, seasonal winds known as monsoons are so predictable and steady that navigation using sailing vessels called dhows° was less difficult and dangerous in ancient times than elsewhere.

The rise of medieval Islam gave Indian Ocean trade an important boost. The great Muslim cities of the Middle East provided a demand for valuable commodities. Even more important were the networks of Muslim traders that tied the region together. Muslim traders shared a common language, ethic, and law and actively spread their religion to distant trading cities. By 1400 there were Muslim trading communities all around the Indian Ocean.

The Indian Ocean traders operated largely independently of the empires and states that they served, but in East Asia imperial China's rulers were growing more and more interested in these wealthy ports of trade. In 1368 the Ming dynasty overthrew Mongol rule and began expansionist policies to reestablish China's predominance and prestige abroad.

Having restored Chinese dominance in East Asia, the Ming next moved to establish direct contacts with

---

dhow (dow)

Chinese Junk   This modern drawing shows how much larger one of Zheng He's ships was than one of Vasco da Gama's vessels. Watertight interior bulkheads made junks the most seaworthy large ships of the fifteenth century. Sails made of pleated bamboo matting hung from the junk's masts and a stern rudder provided steering. European ships of exploration, though smaller, were faster and more maneuverable. (Dugald Stermer)

the peoples around the Indian Ocean. In choosing to send out seven imperial fleets between 1405 and 1433, the Ming may have been motivated partly by curiosity. The fact that most of the ports the fleets visited were important in the Indian Ocean trade suggests that enhancing China's commerce was also a motive. Yet because the expeditions were far larger than needed for exploration or promoting trade, their main purpose probably was to inspire awe of Ming power and achievements.

The Ming expeditions into the Indian Ocean basin were launched on a scale that reflected imperial China's resources and importance. The first consisted of sixty-two specially built "treasure ships," large Chinese junks each about 300 feet long by 150 feet wide (90 by 45 meters). There were also at least a hundred smaller vessels, most of which were larger than the flagship in which Columbus later sailed across the Atlantic. Each treasure ship had nine masts, twelve sails, many decks, and a carrying capacity of 3,000 tons (six times the capacity of Columbus's entire fleet). One expedition carried over 27,000 individuals, including infantry and cavalry troops. The ships would have been armed with small cannon, but in most Chinese sea battles arrows from highly accurate crossbows dominated the fighting.

At the command of the expeditions was Admiral **Zheng He°** (1371–1435). A Chinese Muslim with ancestral connections to the Persian Gulf, Zheng was a fitting emissary to the increasingly Muslim-dominated Indian Ocean basin. The expeditions carried other Arabic-speaking Chinese as interpreters.

One of these interpreters kept a journal recording the customs, dress, and beliefs of the people visited, along with the trade, towns, and animals of their countries. Among his observations were these: exotic animals such as the black panther of Malaya and the tapir of Sumatra; beliefs in legendary "corpse headed barbarians" whose heads left their bodies at night and caused infants to die; the division of coastal Indians into five classes, which correspond to the four Hindu varna and a separate Muslim class; the fact that traders in the rich Indian trading port of Calicut° could perform error-free calculations by counting on their fingers and toes rather than using the Chinese abacus. After his return, the interpreter went on tour in China, telling of these exotic places and "how far the majestic virtue of [China's] imperial dynasty extended."[1]

Zheng He (jung huh)   **Calicut** (KAL-ih-kut)

The Chinese "treasure ships" carried rich silks, precious metals, and other valuable goods intended as gifts for distant rulers. In return those rulers sent back gifts of equal or greater value to the Chinese emperor. Although the main purpose of these exchanges was diplomatic, they also stimulated trade between China and its southern neighbors. For that reason they were welcomed by Chinese merchants and manufacturers. Yet commercial profits could not have offset the huge cost of the fleets.

Interest in new contacts was not confined to the Chinese side. In 1415–1416 at least three trading cities on the Swahili° Coast of East Africa sent delegations to China. The delegates from one of them, Malindi, presented the emperor of China with a giraffe, creating quite a stir among the normally reserved imperial officials. Such African delegations may have encouraged more contacts, for the next three of Zheng's voyages were extended to the African coast. Unfortunately no documents record how Africans and Chinese reacted to each other during these historic meetings between 1417 and 1433. It appears that China's lavish gifts stimulated the Swahili market for silk and porcelain. An increase in Chinese imports of pepper from southern Asian lands also resulted from these expeditions.

Had the Ming court wished to promote trade for the profit of its merchants, Chinese fleets might have continued to play a dominant role in Indian Ocean trade. But some high Chinese officials opposed increased contact with peoples whom they regarded as barbarians with no real contribution to make to China. Such opposition caused a suspension in the voyages from 1424 to 1431, and after the final expedition of 1432 to 1433, no new fleets were sent out. Later Ming emperors focused their attention on internal matters in their vast empire. China's withdrawal left a power vacuum in the Indian Ocean.

The Atlantic Ocean

The greatest mariners of the Atlantic in the early Middle Ages were the Vikings. These northern European raiders and pirates used their small, open ships to attack coastal European settlements for several centuries. They also discovered and settled one island after another in the North Atlantic during these warmer than usual centuries. Like the Polynesians, the Vikings had neither maps nor navigational devices, but they managed to find their way wonderfully well using their knowledge of the heavens and the seas.

The Vikings first settled Iceland in 770. From there some moved on to Greenland in 982, and by accident one group sighted North America in 986. Fifteen years later Leif Ericsson established a short-lived Viking settlement on the island of Newfoundland, which he called Vinland. When a colder climate returned after 1200, the northern settlements in Greenland went into decline, and Vinland became only a mysterious place mentioned in Norse sagas.

Some southern Europeans also used the maritime skills they had acquired in the Mediterranean and coastal Atlantic to explore the Atlantic. In 1291 two Vivaldo brothers from Genoa set out to sail through the South Atlantic and around Africa to India. They were never heard of again. Other Genoese and Portuguese expeditions into the Atlantic in the fourteenth century discovered (and settled) the islands of Madeira°, the Azores°, and the Canaries.

There is also written evidence of African voyages of exploration in the Atlantic in this period. The celebrated Syrian geographer al-Umari (1301–1349) relates that when Mansa Kankan Musa°, the ruler of the West African empire of Mali, passed through Egypt on his lavish pilgrimage to Mecca in 1324, he told of voyages to cross the Atlantic undertaken by his predecessor, Mansa Muhammad. Muhammad had sent out four hundred vessels with men and supplies, telling them, "Do not return until you have reached the other side of the ocean or if you have exhausted your food or water." After a long time one canoe returned, reporting the others had been swept away by a "violent current in the middle of the sea." Muhammad himself then set out at the head of a second, even larger, expedition, from which no one returned.

In addition to sailing up the Pacific coast, early Amerindian voyagers from South America also colonized the West Indies. By the year 1000 Amerindians known as the **Arawak**° had moved up from the small islands of the Lesser Antilles (Barbados, Martinique, Guadaloupe) and into the Greater Antilles (Cuba, Hispaniola, Jamaica, and Puerto Rico) as well as into the Bahamas (see Map 17.2). Their route was followed in later centuries by the Carib, who by the late fifteenth century had overrun most Arawak settlements in the Lesser Antilles and were raiding parts of the Greater Antilles. From the West Indies Arawak and Carib also undertook voyages to the North American mainland.

Swahili (swah-HEE-lee)

Madeira (muh-DEER-uh)   Azores (A-zorz)
Mansa Kankan Musa (MAHN-suh KAHN-kahn MOO-suh)
Arawak (AR-uh-wahk)

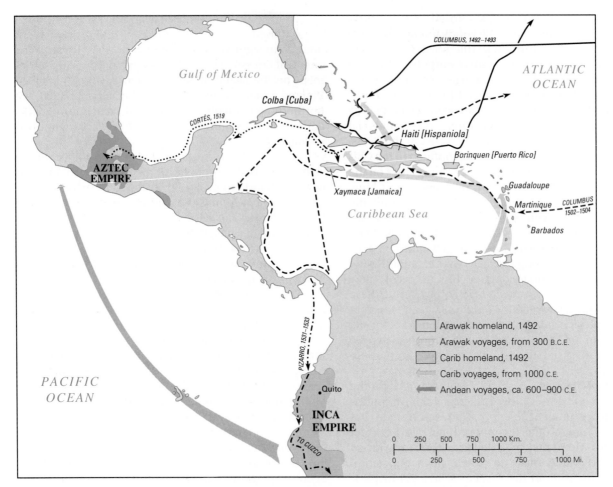

Map 17.2 Middle America to 1533 Early Amerindian voyages from South America brought new settlers to the West Indies and western Mexico. The arrival of Europeans in 1492 soon led to the conquest and depopulation of Amerindians.

EUROPEAN EXPANSION, 1400–1550

The preceding survey shows that maritime expansion occurred in many parts of the world before 1450. The epic sea voyages sponsored by the Iberian kingdoms of Portugal and Spain are of special interest because they began a maritime revolution that profoundly altered the course of world history. The Portuguese and Spanish expeditions ended the isolation of the Americas and increased global interaction. The influence in world affairs of the Iberians and other Europeans who followed them overseas rose steadily in the centuries after 1500.

Iberian overseas expansion was the product of two related phenomena. First, Iberian rulers had strong economic, religious, and political motives to expand their contacts and increase their dominance. Second, improvements in their maritime and military technologies gave them the means to master treacherous and unfamiliar ocean environments, seize control of existing maritime trade routes, and conquer new lands.

Background to European Expansion

Why did Iberian kingdoms decide to sponsor voyages of exploration in the fifteenth century? Part of the answer lies in the individual ambitions and adventurous personalities of these states' leaders. Another part of the answer can be found in long-term tendencies in Europe and the Mediterranean. In many ways these voyages continued four trends evident in the Latin West since about the year 1000: (1) the revival of urban life and trade, (2) a struggle with Islamic powers for dominance of the Mediterranean that mixed religious motives with the desire for trade with distant lands, (3) growing intellectual curiosity about the outside world, and (4) a peculiarly European alliance between merchants and rulers.

The city-states of northern Italy took the lead in all of these developments. By 1450 they had well established trade links to northern Europe, the Indian Ocean, and the Black Sea, and their merchant princes had also sponsored an intellectual and artistic Renaissance. But there were two reasons why Italian states did not take the lead in exploring the Atlantic, even after the expansion of the Ottoman Empire disrupted their trade to the East and led other Christian Europeans to launch new religious wars against the Ottomans in 1396 and 1444. The first was that the trading states of Venice and Genoa preferred to continue the system of alliances with the Muslims that had given their merchants privileged access to the lucrative trade from the East. The second was that the ships of the Mediterranean were ill suited to the more violent weather of the Atlantic. However, many individual Italians played leading roles in the Atlantic explorations.

In contrast, the special history and geography of the Iberian kingdoms led them in a different direction. Part of that special history was centuries of anti-Muslim warfare that dated back to the eighth century when Muslim forces overran most of Iberia. By about 1250 the Iberian kingdoms of Portugal, Castile, and Aragon had conquered all the Muslim lands in Iberia except the southern kingdom of Granada. United by a dynastic marriage in 1469, Castile and Aragon conquered Granada in 1492. These territories were gradually amalgamated into Spain, sixteenth-century Europe's most powerful state.

Christian militancy continued to be an important motive for both Portugal and Spain in their overseas ventures. But the Iberian rulers and their adventurous subjects were also seeking material returns. With only a modest share of the Mediterranean trade, they were much more willing than the Italians to take risks to find new routes through the Atlantic to the rich trades of Africa and Asia. Moreover, both were participants in the shipbuilding changes and the gunpowder revolution that were under way in Atlantic Europe. Though not centers of Renaissance learning, both were especially open to new geographical knowledge. Finally, both states were blessed with exceptional leaders.

Portuguese Voyages

Portugal's decision to invest significant resources in new exploration rested on well-established Atlantic fishing and a history of anti-Muslim warfare. When the Muslim government of Morocco in northwestern Africa showed weakness in the fifteenth century, the Portuguese went on the attack, beginning with the city of Ceuta° in 1415. This assault combined aspects of a religious crusade, a plundering expedition, and a military tournament in which young Portuguese knights displayed their bravery. The capture of this rich North African city, whose splendid homes, they reported, made those of Portugal look like pigsties, also made the Portuguese better informed about the caravans that brought gold and slaves to Ceuta from the African states south of the Sahara. Despite the capture of several more ports along Morocco's Atlantic coast, the Portuguese were unable to push inland and gain access to the gold trade. So they sought more direct contact with the gold producers by sailing down the African coast.

The attack on Ceuta was led by the young Prince Henry (1394–1460), third son of the king of Portugal. Because he devoted the rest of his life to promoting exploration of the South Atlantic, he is known as **Henry the Navigator.** His official biographer emphasized Henry's mixed motives for exploration—converting Africans to Christianity, making contact with existing Christian rulers in Africa, and launching joint crusades with them against the Ottomans. Prince Henry also wished to discover new places and hoped that such new contacts would be profitable. His initial explorations were concerned with Africa. Only later did reaching India become an explicit goal of Portuguese explorers.

Despite being called "the Navigator," Prince Henry himself never ventured much farther from home than North Africa. Instead, he founded a sort of research institute at Sagres° for studying navigation and collecting information about the lands beyond Muslim North Africa. His staff drew on the pioneering efforts of Italian merchants, especially the Genoese, who had learned some of the secrets of the trans-Saharan trade, and of fourteenth-century Jewish cartographers who used information from Arab and European sources to produce remarkably accurate sea charts and maps of distant places. Henry also oversaw the collection of new geographical information from sailors and travelers and sent out ships to explore the Atlantic. His ships established permanent contact with the islands of Madeira in 1418 and the Azores in 1439.

Ceuta (say-OO-tuh)   **Sagres** (SAH-gresh)

Map 17.3 European Exploration, 1420–1542 Portuguese and Spanish explorers showed the possibility and practicality of intercontinental maritime trade. Before 1540 European trade with Africa and Asia was much more important than that with the Americas, but after the Spanish conquest of the Aztec and Inca Empires transatlantic trade began to increase. Notice the Tordesillas line, which in theory separated the Spanish and Portuguese spheres of activity.

Henry also devoted his resources to solving the technical problems faced by mariners sailing in unknown waters and open seas. His staff studied and improved navigational instruments that had come into Europe from China and the Islamic world. These instruments included the magnetic compass, first developed in China, and the astrolabe, an instrument of Arab or Greek invention that enabled mariners to determine their location at sea by measuring the position of the sun or the stars in the night sky. Even with such instruments, however, voyages still depended most on the skill and experience of the navigators.

Another achievement of Portuguese mariners was the design of vessels appropriate for the voyages of exploration. The galleys in use in the Mediterranean were powered by large numbers of oarsmen and were impractical for long ocean voyages. The square sails of the three-masted European ships of the North Atlantic were propelled by friendly winds but could not sail at much of an angle against the wind. The voyages of exploration made use of a new vessel, the **caravel**°. Caravels were small, only one-fifth the size of the largest European ships of their day and of the large Chinese junks. Their size permitted them to enter shallow coastal waters and explore upriver, but they were strong enough to weather ocean storms. When equipped with lateen sails, caravels had great maneuverability and could sail deeply into the wind; when sporting square Atlantic sails, they had great speed. The addition of small cannon made them good fighting ships as well. The caravels' economy, speed, agility, and power justified a contemporary's claim that they were "the best ships that sailed the seas."[2]

To conquer the seas, pioneering captains had to overcome crew's fears that the South Atlantic waters were boiling hot and contained ocean currents that would prevent any ship entering them from ever returning home. It took Prince Henry fourteen years—from 1420 to 1434—to coax an expedition to venture beyond southern Morocco (see Map 17.3). The crew's fears proved unfounded, but the next stretch of coast, 800 miles (1,300 kilometers) of desert, offered little of interest to the explorers. Finally in 1444 the mariners reached the Senegal River and the well-watered and -populated lands below the Sahara beginning at what they named "Cape Verde" (Green Cape) because of its vegetation.

In the years that followed, Henry's explorers made an important addition to the maritime revolution by learning how to return speedily to Portugal. Instead of battling the prevailing northeast trade winds and currents back up the coast, they discovered that by sailing

caravel (KAR-uh-vel)

Astrolabe   This ancient navigational instrument was critical to the fifteenth-century voyages of exploration because it enabled mariners to find their locations at sea from the angle of the sun above the horizon. This unusually elaborate Italian example is from about 1500. (Museum fur Kunst und Gewerbe, Hamburg)

northwest into the Atlantic to the latitude of the Azores, ships could pick up prevailing westerly winds that would blow them back to Portugal. The knowledge that ocean winds tend to form large circular patterns helped explorers discover many other ocean routes.

To pay for the research, the ships, and the expeditions during the many decades before the voyages became profitable, Prince Henry drew partly on the income of the Order of Christ, a military religious order of which he was the governor. The Order of Christ had inherited the properties and crusading traditions of the Order of Knights Templar, which had disbanded in 1314. The Order of Christ received the exclusive right to promote Christianity in all the lands that were discovered, and the Portuguese emblazoned their ships' sails with the crusaders' red cross.

The first financial return from the voyages came from selling into slavery Africans captured by the Portuguese in raids on the northwest coast of Africa and the Canary Islands during the 1440s. The total number of Africans captured or purchased on voyages exceeded eighty thousand by the end of the century and rose steadily thereafter. However, the gold trade quickly became more important than the slave trade as the Portuguese made contact with the trading networks that

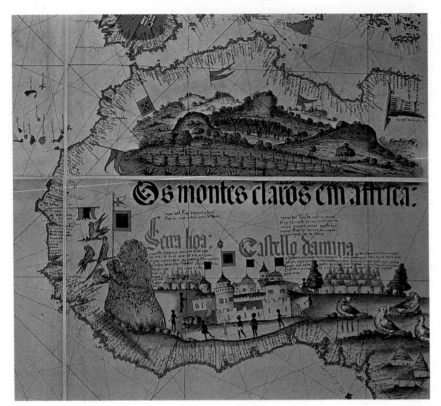

Portuguese Map of Western Africa, 1502
This map shows in great detail a section of
African coastline that Portuguese explorers
charted and named in the fifteenth century.
The cartographer illustrated the African
interior, which was almost completely unknown to Europeans, with drawings of birds
and views of coastal sights: Sierra Leone
(*Serra lioa*), named for a mountain shaped
like a lion, and the Portuguese Castle of the
Mine (*Castello damina*) on the Gold Coast.
(From the American Geographical Society Collection, University of Wisconsin–Milwaukee Library)

flourished in West Africa and reached across the Sahara.
By 1457 enough African gold was coming back to Portugal for the kingdom to issue a new gold coin called the
cruzado (crusade), another reminder of how deeply the
Portuguese entwined religious and secular motives.

By the time of Prince Henry's death in 1460, his explorers had established a secure base of operations in
the uninhabited Cape Verde Islands, explored 600 miles
(950 kilometers) of coast beyond Cape Verde, as far as
what they named Sierra Leone° (Lion Mountain). From
there they knew the coast of Africa curved sharply toward the east. It had taken the Portuguese four decades
to cover the 1,500 miles (2,400 kilometers) from Lisbon
to Sierra Leone; it took only three decades to explore the
remaining 4,000 miles (6,400 kilometers) to the southern
tip of the African continent.

The Portuguese crown continued to sponsor voyages of exploration, but speedier progress resulted from
the growing participation of private commercial interests. In 1469 a prominent Lisbon merchant named Fer-
não Gomes purchased from the Crown the privilege of
exploring 350 miles (550 kilometers) of new coast a year
for five years in return for a monopoly on the trade he

developed there. During the period of his contract,
Gomes discovered the uninhabited island of São Tomé°
on the equator; in the next century it became a major
source of sugar produced with African slave labor. He
also explored what later Europeans called the **Gold
Coast,** which became the headquarters of Portugal's
West African trade.

The final thrust down the African coast was spurred
along by the expectation of finding a passage around
Africa to the rich trade of the Indian Ocean. **Bartolomeu
Dias** was the first Portuguese explorer to round the
southern tip of Africa (in 1488) and enter the Indian
Ocean. In 1497–1498 a Portuguese expedition led by
Vasco da Gama sailed around Africa and reached India
(see Environment and Technology: Vasco da Gama's
Fleet). In 1500 ships in an expedition under Pedro Al-
vares Cabral°, while swinging wide to the west in the
South Atlantic to catch the winds that would sweep them
around southern Africa and on to India, came on the
eastern coast of South America, laying the basis for Portugal's later claim to Brazil. The gamble that Prince
Henry had begun eight decades earlier was about to pay
off handsomely.

Sierra Leone (see- ER-uh lee-OWN

São Tomé (sow toh-MAY)   **Cabral** (kah-BRAHL)

Vasco da Gama's Fleet

The four small ships that sailed from Lisbon in June 1497 for India may seem a puny fleet compared to the sixty-two Chinese vessels that Zheng He had led into the Indian Ocean ninety-five years earlier. But given the fact that China had a hundred times as many people as Portugal, Vasco da Gama's fleet represented at least as great a commitment of resources. In any event, the Portuguese expedition had a far greater impact on the course of history. Having achieved its aim of inspiring awe at China's greatness, the Chinese throne sent out no more expeditions after 1432. Although da Gama's ships seemed more odd than awesome to Indian Ocean observers, that modest fleet began a revolution in global relations.

Portugal spared no expense in ensuring that the fleet would make it to India and back. Craftsmen built extra strength into the hulls to withstand storms at the tip of Africa as powerful as the ones Dias had encountered in 1488. Also, small enough to be able to navigate any shallow harbors and rivers they might encounter, the ships were crammed with specially strengthened casks and barrels of water, wine, oil, flour, meat, and vegetables far in excess of what was required even on a voyage that would take the better part of a year to reach India. Arms and ammunition were also in abundance.

Three of da Gama's ships were rigged with square sails on two masts for speed and a lateen sail on the third mast. The fourth vessel was a caravel with lateen sails. Each ship carried three sets of sails and plenty of extra rigging so as to be able to repair any damages due to storms. The crusaders' red crosses on the sails signaled one of the expedition's motives.

The captains and crew—Portugal's most talented and experienced—received extra pay and other rewards for their service. Yet there was no expectation that the unprecedented sums spent on this expedition would bring any immediate return. According to a contemporary chronicle, the only immediate return the Portuguese monarch received was "the knowledge that some part of Ethiopia and the beginning of Lower India had been discovered." However, the scale and care of the preparations suggest that the Portuguese expected the expedition to open up profitable trade to the Indian Ocean. And so it did.

Vasco da Gama's Flagship
This vessel carried the Portuguese captain on his second expedition to India in 1505. (The Pierpont Morgan Library/Art Resource, NY)

Spanish Voyages

Portugal's century-long efforts to explore the South Atlantic are a testimony to planning and persistence. Spain's early discoveries owed more to haste and blind luck. Throughout most of the fifteenth century, the Spanish kingdoms had been preoccupied with internal affairs: completion of the reconquest of southern Iberia; amalgamation of the various dynasties; the conversion or expulsion of religious minorities. Only in the last decade of the century were Spanish monarchs ready to turn again to overseas exploration, by which time the Portuguese had already found a new route to the Indian Ocean.

The leader of their overseas mission would be **Christopher Columbus** (1451–1506), a Genoese mariner. His three voyages between 1492 and 1498 would reveal the existence of vast lands across the Atlantic, whose existence and whose inhabitants were entirely new to the "old world" peoples of Eurasia and Africa. But Columbus was frustrated rather than fulfilled by his momentous discovery, for his intention had been to find a new route to the Indian Ocean even shorter than the one the Portuguese were pioneering.

As a younger man Columbus had gained considerable experience of the South Atlantic while participating in Portuguese explorations along the African coast, but he had become convinced there was a shorter way to reach the riches of the East than the route around Africa. By his reckoning (based on a serious misreading of a ninth-century Arab authority), the Canaries were a mere 2,400 nautical miles (4,450 kilometers) from Japan. The actual distance was five times as far.

It was not easy for Columbus to find a sponsor willing to underwrite the costs of testing his theory that one could reach Asia by sailing west. Portuguese authorities twice rejected his plan, first in 1485 following a careful study and again in 1488 after Dias had established the feasibility of a route around Africa. Columbus received a more sympathetic hearing in 1486 from Castile's able ruler, Queen Isabella, but no commitment of support. After a four-year study a Castilian commission appointed by Isabella concluded that a westward sea route to the Indies rested on many questionable geographical assumptions, but Columbus's persistence finally won over the queen and her husband, King Ferdinand of Aragon. In 1492 they agreed to fund a modest expedition. Their elation at expelling the Muslims from Granada may have put them in a favorable mood.

Columbus recorded in his log that he and his mostly Spanish crew of ninety men "departed Friday the third day of August of the year 1492," toward "the regions of India." Their mission, the royal contract stated, was "to discover and acquire certain islands and mainland in the Ocean Sea." He carried letters of introduction from the Spanish sovereigns to Eastern rulers, including one to the "Grand Khan" (meaning the Chinese emperor). Also on board was a Jewish convert to Christianity whose knowledge of Arabic was expected to facilitate communication with the peoples of eastern Asia. The expedition traveled in three small ships, the *Santa María*, and two caravels, the *Santa Clara* (nicknamed the *Niña*), and a third vessel now known only by its nickname, the *Pinta*.

The expedition began well. Other attempts to explore the Atlantic west of the Azores had been impeded by unfavorable headwinds. But on earlier voyages along the African coast, Columbus had learned that he could find west-blowing winds in the latitudes of the Canaries, which is why he chose that southern route. After reaching the Canaries, he had the *Niña*'s lateen sails replaced with square sails, for he knew that from then on speed would be more important than maneuverability.

In October 1492 the expedition reached the islands of the Caribbean. Columbus insisted on calling the inhabitants "Indians" because he believed that the islands were part of the East Indies. A second voyage to the Caribbean in 1493 did nothing to change his mind. Even when, two months after Vasco da Gama reached India in 1498, Columbus first sighted the mainland of South America on a third voyage, he stubbornly insisted it was part of Asia. But by then other Europeans were convinced he had discovered islands and continents previously unknown to the Old World. Amerigo Vespucci's explorations, first on behalf of Spain and then for Portugal, led mapmakers to name the new continents "America" after him, rather than "Columbia" after Columbus.

To prevent disputes arising from their efforts to exploit their new discoveries and to spread Christianity among the people there, Spain and Portugal agreed to split the world between them. The Treaty of Tordesillas°, negotiated by the pope in 1494, drew an imaginary line down the middle of the North Atlantic Ocean. Lands east of the line in Africa and southern Asia could be claimed by Portugal; lands to the west in the Americas were reserved for Spain. Cabral's discovery of Brazil, however, gave Portugal a valid claim to the part of South America that bulged east of the line.

But if the Tordesillas line were extended around the earth, where would Spain's and Portugal's spheres of influence divide in the East? Given Europeans' ignorance of the earth's true size in 1494, it was not clear whether the Moluccas°, whose valuable spices had been a goal of the Iberian voyages, were on Portugal's or Spain's side of the line. The missing information concerned the size

---

Tordesillas (tor-duh-SEE-yuhs) **Moluccas** (muh-LOO-kuhz)

of the Pacific Ocean. By chance, in 1513 a Spanish adventurer named Vasco Núñez de Balboa° crossed the isthmus (a narrow neck of land) of Panama from the east and sighted the Pacific Ocean on the other side. And the 1519 expedition of **Ferdinand Magellan** (ca. 1480–1521) was designed to complete Columbus's interrupted westward voyage by sailing around the Americas and across the Pacific, whose vast size no European then guessed. The Moluccas turned out to lie well within Portugal's sphere, as Spain formally acknowledged in 1529.

Magellan's voyage laid the basis for Spanish colonization of the Philippine Islands after 1564. Nor did Magellan's death prevent him from being considered the first person to encircle the globe, for a decade earlier he had sailed from Europe to the East Indies as part of an expedition sponsored by his native Portugal. His two voyages took him across the Tordesillas line, through the separate spheres claimed by Portugal and Spain—at least until other Europeans began demanding a share. Of course, in the year 1500 European claims were largely theoretical. Portugal and Spain had only modest settlements overseas.

Although Columbus failed to find a new route to the East, the consequences of his voyages for European expansion were momentous. Those who followed in his wake laid the basis for Spain's large colonial empires in the Americas and for the empires of other European nations. In turn, these empires promoted, among the four Atlantic continents, the growth of a major new trading network whose importance rivaled and eventually surpassed that of the Indian Ocean network. The more immediately important consequence was Portugal's entry into the Indian Ocean, which quickly led to a major European presence and profit. Both the eastward and the westward voyages of exploration marked a tremendous expansion of Europe's role in world history.

ENCOUNTERS WITH EUROPE, 1450–1550

European actions alone did not determine the consequences of the new contacts that Iberian mariners had opened. The ways in which Africans, Asians, and Amerindians perceived their new visitors and interacted with them also influenced their future relations. Some welcomed the Europeans as potential allies; others

Balboa (bal-BOH-uh)

viewed them as rivals or enemies. In general, Africans and Asians had little difficulty in recognizing the benefits and dangers that European contacts might bring. However, the long isolation of the Amerindians from the rest of the world added to the strangeness of their encounter with the Spanish and made them more vulnerable to the unfamiliar diseases that these explorers inadvertently introduced.

Western Africa

Many Africans along the West African coast were eager for trade with the Portuguese. It would give them new markets for their exports and access to imports cheaper than those that reached them through the middlemen of the overland routes to the Mediterranean. This reaction was evident along the Gold Coast of West Africa, first visited by the Portuguese in 1471. Miners in the hinterland had long sold their gold to African traders, who took it to the trading cities along the southern edge of the Sahara, where it was sold to traders who had crossed the desert from North Africa. Recognizing that they might get more favorable terms from the new sea visitors, coastal Africans were ready to negotiate with the royal representative of Portugal who arrived in 1482 seeking permission to erect a trading fort.

The Portuguese noble in charge and his officers (likely including the young Christopher Columbus, who had entered Portuguese service in 1476) were eager to make a proper impression. They dressed in their best clothes, erected and decorated a reception platform, celebrated a Catholic Mass, and signaled the start of negotiations with trumpets, tambourines, and drums. The African king, Caramansa, staged his entrance with equal ceremony, arriving with a large retinue of attendants and musicians. Through an African interpreter, the two leaders exchanged flowery speeches pledging goodwill and mutual benefit. Caramansa then gave his permission for a small trading fort to be built, assured, he said, by the appearance of these royal delegates that they were honorable persons, unlike the "few, foul, and vile" Portuguese visitors of the previous decade.

Neither side made a show of force, but the Africans' upper hand was evident in Caramansa's warning that if the Portuguese failed to be peaceful and honest traders, he and his people would simply move away, depriving their post of food and trade. Trade at the post of Saint George of the Mine (later called Elmina) enriched both sides. From there the Portuguese crown was soon purchasing gold equal to one-tenth of the world's production at the time. In return, Africans received large quantities of goods that Portuguese ships brought from Asia, Europe, and other parts of Africa.

Afro-Portuguese Ivory   A skilled ivory carver from the kingdom of Benin probably made this saltcellar. Intended for a European market, it depicts a Portuguese ship on the cover and Portuguese nobles around the base. However European the subject, the craftsmanship is typical of Benin. (Courtesy of the Trustees of the British Museum)

Early contacts generally involved a mixture of commercial, military, and religious interests. Some African rulers were quick to appreciate that the European firearms could be a useful addition to their spears and arrows in conflicts with their enemies. Because African religions did not presume to have a monopoly on religious knowledge, coastal rulers were also willing to test the value of Christian practices, which the Portuguese eagerly promoted. The rulers of Benin and Kongo, the two largest coastal kingdoms, invited Portuguese missionaries and soldiers to accompany them into battle to test the Christians' religion along with their muskets.

After a century of aggressive expansion, the kingdom of Benin in the Niger Delta was near the peak of its

power when it first encountered the Portuguese. Its oba (king) presided over an elaborate bureaucracy from a spacious palace in his large capital city, also known as Benin. In response to a Portuguese visit in 1486, the oba sent an ambassador to Portugal to learn more about the homeland of these strangers. Then he established a royal monopoly on trade with the Portuguese, selling pepper and ivory tusks (to be taken back to Portugal) as well as stone beads, textiles, and prisoners of war (to be resold at Elmina). In return, the Portuguese merchants provided Benin with copper and brass, fine textiles, glass beads, and a horse for the king's royal procession. In the early sixteenth century, as the demand for slaves for the Portuguese sugar plantations on the nearby island of São Tomé grew, the oba first raised the price of slaves and then imposed restrictions that limited their sale.

Portuguese efforts to persuade the king and nobles of Benin to accept the Catholic faith ultimately failed. Early kings showed some interest, but after 1538 the rulers declined to receive further missionaries. They also closed the market in male slaves for the rest of the sixteenth century. Exactly why Benin chose to limit its contacts with the Portuguese is uncertain, but the rulers clearly had the power to control how much interaction they wanted.

Farther south, on the lower Congo River, relations between the kingdom of Kongo and the Portuguese began similarly but had a quite different outcome. Like the oba of Benin, the *manikongo*° (king of Kongo) sent delegates to Portugal, established a royal monopoly on trade with the Portuguese, and expressed interest in missionary teachings. Deeply impressed with the new religion, the royal family made Catholicism the kingdom's official faith. But Kongo, lacking ivory and pepper, had less to trade than Benin. So to acquire the goods brought by Portugal and to pay the costs of the missionaries, it had to sell more and more slaves.

Soon the manikongo began to lose his royal monopoly over the slave trade. In 1526 the Christian manikongo, Afonso I (r. 1506–ca. 1540), wrote to his royal "brother," the king of Portugal, begging for his help in stopping the trade because unauthorized Kongolese were kidnapping and selling people, even members of good families. Afonso's appeal that contacts be limited to "some priests and a few people to teach in the schools, and no other goods except wine and flour for the holy sacrament" received no reply. Other subjects took advantage of the manikongo's weakness to rebel against his authority. Indeed, after 1540 the major part of the slave trade from this part of Africa moved farther south.

manikongo (mah-NEE-KONG-goh)

Eastern Africa

Different still were the reactions of the Muslim rulers of the trading coastal states of eastern Africa. As Vasco da Gama's fleet sailed up the coast in 1498, most rulers gave the Portuguese a cool reception, suspicious of the intentions of these visitors who painted crusaders' crosses on their sails. But the ruler of one of the cities, Malindi, saw in the Portuguese an ally who could help him expand their trading position and provided da Gama with a pilot to guide him to India. The suspicions of most rulers were justified seven years later when a Portuguese war fleet bombarded and looted most of the coastal cities of eastern Africa in the name of Christ and commerce, though they spared Malindi.

Another eastern African state that saw potential benefit in an alliance with the Portuguese was Christian Ethiopia. In the fourteenth and early fifteenth centuries, Ethiopia faced increasing conflicts with Muslim states along the Red Sea. Emboldened by the rise of the Ottoman Turks, who had conquered Egypt in 1517 and launched a major fleet in the Indian Ocean to counter the Portuguese, the talented warlord of the Muslim state of Adal launched a furious assault on Ethiopia. Adal's decisive victory in 1529 reduced the Christian kingdom to a precarious state. At that point Ethiopia's contacts with the Portuguese became crucial.

For decades, delegations from Portugal and Ethiopia had been exploring a possible alliance between their states based on their mutual adherence to Christianity. A key figure was Queen Helena of Ethiopia, who acted as regent for her young sons after her husband's death in 1478. In 1509 Helena sent a letter to "our very dear and well-beloved brother," the king of Portugal, along with a gift of two tiny crucifixes said to be made of wood from the cross on which Christ had died in Jerusalem. In her letter she proposed an alliance of her land army and Portugal's fleet against the Turks. No such alliance was completed by the time Helena died in 1522. But as Ethiopia's situation grew increasingly desperate, renewed appeals for help were made.

Finally a small Portuguese force commanded by Vasco da Gama's son Christopher reached Ethiopia in 1539, at a time when what was left of the empire was being held together by another woman ruler. With Portuguese help the queen rallied the Ethiopians to renew their struggle. Christopher da Gama was captured and tortured to death, but the Muslim forces lost heart when their leader was mortally wounded in a later battle. Portuguese aid helped the Ethiopian kingdom save itself from extinction, but a permanent alliance faltered because Ethiopian rulers refused to transfer their Christian affiliation from the patriarch of Alexandria to the Latin patriarch of Rome (the pope) as the Portuguese wanted.

As these examples illustrate, African encounters with the Portuguese before 1550 varied considerably, as much because of the strategies and leadership of particular African states as because of Portuguese policies. Africans and Portuguese might become royal brothers, bitter opponents, or partners in a mutually profitable trade, but Europeans remained a minor presence in most of Africa in 1550. By then the Portuguese had become far more interested in the Indian Ocean trade.

Indian Ocean States

Vasco da Gama's arrival on the Malabar Coast of India in May 1498 did not make a great impression on the citizens of Calicut. After more than ten months at sea, many members of the crew were in ill health. And da Gama's four small ships were far less imposing than the Chinese fleets of gigantic junks that had called at Calicut sixty-five years earlier and no larger than many of the dhows that filled the harbor of this rich and important trading city. The *samorin* (ruler) of Calicut and his Muslim officials showed mild interest in the Portuguese as new trading partners, but the gifts da Gama had brought for the samorin evoked derisive laughter. Twelve pieces of fairly ordinary striped cloth, four scarlet hoods, six hats, and six wash basins seemed inferior goods to those accustomed to the luxuries of the Indian Ocean trade. When da Gama tried to defend his gifts as those of an explorer, not a rich merchant, the samorin cut him short, asking whether he had come to discover men or stones: "If he had come to discover men, as he said, why had he brought nothing?"

Coastal rulers soon discovered that the Portuguese had no intention of remaining poor competitors in the rich trade of the Indian Ocean. Upon da Gama's return to Portugal in 1499 the jubilant King Manuel styled himself "Lord of the Conquest, Navigation, and Commerce of Ethiopia, Arabia, Persia, and India," setting forth the ambitious scope of his plans. Previously the Indian Ocean had been an open sea, used by merchants (and pirates) of all the surrounding coasts. Now the Portuguese crown intended to make it Portugal's sea, the private property of the Portuguese alone, which others might use only on Portuguese terms.

The ability of little Portugal to assert control over the Indian Ocean stemmed from the superiority of its ships and weapons over the smaller and lightly armed merchant dhows. In 1505 the Portuguese fleet of 81 ships and some 7,000 men bombarded Swahili Coast cities. Next on the list were Indian ports. Goa, on the west coast of India, fell to a well-armed fleet in 1510, becoming the base from which the Portuguese menaced the trading

Portuguese in India In the sixteenth century Portuguese men moved to the Indian Ocean basin to work as administrators and traders. This Indo-Portuguese drawing from about 1540 shows a Portuguese man speaking to an Indian woman, perhaps making a proposal of marriage. (Ms. 1889, c. 97, Biblioteca Casanateunse Rome. Photo: Humberto Nicoletti Serra)

cities of Gujarat° to the north and Calicut and other Malabar Coast cities to the south. The port of Hormuz, controlling the entry to the Persian Gulf, was taken in 1515. Aden, at the entrance to the Red Sea, with its intricate natural defenses was able to preserve its independence. The addition of the Gujarati port of Diu in 1535 consolidated Portuguese dominance of the western Indian Ocean.

Meanwhile, Portuguese explorers had been reconnoitering the Bay of Bengal and the waters farther east. The independent city of Malacca° on the strait between the Malay Peninsula and Sumatra became the focus of their attention. During the fifteenth century Malacca had become the main entrepôt° (a place where goods are stored or deposited and from which they are distributed) for the trade from China and Japan, from India, and from the Southeast Asian mainland and the Moluccas. Among the city's more than 100,000 residents an early Portuguese counted eighty-four different languages, including those of merchants from as far west as Cairo, Ethiopia, and the Swahili Coast of East Africa. Many non-Muslim residents supported letting the Portuguese join this cosmopolitan trading community, perhaps to offset the growing solidarity of Muslim traders. In

1511, however, the Portuguese seized this strategic trading center with a force of a thousand fighting men, including three hundred recruited in southern India.

Force was not always necessary. On the China coast local officials and merchants interested in profitable new trade with the Portuguese persuaded the imperial government to allow the Portuguese to establish a trading post at Macao° in 1557. Operating from Macao, Portuguese ships nearly monopolized the trade between China and Japan.

In the Indian Ocean the Portuguese used their control of the major port cities to enforce an even larger trading monopoly. They required all spices to be carried in Portuguese ships, as well as all goods on the major ocean routes such as between Goa and Macao. In addition, the Portuguese also tried to control and tax other Indian Ocean trade by requiring all merchant ships entering and leaving one of their ports to carry a Portuguese passport and to pay customs duties. Portuguese patrols seized vessels that attempted to avoid these monopolies, confiscated their cargoes, and either killed the captain and crew or sentenced them to forced labor.

Reactions to this power grab varied. Like the emperors of China, the Mughal° emperors of India largely ignored Portugal's maritime intrusions, seeing their interests as maintaining control over their vast land possessions. The Ottomans responded more aggressively. From 1501 to 1509 they supported Egypt's fleet of fifteen thousand men against the Christian intruders. Then, having absorbed Egypt into their empire, the Ottomans sent another large expedition against the Portuguese in 1538. Both expeditions failed because the Ottoman galleys were no match for the faster, better-armed Portuguese vessels in the open ocean. However, the Ottomans retained the advantage in the Red Sea and Persian Gulf, where they had many ports of supply.

The smaller trading states of the region were even less capable of challenging Portuguese domination head on, since their mutual rivalry impeded the formation of any common front. Some chose to cooperate with the Portuguese as the best way to maintain their prosperity and security. Others engaged in evasion and resistance. Two examples illustrate the range of responses among Indian Ocean peoples.

The merchants of Calicut put up some of the most sustained local resistance. In retaliation the Portuguese embargoed all trade with Aden, Calicut's principal trading partner, and centered their trade on the port of Cochin, which had once been a dependency of Calicut. Some Calicut merchants became adept at evading the

---

Gujarat (goo-juh-RAHT) **Malacca** (muh-LAH-kuh)
entrepôt (ON-truh-poh)

Macao (muh-COW) **Mughal** (MOO-gahl)

patrol, but the price of resistance was the shrinking of Calicut's importance as Cochin gradually became the major pepper-exporting port on the Malabar Coast.

The traders and rulers of the state of Gujarat farther north had less success in keeping the Portuguese at bay. At first they resisted Portuguese attempts at monopoly and in 1509 joined Egypt's failed effort to sweep the Portuguese from the Arabian Sea. But in 1535, finding his state at a military disadvantage due to Mughal attacks, the ruler of Gujarat made the fateful decision to allow the Portuguese to build a fort at Diu in return for their support. Once established, the Portuguese gradually extended their control, so that by midcentury they were licensing and taxing all Gujarati ships. Even after the Mughals (who were Muslims) took control of Gujarat in 1572, the Mughal emperor Akbar permitted the Portuguese to continue their maritime monopoly in return for allowing one pilgrim ship a year to sail to Mecca without paying the Portuguese any fee.

The Portuguese never gained complete control of the Indian Ocean trade, but their domination of key ports and the main trade routes during the sixteenth century brought them considerable profit, which they sent back to Europe in the form of spices and other luxury goods. The effects were dramatic. The Portuguese sold the large quantities of pepper that they exported for less than the price charged by Venice and Genoa for pepper obtained through Egyptian middlemen, thus breaking the Italian cities' monopoly.

In Asia the consequences were equally startling. Asian and East African traders were at the mercy of Portuguese warships, but their individual responses affected their fates. Some were devastated. Others prospered by meeting the Portuguese demands or evading their patrols. Because the Portuguese were ocean-based, they had little impact on the Asian and African mainland, in sharp contrast to what was occurring in the Americas.

The Americas

In the Americas the Spanish established a vast *territorial* empire, in contrast to the *trading* empires the Portuguese created in Africa and Asia. This outcome had little to do with differences between the two Iberian kingdoms, except for the fact that the Spanish kingdoms had somewhat greater resources to draw on. The Spanish and Portuguese monarchies had similar motives for expansion and used identical ships and weapons. Rather, the isolation of the Amerindian peoples made their responses to outside contacts different from the responses of peoples in Africa and the Indian Ocean cities. In dealing with the small communities in the Caribbean, the first European settlers resorted to conquest and plunder rather than trade. This practice was later extended to the more powerful Amerindian kingdoms on the American mainland. The spread of deadly new diseases among the Amerindians after 1518 weakened their ability to resist.

The first Amerindians to encounter Columbus were the Arawak of Hispaniola (modern Haiti and the Dominican Republic) in the Greater Antilles and the Bahamas to the north (see Map 17.2). They cultivated maize (corn), cassava (a tuber), sweet potatoes, and hot peppers, as well as cotton and tobacco, and they met their other material needs from the sea and wild plants. Although they were skilled at mining and working gold, the Arawak did not trade gold over long distances as Africans did, and they had no iron. The Arawak at first extended a cautious welcome to the Spanish but were unprepared to sell them large quantities of gold. Instead, they told Columbus exaggerated stories about gold in other places to persuade him to move on.

When Columbus made his second trip to Hispaniola, in 1493, he brought with him several hundred settlers from southern Iberia who hoped to make their fortune and missionaries who were eager to persuade the Indians to accept Christianity. The settlers stole gold

Arawak Women Making Tortillas This sixteenth-century woodcut depicts techniques of food preparation in the West Indies. The woman at the left grinds cornmeal on a *metate*. The woman in the center pats cornmeal dough flat and fries the tortillas. The third woman serves tortillas with a bowl of stew. (Courtesy of the John Carter Brown Library at Brown University)

European Male Sexual Dominance Overseas

European expansion and colonization were overwhelmingly the work of men. Missionaries chose to remain celibate; other men did not, as these two letters make clear. The first letter, dated 1495, is from Michele de Cuneo, an officer on Columbus's second voyage across the Atlantic.

While I was in the boat I captured a very beautiful Carib woman, whom the said Lord Admiral [Columbus] gave to me, and with whom, having taken her into my cabin, she being naked according to their custom, I conceived desire to take pleasure. I wanted to put my desire into execution but she did not want it and treated me with her finger nails in such a manner that I wished I had never begun. But seeing that, (to tell you the end of it all), I took a rope and thrashed her well, for which she raised such unheard of screams that you would not have believed your ears. Finally we came to an agreement in such manner that I can tell you that she seemed to have been brought up in a school of harlots.

The second letter, dated 1550, is from an Italian Jesuit missionary in India to Ignatius Loyola, the founder of the Society of Jesus (the Jesuits), in Rome.

Your reverence must know that the sin of licentiousness is so widespread in these regions [India] that no check is placed upon it, which leads to great inconveniences, and to great disrespect of the sacraments. I say this of the Portuguese, who have adopted the vices and customs of the land without reserve, including the evil custom of buying droves of slaves, male and female, just as if they were sheep, large and small. There are countless men who buy droves of girls and sleep with all of them, and subsequently sell them. There are innumerable married settlers who have four, eight, or ten female slaves and sleep with them, as is common knowledge. This is carried to such excess that there was one man in Malacca who had twenty-four women of various races, all of whom were his slaves, and all of whom he enjoyed. I quote this city because it is a thing that everybody knows. Most men, as soon as they can afford to buy a female slave, almost invariably use her as a girl-friend (*amiga*), besides many other dishonesties, in my poor understanding.

What circumstances made it nearly impossible for the women in question to resist the European men's advances? What phrases in the letters suggest that the writers attribute some responsibility for these encounters to the sexual license of the women involved? Are such inferences credible?

Source: The first letter is reprinted from Samuel Eliot Morison, trans. and ed., *Journals and Other Documents in the Life and Voyages of Christopher Columbus* (New York: Heritage Press, 1963), 212. The second letter is from C. R. Boxer, *The Portuguese Seaborne Empire, 1415–1825* (New York: Knopf, 1969). Copyright © 1969 by C. R. Boxer. Reprinted by permission of Alfred A. Knopf, Inc.

---

ornaments, confiscated food, and raped women (see Society and Culture: European Male Sexual Dominance Overseas), provoking the Hispaniola Arawak to war in 1495. In this and later conflicts, horses and body armor gave the Spaniards a great advantage. Tens of thousands of Arawak were slaughtered. Those who survived were forced to pay a heavy tax in gold, spun cotton, and food. Any who failed to meet the quotas were condemned to forced labor. Meanwhile, the cattle, pigs, and goats introduced by the settlers devoured the Arawak's food crops, causing deaths from famine and disease. A governor appointed by the Spanish crown in 1502 forced the Arawak remaining on Hispaniola to be laborers under the control of Spanish settlers.

The actions of the Spanish in the Antilles were reflections of Spanish actions and motives during the wars against the Muslims in Spain in the previous centuries: seeking to serve God by defeating nonbelievers and placing them under Christian control—and becoming rich in the process. Individual **conquistadors**° (conquerors) extended that pattern around the Caribbean. Some attacked the Bahamas to get gold and labor as

---

conquistador (kon-KEY-stuh-dor)

Coronation of Emperor Moctezuma
This painting by an unnamed Aztec artist depicts the Aztec ruler's coronation. Moctezuma, his nose pierced by a bone, receives the crown from a prince in the palace at Tenochtitlan. (Oronz)

both became scarce on Hispaniola. Many Arawak from the Bahamas were taken to Hispaniola as slaves. Juan Ponce de León (1460–1521), who had participated in the conquest of Muslim Spain and the seizure of Hispaniola, conquered the island of Borinquen (Puerto Rico) in 1508 and then in 1513 explored southeastern Florida.

An ambitious and ruthless nobleman, **Hernán Cortés**° (1485–1547), led the most audacious expedition to the mainland. Cortés left Cuba in 1519 with six hundred fighting men and most of the island's stock of weapons to assault the Mexican mainland in search of slaves and to establish trade. But when the expedition learned of the rich Aztec Empire in central Mexico, Cortés brought to the American mainland, on a massive scale, the exploitation and conquest that had begun in the Greater Antilles.

The Aztecs themselves had conquered their vast empire only during the pervious century, and many of the Amerindians they had subjugated were far from loyal subjects. Many resented the tribute they had to pay the Aztecs, the forced labor, and the large-scale human sacrifices to the Aztec gods. Many subject people saw the Spaniards as powerful human allies against the Aztecs and gave them their support. Like the Caribbean people, the Amerindians of Mexico had no precedent by which to judge these strange visitors.

Later accounts suggest that some believed Cortés to be the legendary ruler Quetzalcoatl°, whose return to earth had been prophesied, and treated him with great deference. Another consequence of millennia of isolation was far more significant: the lack of acquired immunity to the diseases of the Old World. Smallpox was the most deadly of the early epidemics that accompanied the Spanish conquistadores. It appeared for the first time on the island of Hispaniola late in 1518. An infected member of the Cortés expedition then transmitted smallpox to Mexico in 1519, where it spread with deadly efficiency.

From his glorious capital city Tenochtitlan°, the Aztec emperor **Moctezuma**° **II** (r. 1502–1520) sent messengers to greet Cortés and figure out whether he was god or man, friend or foe. Cortés advanced steadily toward the capital, Tenochtitlan, overcoming Aztec opposition with cavalry charges and steel swords and gaining the support of thousands of Amerindian allies from among the unhappy subjects of the Aztecs. When the Spaniards were near, the emperor went out in a great procession, dressed in all his finery, to welcome Cortés with gifts and flower garlands.

Cortés (kor-TEZ)

Quetzalcoatl (ket-zahl-COH-ah-tal)
Tenochtitlan (teh-noch-TIT-lan)
Moctezuma (mock-teh-ZOO-ma)

Despite Cortés's initial promise that he came in friendship, Moctezuma quickly found himself a prisoner in his own palace. His treasury was looted, its gold melted down. Soon a battle was raging in and about the capital between the Spaniards (helped by their new Amerindian allies) and the Aztecs and their supporters. Briefly the Aztecs gained the upper hand. They destroyed half of the Spanish force and four thousand of the Spaniards' Amerindian allies, and they sacrificed to their gods fifty-three Spanish prisoners and four horses, displaying their severed heads in rows on pikes. Reinforced by troops from Cuba, Cortés was able to regain the advantage by means of Spanish cannon and clever battle strategies. The capture of Tenochtitlan in 1520 was also greatly facilitated by the spread of smallpox, which weakened and killed more of the city's defenders than died in the fighting. One source remembered that the disease "spread over the people as a great destruction." The bodies of the afficted were covered with oozing sores, and large numbers soon died. It is likely that many Amerindians as well as Europeans saw the devastating spread of this disease as due to supernatural forces.

After the capital fell, the conquistadores took over other parts of Mexico. Then some Spaniards began eyeing the vast Inca Empire, stretching nearly 3,000 miles (5,000 kilometers) south from the equator and containing half of the population in South America. The Inca had conquered the inhabitants of the Andes Mountains and the Pacific coast of South America during the previous century, and their rule was not fully accepted by all of the peoples whom they had defeated.

With the vast Pacific Ocean on one side of their realm and the sparsely inhabited Amazon forests on the other, it is not surprising that Inca rulers believed they controlled most of the world worth controlling. Theirs was a great empire with highly productive agriculture, exquisite stone cities (such as the capital, Cuzco), and rich gold and silver mines. The power of the Inca emperor was sustained by beliefs that he was descended from the Sun God and by an efficient system of roads and messengers that kept him informed about major events in the empire. Yet all was not well.

At the end of the 1520s, before even a whisper of news about the Spanish reached them, smallpox claimed countless Amerindian lives, perhaps including the Inca emperor in 1530. Even more devastating was the threat awaiting the empire from **Francisco Pizarro**° (ca. 1478–1541) and his motley band of 180 men, 37 horses, and two cannon.

With limited education and some military experience, Pizarro had come to the Americas in 1502 at the age of twenty-five to seek his fortune. He had participated in the conquest of Hispaniola and in Balboa's expedition across the isthmus of Panama. By 1520 Pizarro was a wealthy landowner and official in Panama, yet he gambled his fortune on more adventures, exploring the Pacific coast to a point south of the equator, where he learned of the riches of the Inca. With a license from the king of Spain, he set out from Panama in 1531 to conquer them.

In November 1532 Pizarro arranged to meet the new Inca emperor, **Atahualpa**° (r. 1531–1533), near the Andean city of **Cajamarca**°. With supreme boldness and brutality, Pizarro's small band of armed men seized Atahualpa off a rich litter borne by eighty nobles as it passed through an enclosed courtyard. Though surrounded by an Inca army of at least forty thousand, the Spaniards were able to use their cannon to create confusion while their swords sliced the emperor's lightly armed retainers and servants to pieces by the thousands. The strategy to replicate the earlier Spanish conquest of Mexico was working.

Noting the glee with which the Spaniards seized gold, silver, and emeralds, the captive Atahualpa offered them what he thought would satisfy even the greediest among them in exchange for his freedom: a roomful of gold and silver. But when the ransom of 13,400 pounds (6,000 kilograms) of gold and 26,000 pounds (12,000 kilograms) of silver was paid, the Spaniards gave Atahualpa a choice: he could be burned at the stake as a heathen or baptized as a Christian and then strangled. He chose the latter. His death and the Spanish occupation broke the unity of the Inca Empire.

In 1533 the Spaniards took Cuzco and from there set out to conquer and loot the rest of the empire. The defeat of a final rebellion in 1536 spelled the end of Inca rule. Five years later Pizarro himself met a violent death at the hands of Spanish rivals, but the conquest of the mainland continued. Incited by the fabulous wealth of the Aztecs and Inca, conquistadores extended Spanish conquest and exploration in South and North America, dreaming of new treasuries to loot.

Patterns of Dominance

Within fifty years of Columbus's first landing in 1492, the Spanish had located and occupied all of the major population centers of the Americas, and the penetration of the more thinly populated areas was well under way. In no

---

Pizarro (pih-ZAHR-oh)

other part of the world was European dominance so complete. Why did the peoples of the Americas suffer a fate so different from that of peoples in Africa and Asia? Why were the Spanish able to erect a vast land empire in the Americas so quickly? Three factors seem crucial.

First, long isolation from the rest of humanity made the inhabitants of the Americas vulnerable to new diseases. The unfamiliar illnesses first devastated the native inhabitants of the Caribbean islands and then spread to the mainland. Contemporaries estimated that between 25 and 50 percent of those infected with smallpox died. Repeated epidemics inhibited Amerindians' ability to regain control. Because evidence is very limited, estimates of the size of the population before Columbus's arrival vary widely, but there is no disputing the fact that the Amerindian population fell sharply during the sixteenth century. The Americas became a "widowed land," open to resettlement from across the Atlantic.

A second major factor was Spain's superior military technology. Steel swords, protective armor, and horses gave the Spaniards an advantage over their Amerindian opponents in many battles. Though few in number, muskets and cannon also gave the Spaniards a significant psychological edge. However, it should not be forgotten that the Spanish conquests depended heavily on large numbers of Amerindian allies armed with weapons the same as those of the people they defeated. But perhaps the Spaniards' most decisive military advantage came from the no-holds-barred fighting techniques they had developed during a long history of warfare at home.

The third factor in Spain's conquest of the New World was patterns previously established in the Spanish reconquest of Granada in 1492. The reconquest provided precedents for forced labor, forced conversion, and the incorporation of conquered lands into a new empire.

The same three factors help explain the quite different outcomes elsewhere. Because of centuries of contacts before 1500, Europeans, Africans, and Asians shared the same Old World diseases. Only small numbers of very isolated peoples in Africa and Asia suffered the demographic calamity that undercut Amerindians' ability to retain control of their lands. The Iberians enjoyed a military advantage at sea, as the conquest of the Indian Ocean trade routes showed, but on land they had no decisive advantage against more numerous indigenous people who were not weakened by disease. Everywhere, Iberian religious zeal to conquer non-Christians went hand in hand with a desire for riches. In Iberia and America conquest brought wealth. But in Africa and Asia, where existing trading networks were already well established, Iberian desire for wealth from trade restrained or negated the impulse to conquer.

CONCLUSION

Historians agree that the century between 1450 and 1550 was a major turning point in world history. It was the beginning of an age to which they have given various names: the "Vasco da Gama epoch," the "Columbian era," the "age of Magellan," or simply the "modern period." During those years European explorers opened new long-distance trade routes across the world's three major oceans, for the first time establishing regular contact among all the continents. By 1550 those who followed them had broadened trading contacts with sub-Saharan Africa, gained mastery of the rich trade routes of the Indian Ocean, and conquered a vast land empire in the Americas.

As dramatic and momentous as these events were, they were not completely unprecedented. The riches of the Indian Ocean trade that brought a gleam to the eye of many Europeans had been developed over many centuries by the trading peoples who inhabited the surrounding lands. European conquests of the Americas were no more rapid or brutal than the earlier Mongol conquests of Eurasia. Even the crossing of the Pacific had been done before, though in stages.

What gave this maritime revolution unprecedented importance had more to do with what happened after 1550 than with what happened earlier. Europeans' overseas empires would endure longer than the Mongols' and would continue to expand for three-and-a-half centuries after 1550. Unlike the Chinese, the Europeans did not turn their backs on the world after an initial burst of exploration. Not content with dominance in the Indian Ocean trade, Europeans opened in the Atlantic a maritime network that grew to rival the Indian Ocean network in the wealth of its trade. They also pioneered regular trade across the Pacific. The maritime expansion begun in the period from 1450 to 1550 marked the beginning of a new age of growing global interaction.

■ Key Terms

Zheng He	Christopher Columbus
Arawak	Ferdinand Magellan
Henry the Navigator	conquistadors
caravel	Hernán Cortés
Gold Goast	Moctezuma
Bartolomeu Dias	Francisco Pizarro
Vasco da Gama	Atahualpa

■ Suggested Reading

There is no single survey of the different expansions covered by this chapter, but the selections edited by Joseph R. Levenson, *European Expansion and the Counter Example of Asia, 1300–1600* (1967), remain a good introduction to Chinese expansion and Western impressions of China. Janet Abu-Lughod, *Before European Hegemony: The World System, A.D. 1250–1350* (1989), is a stimulating speculative reassessment of the importance of the Mongols and the Indian Ocean trade in the creation of the modern world system; she summarizes her thesis in the American Historical Association (AHA) booklet *The World System in the Thirteenth Century: Dead-End or Precursor?* (1993).

The Chinese account of Zheng He's voyages is Ma Huan, *Ying-yai Sheng-lan: "The Overall Survey of the Ocean's Shores"* [1433], ed. and trans. J. V. G. Mills (1970). A reliable guide to Polynesian expansion is Jesse D. Jennings, ed., *The Prehistory of Polynesia* (1979), especially the excellent chapter "Voyaging," by Ben R. Finney, which encapsulates his *Voyage of Rediscovery: A Cultural Odyssey Through Polynesia* (1994). The medieval background to European intercontinental voyages is summarized by Felipe Fernandez-Armesto, *Before Columbus: Exploration and Colonization from the Mediterranean to the Atlantic, 1229–1492* (1987).

A simple introduction to the technologies of European expansion is Carlo M. Cipolla, *Guns, Sails, and Empires: Technological Innovation and the Early Phases of European Expansion, 1400–1700* (1965; reprint, 1985). More advanced is Roger C. Smith, *Vanguard of Empire: Ships of Exploration in the Age of Columbus* (1993).

The European exploration is well documented and the subject of intense historical investigation. Clear general accounts based on the contemporary records are Boies Penrose, *Travel and Discovery in the Age of the Renaissance, 1420–1620* (1952); J. H. Parry, *The Age of Reconnaissance: Discovery, Exploration, and Settlement, 1450–1650* (1963); and G. V. Scammell, *The World Encompassed: The First European Maritime Empires, c. 800–1650* (1981).

An excellent general introduction to Portuguese exploration is C. R. Boxer, *The Portuguese Seaborne Empire, 1415–1825* (1969). More detail can be found in Bailey W. Diffie and George D. Winius, *Foundations of the Portuguese Empire, 1415–1580* (1977); A. J. R. Russell-Wood, *The Portuguese Empire: A World on the Move* (1998); and Luc Cuyvers, *Into the Rising Sun: The Journey of Vasco da Gama and the Discovery of the Modern World* (1998). John William Blake, ed., *Europeans in West Africa, 1450–1560* (1942), is an excellent two-volume collection of contemporary Portuguese, Castilian, and English sources. Elaine Sanceau, *The Life of Prester John: A Chronicle of Portuguese Exploration* (1941), is a very readable account of Portuguese relations with Ethiopia. *The Summa Oriental of Tomé Pires: An Account of the East, from the Red Sea to Japan, Written in Malacca and India in 1512–1515*, trans. Armando Cortesão (1944), provides a detailed firsthand account of the Indian Ocean during the Portuguese's first two decades there.

The other Iberian kingdoms' expansion is well summarized by J. H. Parry, *The Spanish Seaborne Empire* (1967). Samuel Eliot Morison's *Admiral of the Ocean Sea: A Life of Christopher Columbus* (1942) is a fine scholarly celebration of the epic mariner, also available in an abridged version as *Christopher Columbus, Mariner* (1955). More focused on the shortcomings of Columbus and his Spanish peers is Tzvetan Todorov, *The Conquest of America*, trans. Richard Howard (1985). Marvin Lunenfeld, ed., *1492: Discovery, Invasion, Encounter* (1991), critically examines contemporary sources and interpretations. William D. Phillips and Carla Rhan Phillips, *The Worlds of Christopher Columbus* (1992), examines the mariner and his times in terms of modern concerns. Peggy K. Liss, *Isabel the Queen: Life and Times* (1992), is a sympathetic examination of Queen Isabella of Castile. Detailed individual biographies of each of the individuals in Pizarro's band are the subject of James Lockhart's *Men of Cajamarca: A Social and Biographical Study of the First Conquerors of Peru* (1972). A firsthand account of Magellan's expedition is Antonio Pigafetta, *Magellan's Voyage: A Narrative Account of the First Circumnavigation*, available in a two-volume edition (1969) that includes a facsimile reprint of the manuscript.

The trans-Atlantic encounters of Europe and the Americas are described by J. H. Elliott, *The Old World and the New, 1492–1650* (1970). Alfred W. Crosby, *The Columbian Voyages, the Columbian Exchange, and Their Historians* (1987), available as an AHA booklet, provides a brief overview of the first encounters in the Americas and their long-term consequences. The early chapters of Mark A. Burkholder and Lyman L. Johnson, *Colonial Latin America*, 2d ed. (1994), give a clear and balanced account of the Spanish conquest.

The perceptions of the peoples European explorers encountered are not usually so well documented. John Thornton, *Africa and Africans in the Making of the Atlantic World, 1400–1800*, 2d ed. (1998), examines Africans' encounters with Europeans, importance in the Atlantic economy, and impact in the New World. *The Broken Spears: The Aztec Account of the Conquest of Mexico*, ed. Miguel Leon-Portilla (1962), presents Amerindian chronicles in a readable package, as does Nathan Wachtel, *The Vision of the Vanquished: The Spanish Conquest of Peru Through Indian Eyes* (1977). Anthony Reid, *Southeast Asia in the Age of Commerce, 1450–1680*, 2 vols. (1988, 1993), deals with events in that region.

■ Notes

1. Ma Huan, *Ying-yai Sheng-lan: "The Overall Survey of the Ocean's Shores,"* ed. Feng Ch'eng-Chün, trans. J. V. G. Mills (Cambridge, England: Cambridge University Press, 1970), 180.
2. Alvise da Cadamosto in *The Voyages of Cadamosto and Other Documents*, ed. and trans. G. R. Crone (London: Hakluyt Society, 1937), 2.

THE GLOBE ENCOMPASSED,

1500–1750

European voyages of exploration greatly expanded global commercial, cultural, and biological exchanges between 1500 and 1750. Europeans built new commercial empires that grew stronger with each passing century. The Portuguese had begun the mastery of the seas by opening trade with sub-Saharan Africa and seizing control of maritime trading networks in the Indian Ocean. Then European colonization in the Americas stimulated the growth of a new Atlantic economy. From its colonial base in Mexico, Spain also pioneered new trade routes across the Pacific to the Philippines and China. In time, the Dutch, French, and English expanded these profitable maritime trading networks.

Commerce and colonization led to new interregional demographic and cultural exchanges. The introduction of unfamiliar diseases caused severe population losses in the Americas. To meet the resulting acute labor shortage, Europeans introduced enslaved Africans in ever-growing numbers. Europeans and Africans brought new languages, religious practices, music, and forms of personal adornment to the New World. Some Europeans who spent time overseas adopted new ways and developed new tastes that they later brought back with them when they returned to Europe.

In Asia and Africa, most important changes continued to come from internal causes rather than European expansion. The Islamic world saw the growth of regional empires in the Middle East, South Asia, and West Africa and continued its expansion into sub-Saharan Africa, southeastern Europe, and southern

441

Asia. Secure from external penetration, China experienced military expansion and population growth, and the expansion of educational institutions reinforced traditional values among China's upper classes. In Japan, a strong new national government promoted economic development and stemmed foreign influence, and the development of an indigenous merchant class widened the gap between popular and elite cultures.

Some of the farthest-reaching cultural changes in this period occurred in Europe. Reformers challenged established religious and political institutions, and new scientific discoveries and humanist concerns raised questions about traditional Western values and beliefs.

Important ecological changes occurred in areas of rising population and economic activity. The spread of new plants and animals around the world enhanced food supplies and altered landscapes. Forests were cut down to meet the increasing need for farmland, lumber, and fuel. But the most significant environmental changes resulted from the growing mastery of the winds and currents that propelled European ships across the world's oceans. Europeans' leadership in navigational technology went hand in hand with their emerging dominance in military technology. Lacking an expanding economic base, the great Islamic empires and China fell behind the smaller European nations in military strength. After 1750, the consequences of this widening technological and economic gap were to become momentous.

ARCTIC OCEAN

St. Petersburg

England

Netherlands

EUROPE

R u s s i a n E m p i r e

ASIA

Spain

Ottoman Empire

MIDDLE EAST

Safavid Empire

Korea

Japan

China

Mughal Empire

Calcutta

PACIFIC OCEAN

Songhai

AFRICA

Asante

Dahomey

Swahili Coast

East Indies

INDIAN OCEAN

SOUTH ATLANTIC OCEAN

AUSTRALIA

0   1000   2000   3000 Km.

0   1000   2000   3000 Mi.

1700   1750   1800

• **1664** English take New Netherland from Dutch

West Indies are world's main source of sugar **1700** •

1756–1763 French and Indian War; British take Canada

1780–1782 Revolt of Tupac Armaru in Peru

• **1718** French found New Orleans

1667–1697 Wars of Louis XIV

• **1712** Peter the Great founds St. Petersburg

1700–1800 The Enlightenment

1701–1714 War of the Spanish Succession

• **1755** Lisbon earthquake

• **1680s** Rise of Asante kingdom

• **1720s** Rise of kingdom of Dahomey

1750–1800 Growing slave trade reduces population

• **1683** Last Ottoman siege of Vienna

1718–1730 Tulip Period of Ottoman Empire; Ottoman military decline

Fall of Safavid Empire **1722** •

1736–1747 Nadir Shah reunites Iran

• **1689** Treaty of Nerchinsk

• **1691** British found trading post at Calcutta

• **1792** Russian ships reach Japanese coast

• **1755** Qing conquest of Turkestan

1736–1799 Reign of Qing emperor Qianlong

18

THE TRANSFORMATION OF EUROPE,
1500–1750

Religious and Political Innovations • Building State Power • Urban Society and Commercial Technology • Rural Society and the Environment • The Realm of Ideas

ENVIRONMENT AND TECHNOLOGY: Mapping the World

SOCIETY AND CULTURE: Witchcraft

The Harvesters, **1565, by Pieter Bruegel, the Elder**
A successful wheat harvest was necessary to feed bread- and pasta-eating Europe.

*i*n the winter of 1697–1698 Tsar° Peter I, the young ruler of Russia, traveled in disguise through the Netherlands and England, eager to discover how western European societies were becoming so powerful and wealthy. A practical man, Peter paid special attention to ships and weapons, even working for a time as a ship's carpenter in the Netherlands. With great insight, he perceived that western European success owed as much to trade and toleration as to technology. Trade generated the money to spend on weapons, while toleration attracted talented persons fleeing persecution.

Upon his return to Russia, Peter resolved to "open a window onto Europe," to reform features of his vast empire that he believed were backward. He ended the servile status of women and personally trimmed his noblemen's long beards to conform to Western styles. Peter also put the skilled technical advisers he brought back with him to work on modernizing Russia's industry and military forces. His reformed armies soon gained success against Sweden for possession of a port on the Baltic Sea and against the Ottoman Turks for access to the warm waters of the Black Sea. Then Peter turned to redesigning Russia's government on a German model. He built a new palace like King Louis XIV's and copied the French king's rituals of absolute royal power.

As Peter's actions imply, by the end of the seventeenth century, western European achievements in state administration, warfare, business, and ideas were setting standards that others wished to imitate. Along with maritime expansion (examined in Chapter 17), these internal transformations promoted Western global ascendancy. Yet such achievements did not come smoothly. Warfare, poverty, persecution, and environmental degradation were also widespread in Europe between 1500 and 1750.

As you read this chapter, ask yourself the following questions:

- Was Tsar Peter right in thinking that military, economic, and political changes were moving western Europe ahead of other parts of the world?

- What were the immediate and long-term consequences of those changes and others in European religious and scientific ideas?

- How did the many conflicts and rapid changes of this period affect ordinary men and women in Europe?

RELIGIOUS AND POLITICAL INNOVATIONS

Two bitter struggles in the early sixteenth century marked the end of Europe's medieval era and the beginning of the early modern period. One was the Reformation, a movement that introduced many religious reforms but shattered the ideal of Latin Christian unity. The other was an unsuccessful attempt to unite Christian Europe politically in order to block the inroads of the Muslim armies of the Ottoman Empire.

Instead of achieving unity, early modern Europe was plagued by division and persistent warfare among its national monarchies. Yet such disunity helped foster Europe's growing strength in the world. Competition and conflict promoted technological, administrative, social, and economic changes that propelled western Europe ahead of the more unified and peaceful empires of China and India and even ahead of the militarily aggressive Ottoman Empire.

Religious Reformation, 1517–1563

In 1500 the **papacy,** the central government of Latin Christianity, was simultaneously gaining stature and suffering from corruption and dissent. Economic prosperity produced larger donations and tax receipts, allowing popes to fund ambitious construction projects in Rome, their capital city. During the sixteenth century Rome gained fifty-four new churches and other buildings that showcased the artistic **Renaissance** then under way. However, the church's wealth and power also attracted some ambitious men, some of whose personal lives became the source of scandal.

The jewel of the new building projects was the magnificent new Saint Peter's Basilica in Rome. The unprecedented size and splendor of this church were intended to glorify the Christian faith, display the skill of Renaissance artists and builders, and enhance the standing of

---

tsar (zahr)

Martin Luther   This detail of a painting by Lucas Cranach (1547) shows the Reformer preaching in his hometown church at Wittenberg.   (Church of St. Marien, Wittenberg, Germany/The Bridgeman Art Library, New York and London)

In one German state where the new indulgence was being preached lived a young professor of sacred scripture named Martin Luther (1483–1546), whose personal religious quest had led him to forsake money and marriage for a life of prayer and self-denial in a monastery. Luther had found consolation in the passage in Saint Paul's Epistle to the Romans that argued that salvation came not by "doing certain things" but from religious faith. Thus Luther was very upset by the indulgence preachers, who he thought emphasized the act of giving money more than the faith behind the act. He wrote to Pope Leo, asking him to stop the abuses and challenged the preachers to a debate on the theology of indulgences.

This theological dispute quickly escalated into a contest between two strong-minded men. Largely ignoring Luther's theological objections, Pope Leo regarded his letter as a challenge to papal power and acted to silence him. During a debate in 1519 a papal representative led Luther into open disagreement with some church doctrines, for which the papacy condemned him. Blocked in his effort to reform the church from within, Luther burned the papal bull (document) of condemnation, rejecting the pope's authority and beginning the movement known as the **Protestant Reformation.**

Accusing those whom he called "Romanists" (Roman Catholics) of relying on "good works," Luther insisted that the only way to salvation was through faith in Jesus Christ. He further declared that Christian belief must be based on the word of God in the Bible and on Christian tradition, not on the authority of the pope, as Catholics held. Eventually his conclusions led him to abandon his monastic prayers and penances and to marry a former nun.

Today Roman Catholics and most Lutherans have resolved their differences on many theological issues. But in the sixteenth century, stubbornness on both sides made reconciliation impossible.

Inspired by Luther, others raised their voices to denounce the ostentation and corruption of church leaders and to call for a return to authentic Christian practices and beliefs. John Calvin (1509–1564), a well-educated Frenchman who turned from the study of law to theology after experiencing a religious conversion, became a highly influential Protestant leader. As a young man in 1535, Calvin published *The Institutes of the Christian Religion*, a masterful synthesis of Christian teachings. Much of the *Institutes* was traditional medieval theology, but in two respects Calvin's teaching differed from that of Roman Catholics and Lutherans. First, while agreeing with Luther's emphasis on faith over works, Calvin denied that even human faith could merit salvation. Salvation, said Calvin, was God's free gift to those

the papacy. Such a project required refined tastes and vast sums of money.

The skillful overseer of the design and financing of the new Saint Peter's was Pope Leo X (r. 1513–1521), a member of the wealthy Medici° family of Florence, famous for its patronage of the arts. Pope Leo's artistic taste was superb and his personal life free from scandal, but he was more a man of action than a spiritual leader. One technique that he used to raise funds for the basilica was to authorize an **indulgence**—a forgiveness of the punishment due for past sins, granted by church authorities as a reward for a pious act such as making a pilgrimage, saying a particular prayer, or making a donation to a religious cause.

Medici (MED-ih-chee)

CHRONOLOGY

	Politics and Culture	Environment and Technology	Warfare
1500	**1500s** Spain's golden century **1519** Protestant Reformation begins **1540s** Scientific Revolution begins **1545** Catholic Reformation begins	**Mid-1500s** Improved windmills and increasing land drainage in Holland	**1526–1571** Ottoman wars **1546–1555** German Wars of Religion **1562–1598** French Wars of Religion **1566–1648** Netherlands Revolt
	Late 1500s Witchhunts increase	**1590s** Dutch develop flyboats; Little Ice Age begins	
1600	**1600s** Holland's golden century	**1600s** Depletion of forests growing **1609** Galileo's astronomical telescope	**1618–1648** Thirty Years War **1642–1648** English Civil War **1652–1678** Anglo-Dutch Wars **1667–1697** Wars of Louis XIV **1683–1697** Ottoman wars
1700	**1700s** The Enlightenment begins	**1682** Canal du Midi completed	**1700–1721** Great Northern War **1701–1714** War of the Spanish Succession
		1750 English mine nearly 5 million tons of coal a year **1755** Lisbon earthquake	

God "predestined" for it. Second, Calvin went further than Luther in curtailing the power of ordained clergymen and in simplifying religious rituals. Calvinist congregations elected their own governing committees and in time created regional and national synods (councils) to regulate doctrinal issues. Calvinists also displayed simplicity in dress, life, and worship. In an age of ornate garments, they wore simple black clothes, avoided ostentatious living, and worshiped in churches devoid of statues, most musical instruments, stained-glass windows, incense, and vestments.

The Reformers appealed to religious sentiments, but political and social agendas also inspired many who joined them. Part of the appeal of Lutheranism to German-speakers was in reaction to the power of Italians in the Catholic Church. Peasants and urban laborers sometimes defied their masters by adopting a different faith. Neither tradition had a special attraction for women, since both Protestants and Roman Catholics believed in male dominance in the church and the family. Most Protestants, however, rejected the medieval tradition of celibate priests and nuns and advocated Christian marriage for all adults.

Shaken by the intensity of the Protestant Reformers' appeal, the Catholic Church undertook its own reforms. A council that met at the city of Trent, in northern Italy, in three sessions between 1545 and 1563 issued decrees reforming the education, discipline, and practices of the Roman Catholic clergy. The council also reaffirmed the supremacy of the pope and clarified Catholic beliefs (including those concerning indulgences) in light of Protestant challenges. Also important to this **Catholic Reformation** were the activities of a new religious order—the Society of Jesus, or "Jesuits," that Ignatius of Loyola (1491–1556), a Spanish nobleman, founded in 1534. Well-educated Jesuits helped stem the Protestant tide and win back some adherents by their teaching and preaching (see Map 18.1). Other Jesuits became important missionaries overseas (see Chapters 19 and 22).

Given the complexity of the issues and the intensity of the emotions that the Protestant Reformation stirred, it is not surprising that violence often flared up. Both

Map. 18.1 Religious Reformation in Europe The Reformation brought greater religious freedom but also led to religious conflict and persecution. In many places the Reformation accelerated the trend toward state control of religion and added religious differences to the motives for wars among Europeans.

Predominant Religion in 1555

Lutheran
Calvinist (Reformed)
Church of England
Roman Catholic

▲ Huguenot centers
→ Spread of Calvinism

sides persecuted and sometimes executed those of differing views. Bitter "wars of religion," fought over a mixture of religious and secular issues, continued in parts of western Europe until 1648.

The Failure of Empire, 1519–1556

Meanwhile, there was also trouble in another great medieval institution, the **Holy Roman Empire,** a loose federation of Germanic states and principalities. The threat that the Ottoman Turks posed by their advances into southeastern Europe stirred interest in a pan-European coalition to stop the Muslim advances. Hope centered on a young man named Charles (1500–1557), descended from the powerful **Habsburg°** family of Austria and the rulers of Burgundy on his father's side and from the rulers of Spain on his mother's. After the death of his maternal grandfather in 1516, Charles inherited the Spanish thrones of Castile and Aragon along with their extensive European and American possessions. At the death of his paternal grandfather in 1519, the young king inherited the Austrian Habsburg possessions and also secured election as Emperor Charles V, ruler of the Holy Roman Empire, which the Habsburgs had headed for three generations (see Map 18.2).

A Latin Christian coalition led by Charles eventually halted the Ottomans at the gates of Vienna in 1529, but did not end Ottoman attacks, which continued on and off until 1697. Charles's efforts to forge his several possessions into Europe's strongest state met strong resistance. King Francis I of France, who had lost to Charles in the election for Holy Roman Emperor, openly supported the Muslim Turks to weaken his rival. Nor were the heads of the many states within the Holy Roman Empire eager to share their powers and revenues with the emperor. Luther's Reformation played into their hands. In the imperial Diet (assembly) many German princes, swayed partly by Luther's appeals to German nationalism, also opposed Charles, a French-speaking emperor who defended the papacy. Some Lutheran princes enriched themselves by seizing the church's lands within their states in the name of reform. The new kingdom of Prussia (created in 1701) came into being in lands that a Lutheran prince had seized from a Catholic religious order in 1525.

After decades of bitter squabbles turned to open warfare in 1546 (the German Wars of Religion), Charles V finally gave up his efforts at unification, abdicated control of his various possessions to different heirs, and retired to a monastery. To his son Philip went the throne of Spain, Europe's most powerful state then in the midst of its golden age. Administration of the war-torn Holy Roman Empire went to his brother Ferdinand, who ended the lost war against Lutheranism and the German princes. By the Peace of Augsburg (1555), he recognized the princes' right to choose whether Catholicism or Lutheranism would prevail in their particular states, and he allowed them to keep church lands they had seized before 1552.

Thus two institutions that had symbolized Western unity during the Middle Ages—the papacy and the Holy Roman Empire—were seriously weakened by the mid-sixteenth century. Luther emerged from a monastery to break the papacy; Charles retired to a monastery, broken by opposition to an effective pan-European empire. Both the papacy and the Holy Roman Empire continued to exist, but national kingdoms assumed much of the religious and political leadership in western Europe. Indeed, the collapse of religious and imperial unity was partly the work of ambitious monarchs eager to enhance their own power by bringing all other institutions under their control and preventing the emergence of any imperial superpower.

Royal Centralization, 1500–1750

Talented rulers and their able ministers guided the rise of these European kingdoms. When the system of monarchical succession worked best, it brought to the throne a creative, energetic young person who gained experience and won loyalty over many decades. By good fortune the leading states produced many such talented, hard-working, and long-lived rulers. Spain had only six rulers in the two centuries from 1556 to 1759, and France had but five between 1574 and 1774 (see Table 18.1). The long reigns of the Tudor monarchs Henry VIII and his Protestant daughter Elizabeth I helped stabilize sixteenth-century England, but their Stuart successors were twice overthrown by revolution during the next century.

Successful monarchs depended heavily on their chief advisers, who also eased the transition between rulers. Cardinal Jiménez° guided the nineteen-year-old Charles V's entry to the throne of Spain. Cardinal Richelieu° oversaw the policies of the young Louis XIII in France, and Richelieu's successor Cardinal Mazarin° guided the youthful Louis XIV, who came to the throne at the age of five. By the seventeenth century, kings were beginning to draw on the talents of successful businessmen, such as Jean Baptiste Colbert° (1619–1683), Louis

---

Habsburg (HABZ-berg)

Jiménez (he-MEH-nes)   **Richelieu** (ree-shuh-LYOO)
Mazarin (MAZ-uh-rin, maz-uh-RAN)   **Colbert** (kohl-BEAR)

Map. 18.2 The European Empire of Charles V Charles was Europe's most powerful ruler from 1519 to 1556, but he failed to unify the Christian West. In addition to being the elected head of the Holy Roman Empire, he was the hereditary ruler of the Spanish realms of Castile and Aragon and the possessions of the Austrian Habsburgs in Central Europe. The map does not show his extensive holdings in the Americas and Asia.

Table 18.1   Rulers in Early Modern Western Europe

Spain	France	England/Great Britain
Habsburg Dynasty	**Valois Dynasty**	**Tudor Dynasty**
Charles I (1516–1556) (Holy Roman-Emperor Charles V) Philip II (1556–1598)	Francis I (1515–1547) Henry II (1547–1559) Francis II (1559–1560) Charles IX (1560–1574) Henry III (1574–1589)	Henry VIII (1509–1547) Edward VI (1547–1553) Mary I (1553–1558) Elizabeth I (1558–1603)
	Bourbon Dynasty	**Stuart Dynasty**
Philip III (1598–1621) Philip IV (1621–1665) Charles II (1665–1700)	Henry IV (1589–1610)[a] Louis XIII (1610–1643) Louis XIV (1643–1715)	James I (1603–1625) Charles I (1625–1649)[a, b] (Puritan Republic, 1649–1660) Charles II (1660–1685) James II (1685–1688)[b] William III (1689–1702) and Mary II (1689–1694) Anne (1702–1714)
Bourbon Dynasty		**Hanoverian Dynasty**
Philip V (1700–1746)	Louis XV (1715–1774)	George I (1714–1727) George II (1727–1760)
Ferdinand VI (1746–1759)		

[a]Died a violent death.   [b]Was overthrown.

XIV's able minister of finance. In Great Britain, Robert Walpole, the powerful prime minister from 1721 to 1742, dominated the early Hanoverian kings.

Able monarchs and their advisers worked to enhance royal authority by limiting the autonomy of the church. Well before the Reformation, rulers in Spain, Portugal, and France had gained control over church appointments and had used church revenues to enhance royal power. This absorption of the church into the state helps explain why religious uniformity became a hot political issue. Following the pattern used by his predecessors to suppress Jewish and Muslim practices, King Philip II of Spain used an ecclesiastical court, the Spanish Inquisition, to bring into line those who resisted his authority. It was the one institution common to his three Spanish kingdoms. Suspected Protestants, as well as critics of the king, found themselves accused of heresy, an offense punishable by death. Even those who were acquitted of the charge learned not to oppose the king again.

In France, Prince Henry of Navarre switched his faith from Calvinist to Catholic after gaining the military advantage in the French Wars of Religion (1562–1598), so that, as King Henry IV (the first of the Bourbon kings), he

would share the faith of the majority of his subjects. His son and grandson, Kings Louis XIII and Louis XIV (see Table 18.1), were as devoted to French Catholic religious uniformity as their counterparts in Spain. In 1685 Louis XIV even revoked the Edict of Nantes°, by which his grandfather had granted religious freedom to his Protestant supporters in 1598.

Elsewhere, the Protestant Reformation made it easier for monarchs to increase their control of the church. The church in England lost its remaining autonomy after the pope turned down King Henry VIII's petition for an annulment of his marriage to Katharine of Aragon. Distressed that Katharine had not furnished him with a male heir, Henry had the English archbishop of Canterbury annul the marriage in 1533. The breach with Rome was sealed the next year when Parliament made the English monarch head of the Church of England.

Henry used his authority to disband monasteries and convents. He gave some of their landholdings to his powerful allies and sold others to pay for his new navy. In other respects religion changed little under Henry and his successors, despite growing pressures from English

Nantes (nahnt)

Calvinists known as Puritans to "purify" the Anglican church of Catholic practices and beliefs. In 1603, the first Stuart king, James I, dismissed a Puritan petition to eliminate bishops with the statement "No bishops, no king"—a reminder of the essential role that bishops played in royal administration.

In addition to gaining control of the church, western European kings and queens enhanced their powers by promoting national institutions. In 1500 many of the separate provinces of Spain and France had their own laws and institutions, reflecting their piecemeal acquisition by inheritance and conquest. By 1750 there was more uniformity in law and administration. Seventeenth-century French kings took two steps to decrease local power. They appointed *intendants*°, new royal officials to enforce their orders in the provinces. They also used the army to tear down the fortifications behind which powerful nobles and towns had often asserted their independence.

The growth of a common language, especially among the elites, further strengthened national unity. In Spain the Castilian dialect gained currency. In France people increasingly imitated the speech of Paris. The Protestant emphasis on reading the Bible in vernacular languages (instead of in Latin) speeded up the replacement of many dialects with standardized national languages. Luther's magnificent translation of the Bible into the High German of Saxony laid the basis for modern German. The biblical translation prepared under the direction of King James I did the same for English, as did Calvin's translation for French. Important new secular literatures also helped to standardize national languages. These included the English plays of William Shakespeare (1564–1616), the French satires of François Rabelais° (1483–1553), the Spanish novel *Don Quixote* by Miguel de Cervantes° (1547–1616), and *The Lusiads*, an epic poem celebrating overseas exploration, by the Portuguese poet Luís de Camões° (1524?–1580).

Absolutism and Constitutionalism

The absence of any constitutional check on a ruler's power is called **absolutism.** Many seventeenth- and eighteenth-century European monarchs admired absolutism and tried to put it into practice. But monarchs trying to concentrate power in their own hands had to confront the representative assemblies that traditionally had to approve important royal actions such as making war and levying new taxes. As we have seen, the princes in the imperial Diet of the Holy Roman Empire effectively resisted Charles V. In contrast, French kings succeeded in circumventing the Estates General. In England, Parliament checked royal power and established **constitutionalism,** a system of government that subjects the ruler's power to limits specified by law and custom.

In France the Estates General represented the traditional rights of three groups: the clergy, the nobility, and the towns (that is, townspeople with wealth and high status). The Estates General was able to assert itself during the sixteenth-century French Wars of Religion, when the monarchy was weak. But, except in 1614 when Queen Marie de Medici was ruling in the name of her young son, the Bourbon kings refused to call it into session. Unable to impose new taxes without summoning the Estates General, Louis XIV turned to his astute finance minister, Colbert, who devised new, efficient tax collection methods that tripled the amount of money reaching the royal treasury. To increase the tax base, Colbert also promoted economic development both in France and overseas. When Louis XIV's wars (1667–1697) and high living strained the treasury to the breaking point, the king raised additional sums by selling high offices, again bypassing the Estates General.

Louis XIV's gigantic new palace at Versailles° symbolized the French monarch's triumph over the traditional rights of the nobility. Capable of housing ten thousand people and surrounded by elaborately landscaped grounds and parks, the palace can be seen as a sort of theme park of royal absolutism. Required to spend much of their time at elaborate ceremonies and banquets centered on the king, the nobles who lived at Versailles were kept away from the real politics of the kingdom. According to one of them, the duke of Saint-Simon°, "no one was so clever in devising petty distractions" as the king. So successful was Versailles in taming the nobles that not only Tsar Peter in Russia but other kings, princes, and even a powerful German archbishop built imitations of it.

As eager as his French counterparts to promote royal absolutism, King Charles I of England (see Table 18.1) ruled for eleven years without summoning Parliament, his kingdom's representative body. To raise money, he coerced "loans" from wealthy subjects and twisted tax laws to new uses. Then in 1640, a rebellion in Scotland forced him to summon the members of Parliament to approve new taxes to pay for an army. Noblemen and churchmen sat in the House of Lords. Representatives

---

intendants (in-TEN-dants)   **Rabelais** (RAB-uh-lay)
Cervantes (ser-VAHN-tees)   **Camões** (kuh-MOINSH)

Versailles (vuhr-SIGH)   **Saint-Simon** (san see-MON)

Versailles, 1722   This painting by P.-D. Martin shows the east expanse of buildings and courtyards that make up the palace complex built by King Louis XIV.   (Giraudon/Art Resource, NY)

from the towns and counties sat in the House of Commons. Before authorizing new taxes, Parliament insisted on strict guarantees that the king would never again ignore its traditional rights. These King Charles refused to grant. When he ordered the arrest of his leading critics in the House of Commons in 1642, he plunged the kingdom into civil war.

Defending Parliament's traditional rights were the rich commoners and the well-organized religious Puritans, who had not given up on their plans to cleanse the English church of Catholic traits. Supporting the king were most of the established nobility and the conservative northern parts of the kingdom. When Charles refused to compromise even after being defeated on the battlefield, a "Rump" Parliament purged of his supporters ordered him executed in 1649 and replaced the monarchy with a Puritan Republic under the Puritan general Oliver Cromwell.

Cromwell expanded England's power overseas and imposed firm control over Ireland and Scotland, but he was as unwilling as the Stuart kings to share power with Parliament. After his death the Stuart line was restored in 1660, and for a time it was unclear which side had won the English Civil War.

However, when King James II refused to respect Parliament's rights and had his heir baptized a Roman Catholic, Parliament offered the throne to his Protestant daughter Mary and her Dutch husband, Prince William of Orange. Their triumphal arrival in England forced James into exile in the bloodless Glorious Revolution of 1688. This time, there was no doubt about the outcome. The Bill of Rights of 1689 specified that Parliament had to be called "frequently" and had to consent to changes in laws and to the raising of an army in peacetime. Another law reaffirmed the official status of the Church of England but gave religious toleration to Puritans.

BUILDING STATE POWER

The growing power of early modern European rulers, whether absolutist or constitutional, would have been of modest global significance if they had not achieved notable success in two other important areas. One was developing some of the world's most powerful armed forces. The other was ensuring sufficient economic growth to support the heavy costs of royal administration and warfare.

War and Diplomacy

Warfare was almost constant in early modern Europe (see the Chronology at the beginning of the chapter). These struggles for dominance first produced a dramatic change in the size, skill, and weapons of armed forces and then an advance in diplomacy. The military revolution began in the Late Middle Ages when firearms became the preferred weapons of war: cannon replaced catapults as siege weapons, muskets displaced lances and crossbows, and gun-toting commoners on foot supplanted aristocratic knights on horseback.

The numbers of men in arms increased steadily throughout the early modern period. Spanish armies doubled in size from about 150,000 in the 1550s to 300,000 in the 1630s. French forces, about half the size of the Spanish in the 1630s, grew to 400,000 by the early eighteenth century. Even smaller European states built up impressive armies. Sweden, with under a million people, had one of the finest and best-armed military forces in seventeenth-century Europe. Prussia, with fewer than 2 million inhabitants in 1700, devoted so many resources to building a splendid army that it became one of Europe's major powers. Only England did not maintain a standing army in peacetime, but the Royal Navy protected the island nation from invasion.

Large armies required effective command structures. Long before the development of modern field communications systems, European armies, in the words of a modern historian, "evolved . . . the equivalent of a central nervous system, capable of activating technologically differentiated claws and teeth."[1] New signaling techniques improved control of battlefield maneuvers. Better discipline was achieved by frequent marching drills, which trained troops to obey orders instantly and gave them a close sense of comradeship. First developed in the Netherlands during a long struggle for independence from Spain, the drilling techniques were quickly imitated by the best armies in Europe.

Military victories by the giant armies were not assured, however. New fortifications able to withstand cannon bombardments made cities harder to capture, and battles between evenly matched armies often ended in stalemates, as in the Thirty Years War (1618–1648). Victory in war increasingly depended on naval superiority. Warships were redesigned to accommodate several tiers of cannon that had the power to blow holes in the thick sides of enemy ships. Improved four-wheel carriages made cannon easier to pull back and reload.

The rapid changes in naval warfare are evident in two fleets used by Philip II of Spain. In 1571 a combined Spanish and Italian fleet of 200 ships met an even larger Ottoman force off Lepanto on the Greek coast. Both fleets consisted principally of oar-powered galleys, which had only light armaments. To attack, one galley rammed another so that armed men could climb aboard for hand-to-hand combat. Four hours after the battle began, the remains of 200 Ottoman galleys littered the sea's surface, and the waters were red with the blood of 30,000 slain men. The Christian coalition's victory resulted from the valor of Spanish troops and the superior firepower of a handful of specially built Venetian ships.

A very different Spanish fleet, the Catholic Armada, sailed from Lisbon in 1588 hoping to repeat the Lepanto success over the Protestant enemies of the north. The complex mission of these 130 heavily armed ships was to replace the Protestant ruler of England, Queen Elizabeth, with a Roman Catholic, then put down the rebellion in the Netherlands, and finally intervene on the Catholic side in the French Wars of Religion. But history did not repeat itself. The English could fire more rapidly because of their new cannon carriages, and their smaller, quicker ships successfully evaded the ram-and-board technique, which the Spanish retained from their Mediterranean victory. Moreover, a chance storm, celebrated by the English as a providential "Protestant wind," scattered and sank many Spanish ships that had survived the sea battles, thus dooming Philip's other plans for the armada.

The armada's defeat signaled the end of Spain's military dominance in Europe. By the time of the Thirty Years War, France had recovered from its Wars of Religion to become Europe's most powerful state. With twice the population of Spain at their command, France's forceful kings of the Bourbon dynasty could field Europe's largest armies, whether to squelch domestic unrest, extend France's boundaries, or intervene in the affairs of neighboring states.

After emerging from its own civil conflicts in 1689, England became France's major rival. By then England ruled a North American empire as well as Ireland, and in 1707 England merged with Scotland to become Great

Austrian Siege of Belgrade, 1688   The Ottoman Turks, in control of the Balkan Peninsula since the early sixteenth century, again assaulted the city of Vienna in 1683. Revitalized Austrian Habsburg armies successfully defended their capital and then took the offensive against the Muslim invaders, retaking Hungary and capturing the city of Belgrade, south of the Danube River. Although the Turks soon regained Belgrade, the annexation of Hungary doubled the size of the Austrian Empire and altered the balance of power in southeastern Europe.   (Giraudon/Art Resource, NY)

Britain. England's rise as a sea power had begun in the time of King Henry VIII, who spent heavily on ships and promoted a domestic iron-smelting industry to supply cannon. Queen Elizabeth's victorious fleet of 1588 was considerably improved by the copying of innovative ship designs from the Dutch in the second half of the seventeenth century. The Royal Navy grew in numbers, surpassing the French fleet by the early eighteenth century.

In a series of eighteenth-century wars, beginning with the War of the Spanish Succession (1701–1714), the combination of Britain's naval strength and the land armies of its Austrian and Prussian allies was able to block French expansionist efforts and prevent the Bourbons from uniting the thrones of France and Spain. This defeat of the French monarchy's empire-building efforts illustrated the principle of **balance of power** in international relations: the major European states formed temporary alliances to prevent any one state from becoming too powerful.

Russia emerged as a major power in Europe after Peter the Great's modernized armies defeated Sweden in the Great Northern War (1700–1721). During the next two centuries, though adhering to four different branches of Christianity, the great powers of Europe— Catholic France, Anglican Britain, Catholic Austria, Lutheran Prussia, and Orthodox Russia (see Map 18.3)— maintained an effective balance of power in Europe by shifting their alliances for geopolitical rather than religious reasons.

Politics and the Economy

To pay the extremely heavy military costs of their wars, European rulers had to increase their revenues. The most successful of them after 1600 promoted mutually beneficial alliances with the rising commercial elites. Both parties understood that trade thrived where government taxation and regulation were not excessive, where courts enforced contracts and collected debts, and where military power stood ready to protect overseas expansion by force when necessary.

Spain, sixteenth-century Europe's mightiest state, illustrates how the financial drains of an aggressive military policy and the failure to promote economic development

Map. 18.3 Europe in 1740 By the middle of the eighteenth century the great powers of Europe were France, the Austrian Empire, Great Britain, Prussia, and Russia. Spain, the Holy Roman Empire, and the Ottoman Empire were far weaker in 1740 than they had been two centuries earlier.

could lead to decline. Expensive wars against the Ottomans, northern European Protestants, and rebellious Dutch subjects caused the treasury of King Philip II to default on its debts four times. Moreover, the Spanish rulers' concerns for religious uniformity and traditional aristocratic privilege further undermined the country's economy. In the name of religious uniformity they expelled Jewish merchants, persecuted Protestant dissenters, and forced tens of thousands of skilled farmers and artisans into exile because of their Muslim ancestry. While exempting the landed aristocracy from taxation, Spanish rulers imposed high sales taxes that discouraged manufacturing.

For a time, vast imports of silver and gold bullion from Spain's American colonies filled the government treasury. These bullion shipments also contributed to severe inflation (rising prices), worst in Spain but bad throughout the rest of western Europe as well. A Spanish saying captured the problem: American silver was like rain on the roof—it poured down and washed away. Huge debts for foreign wars drained bullion from Spain to its creditors. More wealth flowed out to purchase manufactured goods and even food in the seventeenth century.

The rise of the Netherlands as an economic power stemmed from opposite policies. The Spanish crown had acquired these resource-poor but commercially successful provinces as part of Charles V's inheritance. But King Philip II's decision to impose Spain's ruinously heavy sales tax and enforce Catholic orthodoxy drove the Dutch to revolt in 1566 and again in 1572. Those measures would have discouraged business and driven away the Calvinists, Jews, and others who were essential to Dutch prosperity. The Dutch fought with skill and ingenuity, raising and training an army and a navy that were among the most effective in Europe. By 1609 Spain was forced to agree to a truce that recognized the autonomy of the northern part of the Netherlands. In 1648, after eight decades of warfare, the independence of these seven United Provinces of the Free Netherlands (to give their full name) became final.

Rather than being ruined by the long war, the United Netherlands emerged in the seventeenth century as the dominant commercial power in Europe and the world's greatest trading nation. During this golden century the wealth of the Netherlands multiplied instead of flowing away. This economic success owed much to a decentralized government. During the long struggle against Spain, the provinces united around the prince of Orange, their sovereign, who served as commander-in-chief of the armed forces. But in economic matters each province was free to pursue its own interests. The maritime province of Holland grew rich by favoring commercial interests.

Holland's many towns and cities were filled with skilled craftsmen. Factories and workshops turned out goods of exceptional quality at a moderate price and on a vast scale. The textile industry concentrated on the highly profitable finishing and printing of cloth, transforming into fine textiles the cloth spun and woven by low-paid workers. Other factories refined West Indian sugar, brewed beer from Baltic grain, cut Virginia tobacco, and made imitations of Chinese ceramics. Holland's printers published books in many languages, free from the censorship imposed by political and religious authorities in neighboring countries. For a small province, barely above sea level, lacking timber and other natural resources, this was a remarkable achievement.

Amsterdam, Holland's major city, was seventeenth-century Europe's financial center and major port. From there Dutch ships dominated the sea trade of Europe, carrying over 80 percent of the trade to Spain from northern Europe, even while Spain and the Netherlands were at war. The Dutch dominance of Atlantic and Indian Ocean trade was such that, by one estimate, they conducted more than half of all the oceangoing commercial shipping in the world (for details see Chapters 20 and 21).

After 1650 the Dutch faced growing competition from the English, who were developing their own close association of business and government. In a series of wars (1652–1678) England used its naval might to break Dutch dominance in overseas trade and to extend England's colonial empire. With government support, the English merchant fleet doubled between 1660 and 1700, and foreign trade rose by 50 percent. As a result, state revenue from customs duties tripled. During the eighteenth century Britain's trading position strengthened still more.

The debts run up by the Anglo-Dutch Wars helped persuade the English monarchy to greatly enlarge the government's role in managing the economy. The outcome has been called a "financial revolution." The government increased revenues by taxing the formerly exempt landed estates of the aristocrats and by collecting taxes directly. Previously private individuals known as tax farmers had advanced the government a fixed sum of money; in return they could keep whatever money they were able to collect from taxpayers. To secure cash quickly for warfare and other emergencies and to reduce the burden of debts from earlier wars, England also followed the Dutch lead in creating a central bank, from which the government was able to obtain long-term loans at low rates.

The French government was also developing its national economy, especially under Colbert. He streamlined tax collection, promoted French manufacturing

Port of Amsterdam Ships, barges and boats of all types are visible in this busy seventeenth–century scene. The large building in the center is the Admiralty House, which housed the headquarters of the Dutch East India Company. (Mansell Collection/Time Inc.)

and shipping by imposing taxes on foreign goods, and improved transportation within France itself. Yet the power of the wealthy aristocrats kept the French government from following England's lead in taxing wealthy landowners, collecting taxes directly, and securing low-cost loans. Nor did France succeed in managing its debt as efficiently as England. (The role of governments in promoting overseas trade is discussed in Chapter 20.)

URBAN SOCIETY AND COMMERCIAL TECHNOLOGY

Just as palaces were early modern Europe's centers of political power, cities were its economic power centers. The urban growth under way since the eleventh century was accelerating and spreading. In 1500, Paris was the only northern European city with over 100,000 inhabitants. By 1700, both Paris and London had populations over 500,000, Amsterdam had burgeoned from a fishing village to a metropolis of some 200,000, and twenty other European cities contained over 60,000 people.

The cities' growth depended primarily on the prosperous merchants who managed the great expansion of regional and overseas commerce. Improved business techniques and manufacturing technologies also added to the cities' prosperity, but wealth was unevenly distributed.

Urban Social Classes

In about 1580 the mayor of the French city of Bordeaux° asked a group of visiting Amerindian chiefs what impressed them most about European cities. The chiefs are said to have expressed astonishment at the disparity between the fat, well-fed people and the poor, half-starved men and women in rags. Why, the visitors wondered, did the poor not grab the rich by the throat or set fire to their homes? The contrasts of wealth in European cities were indeed startling, and social tension often ran high.[2]

Bordeaux (bor-DOH)

The French called the well-off who dominated the cities **bourgeoisie**° (town dwellers). Their wealth came from manufacturing, finance, and especially trade, both regional and overseas.

Grain for bread was brought by carts and barges from the surrounding countryside or, in the largest cities of western Europe, transported by special fleets from the eastern Baltic lands. Other fleets brought wine from southern to northern Europe. Parisians downed 100,000 barrels of wine a year at the end of the seventeenth century. The poor also consumed large amounts of beer. In 1750 Parisian breweries made 23 million quarts (22 million liters) for local consumption, another stimulus to the grain trade. In the seventeenth and eighteenth centuries wealthier urban classes could buy exotic luxuries imported from the far corners of the earth—Caribbean and Brazilian sugar and rum, Mexican chocolate, Virginian tobacco, North American furs, East Indian cotton textiles and spices, and Chinese tea.

As related above, the rise of the bourgeoisie was aided by mutually beneficial alliances with monarchs who saw economic growth as the best means of increasing state revenues. Unlike the old nobility, who shunned productive labor, members of the bourgeoisie devoted long hours to their businesses and poured their profits into new business ventures or other investments rather than spending them. Even so, they still had enough money to live comfortably in large houses with many servants.

Like merchants in the Islamic world, Europe's merchants relied on family and ethnic networks. In addition to families of local origin, many northern European cities contained merchant colonies from Venice, Florence, Genoa, and other Italian cities. In Amsterdam and Hamburg lived Jewish merchants who had fled religious persecution in Iberia. Other Jewish communities expanded out of eastern Europe into the German states, especially after the Thirty Years War. Armenian merchants from Iran were moving into the Mediterranean and became important in Russia in the seventeenth century.

Europe's cities were home not only to the well-off bourgeoisie, but also to craftworkers and many poor people. From 10 to 20 percent of the city dwellers were so poor they were exempt from taxation. This number included only the "deserving poor," whom officials considered permanent residents. Cities contained large numbers of "unworthy poor"—recent migrants from impoverished rural areas, peddlers traveling from place to place, and beggars (many with horrible deformities and sores) who tried to survive on charity. There were also criminals, usually organized in gangs, ranging from youthful pickpockets to highway robbers.

Some people managed to improve their lot in life and others slipped lower, but most followed the careers of their parents.

In contrast to the arranged marriages common in much of the rest of the world, young men and women in early modern Europe generally chose their own spouses and after marriage set up their own households instead of living with their parents. The sons and daughters of craftworkers and the poor had to delay marriage until they could afford to live on their own. Young men had to serve a long apprenticeship to learn a trade. Young women had to work—helping their parents, as domestic servants, or in some other capacity—to save money for the dowry they were expected to bring into the marriage. A dowry was the money and household goods—the amount varied by social class—that enabled a young couple to begin marriage independent of their parents. The typical groom in early modern Europe could not hope to marry before his late twenties, and his bride would be a few years younger—in contrast to the rest of the world, where people usually married in their teens.

Marriage also came late in bourgeois families. One reason for the delay was to allow men to finish their education. Bourgeois parents did not formally arrange their children's marriages, but the fact that nearly all found spouses within their social class strongly suggests that parents promoted marriages that forged business alliances with other families.

Bourgeois parents were very concerned that their children have the education and training necessary for success. They promoted the establishment of municipal schools to provide a solid education, including Latin and perhaps Greek, for their sons, who were then sent abroad to learn modern languages or to a university to earn a law degree. Legal training was useful for conducting business and was a prerequisite for obtaining government judgeships and treasury positions. Daughters were less likely to be groomed for a business career, but wives often helped their husbands as bookkeepers and sometimes inherited businesses.

Besides enabling young people to be independent of their parents, the late age of marriage in early modern Europe also held down the birthrate and thus limited family size. Even so, about one-tenth of the births in a city were to unmarried women, often servants, who generally left their infants on the doorsteps of churches, convents, or rich families. Despite efforts to raise such abandoned children, many perished. Delayed marriage

---

bourgeoisie (boor-zwah-ZEE)

The Fishwife, 1572 Women were essential partners in most Dutch family businesses. This scene by the Dutch artist Adriaen van Ostade shows a woman preparing fish for retail sale. (Rijksmuseum-Stichting)

also had links to the existence of public brothels, where young men could satisfy their lusts in cheap and impersonal encounters with unfortunate young women, often newly arrived from impoverished rural villages. Nevertheless, rape was a common occurrence, usually perpetrated by gangs of young men who attacked young women rumored to be free with their favors. Some historians believe that such gang rapes reflect poor young men's jealousy at older men's easier access to women.

Commercial Techniques and Technology

The expansion of trade in early modern Europe prompted the development of new techniques to manage far-flung business enterprises and invest the profits they produced. As elsewhere in the world, most businesses in Europe operated with family-owned funds or money borrowed from private moneylenders. But a key change in Europe was the rise of large financial institutions to serve the interests of big business and big government. In the seventeenth century, private Dutch banks developed such a reputation for security that wealthy individuals and governments from all over western Europe entrusted them with their money. To make a profit, the banks invested these funds in real estate, local industries, loans to governments, and overseas trade.

Another commercial innovation was the **joint-stock company,** which sold shares to individuals. Often backed by a government charter, such companies offered a way to raise large sums for overseas enterprises while spreading the risks (and profits) among many investors (the operation of chartered joint-stock companies in the overseas trade is examined in Chapter 20). After the initial offerings, investors could buy and sell shares in specialized financial markets called **stock exchanges,** an Italian innovation transferred to the cities of northwestern Europe in the sixteenth century. The greatest stock market in the seventeenth and eighteenth centuries was the Amsterdam Exchange, founded in 1530. Large insurance companies also emerged in this period, and insuring long voyages against loss became a standard practice after 1700 (see Chapter 20).

Changes in technology also facilitated economic growth. As in the case of military developments, this was more an age of technological refinement and multiplication than innovation. For example, water wheels—a traditional source of mechanical energy for mills and factories—gradually increased in size. In the Dutch province of Holland, improved systems of gears made it possible to adapt windmills for new uses, such as driving a saw. Information about new devices was spread by means of printed manuals on machinery, metallurgy, agriculture, and other technical subjects.

Improvements in water transport expanded Europe's superb natural network of seas and navigable rivers for moving bulk items such as grain, wine, and timber. The Dutch built numerous canals to drain the lowlands for agriculture and for transport. Other canals, with elaborate systems of locks to cross hills, were built in France, Germany, Italy, and England. One of the most important was the 150–mile (240–kilometer) Canal du Midi in France, built by the French government between 1661 and 1682 to link the Atlantic and the Mediterranean.

The expansion of maritime trade led to new designs for merchant ships. In this, too, the Dutch played a dominant role. Using timber imported from northern Europe, shipyards in Dutch ports built ships for their own vast fleets and for export. Especially successful was the *fluit*, or "flyboat," a large-capacity cargo ship developed in the 1590s. It was inexpensive to build and required only a small crew. Another successful type of merchant ship, the heavily armed "East Indiaman," helped the Dutch establish their supremacy in the Indian Ocean. The Dutch also excelled at mapmaking (see Environment and Technology: Mapping the World).

Mapping the World

In 1602 the Jesuit missionary Matteo Ricci in China printed an elaborate map of the world. Working from maps produced in Europe and incorporating the latest knowledge gathered by European maritime explorers, Ricci introduced two changes to make the map more appealing to his Chinese hosts. He labeled it in Chinese characters, and he split his map down the middle of the Atlantic so that China lay in the center. This version pleased Chinese elites, who considered China the "Middle Kingdom" surrounded by lesser states. A copy of Ricci's map in six large panels adorned the emperor's Beijing palace.

The stunningly beautiful maps and globes of sixteenth-century Europe were the most complete, detailed, and useful representations of the earth that any society had ever produced. The best mapmaker of the century was Gerhard Kremer, who is remembered as Mercator (the merchant) because his maps were so useful to European ocean traders. By incorporating the latest discoveries and scientific measurements, Mercator could depict the outlines of the major continents in painstaking detail, even if their interiors were still largely unknown to outsiders.

To represent the spherical globe on a flat map, Mercator drew the lines of longitude as parallel lines. Because such lines actually meet at the poles, Mercator's projection greatly exaggerated the size of every landmass and body of water distant from the equator. However, Mercator's rendering offered a very practical advantage: sailors could plot their course by drawing a straight line between their point of departure and their destination. Because of this useful feature the Mercator projection of the world remained in common use until quite recently. To some extent, its popularity came from the exaggerated size this projection gave to Europe. Like the Chinese, Europeans liked to think of themselves as at the center of things. Europeans also understood their true geographical position better than people in any other part of the world.

Dutch World Map, 1641
It is easy to see why the Chinese would not have liked to see their empire at the far right edge of this widely printed map. Besides the distortions caused by the Mercator projection, geographical ignorance exaggerates the size of North America and Antarctica. (Courtesy of the Trustees British Museum)

RURAL SOCIETY AND THE ENVIRONMENT

For all its new political, military, and commercial strengths, early modern Europe rested on a fragile agrarian base. The techniques and efficiency of European agriculture had improved little since 1300. Bad years brought famine; good ones provided only small surpluses. Social tensions and conflicts multiplied as warfare, environmental deterioration, and adverse economic conditions worsened the circumstances of most rural Europeans between 1500 and 1750.

The Struggle for Food

Under the pressure of social and environmental change and inflation, the condition of the average person in western Europe seems to have worsened sharply during the century after 1530. Peasants in England were reduced to a diet of black bread and little else. Elsewhere people starved. Wars and other human-engineered calamities were partly to blame. In Spain the old nobility was responsible for the consolidation of landownership and the impoverishment of the peasantry. By 1600 only 3 percent of the population controlled 97 percent of the land. When Spanish landowners decided that they could increase their incomes by turning cropland into pastures for their sheep, food production and population declined.

Rural Europeans also felt the adverse effects of a century of relatively cool climate that began in the 1590s. During this **Little Ice Age,** average temperatures fell only a few degrees, but the effects were startling. Glaciers in the Alps grew much larger. Rivers and canals important to commerce froze solid from bank to bank. In some places during the coldest years, the growing season shrank by two months. As a result, food crops ripened more slowly during cooler summers and were often damaged by early fall frosts. In spring late frosts withered the tender shoots of newly planted crops.

People could survive a smaller-than-average harvest in one year with reserves left from the year before. But when one cold year followed another, the consequences were devastating. Records show that when average summer temperatures in northern Europe were 2.7°F (1.5°C) lower in 1674 and 1675 and again in 1694 and 1695, deaths due to malnutrition and cold increased sharply.

The cold spell of 1694–1695 caused a famine in Finland that carried off between a quarter and a third of the population.

By 1700, new crops from the Americas were helping the rural poor avoid starvation. At first eaten only in desperate times, potatoes and maize (corn) became staples for the rural poor in the eighteenth century because they yielded more abundant food from small garden plots. Potatoes sustained life in northeastern and Central Europe and in Ireland. Peasants along the Mediterranean who could not afford to eat the wheat they raised for urban markets grew maize for their own consumption.

Deforestation

Another threat to rural life came from **deforestation.** Early modern Europeans cut down their great hardwood forests to provide timbers for ships, lumber for buildings, wagons, and barrels, fuel for heating and cooking, and charcoal for smelting ores and other industrial processes. Each of the three hundred ironworks in England in the late seventeenth century consumed a thousand loads of oak a year. Wood shortages resulting from such high consumption led to increased imports of timber and charcoal from more heavily forested Scandinavian countries and Russia. Sweden used its vast forest resources to become a major iron producer in the seventeenth century. After 1716 Russia was Europe's largest producer of iron.

Because of this consumption of wood for Europe's rising population and expanding economy, forest depletion emerged as a serious issue in the seventeenth and eighteenth centuries. The shortages were particularly acute in England, where one early-seventeenth-century observer lamented: "within man's memory, it was held impossible to have any want of wood in England. But . . . at present, through the great consuming of wood . . . and the neglect of planting of woods, there is a great scarcity of wood throughout the whole kingdom."[3] Shortages in England drove the price of ordinary firewood up five times faster than other prices between the late fifteenth and the mid-seventeenth centuries.

High wood prices encouraged the use of coal as an alternative fuel. England's coal mining increased twelve-fold from 210,000 tons in 1550 to 2.5 million tons in 1700. From 1709, coke—coal refined to remove impurities—gradually replaced charcoal in the smelting of iron. These new demands drove English coal production to nearly 5 million tons a year by 1750.

France was much more forested than England, but increasing consumption there caused Colbert to predict that "France will perish for lack of wood." By the late

Winter in Flanders, 1565   This January scene by the Flemish artist Pieter Bruegel, the Elder, shows many everyday activities. At left, men return from trapping hares, and the women under the sign singe the bristles off a slaughtered pig. On the frozen ponds, people skate and play hockey and curling. An old woman carries a load of faggots across the bridge. A February scene that Bruegel painted as part of this series shows the snow all melted. A few decades later, however, winters became longer and colder.   (Kunsthistorisches Museum, Vienna/The Bridgeman Art Library, New York and London)

eighteenth century, deforestation was becoming an issue even in Sweden and Russia. New laws in France and England designed to protect the forests were largely inspired by fears of shortages for naval vessels, whose keels required high-quality timbers of exceptional size and particular curvature. Although wood consumption remained high, rising prices encouraged some individuals to plant trees for future harvest.

Everywhere in Europe the rural poor felt the depletion of the forests most strongly. For centuries they had depended on woodlands for abundant supplies of wild nuts and berries, free firewood and building materials, and wild game. Many poor men and women flocked to the cities in hopes of finding better jobs, but most were disappointed. As we have seen, begging, theft, and prostitution were the result.

Peasantry and Gentry

The bright side of rural life in western Europe was the remarkable personal freedom of the peasantry in comparison with people of similar status in many other parts of the world. Serfdom, which bound men and women to land owned by a local lord, declined sharply after the great plague of the mid-fourteenth century. Most remaining serfs in western Europe gained their freedom by 1600. By that date slavery in southern Iberia, which had been sustained by large numbers of captives from Africa, had also come to an end. Coincidentally, the disappearance of serfdom in western Europe was paralleled by the introduction of serfdom in much of early modern eastern Europe.

Legal freedom in western Europe did little to make the peasants' lives safe and secure. Peasants with surplus crops to sell benefited from the higher prices brought about by inflation, but the broader trend was for peasants to fall deeper and deeper into debt until they lost their land. This transformation of rural ownership was accelerated by the desire of many successful members of the bourgeoisie to use their wealth to raise their social status. Retiring from their professions and buying country estates gained them admission to the ranks of gentry. These new owners of rural estates affected the lifestyle of the old aristocracy and sometimes received the aristocracy's exemption from taxation, but they did not have titles of nobility.

The gentry loaned money to impoverished peasants and to members of the nobility and in time increased their ownership of land. Some families sought aristocratic husbands for their daughters. The old nobility found such alliances attractive because of the large dowries that rich merchants provided. In France a family could gain the exemption from taxation by living in gentility for three generations. The same family could gain noble status more quickly by purchasing a title. French kings sold so many new patents of nobility that people came to distinguish the new *noblesse de robe*° (dress nobility) from the medieval *noblesse d'épée*° (sword nobility).

Rural misery in early modern Europe provoked many rebellions. For example, in 1525 peasant rebels in the Alps attacked both nobles and clergy as representatives of the privileged and landowning classes. They had no love for merchants either, whom they denounced for lending at interest and charging high prices. Rebellions multiplied as rural conditions worsened. In southwestern France alone some 450 uprisings occurred between 1590 and 1715, many of them set off by food shortages and tax increases. The exemption of the wealthy from taxation was a frequent souce of complaint. A rebellion in southern France in 1670 began when a mob of townswomen attacked the tax collector. It quickly spread to the country, where peasant leaders cried, "Death to the people's oppressors!" Authorities dealt severely with such revolts and executed or maimed their leaders.

In 1750 most Europeans still lived in general wretchedness. Modest improvements in food production in some places were overwhelmed by population growth. Even in the prosperous Dutch towns half of the population lived in acute poverty. Some rural poor in the eighteenth century worked at home spinning yarn and weaving cloth from materials supplied by entrepreneurs. So many single women supported themselves by spinning yarn that *spinster* became the normal English word for an unmarried woman.

---

noblesse de robe (no-BLES deh ROHB)
noblesse d'épée (no-BLES day-PAY)

THE REALM OF IDEAS

New ideas and old beliefs pulled early modern Europeans in several different directions, even after the Reformation controversies subsided. The hold of biblical and traditional folk beliefs on the thinking of most people showed itself in widespread new fears about witches and the power of the Devil. The Renaissance helped sharpen the influence of writings from Greco-Roman antiquity on educated people. A few thinkers broke new scientific ground in deciphering the motion of the planets and constructing mathematical models of the force of gravitation. In time, the new scientific ideas encouraged some to reevaluate traditional social and political systems, with important implications for the period after 1750.

Traditional Thinking and Witch-Hunts

Prevailing European ideas about the natural world blended two distinct traditions. The older was made up of stories and beliefs from local folk cultures and pre-Christian religions, which had not lost their hold on the minds of most Europeans. On to this tradition was grafted the biblical traditions of the Christian and Jewish scriptures, heard by all in church and read by growing numbers in vernacular translations. In the minds of most people ideas of magic and folk spirits mixed with Christian teachings about miracles, saints, and devils.

Like people in other parts of the world, most early modern Europeans believed that natural events could have supernatural causes. When crops failed or domestic animals died unexpectedly, many people blamed unseen spirits. People also attributed human triumphs and tragedies to supernatural causes. When an earthquake destroyed much of Lisbon, Portugal's capital city, in November 1755, for example, both educated and uneducated saw the event as a punishment sent by God. A Jesuit charged it "scandalous to pretend that the earthquake was just a natural event." An English Protestant leader agreed, comparing Lisbon's fate with that of Sodom, the city that God destroyed because of the sinfulness of its citizens, according to the Hebrew Bible.

Nowhere was the belief in unseen forces more evident than in the extraordinary series of **witch-hunts** that swept across northern Europe in the late sixteenth and seventeenth centuries. It is estimated that secular and church authorities tried over a hundred thousand people—some three-fourths of them women—for prac-

Witchcraft

The elderly widow whose account follows was fairly typical of the kind of person accused of witchcraft in the Holy Roman Empire. Her confession, given in 1587, mentions activities commonly associated with witches: fornicating with devils, murdering children, desecrating the Blessed Sacrament, causing destructive storms, and night flying—though on a pitchfork, not a broomstick.

The herein mentioned, malefic and miserable woman, Walpurga Hausmännin, now imprisoned and in chains, has, upon kindly questioning and also torture, . . . confessed her witchcraft and admitted the following. When one-and-thirty years ago, she became a widow, she cut corn for Hans Schlumperger, of this place, together with his former servant, Bis im Pfarrhof, by name. Him she enticed with lewd speeches and gestures and they convened that they should, on an appointed night, meet in her, Walpurga's, dwelling, there to indulge in lustful intercourse. So when Walpurga in expectation of this, sat awaiting him at night in her chamber, meditating upon evil and fleshy thoughts, it was not the said bondsman who appeared unto her, but the Evil One in the latter's guise and raiment and indulged in fornication with her. . . . After the act of fornication she saw and felt the cloven foot of her whoremonger, and that his hand was not natural, but as if made of wood. She was greatly affrighted thereat and called upon the name of Jesus, whereupon the Devil left her and vanished.

On the ensuing night the Evil Spirit visited her again in the same shape and whored with her. . . . Further, the above-mentioned Walpurga confesses that she oft and much rode on a pitchfork by night with her paramour, but not far on account of her duties [as a midwife].

Since she surrendered to the Devil, she had seemingly oft received the Blessed Sacrament of the true Body and Blood of Jesus Christ, apparently by the mouth, but had not partaken of it, but (which once more is terrible to relate) had always taken it out of her mouth again and delivered it up to Federlin, her paramour. At their nightly gatherings she had oft with her other playfellows trodden under foot the Holy and Blessed Sacrament and the image of the Holy Cross. . . . .

He also compelled her to do away with and to kill young infants at birth, even before they had been taken to Holy Baptism. This she did whenever possible. . . . She had used the said little bones to manufacture hail; this she was wont to do once or twice a year. . . .

After all this, the Judges and Jury of the Court of this Town of Dillingen . . . at last unanimously gave the verdict that the aforesaid Walpurga Hausmännin be punished and dispatched from life to death by burning at the stake as being a maleficent and well-known witch and sorceress, convicted according to the context of Common Law and the Criminal Code of the Emperor Charles V and the Holy Roman Empire. All her goods and chattels and estate left after her to go to the Treasury of our Most High Prince and Lord. The aforesaid Walpurga to be led, seated on a cart, to which she is tied, to the place of her execution, and her body first to be torn five times with red-hot irons. . . . But since for nineteen years she was a licensed and pledged midwife of the city of Dillingen, yet has acted so vilely, her right hand with which she did such knavish tricks is to be cut off at the place of execution. Neither are her ashes after burning to remain lying on the ground, but are thereafter to be carried to the nearest flowing water and thrown thereinto.

Under what circumstances did the widow confess to these deeds? Why was she so brutally executed?

Source: *The Fugger News-Letters*, ed. Victor von Klarwill, trans. Pauline de Chary (London: John Lane, The Bodley Head Ltd., 1924); reissued as *News and Rumor in Renaissance Europe: The Fugger Newsletters*, trans. Pauline de Chary (New York: Putnam, 1959), 137–139, 142–143.

ticing witchcraft. Some were acquitted, some recanted, but over half were executed. The trial records make it clear that both the accusers and the accused believed that it was possible for angry and jealous individuals to use evil magic and the power of the Devil to cause people and domestic animals to sicken and die or cause crops to wither in the fields. Torture and badgering questions persuaded many accused witches to confess to casting spells and to describe in vivid detail their encounters with the Devil and their attendance at nighttime assemblies of witches (see Society and Culture: Witchcraft).

Modern historians have sought other explanations for these witch-hunts. The fact that many of the accused were older women, especially widows, may reflect the widespread belief that women not directly under the control of fathers or husbands were likely to turn to evil. The fear of people rebelling against those in authority was well founded.

Modern research, however, also stresses that at least some of those accused in early modern Europe may really have tried to use witchcraft and the powers of the Devil to harm their enemies. The Reformation had focused attention on the Devil and may have helped revive older fears of witchcraft. In parts of the world where belief in witchcraft is still strong, witch-hunts often arise at times of social stress, and people who are marginalized by poverty and by the suspicions of others often relish the celebrity that public confession brings. Self-confessed "witches" may even find release from the guilt they feel for wishing evil on their neighbors.

No single reason can explain the rise in witchcraft accusations and fears in early modern Europe, but, for both the accusers and the accused, there are plausible connections between the witch-hunts and rising social tensions, rural poverty, and environmental strains. Far from being a bizarre aberration, witch-hunts reflected the larger social climate of early modern Europe.

The Scientific Revolution

Ideas about the natural world were influenced by folk and Christian traditions and by writings from Greco-Roman antiquity that had been revived during the Renaissance. Among intellectuals prevailing ideas were based on the physics of Aristotle. The Greek philosopher taught that everything on earth was reducible to four elements. The surface of the earth was composed of the two heavy elements, earth and water. The atmosphere was made up of two lighter elements, air and fire, which floated above the ground. Higher still were the sun, moon, planets, and stars, which, according to Aristotelian physics, were so light and pure that they floated in crystalline spheres. This division between the ponderous, heavy earth and the airy, celestial bodies accorded perfectly with the common-sense perception that all heavenly bodies revolved around the earth.

The prevailing conception of the universe was also influenced by the mathematical tradition derived from the ancient Greek mathematician Pythagoras, who proved the validity of the famous theorem that still bears his name: In a right triangle, the squares of the hy-

potenuse is equal to the sum of the squares of the other two sides ($a^2 + b^2 = c^2$). Pythagoreans attributed to mystical properties the ability of simple mathematical equations to describe physical objects. They attached special significance to the simplest (to them perfect) geometrical shapes: the circle (a point rotated around another point) and the sphere (a circle rotated on its axis). They believed that celestial objects were perfect spheres orbiting the earth in perfectly circular orbits.

In the sixteenth century, however, the careful observations and mathematical calculations of some daring and imaginative European investigators began to challenge these prevailing conceptions of the physical world. These pioneers of the **Scientific Revolution** demonstrated that the workings of the universe could be explained by natural causes.

Over the centuries, observers of the nighttime skies had plotted the movements of the heavenly bodies, and mathematicians had worked to fit these observations into the prevailing theories of circular orbits. To make all the evidence fit, they had come up with eighty different spheres and some ingenious theories to explain the many seemingly irregular movements. Pondering these complications, a Polish monk and mathematician named Nicholas Copernicus (1473–1543) came up with a mathematically simpler solution: switching the center of the different orbits from the earth to the sun would reduce the number of spheres that were needed.

Copernicus did not challenge the idea that the sun, moon, and planets were light, perfect spheres, or that they moved in circular orbits. But his placement of the sun, not the earth, at the center of things began a revolution in understanding about the structure of the heavens and about the central place of humans in the universe. To escape the anticipated controversies, Copernicus delayed the publication of his heliocentric (sun-centered) theory until after his death in 1543.

Other astronomers, including the Danish Tycho Brahe (1546–1601) and his German assistant Johannes Kepler (1571–1630), strengthened and improved on Copernicus's model, showing that planets actually move in elliptical, not circular orbits. The most brilliant of the Copernicans was the Italian Galileo Galilei° (1564–1642). In 1609 Galileo built a telescope through which he took a closer look at the heavens. Able to magnify distant objects thirty times beyond the powers of the naked eye, Galileo saw that heavenly bodies were not the perfectly smooth spheres of the Aristotelians. The moon, he re-

Galileo Galilei (gal-uh-LAY-oh gal-uh-LAY-ee)

ported in *The Starry Messenger* (1610), had mountains and valleys; the sun had spots; other planets had their own moons. In other words, the earth was not alone in being heavy and changeable.

At first, the Copernican universe found more critics than supporters because it so directly challenged not just popular ideas but the intellectual synthesis of classical and biblical authorities. How, demanded Aristotle's defenders, could the heavy earth move without producing vibrations that would shake the planet apart? Is the Bible wrong, asked the theologians, when the Book of Joshua says that, by God's command, "the sun [not the earth] stood still . . . for about a whole day" to give the ancient Israelites victory in their conquest of Palestine? If Aristotle's physics was wrong, worried other traditionalists, would not the theological synthesis built on other parts of his philosophy be open to question?

Intellectual and religious leaders encouraged political authorities to suppress the new ideas. Most Protestant leaders, following the lead of Martin Luther, condemned the heliocentric universe as contrary to the Bible. Catholic authorities waited longer to act. After all, both Copernicus and Galileo were Roman Catholics. Copernicus had dedicated his book to the pope, and another pope, Gregory XIII, in 1582 had used the latest astronomical findings to issue a new and more accurate calendar (still used today). Galileo ingeniously argued that the conflict between scripture and science was only apparent: the word of God revealed in the Bible was expressed in the imperfect language of ordinary people, but in nature God's truth was revealed more perfectly in a language that could be learned by careful observation and scientific reasoning.

Unfortunately, Galileo also ridiculed those who were slow to accept his findings, charging that Copernican ideas were "mocked and hooted at by an infinite multitude . . . of fools." Smarting under Galileo's stinging sarcasm, some Jesuits and other critics got his ideas condemned by the Roman Inquisition in 1616, which put *The Starry Messenger* on the Index of Forbidden Books and prohibited Galileo from publishing further on the subject. (In 1992 the Catholic Church officially retracted its condemnation of Galileo.)

Despite official opposition, printed books spread the new scientific ideas among scholars across Europe. In England, Robert Boyle (1627–1691) used experimental methods and a trial-and-error approach to examine the inner workings of chemistry. He and fellow members of the Royal Society were enthusiastic missionaries of mechanical science and fierce opponents of the Aristotelians.

Galileo in 1624   This engraving by Ottavio Leone shows the Italian scientist in full vigor at age sixty, before he was hounded by the Roman Inquisition.   (British Museum)

Meanwhile, English mathematician Isaac Newton (1642–1727) was carrying Galileo's demonstration that the heavens and earth share a common physics to its logical conclusion. Newton formulated a set of mathematical laws that all physical objects obeyed. It was the force of gravity—not angels—that governed the elliptical orbits of heavenly bodies. It was gravitation (and the resistance of air) that caused cannonballs to fall back to earth. From 1703 until his death Newton served as president of the Royal Society, using his prestige to promote the new science that came to bear his name.

As the condemnation of Galileo demonstrates, many religious and intellectual leaders viewed the new science with suspicion or outright hostility. Yet the principal pioneers of the Scientific Revolution were all convinced that scientific discoveries and revealed religion were not in conflict. At the peak of his fame Newton promoted a series of lectures devoted to proving the validity of Christianity. However, by showing that the Aristotelians and biblical writers held ideas about the natural world that were naive and unfactual, these pioneers opened the door to others who used reason to challenge a broader range of unquestioned traditions and superstitions. The world of ideas was forever changed.

The Early Enlightenment

Advances in scientific thought had few practical applications until long after 1750. But they inspired governments and private groups in many countries to reexamine the reasonableness of everything from agricultural methods to laws, religion, and social hierarchies. The belief that human reason could discover the laws that governed social behavior and were just as scientific as the laws that governed physics energized a movement known as the **Enlightenment.** Like the Scientific Revolution, this movement was the work of a few "enlightened" individuals who often faced bitter opposition from the political, intellectual, and religious establishment. Leading Enlightenment thinkers became accustomed to having their books burned or banned and spent long periods in exile to escape being imprisoned themselves.

Influences besides the Scientific Revolution affected the Enlightenment. The Reformation had aroused many to champion one creed or another, but partisan bickering and bloodshed led others to doubt the superiority of any theological position and to recommend toleration of all religions. The killing of suspected witches also shocked many thoughtful people. The leading French thinker Voltaire (the pen name of François Marie Arouet, 1694–1778) declared: "No opinion is worth burning your neighbor for."

Accounts of cultures in other parts of the world also led some European thinkers to question assumptions about the superiority of European political institutions, moral standards, and religious beliefs. Reports of Amerindian life, though romanticized, led some to conclude that those whom they had called savages were in many ways nobler than European Christians. Matteo Ricci, a Jesuit missionary to China whose journals made a strong impression in Europe, contrasted the lack of territorial ambition of the Chinese with the constant warfare in the West and attributed the difference to the fact that China was wisely ruled by educated men whom he called "Philosophers."

Another influence on the "enlightened" thinkers of the eighteenth century was the English Revolution. In the wake of the Glorious Revolution of 1688 and the English Bill of Rights, the English political philosopher John Locke (1632–1704), who had lived in the Netherlands during the period of Oliver Cromwell's Puritan Republic, published his influential *Second Treatise of Civil Government* (1690). Locke disputed the prevailing idea that government was sacred and that kings ruled by divine right. He argued that rulers derived their power from the consent of the governed, who surrendered some of their rights to the state so that they might better preserve their lives, liberty, and property. Locke challenged the continental monarchs' often-repeated claim that they held absolute authority over their subjects. He believed that absolute monarchy was incompatible with civil society, and he wrote that monarchs, like everyone else, were subject to the law that laid the basis for the compact that brought civil society into existence. If monarchs overstepped the law, Locke argued, citizens had not only the right but the duty to rebel. The consequences of this idea are considered in Chapter 23.

Although many circumstances shaped "enlightened" thinking, the new scientific methods and discoveries provided the clearest model for changing European society. Voltaire posed the issues in these terms: "it would be very peculiar that all nature, all the planets, should obey eternal laws" but a human being, "in contempt of these laws, could act as he pleased solely according to his caprice." The English poet Alexander Pope (1688–1774) made a similar point in verse: "Nature and Nature's laws lay hidden in night; / God said, 'Let Newton be' and all was light."

The Enlightenment was more a frame of mind than a coherent movement. Individuals who embraced it drew inspiration from different sources and promoted different agendas. By 1750 its proponents were clearer about what they disliked than about what new institutions should be created. Some "enlightened" thinkers thought society could be made to function with the mechanical orderliness of planets spinning in their orbits. Nearly all were optimistic that—at least in the long run—human beliefs and institutions could be improved. This belief in progress would help foster political and social revolutions after 1750, as Chapter 23 recounts.

Despite the enthusiasm the Enlightenment aroused in some circles, it was decidedly unpopular with many absolutist rulers and with most clergymen. Europe in 1750 was neither enlightened nor scientific. It was a place where political and religious divisions, growing literacy, and the printing press made possible the survival of the new ideas that profoundly changed life in future centuries.

CONCLUSION

Historians use the word *revolution* to describe many different changes taking place in Europe between 1500 and 1750. The inflation of the sixteenth century has been called a price revolution, the expansion of trade a commercial revolution, the reform of state spending a financial revolution, the changes in weapons and warfare a military revolution. We have also encountered a scientific revolution and the religious revolution of the Reformation.

These important changes in early modern European government, economy, society, and thought were parts of a dynamic process that began in the later Middle Ages and led to even bigger industrial and political revolutions before the eighteenth century was over. Yet the years from 1500 to 1750 were not simply—perhaps not even primarily—an age of progress for Europe. For many, the ferocious competition of European armies, merchants, and ideas was a wrenching experience. The growth of powerful states extracted a terrible price in death, destruction, and misery. The Reformation brought greater individual choice in religion but widespread religious persecution as well. Individual women rose or fell with their social class, but few gained equality with men. The expanding economy benefited members of the emerging merchant elite and their political allies, but most Europeans became worse off as prices rose faster than wages. New scientific and enlightened ideas ignited new controversies long before they yielded any tangible benefits.

The historical significance of this period of European history is clearest when viewed in a global context. What stands out are the powerful and efficient European armies, economies, and governments, which were envied, and sometimes imitated, by other people such as Tsar Peter the Great. Seen from a global perspective, the balance of political and economic power shifted slowly but inexorably in the Europeans' favor from 1500 to 1750. In 1500 the Ottomans threatened Europe. By 1750, as the remaining chapters of Part Five detail, Europeans had brought the world's seas and a growing part of its land and people under their control. No single group of Europeans accomplished this. The Dutch eclipsed the pioneering Portuguese and Spanish; then the English and French bested the Dutch. Competition, too, was a factor in the European success.

Other changes in Europe during this period had no great overseas significance yet. The more representative and financially stable government begun in Britain, the new ideas of the Scientific Revolution and the Enlightenment, and the innovations in agriculture and manufacturing were still of minor importance. Their full effects in furthering Europeans' global dominion were felt after 1750, as Parts Six and Seven will explore.

■ Key Terms

papacy	balance of power
Renaissance (Europe)	bourgeoisie
indulgence	joint-stock company
Protestant Reformation	stock exchange
Catholic Reformation	Little Ice Age
Holy Roman Empire	deforestation
Habsburg	witch-hunt
absolutism	Scientific Revolution
constitutionalism	Enlightenment

■ Suggested Reading

Overviews of this period include Euan Cameron, *Early Modern Europe* (1999), and H. G. Koenigsberger, *Early Modern Europe: Fifteen Hundred to Seventeen Eighty-Nine* (1987). Global perspectives can be found in Fernand Braudel, *Civilization and Capitalism, 15th–18th Century*, trans. Siân Reynolds, 3 vols. (1979), and Immanuel Wallerstein, *The Modern World-System*, vol. 2, *Mercantilism and the Consolidation of the European World-Economy, 1600–1750* (1980).

Excellent introductions to social and economic life are George Huppert, *After the Black Death: A Social History of Early Modern Europe* (1986), and Carlo M. Cipolla, *Before the Industrial Revolution: European Society and Economy, 1000–1700*, 2d ed. (1980). Peter Burke, *Popular Culture in Early Modern Europe* (1978), offers a broad treatment of nonelite perspectives, as does Robert Jütte, *Poverty and Deviance in Early Modern Europe* (1994). For more economic detail see Robert S. DuPlessis, *Transitions to Capitalism in Early Modern Europe* (1997); Myron P. Gutmann, *Toward the Modern Economy: Early Industry in Europe, 1500–1800* (1988); and Carlo M. Cipolla, ed., *The Fontana Economic History of Europe*, vol. 2, *The Sixteenth and Seventeenth Centuries* (1974). Merry E. Wiesner summarizes a body of new research in *Women and Gender in Early Modern Europe* (1994).

Technological and environmental changes are the focus of Geoffrey Parker, *Military Revolution: Military Innovation and the Rise of the West, 1500–1800*, 2d ed. (1996); William H. McNeill, *The Pursuit of Power: Technology, Armed Force, and Society Since A.D. 1000* (1982); Robert Greenhalgh Albion, *Forests and Sea Power: The Timber Problem of the Royal Navy, 1652–1862*

(1965); Emmanuel Le Roy Ladurie, *Times of Feast, Times of Famine: A History of Climate Since the Year 1000*, trans. Barbara Bray (1971); and Jean M. Grove, *The Little Ice Age* (1988). Robert C. Allen, *Enclosure and the Yeoman: The Agricultural Development of the South Midlands, 1450–1850* (1992), focuses on England.

Steven Stapin, *The Scientific Revolution* (1998), and Hugh Kearney, *Science and Change, 1500–1700* (1971) are accessible introductions. Thomas S. Kuhn, *The Structure of Scientific Revolution*, 3d ed. (1996), and A. R. Hall, *The Scientific Revolution, 1500–1800: The Formation of the Modern Scientific Attitude*, 2d ed. (1962), are classic studies. Carolyn Merchant, *The Death of Nature: Women, Ecology and the Scientific Revolution* (1980), tries to combine several broad perspectives. *The Sciences in Enlightened Europe*, ed. W. Clark, J. Golinski, and S. Schaffer (1999), examines particular topics in a sophisticated way. Dorinda Outram, *The Enlightenment* (1995), provides a recent summary of research.

An excellent place to begin examining the complex subject of witchcraft is Brian Levack, *The Witch-Hunt in Early Modern Europe*, 2d ed. (1995). Anne Llewellyn Barstow, *Witchcraft: A New History of the European Witch Hunts* (1994), offers a postmodern interpretation; other up-to-date perspectives can be found in J. Barry, M. Hester, and G. Roberts, eds., *Witchcraft in Early Modern Europe: Studies in Culture and Belief* (1998), and Carlo Ginzburg, *The Night Battles: Witchcraft and Agrarian Cults in the Sixteenth and Seventeenth Centuries*, trans. John and Anne Tedechi (1983). Cross-cultural perspectives are presented by Lucy Mair, *Witchcraft* (1969), and Geoffrey Parrinder, *Witchcraft: European and African* (1963).

Good single-country surveys are J. A. Sharpe, *Early Modern England: A Social History*, 2d ed. (1997); Emmanuel Le Roy Ladurie, *The Royal French State, 1460–1610* (1994) and *The Ancien Régime: A History of France, 1610–1774* (1998); Jonathan Israel, *The Dutch Republic: Its Rise, Greatness and Fall, 1477–1806* (1995); and James Casey, *Early Modern Spain: A Social History* (1999).

▪ Notes

1. William H. McNeill, *The Pursuit of Power: Technology, Armed Force, and Society Since a.d. 1000* (Chicago: University of Chicago Press, 1982), 124.
2. Michel de Montaigne, *Essais*, ch. 31, "Des Cannibales."
3. Quoted by Carlo M. Cipolla, "Introduction," *The Fontana Economic History of Europe*, vol. 2, *The Sixteenth and Seventeenth Centuries* (Glasgow: Collins/Fontana Books, 1974), 11–12.

19

THE DIVERSITY OF AMERICAN COLONIAL SOCIETIES,

1530–1770

The Columbian Exchange • Spanish America and Brazil • English and
French Colonies in North America • Colonial Expansion and Conflict
ENVIRONMENT AND TECHNOLOGY: The Silver Refinery at Potosí, Bolivia, 1700
SOCIETY AND CULTURE: Colonial Wealth and the Exploitation of Indigenous Peoples

Vista de una Máquina, para cernír Tabáco enla R.¹ Fabrica de Sigarros 19.

VIVA EL REY.

Tobacco Factory Machinery in Colonial Mexico City   The tobacco factory in eighteenth-century Mexico City
used a horse-driven mechanical shredder to produce snuff and cigarette tobacco.

hulush Homa—an eighteenth-century Choctaw leader called "Red Shoes" by the English—faced a dilemma. For years he had befriended the French who had moved into the lower Mississippi Valley, protecting their outlying settlements from other indigenous groups and producing a steady flow of deerskins for trade. In return, he received guns and gifts as well as honors previously given only to chiefs. Though born a commoner, he had parlayed his skillful politicking with the French—and the shrewd distribution of the gifts he received—to enhance his position in Choctaw society. Then his fortunes turned. In the course of yet another war between England and France, the English cut off French shipping. Faced with followers unhappy over his sudden inability to supply French guns, Red Shoes decided to make a deal with the English. Unfortunately, the new tactic backfired. His former allies, the French, put a price on his head, which was soon collected. His murder in 1747 launched a Choctaw civil war, a conflict that left French settlements unprotected and the Choctaw people weakened.

The story of Red Shoes reveals a number of themes from the period of European colonization of the Americas. First, although the wars, epidemics, and territorial loss associated with European settlement threatened Amerindians, many adapted the new technologies and new political possibilities to their own purposes and thrived—at least for a time. In the end, though, the best that they could achieve was a holding action. The people of the Old World were coming to dominate the people of the New.

Second, after centuries of isolation, the Americas were being drawn into global events, influenced by the political and economic demands of Europe. The influx of Europeans and Africans resulted in a vast biological and cultural transformation, as the introduction of new plants, animals, diseases, peoples, and technologies fundamentally altered the natural environment of the Western Hemisphere. This was not a one-way transfer, however. The technologies and resources of the New World contributed to profound changes in the Old. Staple crops introduced from the Americas provided highly nutritious foods that helped fuel a population spurt in Europe, Asia, and Africa. As we saw in Chapter 18, riches and products funneled from the Americas changed economic, social, and political relations in Europe.

Third, the fluidity of the Choctaw's political situation reflects the complexity of colonial society, where Amerindians, Europeans, and Africans all contributed to the creation of new cultures. Although similar processes took place throughout the Americas, the particulars varied from place to place, creating a diverse range of cultures. The society that arose in each colony reflected the colony's mix of native peoples, its connections to the slave trade, and the characteristics of the European society establishing the colony. As the colonies matured, new concepts of identity developed, and those living in the Americas began to see themselves as unique.

As you read this chapter, ask yourself the following questions:

- How did the development of European colonies in the Americas alter the natural environment?

- What were the most important differences in the colonial political institutions and economies created by Spain, Portugal, England, and France?

- How important was forced labor to the European colonies?

THE COLUMBIAN EXCHANGE

The term **Columbian Exchange** refers to the transfer of peoples, animals, plants, and diseases between the New and Old Worlds. The European invasion and settlement of the Western Hemisphere opened a long era of biological and technological transfers that altered American environments. Within a century of first settlement, the domesticated livestock and major agricultural crops of the Old World (the known world before Columbus's voyage) had spread over much of the Americas, and the New World's useful staple crops had enriched the agricultures of Europe, Asia, and Africa. Old World diseases

CHRONOLOGY

	Spanish America	Brazil	British America	French America
1500	1518 Smallpox arrives in Caribbean 1535 Creation of Viceroyalty of New Spain 1540s Creation of Viceroyalty of Peru 1542 New Laws outlaw Amerindian enslavement 1545 Silver discovered at Potosí, Bolivia	1540–1600 Era of Amerindian slavery After 1540 Sugar begins to dominate the economy		1524–1554 Jacques Cartier's voyages to explore Newfoundland and Gulf of St. Lawrence
1600	1625 Population of Potosí reaches 120,000	By 1620 African slave trade provides majority of plantation workers	1583 Unsuccessful effort to establish colony on Newfoundland 1607 Jamestown founded 1620 Plymouth founded 1660 Slave population in Virginia begins period of rapid growth 1664 English take New York from Dutch	1608 Quebec founded
1700	1700 Last Habsburg ruler of Spain dies 1713 First Bourbon ruler of Spain crowned	1750–1777 Reforms of marquis de Pombal	1756–1763 French and Indian War	1699 Louisiana founded 1760 English take Canada

that entered the Americas with European immigrants and African slaves devastated indigenous populations. These dramatic population changes weakened native peoples' capacity for resistance and facilitated the transfer of plants, animals, and related technologies. As a result, the colonies of Spain, Portugal, England, and France became vast arenas of cultural and social experimentation.

Demographic Changes

Because of their long isolation from other continents (see Chapter 17), the peoples of the New World lacked immunity to diseases introduced from the Old World. As a result, death rates among Amerindian peoples during the epidemics of the early colonial period were very high. The lack of reliable data has frustrated efforts to measure the deadly impact of these diseases. Scholars disagree about the size of the precontact population but generally agree that, after contact, Old World diseases overwhelmed native populations. According to one estimate, in the century that followed the triumph of Hernán Cortés in 1521, the population of central Mexico fell from a high somewhere between 13 million and 25 million to approximately 700,000. In this same period nearly 75 percent of the Maya population disappeared. In the region of the Inca Empire, population fell from about 9 million to approximately 600,000. Brazil's native population was similarly ravaged, falling from 2.5 million to under a million within a century of the arrival of the Portuguese. The most conservative estimates of population loss begin with smaller precontact populations but accept that epidemics had a catastrophic effect.

Smallpox, which arrived in the Caribbean in 1518, was the most deadly of the early epidemics. In Mexico and Central America, 50 percent or more of the Amerindian population died during the first wave of smallpox epidemics. The disease then spread to South America with equally devastating effects. Measles arrived in the New World in the 1530s and was followed by diphtheria, typhus, influenza, and, perhaps, pulmonary plague. Mortality was often greatest when two or more diseases struck at the same time. Between 1520 and 1521 influenza in combination with other ailments attacked the Cakchiquel of Guatemala. Their chronicle recalls:

> Great was the stench of the dead. After our fathers and grandfathers succumbed, half the people fled to the fields. The dogs and vultures devoured the bodies. . . . So it was that we became orphans, oh my sons! . . . We were born to die![1]

By the mid-seventeenth century, malaria and yellow fever were also present in tropical regions. The deadliest form of malaria arrived with the African slave trade. It ravaged the already reduced native populations and afflicted European immigrants as well. Most scholars believe that yellow fever was also brought from Africa, but new research suggests that the disease was present before the conquest in the tropical low country near present-day Veracruz on the Gulf of Mexico. Whatever its origins, yellow fever killed Europeans in the Caribbean Basin and in other tropical regions nearly as efficiently as smallpox had earlier extinguished Amerindians. Syphilis is the only significant disease believed to have been transferred from the Americas to Europe.

The development of English and French colonies in North America in the seventeenth century led to similar patterns of contagion and mortality. In 1616 and 1617 epidemics nearly exterminated many of New England's indigenous groups. French fur traders transmitted measles, smallpox, and other diseases as far as Hudson Bay and the Great Lakes. Although there is very little evidence that Europeans consciously used disease as a tool of empire, the deadly results of contact clearly undermined the ability of native peoples to resist settlement.

Transfer of Plants and Animals

Even as epidemics swept through the indigenous population, the New and the Old Worlds were participating in a vast exchange of plants and animals that radically altered diet and lifestyles in both regions. All the staples of southern European agriculture—such as wheat, olives,

The Columbian Exchange After the conquest, the introduction of plants and animals from the Old World dramatically altered the American environment. Here an Amerindian woman is seen milking a cow. Livestock sometimes destroyed the fields of native peoples, but cattle, sheep, pigs, and goats also provided food, leather, and wool. (From Martinez Compañon, *Trujillo del Perú*, V.II, E 79. Photo: Imaging services, Harvard College Library)

grapes, and garden vegetables—were being grown in the Americas in a remarkably short time after contact. African and Asian crops—such as rice, bananas, coconuts, breadfruit, and sugar cane—were soon introduced as well. Native peoples remained loyal to their traditional staples but added many Old World plants to their diet. Citrus fruits, melons, figs, and sugar as well as onions, radishes, and salad greens all found a place in Amerindian cuisines.

In return the Americas offered the Old World an abundance of useful plants. The New World staples—

maize, potatoes, and manioc—revolutionized agriculture and diet in parts of Europe, Africa, and Asia (see Environment and Technology: Amerindian Foods in Africa, in Chapter 20). Many experts assert that the rapid growth of world population after 1700 resulted in large measure from the spread of these useful crops, which provided more calories per acre than any of the Old World staples except rice. Beans, squash, tomatoes, sweet potatoes, peanuts, chilies, and chocolate also gained widespread acceptance in the Old World. The New World also provided the Old with plants that provided dyes, medicinal plants, varieties of cotton, and tobacco.

The introduction of European livestock had a dramatic impact on New World environments and cultures. Faced with few natural predators, cattle, pigs, horses, and sheep, as well as pests like rats and rabbits, multiplied rapidly in the open spaces of the Americas. On the vast plains of present-day southern Brazil, Uruguay, and Argentina, herds of wild cattle and horses exceeded 50 million by 1700. Large herds of both animals also appeared in northern Mexico and what became the southwest of the United States.

Where Old World livestock spread most rapidly, environmental changes were most dramatic. Many priests and colonial officials noted the destructive impact of marauding livestock on Amerindian agriculturists. The first viceroy of Mexico, Antonio de Mendoza, wrote to the Spanish king, "May your Lordship realize that if cattle are allowed, the Indians will be destroyed." Sheep, which grazed grasses close to the ground, were also an environmental threat. Yet the viceroy's stark choice misrepresented the complex response of indigenous peoples to these new animals.

Wild cattle on the plains of South America, northern Mexico, and Texas provided indigenous peoples with abundant supplies of meat and hides. In the present-day southwestern United States, the Navajo became sheepherders and expert weavers of woolen cloth. Even in the centers of European settlement, individual Amerindians turned European animals to their own advantage by becoming muleteers, cowboys, and sheepherders.

No animal had a more striking effect on the cultures of native peoples than the horse, which increased the efficiency of hunters and the military capacity of warriors on the plains. The horse permitted the Apache, Sioux, Blackfoot, Comanche, Assiniboine, and others to hunt more efficiently the vast herds of buffalo in North America. The horse also revolutionized the cultures of the Araucanian (or Mapuche) and Pampas peoples in South America.

Spanish America and Brazil

The frontiers of conquest and settlement expanded rapidly. Within one hundred years of Columbus's first voyage to the Western Hemisphere, the Spanish Empire in America included most of the islands of the Caribbean, Mexico, the American southwest, Central America, the Caribbean and Pacific coasts of South America, the Andean highlands, and the vast plains of the Rio de la Plata region (a region that includes the modern nations of Argentina, Uruguay, and Paraguay). Portuguese settlement in the New World developed more slowly. But before the end of the sixteenth century, Portugal occupied most of the Brazilian coast.

Early settlers from Spain and Portugal sought to create colonial societies based on the institutions and customs of their homelands. They viewed society as a vertical arrangement of estates (classes of society), as uniformly Catholic, and as an arrangement of patriarchal extended-family networks. And they moved quickly to establish in the new colonies the religious, social, and administrative institutions that were familiar to them.

Despite the imposition of foreign institutions and the massive loss of life caused by epidemics in the sixteenth century, indigenous peoples exercised a powerful influence on the development of colonial societies. Aztec and Inca elite families sought to protect their traditional privileges and rights through marriage or less formal alliances with the Spanish settlers. They also often used colonial courts to defend their claims to land. In Spanish and Portuguese colonies, indigenous military allies and laborers proved crucial to the development of European settlements. Nearly everywhere, Amerindian religious beliefs and practices survived beneath the surface of an imposed Christianity. Amerindian languages, cuisines, medical practices, and agricultural techniques also survived the conquest and influenced the development of Latin American culture.

The African slave trade added a third cultural stream to colonial Latin American society. At first, African slaves were concentrated in plantation regions of Brazil and the Caribbean (see Chapter 20), but by the end of the colonial era, Africans and their descendants were living throughout Latin America, enriching colonial societies with their traditional agricultural practices, music, religious beliefs, cuisine, and social customs.

State and Church

The Spanish crown moved quickly to curb the independent power of the conquistadors and to establish royal authority over both the defeated native populations and the rising tide of European settlers. Created in 1524, the **Council of the Indies** in Spain supervised all government, ecclesiastical, and commercial activity in the Spanish colonies. Geography and technology, however, limited the Council's real power. Local officials could not be controlled too closely, because a ship needed more than two hundred days to make a roundtrip voyage from Spain to Veracruz, Mexico, and additional months of travel were required to reach Lima, Peru.

As a result of these difficulties of communication, the viceroy of New Spain and the viceroy of Peru, the highest-ranking Spanish officials in the colonies, enjoyed broad power. But the two viceroyalties in their jurisdiction were also vast territories with geographic obstacles to communication. Created in 1535, the Viceroyalty of New Spain, with its capital in Mexico City, included Mexico and the southwest of what is now the United States, Central America, and the islands of the Caribbean. The Viceroyalty of Peru, with its capital in Lima, was formed in the 1540s to govern Spanish South America (see Map 19.1). Each viceroyalty was divided into a number of judicial and administrative districts. Until the seventeenth century, almost all of the officials appointed to high positions in Spain's colonial bureaucracy were born in Spain. Eventually, economic mismanagement in Spain forced the Crown to sell appointments to these positions, and, as a result, local-born members of the colonial elite gained many offices.

In the sixteenth century Portugal concentrated its resources and energies on Asia and Africa. Because early settlers found neither mineral wealth nor rich native empires in Brazil, the Portuguese king hesitated to set up expensive mechanisms of colonial government in the New World. Seeking to promote settlement but limit costs, the king in effect sublet administrative responsibilities in Brazil to court favorites by granting twelve hereditary captaincies in the 1530s. After mismanagement and inadequate investment doomed this experiment, the king appointed a governor-general in 1549 and made Salvador, in the northern province of Bahia, Brazil's capital. In 1720 the first viceroy of Brazil was named.

The government institutions of the Spanish and Portuguese colonies had a more uniform character and were much more extensive and costly than those later established in North America by France and Great Britain. Taxes paid by the silver and gold mines of Spanish America and in Brazil by the sugar plantations and after 1690 by gold mines funded large and intrusive colonial bureaucracies. These institutions made the colonies more responsive to the initiatives of Spain and Portugal, but they also thwarted local economic initiative and political experimentation.

The Catholic Church became the primary agent for the introduction and transmission of Christian belief as well as European language and culture in both Spanish America and Brazil. It undertook the conversion of Amerindians, ministered to the spiritual needs of European settlers and their children, and promoted intellectual life through the introduction of the printing press and formal education.

Spain and Portugal justified their American conquests by assuming an obligation to convert native populations to Christianity. This religious objective was sometimes forgotten, and some members of the clergy were themselves exploiters of native populations. Nevertheless, the effort to convert America's native peoples expanded Christianity on a scale similar to its earlier expansion in Europe at the time of Constantine in the fourth century. In Mexico alone hundreds of thousands of conversions and baptisms were achieved within a few years of the conquest.

The Catholic clergy sought to achieve their evangelical ends by first converting members of the Amerindian elites, in the hope that they could persuade others to follow their example. Franciscan missionaries in Mexico hoped to train members of the indigenous elite for the clergy. These idealistic efforts had to be abandoned when church authorities discovered that many converts were secretly observing old beliefs and rituals. The trial and punishment of two converted Aztec nobles for heresy in the 1530s highlighted this problem. Three decades later, Spanish clergy resorted to torture, executions, and the destruction of native manuscripts to eradicate traditional beliefs and rituals among the Maya. Repelled by these events, the church hierarchy ended both the violent repression of native religious practice and efforts to recruit an Amerindian clergy.

Despite its failures, the Catholic clergy did provide native peoples with some protections against the abuse and exploitation of Spanish settlers. The priest **Bartolomé de Las Casas** (1474–1566) was the most influential defender of the Amerindians in the early colonial

Map. 19.1   Colonial Latin America in the Eighteenth Century Spain and Portugal controlled most of the Western Hemisphere in the eighteenth century. In the sixteenth century they had created new administrative jurisdictions—viceroyalties—to defend their respective colonies against European rivals. Taxes assessed on colonial products helped pay for this extension of governmental authority.

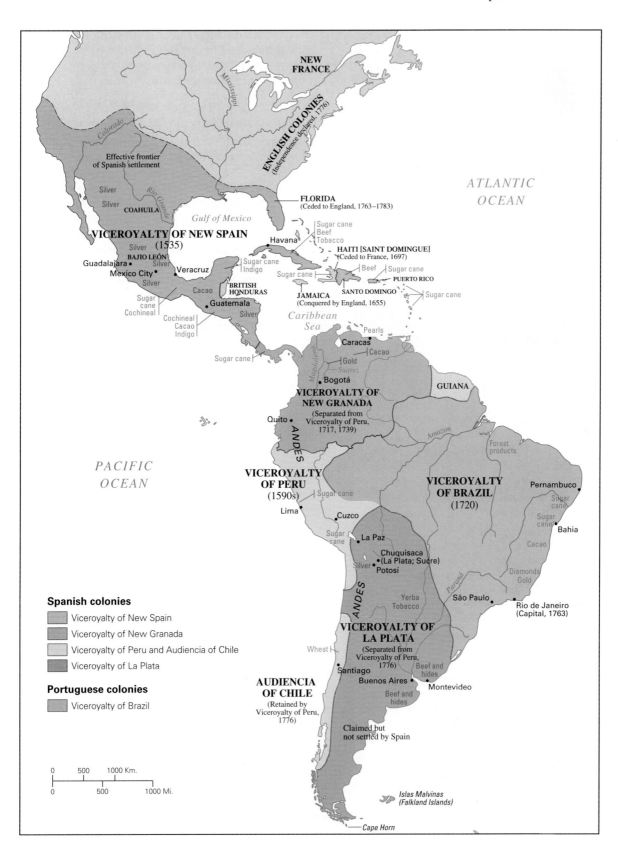

NEW FRANCE

Mississippi

ENGLISH COLONIES
(Independence declared, 1776)

Colorado

Effective frontier
of Spanish settlement

*ATLANTIC
OCEAN*

Silver

Silver

Rio Grande

COAHUILA

FLORIDA
(Ceded to England, 1763–1783)

Gulf of Mexico

VICEROYALTY OF NEW SPAIN (1535)

Silver

Havana

Sugar cane
Beef
Tobacco

HAITI [SAINT DOMINGUE]
(Ceded to France, 1697)

BAJIO LEÓN

Silver

Guadalajara

Beef

Sugar cane

Mexico City

Veracruz

Silver

Sugar cane
Indigo

PUERTO RICO

Sugar cane

SANTO DOMINGO

Cacao

BRITISH
HONDURAS

JAMAICA
(Conquered by England, 1655)

Sugar cane

Sugar
cane
Cochineal

Guatemala

Silver

Cochineal
Cacao
Indigo

*Caribbean
Sea*

Pearls

Sugar cane

Caracas

Cacao

Magdalena

Gold

Suarez

GUIANA

Bogotá

VICEROYALTY OF
NEW GRANADA
(Separated from
Viceroyalty of Peru,
1717, 1739)

Quito

Amazon

Forest
products

*PACIFIC
OCEAN*

VICEROYALTY
OF PERU
(1590s)

Sugar cane

VICEROYALTY
OF BRAZIL
(1720)

Pernambuco

Sugar
cane

Lima

Cuzco

Sugar
cane

Sugar
cane

Bahia

La Paz

Cacao

Chuquisaca
(La Plata; Sucre)

Potosí

Silver

Diamonds
Gold

Paraná

São Paulo

Yerba
Tobacco

Rio de Janeiro
(Capital, 1763)

ANDES

VICEROYALTY OF
LA PLATA
(Separated from
Viceroyalty of Peru,
1776)

Wheat

Beef and
hides

AUDIENCIA
OF CHILE
(Retained by
Viceroyalty of Peru,
1776)

Santiago

Buenos Aires

Montevideo

Beef and
hides

Claimed but
not settled by Spain

Spanish colonies

Viceroyalty of New Spain

Viceroyalty of New Granada

Viceroyalty of Peru and Audiencia of Chile

Viceroyalty of La Plata

Portuguese colonies

Viceroyalty of Brazil

0   500   1000 Km.

0   500   1000 Mi.

*Islas Malvinas
(Falkland Islands)*

Cape Horn

Saint Martín de Porres (1579–1639)　Martín de Porres was the illegitimate son of a Spanish nobleman and his black servant. Eventually recognized by his father, he entered the Dominican Order in Lima, Peru. Known for his generosity, he experienced visions and gained the ability to heal the sick. As was common in colonial religious art, the artist celebrates Martín de Porres's spirituality while representing him doing the type of work assumed most suitable for a person of mixed descent.　(Mint Museum of Art, Charlotte, NC)

period. He arrived in Hispaniola in 1502 as a settler and initially lived off the forced labor and appropriated goods of Amerindians. Deeply moved by the deaths of so many Amerindians and by the misdeeds of the Spanish, Las Casas gave up this way of life and entered the Dominican Order, later becoming the first bishop of Chiapas, in southern Mexico. For the remainder of his long life Las Casas served as the most important advocate for native peoples, writing a number of books that detailed their mistreatment by the Spanish. His most important achievement was the enactment of the New Laws of

1542—reform legislation that outlawed the enslavement of Amerindians and limited other forms of forced labor.

European clergy arrived in the colonies with the intention of transmitting Catholic Christian belief and ritual without alteration. But the large size of Amerindian populations and their geographic dispersal over a vast landscape thwarted this objective. Linguistic and cultural differences among native peoples also inhibited missionary efforts. These problems frustrated Catholic missionaries and sometimes led to repression and cruelty. But the limited success of evangelization permitted the appearance of what must be seen as an Amerindian Christianity that blended Catholic Christian beliefs with important elements of traditional native cosmology and ritual. Most commonly, indigenous beliefs and rituals came to be embedded in the celebration of saints' days or Catholic rituals associated with the Virgin Mary. The Catholic clergy and most European settlers viewed this evolving mixture as the work of the Devil or as evidence of Amerindian inferiority. Instead it was one component of the process of cultural borrowing and innovation that contributed to a distinct and original Latin American culture.

The terrible loss of Amerindian population caused by epidemics and growing signs of resistance to conversion led the Catholic Church to redirect most of its resources from native regions in the countryside to growing colonial cities and towns with large European populations after 1600. One important outcome of this altered mission was the founding of universities and secondary schools and the stimulation of urban intellectual life. Over time, the church became the richest institution in the Spanish colonies, controlling ranches, plantations, and vineyards as well as serving as the society's banker.

Colonial Economies

The silver mines of Peru and Mexico and the sugar plantations of Brazil dominated the economic development of colonial Latin America. The mineral wealth of the New World fueled the early development of European capitalism and funded Europe's greatly expanded trade with Asia. Profits produced in these economic centers also promoted the growth of colonial cities, concentrated scarce investment capital and labor resources, and stimulated the development of livestock raising and agriculture in neighboring rural areas (see Map 19.1). Once established, this colonial dependence on mineral and agricultural exports left an enduring social and economic legacy in Latin America.

Gold worth millions of pesos was extracted from mines in Latin America, but silver mines in the Spanish colonies generated the most wealth and therefore exercised the greatest economic influence. The first important silver strikes occurred in Mexico in the 1530s and 1540s. In 1545 the single richest silver deposit in the Americas was discovered at **Potosí°**, in what is now Bolivia, and until 1680 the silver production of Bolivia and Peru dominated the Spanish colonial economy. After this date Mexican silver production greatly surpassed that of the Andean region.

A large labor force was needed to mine silver. The metal was extracted from deep shafts, and the refining process was complex. Silver mines supported farming, livestock raising, and even textile production, which, in turn, promoted urbanization and the elaboration of regional commercial relations. Silver mining also greatly altered the environment.

At first, silver was extracted from ore by smelting: the ore was crushed in giant stamping mills then packed with charcoal in a furnace and fired. Within a short time this wasteful use of forest resources for fuel destroyed forests near the mining centers. Faced with rising fuel costs, Mexican miners developed an efficient method of chemical extraction that relied on mixing mercury with the silver ore (see Environment and Technology: The Silver Refinery at Potosí, Bolivia, 1700). But this process, too, had severe environmental costs. Mercury was a poison, and its use contaminated the environment and sickened the Amerindian work force. Silver yields and profits increased with mercury amalgamation, but the environmental costs were high.

From the time of Columbus indigenous populations had been compelled to provide labor for European settlers in the Americas. Until the 1540s in Spanish colonies, Amerindian peoples were divided among the settlers and were forced to provide them with labor or with textiles, food, or other goods. This form of forced labor was called the **encomienda°**. As epidemics and mistreatment led to the decline in Amerindian population, reforms such as the New Laws sought to eliminate the encomienda. The discovery of silver in both Peru and Mexico, however, led to new forms of compulsory labor. In the mining region of Mexico, Amerindian populations had been greatly reduced by epidemic diseases. Therefore, from early in the colonial period, Mexican silver miners relied on free-wage laborers. Peru's Amerindian population survived in larger numbers, allowing the Spanish to impose a form of labor called the **mita°**.

Potosí (poh-toh-SEE)   encomienda (in-co-mee-EN-dah)
mita (MEE-tah)

Rural Blacksmiths in Colonial Peru   In colonial Latin America husbands, wives, and older children commonly worked together whether in agriculture or in urban occupations. Because few artisans earned enough to hire help, they often relied on their familes for assistance. In this illustration from Peru a rural blacksmith works alongside his wife.   (From Martinez Compañon, Trujillo del Perú, v.II, E 105. Photo: Imaging Services, Harvard College Library)

Under this system, one seventh of adult male Amerindians were compelled to work for six months each year in mines, or on farms and in textile factories. The most dangerous working conditions existed in the silver mines where workers were forced to carry heavy bags of ore up fragile ladders to the surface.

This colonial institution was a corrupted version of the Inca-era mit'a (see Chapter 12), which had been both a labor tax that supported elites and a reciprocal labor obligation that allowed kin groups to produce surpluses of essential goods that provided for the elderly and incapacitated. In the Spanish mita, few Amerindian workers

The Silver Refinery at Potosí, Bolivia, 1700

The silver refineries of Spanish America were among the largest and most heavily capitalized industrial enterprises in the Western Hemisphere during the colonial period. By the middle of the seventeenth century the mines of Potosí, Bolivia, had attracted a population of more than 120,000.

The accompanying illustration shows a typical refinery (*ingenio*). Aqueducts carried water from large reservoirs on nearby mountainsides to the refineries. The water wheel shown on the right drove two sets of vertical stamps that crushed ore. Each iron-shod stamp was about the size and weight of a telephone pole. Crushed ore was sorted, dried, and mixed with mercury and other catalysts to extract the silver. The amalgam was then separated by a combination of washing and heating. The end result was a nearly pure ingot of silver that was later assayed and taxed at the mint.

Silver production carried a high environmental cost. Forests were cut to provide fuel and the timbers needed to shore up mine shafts and construct stamping mills and other machinery. Unwanted base metals produced in the refining process poisoned the soil. In addition, the need for tens of thousands of horses, mules, and oxen to drive machinery and transport material led to overgrazing and widespread erosion.

A Bolivian Silver Refinery, 1700   The silver refineries of Spanish America were among the largest industrial establishments in the Western Hemisphere.   (Courtesy, Fundacao Biblioteca Nacional, Rio de Janeiro)

could survive on their wages. Wives and children were commonly forced to join the workforce to help meet expenses (see Society and Culture: Colonial Wealth and the Exploitation of Indigenous Peoples). Even those who remained behind in the village were forced to send food and cash to support mita workers.

As the Amerindian population fell with each new epidemic, some of Peru's villages were forced to shorten the period between mita obligations. Instead of serving every seven years, many men were forced to return to mines after only a year or two. Unwilling to accept mita service and the other tax burdens imposed on Amerindian villages, large numbers of Amerindians abandoned traditional agriculture and moved permanently to Spanish mines and farms as wage laborers. The long-term result of these individual decisions weakened Amerindian village life and promoted the assimilation of Amerindians into Spanish-speaking Catholic colonial society.

Before the settlement of Brazil the Portuguese had already developed sugar plantations that depended on slave labor on the Atlantic islands of Madeira, the Azores, the Cape Verdes, and São Tomé. Because of the success of these early experiences, they were able to quickly transfer this profitable form of agriculture to Brazil. After 1550, sugar production expanded rapidly in the northern provinces of Pernambuco and Bahia. By the seventeenth century, sugar dominated the Brazilian economy.

The sugar plantations of colonial Brazil always depended on slave labor. At first the Portuguese sugar planters enslaved Amerindians captured in war or seized from their villages. They used Amerindian men as field hands, although in this indigenous culture women had primary responsibility for agriculture. Any effort to resist or flee led to harsh punishments. Thousands of Amerindian slaves died during the epidemics that raged across Brazil in the sixteenth and seventeenth centuries. This terrible loss of Amerindian life and the rising profits of the sugar planters led to the development of an internal slave trade dominated by settlers from the southern region of São Paulo. To supply the rising labor needs of the sugar plantations of the northeast, slave raiders pushed into the interior, even attacking Amerindian populations in neighboring Spanish colonies. Many of the most prominent slavers were the sons of Portuguese fathers and Amerindian mothers.

Amerindian slaves remained an important source of labor and slave raiding a significant business in frontier regions into the eighteenth century. But sugar planters eventually came to rely more on African than Amerindian slaves. Although African slaves at first cost much more than Amerindian slaves, planters found them to be more productive and more resistant to disease. As profits from the plantations increased, imports of African slaves rose from an average of 2,000 per year in the late sixteenth century to approximately 7,000 per year a century later, outstripping the immigration of free Portuguese settlers. Between 1650 and 1750, for example, more than three African slaves arrived in Brazil for every free immigrant from Europe.

Within Spanish America, the mining centers of Mexico and Peru eventually exercised global economic influence. American silver increased the European money supply, promoting commercial expansion and, later, industrialization. Large amounts of silver also flowed across the Pacific to the Spanish colony of the Philippines, where it was exchanged for Asian spices, silks, and pottery. Spain tried to limit this trade, but the desire for Asian goods in the colonies was so strong that there was large-scale trade in contraband goods.

The rich mines of Peru, Bolivia, and Mexico stimulated urban population growth as well as commercial links with distant agricultural and textile producers. The population of the city of Potosí, high in the Andes, reached 120,000 inhabitants by 1625. This rich mining town became the center of a vast regional market that depended on Chilean wheat, Argentine livestock, and Ecuadorian textiles.

The sugar plantations of Brazil played a similar role in integrating the economy of the south Atlantic region. The ports of Bahia and Rio de Janeiro in Brazil exchanged sugar, tobacco, and reexported slaves from Brazil for yerba (Paraguayan tea), hides, livestock, and silver produced in neighboring Spanish colonies. Portugal's increasing openness to British trade also allowed Brazil to become a conduit for an illegal trade between Spanish colonies and Europe. At the end of the seventeenth century the discovery of gold in Brazil helped overcome this large region's currency shortage and promoted further economic integration.

Both Spain and Portugal attempted to control the trade of their American colonies. Spain's efforts were more ambitious, granting first Seville and then Cádiz monopoly trade rights. Similar monopoly privileges were then awarded to the merchant guilds of Lima, Peru, and Mexico City. Because ships returning to Spain with silver and gold were often attacked by foreign naval forces and pirates, Spain came to rely on convoys escorted by warships to supply the colonies and return with silver and gold. By 1650, Portugal had instituted a similar system of monopoly trade and fleets. The combination of monopoly commerce and convoy systems

SOCIETY & CULTURE

RIO DE JANEIRO, SEGUNDA-FEIRA, 23 DE AG

Colonial Wealth and the Exploitation of Indigenous Peoples

The conditions imposed on indigenous peoples in the Spanish colonies generated contentious debates from the early sixteenth century to the end of the colonial period. Two Spanish naval officers who accompanied a French scientific expedition to South America in the mid-eighteenth century wrote the following description.

Without having to assume anything that cannot be proved absolutely or exaggerating to stretch the truth, we can agree indisputably that all the wealth produced in the Indies [Spain's American colonies], even what is consumed there, stems from the toil of the Indians. From close observation one sees that Indians work the silver and gold mines, cultivate the fields, and raise the livestock. In a word, there is no heavy labor that the Indians do not perform. They are so badly recompensed for their work that if one wanted to find out what the Spaniards paid them, he would discover it to be nothing except consistently cruel punishment, worse than that meted out in the galleys.... The gold and silver which the Spaniards acquire at the expense of the natives' sweat and toil never falls into the hands of the Indians.

[T]hose who contribute most are the ones who enjoy its fruits least and are the most poorly paid for the most arduous tasks....

There are two ways to remedy the abuse perpetrated on the free and mita Indians [the mita was a forced labor system]. The most reasonable and just method would be to eliminate the mita entirely and have free labor work the haciendas, mines, obrajes [textile mills] and everything else....

In the second place it would be fitting to prohibit completely all physical punishment of the Indians in the haciendas and obrajes under severe penalties.

How important were Amerindians to the economy of the Spanish Empire? How did these two visitors judge the treatment of Amerindian peoples? What remedies did these authors suggest?

Source: Jorge Juan and Antonio de Ulloa, *Discourse and Political Reflections on the Kingdom of Peru*, ed. John J. Tepaske and Besse A. Clement (Norman: University of Oklahoma Press, 1978), 126–148.

---

protected shipping and facilitated the collection of taxes, but these measures also slowed the flow of European goods to the colonies and kept prices high. Frustrated by these restraints, colonial populations established illegal commercial relations with the English, French, and Dutch. By the middle of the seventeenth century a majority of European imports were arriving in Latin America illegally.

Society in Colonial Latin America

With the exception of a few early viceroys, few members of Spain's great noble families came to the New World. *Hidalgos°*—lesser nobles—were well represented, as were Spanish merchants, artisans, miners, priests, and lawyers. Small numbers of criminals, beggars, and prostitutes also found their way to the colonies. This flow of immigrants from Spain was never large, and Spanish settlers were always a tiny minority in a colonial society numerically dominated by Amerindians and rapidly growing populations of Africans, **creoles** (whites born in America to European parents), and people of mixed ancestry.

Conquistadors and early settlers who received from the Crown grants of labor and tribute goods (encomienda) from Amerindian communities as rewards for service to Spain dominated colonial society in early Spanish America. These *encomenderos* sought to create a hereditary social and political class comparable to the nobles of Europe. But their systematic abuse of Amerindian communities and the catastrophic loss of Amerindian life during the epidemics of the sixteenth century undermined their position. They also confronted the growing power of colonial viceroys, judges, and bishops appointed by the king.

By the end of the sixteenth century, the elite of Spanish America included both European immigrants and

---

hidalgos (ee-DAHL-goes)

creoles. Europeans dominated the highest levels of the church and government as well as commerce. Creoles commonly controlled colonial agriculture and mining. Wealthy creole families with extensive holdings in land and mines often sought to increase their family prestige by arranging for their daughters to marry successful Spanish merchants and officials. Often richer in reputation than in wealth, immigrants from Spain welcomed the opportunity to forge these connections. Although tensions between Spaniards and creoles were inevitable, most elite families had members from both groups.

Before the Europeans arrived in the Americas, the native peoples were members of a large number of distinct cultural and linguistic groups. Cultural diversity and class distinctions were present even in the highly centralized Aztec and Inca empires. The loss of life provoked by the European conquest undermined this rich social and cultural complexity, and the imposition of Catholic Christianity further eroded ethnic boundaries among native peoples. Colonial administrators and settlers broadly applied the racial label "Indian," which facilitated the imposition of special taxes and labor obligations while at the same time erasing long-standing class and ethnic differences.

Indigenous Amerindian elites survived only briefly in the Spanish colonies and Brazil. Some of the conquistadors and early settlers married or established less formal relations with elite Amerindian women, but fewer of these alliances occurred after European women began to arrive. By 1600 the descendants of the most powerful Amerindian families were indistinguishable from the descendants of the village leaders who had been subordinate to them. Both groups of hereditary leaders, however, had proved indispensable to the first Spanish colonists, helping the Spaniards to organize draft labor and collect taxes. Some descendants of both groups prospered in the colonial period as ranchers, muleteers, and merchants; many others lived in the same materially deprived conditions as Amerindian commoners.

Thousands of blacks participated in the conquest and settlement of Spanish America. The majority were European-born Catholic slaves who came to the New World with their masters. Some free blacks immigrated voluntarily. More than four hundred blacks, most of them slaves, participated in the conquest of Peru and Chile. In the fluid social environment of the conquest era, many slaves gained their freedom. Some simply fled from their masters. Juan Valiente escaped his master in Mexico, participated in Francisco Pizarro's conquest of the Inca Empire, and later became one of the most prominent early settlers of Chile, where he was granted Amerindian laborers in an encomienda.

The status of the black population of colonial Latin America declined with the opening of a direct slave trade with Africa (for details, see Chapter 20). Africans were culturally different from the Afro-Iberian slaves and freedmen who accompanied the conquerors. Afro-Iberians commonly had deep roots in Spain or Portugal, their language was Spanish or Portuguese, and their religion was Catholicism. African slaves were different in language, religious belief, and cultural practice, and these differences were viewed by settlers as signs of inferiority, ultimately serving as a justification for slavery. By 1600 anyone with black ancestry was barred from positions in church and government as well as from many skilled crafts.

The rich mosaic of African identities was retained in colonial Latin America. Many cultural groups struggled in slavery to retain their languages, religious beliefs, and marriage customs. But, in regions with large slave majorities, these cultural and linguistic barriers often divided slaves and made resistance more difficult. Over time, elements from many African traditions blended and mixed with European (and in some cases Amerindian) language and beliefs to forge distinct local cultures. The rapid growth of an American-born slave population accelerated this process of cultural change.

Slave resistance took many forms, including sabotage, malingering, running away, and rebellion. Although many slave rebellions occurred, colonial authorities were always able to reestablish control. Groups of runaway slaves, however, were sometimes able to defend themselves for years. In both Spanish America and Brazil communities of runaways (called *quilombos*° in Brazil and *palenques*° in Spanish colonies) were common. The largest quilombo was Palmares, where thousands of slaves defended themselves against Brazilian authorities for sixty years until they were finally overrun in 1694.

Slaves were skilled artisans, musicians, servants, artists, cowboys, and even soldiers. However, the vast majority worked in agriculture. Conditions for slaves were worst on the sugar plantations of Brazil and the Caribbean, where harsh discipline, brutal punishments, and backbreaking labor were common. Because planters preferred to buy male slaves, there was always a gender imbalance on plantations. As a result, neither the traditional marriage and family patterns of Africa nor those of Europe developed. The disease environment of the tropics, as well as the poor housing, diet, hygiene, and medical care offered to slaves, also weakened slave families.

---

quilombos (key-LOM-bos) *palenques* (pah-LEN-kays)

De Efpañolyd Iudia, Meftifa.

Painting of Castas   This is an example of a common genre of colonial Spanish American painting. In the eighteenth century there was increased interest in ethnic mixing, and wealthy colonials as well as some Europeans commissioned sets of paintings that showed mixed families. Commonly the paintings also indicated what the artist believed was an appropriate class setting. In this painting a richly dressed Spaniard is depicted with his Amerindian wife dressed in European clothing. Notice that the painter has the mestiza daughter look to her European father for guidance.   (Private Collection. Photographer: Camilo Garza/Fotocam, Monterrey, Mexico)

The colonial development of Brazil was distinguished from that of Spanish America by the absence of rich and powerful indigenous civilizations such as those of the Aztecs and Inca and by lower levels of European immigration. Nevertheless, Portuguese immigrants came to exercise the same domination in Brazil as the Spanish exercised in their colonies. The growth of cities and the creation of imperial institutions eventually duplicated in outline the social structures found in Spanish America, but with an important difference. By the early seventeenth century, Africans and their American-born descendants were the largest racial group in Brazil. As a result, Brazilian colonial society (unlike Spanish Mexico and Peru) was influenced more by African culture than by Amerindian culture.

Both Spanish and Portuguese law provided for manumission, the granting of freedom to individual slaves. The majority of those gaining their liberty had saved money and purchased their own freedom. This was easiest to do in cities, where slave artisans and market women had the opportunity to earn and save money. Only a tiny minority of owners freed slaves without demanding compensation. Household servants were the most likely beneficiaries of this form of manumission. Only about 1 percent of the slave population gained freedom each year through manumission. However, because slave women received the majority of manumissions and because children born subsequently were considered free, the free colored population grew rapidly.

Within a century of settlement, groups of mixed descent were in the majority in many regions. There were few marriages between Amerindian women and European men, but less formal relationships were common. Few European or creole fathers recognized their mixed offspring, who were called **mestizos**°. Nevertheless, this rapidly expanding group came to occupy a middle position in colonial society, dominating urban artisan trades and small-scale agriculture and ranching. In frontier regions many members of the elite were mestizos, some proudly asserting their descent from the Amerindian elite. The African slave trade also led to the appearance of new American ethnicities. Individuals of mixed European and African descent—called **mulattoes**—came to occupy intermediate position in the tropics similar to the social position of mestizos in Mesoamerica and the Andean region. In Spanish Mexico and Peru and in Brazil, mixtures of Amerindians and Africans were also common.

All these mixed-descent groups were called *castas*° in Spanish America. Castas dominated small-scale retailing and construction trades in cities. In the countryside, many small ranchers and farmers as well as wage laborers were castas. Members of these mixed groups who gained high status or significant wealth generally spoke Spanish or Portuguese, observed the requirements of Catholicism, and, whenever possible, lived the life of Europeans in their residence, dress, and diet.

---

mestizo (mess-TEE-zoh)   **castas** (CAZ-tahs)

ENGLISH AND FRENCH COLONIES IN NORTH AMERICA

The North American colonial empires of England and France and the colonies of Spain and Portugal had many characteristics in common (see Map 19.1). The governments of England and France hoped to find easily extracted forms of wealth or great indigenous empires like those of the Aztecs or Inca. Like the Spanish and Portuguese, English and French settlers responded to native peoples with a mixture of diplomacy and violence. African slaves proved crucial to the development of all four colonial economies.

Important differences, however, distinguished North American colonial development from the Latin American model. The English and French colonies were developed nearly a century after Cortés's conquest of Mexico and initial Portuguese settlement in Brazil. The intervening period witnessed significant economic and demographic growth in Europe. It also witnessed the Protestant Reformation, which helped to propel English and French settlement in the Americas. By the time England and France secured a foothold in the Americas, the regions of the world were also more interconnected commercially. Distracted by ventures elsewhere and by increasing military confrontation in Europe, neither England nor France imitated the large and expensive colonial bureaucracies established by Spain and Portugal. As a result, private companies and individual proprietors played a much larger role in the development of English and French colonies. Particularly in the English colonies, this practice led to greater regional variety in economic activity, political institutions and culture, and social structure than was evident in the colonies of Spain and Portugal.

Early English Experiments

England's first efforts to gain a foothold in the Americas produced more failures than successes. The first attempt was made by a group of West Country gentry and merchants led by Sir Humphrey Gilbert. Their effort in 1583 to establish a colony in Newfoundland, off the coast of Canada, quickly failed. After Gilbert's death in 1584, his half-brother Sir Walter Raleigh organized private financing for a new colonization scheme. A year later, 108 men attempted a settlement on Roanoke Island, off the coast of present-day North Carolina. Afflicted with poor leadership, undersupplied, and threatened by Amerindian groups, the colony was abandoned within a year. Another effort to settle Roanoke was made in 1587. Because the Spanish Armada was threatening England, no relief expedition was sent to Roanoke until 1590. When help finally arrived, there was no sign of the 117 men, women, and children who had attempted settlement. Raleigh's colonial experiment was abandoned.

In the seventeenth century, England renewed its effort to establish colonies in North America. England continued to rely on private capital to finance settlement and continued to hope that the colonies would become sources of high-value products such as silk, citrus, and wine. New efforts to establish American colonies were influenced also by English experience in colonizing Ireland after 1566. In Ireland land had been confiscated, cleared of its native population, and offered for sale to English investors. The city of London, English guilds, and wealthy private investors all purchased Irish "plantations" and then recruited "settlers." By 1650 investors had sent nearly 150,000 English and Scottish immigrants to Ireland. Indeed, Ireland attracted six times as many colonists in the early seventeenth century as did New England.

The South

London investors, organized as the privately funded Virginia Company, took up the challenge of colonizing Virginia in 1606. A year later 144 settlers disembarked at Jamestown, an island 30 miles (48 kilometers) up the James River in the Chesapeake Bay region. Additional settlers arrived in 1609. The investors and settlers hoped for immediate profits, but these unrealistic dreams were soon dashed. Although the location was easily defended, it was a swampy and unhealthy place; nearly 80 percent of all settlers in Jamestown in the first fifteen years died from disease or Amerindian attacks. There was no mineral wealth, no passage to Asia, and no docile and exploitable native population. By concentrating their energies on the illusion of easy wealth, settlers failed to grow enough food and were saved on more than one occasion by the generosity of neighboring Amerindian peoples.

In 1624 the English crown was forced to dissolve the Virginia Company because of its mismanagement of the colony. Freed from the company's commitment to Jamestown's unhealthy environment, colonists pushed deeper into the interior, developing a sustainable economy based on furs, timber, and, increasingly, tobacco. The profits from tobacco soon attracted new immigrants and new capital. Along the shoreline of Chesapeake Bay and the rivers that fed it, settlers spread out, developing plantations and farms. Colonial Virginia's population remained dispersed. In Latin America, large and powerful cities dominated by viceroys and royal courts and networks of secondary towns flourished. In contrast, in colonial Virginia no city of any significant size developed.

Colonists in Latin America had developed systems of forced labor to develop the region's resources. Encomienda, mita, and slavery were all imposed on indigenous peoples, and later the African slave trade compelled the migration of millions of additional forced laborers to the colonies of Spain and Portugal. The English settlement of the Chesapeake Bay region added a new system of compulsory labor to the American landscape: **indentured servants.** Ethnically indistinguishable from free settlers, indentured servants eventually accounted for approximately 80 percent of all English immigrants to Virginia and the neighboring colony of Maryland. Young men and women unable to pay for their transportation to the New World accepted indentures (contracts) that bound them to a term ranging from four to seven years of labor in return for passage, a small parcel of land, and some tools and clothes. During the seventeenth century, approximately fifteen hundred indentured servants, mostly male, arrived each year (see Chapter 20 for details on the indentured labor system). Planters were less likely to lose money if they purchased the cheaper limited contracts of indentured servants instead of purchasing African slaves during the period when both groups suffered high mortality rates. As life expectancy in the colony improved, planters began to purchase more slaves. They calculated that greater profits could be secured by paying the higher initial cost of slaves owned for life than by purchasing the contracts of indentured servants bound for short periods of time. As a result, Virginia's slave population grew rapidly from 950 in 1660 to 120,000 by 1756.

By the 1660s many of the elements of the mature colony were in place in Virginia. Colonial government was administered by a Crown-appointed governor and his council, as well as by representatives of towns meeting together as the **House of Burgesses.** When these representatives began to meet alone as a deliberative body, they initiated a form of democratic representation that distinguished the English colonies of North America from the colonies of other European powers. Ironically, this expansion in colonial liberties and political rights occurred along with the dramatic increase in the colony's slave population. The intertwined evolution of American freedom and American slavery gave England's southern colonies a unique and conflicted political character that endured even after independence.

At the same time, the English colonists were expanding settlements to the South. The Carolinas at first prospered from the profits of the fur trade. Fur traders pushed into the interior, eventually threatening the French trading networks based in New Orleans and Mobile. Native peoples eventually provided over a hundred thousand deerskins annually to this profitable commerce. The environmental and cultural costs of the fur trade were little appreciated at the time. As Amerindian peoples hunted more intensely, the natural balance of animals and plants was disrupted in southern forests. The profits of the fur trade altered Amerindian culture as well, leading villages to place less emphasis on subsistence hunting and fishing and traditional agriculture. Deepening dependencies on European products, including firearms, metal tools, textiles and alcohol, further altered Amerindian life.

Although increasingly brought into the commerce and culture of the Carolina colony, indigenous peoples were being weakened by epidemics, alcoholism, and a rising tide of ethnic conflicts generated by competition for hunting grounds. Conflicts among indigenous peoples—now armed with firearms—became more deadly. Many Amerindians captured in these wars were sold as slaves to local colonists, who used them as agricultural workers or exported them to the sugar plantations of the Caribbean islands. Dissatisfied with the terms of trade imposed by fur traders and angered by this slave trade, Amerindians launched attacks on English settlements in the early 1700s. Their defeat by colonial military forces led inevitably to new seizures of Amerindian land by European settlers.

The northern part of the Carolinas had been settled from Virginia and followed that colony's mixed economy of tobacco and forest products. Slavery expanded slowly in this region. Charleston and the interior of South Carolina followed a different path. Settled first by planters from the Caribbean Island of Barbados in 1670, this colony soon developed an economy based on plantations and slavery in imitation of the colonies of the Caribbean and Brazil. In 1729 North and South Carolina became separate colonies.

Despite an unhealthy climate, the prosperous rice and indigo plantations near Charleston attracted a diverse array of immigrants and an increasing flow of African slaves. African slaves were present from the founding of Charleston. They were instrumental in introducing irrigated rice agriculture along the coastal lowlands and in developing indigo (a plant that produced a blue dye) plantations at higher elevations away from the coast. Slaves were often given significant responsibilities. As one planter sending two slaves and their families to a frontier region put it: "[They] are likely young people, well acquainted with Rice & every kind of plantation business, and in short [are] capable of the management of a plantation themselves."[2]

As profits from rice and indigo rose, the importation of African slaves created a black majority in South Carolina. African languages and Gullah (a dialect with African and English roots), as well as African religious beliefs and diet, strongly influenced this unique colonial culture. African slaves were more likely than American-born slaves to rebel or run away. In South Carolina's largest slave uprising, the Stono Rebellion of 1739, Africans played a major role. After a group of about twenty slaves, many of them African Catholics who sought to flee south to Spanish Florida, seized firearms, about a hundred slaves from nearby plantations joined them. The colonial militia soon defeated the rebels and executed many of them, but the rebellion shocked slave owners throughout England's southern colonies and led to greater repression.

Colonial South Carolina was the most hierarchical society in British North America. Planters controlled the economy and political life. The richest maintained households both in the countryside and in Charleston, the largest city in the southern colonies. Small farmers, cattlemen, artisans, merchants, and fur traders held an intermediate but clearly subordinate social position. Native peoples remained influential participants in colonial society through commercial contacts and alliances, but they were increasingly marginalized. As had occurred in colonial Latin America, the growth of a large mixed population blurred racial and cultural boundaries. On the frontier, the children of white men and Indian women held an important place in the fur trade. In the plantation regions and Charleston, the offspring of white men and black women often held preferred positions within the slave work force or, if they had been freed, as carpenters, blacksmiths, or in other skilled trades.

New England

The colonization of New England by two separate groups of Protestant dissenters, Pilgrims and Puritans, put the settlement of this region on a different course. The **Pilgrims,** who came first, wished to break completely with the Church of England, which they believed was still essentially Catholic. Unwilling to confront the power of the established church and the monarch, they sought an opportunity to pursue their spiritual ends in a new land. As a result, in 1620 approximately one hundred settlers—men, women, and children—established the colony of Plymouth on the coast of present-day Massachusetts. Although nearly half of the settlers died during the first winter, the colony survived. Plymouth benefited from strong leadership and the discipline and cooperative nature of the settlers. Nevertheless, this experiment in creating a church-directed community failed. The religious enthusiasm and purpose that at first sustained the Pilgrims was dissipated by new immigrants who did not share the founders' religious beliefs, and by geographic dispersal to new towns. In 1691, Plymouth was absorbed into the larger Massachusetts Bay Colony of the Puritans.

The **Puritans** wished to "purify" the Church of England, not break with it. They wanted to abolish its hierarchy of bishops and priests, free it from governmental interference, and limit membership to people who shared their beliefs. Subjected to increased discrimination in England for their efforts to transform the church, large numbers of Puritans began emigrating from England in 1630.

The Puritan leaders of the Massachusetts Bay Company—the joint-stock company that had received a royal charter to finance the Massachusetts Bay Colony—carried with them from England to Massachusetts the company charter, which spelled out company rights and obligations as well as the direction of company government. By bringing the charter with them, they limited Crown efforts to control them; the Crown could revoke but not alter the terms of the charter. By 1643, more than 20,000 Puritans had settled in the Bay Colony.

Immigration to Massachusetts differed from immigration to the Chesapeake and to South Carolina. Most newcomers to Massachusetts arrived with their families. Whereas 84 percent of Virginia's population in 1625 was male, Massachusetts had a normal gender balance in its population almost from the beginning. It was also the healthiest of England's colonies. The result was a rapid natural increase in population. The population of Massachusetts quickly became more "American" than the population of the colonies to the south or in the Caribbean, whose survival depended on a steady flow of new English immigrants to counter the high mortality rates. Massachusetts also was more homogeneous and less hierarchical than the southern colonies.

Political institutions evolved out of the terms of the company charter. A governor was elected, along with a council of magistrates drawn from the board of directors of the Massachusetts Bay Company. Disagreements between this council and elected representatives of the towns led, by 1650, to the creation of a lower legislative house that selected its own speaker and began to develop procedures and rules similar to those of the House of Commons in England. The result was greater autonomy and greater local political involvement than in the colonies of Latin America.

Economically, Massachusetts differed dramatically from the southern colonies. Agriculture met basic needs, but poor soils and harsh climate offered no opportunity to develop cash crops like tobacco or rice. To pay for imported tools, textiles, and other essentials, the colonists needed to discover some profit-making niche in the growing Atlantic market. Fur, timber and other forest products, and fish provided the initial economic foundation, but New England's economic well-being soon depended on providing commercial and shipping services in a dynamic and far-flung commercial arena that included the southern colonies, the smaller Caribbean islands, Africa, and Europe.

In Spanish and Portuguese America, heavily capitalized monopolies (companies or individuals given exclusive economic privileges) dominated international trade. In New England, by contrast, merchants survived by discovering smaller but more sustainable profits in diversified trade across the Atlantic. The colony's commercial success rested on market intelligence, flexibility, and streamlined organization. The success of this development strategy is demonstrated by urban population growth. With 16,000 inhabitants in 1740, Boston, capital of Massachusetts Bay Colony, was the largest city in British North America. This coincided with the decline of New England's once-large indigenous population, which had been dramatically reduced by a combination of epidemics and brutal military campaigns.

Lacking a profitable agricultural export like tobacco, New England did not develop the extreme social stratification of the southern plantation colonies. Slaves and indentured servants were present, but in very small numbers. New England was ruled by the richest colonists and shared the racial attitudes of the southern colonies, but it also was the colonial society with fewest differences in wealth and status and with the most uniformly British and Protestant population in the Americas.

The Middle Atlantic Region

Much of the future success of English-speaking America was rooted in the rapid economic development and remarkable cultural diversity that appeared in the Middle Atlantic colonies—diversity that grew in part from non-European origins. In 1624 the Dutch West India Company established the colony of New Netherland and located its capital on Manhattan Island. The colony was poorly managed and underfinanced from the start, but its location commanded the potentially profitable and strategically important Hudson River. Dutch merchants established with the **Iroquois Confederacy**—an alliance among the Mohawk, Oneida, Onondaga, Cayuga, and Seneca peoples—and with other native peoples alliances and trading relationships that gave them access to the rich fur trade of Canada. When confronted by an English military expedition in 1664, the Dutch surrendered without a fight. James, duke of York and later King James II of England, became proprietor of the colony, which was renamed New York.

New York was characterized by tumultuous politics and corrupt public administration. The colony's success was guaranteed in large measure by the development of New York City as a commercial and shipping center. Located at the mouth of the Hudson River, the city played an essential role in connecting the region's grain farmers to the booming markets of the Caribbean and southern Europe. By the early eighteenth century, New York Colony had a diverse population that included (in addition to English colonists) Dutch, German, and Swedish settlers as well as a large slave community.

Pennsylvania began as a proprietary colony and as a refuge for Quakers, a persecuted religious minority. In 1682 William Penn secured an enormous grant of territory (nearly the size of England) because the English king Charles II was indebted to Penn's father. As proprietor (owner) of the land, Penn had sole right to establish a government, subject only to the requirement that he provide for an assembly of freemen.

Penn quickly lost control of the colony's political life, but the colony enjoyed remarkable success. By 1700 Pennsylvania had a population of more than 21,000, and Philadelphia, its capital, soon passed Boston to become the largest city in the British colonies. Healthy climate, excellent land, relatively peaceful relations with native peoples (prompted by Penn's emphasis on negotiation rather than warfare), and access through Philadelphia to good markets led to rapid economic and demographic growth in the colony.

Both Pennsylvania and South Carolina were grain-exporting colonies, but they were very different societies. South Carolina's rice plantations required large numbers of slaves. In Pennsylvania, free workers, including a large number of German families, produced the bulk of the colony's grain crops on family farms. As a result, Pennsylvania's economic expansion in the late seventeenth century occurred without reproducing South Carolina's hierarchical and repressive social order. By the early eighteenth century, however, the prosperous city of Philadelphia did have a large population of black slaves and freedmen. Many were servants in the homes of wealthy merchants, but the fast-growing economy offered many opportunities in skilled trades as well.

The Home of Sir William Johnson, British Superintendent for Indian Affairs, Northern District   As the colonial era drew to a close, the British attempted to limit the cost of colonial defense by negotiating land settlements between native peoples and settlers. These agreements were doomed by the growing tide of western migration. William Johnson (1715–1774) maintained a fragile peace along the northern frontier by building strong personal relations with influential leaders of the Mohawk and other members of the Iroquois Confederacy. His home in present-day Johnstown, New York, shows the mixed nature of the frontier—the relative opulence of the main house offset by the two defensive blockhouses built for protection.   ("Johnson Hall," by E. L. Henry. Courtesy, Albany Institute of History and Art)

French America

Patterns of French settlement more closely resembled those of Spain and Portugal than of England. The French were committed to missionary activity among Amerindian peoples and emphasized the extraction of natural resources—furs rather than minerals. The navigator and promoter Jacques Cartier first stirred France's interest in North America. In three voyages between 1524 and 1542, he explored the region of Newfoundland and the Gulf of St. Lawrence. A contemporary of Cortés and Pizarro, Cartier also hoped to find mineral wealth, but the stones he brought back to France turned out to be quartz and iron pyrite, "fool's gold."

The French waited more than fifty years before establishing settlements in North America. Coming to Canada after spending years in the West Indies, Samuel de Champlain founded the colony of **New France** at Quebec°, on the banks of the St. Lawrence River, in 1608. This location provided ready access to Amerindian trade routes, but it also compelled French settlers to take sides in the region's ongoing warfare. Champlain allied New France with the Huron and Algonkian peoples, traditional enemies of the powerful Iroquois Confederacy. Although French firearms and armor at first tipped the balance of power to France's native allies, the members of the Iroquois Confederacy proved to be resourceful and persistent enemies.

The European market for fur, especially beaver, fueled French settlement. Young Frenchmen were sent to live among native peoples to master their languages and customs. These **coureurs de bois°**, or runners of the woods, often began families with indigenous women,

---

Quebec (kwuh-BEC)   coureurs de bois (koo-RUHR day BWA)

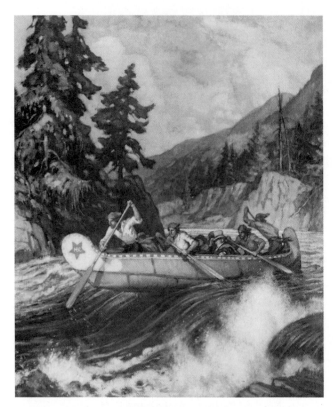

Canadian Fur Trader   The fur trade provided the economic foundation of early Canadian settlement. The trade depended on a mix of native and European skills and resources. The fur trader's canoe was developed from native technology to carry large loads over great distances.   (Hudson's Bay Company Archives, Provincial Archives of Manitoba)

flicted a series of humiliating defeats on the French. At the high point of their power in the early 1680s, Iroquois hunters and military forces gained control of much of the Great Lakes region and the Ohio River Valley. A large French military expedition and a relentless attack focused on Iroquois villages and agriculture finally checked Iroquois power in 1701.

Spain had effectively limited the spread of firearms in its colonies. But the fur trade, together with the growing military rivalry between Algonkian and Iroquois peoples and their respective French and English allies, led to the rapid spread of firearms in North America. Use of firearms in hunting and warfare moved west and south, reaching indigenous plains cultures that previously had adopted the horse introduced by the Spanish. This intersection of horse and gun frontiers in the early eighteenth century dramatically increased the military power and hunting efficiency of the Sioux, Comanche, Cheyenne, and other indigenous peoples, and slowed the pace of European settlement in the North American west.

In French Canada, the Jesuits led the effort to convert native peoples to Christianity. Building on earlier evangelical efforts in Brazil and Paraguay, French Catholic missionaries mastered native languages, created boarding schools for young boys and girls, and set up model agricultural communities for converted Amerindians. The Jesuits' greatest successes coincided with a destructive wave of epidemics and renewed warfare among native peoples in the 1630s. Eventually, churches were established throughout Huron and Algonkian territories. Nevertheless, local culture persisted. In 1688 a French nun who had devoted her life to instructing Amerindian girls expressed the frustration of many missionaries with the resilience of indigenous culture:

> We have observed that of a hundred that have passed through our hands we have scarcely civilized one. . . . When we are least expecting it, they clamber over our wall and go off to run with their kinsmen in the woods, finding more to please them there than in all the amenities of our French house.[3]

As epidemics undermined conversion efforts in mission settlements and evidence of indigenous resistance to conversion mounted, the church redirected some of its resources from the evangelical effort to the larger French settlements, founding schools, hospitals, and churches.

Responsibility for finding settlers and supervising the colonial economy was first granted to a monopoly company chartered in France. Even though the fur trade flourished, population growth was slow. Founded at about the same time as French Canada, Virginia had twenty times as many European residents as Canada by

and they and their children, who were called *métis*°, helped to direct the fur trade, guiding French expansion to the west and south. Amerindians actively participated in this trade because they quickly came to depend on the goods they received in exchange for furs—firearms, metal tools and utensils, textiles, and alcohol. This change in the material culture of the native peoples led to overhunting, which rapidly transformed the environment and led to the depletion of beaver and deer populations. It also increased competition among native peoples for hunting grounds, thus promoting warfare.

The proliferation of firearms made indigenous warfare more deadly. The Iroquois Confederacy responded to the increased military strength of France's Algonkian allies by forging commercial and military links with Dutch and later English settlements in the Hudson River Valley. Well armed by the Dutch and English, the Iroquois Confederacy nearly eradicated the Huron in 1649 and in-

métis (may-TEES)

1627. After the establishment of royal authority in the 1660s, Canada's French population increased but remained at only 7,000 in 1673. Although improved fiscal management and more effective colonial government did promote a limited agricultural expansion, the fur trade remained important. It is clear that Canada's small settler population and the fur trade's dependence on the voluntary participation of Amerindians allowed indigenous peoples to retain greater independence and more control over their traditional lands than was possible in the colonies of Spain, Portugal, or England. Unlike these colonial regimes, which sought to transform ancient ways of life or force the transfer of native lands, the French were compelled to treat indigenous peoples as allies and trading partners. This permitted indigenous peoples to more gradually adapt to new religious, technological, and market realities.

Despite Canada's small population, limited resources, and increasing vulnerability to attack by the English and their indigenous allies, the French aggressively expanded to the west and south. Louisiana was founded in 1699, but by 1708 there were fewer than 300 soldiers, settlers, and slaves in the territory. Like Canada, Louisiana depended on the fur trade, exporting more than 50,000 deerskins in 1726. And also as in Canada, Amerindians, driven by a desire for European goods, eagerly embraced this trade. In 1753 a French official reported a Choctaw leader as saying, "[The French] were the first . . . who made [us] subject to the different needs that [we] can no longer now do without."[4]

France's North American colonies were threatened by a series of wars fought by France and England and by the population growth and increasing prosperity of neighboring English colonies. The "French and Indian War" (also known as the Seven Years War, 1756–1763), however, proved to be the final contest for North American empire (see Map 19.2). England committed a larger military force to the struggle and, despite early defeats,

Map. 19.2 European Claims in North America, 1755–1763 The results of the French and Indian War dramatically altered the map of North America. France's losses precipitated conflicts between Amerindian peoples and the rapidly expanding population of the British colonies.

took the French capital of Quebec in 1759. Although resistance continued briefly, French forces in Canada surrendered in 1760. The peace agreement forced France to yield Canada to the English and cede Louisiana to Spain. The differences between French and English colonial realities were suggested by the petition of one Canadian indigenous leader to a British officer after the French surrender. "[W]e learn that our lands are to be given away not only to trade thereon but also to them in full title to various [English] individuals. . . . We have always been a free nation, and now we will become slaves, which would be very difficult to accept after having enjoyed our liberty so long."[5] With the loss of Canada the French concentrated their efforts on their sugar-producing colonies in the Caribbean (see Chapter 20).

COLONIAL EXPANSION AND CONFLICT

In the last decades of the seventeenth century, all of the European colonies in the Americas began to experience a long period of economic and demographic expansion. The imperial powers responded by strengthening their administrative and economic controls in the colonies. They also sought to force colonial populations to pay a larger share of the costs of administration and defense. These efforts at reform and restructuring coincided with a series of imperial wars fought along Atlantic trade routes and in the Americas. France's loss of its North American colonies was one of the most important results of these struggles. Equally significant, colonial populations throughout the Americas became more aware of separate national identities and more aggressive in asserting local interests against the will of distant monarchs.

Imperial Reform in Spanish America and Brazil

Spain's Habsburg dynasty ended when the Spanish king Charles II died without an heir in 1700 (see Table 18.1). After thirteen years of conflict involving the major European powers and factions within Spain, Philip of Bourbon, grandson of Louis XIV of France, gained the Spanish throne. Under Philip V and his Bourbon heirs, Spain's colonial administration and tax collection were reorganized. Spain's reliance on convoys protected by naval vessels was abolished, more colonial ports were permitted to trade with Spain, and intercolonial trade was expanded. Spain also created new commercial monopolies to produce tobacco, some alcoholic beverages, and chocolate. Also, the Spanish navy was strengthened, and trade in contraband was more effectively policed.

For most of the Spanish Empire, the eighteenth century was a period of remarkable economic expansion associated with population growth. Amerindian populations began to recover from the early epidemics, the flow of Spanish immigrants increased, and the slave trade to the plantation colonies was expanded. Mining, the heart of the Spanish colonial economy, increased as silver production in Mexico and Peru rose steadily into the 1780s. Agricultural exports also expanded: tobacco, dyes, hides, chocolate, cotton, and sugar joined the flow of goods to Europe.

But these reforms carried unforeseen consequences that threatened the survival of the Spanish Empire. Despite expanded silver production, the economic growth of the eighteenth century was led by the previously minor agricultural and grazing economies of Cuba, the Rio de la Plata region, Venezuela, Chile, and Central America. These export economies were less able than the mining economies of Mexico and Peru to weather breaks in trade caused by imperial wars. Each such disruption forced landowning elites in Cuba and the other regions to turn to alternative, often illegal, trade with English, French, or Dutch merchants. By the 1790s, the wealthiest and most influential sectors of Spain's colonial society had come to view the Spanish Empire as an impediment to prosperity and growth.

Bourbon political and fiscal reforms also contributed to a growing sense of colonial grievance by limiting creoles' access to colonial offices and by imposing new taxes and monopolies on colonial production. Consumer and producer resentment, for example, led to rioting when the Spanish established monopolies on tobacco, cacao (chocolate), and brandy. Because these reforms produced a more intrusive and expensive colonial government that interfered with established business practices, many colonists saw these changes as an abuse of the informal constitution that had long governed the empire. Only in the Bourbon effort to expand colonial militias in the face of English threats did creoles find opportunity for improved status and greater responsibility.

In addition to tax rebellions and urban riots, colonial policies also provoked Amerindian uprisings. Most spectacular was the rebellion initiated in 1780 by the Peruvian Amerindian leader José Gabriel Condorcanqui. Once in rebellion, he took the name of his Inca ancestor

Market in Rio de Janeiro   In many of the cities of colonial Latin America female slaves and black free women dominated retail markets. In this scene from late colonial Brazil, Afro–Brazilian women sell a variety of foods and crafts.   (Sir Henry Chamberlain, *Views and Costumes of the City and Neighborhoods of Rio de Janeiro*, London, 1822)

Tupac Amaru°, who had been executed as a rebel in 1572. **Tupac Amaru II** was well connected in Spanish colonial society. He had been educated by the Jesuits and was actively involved in trade with the silver mines at Potosí. Despite these connections, he still resented the abuse of Amerindian villagers.

Historians still debate the objectives of this rebellion. Tupac Amaru's own pronouncements did not clearly state whether he sought to end local injustices or overthrow Spanish rule. It appears that a local Spanish judge who challenged Tupac Amaru's hereditary rights provided the initial provocation, but that Tupac Amaru was ultimately driven by the conviction that colonial authorities were oppressing the indigenous people. As thousands joined him, he dared to contemplate the overthrow of Spanish rule.

Amerindian communities suffering under the mita and tribute obligations provided the majority of Tupac Amaru's army. He also received some support from creoles, mestizos, and slaves. After his capture, he was brutally executed, as were his wife and fifteen other

family members and allies. Even after his execution Amerindian rebels continued the struggle for more than two years. By the time Spanish authority was firmly reestablished, more than a hundred thousand lives had been lost and enormous amounts of property destroyed.

Brazil experienced a similar period of expansion and reform after 1700. Portugal created new administrative positions and gave monopoly companies exclusive rights to little-developed regions. Here, too, a more intrusive colonial government led to rebellions and plots, including open warfare in 1707 between "sons of the soil" and "outsiders" in São Paulo. The most aggressive period of reform occurred during the ministry of the marquis of Pombal (1750–1777). The Pombal reforms were made possible by an economic expansion fueled by the discovery of gold in the 1690s and diamonds after 1720 as well as by the development of markets for coffee and cotton. This new wealth paid for the importation of nearly 2 million African slaves. In Spanish America, a reinvigorated Crown sought to eliminate contraband trade. Portugal, however, had fallen into the economic orbit of England, and Brazil's new prosperity fueled a new wave of English imports.

Tupac Amaru (TOO-pack a-MAH-roo)

Reform and Reorganization in British North America

England's efforts to reform and reorganize its North American colonies began earlier than the Bourbon initiative in Spanish America. After the period of Cromwell's Puritan Republic, the restored Stuart king, Charles II, undertook an ambitious campaign to establish greater Crown control over the colonies. Between 1651 and 1673 a series of Navigation Acts sought to severely limit colonial trading and colonial production that competed directly with English manufacturers. James II also attempted to increase royal control over colonial political life. Royal governments replaced orginal colonial charters as in Massachusetts and proprietorships as in the Carolinas. Because the New England colonies were viewed as centers of smuggling, the king temporarily suspended their elected assemblies. At the same time, he appointed colonial governors and granted them new fiscal and legislative powers.

James II's overthrow in the Glorious Revolution of 1688 ended this confrontation, but not before colonists were provoked to resist and, in some cases, rebel. They overthrew the governors of New York and Massachusetts and removed the Catholic proprietor of Maryland. William and Mary restored relative peace, but these conflicts alerted the colonists to the potential for aggression by the English government. Colonial politics would remain confrontational until the American Revolution.

During the eighteenth century the English colonies experienced renewed economic growth and attracted a new wave of European immigration, but social divisions were increasingly evident. The colonial population in 1770 was more urban, more clearly divided by class and race, and more vulnerable to economic downturns. Crises were provoked when imperial wars with France and Spain disrupted trade in the Atlantic, increased tax burdens, forced military mobilizations, and provoked frontier conflicts with the Amerindians. On the eve of the American Revolution, England defeated France and weakened Spain. The cost, however, was great. Administrative, military, and tax policies imposed to gain empirewide victory alienated much of the American colonial population.

CONCLUSION

The New World colonial empires of Spain, Portugal, France, and England had many characteristics in common. All subjugated Amerindian peoples and introduced large numbers of enslaved Africans. Within all four empires, forests were cut down, virgin soils were turned with the plow, and Old World animals and plants were introduced. Colonists in all four applied the technologies of the Old World to the resources of the New, producing wealth and exploiting the commercial possibilities of the emerging Atlantic market.

Each of the New World empires also reflected the distinctive cultural and institutional heritages of its colonizing power. Mineral wealth allowed Spain to develop the most centralized empire. Political and economic power was concentrated in the great capital cities of Mexico City and Lima. Portugal and France pursued objectives similar to Spain's in their colonies. However, neither Brazil's agricultural economy nor France's Canadian fur trade produced the financial resources that made possible the centralized control achieved by Spain. Nevertheless, all three of these Catholic powers were able to impose and enforce significant levels of religious and cultural uniformity, relative to the British.

Greater cultural and religious diversity characterized British North America. Colonists were drawn to British North America from throughout the British Isles and included participants in all of Britain's numerous religious traditions. They were joined by German, Swedish, French Huguenot, and Dutch immigrants. British colonial government varied somewhat from colony to colony and was more responsive to local interests. Thus colonists in British North America were better able than colonists in the areas controlled by Spain, Portugal, and France to respond to changing economic and political circumstances. Most important, the British colonies attracted many more European immigrants than did the other New World colonies. Between 1580 and 1760, French colonies received 60,000 immigrants, Brazil 523,000, and the Spanish colonies 678,000. Within a shorter period—between 1600 and 1760—the British settlements welcomed 746,000. Population in British North America—free and slave combined—then reached an extraordinary 2.5 million by 1775.

By the eighteenth century, colonial societies across the Americas had matured as wealth increased, populations grew, and contacts with the rest of the world became more common (see Chapter 20). Colonial elites were more confident of their ability to define and defend local interests. Colonists were in general increasingly aware of their unique and distinctive cultural identities and willing to defend American experience and practice in the face of European presumptions of superiority. Moreover, influential groups in all the colonies were drawn toward the liberating ideas of Europe's Enlightenment. In the open and less inhibited spaces of the Western Hemisphere, these ideas (as Chapter 23 examines) soon provided a potent intellectual basis for opposing the continuation of empire.

■ Key Terms

Columbian Exchange	indentured servant
Council of the Indies	House of Burgesses
Bartolomé de Las Casas	Pilgrims
Potosí	Puritans
encomienda	Iroquois Confederacy
creoles	New France
mestizo	coureurs de bois
mulatto	Tupac Amaru II

■ Suggested Reading

Alfred W. Crosby, Jr., is justifiably the best-known student of the Columbian Exchange. See his *The Columbian Exchange: Biological and Cultural Consequences of 1492* (1972) and *Ecological Imperialism* (1986). William H. McNeill, *Plagues and People* (1976), puts the discussion of the American exchange in a world history context. Elinor G. K. Melville, *A Plague of Sheep: Environmental Consequences of the Spanish Conquest of Mexico* (1994), is the most important recent contribution to this field.

Colonial Latin America, 2d ed. (1994), by Mark A. Burkholder and Lyman L. Johnson, provides a good introduction to colonial Latin American history. *Early Latin America* (1983) by James Lockhart and Stuart B. Schwartz and *Spain and Portugal in the New World, 1492–1700* (1984) by Lyle N. McAlister are both useful introductions as well.

The specialized historical literature on the American colonial empires is extensive and deep. A sampling of useful works follows. For the early colonial period see Inga Clendinnen, *Ambivalent Conquests* (1987); James Lockhart, *The Nahuas After the Conquest* (1992); and John Hemming, *Red Gold: The Conquest of the Brazilian Indians* (1978). Nancy M. Farriss, *Maya Society Under Spanish Rule: The Collective Enterprise of Survival* (1984), is also one of the most important books on colonial Spanish America. For the Catholic Church see William Taylor, *Magistrates of the Sacred: Priests and Parishioners in Eighteenth-Century Mexico* (1996). Lyman L. Johnson and Sonya Lipsett-Rivera, *The Faces of Honor* (1999), provides a good introduction to the culture of honor. For the place of women see Asunción Lavrin, ed., *Sexuality and Marriage in Colonial Latin America* (1989). On issues of class R. Douglas Cope, *The Limits of Racial Domination* (1994), is recommended. On the slave trade, Herbert S. Klein, *The Middle Passage* (1978), and Philip D. Curtin, *The Atlantic Slave Trade: A Census* (1969), are indispensable. Frederick P. Bowser, *The African Slave in Colonial Peru, 1524–1650* (1973); Mary C. Karasch, *Slave Life and Culture in Rio de Janeiro, 1808–1850* (1986); and Stuart B. Schwartz, *Sugar Plantations in the Formation of Brazilian Society: Bahia, 1550–1835* (1985), are excellent introductions to the African experience in two very different Latin American societies.

Among the useful general studies of the British colonies are Charles M. Andrews, *The Colonial Period of American History: The Settlements*, 3 vols. (1934–1937); David Hackett Fischer, *Albion's Seed: Four British Folkways in America* (1989); and Gary B. Nash, *Red, White, and Black: The Peoples of Early America*, 2d ed. (1982). On the economy see John J. McCusker and Russell R. Menard, *The Economy of British America, 1607–1789* (1979). For slavery see David Brion Davis, *The Problem of Slavery in Western Culture* (1966); Allan Kulikoff, *Tobacco and Slaves: The Development of Southern Cultures in the Chesapeake, 1680–1800* (1986); and Peter H. Wood, *Black Majority: Negroes in Colonial South Carolina from 1670 Through the Stono Rebellion* (1974). Two very useful works on the relations between Europeans and Indians are James Merrill, *The Indians' New World: Catawbas and Their Neighbors from European Contact Through the Era of Removal* (1989); and Daniel H. Usner, Jr., *Indians, Settlers, and Slaves in a Frontier Exchange Economy: The Lower Mississippi Valley Before 1783* (1992).

For late colonial politics see Gary B. Nash, *Urban Crucible: Social Change, Political Consciousness, and the Origins of the American Revolution* (1979); Bernard Bailyn, *The Origins of American Politics* (1986); Jack P. Greene, *The Quest for Power: The Lower Houses of Assembly in the Southern Royal Colonies* (1963); and Richard Bushman, *King and People in Provincial Massachusetts* (1985). On immigration see Bernard Bailyn, *The Peopling of British North America* (1986).

On French North America, William J. Eccles, *France in America*, rev. ed. (1990), is an excellent overview; see also his *The Canadian Frontier, 1534–1760* (1969). G. F. G. Stanley, *New France, 1701–1760* (1968), is also an important resource. R. Cole Harris, *The Seigneurial System in Canada: A Geographical Study* (1966), provides an excellent analysis of the topic. Harold Innis, *The Fur Trade in Canada: An Introduction to Canadian Economic History* (1927), remains indispensable. Also of value are Cornelius Jaenen, *The Role of the Church in New France* (1976), and Alison L. Prentice, *Canadian Women: A History* (1988).

■ Notes

1. Quoted in Alfred W. Crosby, Jr., *The Columbian Exchange: Biological and Cultural Consequences of 1492* (Westport, CT: Greenwood, 1972), 58.
2. Quoted ibid.
3. Quoted in R. Douglas Francis, Richard Jones, and Donald B. Smith, *Origins: Canadian History to Confederation* (Toronto: Holt, Rinehart, and Winston of Canada, 1992), 52.
4. Quoted in Daniel H. Usner, Jr., *Indians, Settlers and Slaves in a Frontier Exchange Economy: The Lower Mississippi Valley Before 1783*, Institute of Early American History and Culture Series (Chapel Hill: University of North Carolina Press, 1992), 96.
5. Quoted in Cornelius J. Jaenen, "French and Native Peoples in New France," in J. M. Bumsted, *Interpreting Canada's Past*, vol. 1, 2d ed. (Toronto: Oxford University Press, 1993), 73.

20

THE ATLANTIC SYSTEM AND AFRICA,

1550–1800

**Plantations in the West Indies • Plantation Life in the Eighteenth Century •
Creating the Atlantic Economy • Africa, the Atlantic, and Islam**

ENVIRONMENT AND TECHNOLOGY: Amerindian Foods in Africa

SOCIETY AND CULTURE: A Maroon Village in French Guiana, 1748

Caribbean Sugar Mill   The wind mill crushes sugar cane whose juice
is boiled down in the smoking building next door.

As the ship bearing a cargo of slaves from West Africa neared the West Indian island of Barbados in 1757, the English crew gave a joyful shout, glad that this leg of their trading tour around the Atlantic was over. Since leaving England, some of their number had died of African tropical diseases, and one crewman had been flogged to death for insubordination. The survivors, thankful to put the risk of disease and slave insurrection behind them, looked forward to returning to England.

However, one of the slaves on board, Olaudah Equiano°, recorded in his biography that the sight of Barbados filled the shackled Africans with apprehension. Although fortunate to have survived long weeks of suffocating heat and loathsome smells packed side by side in the cargo hold, the captive African men, women, and children feared they were going to be eaten by the white people who rushed to inspect them after the ship anchored in the harbor of Bridgetown. To ease the new arrivals' panic, local sugar planters sent veteran slaves on board to assure them in several African languages that they would not be eaten. Instead, most were destined to work on the island's sugar plantations. After landing, Equiano relates, he and his companions were relieved to discover that most of the island's inhabitants were Africans. The eleven-year-old Equiano found many of his own Igbo° people there.

After examining the slaves for physical defects, the local merchants divided them into "parcels" of several slaves each and penned them in a yard, in Equiano's words, "like so many sheep in a fold without regard to sex or age." A few days later they were sold to the planters, not by auction but in a terrifying "scramble." At the beat of a drum, buyers rushed into the yard and seized the parcel of slaves they wanted. "In this manner," Equiano commented, "without scruple, are relations and friends separated, most of them never to see each other again."

By the 1750s, Barbados was past its prime as a sugar colony, so Equiano and some companions were shipped to the colony of Virginia. There for a time he was put to work weeding; he later worked on a ship. In 1766 at the age of twenty-one, Equiano was able to buy his freedom with money he earned in private trading. He worked as a seaman and then resided in England, where he married and joined the campaign against the slave trade.

The slave trade and the plantations in the West Indies, Virginia, and elsewhere in the Americas were crucial pieces of a new **Atlantic system.** This network of trading links moved not only goods and wealth but also people and cultures around the Atlantic world.

As you read this chapter, ask yourself the following questions:

- How did participation in the Atlantic system affect Europe, Africa, and the Americas?
- How and why did European businessmen, with the help of their governments, put this trading system together?
- How and why did the West Indies and other places in the Americas become centers of African population and culture?
- How did sub-Saharan Africa's expanding contacts in the Atlantic compare with its contacts with the Islamic world?

PLANTATIONS IN THE WEST INDIES

The West Indies was the first place in the Americas reached by Columbus and the first part of the Americas where native populations collapsed. It took a long time to repopulate these islands from abroad and forge new economic links between them and other parts of the Atlantic. But after 1650, sugar plantations, African slaves, and European capital made these islands a major center of the Atlantic economy.

Olaudah Equiano (oh-LAU-duh ay-kwee-AHN-oh)
Igbo (EE-boh)

Colonization Before 1650

Spanish settlers introduced sugar-cane cultivation into the West Indies shortly after 1500, but soon these colonies fell into neglect as attention shifted to colonizing the American mainland. After 1600 the West Indies revived as a focus of colonization, this time by northern Europeans interested in growing tobacco and other crops. In the 1620s and 1630s English colonization societies founded small European settlements on Montserrat°, Barbados°, Trinidad°, and other Caribbean islands, while the French colonized Martinique°, Guadeloupe°, and some other islands. Because of greater support from their government, the English colonies prospered first, largely by growing tobacco for export.

This New World leaf, long used by Amerindians for recreation and medicine, was finding a new market among seventeenth-century Europeans. Despite the opposition of individuals like King James I of England, who condemned tobacco smoke as "dangerous to the eye, hateful to the nose, harmful to the brain, and dangerous to the lungs," the habit spread. By 1614 tobacco was reportedly being sold in seven thousand shops in and around London, and some English businessmen were dreaming of a tobacco trade as valuable as Spain's silver fleets.

Turning such pipe dreams into reality was not easy. Diseases, hurricanes, and attacks by the Carib and the Spanish scourged the early French and English West Indies colonists. They also suffered from shortages of supplies from Europe and shortages of labor sufficient to clear and plant virgin land with tobacco. Two changes improved the colonies' prospects. One was the formation of **chartered companies.** To promote national claims without government expense, France and England gave groups of private investors monopolies over trade to their West Indies colonies in exchange for the payment of an annual fee. The other change was that the companies began to provide free passage to the colonies for poor Europeans. These indentured servants paid off their debt by working three or four years for the established colonists (see Chapter 19).

Under this system the French and English population on several tobacco islands grew rapidly in the 1630s and 1640s. By the middle of the century, however, the Caribbean colonies were in crisis because of stiff competition from milder Virginia-grown tobacco, also cultivated by indentured servants. The cultivation of sugar cane, introduced in the 1640s by Dutch investors expelled from Brazil, provided the Caribbean colonies a way out of this crisis. In the process their labor force changed from mostly European to mostly African.

The Portuguese had introduced sugar cultivation into Brazil from islands along the African coast after 1550 and had soon introduced enslaved African labor as well (see Chapter 19). By 1600 Brazil was the Atlantic world's greatest sugar producer. Some Dutch merchants invested in Brazilian sugar plantations so that they might profit from transporting the sugar across the Atlantic and distributing it in Europe. However, in the first half of the seventeenth century the Dutch were fighting for their independence from the Spanish crown, which then ruled Portugal and Brazil. As part of that struggle, the Dutch government chartered the **Dutch West India Company** in 1621 to carry the conflict to Spain's overseas possessions.

Not just a disguised form of the Dutch navy, the Dutch West India Company was a private trading company. Its investors expected the company's profits to cover its expenses and pay them dividends. After the capture of a Spanish treasure fleet in 1628, the company used some of the windfall to pay its stockholders a huge dividend and the rest to finance an assault on Brazil's valuable sugar-producing areas. By 1635 the Dutch company controlled 1,000 miles (1,600 kilometers) of northeastern Brazil's coast. Over the next fifteen years the new Dutch owners improved the efficiency of the Brazilian sugar industry, and the company prospered by supplying the plantations with enslaved Africans and European goods and carrying the sugar back to Europe.

Like its assault on Brazil, the Dutch West India Company's entry into the African slave trade combined economic and political motives. It seized the important West African trading station of Elmina from the Portuguese in 1638 and took their port of Luanda° on the Angolan coast in 1641. From these coasts the Dutch shipped slaves to Brazil and the West Indies. Although the Portuguese were able to drive the Dutch out of Angola after a few years, Elmina remained the Dutch West India Company's headquarters in West Africa.

Once free of Spanish rule in 1640, the Portuguese crown turned its attention to reconquering Brazil. By 1654 Portuguese armies had driven the last of the Dutch sugar planters from Brazil. Some of the expelled planters transplanted their capital and knowledge of sugar production to small colonies, which the Dutch had founded earlier as trading bases with Spanish colonies; others in-

---

Montserrat (mont-suh-RAHT)   Barbados (bahr-BAY-dohs)
Trinidad (TRIN-ah-dad)   Martinique (mahr-tee-NEEK)
Guadeloupe (gwah-duh-LOOP)

Luanda (loo-AHN-duh)

CHRONOLOGY

	West Indies	Atlantic	Africa
1500	**ca. 1500** Spanish settlers introduce sugar-cane cultivation	**1530** Amsterdam Exchange opens	**1500–1700** Gold trade predominates
			1591 Morocco conquers Songhai
1600	**1620s and 1630s** English and French colonies in Caribbean	**1621** Dutch West India Company chartered	**1638** Dutch take Elmina
	1640s Dutch bring sugar plantation system from Brazil		
	1655 English take Jamaica		
		1660s English Navigation Acts	
	1670s French occupy western half of Hispaniola	**1672** Royal African Company chartered	**1680s** Rise of Asante
		1698 French *Exclusif*	
1700	**1700** West Indies surpass Brazil in sugar production	**1700 to present** Atlantic system flourishing	**1700–1830** Slave trade predominates
			1720s Rise of Dahomey
			1730 Oyo makes Dahomey pay tribute
	1760 Tacky's rebellion in Jamaica		
	1795 Jamaican Maroon rebellion		

troduced the Brazilian system into English and French Caribbean islands. This was a momentous turning point in the history of the Atlantic economy.

Sugar and Slaves The Dutch infusion of expertise and money revived the French colonies of Guadeloupe and Martinique, but the English colony of Barbados best illustrates the dramatic transformation that sugar brought to the seventeenth-century Caribbean. In 1640 Barbados's economy depended largely on tobacco, mostly grown by European settlers, both free and indentured. By the 1680s sugar had become the colony's principal crop, and enslaved Africans were three times as numerous as Europeans. Exporting up to 15,000 tons of sugar a year, Barbados had become the wealthiest and most populous of England's American colonies. By 1700, the West Indies had surpassed Brazil as the world's principal source of sugar.

The expansion of sugar plantations in the West Indies required a sharp increase in the volume of the slave trade from Africa (see Figure 20.1). During the first half of the seventeenth century about 10,000 slaves a year had arrived from Africa. Most were destined for Brazil and the mainland Spanish colonies. In the second half of the century the trade averaged 20,000 slaves a year. More than half were intended for the English, French, and Dutch West Indies and most of the rest for Brazil. A century later the volume of the Atlantic slave trade was three times larger.

The shift in favor of African slaves was a product of many factors. Recent scholarship has cast doubt on the once-common assertion that Africans were more suited than Europeans to field labor, since newly arrived Africans and Europeans both died in large numbers in the American tropics. Africans' slightly higher survival rate was not decisive because mortality was about the same among later generations of blacks and whites born in the West Indies and acclimated to its diseases.

The West Indian historian Eric Williams also refuted the idea that the rise of African slave labor was primarily motivated by prejudice. Citing the West Indian colonies' prior use of enslaved Amerindians and indentured Europeans, along with European convicts and prisoners of war, he argued, "Slavery was not born of racism: rather, racism was the consequence of slavery."[1] Williams suggested the shift was due to the lower cost of African labor.

Yet slaves were far from cheap. Cash-short tobacco planters in the seventeenth century preferred indentured

Figure 20.1   Transatlantic Slave Trade from Africa, 1551–1850

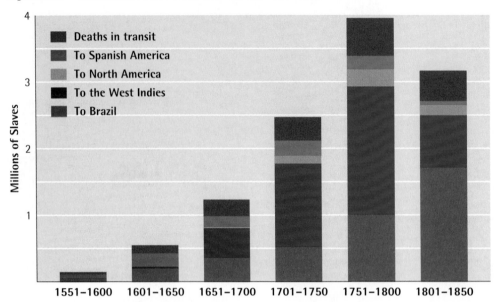

Source: Philip D. Curtin, *The Atlantic Slave Trade: A Census* (Madison: University of Wisconsin Press, 1969), tables 33, 34, 65; Paul E. Lovejoy, "The Volume of the Atlantic Slave Trade: A Synthesis," *Journal of African History* 23 (1982): 473–501; David Eltis, *Economic Growth and the Ending of the Transatlantic Slave Trade* (New York: Oxford University Press, 1987), table A8.

Europeans because they cost half as much as African slaves. Poor European men and women were willing to work for little in order to get to the Americas, where they could acquire their own land cheaply at the end of their term of service. However, as the cultivation of sugar spread after 1750, rich speculators drove the price of land in the West Indies up so high that end-of-term indentured servants could not afford to buy it. As a result, poor Europeans chose to indenture themselves in the mainland North American colonies, where cheap land was still available. Rather than raise wages to attract European laborers, Caribbean sugar planters switched to slaves.

Rising sugar prices helped the West Indian sugar planters afford the higher cost of African slaves. The fact that the average slave lived seven years, while the typical indentured labor contract was for only three or four years, also made slaves a better investment. The planters could rely on the Dutch and other traders to supply them with enough new slaves to meet the demands of the expanding plantations. Rising demand for slaves (see Figure 20.1) drove their sale price up steadily during the eighteenth century. These high labor costs were one more factor favoring large plantations over smaller operations.

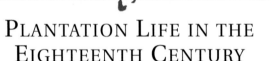

PLANTATION LIFE IN THE EIGHTEENTH CENTURY

To find more land for sugar plantations, France and England founded new Caribbean colonies. In 1655 the English had wrested the island of Jamaica from the Spanish (see Map 19.1). The French seized the western half of the large Spanish island of Hispaniola in the 1670s. During the eighteenth century this new French colony of Saint Domingue° (present-day Haiti) became the greatest producer of sugar in the Atlantic world, while Jamaica surpassed Barbados as England's most important sugar colony. The technological, environmental, and social transformation of these island colonies illustrates the power of the new Atlantic system.

Saint Domingue (san doh-MANGH)

Plantation Scene, Antigua, British West Indies   Even in this romanticized painting the slave's simple earthen huts contrast sharply with the planter's elegant great house on the rising ground on the left. Notice the large church in the center background and the women performing domestic tasks.   (West India Committee)

Technology and Environment

The cultivation of sugar cane was fairly straightforward. From fourteen to eighteen months after planting, the canes were ready to be cut. The roots continued to produce new shoots that could be harvested about every nine months. Only simple tools were needed: spades for planting, hoes to control the weeds, and sharp machetes to cut the canes. What made the sugar plantation a complex investment was that it had to be a factory as well as a farm. Freshly cut canes needed to be crushed within a few hours to extract the sugary sap. Thus, for maximum efficiency, each plantation needed its own expensive crushing and processing equipment.

At the heart of the sugar works was the mill where canes were crushed between sets of heavy rollers. Small mills could be turned by animal or human power, but larger, more efficient mills needed more sophisticated sources of power. Eighteenth-century Barbados went in heavily for windmills, and the French sugar islands and Jamaica used costly water-powered mills often fed by elaborate aqueducts.

From the mill, lead-lined wooden troughs carried the cane juice to a series of large copper kettles in the boiling shed, where the excess water boiled off, leaving a thick syrup. Workers poured the syrup into conical molds in the drying shed. The sugar crystals that formed in the molds were packed in wooden barrels for shipment to Europe. The dark molasses that drained off was made into rum in yet another building, or it was barreled for export.

To make their operation more efficient and profitable, investors gradually increased the size of the typical West Indian plantation from around 100 acres (40 hectares) in the seventeenth century to at least twice that size in the eighteenth century. Some plantations were even larger. In 1774 Jamaica's 680 sugar plantations averaged 441 acres (178 hectares) each; some spread over 2,000 acres (800 hectares). Jamaica specialized so heavily in sugar production that the island had to import most of its food. Saint Domingue had a comparable number of plantations of smaller average size but generally higher productivity. The French colony was also more diverse in its economy. Although sugar production was paramount, some planters raised provisions for local consumption of crops such as coffee and cacao for export.

In some ways the mature sugar plantation was environmentally responsible. The crushing mill was powered by water, wind, or animal power, not fossil fuels. The boilers were largely fueled by burning the crushed canes, and the fields were fertilized by manure of the cattle. In two respects, however, the plantation was very damaging to the environment: soil exhaustion and deforestation.

Repeated cultivation of a single crop removes from the soil more nutrients than animal fertilizer and fallow periods can restore. Instead of rotating sugar with other crops in order to restore the nutrients naturally, planters found it more profitable to clear new lands when yields declined too much in the old fields. When land close to the sea was exhausted, planters moved on to new islands. Many of the English who first settled Jamaica were from Barbados, and the pioneer planters on Saint Domingue came from older French sugar colonies. In the second half of the eighteenth century Jamaican sugar production began to fall behind that of Saint Domingue, which still had access to virgin land. Thus the plantations of this period were not a stable form of agriculture but one that gradually laid waste to the landscape.

Deforestation, the second form of environmental damage, continued a trend begun in the sixteenth century. The Spanish had cut down some forests in the Caribbean to make pastures for the cattle they introduced. Sugar cultivation rapidly accelerated land clearing. Forests near the coast were the first to disappear, and by the end of the eighteenth century only land in the interior of the islands retained dense forests.

Other changes, combined with soil exhaustion and deforestation, profoundly altered the ecology balance of the West Indies. By the eighteenth century nearly all of the domesticated animals and cultivated plants in the Caribbean were ones that Europeans had introduced. The Spanish had brought cattle, pigs, and horses, all of which multiplied so rapidly that no new imports had been necessary after 1503. They had also introduced new plants. Of these, bananas and plantain from the Canary Islands were a valuable addition to the food supply, and sugar and rice formed the basis of plantation agriculture, along with native tobacco. Other food crops arrived with the slaves from Africa, including okra, black-eyed peas, yams, grains such as millet and sorghum, and mangoes. Many of these new animals and plants were useful additions to the islands, but they crowded out indigenous species.

The most tragic and dramatic transformation in the West Indies occurred in the human population. Chapter 17 detailed how the indigenous Arawak peoples of the large islands were wiped out by disease and abuse within fifty years of Columbus's first voyage. As the plantation economy spread, the Carib surviving on the smaller islands were also pushed to the point of extinction. Far earlier and more completely than in any mainland colony, the West Indies were repeopled from across the Atlantic—first from Europe and then from Africa.

Slaves' Lives

During the eighteenth century, West Indian plantation colonies were the world's most polarized societies. On most islands 90 percent or more of the inhabitants were slaves. Power resided in the hands of a **plantocracy,** a small number of very rich men who owned most of the slaves and most of the land as well. Between the slaves and the masters might be found only a few others—a few estate managers and government officials and, in the French islands, some small farmers, both white and black. Thus it is only a slight simplification to describe eighteenth-century Caribbean society as being made up of a large, abject class of slaves and a small, powerful class of masters.

The profitability of a Caribbean plantation depended on extracting as much work as possible from the slaves. Their long workday might stretch to eighteen hours or more when the cane harvest and milling were in full swing. Sugar plantations achieved exceptional productivity through the use of force and the threat of force. As Table 20.1 shows, on a typical Jamaican plantation about 80 percent of the slaves actively engaged in productive tasks; the only exceptions were infants, the seriously ill, and the very old. Everyone on the plantation, except those disabled by age or infirmity, had an assigned task.

Table 20.1 also illustrates how slave labor was organized by age, sex, and ability. As in other Caribbean colonies, only 2 or 3 percent of the slaves served as house servants. About 70 percent of the able-bodied slaves worked in the fields, generally in one of three labor gangs. A "great gang," made up of the strongest slaves in the prime of life, did the heaviest work, such as breaking up the soil at the beginning of the planting season. A second gang of youths, elders, and less fit slaves did somewhat lighter work. A "grass gang," composed of children under the supervision of an elderly slave, was responsible for weeding and other simple work, such as collecting grass for the animals. Women formed the majority of the field laborers, even in the great gang. Nursing mothers took their babies with them to the fields. Slaves too old for field labor tended the toddlers.

Because slave ships brought twice as many males as females from Africa, men outnumbered women on Caribbean plantations. As Table 20.1 shows, a little over half of the adult males were employed in nongang work. Some tended the livestock, including the mules and oxen that did the heavy carrying work; others were skilled tradesmen, such as blacksmiths and carpenters. The most important artisan slave was the head boiler, who oversaw the delicate process of reducing the cane sap to crystallized sugar and molasses.

Table 20.1   Slave Occupations on a Jamaican Sugar Plantation, 1788

Occupations and Conditions	Men	Women	Boys and Girls	Total
Field laborers	62	78		140
Tradesmen	29			29
Field drivers	4			4
Field cooks		4		4
Mule-, cattle-, and stablemen	12			12
Watchmen	18			18
Nurse		1		1
Midwife		1		1
Domestics and gardeners		5	3	8
Grass-gang			20	20
Total employed	**125**	**89**	**23**	**237**
Infants			23	23
Invalids (18 with yaws)				32
Absent on roads				5
Superannuated [elderly]				7
Overall total				**304**

Source: Adapted from "Edward Long to William Pitt," in Michael Craton, James Walvin, and David Wright, eds., *Slavery, Abolition, and Emancipation* (London: Longman, 1976), 103. Used by permission of Pearson Education Limited.

Punishment for Slaves   In addition to whipping and other cruel punishments, slave owners devised other ways to shame and intimidate slaves into obedience. This metal face mask prevented the wearer from eating or drinking.   (By permission of the Syndics of Cambridge University Library)

Skilled slaves received rewards of food and clothing or time off for good work, but the most common reason for working hard was to escape punishment. A slave gang was headed by a privileged male slave, appropriately called the **"driver,"** whose job was to ensure that the gang completed its work. Since production quotas were high, slaves toiled in the fields from sunup to sunset, except for meal breaks. Those who fell behind due to fatigue or illness soon felt the sting of the whip. Openly rebellious slaves, who refused to work, disobeyed orders, or tried to escape, were punished with flogging, confinement in irons, or mutilation. On a Virginia plantation Equiano was shocked to see a woman slave being punished with an "iron muzzle" that "locked her mouth so fast that she could scarcely speak, and could not eat nor drink."

Even though slaves did not work in the fields on Sunday, it was no day of rest, for they had to farm their own provisioning grounds, maintain their dwellings, and do other chores, such as washing and mending their rough clothes. Sunday markets, where slaves sold small amounts of produce or animals they had raised to get a little spending money, were common in the British West Indies.

Except for occasional holidays—including the Christmas-week revels in the British West Indies—there was little time for recreation and relaxation. Slaves might sing in the fields, but singing was simply a way to distract themselves from their fatigue and the monotony of the work. There was certainly no time for schooling, and no willingness to educate slaves, beyond skills useful to the plantation.

Time for family life was also inadequate. Although the large proportion of young adults in plantation colonies ought to have led to a high rate of natural increase, the opposite occurred. Poor nutrition and overwork lowered fertility. A woman who did become pregnant found it difficult to carry a child to term while continuing heavy fieldwork or to ensure her infant's survival. As a result of these conditions, along with disease and accidents from dangerous mill equipment, deaths heavily outnumbered births on West Indian plantations (see Table 20.2). Life expectancy for slaves in nineteenth-century Brazil was only 23 years of age for males and 25.5 years for females. The figures were probably similar for the eighteenth-century Caribbean. A callous opinion, common among slave owners in the Caribbean and in parts of Brazil, held that it was cheaper to import a youthful new slave from Africa than to raise one to the same age on a plantation.

The harsh conditions of plantation life played a major role in shortening slaves' lives, but the greatest killer was disease. The very young were carried off by dysentery caused by contaminated food and water. Slaves newly arrived from Africa went through the period of adjustment to a new environment, known as **seasoning,** during which one-third on average died of unfamiliar diseases. Slaves also suffered from diseases brought with them, including malaria. On the plantation profiled in Table 20.1, for example, more than half of the slaves incapacitated by illness had yaws, a painful and debilitating skin disease common in Africa. As a consequence, only slave populations in the healthier temperate zones of North America experienced natural increase; those in tropical Brazil and the Caribbean had a negative rate of growth.

Such high mortality greatly added to the volume of the Atlantic slave trade, since plantations had to purchase new slaves every year or two just to replace those who died (see Table 20.2). The additional imports of slaves to permit the expansion of the sugar plantations meant that the majority of slaves were African-born on most West Indian plantations. As a result, African religious beliefs, patterns of speech, styles of dress and adornment, and music were prominent parts of West Indian life.

Given the harsh conditions of their lives, it is not surprising that slaves in the West Indies often sought to regain the freedom into which most had been born. Individual slaves often ran away, hoping to elude the men and dogs who would track them. Sometimes large groups of plantation slaves rose in rebellion against their bondage and abuse. For example, a large rebellion in Jamaica in 1760 was led by a slave named Tacky, who had been a chief on the Gold Coast of Africa. One night his followers broke into a fort and armed themselves. Joined by slaves from other nearby plantations, they stormed several plantations, setting them on fire and killing the planter families. Tacky died in the fighting that followed, and three other rebel leaders stoically endured cruel deaths by torture that were meant to deter others from rebellion.

Because they believed rebellions were usually led by slaves with the strongest African heritage, European planters tried to curtail African cultural traditions. They required slaves to learn the colonial language and discouraged the use of African languages by deliberately mixing slaves from different parts of Africa. In French and Portuguese colonies, slaves were encouraged to adopt Catholic religious practices, though African deities and beliefs also survived. In the British West Indies, where only Quaker slave owners encouraged Christianity among their slaves before 1800, African herbal medicine remained strong, as did African beliefs concerning nature spirits and witchcraft.

Table 20.2   Birth and Death on a Jamaican Sugar Plantation, 1779–1785

| Year | Born | | | Died | | |
	Males	Females	Purchased	Males	Females	Proportion of Deaths
1779	5	2	6	7	5	1 in 26
1780	4	3	–	3	2	1 in 62
1781	2	3	–	4	2	1 in 52
1782	1	3	9	4	5	1 in 35
1783	3	3	–	8	10	1 in 17
1784	2	1	12	9	10	1 in 17
1785	2	3	–	0	3	1 in 99
Total	19	18	27	35	37	
	Born 37			Died 72		

Source: From "Edward Long to William Pitt," in Michael Craton, James Walvin, and David Wright, eds., *Slavery, Abolition, and Emancipation* (London: Longman, 1976), 105. Used by permission of Pearson Education Limited.

Free Whites and Free Blacks

The lives of the small minority of free people were very different from the lives of slaves. In the French colony of Saint Domingue, which had nearly half of the slaves in the Caribbean in the eighteenth century, free people fell into three distinct groups. First, at the top of free society were the wealthy owners of large sugar plantations (the *grand blancs°*, or "great whites"), who dominated the economy and society of the island. Second came less-well-off Europeans (*petits blancs°*, or "little whites"). Most of them raised provisions for local consumption and crops such as coffee, indigo, and cotton for export, relying on their own and slave labor. Third came the free blacks. Though nearly as numerous as the free whites and engaged in similar occupations, they ranked below whites socially. A few free blacks became wealthy enough to own their own slaves.

The dominance of the plantocracy was even greater in British colonies. Whereas sugar constituted about half of Saint Domingue's exports, in Jamaica the figure was over 80 percent. Such concentration on sugar cane left much less room for small cultivators, white or black, and confined most landholding to a few larger owners. Three-quarters of the farmland in Jamaica at mid-century belonged to individuals who owned 1,000 acres (400 hectares) or more.

One source estimated that a planter had to invest nearly £20,000 ($100,000) to acquire even a medium-size Jamaican plantation of 600 acres (240 hectares) in 1774. A third of this money went for land on which to grow sugar and food crops, pasture animals, and cut timber and firewood. A quarter of the expense was for the sugar works and other equipment. The largest expense was to purchase 200 slaves at about £40 ($200) each. In comparison, the wage of an English rural laborer at this time was about £10 ($50) a year (one-fourth the price of a slave), and the annual incomes in 1760 of the ten wealthiest noble families in Britain averaged only £20,000 each.

Reputedly the richest Englishmen of this time, West Indian planters often translated their wealth into political power and social prestige. The richest planters put their plantations under the direction of managers and lived in Britain, often on rural estates that once had been the preserve of country gentlemen. Between 1730 and 1775 seventy of these absentee planters secured election to the British Parliament, where they formed an influential voting bloc. Those who resided in the West Indies had political power as well, for the British plantocracy controlled the colonial assemblies.

The Unknown Maroon of Saint-Domingue This modern sculpture by Albert Mangonès celebrates the brave but perilous life of a run-away slave, who is shown drinking water from a seashell. (Albert Mangonès, "The Unknown Maroon of Saint-Domingue." From Richard Price, *Maroon Societies*, Johns Hopkins University Press. Reproduced with permission.)

Most Europeans in plantation colonies were single males. Many of them took advantage of slave women for sexual favors or took slave mistresses. A slave owner who fathered a child by a female slave often gave both mother and child their freedom. In some colonies such **manumission** (a legal grant of freedom to an individual slave) produced a significant free black population. By the late eighteenth century, free blacks were more numerous than slaves in most of the Spanish colonies. They were almost 30 percent of the black population of Brazil, and they existed in significant numbers in the French colonies. Free blacks were far less common in the British colonies and the United States, where manumission was rare.

As in Brazil (see Chapter 19), escaped slaves constituted another part of the free black population. In the Caribbean runaways were known as **maroons,** Maroon communities were especially numerous in the mountainous interiors of Jamaica and Hispaniola as well as in the island parts of the Guianas° (see Society and Culture:

grands blancs (grawn blawnk)   *petits blancs* (pay-TEE blawnk)

Guianas (guy-AHN-uhs)

A Maroon Village in French Guiana). The Jamaican Maroons, after withstanding several attacks by the colony's militia, signed a treaty in 1739 that recognized their independence in return for their cooperation in stopping new runaways and suppressing slave revolts. Similar treaties with the large maroon population in the Dutch colony of Surinam (Dutch Guiana) recognized their possession of large inland regions.

CREATING THE ATLANTIC ECONOMY

At once archaic in their cruel system of slavery and oddly modern in their specialization in a single product, the West Indian plantation colonies were the bittersweet fruits of a new Atlantic trading system. Changes in the type and number of ships crossing the Atlantic illustrate the rise of this new system. The Atlantic trade of the sixteenth century calls to mind the treasure fleet, an annual convoy of from twenty to sixty ships laden with silver and gold bullion from Spanish America. Two different vessels typify the far more numerous Atlantic voyages of the late seventeenth and eighteenth centuries. One was the sugar ship, returning to Europe from the West Indies or Brazil crammed with barrels of brown sugar destined for further refinement. At the end of the seventeenth century an average of 266 sugar ships sailed every year just from the small island of Barbados. The second type of vessel was the slave ship. At the trade's peak between 1760 and 1800, some 300 ships, crammed with an average of 250 African captives each, crossed the Atlantic to the Americas each year.

Many separate pieces went into the creation of the new Atlantic economy. Besides the plantation system itself, three other elements merit further investigation: new economic institutions, new partnerships between private investors and governments in Europe, and new working relationships between European and African merchants. The new trading system is a prime example of how European capitalist relationships were reshaping the world.

Capitalism and Mercantilism

The Spanish and Portuguese voyages of exploration in the fifteenth and sixteenth centuries were government ventures, and both countries tried to keep their overseas trade and colonies royal monopolies (see Chapters 17 and 18). Monopoly control, however, proved both expensive and inefficient. The success of the Atlantic economy in the seventeenth and eighteenth centuries owed much to private enterprise, which made trading venues more efficient and profitable. European private investors were attracted by the profits they could make from an established and growing trading and colonial system, but their successful participation in the Atlantic economy depended on new institutions and a significant measure of government protection that reduced the likelihood of catastrophic loss.

Two European innovations enabled private investors to fund the rapid growth of the Atlantic economy. One was the ability to manage large financial resources through mechanisms that modern historians have labeled **capitalism.** The essence of early modern capitalism was a system of large financial institutions—banks, stock exchanges, and chartered trading companies—that enabled wealthy investors to reduce risks and increase profits. Originally developed for business dealings within Europe, the capitalist system expanded overseas in the seventeenth century, when slow economic growth in Europe led many investors to seek greater profits abroad.

Banks were a central capitalist institution. By the early seventeenth century, Dutch banks had developed such a reputation for security that individuals and governments from all over western Europe entrusted them with large sums of money. To make a profit, the banks invested these funds in real estate, local industries, loans to governments, and overseas trade.

Individuals seeking returns higher than the low rate of interest paid by banks could purchase shares in a joint-stock company, a sixteenth-century forerunner of the modern corporation. Shares were bought and sold in specialized financial markets called stock exchanges. The Amsterdam Exchange, founded in 1530, became the greatest stock market in the seventeenth and eighteenth centuries. To reduce risks in overseas trading, merchants and trading companies bought insurance on their ships and cargoes from specialized companies that agreed to cover losses.

The capitalism of these centuries was buttressed by **mercantilism,** policies adopted by European states to promote their citizens' overseas trade and accumulate capital in the form of precious metals. Mercantilist policies strongly discouraged citizens from trading with foreign merchants and used armed force when necessary to secure exclusive relations.

Chartered companies were one of the first examples of mercantilist capitalism. A charter issued by the government of the Netherlands in 1602 gave the Dutch East India Company a legal monopoly over all Dutch trade in the Indian Ocean. This privilege encouraged private in-

A Maroon Village in French Guiana, 1748

Runaway slaves, called maroons, *were common in planta- tion colonies. Colonial officials regularly tried to recapture them and destroy their villages. In 1748 a captured maroon youth named Louis gave the following testimony to officials in French Guiana in South America.*

He declared and admitted that he has been a maroon for about eighteen moons [lunar months] with Rémy, his fa- ther, and other Negroes belonging to [M. Gourgues]; that Rémy having displeased the said M. Gourgues and having been whipped by him, had planned this marronage having first gotten together a supply of . . . cassava and bananas for the trip . . . ; that after an unknown number of weeks, a cer- tain André [guided them] to the maroon village . . . ; that in the said village there are twenty-seven houses and three open sheds . . .; that the said houses belong to and are in- habited by twenty-nine strong male Negroes . . . , twenty- two female Negroes . . . , nine Negro boys, and twelve Negro girls, making in all seventy-two slaves. . . .

[Louis further declared that the captain of the village,] Bernard, nicknamed Couacou, . . . takes care of wounds [with herbal medicines,] baptizes with holy water and recites daily prayer. . . . That no member of the troop has died during the past two years.

That the captain's orders are obeyed perfectly; it is in his yard that prayers are recited in the morning and evening, as they are on well-run plantations; those who are sick recite their prayers in their houses.

That André either whips or has whipped those who de- serve punishment. . . . That André and some of his trusted followers make sorties from time to time to recruit new members in the area. . . . That no whites ever entered the vil- lage, nor any Negroes other than the ones who are re- cruited . . . and who promise never to betray them nor to run away, under penalty of being hunted down and killed. . . .

That whenever land has to be cleared, everyone works to- gether, and that once a large area has been burned, everyone is allotted a plot according to the needs of the family to plant and maintain. That the wild pigs that they kill fre- quently are divided among them, as is other large game, even fish that they dry when there are large numbers of them. . . .

That . . . they maintain and repair their arms themselves, keeping them in good condition at all times, but that when having hunted a great deal they are without powder and shot, . . . they use tiny stones, which . . . are found in abun- dance in the area. . . .

That the women spin cotton when the weather is bad and work in the fields in good weather. That [men] weave cotton cloth, which serves to make skirts for the women and loin- cloths for the men; that this cotton material is woven piece by piece and then assembled and decorated with Siamese cotton thread. . . .

That they get salt from the ashes of the Maracoupy palm. That they make a beverage out of sweet potatoes, yams, ba- nanas, and various grains, in addition to their [cassava beer].

That they store all their belongings in [baskets, and they all] are equipped with axes and machetes and that there are spares . . . and that they have no tools other than a few files, gimlets, and hammers; that they have no saws or adzes [wood-working axes]. That they had at the said Negro village two Negro drums, which they played on certain holidays.

What is the significance of the maroons employing African forms of communal ownership, herbal medicine, brewing, cloth making, and musical instruments? How much did they rely on tools, weapons, beliefs, and practices that they acquired from the French?

Source: Richard Price, ed., *Maroon Societies: Rebel Slave Communities in the Americas,* 2d ed. (Baltimore: Johns Hopkins University Press, 1979), 313– 318. Reprinted by permission of the Johns Hopkins University Press.

vestors to buy shares in the company. They were amply rewarded when Dutch East India Company captured control of the long-distance trade routes in the Indian Ocean from the Portuguese (see Chapter 21). As we have seen, a sister firm, the Dutch West India Company, was chartered in 1621 to engage in the Atlantic trade and to seize sugar-producing areas in Brazil and African slaving ports from the Portuguese.

Such successes inspired other governments to set up their own chartered companies. In 1672, a royal char- ter placed all English trade with West Africa in the hands of a new **Royal African Company,** which established its headquarters at Cape Coast Castle, just east of Elmina on the Gold Coast. The French government also played an active role in chartering companies and promoting overseas trade and colonization. Jean Baptiste Colbert°, King Louis XIV's minister of finance from 1661 to 1683, chartered French East India and French West India Companies to reduce French colonies' dependence on Dutch and English traders.

French and English governments also used military force in pursuit of commercial dominance, especially to break the trading advantage of the Dutch in the Americas. Restrictions on Dutch access to French and English colonies provoked a series of wars with the Netherlands between 1652 and 1678 (see Chapter 18), during which the larger English and French navies defeated the Dutch and drove the Dutch West India Company into bankruptcy.

With Dutch competition in the Atlantic reduced, the French and English governments moved to revoke the monopoly privileges of their chartered companies. England opened trade in Africa to any English subject in 1698 on the grounds that ending monopolies would be "highly beneficial and advantageous to this kingdom." It was hoped that such competition would also cut the cost of slaves to West Indian planters, though the demand for slaves soon drove the prices up again.

Such new mercantilist policies fostered competition among a nation's own citizens, while using high tariffs and restrictions to exclude foreigners. In the 1660s England had passed a series of Navigation Acts that confined trade with its colonies to English ships and cargoes. The French called their mercantilist legislation, first codified in 1698, the *Exclusif*°, highlighting its exclusionary intentions. Other mercantilist laws defended manufacturing and processing interests in Europe against competition from colonies, imposing prohibitively high taxes on any manufactured goods and refined sugar imported from the colonies.

As a result of such mercantilist measures, the Atlantic became Britain, France, and Portugal's most important overseas trading area in the eighteenth century. Britain's imports from its West Indian colonies in this period accounted for over one-fifth of the value of total British imports. The French West Indian colonies played an even larger role in France's overseas trade. Only the Dutch, closed out of much of the American trade, found Asian trade of greater importance (see Chapter 21). Profits from the Atlantic economy, in turn, promoted further economic expansion and increased the revenues of European governments.

Colbert (kohl-BEAR)
Exclusif (ek-skloo-SEEF)

The Great Circuit and the Middle Passage

At the heart of the Atlantic system was a great clockwise network of trade routes known as the **Great Circuit** (see Map 20.1). It began in Europe, ran south to Africa, turned west across the Atlantic Ocean to the Americas, and then swept back to Europe. Like Asian sailors in the Indian Ocean, Atlantic mariners depended on the prevailing winds and currents to propel their ships. What drove the ships as much as the winds and currents was the desire for the profits that each leg of the circuit was expected to produce.

The first leg, from Europe to Africa, carried European manufactures—notably metal bars, hardware, and guns—as well as great quantities of cotton textiles brought from India. Some of these goods were traded for West African gold, timber, and other products, which were taken back to Europe. More goods went to purchase slaves, who were transported across the Atlantic to the plantation colonies in the part of the Great Circuit known as the **Middle Passage.** On the third leg, plantation goods from the colonies returned to Europe. Each leg of the circuit carried goods from where they were abundant and relatively cheap to where they were scarce and therefore more valuable. Thus, in theory, each leg of the Great Circuit could earn much more than its costs, and a ship that completed all three legs could return a handsome profit to its owners. In practice, shipwrecks, deaths, piracy, and other risks could turn profit into loss.

The three-sided Great Circuit is only the simplest model of Atlantic trade. Many other trading voyages supplemented the basic circuit. Cargo ships made long voyages from Europe to the Indian Ocean, passed southward through the Atlantic with quantities of African gold and American silver, and returned with the cotton textiles necessary to the African trade. Other sea routes brought to the West Indies manufactured goods from Europe or foodstuffs and lumber from New England. In addition, some Rhode Island and Massachusetts merchants participated in a "Triangular Trade" that carried rum to West Africa, slaves to the West Indies, and molasses and rum back to New England. There was also a considerable two-way trade between Brazil and Angola, which exchanged Brazilian liquor and other goods for slaves. On another route, Brazil and Portugal exchanged sugar and gold for European imports.

Map. 20.1 The Atlantic Economy   By 1700 the volume of maritime exchanges among the Atlantic continents had begun to rival the trade of the Indian Ocean basin. Notice the trade in consumer products, slave labor, precious metals, and other goods. A silver trade to East Asia laid the basis for a Pacific Ocean economy.

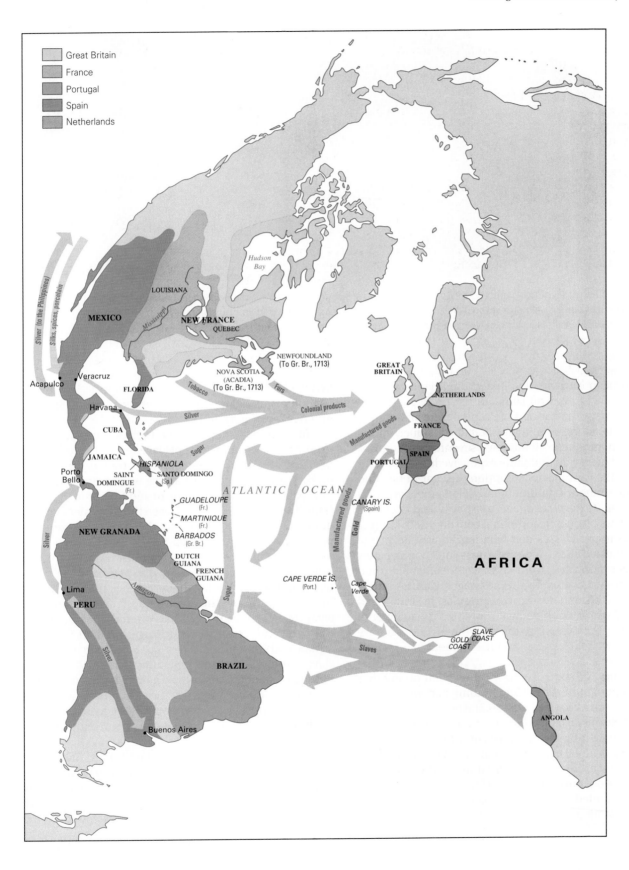

Great Britain
France
Portugal
Spain
Netherlands

Hudson Bay

LOUISIANA

MEXICO

NEW FRANCE
QUEBEC

Mississippi

NEWFOUNDLAND
(To Gr. Br., 1713)

NOVA SCOTIA
(ACADIA)
(To Gr. Br., 1713)

GREAT
BRITAIN

NETHERLANDS

FRANCE

Acapulco
Veracruz
FLORIDA

Tobacco

Furs

PORTUGAL   SPAIN

Havana

Silver

Colonial products

Manufactured goods

CUBA

Sugar

JAMAICA

HISPANIOLA

Porto
Bello

SAINT
DOMINGUE
(Fr.)

SANTO DOMINGO
(Sp.)

ATLANTIC   OCEAN

CANARY IS.
(Spain)

Manufactured goods

Gold

GUADELOUPE
(Fr.)

MARTINIQUE
(Fr.)

Silver

NEW GRANADA

BARBADOS
(Gr. Br.)

DUTCH
GUIANA

AFRICA

FRENCH
GUIANA

Sugar

CAPE VERDE IS.
(Port.)

Cape
Verde

Amazon

Lima

PERU

SLAVE
COAST

GOLD
COAST

Silver

Slaves

BRAZIL

ANGOLA

Buenos Aires

Silver (to the Philippines)

Silks, spices, porcelain

Slave Ship This model of the English vessel *Brookes* shows the specially built section of the hold where enslaved Africans were packed together during the Middle Passage. Girls, boys, and women were confined separately. (Wilberforce House Museum, Hull, Humberside, UK/The Bridgeman Art Library, London and New York)

European interests dominated the Atlantic system. The manufacturers who supplied the trade goods and the investors who provided the capital were all based in Europe, but so too were the principal consumers of the plantation products. Before the seventeenth century, sugar had been rare and fairly expensive in western Europe. By 1700 annual consumption of sugar in England had risen to about 4 pounds (nearly 2 kilograms) per person. Rising western European prosperity and declining sugar prices promoted additional consumption, starting with the upper classes and working its way down the social ladder. People spooned sugar into popular new beverages imported from overseas—tea, coffee, and chocolate—to overcome the beverages' natural bitterness. By 1750 annual sugar consumption in Britain had doubled, and it doubled again to about 18 pounds (8 kilograms) per person by the early nineteenth century (well below the American average of about 100 pounds [45 kilograms] a year in 1960).

The flow of sugar to Europe depended on another key component of the Atlantic trading system: the flow of slaves from Africa (see Map 20.2). The rising volume of the Middle Passage also measures the Atlantic system's expansion. During the first 150 years after the European discovery of the Americas, some 800,000 Africans had begun the journey across the Atlantic. During the boom in sugar production between 1650 and 1800, the slave trade amounted to nearly 7,500,000. Of the survivors, over half landed in the West Indies and nearly a third in

Brazil. Plantations in North America imported another 5 percent, and the rest went to other parts of Spanish America (see Figure 20.1).

In these peak decades, the transportation of slaves from Africa was a highly specialized trade, although it regularly attracted some amateur traders hoping to make a quick profit. Most slaves were carried in ships that had been specially built or modified for the slave trade by the construction between the ships' decks of additional platforms on which the human cargo was packed as tightly as possible.

Seventeenth-century mercantilist policies placed much of the Atlantic slave trade in the hands of chartered companies. During their existence the Dutch West India Company and the English Royal African Company each carried about 100,000 slaves across the Atlantic. In the eighteenth century, private English traders from Liverpool and Bristol controlled about 40 percent of the slave trade. The French, operating out of Nantes and Bordeaux, handled about half as much, but the Dutch hung on to only 6 percent. The Portuguese supplying Brazil and other places had nearly 30 percent of the Atlantic slave trade, in contrast to the 3 percent carried in North American ships.

To make a profit, European slave traders had to buy slaves in Africa for less than the cost of the goods they traded in return. Then they had to deliver as many healthy slaves as possible across the Atlantic for resale in the plantation colonies. The treacherous voyage to the

Map. 20.2 The African Slave Trade, 1500–1800 After 1500 a vast new trade in slaves from sub-Saharan Africa to the Americas joined the ongoing slave trade to the Islamic states of North Africa, the Middle East, and India. The West Indies were the major destination of the Atlantic slave trade, followed by Brazil.

Americas lasted from six to ten weeks. Some ships completed it with all of their slaves alive, but large, even catastrophic, losses of life were common. On average between 1650 and 1800, about one slave in every six perished during the Middle Passage (see Figure 20.1).

Some deaths resulted from the efforts of the captives to escape. On his voyage Equiano witnessed two of his Igbo countrymen, who were chained together, jump into the sea, "preferring death to such a life of misery." To inhibit such attempts, African men were confined below deck during most of the voyage, and special netting was installed around the outside of the ship. Some slaves fell into deep psychological depression, known to contemporaries as "fixed melancholy," from which many perished. Others, including Equiano, refused to eat, so forced feeding was used to keep slaves alive. When opportunities presented themselves (nearness to land,

illness among the crew), some cargoes of enslaved Africans tried to overpower their captors. Such "mutinies" were rarely successful and were put down with brutality that occasioned further losses of life.

Other deaths during the Middle Passage were due to the ill treatment slaves received. Although it was in the interests of the captain and crew to deliver their slave cargo in good condition, whippings, beatings, and even executions were used to maintain order and force the captives to take nourishment. Moreover, the dangers and brutalities of the slave trade were so notorious that many ordinary seamen shunned such work. As a consequence, cruel and brutal characters abounded among the officers and crews on slave ships.

Although examples of unspeakable cruelties are common in the records, most deaths in the Middle Passage were the result of disease rather than abuse, just as on the plantations. Dysentery spread by contaminated food and water caused many deaths. Others died of contagious diseases such as smallpox carried by persons whose infections were not detected during the medical examinations of slaves prior to boarding. Such maladies spread quickly in the crowded and unsanitary confines of the ships, claiming the lives of many slaves already physically weakened and mentally traumatized by their ordeals.

Crew members who were in close contact with the slaves were equally exposed to the epidemics and regularly suffered heavy losses. Moreover, sailors often fell victim to tropical diseases, such as malaria, to which Africans had acquired resistance. It is a measure of the callousness of the age, as well as the cheapness of European labor, that over the course of a Great Circuit voyage the proportion of crew deaths could be as high as the slave deaths on the Middle Passage.

AFRICA, THE ATLANTIC, AND ISLAM

The Atlantic system took a terrible toll in African lives both during the Middle Passage and under the harsh conditions of plantation slavery. Many other Africans died while being marched to African coastal ports for sale overseas. The overall effects on Africa of these losses and of other aspects of the slave trade have been the subject of considerable historical debate. It is clear that the trade's impact depended on the intensity and terms of different African regions' involvement.

Any assessment of the Atlantic system's effects in Africa must also take into consideration the fact that some Africans profited from the trade by capturing and selling slaves. They chained the slaves together or bound them to forked sticks for the march to the coast, then bartered them to the European slavers for trade goods. The effects on the enslaver were different from the effects on the enslaved. Finally, a broader understanding of the Atlantic system's effects in sub-Saharan Africa comes from comparisons with the effects of Islamic contacts.

The Gold Coast and the Slave Coast

As Chapter 17 showed, early European visitors to Africa's Atlantic coast were interested more in trading than in colonizing or controlling the continent. As the Africa trade mushroomed after 1650, this pattern continued. African kings and merchants sold slaves and other goods at many new coastal sites, but the growing slave trade did not lead to any substantial European colonization.

The transition to slave trading was not sudden. Even as slaves were becoming Atlantic Africa's most valuable export, nonslave goods such as gold, ivory, and timber remained a significant part of the total trade. For example, during its eight decades of operation from 1672 to 1752, the English Royal African Company made 40 percent of its profits from dealings in gold, ivory, and forest products. In some parts of West Africa, such nonslave exports remained predominant even at the peak of the trade.

African merchants were very discriminating about what merchandise they received in return for slaves or other goods. A European ship that arrived with goods of low quality or not suited to local tastes found it hard to purchase a cargo at a profitable price. European guidebooks to the African trade carefully noted the color and shape of beads, the pattern of textiles, the type of guns, and the sort of metals that were in demand on each section of the coast. In the early eighteenth century, the people of Sierra Leone had a strong preference for large iron kettles, brass pans were preferred on the Gold Coast, and iron and copper bars were in demand in the Niger Delta, where smiths turned them into useful objects (see Map 20.3).

Although preferences for merchandise varied, Africans' greatest demands were for textiles, hardware, and guns. Of the goods the Royal African Company traded in West Africa in the 1680s, over 60 percent were Indian and European textiles, 30 percent hardware and weaponry. Beads and other jewelry formed 3 percent. The rest consisted of cowrie shells that were used as money. In the eighteenth century, tobacco and rum from the Americas became welcome imports.

Both Europeans and Africans naturally attempted to drive the best bargain for themselves and sometimes engaged in deceitful practices. The strength of the African bargaining position, however, may be inferred from the fact that as the demand for slaves rose, so too did their price in Africa. In the course of the eighteenth century the goods needed to purchase a slave on the Gold Coast doubled and in some places tripled or quadrupled.

West Africans' trading strengths were reinforced by African governments on the Gold and Slave Coasts that made Europeans observe African trading customs and prevented them from taking control of African territory. Rivalry among European nations, each of which established its own trading "castles" along the Gold Coast, also reduced Europeans' bargaining strength. In 1700 the head of the Dutch East India Company in West Africa,

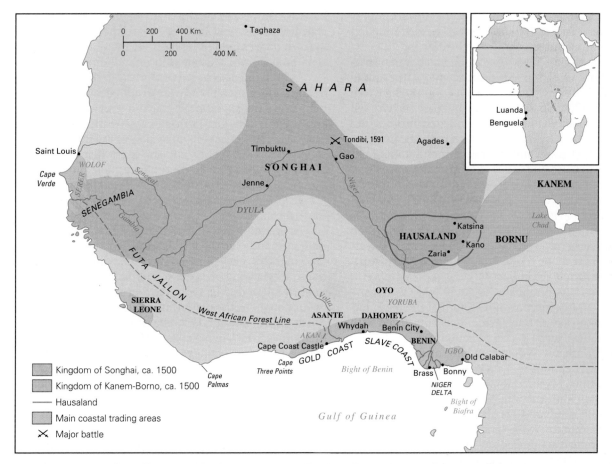

Map. 20.3   West African States and Trade, 1500–1800   The Atlantic and the trans-Saharan trade brought West Africans new goods and promoted the rise of powerful states and trading communities. The Moroccan invasion of Songhai and Portuguese colonization of the Angolan ports of Luanda and Benguela showed the political dangers of such relations.

Willem Bosman°, bemoaned the fact that, to stay competitive against the other European traders, his company had to include large quantities of muskets and gunpowder in the goods it exchanged, thereby adding to Africans' military power.

Bosman also related that before being allowed to buy slaves at Whydah on the Slave Coast his agents first had to pay the king a substantial customs duty and buy at a premium price whatever slaves the king had to sell. By African standards, Whydah was a rather small kingdom controlling only that port and its immediate hinterland. In 1727 it was annexed by the larger kingdom of Dahomey°, which maintained a strong trading position with Europeans at the coast. Dahomey's rise in the 1720s depended heavily on the firearms that the slave trade supplied for its well-trained armies of men and women.

In the cases of two of Dahomey's neighbors, the connections between state growth and the Atlantic trade were more complex. One was the inland Oyo° kingdom to the northeast. Oyo cavalry overran Dahomey in 1730 and forced it to pay an annual tribute to keep its independence. The other was the newer kingdom of Asante°, west of Dahomey along the Gold Coast, which expanded rapidly after 1680. Both Oyo and Asante participated in the Atlantic trade, but neither kingdom was so dependent on it as Dahomey. Overseas trade formed a relatively modest part of the economies of these large and populous states and was balanced by their extensive overland trade with their northern neighbors and with

---

Willem Bosman (VIL-uhm boos-MAHN)
Dahomey (dah-HOH-mee)

Oyo (aw-YOH)   **Asante** (uh-SHAN-tee)

states across the Sahara. Like the great medieval empires of the western Sudan, Oyo and Asante were stimulated by external trade but not controlled by it.

How did African kings and merchants obtain slaves for sale? Bosman dismissed misconceptions prevailing in Europe in his day. "Not a few in our country," he wrote to a friend in 1700, "fondly imagine that parents here sell their children, men their wives, and one brother the other. But those who think so, do deceive themselves; for this never happens on any other account but that of necessity, or some great crime; but most of the slaves that are offered to us are prisoners of war, which are sold by the victors as their booty."[2] Other accounts agree that prisoners taken in war were the greatest source of slaves for the Atlantic trade, but it is difficult to say how often capturing slaves for export was the main cause of warfare. "Here and there," conclude two respected historians of Africa, "there are indications that captives taken in the later and more peripheral stages of these wars were exported overseas, but it would seem that the main impetus of conquest was only incidentally concerned with the slave-trade in any external direction."[3]

An early-nineteenth-century king of Asante had a similar view: "I cannot make war to catch slaves in the bush, like a thief. My ancestors never did so. But if I fight a king, and kill him when he is insolent, then certainly I must have his gold, and his slaves, and his people are mine too. Do not the white kings act like this?"[4] English rulers had indeed sentenced seventeenth-century Scottish and Irish prisoners to forced labor in the West Indies. One may imagine that the African and the European prisoners did not share their kings' view that such actions were legitimate.

The Bight of Biafra and Angola

In the eighteenth century the slave trade expanded eastward to the Bight (bay) of Biafra. In contrast to the Gold and Slave Coasts, where strong kingdoms predominated, the densely populated interior of the Bight of Biafra contained no large states. Even so, the powerful merchant princes of the coastal ports still made European traders give them rich presents. Because of the absence of sizable states, there were no large-scale wars and consequently few prisoners of war. Instead, kidnapping was the major source of slaves, as Equiano's autobiography indicates. In about 1756, while their parents were away working in the fields, the eleven-year-old Equiano and his younger sister were snatched from their yard by two men and a woman. After passing through many hands, Equiano finally reached a coastal port, where, he relates,

he was astonished at the sight of the slave ship and alarmed at his first sight of "white men with horrible looks, red faces, and loose hair." By then he had become separated from his sister, whose fate he never learned.

As Equiano discovered on his way to the coast, some inland African merchants were experienced in procuring debtors, victims of kidnapping, and convicted criminals and shepherding them through a network of markets to the coast. The largest inland traders of the Bight of Biafra were the Aro of Arochukwu, who used their control of a famous religious oracle to enhance their prestige. The Aro cemented their business links with powerful inland families and the coastal merchants through gifts and marriage alliances.

As the volume of the Atlantic trade along the Bight of Biafra expanded in the late eighteenth century, some inland markets evolved into giant fairs with different sections specializing in slaves and imported goods. An English ship's doctor reported that in the 1780s slaves were "bought by the black traders at fairs, which are held for that purpose, at a distance of upwards of two hundred miles from the sea coast." He reported seeing from twelve hundred to fifteen hundred enslaved men and women arriving at the coast from a single fair.[5]

The local context of the Atlantic trade was different south of the Congo estuary at Angola, the greatest source of slaves for the Atlantic trade (see Map 20.2). This was also the one place along the Atlantic coast where a single European nation, Portugal, controlled a significant amount of territory. Except when overrun by the Dutch for a time in the seventeenth century, Portuguese residents of the main coastal ports of Luanda and Benguela° served as middlemen between the caravans that arrived from the far interior and the ships that crossed from Brazil. From the coastal cities Afro-Portuguese traders guided large caravans of trade goods inland to exchange for slaves at special markets. Some markets met in the shadow of Portuguese frontier forts; powerful African kings controlled others.

Many of the slaves sold at these markets were prisoners of war captured by expanding African states. By the late eighteenth century, slaves sold from Angolan ports were prisoners of wars fought from as far as 600 to 800 miles (1,000 to 1,300 kilometers) inland. Many were victims of wars of expansion fought by the giant federation of Lunda kingdoms. As elsewhere in Africa, such prisoners usually seem to have been a byproduct of African wars rather than the purpose for which the wars were fought.

Benguela (ben-GWAY-luh)

Queen Nzinga of Angola, 1622   This formidable African woman went to great lengths to maintain her royal dignity when negotiating a treaty for her brother with the Portuguese governor of Luanda. To avoid having to stand in his presence, she had one of her women bend herself into a human seat. Nzinga later ruled in her own name and revolted against the Portuguese with the aid of Dutch and African allies.   (Jean-Loup Charmet)

Recent research has linked other enslavement with environmental crises in the hinterland of Angola.[6] During the eighteenth century these southern grasslands periodically suffered severe droughts, which drove famished refugees to better-watered areas. Powerful African leaders gained control of such refugees in return for supplying them with food and water. These leaders built up their followings by assimilating refugee children, along with adult women, who were valued as food producers and for reproduction. However, they often sold into the Atlantic trade the adult make refugees, who were more likely than the women and children to escape or challenge the ruler's authority. Rising Angolan leaders parceled out the Indian textiles, weapons, and alcohol they received in return for such slaves as gifts to attract new followers and to cement the loyalty of their established allies.

The most successful of these inland Angolan leaders became heads of powerful new states that stabilized areas devastated by war and drought and repopulated them with the refugees and prisoners they retained. The slave frontier then moved farther inland. This cruel system worked to the benefit of a few African rulers and merchants at the expense of the many thousands of Africans who were sent to death or perpetual bondage in the Americas.

Although the organization of the Atlantic trade in Africa varied, it was based on a partnership between European and African elites. To obtain foreign textiles, metals, and weapons, African rulers and merchants sold slaves and many other products. Most of the exported slaves were prisoners taken in wars associated with African state growth. But strong African states also helped offset the Europeans' economic advantage and hindered them from taking control of African territory. Even in the absence of strong states, powerful African merchant communities everywhere dominated the movement of goods and people. The Africans who gained from these exchanges were the rich and powerful few. Many more Africans were losers in these exchanges.

Comparing European and Islamic Contacts

The growing European influence in Atlantic Africa has a parallel in the continuing Islamic influence along the southern border of the Sahara and in eastern Africa. There are striking similarities and differences in the political, commercial, and cultural impacts of these two external influences on sub-Saharan Africa between 1500 and 1800.

Despite all their commercial expansion in the centuries before 1800, Europeans had acquired control of little African territory. Their trading posts along the Gold and Slave Coasts were largely dependent on the goodwill of local African rulers. Only on islands and in Angola did the Atlantic trade lead to significant European colonies. Ironically, the largest European colony in Africa before 1800, the Dutch East India Company's Cape Colony at the southern tip of the continent, was tied to the Indian Ocean trade, not to the Atlantic trade. The Cape Colony did not export slaves; rather the 25,750 slaves in its population were mostly derived from persons *imported* from Madagascar, South Asia, and the East Indies.

Muslim territorial dominance was more extensive. Arab conquests in the seventh century permanently brought North Africa into the Muslim world. Muslim practices and traders spread south of the Sahara, but Arab and North African Muslims had little success in extending their territorial dominance southward before 1500. During the sixteenth century, all of North Africa except Morocco was annexed to the new Ottoman Islamic empire, while Ethiopia lost extensive territory to other Muslim conquerors (see Chapter 17).

In the 1580s Morocco began a southward expansion aimed at gaining control of the Saharan trade. To that end it sent a military expedition of 4,000 men and 10,000 camels from Marrakesh to attack the indigenously ruled Muslim empire of Songhai° in the western Sudan. Half of the men perished on their way across the desert. The remainder, armed with 2,500 muskets, succeeded in besting Songhai's army of 40,000 cavalry and foot soldiers in 1591, reducing the empire to a shadow of its former self. Although Morocco was never able to annex the western Sudan, for the next two centuries the occupying troops extracted a massive tribute of slaves and goods from the local population and collected tolls from passing merchants.

Morocco's destruction of Songhai weakened the trans-Saharan trade in the western Sudan. Caravans continued to cross the desert bringing textiles, hard-

ware, and weapons, but much of the trade shifted eastward to the central Sudan. Except for the absence of alcohol (which was prohibited to Muslims), these goods were similar to those in the Atlantic trade. There was also a continuation of the salt trade southward from Saharan mines. Communities of Dyula° traders in the western Sudan and Hausa traders in the central Sudan distributed these imports and local goods throughout West Africa. They also collected goods for shipment northward, including gold, caffeine-rich kola nuts from Asante and other parts of the forest (a stimulant allowed by Muslim law), African textiles and leather goods, as well as slaves.

Fewer slaves crossed the Sahara than crossed the Atlantic, but their numbers were substantial. It is estimated that between 1600 and 1800 about 850,000 slaves trudged across the desert's various routes (see Map 20.2). A nearly equal number of slaves from sub-Saharan Africa entered the Islamic Middle East and India by way of the Red Sea and the Indian Ocean.

The tasks that African slaves performed in the Islamic world were very different from their tasks in the Americas. In the late seventeenth and eighteenth centuries, Morocco's rulers employed an army of 150,000 slaves obtained from the south to keep them in power. Other slaves worked for Moroccans on sugar plantations, as servants, and as artisans. In contrast to the makeup of the Atlantic slave trade, the majority of the slaves crossing the desert were women, intended to serve wealthy households as concubines and servants. The trans-Saharan slave trade also included a much higher proportion of children than did the Atlantic trade, including eunuchs meant for eventual service as harem guards. It is estimated that only one in ten of these boys survived the surgical removal of their genitals.

The central Sudanese kingdom of Bornu illustrates some aspects of trans-Saharan contacts. This ancient Muslim state had grown and expanded in the sixteenth century as the result of guns imported from the Ottoman Empire. Bornu retained many captives from its wars, or sold them as slaves to the north in return for the firearms and horses that underpinned the kingdom's military power. Bornu's king, Mai Ali, conspicuously displayed his kingdom's new power and wealth while on four pilgrimages to Mecca between 1642 and 1667. On the last, an enormous entourage of slaves—said to number fifteen thousand—accompanied him.

Like Christians, Muslims of this period saw no moral impediment to owning and trading in slaves. Indeed, Is-

---

Songhai (song-GAH-ee)

Dyula (JOO-lah)

lam recognized the *jihad* (holy war) as a means by which their religion could be spread and considered enslaving "pagans" to be a meritorious act because it brought them into the faith. Although Islam forbade the enslavement of Muslims, some Muslim states south of the Sahara did not strictly observe that law. Ahmad Baba, a Muslim scholar of Timbuktu, in a 1614 treatise on slavery lamented that the enslavement of free Muslims was much practiced, notably by Muslim Hausa rulers.

A West African named Ayuba Suleiman Diallo° may serve as a revealing example of an enslaved Muslim. In 1730 his father, a prominent Muslim scholar, sent Ayuba to sell two slaves to an English ship on the Gambia River so as to buy paper and other necessities. On his way home a few days later, other Africans kidnapped Ayuba, shaved his head to make him appear to have been a war captive, and sold him to the same English ship. A planter from Maryland purchased Ayuba. Soon after, an English scholar, impressed by Ayuba's knowledge of Arabic and his elevated social origins, bought his freedom and arranged for him to return home.[7]

Because of sub-Saharan Africa's long and deep exposure to Islam, Muslim cultural influences were much greater than European ones before 1800. The Arabic language, long dominant in North Africa, continued to expand as a means of communication among scholars and merchants south of the Sahara. The Islamic religion also increased the number of its adherents south of the desert, reaching well beyond the urban centers that had been its medieval strength.

In contrast, African conversion to Christianity was limited to coastal Angola and the immediate vicinity of small European trading posts. The use of European languages was also largely confined to the trading coasts. Still it is notable that some African merchants sent their sons to Europe to learn European ways. One of these young men, Philip Quaque°, was educated in England and ordained as a priest in the Church of England and became the official chaplain of the Cape Coast Castle from 1766 until his death in 1816. Not only men of Quaque's stature but many African merchants learned to write a European language. A leading trader of Old Calabar on the Bight of Biafra kept a diary in pidgin English in the late eighteenth century.

The interesting details of the lives of elite and culturally sophisticated individuals such as Ayuba Suleiman and Philip Quaque must not distract us from the grim, sordid details of this era of slave trading. It is easy to re-

---

Ayuba Suleiman Diallo (ah-YOO-bah SOO-lay-mahn JAH-loh)
Quaque (KWAH-kay)

Ayuba Suleiman Diallo (1701–??)   Known as Job ben Solomon to the Maryland planter who owned him as a slave from 1731 to 1735, this Muslim from the West African state of Bondu was able to regain his freedom and return to Africa. Notice the booklet of Quranic verses around his neck.   (British Library)

joice in Ayuba's return to Africa while forgetting the unrecorded fates of the two persons whom he sold into slavery. In admiring Quaque's achievement of a position second only to the British governor on the Gold Coast, we should not overlook that his principal duties were to tend the spiritual needs of the slave traders, not the slaves. Unfortunately, surviving records tell us much less about the large number of Africans who suffered than about the small number who prospered from the European and Muslim trades.

Despite uncertainty over many details, it is still possible to assess some of the effects of the Atlantic and Islamic trades on sub-Saharan Africa. One key issue is how the European and Islamic slave trades affected Africa's population. Most scholars who have looked deeply into the question agree on two points: (1) the effect of slave exports could not have been large when measured against the population of the entire continent, but (2) losses in regions that contributed heavily to the slave trade were severe. The lands behind the Slave Coast are thought to have been acutely affected. The large slave

Amerindian Foods in Africa

The migration of European plants and animals across the Atlantic to the New World was one side of the Columbian Exchange (see Chapter 19). The Andean potato, for example, became a staple crop of the poor in Europe, and cassava (a Brazilian plant cultivated for its edible roots) and maize (corn) moved across the Atlantic to Africa.

Maize was a high-yielding grain that could produce much more food per acre than many grains indigenous to Africa. The varieties of maize that spread to Africa were not modern high-bred "sweet corn" but starchier types found in white and yellow corn meal. Cassava—not well known to modern North Americans except perhaps in the form of tapioca—became the most important New World food in Africa. Truly a marvel, cassava had the highest yield of calories per acre of any staple food and thrived even in poor soils and during droughts. Both the leaves and the root could be eaten. Ground into meal, the root could be made into a bread that would keep for up to six months, or it could be fermented into a beverage.

Cassava Plant   Both the leaves and the starchy root of the cassava plant could be eaten. (Engraving from André Thevet, *Les Singularitez de la Franc Antarctique*. Paris: Maurice de la Porte, 1557). Courtesy of the James Bell Library, University of Minnesota)

Cassava and maize were probably introduced accidentally into Africa by Portuguese ships from Brazil that discarded leftover supplies after reaching Angola. It did not take long for local Africans to recognize the food value of these new crops, especially in drought-prone areas. As the principal farmers in Central Africa, women must have played an important role in learning how to cultivate, harvest, and prepare these foods. By the eighteenth century, Lunda rulers hundreds of miles from the Angolan coast were actively promoting the cultivation of maize and cassava on their royal estates in order to provide a more secure food supply.

Some historians of Africa believe that in the inland areas these Amerindian food crops provided the nutritional base for a population increase that partially offset losses due to the Atlantic slave trade. By supplementing the range of food crops available and by enabling populations to increase in once lightly settled or famine-prone areas, cassava and maize, along with peanuts and other New World legumes, permanently altered Africans' environmental prospects.

---

trade may also have caused serious depopulation in Angola. To some extent, however, losses from famine in this region may have been reduced by the increasing cultivation of high-yielding food plants from the Americas (see Environment and Technology: Amerindian Foods in Africa).

Although both foreign Muslims and Europeans obtained slaves from sub-Saharan Africa, there was a significant difference in the numbers they obtained and thus in the overall effects of the two slave trades. Between 1550 and 1800 some 8 million Africans were exported into the Atlantic trade, four times as many as were taken from sub-Saharan Africa to North Africa and the Middle East. The families of all those sent abroad suffered from their individual loss, but the ability of the population to replenish its numbers through natural increase depended on the proportion of women lost to these slave trades. The much higher proportion of women in the Muslim slave trade would have multiplied its lasting effects on sub-Saharan African populations.

It is impossible to assess with precision the complex effects of the goods received in sub-Saharan Africa from these trades. Africans were very particular about what they received, so it is unlikely that they could have been consistently cheated. Some researchers have suggested that imports of textiles and metals undermined African weavers and metalworkers, but most economic historians calculate that on a per capita basis the volume of these imports was too small to have idled many African artisans. Imports supplemented rather than replaced local production. The goods received in sub-Saharan Africa were intended for consumption and thus did not serve to develop the economy. Likewise, the sugar, tea, and chocolate Europeans consumed did little to promote economic development in Europe. However, both African and European merchants profited from trading these consumer goods. Because they directed the whole Atlantic system, Europeans gained far more wealth than Africans.

Historians disagree in their assessment of how deeply European capitalism dominated Africa before 1800, but Europeans clearly had much less political and economic impact in Africa than in the West Indies or in other parts of the Americas. Still, it is significant that Western capitalism was expanding rapidly in the seventeenth century, while the Ottoman Empire, the dominant state of the Middle East, was entering a period of economic and political decline (see Chapter 27). The tide of influence in Africa was thus running in the Europeans' direction.

Conclusion

The new Atlantic trading system had great importance and momentous implications for world history. In the first phase of their expansion Europeans had conquered and colonized the Americas and captured major Indian Ocean trade routes. The development of the Atlantic system showed Europeans' ability to move beyond the conquest and capture of existing systems to create a major new trading system that could transform a region almost beyond recognition.

The West Indies felt the transforming power of capitalism more profoundly than did any other place outside Europe in this period. The establishment of sugar plantation societies was not just a matter of replacing native vegetation with alien plants and native peoples with Europeans and Africans. More fundamentally it made these once-isolated islands part of a dynamic trading system controlled from Europe. To be sure, the West Indies was not the only place affected. Parts of northern Brazil were touched as deeply by the sugar revolution, and other parts of the Americas were yielding to the power of European colonization and capitalism.

Africa played an essential role in the Atlantic system, importing trade goods and exporting slaves to the Americas. Africa, however, was less dominated by the Atlantic system than were Europe's American colonies. Africans remained in control of their continent and interacted culturally and politically with the Islamic world more than with the Atlantic.

Historians have seen the Atlantic system as a model of the kind of highly interactive economy that became global in later centuries. For that reason the Atlantic system was a milestone in a much larger historical process, but not a monument to be admired. Its transformations were destructive as well as creative, producing victims as well as victors. Yet one cannot ignore that the system's awesome power came from its ability to create wealth. As the next chapter describes, southern Asia and the Indian Ocean basin were also beginning to feel the effects of Europeans' rising power.

■ Key Terms

Atlantic system	maroon
chartered company	capitalism
Dutch West India Company	mercantilism
plantocracy	Royal African Company
driver	Great Circuit
seasoning	Middle Passage
manumission	

■ Suggested Reading

The global context of early modern capitalism is examined by Immanuel Wallerstein, *The Modern World-System*, 3 vols. (1974–1989); by Fernand Braudel, *Civilization and Capitalism, 15th–18th Century*, 3 vols. (1982–1984); and in two volumes of scholarly papers edited by James D. Tracy: *The Rise of Merchant Empires* (1990) and *The Political Economy of Merchant Empires* (1991). Especially relevant are the chapters in *The Rise of Merchant Empires* by Herbert S. Klein, summarizing scholarship on the Middle Passage, and by Ralph A. Austen, on the trans-Saharan caravan trade between 1500 and 1800.

The best general introductions to the Atlantic system are Philip D. Curtin, *The Rise and Fall of the Plantation Complex* (1990), and Herbert S. Klein, *The Atlantic Slave Trade* (1999) and David

Ellis, *The Rise of African Slavery in the Americas* (2000). Recent scholarly articles on subjects considered in this chapter are available in *The Atlantic Slave Trade: Effects on Economies, Societies, and Peoples in Africa, the Americas and Europe,* ed. Joseph E. Inikori and Stanley L. Engerman (1992); in *Slavery and the Rise of the Atlantic System,* ed. Barbara L. Solow (1991); and in *Africans in Bondage: Studies in Slavery and the Slave Trade,* ed. Paul Lovejoy (1986). Pieter Emmer has edited a valuable collection of articles on *The Dutch in the Atlantic Economy, 1580–1880: Trade, Slavery, and Emancipation* (1998).

Edward Reynolds, *Stand the Storm: A History of the Atlantic Slave Trade* (1993), provides a brief overview of research on that subject. A useful collection of primary and secondary sources is David Northrup, ed., *The Atlantic Slave Trade* (1994). Hugh Thomas's *The Slave Trade: The Story of the Atlantic Slave Trade, 1440–1870* (1999), and Basil Davidson's *The Atlantic Slave Trade,* rev. ed. (1980), are other useful historical narratives.

The cultural connections among African communities on both sides of the Atlantic are explored by John Thornton, *Africa and Africans in the Making of the Atlantic World, 1400–1800,* 2d ed. (1998), and Margaret E. Crahan and Franklin W. Knight, eds., *Africa and the Caribbean: The Legacies of a Link* (1979). See also the collection edited by Richard Price, *Maroon Societies: Rebel Slave Communities in the Americas,* 2d ed. (1979).

Herbert S. Klein's *African Slavery in Latin America and the Caribbean* (1986) is an exceptionally fine synthesis of recent research on New World slavery, including North American slave systems. The larger context of Caribbean history is skillfully surveyed by Eric Williams, *From Columbus to Castro: The History of the Caribbean* (1984), and more simply surveyed by William Claypole and John Robottom, *Caribbean Story,* vol. 1, *Foundations,* 2d ed. (1990). Michael Craton, James Walvin, and David Wright, eds., *Slavery, Abolition, and Emancipation* (1976), is a valuable collection of primary sources about slavery in the British West Indies.

Roland Oliver and Anthony Atmore, *The African Middle Ages, 1400–1800* (1981), summarize African history in this period. Students can pursue specific topics in more detail in Richard Gray, ed., *The Cambridge History of Africa,* vol. 4 (1975), and B. A. Ogot, ed., *UNESCO General History of Africa,* vol. 5 (1992).

For recent research on slavery and the African, Atlantic, and Muslim slave trades with Africa see Paul Lovejoy, *Transformations in Slavery: A History of Slavery in Africa* (1983); Claire C. Robertson and Martin A. Klein, eds., *Women and Slavery in Africa* (1983); and Patrick Manning, *Slavery and African Life: Occidental, Oriental, and African Slave Trades* (1990). Case studies are found in J. E. Inikori, ed., *Forced Migration: The Impact of the Export Slave Trade on African Societies* (1982). *The Interesting Narrative of the Life of Olaudah Equiano* (1789) exists in several old and modern editions, and a critical edition of the portion relevant to the slave trade is reprinted in Philip D. Curtin, ed., *Africa Remembered: Narratives by West Africans from the Era of the Slave Trade* (1968, 1997), along with other African voices.

Those interested in Islam's cultural and commercial contacts with sub-Saharan Africa will find useful information in James L. A. Webb, Jr., *Desert Frontier: Ecological and Economic Change along the Western Sahel, 1600–1850* (1995); Elizabeth Savage, ed., *The Human Commodity: Perspectives on the Trans-Saharan Slave Trade* (1992); and J. Spencer Trimingham, *The Influence of Islam upon Africa* (1968).

■ Notes

1. Eric Williams, *Capitalism and Slavery* (Charlotte: University of North Carolina Press, 1944), 7.
2. Willem Bosman, *A New and Accurate Description of Guinea, etc.* (London, 1705), quoted in David Northrup, ed., *The Atlantic Slave Trade* (Lexington, MA: D. C. Heath, 1994), 72.
3. Roland Oliver and Anthony Atmore, *The African Middle Ages, 1400–1800* (Cambridge, England: Cambridge University Press, 1981), 100.
4. King Osei Bonsu, quoted in Northrup, ed., *The Atlantic Slave Trade,* 93.
5. Alexander Falconbridge, *Account of the Slave Trade on the Coast of Africa* (London: J. Phillips, 1788), 12.
6. Joseph C. Miller, "The Significance of Drought, Disease, and Famine in the Agriculturally Marginal Zones of West-Central Africa," *Journal of African History* 23 (1982) 17–61.
7. In Philip D. Curtin, ed., *Africa Remembered: Narratives by West Africans from the Era of the Slave Trade* (Madison: University of Wisconsin Press, 1968).

21

SOUTHWEST ASIA AND THE INDIAN OCEAN,

1500–1750

The Ottoman Empire, to 1750 • **The Safavid Empire, 1502–1722** •
The Mughal Empire, 1526–1761 • **Trade Empires in the Indian Ocean, 1600–1729**

ENVIRONMENT AND TECHNOLOGY: Metal Currency and Inflation

SOCIETY AND CULTURE: Indian Merchants in Russia

Ottoman Astronomers   Instruments shown include an astrolabe, a quadrant, and an hourglass.

Anthony Jenkinson, merchant-adventurer for the Muscovy Company, founded in 1555 to develop trade with Russia, was the first Englishman to set foot in Iran. Eight years after the first English ship dropped anchor at Archangel on the White Sea in Russia's frigid north, Jenkinson made his way through Russia, down the Volga River, and across the Caspian Sea. The local ruler he met when he disembarked in 1561 in northwestern Iran was an object of wonder, "richly apparelled with long garments of silk, and cloth of gold, embroidered with pearls of stone; upon his head was a *tolipane* [headdress shaped like a tulip] with a sharp end pointing upwards half a yard long, of rich cloth of gold, wrapped about with a piece of India silk of twenty yards long, wrought in gold richly enameled, and set with precious stones; his earrings had pendants of gold a handful long, with two rubies of great value, set in the ends thereof."

Moving on to Qazvin°, Iran's capital, Jenkinson met the shah, whom the English referred to as the "Great Sophie" (apparently from Safavi°, the name of the ruling family). "In lighting from my horse at the Court gate, before my feet touched the ground, a pair of the Sophie's own shoes . . . were put upon my feet, for without the same shoes I might not be suffered to tread upon his holy ground."[1] After presenting a letter from Queen Elizabeth in Latin, English, Hebrew, and Italian but finding no one capable of reading it, he managed nevertheless to propose trade between England and Iran. The shah rejected the idea, since diverting Iranian silk from the markets of the Ottoman sultans, with whom he was negotiating a truce after a half-century of intermittent war, would have been undiplomatic.

Though Central Asia's bazaars were only meagerly supplied with goods, as Jenkinson and later merchants discovered, the idea of bypassing the Ottomans in the eastern Mediterranean and trading directly with Iran through Russia remained tempting. By the same token, the Ottomans were tempted by the idea of outflanking Safavid Iran. In 1569, an Ottoman army tried unsuccessfully to dig a 40-mile (64-kilometer) canal between the Don River, which opened into the Black Sea, and the Volga, which flowed into the Caspian. Their objective was to enable Ottoman ships to reach the Caspian and attack Iran from the north.

The Ottomans' foe was Russia, then ruled by Tsar Ivan IV (r. 1533–1584), known as Ivan the Terrible or Awesome. Ivan transformed his principality from a second-rate power into the sultan's primary competitor in Central Asia. In the river-crossed steppe, where Turkic nomads had long enjoyed uncontested sway, Slavic Christian Cossacks from the region of the Don and Dnieper Rivers used armed wagon trains and river craft fitted with small cannon to push southward and establish a Russian presence.

A contest for trade with or control of Central Asia was natural after the centrality conferred on the region by three centuries of Mongol and Turkic conquest, highlighted by the campaigns of Genghis Khan and Timur. But as we shall see, changes in the organization of trade were sapping the vitality of the Silk Road. Wealth and power were shifting to European seaborne empires linking the Atlantic with the Indian Ocean. Though the Ottomans were a formidable naval power in the Mediterranean, neither they nor the Safavid shahs in Iran nor the Mughal emperors of India deployed more than a token navy in the southern seas.

As you read this chapter, ask yourself the following questions:

- What were the advantages and disadvantages of a land as opposed to a maritime empire?
- What role did religion play in political alliances and rivalries and in the formation of states?
- How did trading patterns change between 1500 and 1750?

THE OTTOMAN EMPIRE, TO 1750

The most long-lived of the post-Mongol Muslim empires was the **Ottoman Empire,** founded around 1300. By extending Islamic conquests into eastern Europe, starting in the late fourteenth century, and by taking Syria and Egypt from the Mamluk rulers in the early

---

Qazvin (kaz-VEEN)   **Safavi** (SAH-fah-vee)

CHRONOLOGY

	Ottoman Empire	Safavid Empire	Mughal Empire	Europeans in the Indian Ocean States
1500		**1502–1524** Shah Ismail establishes Safavid rule in Iran		**1511** Portuguese seize Malacca from local Malay ruler
	1514 Selim I defeats Safavid shah at Chaldiran; conquers Egypt and Syria (1516–1517)	**1514** Defeat by Ottomans at Chaldiran limits Safavid growth		
	1520–1566 Reign of Suleiman the Magnificent; peak of Ottoman Empire			
	1529 First Ottoman siege of Vienna		**1526** Babur defeats last sultan of Delhi at Panipat	
			1539 Death of Nanak, founder of Sikh religion	
	1571 Ottoman naval defeat at Lepanto	**1587–1629** Reign of Shah Abbas the Great; peak of Safavid Empire	**1556–1605** Akbar rules in Agra; peak of Mughal Empire	**1565** Spanish establish their first fort in the Philippines
1600				**1600** English East India Company founded
				1602 Dutch East India Company founded
				1606 Dutch reach Australia
	1610 End of Anatolian revolts	**1622** Iranians oust Portuguese from Hormuz after 108 years		**1641** Dutch seize Malacca from Portuguese
				1650 Omani Arabs capture Musqat from Portuguese
			1658–1707 Aurangzeb imposes conservative Islamic regime	
			1690 British found city of Calcutta	
1700				**1698** Omani Arabs seize Mombasa from Portuguese
	1718–1730 Tulip Period; military decline apparent to Austria and Russia	**1722** Afghan invaders topple last Safavid shah		
		1736–1747 Nadir Shah temporarily reunites Iran; invades India (1739)	**1739** Iranians under Nadir Shah sack Delhi	**1742** Expansion of French Power in India

sixteenth, the Ottomans seemed to recreate the might of the original Islamic caliphate, the empire established by the Muslim Arab conquests in the seventh century. However, the empire was actually more similar to the new centralized monarchs of France and Spain (see Chapter 18) than to any medieval model.

Enduring more than five centuries, until 1922, the Ottoman Empire survived several periods of wrenching change, some caused by internal problems, others by the growing power of European adversaries. These periods of change reveal the problems faced by huge, land-based empires around the world.

Map 21.1   Muslim Empires in the Sixteenth and Seventeenth Centuries   Iran, a Shi'ite state flanked by Sunni Ottomans on the west and Sunni Mughals on the east, had the least exposure to European influences. Ottoman expansion across the southern Mediterranean Sea intensified European fears of Islam. The areas of strongest Mughal control dictated that Islam's spread into southeast Asia would be heavily influenced by merchants and religious figures from Gujarat instead of from eastern India.

Aya Sofya Mosque in Istanbul   Orginally a Byzantine cathedral, Aya Sofya (in Greek, Hagia Sophia) was transformed into a mosque after 1453, and four minarets were added. It then became a model for subsequent Ottoman mosques. To the right behind it is the Bosporus strait dividing Europe and Asia, to the left the Golden Horn inlet separating the old city of Istanbul from the newer parts. The gate to the Ottoman sultan's palace is to the right of the mosque. The pointed tower to the left of the dome is part of the palace.   (Robert Frerck/Woodfin Camp & Associates)

Expansion and Frontiers

The Ottoman Empire grew from a tiny state in northwestern Anatolia established around 1300 on the strength of Turkish nomad warriors and a few Christian converts to Islam (see Map 21.1). The empire grew because of three factors: (1) the shrewdness of its founder Osman (from which the name "Ottoman" comes) and his descendants, (2) control of a strategic link between Europe and Asia at Gallipoli° on the Dardanelles strait, and (3) the creation of an army that took advantage of the traditional skills of the Turkish cavalryman and the new military possibilities presented by gunpowder.

At first, Ottoman armies concentrated on Christian enemies in Greece and the Balkans, in 1389 conquering a strong Serbian kingdom at the Battle of Kosovo° (in present-day Yugoslavia). Much of southeastern Europe and Anatolia was under the control of the sultans by 1402, when Bayazid° I, "the Thunderbolt," confronted Timur's challenge from Central Asia. After Timur defeated and captured Bayazid at the Battle of Ankara (1402), a generation of civil war followed, until Mehmed° I reunified the sultanate.

During a century and a half of fighting for territory both east and west of Constantinople, the sultans had repeatedly eyed the heavily fortified capital of the slowly dying Byzantine Empire. In 1453, Sultan Mehmed II, "the Conqueror," laid siege to Constantinople. His forces used enormous cannon to bash in the city's walls, dragged warships over a high hill from the Bosporus strait to the city's inner harbor to get around its sea defenses, and finally penetrated the city's land walls through a series of direct infantry assaults. The fall of Constantinople—henceforth commonly known as Istanbul—brought to an end over eleven hundred years of Byzantine rule and made the Ottomans seem invincible.

In 1514, at the Battle of Chaldiran (in Armenia), Selim° I, "the Inexorable," ended a potential threat on his eastern frontier from the new and expansive realm of the Safavid shah in Iran (see below). Although further wars were to be fought with Iran, the general border between the Ottomans and their eastern neighbors was essentially established at this time, leaving Iraq a contested and repeatedly ravaged frontier province.

When Selim conquered the Mamluk Sultanate of Egypt and Syria in 1516 and 1517, the Red Sea became the Ottomans' southern frontier. As for the Ottomans'

Gallipoli (gah-LIP-po-lee)   Kosovo (KO-so-vo)
Bayazid (BAY-yan-zeed)   Mehmed (MEH-met)

Selim (seh-LEEM)

western frontier, the rulers of the major port cities of Algeria and Tunisia, some of them Greek or Italian converts to Islam, voluntarily joined the empire in the early sixteenth century, thereby greatly strengthening its Mediterranean fleets.

The sultan who presided over the greatest Ottoman assault on Christian Europe was **Suleiman° the Magnificent** (r. 1520–1566), known to his subjects as Suleiman Kanuni, "the Lawgiver." The son of Selim I, Suleiman seemed unstoppable as he conquered Belgrade in 1521, expelled the Knights of the Hospital of St. John from the island of Rhodes the following year, and laid siege to Vienna in 1529. Vienna was saved by the lateness of the season and the need to retreat before the onset of winter more than by military action. In later centuries, Ottoman historians looked back on the reign of Suleiman as the period when the imperial system worked to perfection and spoke of it as the golden age of Ottoman greatness.

While Ottoman armies pressed deeper and deeper into eastern Europe, the sultans also sought to control the Mediterranean. Between 1453 and 1502, the Ottomans fought the opening rounds of a two-century war with Venice, the most powerful of Italy's commercial city-states. From the Fourth Crusade of 1204 onward, Venice had assembled a profitable maritime empire that included major islands such as Crete and Cyprus along with strategic coastal strongpoints in Greece. Venice thereby became more than just a trading nation. Its island sugar plantations, exploiting cheap slave labor, competed favorably with Egypt in the international trade of the fifteenth century. With their rivals the Genoese, trading through the strategic island of Chios, the Venetians stifled Ottoman maritime activities in the Aegean Sea.

The initial fighting left Venice in control of its lucrative islands for another century. But it also left Venice a reduced military power compelled to pay tribute to the Ottomans. The Ottomans, like the Chinese, were willing to let other nations carry trade to and from their ports— they preferred trade of this sort—so long as those other nations acknowledged Ottoman authority. It never occurred to them that a sea empire held together by flimsy ships could truly rival a great land empire fielding an army of a hundred thousand men.

In the south, Muslims of the Red Sea and Indian Ocean region were accustomed to trading by way of Egypt and Syria. In the early sixteenth century, merchants from southern India and Sumatra sent emissaries to Istanbul requesting naval support against the Portuguese. The Ottomans responded vigorously to Portuguese threats close to their territories, such as at Aden at the southern entrance to the Red Sea, but their efforts farther afield were insufficient to stifle growing Portuguese domination.

Eastern luxury products still flowed to Ottoman markets. Portuguese power was territorially limited to fortified coastal points, such as Hormuz at the entrance to the Persian Gulf, Goa in western India, and Malacca in Malaya (see Chapter 17). Why commit major resources to subduing an enemy whose main threat was a demand that merchant vessels, mostly belonging to non-Ottoman Muslims, buy protection from Portuguese attack? The Ottomans did send a small naval force to Indonesia, but they never formulated a consistent or aggressive policy with regard to political and economic developments in the Indian Ocean.

Central Institutions

Heirs of the military traditions of Central Asia, the Ottoman army originally consisted of lightly armored mounted warriors skilled at shooting a short bow made of compressed layers of bone, wood, and leather. The conquest of Christian territories in the Balkans in the late fourteenth century, however, gave the Ottomans access to a new military resource: Christian prisoners of war induced to serve as military slaves.

Slave soldiery had a long history in Islamic lands. The Mamluk Sultanate of Egypt and Syria was built on that practice. The Mamluks, however, acquired their new blood from slave markets in Central Asia. Enslaving Christian prisoners, an action of questionable legality in Islamic law, was an Ottoman innovation. Converted to Islam, these "new troops," called *yeni cheri* in Turkish and "**Janissary**"° in English, gave the Ottomans unusual military flexibility.

Christians by upbringing, the Janissaries had no misgivings about fighting against Turks and Muslims when the sultans wished to expand in western Asia. Since horseback riding and bowmanship were not part of their cultural backgrounds, they readily accepted the idea of fighting on foot and learning to use guns, which at that time were still too heavy and awkward for a horseman to load and fire. The Janissaries lived in barracks and trained all year round. Up to the middle of the sixteenth century, they were barred both from holding jobs and from marrying.

The process of selection for Janissary training changed early in the fifteenth century. The new system, called the **devshirme°** (literally "selection"), imposed a regular levy of male children on Christian villages in the Balkans and occasionally elsewhere. Devshirme children

---

Suleiman (SOO-lay-man)

Janissary (JAN-nih-say-ree)   *devshirme* (dev-sheer-MEH)

were placed with Turkish families to learn their language and then were sent to the sultan's palace in Istanbul for an education that included instruction in Islam, military training, and, for the most talented, what we might call liberal arts. This regime, sophisticated for its time, produced not only the Janissary soldiers but also, from among the chosen few who received special training in the inner service of the palace, senior military commanders and heads of government departments up to the rank of grand vizier.

The Ottoman Empire became cosmopolitan in character. The sophisticated court language, Osmanli° (the Turkish form of *Ottoman*), shared basic grammar and vocabulary with the Turkish spoken by Anatolia's nomads and villagers, but Arabic and Persian elements made it as distinct from that language as the Latin of educated Europeans was from the various Latin-derived Romance languages. Everyone who served in the military or the bureaucracy and conversed in Osmanli was considered to belong to the *askeri*°, or "military," class. Members of this class were exempt from taxes and owed their well-being to the sultan. The mass of the population, whether Muslims, Christians, or Jews—Jews flooded into Ottoman territory after their expulsion from Spain in 1492 (see Chapter 17)—constituted the *raya*°, literally "flock of sheep."

By the beginning of the reign of Sultan Suleiman the Magnificent, the Ottoman Empire was the most powerful and best-organized state in either Europe or the Islamic world. Its military was balanced between mounted archers, primarily Turks supported by grants of land in return for their military service, and Janissaries, Turkified Albanians, Serbs, and Macedonians paid from the central treasury and trained in the most advanced weaponry. The galley-equipped navy was manned by Greek, Turkish, Algerian, and Tunisian sailors, usually under the command of an admiral from one of the North African ports.

The balance of the Ottoman land forces brought success to Ottoman arms in recurrent wars with the Safavids, who were much slower to adopt firearms, and in the inexorable conquest of the Balkans. Expansion by sea was less dramatic. A major expedition against Malta that would have given the Ottomans a foothold in the western Mediterranean failed in 1565. Combined Christian forces also achieved a massive naval victory at the Battle of Lepanto, off Greece, in 1571. But Ottoman resources were so extensive that in a year's time they had replaced all of the galleys sunk in that battle.

Under the land-grant system, resident cavalrymen administered most rural areas in Anatolia and the

Ottoman Glassmakers on Parade   *Celebrations of the circumcisions of the sultan's sons featured parades organized by the craft guilds of Istanbul. This float features glassmaking, a common craft in Islamic realms. The most elaborate glasswork included oil lamps for mosques and colored glass for the small stained-glass windows below mosque domes.* (Topkapi Saray Museum)

Balkans. They maintained order, collected taxes, and reported for each summer's campaign with their horses, retainers, and supplies, all paid for from the taxes they collected. When not campaigning, they stayed at home. Some historians maintain that these cavalrymen, who did not own their land, had little interest in encouraging production or introducing new technologies, but since a militarily able son often succeeded his father, the grant holders did have some interest in productivity.

The Ottoman conception of the world saw the sultan providing justice for his "flock of sheep" (raya) and the military protecting them. In return, the raya paid the taxes that supported both the sultan and the military. In reality, the sultan's government, like most large territorial governments in premodern times, remained comparatively isolated from the lives of most subjects. Arab, Turkish, and Balkan townsfolk depended on local notables and religious leaders to represent them before Ottoman provincial governors and their staffs. Islam was the ruling religion and gradually became the majority religion in Balkan regions such as Albania and Bosnia that had large numbers of converts. Thus the law of Islam (the Shari'a°), as interpreted by local *ulama*° (religious

---

Osmanli (os-MAHN-lee)   *askeri* (AS-keh-ree)   *raya* (RAH-yah)   **Shari'a** (sha-REE-ah)   *ulama* (oo-leh-MAH)

Metal Currency and Inflation

Inflation occurs when the quantity of goods and services available for purchase remains stable while the quantity of money in circulation increases. With more money in their pockets, people are willing to pay more to get what they want. Prices go up, and what people think of as the value of money goes down.

Today, with paper money and electronic banking, governments try to control inflation by regulating the printing of money or by other means. Prior to the nineteenth century, money consisted of silver and gold coins, and governments did not keep track of how much money was in circulation. As long as the annual production of gold and silver mines was quite small, inflation was not a worry. In the sixteenth and seventeenth centuries, however, precious metal poured into Spain from silver and gold mines in the New World, but there was no increase in the availability of goods and services. The resulting inflation triggered a "price revolution" in Europe—a general tripling of prices between 1500 and 1650. In Paris in 1650, the price of wheat and hay was fifteen times higher than the price had been in 1500.

This wave of inflation worked its way east, contributing to social disorder in the Ottoman Empire. European traders had more money available than Ottoman merchants and could outbid them for scarce commodities. Lacking silver and gold mines,

the Ottoman government reduced the amount of precious metal in Ottoman coins. This made the problem worse. Hit hardest were people who had fixed incomes. Cavalrymen holding land grants worth a set amount each year were unable to equip themselves for military campaigns. Students living on fixed scholarships went begging.

Safavid Iran needed silver and gold to pay for imports from Mughal India, which imported few Iranian goods. Iranians sold silk to the Ottoman Empire for silver and gold, worsening the Ottoman situation, and then passed the precious metal on to India. Everyday life in Iran depended on barter or locally minted copper coinage, both more resistant to inflation. Copper for coins was sometimes imported from China.

Though no one then grasped the connection between silver production in Mexico and the trade balance between Iran and India, the world of the sixteenth and seventeenth centuries was becoming more closely linked economically than it had ever been before.

Set of Coin Dies The lower die, called the anvil die, was set in a piece of wood. A blank disk of gold, silver, or copper was placed on top of it. The hammer die was placed on top of the blank and struck with a hammer to force the coin's image onto it. (Courtesy, Israel Museum, Jerusalem)

---

scholars), conditioned urban institutions and social life. Local customs prevailed among non-Muslims and in many rural areas; and non-Muslims looked to their own religious leaders for guidance in family and spiritual matters.

Crisis of the Military State, 1585–1650

As military technology evolved, cannon and lighter-weight firearms played an ever-larger role on the battlefield. Accordingly, the size of the Janissary corps—and its cost to the government—grew steadily, and the role of the Turkish cavalry, which continued to disdain firearms even as they became lighter and easier to use, diminished. To fill state coffers and pay the Janissaries, in the mid-sixteenth century the sultan started reducing the number of landholding cavalrymen. Revenues previously spent on their living expenses and military equipment went directly into the imperial treasury. Some of the displaced cavalrymen, armed and unhappy, became a restive element in rural Anatolia.

At about the same time, in the late sixteenth century, inflation caused a flood of cheap silver from the New World (see Environment and Technology: Metal Currency and Inflation) affected many of the remaining landholders restricted by law to collecting a fixed amount of taxes. Their purchasing power declined so much that they were unable to report for military service. This delinquency, however, played into the hands of the sultan's government, which wanted to reduce the cavalry and increase the Janissary corps and thus made no reforms to allow landholders to keep their land grants. As land was returned to the state, more and more cavalrymen joined the ranks of dispossessed troopers. Students and professors in *madrasas* (religious colleges) similarly found it impossible to live on fixed stipends from madrasa endowments.

Constrained by religious law from fundamentally changing the tax system, the government levied emergency surtaxes to obtain enough funds to pay the Janissaries and bureaucrats. For additional military strength, particularly in its wars with Iran, the government reinforced the Janissary ranks with partially trained, salaried soldiers hired for the duration of a campaign. Once the summer campaign season was over, however, these soldiers found themselves out of work and short on cash.

This complicated situation resulted in revolts that devastated Anatolia between 1590 and 1610. Former landholding cavalrymen, short-term soldiers released at the end of the campaign season, peasants overburdened by emergency taxes, and even impoverished students of religion formed bands of marauders. Anatolia experienced the worst of the rebellions and suffered greatly from emigration and the loss of agricultural production. But an increase in banditry, made worse by the government's inability to stem the spread of muskets among the general public, beset other parts of the empire as well.

In the meantime, the Janissaries took advantage of their growing influence to gain relief from prohibitions on their marrying and engaging in business. Janissaries who involved themselves in commerce lessened the burden on the state budget, and married Janissaries who enrolled sons or relatives in the corps made it possible in the seventeenth century for the government to save state funds by abolishing the devshirme system with its traveling selection officers. These savings, however, were more than offset by the increase in the total number of Janissaries and in their steady deterioration as a military force, which necessitated the hiring of more and more supplemental troops.

Economic Change and Growing Weakness, 1650–1750

A very different Ottoman Empire emerged from this period of crisis. The sultan once had led armies. Now he mostly resided in his palace and had little experience of the real world. This manner of living resulted from a gradually developed policy of keeping the sultan's male relatives confined to the palace to prevent them from plotting coups or meddling in politics. The sultan's mother and the chief eunuch overseeing the private quarters of the palace thus became important arbiters of royal favor, and even of succession to the sultanate, and the affairs of government were overseen more and more by the chief administrators—the grand viziers. (Ottoman historians draw special attention to the negative influence of women in the palace after the time of Suleiman, but to some degree they are reflecting traditional male, and Muslim, fears about women in politics.)

The devshirme had been discontinued, and the Janissaries had taken advantage of their increased power and privileges to make membership in their corps hereditary. Together with several other newly prominent infantry regiments, they involved themselves in crafts and trading, both in Istanbul and in provincial capitals such as Cairo, Aleppo, and Baghdad. This activity took a toll on their military skills, but they continued to be a powerful faction in urban politics that the sultans could neither ignore nor reform.

Land grants in return for military service also disappeared. Tax farming arose in their place. Tax farmers paid specific taxes, such as customs duties, in advance in return for the privilege of collecting a greater amount from the actual taxpayers. In one instance, two tax farmers advanced the government 18 million akches (small silver coins) for the customs duties of the Aegean port of Izmir°, and collected a total of 19,169,203 akches for a profit of 6.5 percent.

Rural administration, already disrupted by the rebellions, suffered from the transition to tax farms. The former landholders had been military men who readily kept order on their lands in order to maintain their incomes. Tax farmers were less likely to live on the land, and their tax collection rights could vary from year to year. The imperial government, therefore, faced greater administrative burdens and came to rely heavily on powerful provincial governors or on wealthy men who purchased lifelong tax collection rights that prompted them to behave more or less like private landowners.

Rural disorder and decline in administrative control sometimes opened the way for new economic opportunities. The port of Izmir, known to Europeans by the ancient name "Smyrna," had a population of around 2,000 in 1580. By 1650 the population had increased almost twentyfold to between 30,000 and 40,000. Along with refugees from the Anatolian uprisings and from European pirate attacks along the coast came European merchants and large colonies of Armenians, Greeks, and Jews. A French traveler in 1621 wrote: "At present, Izmir

Izmir (IZ-meer)

has a great traffic in wool, beeswax, cotton, and silk, which the Armenians bring there instead of going to Aleppo . . . because they do not pay as many dues.[2]

Izmir was able to transform itself between 1580 and 1650 from a small Muslim Turkish town into a multiethnic, multireligious, multilinguistic entrepôt because of the Ottoman government's inability to control trade and the slowly growing dominance of European traders in the Indian Ocean. Spices from the East, though still traded in Aleppo and other long-established Ottoman centers, were not to be found in Izmir. Aside from Iranian silk brought in by caravan, European traders at Izmir purchased local agricultural products—dried fruits, sesame seeds, nuts, and olive oil. As a consequence local farmers who previously had grown grain for subsistence shifted their plantings more and more to cotton and other cash crops, including, after its introduction in the 1590s, tobacco, which quickly became popular in the Ottoman Empire despite government prohibitions. In this way the agricultural economy of western Anatolia, the Balkans, and the Mediterranean coast—the Ottoman lands most accessible to Europe (see Map 21.1)—became enmeshed in the seventeenth century in a growing European commercial network.

At the same time, Ottoman military power slowly ebbed. The ill-trained Janissaries sometimes resorted to hiring substitutes to go on campaign, and the sultans relied on partially trained seasonal recruits and on armies raised by the governors of frontier provinces. By the middle of the eighteenth century, it was obvious to the Ottomans' Austrian and Russian opponents that the empire was in decline. On the eastern front, however, Ottoman exhaustion after many wars was matched by the demise in 1722 of their perennial adversary, the Safavid state of Iran.

The Ottoman Empire lacked both the wealth and the inclination to match European economic advances. Overland trade from the east dwindled as political disorder in Safavid Iran cut deeply into Iranian silk production (see below). Coffee, an Arabian product that rose from obscurity in the fifteenth century to become the rage first in the Ottoman Empire and then in Europe, was grown in the highlands of Yemen and exported by way of Egypt. By 1770, however, Muslim merchants trading in the Yemeni port of Mocha° (literally "the coffee place") were charged 15 percent in duties and fees. But European traders, benefiting from trade agreements with the Ottoman Empire going back to the time of Mehmed the Conqueror, paid little more than 3 percent. Such trade agreements led to European domination of Ottoman import and export trade by sea. Neverthe-

less, the Europeans did not control strategic ports in the Mediterranean comparable to Malacca in the Indian Ocean and Hormuz on the Persian Gulf, so their economic power stopped short of colonial settlement and direct political administration in Ottoman territories.

A few astute Ottoman statesmen observed the growing disarray of the empire and advised the sultans to reestablish the land-grant and devshirme systems of Suleiman's reign. But to most people the downward course of imperial power was far from evident, much less the reasons behind it. Ottoman historians named the period between 1718 and 1730 the "**Tulip Period**" because of the craze for high-priced tulip bulbs that swept Ottoman ruling circles. The craze replicated a Dutch tulip mania that had begun in the mid-sixteenth century, when the flower was introduced into Holland from Istanbul, and peaked in 1636 with particularly rare bulbs going for 2,500 florins apiece—the value of twenty-two oxen. Far from seeing Europe as the enemy that eventually would dismantle the weakening Ottoman Empire, the Istanbul elite experimented with European clothing and furniture styles and purchased printed books from the empire's first (and short-lived) press.

In 1730, however, the gala soirees, at which guests watched turtles with candles on their backs wander in the dark through massive tulip beds, gave way to a conservative Janissary revolt with strong religious overtones. Sultan Ahmed III abdicated, and the leader of the revolt, Patrona Halil°, an Albanian former seaman and stoker of the public baths, swaggered around the capital for several months dictating government policies before he was seized and executed.

The Patrona Halil rebellion confirmed the perceptions of a few that the Ottoman Empire was facing severe difficulties. But decay at the center spelled benefit elsewhere. In the provinces, ambitious and competent governors, wealthy landholders, urban notables, and nomad chieftains were well placed to take advantage of the central government's weakness. By the middle of the eighteenth century, groups of Mamluks had regained a dominant position in Egypt, and Janissary commanders had become virtually independent rulers in Baghdad. In central Arabia, Muhammad ibn Abd al-Wahhab's conservative Sunni movement had begun its remarkable rise beyond the reach of Ottoman power. Although no region declared full independence, the sultan's power was slipping away to the advantage of a broad array of lower officials and upstart chieftains in all parts of the empire, and the Ottoman economy was reorienting itself toward Europe.

Mocha (MOH-kuh)

Patrona Halil (pa-TROH-nuh ha-LEEL)

Safavid Shah with Attendants and Musicians   This painting by Ali-Quli Jubbadar, a European convert to Islam working for the Safavid armory, reflects Western influences. Notice the use of light and shadow to model faces and the costume of the attendant to the shah's right. The shah's waterpipe indicates the spread of tobacco, a New World crop, to the Middle East.   (Courtesy of Oriental Institute, Academy of Sciences, Leningrad. Reproduced from *Album of Persian and Indian Miniatures* [Moscow, 1962], ill. no. 98)

THE SAFAVID EMPIRE, 1502–1722

The **Safavid Empire** of Iran (see Map 21.1) resembled its long-time Ottoman foe in many ways: it initially relied militarily on cavalry paid through land grants; its population spoke several different languages; it was oriented inward away from the sea; and urban notables, nomadic chieftains, and religious scholars served as intermediaries between the people and the government. It also had distinct qualities that to this day set Iran off from its neighbors: it derived part of its legitimacy from the pre-Islamic dynasties of ancient Iran, and it adopted the Shi'ite form of Islam.

The Rise of the Safavids

Timur had been a great conqueror. But his children and grandchildren contented themselves with modest realms in Afghanistan and Central Asia, while a number of would-be rulers vied for control elsewhere. In Iran itself, the ultimate victor in a complicated struggle for power among Turkish chieftains was Ismail°, a boy of Kurdish, Iranian, and Greek ancestry, the hereditary leader of a militant Sufi brotherhood named "Safaviya" for his ancestor Safi

al-Din. In 1502, at the age of sixteen, Ismail proclaimed himself shah of Iran. At around the same time, he declared that from that time forward his realm would be devoted to **Shi'ite Islam,** which revered the family of Muhammad's son-in-law Ali, and he called on all his subjects to abandon their Sunni beliefs.

Most of the members of the Safavi brotherhood were Turkish-speakers from nomadic groups known as *qizilbash*°, or "redheads," because of their distinctive turbans. They believed that Ismail was practically a god incarnate, and they fought ferociously on his behalf. If Ismail wished his state to be Shi'ite, his word was law to the qizilbash. The Iranian subject population, however, was not so easily persuaded. Neighboring lands received Sunni refugees from Safavid rule. Their preaching and intriguing helped stoke the fires that kept Ismail (d. 1524) and his son Tahmasp° (d. 1576) engaged in war after war. It took a century and a series of brutal persecutions to make Iran an overwhelmingly Shi'ite land. The transformation also required the importation of Arab Shi'ite scholars from Lebanon and Bahrain to institute Shi'ite religious education at a high level.

Although Ismail's reasons for compelling Iran's conversion to Shi'ism are unknown, the effect of this radical act was to create a deep chasm between Iran and its neighbors, all of which were Sunni. Iran became a truly separate country for the first time since its incorporation into the Islamic caliphate in the seventh century.

Ismail (IS-ma-eel)

qizilbash (KIH-zil-bahsh)   Tahmasp (tah-MAHSP)

Society and Religion

The imposition of Shi'ite belief made permanent the split between Iran and its neighbors, but differences between them had long been in the making. Persian, written in the Arabic script from the tenth century onward, had emerged as the second language of Islam. By 1500, an immense library of legal and theological writings; epic, lyric, and mystic poetry; histories; and drama and fiction had come into being. Iranian scholars and writers normally read Arabic as well as Persian and sprinkled their writings with Arabic phrases, but their Arab counterparts were much less inclined to learn Persian. Even handwriting styles differed, Iranians preferring highly cursive forms of the Arabic script.

This divergence between the two language areas had intensified after the Mongols destroyed Baghdad, the capital of the Islamic caliphate, in 1258 and diminished the importance of Arabic-speaking Iraq. Syria and Egypt had become the heartland of the Arab world while Iran developed largely on its own, having more extensive contacts with India—where Muslim rulers favored the Persian language—than with the Arabs.

In the heyday of the Islamic caliphate in the seventh through ninth centuries, cultural styles had radiated in all directions from Baghdad. In the post-Mongol period—a time of immense artistic creativity and innovation in Iran, Afghanistan, and Central Asia—styles in the East went their own separate ways. Painted and molded tiles and tile mosaics, often in vivid turquoise blue, became the standard exterior decoration of mosques in Iran but never were used in Syria and Egypt. Persian poets raised morally instructive and mystical-allegorical verse to peaks of perfection that had no reflection in Arabic poetry, generally considered to be in a state of decline.

The Turks, who steadily came to dominate the political scene from Bengal to Algeria, generally preferred Persian as a vehicle for literary or religious expression. The Mamluks in Egypt and Syria showed greatest respect for Arabic. The Turkish language, which had a vigorous tradition of folk poetry, developed only slowly, primarily in the Ottoman Empire, as a language of literature and administration. Ironically, Ismail Safavi was a noted religious poet in the Turkish language of his qizilbash followers, and his mortal adversary, the Ottoman Selim I (r. 1512–1520), was known for the elegance of his Persian poetry.

To be sure, Islam itself provided a tradition that crossed ethnic and linguistic borders. Mosque architecture differed, but Iranians, Arabs, and Turks, as well as Muslims in India, all had mosques. They also had madrasas that trained the ulama to sustain and interpret the Shari'a as the all-encompassing law of Islam. Yet local understandings of the common tradition differed substantially.

All Sufi orders had distinctive rituals and concepts of mystical union with God. These orders also were present in pre-Safavid Iran, but Iran stood out as the land where Sufism most often fused with militant political objectives. The Safavi Order was not the first to deploy armies and use the point of a sword to promote love of God. The Safavid shahs were unique, however, in eventually banning, somewhat ineffectively, all Sufi orders from their domain.

Even prior to Shah Ismail's imposition of Shi'ism, therefore, Iran had become a distinctive society. Nevertheless, the impact of Shi'ism was significant. Shi'ite doctrine says that all temporal rulers, regardless of title, are temporary stand-ins for the **"Hidden Imam"**: the twelfth descendant of Ali, who was the prophet Muhammad's cousin and son-in-law. Shi'ites believe that leadership of the Muslim community rests solely with divinely appointed Imams from Ali's family, that the twelfth descendant (the Hidden Imam) disappeared as a child in the ninth century, and that the Shi'ite community will lack a proper religious authority until he returns. Some Shi'ite scholars concluded that the faithful should calmly accept the world as it was and wait quietly for the Hidden Imam's return. Others maintained that they themselves should play a stronger role in political affairs because they were best qualified to know the Hidden Imam's wishes. These two positions, which still play a role in Iranian Shi'ism, tended to enhance the self-image of the ulama as independent of imperial authority and stood in the way of religious scholars becoming subordinate government functionaries, as happened with many Ottoman ulama.

Shi'ism also affected the psychological life of the people. Commemoration of the martyrdom of Imam Husayn (d. 680), Ali's son and the third Imam, during the first two weeks of every lunar year regularized an emotional outpouring with no parallel in Sunni lands. Day after day for two weeks (as they do today) preachers recited the woeful tale to crowds of weeping believers, and elaborate street processions, often organized by craft guilds, paraded chanting and self-flagellating men past crowds of reverent onlookers. Passion plays in which Husayn and his family are mercilessly killed by the agents of the caliph became a unique form of Iranian public theater.

Of course, Shi'ites elsewhere observed some of the same rites of mourning for Imam Husayn, particularly in the Shi'ite pilgrimage cities of Karbala and Najaf° in

---

Najaf (NAH-jaf)

Ottoman Iraq. But the impact of these rites on society as a whole was especially great in Iran, where 90 percent of the population was Shi'ite. Over time, the subjects of the Safavid shahs came to feel more than ever a people apart, even though many of them had been Shi'ite for only two or three generations.

A Tale of Two Cities: Isfahan and Istanbul

Isfahan° became Iran's capital in 1598 by decree of **Shah Abbas I** (r. 1587–1629). Outwardly, Istanbul and Isfahan looked quite different. Built on seven hills on the south side of the narrow Golden Horn inlet, Istanbul boasted a skyline punctuated by the gray stone domes and thin, pointed minarets of the great imperial mosques. Their design was inspired by Hagia Sophia, the Byzantine cathedral converted to a mosque and renamed Aya Sofya after 1453 (see page 525). The mosques surrounding the royal plaza in Isfahan, in contrast, had unobtrusive minarets and brightly tiled domes that rose to gentle peaks. High walls surrounded the sultan's palace in Istanbul. Shah Abbas in Isfahan focused his capital on the giant royal plaza, which was large enough for his army to play polo, and he used an airy palace overlooking the plaza to receive dignitaries and review his troops. This public image contributed to Shah Abbas being called "the Great."

The harbor of Istanbul, the primary Ottoman seaport, teemed with sailing ships and smaller craft, many of them belonging to a colony of European merchants perched on a hilltop on the north side of the Golden Horn. Isfahan, far from the sea, was only occasionally visited by Europeans. Most of its trade was in the hands of Jews, Hindus, and especially a colony of Armenian Christians brought in by Shah Abbas and settled in a suburb of the city.

Beneath these superficial differences, the two capitals had much in common. Wheeled vehicles were scarce in hilly Istanbul and nonexistent in Isfahan, which was within the broad zone where camels supplanted wheeled transport after the rise of the Arab caravan cities in the pre-Islamic centuries. In size and layout both cities were built for walking and, aside from the royal plaza in Isfahan, lacked the open spaces common in contemporary European cities. Away from the major mosque complexes, streets were narrow and irregular. Houses crowded against each other in dead-end lanes. Open areas were interior courtyards where residents could enjoy their privacy. Artisans and merchants organized themselves into guilds that had strong social and

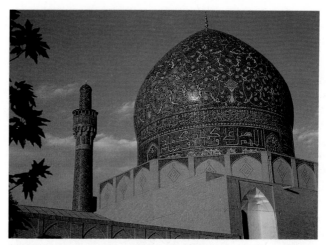

Masjid–i Shah (Royal Mosque) in Isfahan   This masterpiece of Safavid architecture reflects several highlights of Iranian craftsmanship. The tile mosaics include different styles of Arabic calligraphy: a cursive version with long uprights in a band around the dome; below that, a partially squared-off script between the window grills; and below that, and on the minaret, completely orthogonal words set within polygons. The flowery pattern on the dome recalls the designs of Persian carpets. Notice the difference between this minaret and the Ottoman minarets in the illustration on page 525.   (Walter H. Hodge/Peter Arnold, Inc.)

religious as well as economic bonds. The shops of each guild adjoined each other in the markets.

Women were seldom seen in public, even in Istanbul's mazelike covered market or in Isfahan's long, serpentine bazaar. At home, the women's quarters—called *anderun*°, or "interior," in Iran and *harem*, or "forbidden area," in Istanbul—were separate from the public rooms where the men of the family received visitors. In both areas, low cushions, charcoal braziers for warmth, carpets, and small tables constituted most of the furnishings. In Iran and the Arab provinces, shelves and niches for books could be cut into the thick, mud-brick walls. Residences in Istanbul were usually built of wood. Glazed tile in geometric or floral patterns covered the walls of wealthy men's reception areas.

The private side of family life has left few traces, but it is apparent that women's society—consisting of wives, children, female servants, and sometimes one or more eunuchs—was not entirely cut off from the outside world. Ottoman court records reveal that women, using male agents, were very active in the urban real estate market. Often they were selling inherited shares of their father's estate, but some both bought and sold real estate on a regular basis and even established religious

Isfahan (is-fah-HAHN)

anderun (an-deh-ROON)

Istanbul Family on the Way to a Bath House Public baths, an important feature of Islamic cities, set different hours for men and women. Young boys, such as the lad in the turban shown here, went with their mothers and sisters. Notice that the children wear the same styles as the adults. (Osterreichische Nationalbibliothek)

endowments for pious purposes. The fact that Islamic law, unlike some European codes, permitted a wife to retain her property after marriage gave some women a stake in the general economy and a degree of independence from their spouses. Women also appeared in other types of court cases, where they often testified for themselves, for Islamic courts did not recognize the role of attorney. Although comparable Safavid court records do not survive, historians assume that a parallel situation prevailed in Iran.

European travelers commented on the veiling of women outside the home, but miniature paintings indicate that ordinary female garb consisted of a long, ample dress with a scarf or long shawl pulled tight over the forehead to conceal the hair. Lightweight trousers, either close-fitting or baggy, were often worn under the dress. This mode of dress was not far different from that of men. Poor men wore light trousers, a long shirt, a jacket, and a hat or turban. Wealthier men wore over their trousers ankle-length caftans, often closely fitted around the chest. The norm for both sexes was complete coverage of arms, legs, and hair.

Public life was almost entirely the domain of men. Poetry and art, both somewhat more elegantly developed in Isfahan than in Istanbul, were as likely to extol the charms of beardless boys as pretty women. Despite religious disapproval of homosexuality, attachments to adolescent boys were neither unusual nor hidden. Women who appeared in public—aside from non-Muslims, the aged, and the very poor—were likely to be slaves. Miniature paintings frequently depict female dancers, musicians, and even acrobats in attitudes and costumes that range from decorous to decidedly erotic.

Despite social similarities, the overall flavors of Isfahan and Istanbul were not the same. Isfahan had its prosperous Armenian quarter across the river from the city's center, but it was not a truly cosmopolitan capital, just as the peoples of the Safavid realm were not remarkably diverse. Like other rulers of extensive land empires, Shah Abbas located his capital toward the center of his domain within comparatively easy reach of any threatened frontier. Istanbul, in contrast, was a great seaport and crossroads located on the straits separating the sultan's European and Asian possessions. People of all sorts lived or spent time in Istanbul—Venetians, Genoese, Arabs, Turks, Greeks, Armenians, Albanians, Serbs, Jews, Bulgarians, and more. In this respect Istanbul conveyed the cosmopolitan character of major seaports from London to Canton (Guangzhou) and belied the fact that its prosperity rested on the vast reach of the sultan's territories rather than on the voyages of its merchants.

Economic Crisis and Political Collapse

The silk fabrics of northern Iran, monopolized by the shahs, were the mainstay of the Safavid Empire's foreign trade. However, the manufacture that eventually became most powerfully associated with Iran was the deep-pile carpet made by knotting colored yarns around stretched warp threads. Different cities produced distinctive carpet designs. Women and girls did much of the actual knotting work.

Carpets with geometrical or arabesque designs appear in Timurid miniature paintings, but no knotted "Persian rug" survives from the pre-Safavid era. One of the earliest dated carpets was produced in 1522 to adorn the tomb of Shaikh Safi al-Din, the fourteenth-century founder of the Safavi Order. This use indicates the high value accorded these products within Iran. One German visitor to Isfahan remarked: "The most striking adornment of the banqueting hall was to my mind the carpets laid out over all three rostra in a most extravagant fashion, mostly woolen rugs from Kirman with animal patterns and woven of the finest wool."[3]

Overall, Iran's manufacturing sector was neither large nor notably productive. Most of the shah's subjects, whether Iranians, Turks, Kurds, or Arabs, lived by subsistence farming or herding. Neither area of activity recorded significant technological advances during the Safavid period. Large sections of the country were granted to the qizilbash nomads in return for their furnishing mounted warriors for the army. These lands were held by the groups in common, however, and were not subdivided into individual landholdings as in the Ottoman Empire. Thus many people in rural areas lived according to the will of a nomad chieftain who had little interest in building the agricultural economy.

The Safavids, like the Ottomans, had difficulty finding the money to pay troops armed with firearms. This crisis occurred somewhat later in Iran because of its greater distance from Europe. By the end of the sixteenth century, it was evident that a more systematic adoption of cannon and firearms in the Safavid Empire would be needed to hold off the Ottomans and the Uzbeks° (Turkish rulers who had succeeded the Timurids on Iran's Central Asian frontier; see Map 21.1). Like the Ottoman cavalry a century earlier, however, the warriors furnished by the nomad leaders were not inclined to trade in their bows for firearms. Shah Abbas responded by establishing a slave corps of year-round soldiers and arming them with guns.

The Christian converts to Islam who initially provided the manpower for the new corps were mostly captives taken in raids on Georgia in the Caucasus°. Some became powerful members of the court. They formed a counterweight to the nomad chiefs just as the Janissaries had earlier challenged the landholding Turkish cavalry in the Ottoman Empire. Under the strong hand of Shah Abbas, the inevitable rivalries and intrigues between the factions were kept under control. His successors were less fortunate.

In the late sixteenth century, the inflation caused by cheap silver spread into Iran; then overland trade through Safavid territory declined because of mismanagement of the silk monopoly after Shah Abbas's death in 1629. As a result, the country faced the unsolvable problem of finding money to pay the army and bureaucracy. Trying to unseat the nomads from their lands to regain control of taxes was more difficult and more disruptive militarily than the piecemeal dismantlement of the land-grant system in the Ottoman Empire. The nomads were still a cohesive military force, and pressure from the center simply caused them to withdraw to their mountain pastures until the pressure subsided. By 1722, the government had become so weak and commanded so little support from the nomadic groups that an army of marauding Afghans was able to capture Isfahan and effectively end Safavid rule.

Despite Iran's long coastline, the Safavids never possessed a navy. The Portuguese seized the strategic Persian Gulf island of Hormuz in 1517 and were expelled only in 1622, when the English ferried Iranian soldiers to the attack. Land-oriented rulers, the shahs relied on the English and Dutch for naval support and never considered competing with them at sea. Nadir Shah, a general who emerged from the confusion of the Safavid fall to reunify Iran briefly between 1736 and 1747, purchased some naval vessels from the English and used them in the Persian Gulf. But his navy decayed after his death, and Iran did not have a navy again until the twentieth century.

THE MUGHAL EMPIRE, 1526–1761

What distinguished the Indian empire of the Mughal° sultans from the empires of the Ottomans and Safavids was the fact that India was a land of Hindus ruled by a Muslim minority. To be sure, the Ottoman provinces in the Balkans, except for Albania and Bosnia, remained mostly Christian, but the remainder of the Ottoman Empire was overwhelmingly Muslim with small Christian and Jewish minorities. The Ottoman sultans made much of their control of Mecca and Medina and resulting supervision of the annual pilgrimage caravans just as the Safavids fostered pilgrimages to a shrine in Mashhad in northeastern Iran for their overwhelmingly Shi'ite subjects.

India, in contrast, was far from the Islamic homelands (see Map 21.1). Muslim dominion in India was the result of repeated military campaigns from the early eleventh century onward, and the Mughals had to contend with the Hindus' long-standing resentment of the destruction of their culture by Muslims. The Balkan peoples had struggled to maintain their separate identities in relation to the Byzantines, the crusaders, and one another before arrival of the Turks. The peoples of the Indian subcontinent, in contrast, had used centuries of freedom from foreign intrusion to forge a distinctive Hindu civilization that could not easily accommodate the world-view of Islam. Thus the challenge facing the Mughals was not just conquering and organizing a large territorial state but also finding a formula for Hindu-Muslim coexistence.

Uzbeks (UHZ-bex)   **Caucasus** (CAW-kuh-suhs)

Mughal (MOH-guhl)

New Year Celebration at the Court of Shah Jahan (r. 1628–1658) The Pre-Islamic Iranian tradition of celebrating the New Year (in Persian *No Ruz*, "New Day") on March 21, the vernal equinox, spread with Islamic rule. The dancing girls are a characteristically Indian aspect of the celebration. (The Royal Collection © Her Majesty Queen Elizabeth II)

Political Foundations

Babur° (1483–1530), the founder of the **Mughal Empire,** was a Muslim descendant of Timur. Though *Mughal* is Persian for "Mongol," the Timurids were of Turkic rather than Mongol origin. Timur's marriage to a descendant of Genghis Khan had earned him the Mongol designation "son-in-law," but he and his descendants, like the Ottomans, could never claim the mantle of Genghisid political legitimacy that came naturally to lesser rulers in Central Asia and in the Crimea north of the Black Sea.

Invading from Central Asia, Babur defeated the last Muslim sultan of Delhi at the Battle of Panipat in 1526. But even though this victory marked the birth of a brilliant and powerful state in India, Babur's descendants continued to think of Central Asia as their true home, from time to time expressing intentions of recapturing Samarkand and referring to its Uzbek ruler—a genuine descendant of Genghis Khan—as a governor rather than an independent sovereign.

India proved to be the primary theater of Mughal accomplishment, however. Babur's grandson **Akbar** (r. 1556–1605), a brilliant but mercurial man whose life-long illiteracy betrayed his upbringing in the wilds of Afghanistan, established the central administration of the expanding state. Under him and his three successors—the last of whom died in 1707—all but the southern tip of India fell under Mughal rule, administered first from Agra and then from Delhi°.

Akbar granted land revenues to military officers and government officials in return for their service. Ranks, called *mansabs*°, some high and some low, entitled their holders to revenue assignments. As in the other Islamic empires, revenue grants were not considered hereditary, and the central government kept careful track of their issuance.

With a population of 100 million, a thriving trading economy based on cotton cloth, and a generally efficient administration, India under Akbar was probably the most prosperous empire of the sixteenth century (see Society and Culture: Indian Merchants in Russia). He and his successors faced few external threats and experienced generally peaceful conditions in their northern Indian heartland. Nevertheless, they were capable of squandering immense amounts of blood and treasure to subdue Hindu kings and rebels in the Deccan region or Afghans on their western frontier (see Map 21.1).

Foreign trade boomed at the port of Surat in the northwest, which also served as an embarkation point for pilgrims on their way to Mecca. Like the Safavids, the Mughals had no navy or merchant ships. The government saw the Europeans—now primarily Dutch and English, the Portuguese having lost most of their Indian ports—less as enemies than as shipmasters whose naval support could be procured as needed in return for trading privileges. It never questioned the wisdom of selling Indian cottons for European coin—no one understood how cheap silver had become in Europe—and shipping them off to European customers in English and Dutch vessels.

Babur (BAH-bur)

Delhi (DEL-ee) *mansabs* (MAN-sabz)

SOCIETY & CULTURE

Indian Merchants in Russia

Overland commerce through Central Asia continued throughout this period. Few traders from eastern lands reached western Europe, but trading missions from India visited Russia, and a small but important colony of Indian merchants developed in Astrakhan, at the mouth of the Volga River, where they dealt primarily in cotton and silk cloth.

In 1675, Indian merchants in Moscow informed Russian officials that:

In the Indian state the highest demand for Russian goods is for high-priced sables—10, 20, 30 roubles a pair, good, red broad cloth and green broad cloth, red leather, walrus teeth, coral, large middle sized and small mirrors, gold and silver velvet and Turkish velvet. . . . And the Indian rulers love Borzoi dogs. (p. 91)

One Indian merchant of Astrakhan, Marwar Bara, wrote in 1735:

Previously there were favorable conditions for trade from India to Russia and merchants comfortably went [abroad]. Each year about two hundred exported . . . goods, and then when disturbances occurred in Persia and passage became difficult because of robbers the number of merchants declined year by year. Now exceedingly few came, less than eighty. (p. 128)

Nevertheless, in 1777 the Russian governor of Astrakhan complained:

It is not a secret that they, the Indians, having trade with Russian subjects, attempt, in exchange for Russian money and for goods, to receive Russian silver money, and especially heavy silver of the best kind with the portrait of Peter the Great. . . . Silver is in short supply in Russia and is aggravated by these noncitizens, the Indians. (p. 111)

How do the circumstances of Indian traders in Russia compare with those of Europeans in India? How do the goods exchanged between India and Russia compare with goods exchanged across the Indian Ocean?

Source: Stephen Frederic Dale, *Indian Merchants and Eurasian Trade, 1600–1750* (Cambridge: Cambridge University Press, 1994).

Hindus and Muslims

India had not been dominated by a single ruler since the time of Harsha Vardhana (r. 606–647). Hindus were horrified by Muslim destruction of Hindu cultural monuments, the expansion of Muslim territory, and the practice, until Akbar's time, of enslaving prisoners of war and compelling them to convert to Islam. But Hindu efforts to oppose Muslim rule were piecemeal rather than concerted. The Mughal state, in contrast, inherited traditions of unified imperial rule both from the Islamic caliphate and from the more recent examples of Genghis Khan and Timur.

Those Mongol-based traditions did not necessarily mean religious intolerance. Seventy percent of the *mansabdars*° (officials holding land revenues) appointed under Akbar were Muslim soldiers born outside India, but 15 percent were Hindus. Most of the Hindu appointees were warriors from the north called **Rajputs**°, one of whom rose to be a powerful revenue minister. Their status as mansabdars was a manifestation of the policy of religious accommodation adopted by Akbar and his successors.

Akbar was the most illustrious ruler of his dynasty. He differed from his Ottoman and Safavid counterparts—Suleiman the Magnificent and Shah Abbas the Great—in his striving for social harmony and not just for more territory and revenue. He succeeded to the throne at the age of thirteen, and his actions at first were dominated by a regent and then by his strong-minded childhood nurse. At the age of twenty, he took command of the government. He married a Rajput princess, whose name is not recorded, and welcomed her father and brother to the court in Agra.

---

mansabdars (man-sab-DAHRZ)

Rajputs (RAHJ-putz)

Other rulers might have used such a marriage as a means of humiliating a subject group. But Akbar signaled by this marriage his desire for reconciliation and even intermarriage between Muslims and Hindus. A year later he rescinded the head tax that Muslim rulers traditionally levied on tolerated non-Muslims. This measure was more symbolic than real because the tax had not been regularly collected, but the gesture helped cement the allegiance of the Rajputs.

Akbar longed for an heir. Much to his relief, his Rajput wife gave birth to a son in 1569, ensuring that future rulers would have both Muslim and Hindu ancestry.

Akbar ruled that in legal disputes between two Hindus, decisions would be made according to village custom or Hindu law as interpreted by local Hindu scholars. Shari'a law was in force for Muslims. Akbar made himself the legal court of last resort in a 1579 declaration that he was God's infallible earthly representative. Thus appeals could be made to Akbar personally, a possibility not usually present in Islamic jurisprudence.

Akbar also made himself the center of a new "Divine Faith" incorporating Muslim, Hindu, Zoroastrian, Sikh°, and Christian beliefs. He was strongly attracted by Sufi ideas, which permeated the religious rituals he instituted at his court. To promote serious consideration of his religious principles, he oversaw, from a catwalk high above the audience, debates among scholars of all religions assembled in his octagonal private audience chamber. When courtiers uttered the Muslim exclamation "Allahu Akbar"—"God is great"—they also understood it in its second grammatical meaning: "God is Akbar." Akbar's religious views did not survive him, but the court culture he fostered, reflecting a mixture of Muslim and Hindu traditions, flourished until his zealous great-grandson Aurangzeb° (r. 1658–1707) reinstituted many restrictions on Hindus.

Mughal and Rajput miniature paintings reveled in precise portraits of political figures and depictions of scantily clad women, even though they brought frowns to the faces of pious Muslims, who deplored the representation of human beings in art. Most of the leading painters were Hindus. In poetry, in addition to the florid style of Persian verse favored at court, a new taste developed for poetry and prose in the popular language of the Delhi region. The Turkish word *ordu,* meaning "army," led to the modern descendant of this language being called *Urdu* in Pakistan (in India it is called *Hindi*).

Akbar's policy of toleration does not explain the pattern of conversion to Islam in Mughal India. Some scholars maintain that most converts came from members of the lowest Hindu social groups, or castes, who hoped to improve their lot in life, but there is little data to confirm this theory. Others argue that Sufi brotherhoods, which developed strongly in India, led the way in converting people to Islam, but this proposition has not been proved. The most heavily Muslim regions were in the valley of the Indus River and east Bengal. The Indus center dates from the establishment of Muslim rule there as early as the eighth century.

A careful study of local records and traditions from east Bengal indicates that the eastward movement of the delta of the Ganges River and the spread of rice cultivation into forest clearings played the primary role in conversions to Islam there. Mansabdars (mostly Muslims) with land grants in east Bengal contracted with local entrepreneurs to collect a labor force, cut down the forest, and establish rice paddies. Some of the entrepreneurs were Hindus, but most were non-Sufi Muslim religious figures. Like the Hindus, those Muslims used religion, represented by the construction of mosques and shrines, as a cement to maintain their farming communities. Most natives of the region were accustomed to worshiping local forest deities rather than the main Hindu gods. So the shift to Islam represented a move to a more sophisticated, literate culture appropriate to their new status as farmers producing for the commercial rice market. Gradual religious change of this kind often produced Muslim communities whose social customs differed little from those in neighboring Hindu communities. In east Bengal, common Muslim social institutions, such as madrasas, the ulama, and law courts, were little in evidence.

Another change in Indian religious life in the Mughal period was the appearance of **Sikhism** in the Punjab region of northwest India. Nanak (1469–1539), the religion's first *guru* (spiritual teacher), stressed meditation as a means of seeking enlightenment and drew from both Muslim and Hindu imagery in his teachings. His followers formed a single community without differences of caste. However, after Aurangzeb ordered the ninth guru beheaded in 1675 for refusing to convert to Islam, the tenth and final guru dedicated himself to avenging his father's death and reorganized his followers into "the army of the pure," a religious order dedicated to defending Sikh beliefs. These devotees signaled their faith by leaving their hair uncut; carrying a comb, a steel bracelet, and a sword or dagger; and wearing military-style breeches. By the eighteenth century, the Mughals were encountering fierce opposition from the Sikhs as well as from Hindu guerrilla forces in the rugged and ravine-scarred province of Maharashtra on India's west coast.

Sikh (sick)   **Aurangzeb** (ow-rang-ZEB)

Central Decay and Regional Challenges 1707–1761

Mughal power did not long survive Aurangzeb's death in 1707. Some historians consider the land-grant system a central element in the rapid decline of imperial authority, but other factors were at play as well. Aurangzeb's additions to Mughal territory in southern India were not all well integrated into the imperial structure, and a number of strong regional powers arose to challenge Mughal military supremacy. The Marathas proved a formidable enemy as they carved out a swath of territory across India's middle, and Sikhs, Hindu Rajputs, and Muslim Afghans exerted intense pressure from the northwest. A climax came in 1739 when Nadir Shah, the warlord who had seized power in Iran after the fall of the Safavids, invaded the subcontinent and sacked Delhi, which Akbar's grandson had rebuilt and beautified as the Mughal capital some decades before. The "peacock throne," the priceless, jewel-encrusted symbol of Mughal gandeur, was carried off to Iran as part of the booty. Another throne was found for the later Mughals to sit on; but their empire, which survived in name to 1857, was finished.

In 1723, Nizam al-Mulk°, the powerful vizier of the Mughal sultan, gave up on the central government and established his own nearly independent state at Hyderabad in the eastern Deccan. Other officials bearing the title *nawab*°, Anglicized as "nabob," became similarly independent in Bengal and Oudh° in the northeast, as did the Marathas farther west. In the northwest, simultaneous Iranian and Mughal weakness allowed the Afghans to establish an independent kingdom.

Some of these regional powers, and the smaller princely states that arose on former Mughal territory, were prosperous and benefited from the removal of the sultan's heavy hand. Linguistic and religious communities, freed from the religious intolerance instituted during the reign of Aurangzeb, similarly enjoyed greater opportunity for political expression. However, this disintegration of central power favored the intrusion of European adventurers.

Joseph François Dupleix° took over the presidency of the French stronghold of Pondicherry° in 1741 and began a new phase of European involvement in India. He captured the English trading center of Madras and used his small contingent of European and European-trained Indian troops to become a power broker in southern India. Though offered the title *nawab,* Dupleix preferred to operate behind the scenes, using Indian princes as puppets. His career ended in 1754 when he was called home. Deeply involved in wars in Europe, the French government was unwilling to pursue further adventures in India. Dupleix's departure opened the way for the British, whose ventures in India are described in Chapter 26.

TRADE EMPIRES IN THE INDIAN OCEAN, 1600–1729

It is no coincidence that the Mughal, Safavid, and Ottoman Empires declined simultaneously in the seventeenth and eighteenth centuries. Complex changes in military technology and in the world economy, along with the increasing difficulty of basing an extensive land empire on military forces paid through land grants, affected them all adversely. The opposite was true for seafaring countries intent on turning trade networks into maritime empires. Improvements in ship design, navigation accuracy, and the use of cannon gave an ever-increasing edge to European powers competing with local seafaring peoples. Moreover, the development of joint-stock companies in which many merchants pooled their capital provided a flexible and efficient financial instrument for exploiting new possibilities. The English East India Company was founded in 1600, the Dutch East India Company in 1602.

Although the Ottomans, Safavids, and the Mughals did not seriously contest the growth of Portuguese and then Dutch, English, and French maritime power, the majority of non-European shipbuilders, captains, sailors, and traders were Muslim. Groups of Armenian, Jewish, and Hindu traders were also active, but they remained almost as aloof from the Europeans as the Muslims did. The presence in every port of Muslims following the same legal traditions and practicing their faith in similar ways cemented the Muslims' trading network. Islam, from its very outset in the life and preachings of Muhammad (570–632), was always congenial to trade and traders. Unlike Hinduism, it was a proselytizing religion, a factor that encouraged the growth of coastal Muslim communities as local non-Muslims were drawn into Muslim commercial activities, converted, and intermarried with Muslims from abroad.

Although European missionaries, particularly the Jesuits, tried to extend Christianity into Asia and Africa

---

Nizam al-Mulk (nee-ZAHM al-MULK)   *nawab* (NAH-wab)
Oudh (OW-ad)   **Dupleix** (doo-PLAY)
Pondicherry (pon-dir-CHEH-ree)

Map 21.2   European Colonization in the Indian Ocean to 1750   Since Portuguese explorers were the first Europeans to reach India by rounding Africa, Portugal gained a strong foothold in both areas. Rival Spain was barred from colonizing the region by the Treaty of Tordesillas in 1494, which limited Spanish efforts to lands west of a line drawn through the mid-Atlantic Ocean. The line carried around the globe provided justification of Spanish colonization in the Philippines. French, British, and Dutch colonies date from after 1600 when joint stock companies provided a new stimulus for overseas commerce.

(see Chapters 17 and 22), most Europeans, the Portuguese excepted, were less inclined than the Muslims were to treat local converts or the offspring of mixed marriages as full members of their communities. As a consequence, Islam spread extensively into East Africa and Southeast Asia during precisely the time of rapid European commercial expansion. Even without the support of the Muslim land empires, Islam became a source of resistance to growing European domination.

Muslims in the East Indies

Historians disagree about the chronology and manner of Islam's spread in Southeast Asia. Arab traders were well known in southern China as early as the eighth century, so Muslims probably reached the East Indies at a similarly early date. Nevertheless, the dominance of Indian cultural influences in the area for several centuries thereafter indicates that early Muslim visitors had little impact on local beliefs. Clearer indications of conversion and the formation of Muslim communities date from roughly the fourteenth century. The strongest overseas linkage is to the port of Cambay in India (see Map 21.2) rather than to the Arab world. Islam took root first in port cities and in some royal courts and spread inland slowly, possibly transmitted by itinerant Sufis.

Although appeals to the Ottoman sultan for support against the Europeans ultimately proved of little use, Islam as a political ideology strengthened resistance to Portuguese, Spanish, and Dutch intruders. When the Spaniards conquered the Philippines during the decades following the establishment of their first fort in 1565 (see Chapter 17), they encountered Muslims on the southern island of Mindanao° and the nearby Sulu archipelago. They called them "Moros," the Spanish term for their old enemies, the Muslims of North Africa. In the ensuing Moro wars, the Spaniards portrayed the Moros as greedy pirates who raided non-Muslim territories for slaves. In fact, they were political, religious, and commercial competitors whose perseverance enabled them to establish the Sulu Empire based in the southern Philippines, one of the strongest states in Southeast Asia from 1768 to 1848.

Other local kingdoms that looked on Islam as a force to counter the aggressive Christianity of the Europeans included the actively proselytizing Brunei° Sultanate in northern Borneo and the **Acheh° Sultanate** in northern Sumatra. At its peak in the early seventeenth century, Acheh succeeded Malacca as the main center of Islamic expansion in Southeast Asia. It prospered from trade in pepper and cotton cloth from Gujarat in India. Acheh declined after the Dutch seized Malacca from Portugal in 1641.

How well Islam was understood in these Muslim kingdoms is open to question. In Acheh, for example, a series of women ruled between 1641 and 1699. This practice came to an end when local Muslim scholars obtained a ruling from scholars in Mecca and Medina that Islam did not approve of female rulers. This ruling became a turning point after which scholarly understandings of Islam gained greater prominence in the East Indies.

Historians have theorized that the first propagators of Islam in Southeast Asia were merchants, Sufi preachers, or both. The scholarly vision of Islam, however, took root in the sixteenth century by way of pilgrims returning from years of study in Mecca and Medina. Islam was the primary force in the dissemination of writing in the region. Some of the returning pilgrims wrote in Arabic, others in Malay or Javanese. As Islam continued to spread, *adat,* a form of Islam rooted in pre-Muslim religious and social practices, retained its preeminence in rural areas over practices centered on the Shari'a, the religious law. But the royal courts in the port cities began to heed the views of the pilgrim teachers, as in their condemnation of female rulers. Though different in many ways, both varieties of Islam provided believers with a firm basis of identification in the face of the growing European presence. Christian missionaries gained most of their converts in regions that had not yet converted to Islam, such as the northern Philippines.

Muslims in East Africa

The East African ports that the Portuguese began to visit in the fifteenth century were governed by Muslim rulers but were not linked politically (see Map 21.2). People living in the millet and rice lands of the Swahili Coast—from the Arabic *sawahil°* meaning "coasts"—had little contact with those in the dry hinterlands. Throughout this period, the East African lakes region and the highlands of Kenya witnessed unprecedented migration and relocation of peoples because of drought conditions that persisted from the late sixteenth through most of the seventeenth century.

Cooperation among the trading ports of Kilwa, Mombasa, and Malindi was hindered by the thick bush country that separated the cultivated tracts of coastal

---

Mindanao (min-duh-NOW)   Brunei (BROO-nie)
Acheh (AH-cheh)

sawahil (suh-WAH-hil)

Portuguese Fort Guarding Musqat Harbor   Musqat in Oman and Aden in Yemen, the best harbors in southern Arabia, were targets for imperial navies trying to establish dominance in the Indian Ocean. Mosqat's harbor is small and circular with one narrow entrance overlooked by this fortress. The palace of the sultan of Oman is still located at the opposite end of the harbor. (Robert Harding Picture Library)

land and by the fact that the ports competed with one another in the export of ivory; ambergris° (a whale byproduct used in perfumes); and forest products such as beeswax, copal tree resin, and wood (Kilwa also exported gold). In the eighteenth century, slave trading, primarily to Arabian ports but also to India, increased in importance. Because Europeans—the only peoples who kept consistent records of slave-trading activities—played a minor role in this slave trade, few records have survived to indicate its extent. Perhaps the best estimate is that 2.1 million slaves were exported between 1500 and 1890, a little over 12.5 percent of the total traffic in African slaves during that period (see Chapter 20).

The Portuguese conquered all of the coastal ports from Mozambique northward except Malindi, with whose ruler Portugal cooperated. A Portuguese description of the ruler indicates some of the cloth and metal goods that Malindi imported, as well as some local manufactures:

> The King wore a robe of damask trimmed with green satin and a rich [cap]. He was seated on two cushioned chairs of bronze, beneath a rough sunshade of crimson satin attached to a pole. An old man, who attended him as a page, carried a short sword in a silver sheath. There were many players on [horns], and two trumpets of ivory richly carved and of the size of a man, which were blown through a hole in the side, and made sweet harmony with the [horns].[4]

Initially, the Portuguese favored the port of Malindi, which caused the decline of Kilwa and Mombasa. Repeatedly plagued by local rebellion, Portuguese power suffered severe blows when the Arabs of **Oman** in southeastern Arabia captured their south Arabian stronghold at Musqat (1650) and then went on in support of African resistance to seize Mombasa (1698), which had become the Portuguese capital in East Africa. The Portuguese briefly retook Mombasa but lost control permanently in 1729. From then on, the Portuguese had to content themselves with Mozambique in Africa and a few remaining ports in India (Goa) and farther east (Macao and Timor).

The Omanis created a maritime empire of their own, but one that worked in greater cooperation with the African populations. The Bantu language of the coast, broadened by the absorption of Arabic, Persian, and Portuguese loanwords, developed into **Swahili°,** which was spoken throughout the region. Arabs and other Muslims who settled in the region intermarried with local families, giving rise to a mixed population that played an important role in developing a distinctive Swahili culture.

Islam also spread in the southern Sudan in this period, particularly in the dry areas away from the Nile River. This growth coincided with a waning of Ethiopian power as a result of Portugal's stifling of trade in the Red Sea. Yet no significant contact developed between the emerging Muslim Swahili culture and that of the Muslims in the Sudan, to the north.

---

ambergris (AM-ber-grees)

Swahili (swah-HEE-lee)

The Coming of the Dutch

The Dutch played a major role in driving the Portuguese from their possessions in the East Indies. They were better organized than the Portuguese through the Dutch East India Company (see Chapter 20). Just as the Portuguese had tried to dominate the trade in spices, so the Dutch concentrated at first on the spice-producing islands of Southeast Asia. The Portuguese had seized Malacca, a strategic town on the narrow strait at the end of the Malay Peninsula, from a local Malay ruler in 1511 (see Chapter 17). The Dutch took it away from them in 1641, leaving Portugal little foothold in the East Indies except the islands of Ambon° and Timor (see Map 21.2).

Although the United Netherlands was one of the least autocratic countries of Europe, the governors-general appointed by the Dutch East India Company deployed almost unlimited powers in their efforts to maintain their trade monopoly. They could even order the execution of their own employees for "smuggling"—that is, trading on their own. Under strong governors-general, the Dutch fought a series of wars against Acheh and other local kingdoms on Sumatra and Java. In 1628 and 1629, their new capital at **Batavia,** now the city of Jakarta on Java, was besieged by a fleet of fifty ships belonging to the sultan of Mataram°, a Javanese kingdom. The Dutch held out with difficulty and eventually prevailed when the sultan was unable to get effective help from the English.

Suppressing local rulers, however, was not enough to control the spice trade once other European countries adopted Dutch methods, became more knowledgeable about where goods might be acquired, and started to send more ships to Southeast Asia. In the course of the eighteenth century, therefore, the Dutch gradually turned from being a middleman for Southeast Asian producers and European buyers to being a producer of crops in areas they controlled, notably in Java. Javanese teak forests yielded high-quality lumber, and coffee, transplanted from Yemen, grew well in the hilly regions of western Java. In this new phase of colonial export production, Batavia developed from being the headquarters town of a far-flung enterprise to being the administrative capital of a conquered land.

Beyond the East Indies, the Dutch utilized their discovery of a band of powerful eastward-blowing winds (called the "Roaring Forties" because they blow throughout the year between 40 and 50 degrees south latitude) to reach Australia in 1606. In 1642 and 1643 Abel Tasman became the first European to set foot on Tasmania and New Zealand and to sail around Australia, signaling European involvement in that region (see Chapter 26).

Ambon (am-BOHN)   Mataram (MAH-tah-ram)

CONCLUSION

That a major shift in world economic and political alignments was well under way by the late seventeenth century was scarcely perceivable in those parts of Asia and Africa ruled by the Ottoman and Mughal sultans and the Safavid shahs. They focused their efforts on conquering more and more land, sometimes at the expense of Christian Europe or Hindu India, but also at one another's expense since the Sunni-Shi'ite division justified Iranian attacks on its neighbors and vice versa.

To be sure, more and more trade was being carried in European vessels, particularly after the advent of joint-stock companies in 1600; and Europeans had enclaves in a handful of port cities and islands. But the age-old tradition of Asia was that imperial wealth came from control of broad expanses of agricultural land. Except in the case of state monopolies, such as Iranian silk, governments did not greatly concern themselves with what farmers planted. They relied mostly on land taxes, usually indirectly collected via holders of land-grants or tax farmers, rather than on customs duties or control of markets to fill the government coffers.

With ever-increasing military expenditures, these taxes fell short of the rulers' needs. Few people realized, however, that this was a problem basic to the entire economic system rather than a temporary revenue shortfall. Imperial courtiers pursued their luxurious ways, poetry and the arts continued to flourish, and the quality of manufacturing and craft production remained generally high. Eighteenth century European observers, luxuriating in the prosperity gained from their ever increasing control of the Indian Ocean, marvelled no less at the riches and industry of these eastern lands than at the fundamental weakness of their political and military systems.

■ Key Terms

Ottoman Empire	Mughal Empire
Suleiman the Magnificent	Akbar
Janissary	*mansabs*
devshirme	Rajputs
Tulip Period	Sikhism
Safavid Empire	Acheh Sultanate
Shi'ite Islam	Oman
Hidden Imam	Swahili
Shah Abbas I	Batavia

■ Suggested Reading

The best comprehensive and comparative account of the post-Mongol Islamic land empires, with an emphasis on social history, is Ira Lapidus, *A History of Islamic Societies* (1988). For a work of similar scope concentrating on intellectual history see Marshall G. S. Hodgson, *The Venture of Islam*, vol. 3, *The Gunpowder Empires and Modern Times* (1974).

Ottoman origins are well covered in Cemal Kafadar, *Between Two Worlds* (1995). On the Ottoman Empire, the standard political history is Stanford J. Shaw, *History of the Ottoman Empire and Modern Turkey*, vol. 1, *Empire of the Ghazis: The Rise and Decline of the Ottoman Empire, 1280–1808* (1976). Jason Goodwin, *Lords of the Horizons: A History of the Ottoman Empire* (1999), offers a more readable and journalistic account. For a collection of articles on nonpolitical matters see Halil Inalcik and Donald Quataert, eds., *An Economic and Social History of the Ottoman Empire, 1300—1914* (1994).

The world's foremost Ottoman historian, Halil Inalcik, analyzes the history and structure of the empire in *The Ottoman Empire: The Classical Age, 1300–1600* (1989). For a sociological analysis of change in the seventeenth century see Karen Barkey, *Bandits and Bureaucrats* (1994).

Among the specialized studies of cities and regions that give a good sense of some of the major changes in Ottoman society and economy after the sixteenth century are Daniel Goffman, *Izmir and the Levantine World, 1550–1650* (1990); Abraham Marcus, *The Middle East on the Eve of Modernity: Aleppo in the Eighteenth Century* (1989); and Bruce McGowan, *Economic Life in the Ottoman Empire: Taxation, Trade, and the Struggle for Land, 1600–1800* (1981).

Questions relating to religious minorities in the Ottoman Empire are best covered by the articles in Benjamin Braude and Bernard Lewis, eds., *Christians and Jews in the Ottoman Empire: The Functioning of a Plural Society* (1982). The role of women in the governance of the empire is skillfully treated by Leslie Pierce, *The Imperial Harem: Women and Sovereignty in the Ottoman Empire* (1993). Ralph S. Hattox, *Coffee and Coffeehouses: The Origins of a Social Beverage in the Medieval Near East* (1988), is an excellent contribution to Ottoman social history.

The most comprehensive treatment of the history of Safavid Iran is in the articles in Peter Jackson and Laurence Lockhart, eds., *The Cambridge History of Iran*, vol. 6, *The Timurid and Safavid Periods* (1986). The articles by Hans Roemer in this volume provide the best political narratives of the pre-Safavid and Safavid periods. Roger Savory's important article on the structure of the Safavid state is available in a more extensive form in his *Iran Under the Safavids* (1980).

For the artistic side of Safavid history, abundantly illustrated, see Anthony Welch, *Shah Abbas and the Arts of Isfahan* (1973). Said Amir Arjomand, *The Shadow of God and the Hidden Imam: Religion, Political Order, and Societal Change in Shiite Iran from the Beginning to 1890* (1984), contains the best analysis of the complicated relationship between Shi'ism and monarchy. Safavid economic history is not well developed, but useful studies have been published by Ann K. S. Lambton, *Landlord and Peasant in Persia: A Study of Land Tenure and Land Revenue Administration*, rev. ed. (1991), and Mehdi Keyvani, *Artisans and Guild Life in the Later Safavid Period: Contribution to the Social-Economic History of Persia* (1982).

A highly readable work that situates the Mughal Empire within the overall history of the subcontinent is Stanley Wolpert, *A New History of India*, 4th ed. (1993). For a broad treatment of the entire development of Islamic society in India with emphasis on the Mughal period see S. M. Ikram, *History of Muslim Civilization in India and Pakistan* (1989). Wheeler Thackston has made a lively translation of Babur's autobiography in *The Baburnama: Memoirs of Babur, Prince and Emperor* (1996). For a comprehensive history of the Mughals see John F. Richards, *The Mughal Empire* (1993). Irfan Habib has edited an extensive collection of articles on the Mughal Empire in its prime entitled *Akbar and His India* (1997). For the history of the Sikhs see W. H. McLeod *The Sikhs: History, Religion, and Society* (1989). Two specialized works on the economic and trading history of India are Ashin Das Gupta and M. N. Pearson, eds., *India and the Indian Ocean, 1500–1800* (1987), and Stephen Frederic Dale, *Indian Merchants and Eurasian Trade, 1600–1750* (1994).

The history of East Africa in this period is not well documented, but B. A. Ogot, ed., *UNESCO General History of Africa*, vol. 5, *Africa from the Sixteenth to the Eighteenth Century* (1992), provides a useful collection of articles. See also Tom Spear *The Swahili*, (1984) and James de Vere Allen, *Swahili Origins* (1993).

For a brief, general introduction to the relations between the Muslim land empires and the development of Indian Ocean trade see Patricia Risso, *Merchants and Faith: Muslim Commerce and Culture in the Indian Ocean* (1995). Esmond Bradley Martin and Chryssee Perry Martin have written a popular and well-illustrated work on the western Indian Ocean entitled *Cargoes of the East: The Ports, Trade and Culture of the Arabian Seas and Western Indian Ocean* (1978). C. R. Boxer, *The Dutch Seaborne Empire, 1600–1800* (1973), is a classic account of all aspects of Dutch maritime expansion.

■ Notes

1. Quoted in Sarah Searight, *The British in the Middle East* (New York: Atheneum 1970), 36.
2. Daniel Goffman, *Izmir and the Levantine World, 1550–1650* (Seattle: University of Washington Press, 1990), 52.
3. Quoted in Peter Jackson and Laurence Lockhart, eds., *The Cambridge History of Iran*, vol. 6, *The Timurid and Safavid Periods* (New York: Cambridge University Press, 1986), 703.
4. Esmond Bradley Martin and Chryssee Perry Martin, *Cargoes of the East: The Ports, Trade and Culture of the Arabian Seas and Western Indian Ocean* (1978), 17.

22

EASTERN EURASIA,

1500–1800

New Patterns of Contact in Eurasia • The Triumph of the Russian Empire •
The Late Ming and Early Qing Empires, 1500–1800 • Decentralization and
Innovation in Tokugawa Japan, to 1800

ENVIRONMENT AND TECHNOLOGY: Women and Tokugawa Technology

SOCIETY AND CULTURE: Style and Conversion: Christian Rivalries in Beijing

Russian Ambassadors to Holland Display Their Furs, 1500s   Representatives from Muscovy impressed
the court of the German prince Maximillian II of Regensburg with their sable coats and caps.

n the 1650s, two enormous and expanding empires battled for control of Siberia, the Amur° River basin, and the Pacific coast of northern Asia. Hardy Russian scouts, mostly Cossacks, came east across the tundra, hoping to stake an early claim to the great Amur waterway. They built wooden forts on its northern bank, but they were countered by Manchu agents of the Qing° Empire based in China, which hoped to secure Qing territories north of Korea and to secure the same stretch of Pacific coast the Russians sought. The Manchus built wooden forts on the southern bank of the Amur.

Neither empire sent large forces into the Amur territories, and the contest was mostly a struggle for the goodwill of the local Evenk and Dagur peoples. The Qing emperor emphasized the importance of treading lightly in the struggle and well understood the principles of espionage:

> Upon reaching the lands of the Evenks and the Dagurs you will send to announce that you have come to hunt deer. Meanwhile, keep a careful record of the distance and go, while hunting, along the northern bank of the Amur until you come by the shortest route to the town of Russian settlement at Albazin. Thoroughly reconnoitre its location and situation. I don't think the Russians will take a chance on attacking you. If they offer you food, accept it and show your gratitude. If they do attack you, don't fight back. In that case, lead your people and withdraw into our own territories. For I have a plan of my own.[1]

That delicacy gives a false impression of the intensity of the struggle between these two great empires. The contest was partly for dominance in the new northeast Asian economy of furs, timber, and metals concentrated in Siberia, Manchuria, and Yakutsk. But even without the attraction of those specific resources, the Amur River would have been critical in the interplay of the two empires, because each had an overriding need to protect itself against the other. The kingdoms of Europe, and even Europe's emerging sea-based empires, were small in territory and weak in economic influence in comparison with these titanic Eurasian empires.

Where the Russian and Qing Empires faced each other—in Central Asia, in Mongolia, and in Northeast Asia—they had to expend great resources conquering and defending lands that in the long run yielded very little profit. But for either to have flinched would have meant disaster at the hands of the other.

In 1689, the Qing and Russian Empires formalized their stand-off with a treaty establishing a border and a set of customs regulations. Russia was denied access to the Pacific coast east of the Amur, but the Russians exploited a more northerly route to explore the North Pacific and colonize the northwestern coast of North America. The Russian and Qing Empires still sought ways around each other but apparently were evenly matched. Only the intrusion of the smaller, product-poor empires of Europe eventually upset the balance and permitted one of the Eurasian giants to outflank the other.

The Russian and Qing Empires were part of a regional power system in which size, agriculture, and infrastructure for overland communication and transport were of the greatest importance. In their struggle to maintain their power when challenged by the new empires of Europe, the Russian and Qing Empires faced common problems and experienced similar outcomes. The response of Japan was spectacularly different. That small, relatively remote nation had been a minor player in Asian affairs but was able to withstand economic and political changes more effectively than Asia's greatest empires.

As you read this chapter, ask yourself the following questions:

- What did the Russian and Qing Empires have in common? How do their similarities explain the tensions between them?

- What were the Russian and Qing attitudes toward Europe in the times of Peter the Great and Emperor Kangxi? What were the long-term consequences of these attitudes?

- What explains the comparative speed of Japanese economic and technological development in the 1700s?

Amur (AH-moor) Qing (ching)

CHRONOLOGY

	Russia	China and Central Asia	Korea and Japan
1500	**1547** Ivan IV tsar		
	1582 Cossacks conquer Khanate of Sibir		**1582** Japanese invasion of Korea
1600		**1601** Matteo Ricci active in Ming China	**1600** Decisive battle begins Tokugawa Shogunate
	1613–1645 Rule of Mikhail, the first Romanov tsar	**1644** Qing conquest of Beijing	**1649** Closing of Japan
		1662–1722 Rule of Emperor Kangxi	
	1689–1725 Rule of Peter the Great	**1689** Treaty of Nerchinsk with Russia	
		1691 Qing control of Inner Mongolia	**1702** Trial of the Forty-seven Ronin
1700	**1712** St. Petersburg becomes Russia's capital	**1736–1795** Rule of Emperor Qianlong	
	1762–1796 Rule of Catherine the Great	**1755** Qing conquest of Turkestan	**1792** Russian ships first spotted off the coast of Japan
	1799 Alaska becomes a Russian colony		

NEW PATTERNS OF CONTACT IN EURASIA

Between 1500 and 1800 several fundamental factors transformed the routes of contact and commerce in Eurasia. During the period of Mongol domination of Eurasia in the thirteenth century, overland trade connecting Iran, southern Russia, and China had thrived. But the Ming rulers, who came to power in China in 1368, did not control Central Asia as the Mongols had done. Instead, local leaders in Central Asia fought for dominance over the trading routes and commercial centers. After 1500, no single power controlled all of Central Asia, and no unified economic policy protected and promoted trade. Large and ambitious empires based in the Middle East, in Russia, and in China competed for control of parts of Central Asia, and this competition deepened their conflicts with the remaining Mongol groups and further depressed both travel and profitable trade.

Samarkand°, Bukhara°, Kashgar° and other oasis cities that had been rich and cosmopolitan in the days when overland trade was vigorous became isolated. Their governors were often hostile to outside influences. As the 1500s passed, the transporting of many goods by caravan between East Asia and the Middle East was neither cheap nor reliable.

The troubles afflicting Central Asia in this period might have been overcome in the interests of profitable trade, but a new venue of commerce had opened: Along the southern and eastern coasts of Eurasia, merchants from Europe, the Middle East, and Asia were taking advantage of the new global trade connections. Seaborne trade was now cheaper, faster, and more reliable than overland trade. Goods once transported across the interior of Eurasia could be moved more efficiently around its edges, and many new goods were available from the sea-connected economies.

Samarkand (SAM-mar-kahnd)   **Bukhara** (boo-CAR-ruh)
Kashgar (kahsh-gar)

Ancient Asian ports that had become rich from centuries of trade found new economic stimulation from the development of European commerce. China, and later Japan, were also beneficiaries of this new trade in the old ports. And after 1700, the development of a global commercial interest in the Pacific magnified the importance of the sea and control of its main trade routes. China, Japan, and other coastal economies of East Asia participated in the trade and sought means of cushioning the effects of globalization on their own economies and societies. Russia, in contrast, had to enter a period of renewed and more militant expansion or risk being left out of the Pacific trade.

The Land-Based Empires of Eurasia

The Portuguese, Spanish, and Dutch Empires relied on the sea for contact with their colonies. As relatively small empires, they had few major strategic worries and could exercise a wide range of options in their territorial roamings and commercial and military activities. For the Ottoman, Russian, Mughal, and Ming Empires, things were very different. They were land-based empires and much larger than the sea-based empires of Europe. Their self-defense was extremely expensive, they had fewer choices than their smaller European contemporaries about where to expand and how to enrich themselves after they expanded.

Even though the commercial importance of Central Asia had declined steeply by 1500, the region remained the strategic center of gravity for the land-based Eurasian empires, because this was where each was most vulnerable to attack by an ambitious rival. Much of Central Asia, however, was arid steppes or desert, crossed by formidable mountain ranges. Maintaining garrisons in these regions was extremely expensive, for food, weapons, animals, and even building materials had to be brought in from far away. The best hope of eventually making these territories self-supporting lay in the development of agriculture and mining, which required the introduction of large-scale irrigation, crops able to thrive in cold, dry climates, extensive new roads, and large numbers of settlers or prisoners to serve as laborers. All the land-based empires achieved some success in agriculture and mining, but the costs were so steep that often there was no profit.

The challenge to make large, unprofitable areas in the land-based Eurasian empires self-supporting through environmental change strengthened two tendencies that were already strong. First, it reinforced the emphasis on agriculture as the predominant source of wealth and government tax revenues. Although these empires were interested in new industries and sea communications, they had little choice but to concentrate on agriculture. Second, it reinforced the tendency toward political centralization, which was to be important in the Russian and Qing Empires in the late 1600s. If the herculean task of environmental transformation across Central Asia and parts of northern Asia was to be achieved, imperial governments had to be in full command of the massive resources necessary for development of the infrastructure. Forced labor by the domestic population persisted in the Russian and Qing Empires after it was abandoned in Europe; in Russia serfdom became more brutal and widespread in the seventeenth and eighteenth centuries than ever before. Rulers and their advisers believed that the strategic concerns were so great that there could be no interference in policy-making from the aristocracy, low-level bureaucrats, or anyone else.

In the long run, these empires were at a disadvantage in the competition with the sea-based empires of Europe. The Europeans concentrated on the colonization of profitable areas, linked the development of commerce to the enrichment of their central governments, and enlisted the aid of joint-stock companies and other semiprivate organizations to acquire and develop territories. Between 1500 and about 1800, the land-based empires of Eurasia were the largest administrative and economic systems in the world, but they posed more of a danger to each other than they faced from any of the sea-based empires of Europe.

New Global Influences: The Society of Jesus and the East India Companies

The European entry into sea trade and communications that so challenged Russia and the Qing was not at first a project of empires or even of states. In the sixteenth and seventeenth centuries, new global organizations such as the Society of Jesus and the East India Companies created ties between Asia, Europe, and the Americas. The **Jesuits** often preceded traders, explorers, and conquerors to those regions that were newly known to Europe. One of the first Jesuits, Francis Xavier, went to India in the mid-sixteenth century looking for converts and later traveled throughout Southeast and East Asia. He spent two years in Japan and died in 1552 in China. Following Xavier, other Jesuits had a significant influence in China and presented to Europeans an intriguing picture of Asian life.

China reaped some material benefits from contact with the Jesuits. Chinese converts to Catholicism were important in introducing European techniques of crop

TROMBE. DA ROTA PER CAVAR AQVA

圖 八 第

From the Jesuit Library at Beijing
Jesuits such as Matteo Ricci were willing to share books on technology and science with Chinese scholars. But without firsthand experience it was impossible for Chinese translators to convey how the devices actually worked. Here, a man walking in a wheel drives a shaft that changes the pressure inside two pumps. In the Chinese translation of the drawing, the mechanisms were all lost. (Left: From Zonca, *Trombe da Rota per Vavar Aqua* [1607]. Right: "Diagram Number Eight" from *Qi tushuo* [*Illustrations on Energy*] [1627]. Both courtesy of Joseph Needham, *Science and Civilization in China*, vol. 4)

production, irrigation, and engineering. The outstanding Jesuit of late Ming China, Matteo Ricci° (1552–1610), became expert in the Chinese language and an accomplished scholar of the Confucian classics. He and other Jesuits in China made a deep impression on the Ming elites at Beijing° and also in the wealthy, cosmopolitan cities of the Yangzi River delta and the southern China coast. Ricci himself was deeply affected by Chinese literature and philosophy. In his time and after, Jesuits remained important in transmitting to Europe knowledge of Chinese classical culture and translations of Chinese philosophical works. The high regard in which many European thinkers of the 1600s and early 1700s held the rulers of China was very much due to the activities of the Jesuits. The Society of Jesus was the most prominent transmitter of European science and technology to China, and of Chinese philosophy and literature to Europe.

European merchants arrived in East Asia by the time of the Jesuits arrival. First came the Portuguese, who after 1500 dominated the spice trade of the Moluccas and Java and the trade routes around India. The Spanish also were interested in the trade and established a small base on the island of Taiwan, off the coast of southeast China

(and not at the time part of the Ming Empire). Soon after 1600, the Dutch dislodged the Portuguese and Spanish from Taiwan. To secure their influence in East Asia and to discredit their rivals, representatives of the Dutch East India company (VOC) willingly complied with Chinese rituals by which foreigners were supposed to acknowledge the moral superiority of the emperor of China. They performed the ritual *kowtow* (in which the visitor knocked his head on the floor while crawling toward the throne) to the Ming emperor in China. The Dutch also got along well with the rulers of Japan and retained exclusive permission to live on the island of Deshima°, off Nagasaki°, after other Europeans were banned from the country. Outside Japan, however, the VOC faced a strong rival in the East India Company of England, chartered by Queen Elizabeth I in 1600.

The European trading companies and the Jesuits are examples of the global organizations that became conduits of trade and knowledge between Asia and Europe. The two-way communication that they made possible sparked enormous changes in how the opposite ends of Eurasia related to each other. But in the 1700s these organizations were viewed with suspicion by imperial authorities in Europe as well as in Asia.

Matteo Ricci (ma-TAY-o REE-chee) **Beijing** (bay-JING) **Deshima** (DUH-shee-ma) **Nagasaki** (nah-gah-SAH-kee)

The Russian Empire

Russia in 1533
Russia in 1598
Russia in 1721
Russia in 1796

■ Fort

PACIFIC OCEAN

Novo Arkhangelsk (Sitka)
TLINGIT

BRITISH NORTH AMERICA (CANADA)

RUSSIAN AMERICA (ALASKA)

ALEUTS

INUIT

INUIT

Bering Strait

INUIT

CHUKCHI

Bering Sea

50°
60°

KORYAKS

Petropavlovsk
ALEUTS
Kamchatka Peninsula

GREENLAND

ARCTIC OCEAN

100° 120° 140°
180°
160°
160°
140°
120°
100°

80°

70°

80°

Zashiversk

Okhotsk

Sea of Okhotsk

Sakalin

SIBERIA

Zhigansk
Yakutsk

EVENKI

YAKUTS

LAMUTS

Novaya Zemlya

Kara Sea

Barents Sea

SWEDEN

FINLAND

Baltic Sea

Arkhangelsk

Obdorsk

SAMOYEDS

TUNGUSY

EVENKI

Amur
Nerchinsk

MANCHURIA

St. Petersburg
Novgorod
Riga

URAL MOUNTAINS

Verkhoturye

OSTYAKS

Surgut

TARTARS

OSTYAKS

Bratsk

Krasnoyarsk
Irkutsk

PRUSSIA

Moscow
Smolensk
Nizhni Novgorod
Samara

Kama

Biysk

MONGOLIA

POLAND

Kiev
Saratov

COSSACKS

Omsk

AUSTRIA

UKRAINIANS

COSSACKS

Volga

KAZAKS

QING EMPIRE

OTTOMAN EMPIRE

Black Sea

GEORGIA

Aral Sea

Caspian Sea

TIBET

BHUTAN

AFGHANISTAN

NEPAL

BURMA

PERSIA

INDIA

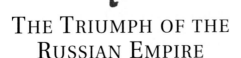

THE TRIUMPH OF THE RUSSIAN EMPIRE

The shift in intensity of exchange toward the seas and away from inland Asia presented both challenges and opportunities to the rising Russian Empire. The fragmentation of political power in Central Asia lessened the pressure on the Russian rulers to defend themselves on their southern border with Turkestan. Instead, they could turn their attention toward eastern Eurasia, including Mongolia and **Siberia,** and even to the Pacific coast. It was still necessary to maintain western and southern boundaries against the Ottoman Empire. But the rise of the European empires diminished this need somewhat, because the Europeans not only held the line against further Ottoman expansion in the Balkans but began to challenge and distract the Ottomans in the eastern Mediterranean.

The Rise of Romanov Power

After the dissolution of Mongol power in Russia, the city of Moscow became the foundation for a new state, **Muscovy°,** the territory surrounding the city of Moscow. By 1500, Muscovy was the dominant political force in the lands that had been controlled by the Kievan state. The process of unification forced by Muscovy was very difficult. By the mid-sixteenth century, Novgorod, which had been independent since the twelfth century and had maintained close connections with Sweden, was absorbed. To mark the extension of Muscovy and of his personal power, the Muscovite ruler Ivan IV ("the Terrible") assumed the title **tsar** (from "caesar") in 1547. Within a few years Ivan expanded Russia's borders far to the east through the conquest of the Khanates of Kazan and Astrakhan and the northern Caucausus region (see Map 22.1).

The westward extension of the territories ruled by Ivan IV and his successors did not progress much thereafter. Sweden and Poland, the dominant powers in north-eastern Europe, prevented Russian expansion westward. Instead, Russia had to defend itself more strenuously on the European front. In the early seventeenth century Swedish and Polish forces briefly occupied Moscow on separate occasions, and Russian politics were rent by prolonged and deadly rivalries for the tsarship.

In the midst of this "Time of Troubles" the old line of Muscovite rulers was finally deposed, and the Russian aristocracy—the *boyar*s°—allowed one of their own, **Mikhail Romanov°,** to become tsar (r. 1613–1645). But this dynastic change did not resolve the social and political tensions resulting from boyar resistance to further centralization of political power. Equally destabilizing were attacks from Sweden, Poland, and the Ottoman Empire.

The early Romanov rulers realized that consolidation of their own authority and successful competition with neighboring powers went together. Options for Russian expansion were limited. The Ottoman Empire controlled the Balkans, and the Safavid rulers of Iran dominated southern Central Asia. Trade with Europe was blocked as well because Sweden controlled the Baltic Sea, the Ottomans the Black Sea, and Iran the access to the surviving overland routes. As we will see, the obvious direction for expansion—east—provided the Russian Empire both its greatest possibilities for conquest and its greatest conflicts with old and new powers.

Russians and Turks

Most of the peoples who defined themselves as "Russian" during the Kievan period were speakers of a language closely related to other Slavic languages, and they tended to live as farmers, hunters, builders, scribes, or merchants. Surrounding Russia to the north, east, and parts of the south were speakers of Turkic languages who tended to live as herders, caravan workers, and soldiers. Language was not a solid defining line between peoples: Turkic-speakers had lived among Russian-speakers for centuries and in many instances were indistinguishable from Russians. Nevertheless, despite instances of cooperation, suspicion between Russian and Turkic peoples remained strong. Hostility increased when the Ottoman Empire emerged as a great power in the Caucasus and in the Balkans. The Romanovs felt those two regions were critical to Russia's security and were eager to control them.

Under the Romanov dynasty, the divisions between Russians and Turks tended to be represented as conflicts

Map 22.1   The Expansion of Russia, 1500–1800   Sweden and Poland initially blocked Russian expansion in Europe, while the Ottoman Empire blocked the southwest. In the sixteenth century, Russia began to expand east, toward Siberia and the Pacific Ocean. By the end of the rule of Catherine the Great in 1796, Russia encompassed all of northern and northeastern Eurasia.

Muscovy (MUSS-koe-vee)   *boyar* (BOY-ar)
Romanov (ROE-man-off or roe-MAN-off)

between Christians and "infidels" or between the civilized and the "barbaric". Despite this rhetoric, it is important to understand that the interplay of Turkic (Central Asian) Russian (Slavic) influences was what produced the Russian Empire. These cultural groups were defined not by blood ties but by the way in which they lived.

A revealing example is the **Cossacks.** Their name comes from a Turkic word for a warrior or mercenary and is related to the modern name Kazakh. The word *Cossack* in various forms seems to have first emerged in the Ukraine, where it referred to bands of people living on the steppes, herding or robbing for their livelihoods. But the Cossacks of the Ukraine were a diverse group. Many were escaped serfs from Muscovy or Lithuania; others were wandering Turks or Cumans, Poles, Hungarians, or Mongols. Who their ancestors were was irrelevant. What mattered was that they lived in close-knit bands, were superb riders and fighters, and were feared by both the villagers and the legal authorities. Poland enlisted Cossacks to be the front line against the Ottomans. The Cossacks also proved to be a danger to their Polish patrons.

The Muscovite and early Romanov rulers decided to take no chances with the Cossacks and moved to crush them as an independent political force in the Ukraine. But Russia also desired to exploit the Cossacks' extraordinary military spirit and skills. The empire reached an accommodation with them, enrolling them in special military regiments and allowing them to live in autonomous villages. In return the Cossacks performed distinctive service for Russia, not only defending against Swedish and Ottoman incursions in the west but leading campaigns for exploration, conquest, and settlement in the east.

The Cossacks were an example of the ways in which Russia combined elements considered "Turk" with those considered "Russian." They displayed the military skills of Asian horsemen but were Russian-speakers, Christians, and in most cases willing participants in the building of the Russian Empire. Although Russian rulers and churchmen often tried to draw a strong line between the realm of the Russian and the realm of the Turk, this artificial distinction was at odds with the historical realities of the Russian Empire.

Peter the Great, r. 1689–1725

Much of the rhetoric that drew distinctions between "Russians" and "Turks" was connected to the age of **Peter the Great,** who ruled Russia from 1689 to 1725 (see Chapter 18). Peter was determined to secure a warm-water port on the Black Sea, and his first priority was to build a small but formidable navy that could blockade Ottoman ports. Peter described his wars with the Ottoman Empire as a new crusade to liberate Constantinople (now Istanbul) from the Muslim sultans. He also claimed the right to function as the legal protector of Orthodox Christians living in the Balkan territories under Ottoman rule. Peter's forces seized the port of Azov in 1696, but the fortress was lost again in 1713 and Russian expansion southward was blocked for the rest of Peter's reign. The need for a Black Sea port and Russia's role as the protector of Orthodox Christians, however, were not forgotten.

Peter was more successful in his campaigns in the west. In the long and costly Great Northern War (1700–1721), Peter's modernized armies broke Swedish control of the Baltic Sea, establishing direct contacts between Russia and Europe. Previously the courts of western Europe had regarded Russia as backward, brutal, and alien. But Peter's striking intelligence, his imposing physical presence, his open admiration of European architecture, art, and military technology, and his disarming willingness to engage in physical labor while learning carpentry, shipbuilding, and architecture had made him a European celebrity and generally improved the European opinion of Russia.

Peter's victory in the Great Northern War forced the European powers to recognize Russia as a major power for the first time. Taking advantage of his new prestige in Europe, he built a new city, St. Petersburg, on land captured from Sweden. In 1712 the city became Russia's capital. Peter intended St. Petersburg to be a model to Russian elites seeking to absorb European culture and a demonstration to Europeans of Russian sophistication. Houses were to be built of stone and brick, in the baroque style then fashionable in western Europe. Nobles were ordered to wear western styles and shave their beards. Peter attempted to end the traditional seclusion of upper-class Russian women, by requiring officials, officers, and merchants to bring their wives to the social gatherings he organized in the capital.

There was also a political objective in building the new capital: Peter intended to break the power of the boyars by sharply reducing their traditional roles in government and the army. The old boyar council of Moscow was replaced by a group of advisers in St. Petersburg whom the tsar appointed. Members of the traditional nobility continued to serve as generals and admirals, but officers in Peter's modern, professional army and navy were promoted according to merit, not birth.

Peter was interested in European technology and in some of Europe's culture, but he had no intention of following the movement of the Netherlands and Britain toward political liberalization. The goal of westernization was to strengthen the Russian state and the institutions of personal power that the Russians called **autocracy.** A decree of 1716 proclaimed that the tsar "is not obliged to answer to anyone in the world for his doings, but possesses power and authority over his kingdom and land, to rule them at his will and pleasure as a Christian ruler." Under this expansive definition of his role, Peter brought the Russian Orthodox Church firmly under state control, built factories and iron and copper foundries to provide munitions and supplies for the military, and increased the burdens of taxes and forced labor on the serfs. **Serfs**— the great mass of Russian people, forced by law and custom to work the land of their overlords—could have been freed as part of Peter's reform. But there was no move to abolish serf status, because the Russian Empire was dependent on serfs for the production of basic foodstuffs. It was locked in the struggle of the Eurasian land empires, and political centralization remained critical to the strategic challenges it faced.

The Russian Drive Eastward

Long before Peter's time, Russian rulers realized that the eastern frontier was wide open to Russian expansion because no other great empire controlled the northern tier of Asia. Living there were small groups of native peoples who relied on hunting and fishing for their survival and who had not assembled the complex military organizations and weaponry of the empires to the west and south. Russian exploration of Siberia began in the time of Ivan IV and was led by a Cossack, Yermak Timofeyovich°. Yermak's troops attacked the only political power in the region, the Khanate of Sibir, and by force of their rifles destroyed the khanate in 1582. Yermak himself did not survive to return to Moscow, but Cossacks remained in the forefront of Russian campaigns to conquer and settle Siberia. Most historians believe that Cossacks founded all the major towns of Russian Siberia.

Siberian furs and timber were the first valued resources; after 1700, gold, coal, and iron also became important. From the early seventeenth century the tsar used Siberia as a penal colony for criminals and political prisoners. By the 1650s, Cossack explorers had claimed the Amur Valley for the Russian Empire, and many villages along the Amur River were rendering tribute to Russian officials. Through the 1650s, clashes occurred between

---

Yermak Timofeyovich (YAIR-mak tih-mo-FAY-oh-vich *or* tih-mo-fay-OH-vich)

these soldiers and soldiers of the Qing Empire stationed near the river. To deprive the Russians of the goods rendered by the Amur villagers, the Qing Empire forcibly resettled native peoples westward in Qing territory.

By the late 1600s the Russian and Qing Empires also were competing for influence in Mongolia and Central Asia. The Mongol federations were attempting to maintain their independence by playing the Russians and Qing against each other. Both the Russian and the Qing rulers saw that their interests lay in a diplomatic agreement that would delineate their borders in Mongolia, Siberia, and the Amur River Valley, as well as fix trade and tariff regulations across their borders. The Treaty of Nerchinsk in 1689 was a strategic coup for both empires, and it was reinforced in the Treaty of Kiakhta in 1727.

The immediate results were two. First, Mongol groups lost the leverage they had gained by exploiting Russian and Qing competition. Thereafter, the Mongols steadily declined as a power, and the Qing Empire quickly consolidated its control over Mongolia and Central Asia. Second, with a fixed boundary and Siberia inside it, Russia could concentrate on further eastern expansion, all the way to the Pacific and, by logical extension, into North America.

The ramifications of Russia's arrival at the Pacific were apparent by the mid-1700s, as British expeditions explored not only the Hawaiian Islands but also the Alaskan coast. They were alert to the extraordinary possibilities of pelt gathering in the American northwest. Sable and fox furs were precious goods in both Europe and China, and the British looked for ways to add seal and beaver furs to the markets. Furs from the eastern part of North America had traded in Europe for a century and become the foundation of the charter companies. But to exploit the fur market in China without a ruinous overhead, traders would have to secure and process furs on the west coast of America. The economic possibilities of the fur trade in northwestern America fired the imagination of English and American entrepreneurs. But within a few decades Russia dominated Alaska, and Russian traders were active along the entire western coast of North America.

The drive to the east brought Russia control of the rich natural resources of Siberia and the strategically important Amur River and put Russia into a position to dominate the lucrative fur and shipping industries of the North Pacific. This expansion of the empire was started by the rulers of Muscovy, had its most dramatic developments under Peter, and was sustained by Peter's successors. When Catherine the Great (r. 1762–1796) died, Russian reach extended from Poland in the west to Alaska in the east, from the Barents Sea in the north to the

Power and Youth   Emperor Kangxi (left) and Peter the Great (right) were contemporaries, great rulers, and rivals for control of Central and Northeast Asia. Both were child-emperors who outwitted their elders to achieve personal rule and then pursued all avenues of knowledge to strengthen their empires. But their youthful portraits show differences: Peter is depicted here while he was a student in Holland in 1697, learning engineering and shipbuilding. Kangxi, in a portrait from about 1690, preferred to be portrayed as a refined scholar. (left: The Palace Museum, Beijing; right: Collection, Countess Bobrinskoy/Michael Holford)

Caspian Sea in the south, and was still growing. Catherine ruled the world's largest land empire, the survivor of a form of Eurasian empire that had prized large territories, agriculture, logging, fishing, and furs. It shared these qualities with its old rival, the Qing Empire.

THE LATER MING AND EARLY QING EMPIRES, 1500–1800

By the time the Qing Empire was fighting Russia for control of Northeast Asia, it was in its own right a very large and growing empire. Only a half-century earlier, however, the ancestors of the Qing rulers were local chiefs trying to protect the economic enterprises of their followers in Manchuria from regulation by the **Ming Empire** based in China. Though the Ming Empire did not control Mongolia, Turkestan, or Tibet, it was a large empire with a rich and complex economy. It was militarily

and politically influential, positioned at the center of an international tributary system, mounting effective military campaigns against Vietnam and the Mongols, and defending Korea against Japanese invasion. It would have been difficult for anybody to predict that in such a short period the Ming Empire would be destroyed and the Qing would assume control of China. Was the achievement due primarily to Ming weakness or to Qing strengths?

The End of the Ming

Historians are puzzled by the Ming decline because of the brilliance of the earlier Ming period. The unusual economic and cultural achievements of the Ming period continued until 1600. Ming manufacturers had transformed the global economy with their techniques for the assembly-line production of porcelain. By the 1500s Europe knew about the high-grade blue-on-white porcelain commonly used by the elites of China. Portuguese merchants not only began importing the products to Europe but requested special designs that imitated European pitchers and bowls that otherwise would have been made of metal or wood. Many of these commissioned items featured distinctive gold fittings and designs that Chinese artisans copied from European paintings. By 1600 the Dutch were also heavily involved in this trade, and wealthy families in Europe were becoming accustomed to the fine new porcelain, which they called "china." An international market eager for Ming porcelain, as well as for silk and lacquered furniture, stimulated the commercial development of East Asia, the Indian Ocean, and Europe.

This apparent golden age, however, was beset by serious problems that by the year 1600 left the Ming Empire economically exhausted, politically deteriorating, and technologically lagging behind both its East Asian neighbors and Europe. Some of these problems were the result of natural disasters associated with climate change and disease. There is evidence of climate change in the seventeenth century. Annual temperatures dropped, reached a low point about 1645, then remained low until the early 1700s. The last decades of the Ming were a time of agricultural distress, migration of peoples out of less productive areas, and the spread of epidemic diseases. Large uprisings that speeded the end of the Ming Empire were fueled by the dissatisfaction of tenant farmers and day workers squeezed by high rents, low wages, and poor crop yields. The devastation caused by these uprisings resulted in steep declines in local populations and grinding distress for individuals who were left. Climate change also may have contributed to external pressure on the Ming, as Manchus and Mongols sought to protect their productive lands from Ming control and to acquire land along the Ming borders.

Other kinds of global change also affected China. As Europeans colonized Mexico and Central America, they exploited the new sources of silver and flooded the global trade networks with silver coins. As China became more involved in this trade in the 1500s and early 1600s, silver flowed into China in exchange for goods sold to Europe. Silver dollars from the Spanish Empire were fully accepted in the Chinese economy, and the Chinese government began to mint its own silver coins and remint foreign silver in imitation of the Spanish design.

As the amount of silver in circulation rose, its relative value fell. Nevertheless, the Ming government maintained a strict ratio in price between silver coins and copper coins. Taxes and the prices of commodities were tied to the vlaue of silver, and most transactions required the conversion of copper coinage to silver. As silver declined in value, more and more copper was needed to make purchases and pay taxes. In a time of worsening economic and population conditions, the decline in the

value of silver and consequent inflation in prices and taxes hit the rural population especially hard. The Ming government found it increasingly difficult to maintain order and eventually was overwhelmed by rebellious forces.

Environmental and economic stress do not in themselves destroy societies. Indeed both the eastern Mongols and the Manchus centralized their political systems and increased the territories under their control in the 1600s, all at the expense of the Ming Empire. The importance of global factors in the demise of the Ming must be placed in the context of the special factors operating on China.

Ming cities were culturally and commercially vibrant. Many large landowners and absentee landlords lived in the cities, as well as officials, artists, and rich merchants who had purchased ranks or prepared their sons for the examinations. The elites had created a brilliant culture in which novels, operas, poetry, porcelain, and painting were all closely interwoven. Owners of small businesses catering to the urban elites could make money through printing, tailoring, running restaurants, or selling paper, ink, ink-stones, and writing brushes. The imperial government also marketed to the urban elites by operating factories for the production of ceramics and silks. Enormous government complexes at Jingdezhen° and at Dehua° invented assembly-line techniques and produced large quantities of high-quality ceramics for sale in China and abroad. But by the end of the Ming period the factories were plagued by disorder and inefficiency. The situation became so bad during the late sixteenth and seventeeth centuries that workers held strikes with increasing frequency. During a work action at Jingdezhen in 1601, workers threw themselves into the kilns to protest working conditions.

Yet the urban and industrial sectors of later Ming society fared much better than the rural, agricultural sector. After a period of economic growth and recovery from the population decline of the thirteenth century, the rural Ming economy did not continue strong growth. After the beginning of the sixteenth century, China had knowledge, gained from European traders, of new crops from Africa and America. But they were introduced very slowly, and neither rice-growing regions in southern China nor wheat-growing regions in northern China experienced a meaningful increase in productivity during the second half of the Ming period. After 1500, economic depression in the countryside, combined with recurring epidemics in central and southern China, kept population growth in check. The Ming population—about a

---

Jingdezhen (JING-deh-JUHN)   **Dehua** (duh-HUA)

hundred million—at its height probably did not much surpass that of the Song dynasty four hundred years earlier.

The Ming also were under constant pressure from the powerful Mongol federations of Central Asia. In the late 1500s large numbers of Mongols were unified again. This time, Tibetan religion was used to centralize power in the hands of a Mongol khan. To legitimate his power, the khan designated for the first time a **dalai lama°**, or universal teacher, of Tibetan Buddhism. The unification of the Mongols in the 1500s was a significant step in the reemergence of Mongolia as a regional military power around 1600. In its last decades the Ming Empire was squeezed by Mongol forces on the west and north.

In 1582 Japanese warriors invaded Korea, which was a Ming tributary state. The invasions threw East Asia into crisis. The **Manchus,** an agriculturally based people who controlled the region north of Korea, contributed troops to an international force under Ming leadership. The Koreans employed all the technological and military skill for which the Yi period was renowned. General Yi Sonsin devised and employed the covered warships, or "turtle boats," that intercepted a portion of Japanese fleet.

The effects of the Japanese invasion were lasting. The impoverished Ming had to pay a high price to bring the Manchus into the struggle. In addition, the strain of repelling the invasions hastened the Ming decline in military strength. In Korea, the factionalism afflicting the Yi court before the Japanese arrived was worsened by the devastation resulting from the invasion and the struggle for leadership after the invaders were turned back. Korea was so weakened that the Manchus soon brought the country under their sway.

For the entire later Ming period, the boundaries of the empire were critical to its health, and conditions at the boundaries are an indication of the difficulties the later Ming Empire endured. The Mongols remained strong in the north. The Manchus grew stronger in the northeast and severed the traditional relationship between China and Korea. In the southwest, there were repeated uprisings among native peoples crowded by the immigration of Chinese farmers. The Ming could not look to the seas for relief. Pirates, often of Japanese or partial Japanese ancestry, based themselves in Okinawa and in Taiwan and roamed the southeastern coast of China, frequently looting inadequately protected trading towns. Ming military resources, concentrated against the Mongols and the Manchus in the north, could not be deployed to make the coasts hospitable to Chinese traders who were not themselves connected to the pirates. Frus-

trated by conditions and despairing of ever making a living at home, many southern Chinese migrated to all areas of Southeast Asia, where they began to profit from the sea trading networks of the Indian Ocean.

After decades of weakening control, the Ming ruler was deposed when rebellious forces under the leadership of Li Zicheng° captured Beijing. The imperial family left the city, but a Ming general entered into an agreement with Manchu leaders, inviting them to take Beijing from the rebels. The Qing did so in the summer of 1644 but did not restore the Ming. They claimed China for their own and began a forty-year conquest of the rest of the Ming territories.

It was some years before all hope was lost for the Ming. The Ming imperial family thought they could appeal to the Catholic Church for help in resisting the invaders. On November 4, 1650, from the remote highlands of Southeast Asia, Grand Dowager Empress Wang° sent a delegation of Jesuits to Rome to ask the pope to "take pity on us sinners in God's presence and, when we die, to bestow a special absolution." Wang noted that all members of the imperial family had been converted and said that if the papacy would help repel the Manchus "ambassadors will be dispatched to perform proper ceremonies at the altars of Saints Peter and Paul." Michel Boym°, the Jesuit priest acting as Wang's envoy, did not reach Rome until 1652 and could gain no papal audience until 1656. Then, with an encouraging letter from Pope Alexander VI, Boym returned to a China nearly conquered by the Manchus, who refused to let him travel inland from Canton. By that time Wang and her family were dead. Boym himself died attempting to contact them and was buried in the highlands between China and Vietnam in 1659.[2]

Power and Trade in the Early Qing

The **Qing Empire** was ruled by a Manchu imperial family, and Manchus were the leaders of the military forces. But Manchus were a very small portion of the population, and from its beginnings the empire was dependent on diverse peoples for its achievements. Peoples of Mongol, Korean, Cossack, and Turkic descent were all important in one way or another. Some Jesuits also were helpers, particularly after the collapse of Ming resistance. But the most important population in the Qing Empire was the Chinese, particularly the millions who deserted the Ming as Qing forces entered the country. Though the Qing style

---

dalai lama (DAH-lie LAH-mah)

Li Zicheng (lee ZUH-cheng)   **Wang** (wahng)
Michel Boym (mee-SHELL bwam)

Map 22.2   The Qing Empire, 1644–1783   The Qing Empire began in Manchuria and captured north China in 1644. Between 1644 and 1783 the Qing conquered all the former Ming territories and added Taiwan, the lower Amur River basin, Inner Mongolia, eastern Turkestan, and Tibet. The resulting state was more than twice the size of the Ming Empire.

of rule was multilingual and international and the Qing were keenly focused on large strategic issues relating to competition with the Russian Empire, the overwhelming majority of officials, soldiers, merchants, and farmers were Chinese.

Before the year 1700 the Qing gained south China, and for the first time the island of Taiwan was incorporated into an empire based in China (see Map 22.2). At the time, the Qing Empire was also conquering Mongolia and Central Asia. The seventeenth and eighteenth centuries in China—particularly the reigns of the Kangxi° (r. 1662–1722) and Qianlong° (r. 1736–1796) emperors—were the period of greatest economic, military, and cultural achievement.

The early Qing emperors wished to foster economic and demographic recovery in China. They repaired the

roads and waterworks, lowered transit taxes, mandated comparatively low rents and interest rates, and established economic incentives for resettlement of the areas devastated during the peasant rebellions of the late Ming period. Foreign trade was encouraged. Korean ambassadors and students were numerous in Beijing and readily absorbed the tastes of the Qing elite. Vietnam, Burma, and Nepal sent regular embassies to the Qing tribute court and carried the latest Chinese fashions back home. Overland routes of communication from Samarkand to Korea were revived, though their economic and cultural influence was a shadow of what it had been under the Mongols in the 1200s. Nevertheless, through its Central Asian conquests the Qing Empire gained access to the superior horses of Afghanistan, gained new sources of coal, iron, gold, and silver, and eventually was able to eliminate the military danger of the Mongols.

Kangxi (KAHNG-shee)   **Qianlong** (chee-YEN-loong)

Style and Conversion: Christian Rivalries in Beijing

The Treaty of Nerchinsk (1689) presented new opportunities for Russian missionaries in Beijing to continue their work of ministering to Russians in Beijing as well as spreading Orthodox Christianity in China. They failed to gain converts, largely because they did not learn Chinese. But they believed their failure was due to the interference of the Jesuits, who had arrived before them, knew Chinese, and made themselves indispensable in diplomatic communications between the Qing and Russian courts. In 1722 leaders of the Orthodox Church wrote the following comment to the new head of the Russian mission in Beijing.

It would be prudent if you kept your rank of bishop a secret, because your status might arouse opposition among our enemies—especially our main enemies, the Jesuits. They are constantly creating troubles between us and others, as well as strife among ourselves, in order to frustrate our good works. Of course it could not be otherwise, for remember that Jesus cried out to the Father, "Lord, have I not sown good seed? Where have these weeds come from?" And the Lord said, "The Devil has done this."

For their part, the Jesuits considered the Russian missionaries hopelessly unpersuasive, not only because of their limitations of language but also because of their poverty. Russians traveled overland, by caravan, to Beijing, which was very expensive. Once there, they lived on a very small allowance from the Qing court, and they were often short of food and fuel, not to mention new clothes. The relatively independent and wealthy Jesuits considered the Russian missionaries unprepared for international experience, as Matteo Ripa made clear in his report to the Vatican on the Russian mission in Beijing, probably in 1718.

I sent a present to the head of the mission, then visited him. His manners were courteous and dignified, and his dress remarkably neat. With me, he pretended to be a Roman Catholic (despite the fact he was obviously Orthodox), speaking just enough Latin to be understood. He told me that a priest who was ill and in bed could speak Latin, and so I went to visit him, but all I could get out of him was the word "intelligit, intelligit, [he understands, he understands]" over and over. The head of the mission told me that the congregation is limited to descendants of Russian prisoners of war. They cannot convert the Chinese because they don't speak Chinese, and besides they have so few priests that they have no time for any but their flock of Russians.

The truth is, their church services have no ceremony at all, and they allow men and women to worship together, which in China is considered abominable. And though the head of the mission looks elegant, the priests on his staff look very shabby. To make matters worse, the priests play in the streets in front of the mission. In China this is absolutely uncouth, and no respectable person would do it.

What do you think accounts for the tensions between the Jesuits and Russian Orthodox churchmen in China? What were they really competing for?

Source: Eric Widmer, *The Russian Ecclesiastical Mission in Peking During the Eighteenth Century* (Cambridge, MA: Harvard East Asian Research Center, 1976), 44, 63. © The President and Fellows of Harvard College 1976. Reproduced by permission of the Harvard University Asia Center.

Emperor Kangxi

The early Qing conquest of Beijing and north China was carried out under the leadership of a group of Manchu aristocrats who dominated the first Qing emperor based in China and were regents for his young son, who was declared emperor in 1662. This child-emperor, Kangxi, spent several years doing political battle with his regents, and in 1669 he gained real as well as formal control of the government by executing his chief regent. **Kangxi** was then sixteen. He was an intellectual prodigy who mastered classical Chinese, Manchu, and Mongolian at an early age and memorized the Chinese classics. He was a successful military commander who personally led troops in the great campaigns that brought Mongolia under Qing control by 1691. He battled with and then made peace with the Russian Empire and negotiated complex domestic political crises. His reign, lasting until his death in 1722, was marked not only by great expansion of the empire but by great stability as well.

Part of the effectiveness of Qing expansion in the Kangxi era was due to Qing willingness to incorporate ideas and technologies from different regions. Before the invasion of China, the Qing already were using the Mongol system of political organization. They also adapted a program of religious legitimation of the emperor's power that was Tibetan in origin but had been used by Mongol emperors. Many of the agricultural policies of the early Qing state were influenced by Korean and Chinese practices.

As the Qing conquest was consolidated in north China, south China, and Northeast Asia, maps in the European style—reflecting the century of Jesuit influence at the Ming court—were created as practical guides to the newly conquered regions and as symbols of Qing dominance. Kangxi considered introducing the European calendar, but protests were so strong that an anti-Jesuit backlash developed among the Confucian elites, and the plan was dropped. The emperor himself remained friendly with the Jesuits and frequently discussed scientific and philosophical issues with them (see Society and Culture: Style and Conversion: Christian Rivalries in Beijing). When he fell ill with malaria in the 1690s, he relied on Jesuit medical expertise (in this case, the use of quinine) for his recovery. He ordered the creation of illustrated books in Manchu detailing European anatomical and pharmaceutical knowlege. The Jesuits also lectured Kangxi on mathematics, astronomy, and European civilization generally.

To gain converts among the Chinese elite, the Jesuits made important compromises in their religious teaching. The most important was their toleration of Confucian ancestor worship. The matter caused great controversy between the Jesuits and their Catholic rivals in China, the Franciscans and Dominicans, and also between the Jesuits and the pope. In 1690 the disagreement reached a high pitch. Kangxi wrote to Rome supporting the Jesuit position, but the matter was dropped, inconclusively, in the early 1700s. By that time, the influx of Jesuits to China had slowed, and for the remainder of the 1700s a very small population of Jesuits remained at the Qing court.

The exchange of information between the Qing and the Europeans that Kangxi had fostered was never one-way. When the Jesuits informed the Qing court on matters of anatomy, for instance, the Qing were able to demonstrate to the Jesuits an early form of inoculation, called **variolation,** that had been used to stem the spread of smallpox after the Qing conquest of Beijing. The technique was the inspiration for the vaccines later developed by Europeans. Similarly, the enormous imperial factories that produced porcelain inspired the industrial management of practices of Josiah Wedgwood in England.

Transferring European Designs, Canton   By 1750, both Chinese and European merchants at Canton were dependent on the expansion of commerce between Europe and the Qing Empire for their fortunes. For centuries Chinese factories had produced special products in porcelain, silk, and lacquerware for European markets. By the end of the 1700s, even the trade itself was an object of commercialization: Here, a painting specially made for export shows a Canton artisan carefully transferring European designs to a glass painting that is itself specially made for export.   (V & A Picture Library)

Tea and Diplomacy

The brilliant successes of the Qing in conquest and trade excited admiration in Europe. Things Chinese—or things that looked to Europeans as if they could be Chinese—were demanded by the wealthy and the aspiring middle classes of Europe. Not only silk, porcelain, and tea were being avidly consumed, but also cloisonné jewelry, tableware and decorative items, lacquered and jeweled room dividers, painted fans, carved jade and ivory (which originated in Africa and was finished in China). Perhaps the most striking Chinese influence on the transformation of European interior life in this period was wallpaper—an adaptation of the Chinese practice of covering walls with enormous loose-hanging watercolors or calligraphy scrolls. By the mid-1700s, special workshops throughout China were producing wallpaper and other consumer items according to the specifications of European merchants. The items were shipped to Canton for export to Europe.

In political philosophy, too, the Europeans felt they had something to learn from the early Qing emperors. In the late 1770s, poems supposedly written by Emperor Qianlong were translated into French and disseminated through the intellectual circles of western Europe. These works depicted the Qing emperors as benevolent despots who campaigned against superstition and ignorance, curbed the excesses of the aristocracy, and patronized science and the arts. European intellectuals who were questioning the political systems of their own societies found the image of a practical, secular, compassionate ruler intriguing. Voltaire proclaimed the Qing emperors model philosopher-kings and advocated such rulership as a protection against the growth of aristocratic privilege. Though Jesuit interest in China was in decline by this time, the works of the Jesuits stimulated interest in the languages and civilizations of East Asia and an intensification of European efforts to establish communications with China.

The Qing were eager to expand China's economic influence but were determined to control the trade very strictly. The purposes of this regulation were to allow the imperial family to enjoy the benefits of taxation of the trade and to limit piracy on the seas and smuggling inland. The system that the Qing used for regulating trade permitted only one market point for each foreign sector. Overland trade from Central Asia was directed to Kashgar, trade from Japan was directed to a city on the eastern coast near Shanghai, and all trade from the South China Sea was directed to Canton on the southern coast. Since Europeans came to China by way of the Indian Ocean and Southeast Asia, they were included in the South China Sea sector and permitted to trade only at Canton.

This system worked well enough for European traders until the late 1700s. Britain had become an important presence in East Asia, using its bases in India and Singapore to move eastward to China. The directors of the East India Company (EIC) believed that China's technological achievements and gigantic potential markets made China the key to limitless profit. China had tea, rhubarb, porcelain, and silk to offer. Dutch merchants enriched themselves by transporting these goods to Europe for centuries, but by the early 1700s the EIC dominated the community of European "factories"—the combined residences and offices of the European merchants residing in Canton—and British families such as the Barings, Jardines, and Mathesons had established themselves as quasi-political powers.

Tea from China became enormously popular in England. It had earlier been a prized import to Russia, Central Asia, and the Middle East, all of which knew it by its northern Chinese name, *cha*, and all of which acquired it by the overland Eurasian routes of medieval and early modern times. Western Europe, however, acquired tea from sea routes first exploited by the Portuguese and Dutch and thus knew it by its name in the Fujian province of coastal China and Taiwan: *te*. From the time of its introduction to England in the mid-1600s, tea displaced chocolate and coffee as the preferred drink.

English traders, whether members of the EIC or independent businessmen, considered the potential of trade with China to be obstructed by the Qing trade system. Great fortunes were being made in the tea trade, but the English had not found a product to sell to China. They believed that China was a vast unexploited market, with hundreds of millions of potential consumers of lamp oil made from whale blubber, cotton grown in India or the American south, or guns manufactured in London or Connecticut. Particularly after the loss of the thirteen American colonies, Britain feared that its markets would diminish and believed that only the Qing trade system—the "Canton system," as the British called it—stood in the way of opening new paths for commerce.

The British government worried about Britain's massive trade deficit with China. Because the Qing Empire rarely bought anything from Britain, British silver poured into China to pay for the imported tea and other products. The Qing government, whose revenues were declining in the later 1700s while its expenses rose, needed the silver. But in Britain the imbalance of payments stirred anxiety and anger over the allegedly unfair restrictions that the Qing Empire placed on the import of foreign goods. To make matters worse, the East India Company had managed its worldwide holdings badly, and as it teetered on bankruptcy, its attempts to manipulate Parliament became increasingly intrusive. The British government attempted to limit the actions and privileges of the EIC but thought that only the opening of the China trade and increasing competition from British merchants would finally dissolve the outmoded EIC. In 1792 George Macartney was dispatched to China to open diplomatic relations with the Qing Empire and attempt to revise the trade system.

The **Macartney mission** to China, which extended into 1793, was a fiasco. Qing officials were not expecting Macartney and would not allow him to travel from Canton to Beijing. Moreover, they did not accept his credentials, and Macartney did not know how to make any headway through the Qing bureaucracy. There were prolonged disputes about rituals. Macartney was ordered to perform the kowtow, but he refused. He asked Qing officials to bow before a portrait of the king of England, and they refused. The basic issues were unresolvable. Britain wished the Qing Empire to abandon its trade system because it was benefiting only the troublesome EIC. Britain wished the Qing to open Chinese ports to a wide range of competing British firms, one of which might eventually find a product that would be popular in China and help to reverse the trade imbalance. The Qing, however, had no interest in changing the system. The EIC was not a Qing problem; the Qing were submitting British traders to no restrictions that did not also apply to all other foreign merchants; the system provided revenue to the imperial family and lessened serious piracy problems. Macartney left China humiliated by his inability to persuade the Qing to make changes. Many people at home suspected he had in fact performed the kowtow, humiliating not only himself but all of Britain.

Dutch, French, and Russian embassies soon attempted to achieve what Macartney had failed to do, When they failed also, European frustration with the Qing mounted. The great European admiration for China of the early 1700s faded, and China was considered despotic, self-satisfied, and unrealistic. Political solutions seemed impossible because the Qing court would not communicate with foreign envoys or observe the simplest rules of the diplomatic system familiar to Europeans.

There occurred here a subtle shift in the position of Russia. In the time of Peter the Great and of the Emperor Kangxi, the two great empires had faced each other in a special contest and had found a sophisticated means of resolving or at least suspending their differences. They had used a diplomatic system, relying on Jesuits as interpreters, to create treaties establishing formal borders and customs procedures. But in those times Russia and the Qing were struggling for control of Central Asia and Mongolia and had similar strengths and weaknesses. By the last decade of the eighteenth century, Russia was committed to sea exploration, colonization of overseas territories, and the creation of a European-style empire. It had moved beyond its Eurasian land empire context, and was leaning toward the European consensus that the Qing Empire was keeping in place an unreasonable and outdated trade system. The Qing emperors at the end of the 1700s did not understand the importance of this Russian shift or anticipate the ways in which it would work to destroy the status quo that the two gigantic empires had once enjoyed.

Population and Social Stress

When Macartney and his entourage visited China in 1792–1793, they were carefully guided through the most prosperous cities and the most productive farmland. They did not see evidence of the economic and environmental decline that had begun to affect China in the last decades of the 1700s. The population explosion had intensified demand for rice and wheat, for land to be opened for the planting of crops imported from Africa and the Americas, and for more thorough exploitation of land already in use.

The narratives of Marco Polo's adventures in the 1200s had already fixed in the European imagination the image of packed, affluent Chinese cities, and between the time of Marco Polo and the time of the Macartney mission the Chinese population tripled.

This growth was partly the result of the peace that the Qing enforced. In addition, foreign crops known in the late Ming but not widely exploited then were commonly used in the Qing period to supplement or replace traditional crops. For instance, in regions of northern China, years of planting wheat and barley had exhausted the soil near the surface. In these areas, the introduction of corn from America temporarily revived agricultural productivity because the roots of corn extend deep into the soil to seek their nutrients. In central and southern China, the use of sweet potatoes and other crops from Africa made possible the cultivation of land not suitable for rice or wheat. As Macartney observed, field crops were sown in neat rows by mechanical seeders—at a time when most farmers in Europe still used the broadcast method, which wasted much of the seed.

The early Qing population exploded and reached between 350 million and 400 million by the end of the 1700s. But because of the efficiency of Chinese agriculture, population growth that had driven the per capita area of arable land to one-third of what it had been a century before had not yet created general poverty.

Whatever woodlands remained in China at the beginning of the 1700s were rapidly diminishing by the end of the century. Houses could be built of brick, but erosion became a serious problem because of deforestation. As erosion advanced, the danger of flooding grew, but government corruption and general inefficiency limited efforts to prevent flooding or recover from its effects. Dams and dikes were not maintained, and silted-up river channels were not dredged. By the end of the eighteenth century the Grand Canal was nearly unusable, and the towns that bordered it were starved for commerce.

The result was localized misery in many parts of interior China by the year 1800. Environmental deterioration and the decline of agriculture prompted many people to move. They sought seasonal jobs in better-off agricultural areas, or they worked in low-status jobs such as barge puller, charcoal burner, or nightsoil carrier. Many drifted to the cities to make their way by begging, prostitution, or theft. In central and southwestern China, where farmers had been impoverished by serious flooding, rebellions became endemic. Often joining in revolt were various indigenous peoples, who were largely concentrated in the less fertile lands in the south and in the northern and western borderlands of the empire (see Map 22.3).

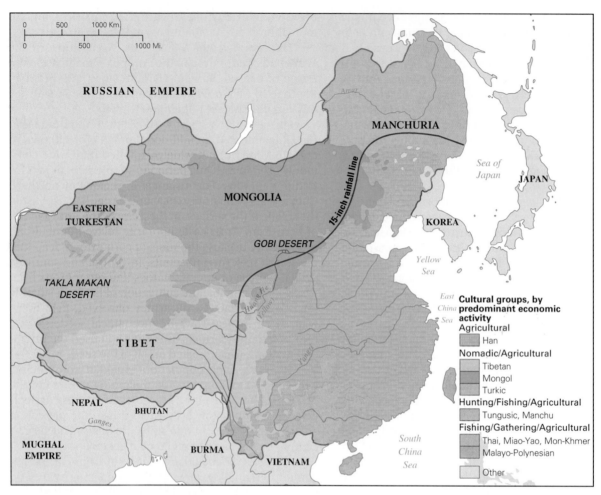

Map 22.3   Climate and Diversity in the Qing Empire   The Qing Empire encompassed different environmental zones, and the climate differences corresponded to population density and cultural divisions. Wetter regions to the east of the 15-inch rainfall line also contained the most densely populated 20 percent of Qing land. The drier, less densely populated 80 percent of the Empire was home to the greatest portion of peoples who spoke languages other than Chinese. Many were nomads, fishermen, hunters, or farmers who raised crops other than rice.

The Qing Empire was outgrowing the state's control. The Qing government employed about the same number of officials as the Ming even though the Qing Empire was twice the size of the Ming geographically and nearly four times its size in terms of population. To maintain local control, the Qing depended on working alliances with local elites, including gentry and aspiring official families. But this dependence undercut the government's ability to enforce tax regulations and to control standards for admission to government service. The resulting semi-privatization of governance in the late 1700s promoted a situation in which corruption was widespread, military policies were inconsistent and ineffective, banditry was growing, and government revenues were shrinking.

The Qing fell victim to some of the basic characteristics of the land-based empires. To defend itself against Russia, it had conquered a huge stretch of territory extending from Turkestan—brought under military occupation in 1755—to Northeast Asia, and the costs of maintaining it were enormous. Population growth and the need to transport food to nonagricultural areas stressed the food and grain systems. The need to invest in agriculture and in transport infrastructure limited investment in new industries and heightened government interest in taxing foreign trade. Russia was attempting to move out of that mode by turning toward European-style imperialism and industrialization. Japan, China's neighbor, was poised for an entirely different response.

DECENTRALIZATION AND INNOVATION IN TOKUGAWA JAPAN, TO 1800

Like East Asia under the Qing rulers, Japan under the Tokugawa° shoguns had to deal with the transition from the intense militarization of the early 1600s to the comparative peace of the 1700s, while at the same time facing a decrease in state revenues and mounting European pressure for contact. In nearly every respect, the Japanese reaction to these problems strongly contrasted with the Qing response, with lasting consequences for Japan.

Shogunate and Economy

Japan's centralized political system had broken down in the twelfth century, when the first of the decentralized military governments—the shogunates—had been created. By 1500, civil war had brought a new warrior class to power, and the second of Japan's shogunates—the Ashikaga—was a loosely organized system of regional lords giving their loyalty to their leader, the shogun, who gave his loyalty to the secluded emperor. The extreme decentralization of the Ashikaga period fostered wars among ambitious local lords, and during the later 1500s infighting among the leaders engulfed the country.

In 1600 a new shogun, Tokugawa Ieyasu°, declared victory. Though Japan was brought under a single military government, the structure of the **Tokugawa Shogunate** had a very important influence over the development of the Japanese economy in the early modern period. The regional lords who fought for Tokugawa Ieyasu in the final battle in 1600 were understood to have an especially close relationship with the shogun. The shogun's original intention was to reward the lords who had supported him with well-developed rice lands in central Japan—relatively close to the shogunal capital—and to punish those who had not supported him by granting them remote, undeveloped lands at the northern and southern extremes of the Japanese islands.

The emperor of Japan had no political power; he remained at Kyoto°, the medieval capital. The Tokugawa shoguns built a new capital for themselves at Edo° (now Tokyo). A well-maintained road connected Kyoto and Edo, and trade and trading centers developed along this route.

The shogun was served by the regional lords, each of whom maintained a castle town, a small bureaucracy, a population of warriors—**samurai**°—and military support personnel, and often an academy. The result of this controlled decentralization was the establishment of well-spaced urban centers, between which there was frequent traffic. Because Tokugawa shoguns required the lords to visit Edo frequently, good roads, traffic, and commerce linked Edo to three of the four main islands of Japan. The shogun paid the lords in rice, and the lords paid their followers in rice. To meet their personal expenses, recipients of rice had to convert a large portion of it into cash. This transaction stimulated the development of rice exchanges at Edo and at Osaka°, where merchants speculated in rice prices.

Because of the domestic peace of the Tokugawa era, the warrior class had to adapt itself to the growing bureaucratic needs of the state. As the samurai became better educated, more attuned to the tastes of the civil elite, and more interested in conspicuous consumption, merchants dealing in silks, *sake*° (rice wine), fans, porcelain, lacquerware, books, and loans were well positioned to exploit the new opportunities. The state attempted—unsuccessfully—to curb the independence of the merchants when the economic well-being of the samurai was threatened, particularly when rice prices went too low or interest rates on loans were too high.

The 1600s and 1700s were centuries of high achievment in artisanship and commerce (see Environment and Technology: Women and Tokugawa Technology). Japanese skills in steel making, pottery, and lacquerware were joined by excellence in the production and decoration of porcelain, thanks in no small part to Korean experts brought back to Japan after the invasion of 1582. In the early 1600s manufacturers and merchants amassed enormous family fortunes. Several of the most important industrial and financial companies—for instance, the Mitsui° companies—had their origins in *sake* or beer breweries of the early Tokugawa period, then branched out into manufacturing, finance, and transport.

Wealthy industrial families usually cultivated close alliances with their regional lords and, if possible, with the shogun himself. In this way they could weaken the strict control of merchant activity that was an official part of Tokugawa policy. By the end of the 1700s, the industrial families of Tokugawa Japan held the key to modernization and the development of heavy industry, particularly in the prosperous provinces. Their political

---

Tokugawa (toe-koo-GAH-wah) Ieyasu (ee-yeh-YAH-soo)
Kyoto (kee-YO-toe) Edo (ED-doe)

samurai (SAH-moo-rie) Osaka (OH-sah-kah) sake (SAH-kay)
Mitsui (MIT-soo-ee)

Women and Tokugawa Technology

In the early modern period, the balance between available resources and demand was better in Japan than in China. In Qing China, population rapidly outstripped farmers' ability to increase agricultural output. In addition, the population of China was unevenly distributed, and when the population far exceeded the demand for labor, not everyone who needed work could find it. In such circumstances, social expectations forced many working women to relinquish skilled, specialized jobs to men and to consider themselves lucky if they were able to find low-paying, unskilled work.

In Tokugawa Japan, by contrast, women's labor remained valuable through the 1700s and became increasingly specialized. Women were regularly employed in the countryside and in the industries of the towns. In Japan as in China, they were indispensable in agricultural labor. But in Japan, because of social coherence and the comparative uniformity of the work in all regions, women's roles were well integrated with those of men, and women maintained a role in both the political and the economic life of the village. As mechanization was introduced, the value of women's work did not decline. Indeed, women's skills actually became more specialized, and mechanization became a normal part of their work.

The silk industry traditionally had been dominated by women working at home, where they oversaw the breeding and feeding of silkworms and the production of raw silk. In the Tokugawa period, these skills were mechanized—sometimes on so large a scale that the making of silk could no longer be considered a cottage industry. Nevertheless, the demand for labor remained so high that women were able to maintain their role in silk weaving.

Women also were important in mining. They were believed to have special intuition for separating desired metals from the surrounding stone, and certainly their skills at this task were very well developed. Mining was a lowly trade that was expected to attract humble workers. But as the Tokugawa economy grew, the demand for iron, copper, silver, and gold increased, and women workers remained critical to the advancement of industry, despite their low social standing. Watercolors and drawings of the period commonly depict the integration of women into the Tokugawa economic scene.

There was, however, a firm ceiling above which Tokugawa women could not rise. Although they enjoyed more economic leverage than their equally hard-working counterparts in China and Korea, they had no property rights. Moreover, despite the fact that Tokugawa women maintained their position in mechanized trades, they generally were not instructed in the most advanced techniques until after they married, because if a girl were instructed at a very young age, and then married, for the remainder of her life her skills would benefit not her own birth family but the family of her husband. Thus, when increasing complexity demanded earlier and more prolonged training in some trades, women in Japan began to lose their place in industry.

Silk Weaving by Japanese Women   Before the emergence of large factories, this sort of work could be done in the home or at a shared village site. (From Hishikawa Moronobu *Wakoku hyakujo* [1695]. Reproduced courtesy of the Harvard-Yenching Library)

Comprehensive Map of the Myriad Nations Thanks to the "Dutch studies" scholars and to overseas contacts, many Japanese were well informed about the cultures, technologies, and political systems of various parts of the world. This combination map and ethnographic text of 1671 enthusiastically explores the differences among the many peoples living or traveling in Asia. The map of the Pacific hemisphere has the north pole on the left and south pole on the extreme right of the drawing. (British Museum/Fotomas Index)

influence was critical to the later transformation of Japan into an industrialized society.

The "Closing" of Japan

Like China, Japan at the end of the 1500s was a target of missionary activity by the Jesuits. But while members of the Chinese elite were open to the Jesuits so long as they accommodated Confucian values and became acquainted with Chinese culture, Japanese elite converts to Catholic Christianity were comparatively few. Missionaries could selectively gain the favor of regional lords while bypassing the shogunal court in Edo, which was consistently hostile to Christianity. This was the case with Date Masamuni°, the fierce and independent warlord of northern Honshu°, who sent his own embassy to the Vatican in 1613, by way of the Philippines (where there were significant communities of Japanese merchants and pirates) and Mexico City.

Generally, Christianity was more successful among farmers in the countryside. Jesuits had their greatest success in the southern and eastern regions of Japan. But in the late 1630s these regions were the scenes of massive uprisings by farmers impoverished by local rents and taxes. The rebellions, which were ruthlessly suppressed, were blamed on Christian influence. Hundreds of Japanese Christians were crucified as a warning to others; be-

lief in Christianity was banned by law; and in 1649 the shogunate ordered the closing of the country, making it illegal and punishable by death for foreigners to come in or for Japanese to leave.

The purpose of the closing was to prevent the spread of foreign influence in Japan, not necessarily to exclude from Japan knowledge of foreign cultures. A few Europeans, primarily the Dutch, were permitted to reside on the small island of Deshima near Nagasaki, and a few Japanese were licensed to supply their needs. Curious about Western ways, these intermediaries concentrated first on learning Dutch, so the knowledge that they acquired and that eventually spread from Nagasaki was known as "Dutch studies." It included information about European weapons technology, shipbuilding, mathematics and astronomy, anatomy and medicine, and geography. In the 1700s some Japanese theorists advocated that Japan should abandon its decentralized, agriculturally oriented system in favor of the more centralized, mercantilistic systems used by European empires.

The closing of Japan was ignored by some of the regional lords whose fortunes depended on overseas trade with Korea, Okinawa°, Taiwan, China, and Southeast Asia. The "outer" lords at the northern and southern extremes of Japan tended to be under less control by the shoguns. Many of them not only pursued overseas trade and piracy but also claimed dominion over islands between Japan

---

Date Masamuni (dah-tay mah-sah-moo-nee)   **Honshu** (hahn-shoo)   **Okinawa** (oh-kee-NAH-wah)

and Korea to the east and over islands between Japan and Taiwan to the south, including present-day Okinawa. The southern Japanese lords became wealthy and powerful by controlling sea trade—so powerful that the shogunate could no longer master them.

Elite Decline and Social Crisis

Sea trade was only one factor in the reversal of the relative fortunes of the "inner" and the "outer" lords. Population growth was putting a great strain on the well-developed lands of central Japan. In the remote provinces, where the lords had sponsored programs to settle and develop new agricultural lands, the rate of economic growth far outstripped the growth rate in centrally located domains.

Also destabilizing the Tokugawa government in the 1700s was the shogunate's inability to stabilize rice prices and halt the economic decline of the samurai. To finance their living, the samurai had to convert their rice to cash in the market. The Tokugawa government realized that the rice brokers might easily enrich themselves at the expense of the samurai if the price of rice, and the rate of interest, were not strictly controlled. Laws designed to regulate both had been passed early in the Tokugawa period, and laws requiring moneylenders to forgive samurai debts were added later. But these laws were not always enforced, sometimes because neither the lords nor the samurai wished them to be. By the early 1700s members of both groups were dependent on the willingness of merchants to provide them credit.

The Tokugawa shoguns strongly resisted the forces tending to weaken the samurai and to strengthen the merchant class. Their legitimacy rested on their ability to reward and protect the interests of the lords and samurai who had supported the Tokugawa conquest. But the Tokugawa government, like the governments of the Qing Empire, Korea, and Vietnam, accepted the Confucian idea that agriculture should be the basis of state wealth and that merchants should occupy lowly positions in society because of their reputed lack of moral character.

Governments throughout East Asia used Confucian philosophy to attempt to limit the influence and power of merchants. The Tokugawa government, however, was at a special disadvantage. Its decentralized system limited its ability to regulate merchant activities and actually stimulated the growth of commercial activities. In the first two centuries of the Tokugawa Shogunate—from 1600 to 1800—the economy grew faster than the population. Household amenities and cultural resources that in China were found only in the cities were common in the Japanese countryside. Despite official disapproval, merchants and others involved in the growing

Woodblock Print of the "Forty-Seven Ronin" Story The saga of the forty-seven ronin and the avenging of their fallen leader has fascinated the Japanese public since the event occurred in 1702. This watercolor from the Tokugawa period shows the leaders of the group pausing on the snowy banks of the Sumida River in Edo (Tokyo) before storming their enemy's residence. (Jean-Pierre Hauchecorne Collection)

economy enjoyed relative freedom and influence in eighteenth-century Japan. They produced a vivid culture of their own, fostering the development of *kabuki* theater, colorful woodblock prints and silkscreened fabrics, and restaurants.

The ideological and social crisis of Tokugawa Japan's transformation from a military to a civil society is captured in the "Forty-seven Ronin°" incident of 1702. A young regional lord was provoked by a senior minister into drawing his sword at the shogun's court. For this offense the young lord was sentenced to commit *seppuku°*, the ritual suicide of the samurai. His own followers then became *ronin*, "masterless samurai," obliged by the traditional code of the warrior to avenge their deceased master. They broke into the house of the senior minister who had provoked their own lord, and they killed him and others in his household. Then they withdrew to a temple

---

ronin (ROH-neen) *seppuku* (SEP-poo-koo)

in Edo and petitioned the shogun to acknowledge their obligation to be loyal to their lord and avenge his death.

A legal debate began in the shogun's government. To deny the righteousness of the ronin would be to deny samurai values. But to approve their actions would create social chaos, undermine laws against murder, and deny the shogunal government itself the right to try cases of samurai violence. The shogun ruled that the ronin had to die but would be permitted to die honorably by committing *seppuku*.

This solution exposed a fatal contradiction in the structure of shogunal government. To maintain a state based on military values, the state must place the military itself outside the law. Centralization, standardization of laws, and the ability of the state to enforce law for protection of the public would be impossible. The purity of purpose of the ronin is still celebrated in Japan, but since the time of the case of 1702, Japanese writers, historians, and teachers have recognized that the self-sacrifice of the ronin for the sake of upholding civil law was necessary.

The Tokugawa Shogunate put into place a political and economic system that fostered innovation, but the government itself could not exploit it. Thus during the Tokugawa period the government remained quite traditional while other segments of society developed new methods of productivity and management.

CONCLUSION

In the early eighteenth century Eurasia was dominated by the struggle of two enormous, land-based empires to defend themselves against each other and to acquire lands that would be at least marginally profitable. Because their needs were so similar, they often competed for the same resources, from Turkestan to Northeast Asia. Russia and the Qing Empire depended on large transportation systems, intense agricultural production, and coerced labor from their domestic populations. They preserved social systems that obligated a majority of the population to work the land but withheld the right to landownership. At the center of their political structures were powerful emperors with the economic and legal resources to command armies, engineering teams, and explorers at a distance. Not surprisingly, each empire had its most brilliant period—under Peter the Great and Emperor Kangxi—when the throne was occupied by a talented, energetic, and far-sighted ruler.

There were also distinct differences between these empires. The Qing court was generally open to many kinds of foreign influences and used ideas, institutions, and technologies from a wide range of sources. But distance and circumstance limited Qing contact with Europe. The Qing could not control which Europeans came to the Qing territories and thus encountered only merchants and missionaries. The merchants did not make much of an impression. The Jesuits were influential in philosophy, mathematics, astronomy, and other issues of concern to them. But they were not an inexhaustible resource for the Kangxi emperor, who was brilliant and inquisitive. From the Jesuits he got very little insight into the emergence of European empires, their tactics, or their goals.

Peter the Great banned the Jesuits from Russia, considering them a subversive and backward influence. St. Petersburg gave Peter a "window" into Europe, and from that vantage point his choices of what to learn from the Europeans and what to reject were unlimited. Among his choices were architecture, engineering, shipbuilding, and military technologies of all kinds. He knew how to exploit the symbolism of European emperorship, and perhaps he knew how to avoid tendencies toward liberalization represented by some Enlightenment thinkers. He understood the meaning of the new European use of the sea, and he foresaw the importance of America in the developing global economy. He set Russian rulers on a path tending toward European practices of diplomacy and imperialism and away from the static values of the huge land empires.

Russia and the Qing represent variations on an imperial pattern not shared by their neighbor Japan. Instead of pursuing centralization, standardization, and strengthening of the ruler, Japan was decentralized. Each local lord developed his own economic and political center, but there was enough connection at the level of the shogun's court for nationwide roadways and trade systems to thrive. Local lords had great incentive to develop their lands, and many turned to overseas opportunities in legitimate trade or in piracy. Despite the official policy of keeping merchants down, in practice merchants worked with the regional lords to develop local enterprises, sustain local samurai, and outfit local soldiers. Many regions of Tokugawa Japan created innovative means of financing local industry and developed unique relationships with other countries, particularly the islands of the western Pacific. In 1792, when Russian ships exploring the North Pacific turned toward the Japanese coast, the local lord used his own forces to chase them away. All local lords understood that they would be on their own as foreign incursions increased. After centuries of competition with, independence from, and often disobedience to the shogunate, they were to have a very different response to foreign challenges from either of their huge imperial neighbors.

◼ Key Terms

Jesuits	Peter the Great	Qing Empire
Siberia	autocracy	Kangxi
Muscovy	serfs	variolation
tsar	Ming Empire	Macartney Mission
Mikhail Romanov	dalai lama	Tokugawa Shogunate
Cossacks	Manchus	*samurai*

◼ Suggested Reading

There is a great deal of literature focused on the Jesuits' history in various countries. See these general histories: Christopher Hollis, *The Jesuits: A History* (1968), and Georg Schurhammer, *Francis Xavier: His Life, His Times,* trans. M. Joseph Costelloe, (1973–1982). For East Asia in the sixteenth and seventeenth centuries see Michael Coopers, S.J., *Rodrigues the Interpreter: An Early Jesuit in Japan and China* (1974). For China see David E. Mungello, *Curious Land: Jesuit Accommodation and the Origins of Sinology* (1985), and Jonathan D. Spence, *The Memory Palace of Matteo Ricci* (1984). For Japan see C. R. Boxer, *The Christian Century in Japan, 1549–1650* (1951). See also Cornelius Wessels, *Early Jesuit Travellers in Central Asia, 1603–1721* (1924). On European images of and interactions with China connected to the Jesuits, see the relevant portions of Jonathan D. Spence, *The Chan's Great Continent: China in Western Minds* (1998), and Joanna Waley-Cohen, *The Sextants of Beijing: Global Currents in Chinese History* (1999).

On the East India companies see John E. Wills, *Pepper, Guns, and Parleys: The Dutch East India Company and China, 1662– 1681* (1974); Dianne Lewis, *Jan Compagnie in the Straits of Malacca, 1641–1795* (1995); John Keay, *The Honourable Company: A History of the English East India Company* (1991); Brian Gardner, *The East India Company* (1971); and Lucy Stuart Sutherland, *The East India Company in Eighteenth-Century Politics* (1952). On the development of global commerce in tea, coffee, and cocoa see the relevant chapters in Roy Porter and Mikulås Teich, *Drugs and Narcotics in History* (1995).

On early modern Russian history, see W. E. Brown, *A History of Eighteenth-Century Russia* (1980), and Robert O. Crummey, *Aristocrats and Servitors: The Boyar Elite in Russia, 1613–1689* (1983). On Peter the Great there is a very extensive collection of works. Among the best-known recent books are Matthew Smith Anderson, *Peter the Great* (1978); Robert K. Massie, *Peter the Great: His Life and World* (1980); and Lindsey Hughes, *Russia in the Age of Peter the Great: 1682–1725* (1998). On the effect of Peter's reforms on the serfs and on the military see Elise K. Wirtschafter, *From Serf to Russian Soldier* (1990). For Russian naval development and Russian influence in the Pacific and in America see Glynn Barratt, *Russia in Pacific Waters, 1715–1825: A Survey of the Origins of Russia's Naval Presence in the North and South Pacific* (1981), and Howard I. Kushner, *Conflict on the Northwest Coast: American-Russian Rivalry in the Pacific Northwest, 1790–1867* (1975).

For China during the transition from the Ming to Qing periods see James W. Tong, *Disorder Under Heaven: Collective Violence in the Ming Dynasty* (1991); Frederic Wakeman, *The Great Enterprise* (1985); and Lynn Struve, *Voices from the Ming-Qing Cataclysm: In Tiger's Jaws* (1993). On the history of the Manchus and of the Qing Empire see Evelyn Sakakida Rawski, *The Last Emperors* (1999), and Pamela Kyle Crossley, *The Manchus* (1997).

On Chinese society generally in this period see two classic (though slightly dated) works by Ping-ti Ho: *The Ladder of Success in Imperial China: Aspects of Social Mobility, 1368–1911* (1962), and *Studies in the Population of China 1368–1953* (1959); and see the general study by Susan Naquin and Evelyn S. Rawski, *Chinese Society in the Eighteenth Century* (1987). On the two greatest of the Qing emperors and their times see Jonathan D. Spence, *Emperor of China; Self Portrait of K'ang Hsi, 1654–1722,* (1974). For a more scholarly treatment see Lawrence D. Kessler, *K'ang-hsi and the Consolidation of Ch'ing Rule, 1661–1684* (1976); Jonathan D. Spence, *Ts'ao Yin and the K'ang-hsi Emperor: Bondservant and Master* (1966); and Harold Kahn, *Monarchy in the Emperor's Eyes: Image and Reality in the Ch'ien-lung Reign* (1971).

On the Qing trade systems see John E. Wills, *Embassies and Illusions: Dutch and Portuguese Envoys to K'ang-hsi, 1666–1687* (1984), and Craig Clunas, *Chinese Export Art and Design* (1987).

There is a great deal published on the Macartney mission, much of it originating in the diaries and memoirs of the participants. See the exhaustively detailed Alain Peyrefitte, *The Immobile Empire,* trans. Jon Rothschild (1992). For a more theoretical discussion see James L. Hevia, *Cherishing Men from Afar: Qing Guest Ritual and the Macartney Embassy of 1793* (1995).

On Japan in this period see Chie Nakane and Shinzaburo Oishi *Tokugawa Japan: The Social and Economic Antecedents of Modern Japan,* trans. Conrad Totman (1990), and Tessa Morris-Suzuki, *The Technological Transformation of Japan from the Seventeenth to the Twenty-First Century* (1994). Mary Elizabeth Berry, *Hideyoshi* (1982), is an account of the reunification of Japan at the end of the sixteenth century and the invasion of Korea. On technological advancement, capital formation, and competition in the Tokugawa period see the classic by Thomas C. Smith, *Agrarian Origins of Modern Japan* (1959); the first chapter of Albert Craig, *Choshu in the Meiji Restoration* (1961); John Whitney Hall and Marius B. Jansen, eds., *Studies in the Institutional History of Early Modern Japan* (1968); and John G. Roberts, *Mitsui: Three Centuries of Japanese Business* (1973).

◼ Notes

1. Adapted from G. V. Melikhov, "Manzhou Penetration into the Basin of the Upper Amur in the 1680s," in S. L. Tikhvinshii, ed., *Manzhou Rule in China* (Moscow: Progress Publishers, 1983).
2. See Lynn Struve, *Voices from the Ming-Qing Cataclysm: In Tiger's Jaws* (New Haven, CT: Yale University Press, 1993), 235–237.

PART SIX

REVOLUTIONS RESHAPE THE WORLD,

1750–1870

Between 1750 and 1870, dramatic political, economic, and social changes affected nearly every part of the world. The beginnings of industrialization, the American and French Revolutions, and revolutions for independence in Latin America challenged the existing order in the West. In Africa, Asia, and the Middle East, the expansion of European commercial and military power combined with powerful internal transformations to challenge long-established institutions.

In the West, the American, French, and Haitian Revolutions unleashed forces of nationalism and social reform. At this time, the Industrial Revolution introduced technologies and patterns of work that made industrial societies wealthier, more socially fluid, and militarily more powerful than nonindustrial, traditional societies. Even while Europe's colonial empires in the Western Hemisphere were being dismantled, the Industrial Revolution was fueling European economic expansion, which undermined traditional producers in distant places such as Asia and Africa. When this economic penetration was resisted, as it was in East Asia, the industrializing nations of the West used military force to open markets.

Great Britain expanded its empire by establishing colonial rule in distant Australia, New Zealand, and India. India alone had a population larger than the combined populations of all the colonies that Europe lost in the Americas. The Atlantic slave trade was ended by an international abolitionist movement and by Great Britain's use of diplomacy and naval power. European economic influence expanded in Africa. Invigorated by this exchange, some African states created new institutions and introduced new economic sectors.

The Ottoman Empire, the Qing Empire, and Japan were deeply influenced by the expansion of Europe and the United States. Each society met the Western challenge with reform programs that preserved traditional structures while adopting elements of Western technology and organization. The Ottoman court introduced reforms in education, the military, and law and created the first constitution in an Islamic state. The Qing Empire survived the period of European expansion, but a series of military defeats and civil war seriously compromised China's centralization efforts. Japan experienced the most revolutionary change, abolishing its ancient political system and initiating radical top-down transformations.

The economic, political, and social revolutions that began in the mid-eighteenth century shook the foundations of European culture and led to the expansion of Western power across the globe. Societies throughout Asia, Africa, and Latin America responded to cross-cultural contacts. Some resisted foreign intrusion by using local culture and experience as a guide. Others adopted Western commercial policies, industrial technologies, and government institutions.

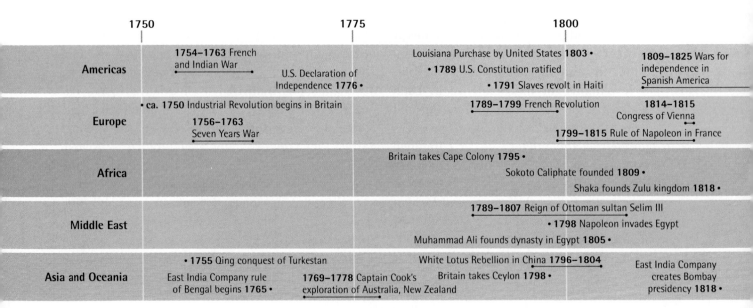

	1750		1775		1800	
Americas		1754–1763 French and Indian War	U.S. Declaration of Independence 1776 •	Louisiana Purchase by United States 1803 • • 1789 U.S. Constitution ratified • 1791 Slaves revolt in Haiti		1809–1825 Wars for independence in Spanish America
Europe	• ca. 1750 Industrial Revolution begins in Britain 1756–1763 Seven Years War			1789–1799 French Revolution 1799–1815 Rule of Napoleon in France		1814–1815 Congress of Vienna
Africa				Britain takes Cape Colony 1795 • Sokoto Caliphate founded 1809 • Shaka founds Zulu kingdom 1818 •		
Middle East				1789–1807 Reign of Ottoman sultan Selim III • 1798 Napoleon invades Egypt Muhammad Ali founds dynasty in Egypt 1805 •		
Asia and Oceania	• 1755 Qing conquest of Turkestan East India Company rule of Bengal begins 1765 •		1769–1778 Captain Cook's exploration of Australia, New Zealand	White Lotus Rebellion in China 1796–1804 Britain takes Ceylon 1798 •		East India Company creates Bombay presidency 1818 •

ARCTIC OCEAN

Britain

R u s s i a n   E m p i r e

EUROPE

France

ASIA

Ottoman Empire

Spain

Algeria

Japan

C h i n a

MIDDLE EAST

Egypt

I n d i a

Burma

AFRICA

Sokoto Caliphate

PACIFIC OCEAN

Liberia

Ceylon

INDIAN OCEAN

SOUTH ATLANTIC OCEAN

AUSTRALIA

Zulu Kingdom

Cape Colony

New Zealand

0	1000	2000	3000 Km.
0	1000	2000	3000 Mi.

1825

1850

1875

- **1822** Independence of Brazil

- **1848** Women's Rights Convention in Seneca Falls New York

- **1862–1867** French invasion of Mexico
- **1867** Creation of Dominion of Canada
- **1861–1865** U.S. Civil War

- **1830** Revolutions of 1830
- **1834** Abolition of slavery in British Empire

- **1852–1870** Rule of Napoleon III in France
- **1853–1856** Crimean War
- **1848** Revolutions of 1848

- **1821** Republic of Liberia founded

- **1869** Jaja founds Opobo
- **1836–1839** Afrikaners' Great Trek

- **1826** Ottoman ruler dissolves Janissary corps
- **1831–1847** Algerians resist French takeover
- **1839** Ottoman ruler Abdul Mejid launches Tanzimat reforms

- **1860s** Beginning of Young Turk movement
- **1869** Suez Canal opens

- **1826** East India Company annexes Assam, northern Burma
- **1839–1842** Opium War

- **1850–1864** Taiping Rebellion in China
- **1857–1858** Sepoy Rebellion in India
- **1868** Meiji Restoration in Japan

23

REVOLUTIONARY CHANGES IN THE ATLANTIC WORLD,

1750–1850

Prelude to Revolution: The Eighteenth-Century Crisis •
The American Revolution, 1775–1800 • The French Revolution, 1789–1815 •
Revolution Spreads, Conservatives Respond, 1789–1850
ENVIRONMENT AND TECHNOLOGY: The Pencil
SOCIETY AND CULTURE: The Women of Revolutionary France

Execution of Louis XVI The execution of the French king in 1793 was the most shocking
and dramatic signal that the "Old Order" was about to be swept away.

On the evening of August 14, 1791, more than two hundred slaves and black freedmen met in secret in the plantation district of northern Saint Domingue° (present-day Haiti) to set the date for an armed uprising against local slave owners. Although the delegates agreed to delay the attack for a week, violence began almost immediately. During the following decade, slavery was abolished, military forces from Britain and France were defeated, and Haiti achieved independence.

This meeting was provoked by news and rumors about revolutionary events in France that had spread through the island's slave community. Events in France also had divided the island's white population into competing camps of royalists (supporters of France's King Louis XVI) and republicans (supporters of democracy). The free mixed-race population initially gained some political rights from the French Assembly but was then forced to rebel when the slave-owning elite reacted violently.

Among those planning the insurrection was a black freedman named François Dominique Toussaint. He proved to be one of the most remarkable representatives of the revolutionary era, later taking the name Toussaint L'Ouverture°. He organized the rebels into a potent military force, negotiated with the island's royalist and republican factions and with representatives of Great Britain and France, and wrote his nation's first constitution. Commonly portrayed as a fiend by slave owners throughout the Western Hemisphere, Toussaint became for slaves a towering symbol of resistance to oppression.

The Haitian slave rebellion was an important episode in the long and painful political and cultural transformation of the modern Western world. Economic expansion and the growth of trade were creating unprecedented wealth. The first stage of the Industrial Revolution (see Chapter 24) increased manufacturing productivity and led to greater global interdependence, new patterns of consumerism, and altered social structures. At the same time, intellectuals were questioning the traditional place of monarchy and religion in society. An increasingly powerful class of merchants, professionals, and manufacturers created by the emerging economy provided an audience for these new intellectual currents and began to press for a larger political role.

This revolutionary era turned the Western world "upside down." The *ancien régime*°, the French term for Europe's old order, rested on medieval principles: politics dominated by powerful monarchs, intellectual and cultural life dominated by religion, and economics dominated by a hereditary agricultural elite. In the West's new order, politics was opened to vastly greater participation, science and secular inquiry took the place of religion in intellectual life, and economies were increasingly opened to competition.

This radical transformation did not take place without false starts and temporary setbacks. Imperial powers resisted the loss of colonies; monarchs and nobles struggled to retain their ancient privileges; and the church fought against the claims of science. Revolutionary steps forward were often matched by reactionary steps backward. The liberal and nationalist ideals of the eighteenth-century revolutionary movements were only imperfectly realized in Europe and the Americas in the nineteenth century. Despite setbacks, belief in national self-determination and universal suffrage, and a passion for social justice continued to animate reformers into the twentieth century.

As you read this chapter, ask yourself the following questions:

- How did imperial wars among European powers provoke revolution?
- In what ways were the revolutions, expanded literacy, and new political ideas linked?
- How did revolution in one country help to incite revolution elsewhere?
- Why were the revolutions in France and Haiti more violent than the American Revolution?

Saint Domingue (san doe-MANG)
Toussaint L'Ouverture (too-SAN loo-ver-CHORE)

---

ancien régime (ahn-see-EN ray-ZHEEM)

PRELUDE TO REVOLUTION: THE EIGHTEENTH-CENTURY CRISIS

In large measure, the cost of wars fought among Europe's major powers over colonies and trade precipitated the revolutionary era that began in 1775 with the American Revolution. Britain, France, and Spain were the central actors in these global struggles, but other imperial powers were affected as well. Unpopular and costly wars had been fought earlier and paid for with new taxes. But changes in the Western intellectual and political environments led to a much more critical response. Any effort to extend the power of a monarch or impose new taxes now raised questions about the rights of individuals and the authority of political institutions.

Colonial Wars and Fiscal Crises

The rivalry among European powers intensified in the early 1600s when the newly independent Netherlands began an assault on the American and Asian colonies of Spain and Portugal. The Dutch attacked Spanish treasure fleets in the Caribbean and Pacific and seized parts of Portugal's colonial empire in Brazil and Angola. Europe's other emerging sea power, Great Britain, also attacked Spanish fleets and seaports in the Americas. By the end of the seventeenth century, expanding British sea power had checked Dutch commercial and colonial ambitions and ended the Dutch monopoly of the African slave trade.

As Dutch power ebbed, Britain and France began a long struggle for political preeminence in western Europe and for territory and trade outlets in the Americas and Asia. Both the geographic scale and the expense of this conflict expanded during the eighteenth century. Nearly all of Europe's great powers were engaged in the War of the Spanish Succession (1701–1714). War between Britain and Spain, begun in 1739 over smuggling in the Americas, quickly broadened into a generalized European conflict, the War of the Austrian Succession (1740–1748). Conflict between French and English settlers in North America then helped ignite a long war that altered the colonial balance of power. When Britain finally won the Seven Years War (1756–1763), known as the French and Indian War in America, it not only gained undisputed control of North America east of the Mississippi River but also forced France to surrender most of its holdings in India.

The enormous costs of these conflicts distinguished them from earlier wars. Traditional taxes collected in traditional ways no longer covered the obligations of governments. For example, at the end of the Seven Years War in 1763, Britain's war debt had reached £137 million. Although Britain's total budget before the war had averaged only £8 million, annual interest on the war debt alone came to exceed £5 million. Even as European economies expanded because of increased trade and the early stages of the Industrial Revolution, fiscal crises overtook one European government after another. In an intellectual environment transformed by the Enlightenment, the need for new revenues provoked debate and confrontation within a vastly expanded and more critical public.

The Enlightenment and the Old Order

The complex and diverse intellectual movement called the **Enlightenment** applied the methods and questions of the Scientific Revolution of the seventeenth century to the study of human society. Dazzled by Copernicus's ability to explain the structure of the solar system and Newton's representation of the law of gravity, European intellectuals began to apply the logical tools of scientific inquiry to other questions. Some labored to systematize knowledge or organize reference materials. For example, Carolus Linnaeus° (a Swedish botanist known by the Latin form of his name) sought to categorize all living organisms, and Samuel Johnson published a comprehensive English dictionary with over forty thousand definitions. In France Denis Diderot° worked with other Enlightenment thinkers to create a compendium of human knowledge, the thirty-five-volume *Encyclopédie*.

Other thinkers pursued lines of inquiry that challenged long-established religious and political institutions. Some argued that if scientists could understand the laws of nature then surely similar forms of disciplined investigation might reveal laws of human nature. Others wondered whether society and government might be better regulated and more productive if guided by science rather than by hereditary rulers and the church. These new perspectives and the intellectual optimism that fed them were to help guide the revolutionary movements of the late eighteenth century.

The English political philosopher John Locke (1632–1704) argued in 1690 that governments were created to protect life, liberty, and property and that the people had

---

Carolus Linnaeus (kar-ROLL-uhs lin-NEE-uhs)
Denis Diderot (duh-nee DEE-duh-roe)

CHRONOLOGY

	The Americas	Europe
1750		
	1756–1763　French and Indian War	1756–1763　Seven Years War
1775	1770　Boston Massacre 1776　American Declaration of Independence 1778　United States alliance with France 1783　Treaty of Paris ends American Revolution	
	1791　Slaves revolt in Saint Domingue (Haiti)	1789　Storming of Bastille begins French Revolution 1793–1794　Reign of Terror in France 1795–1799　The Directory rules France 1799　Napoleon overthrows the Directory
1800	1798　Toussaint L'Ouverture defeats British in Haiti 1804　Haitians defeat French invasion and declare independence	1804　Napoleon crowns himself emperor 1814　Napoleon abdicates; Congress of Vienna opens 1815　Napoleon defeated at Waterloo
		1830　Greece gains independence; revolution in France overthrows Charles X 1848　Revolutions in France, Austria, Germany, Hungary, and Italy

a right to rebel when a monarch violated these natural rights. Locke's closely reasoned theory began with the assumption that individual rights were the foundation of civil government. In *The Social Contract,* published in 1762, the French-Swiss intellectual Jean-Jacques Rousseau° (1712–1778) asserted that the will of the people was sacred and that the legitimacy of the monarch depended on the consent of the people. Although both men beleived that government rested on the will of the people rather than divine will, Locke emphasized the importance of individual rights, and Rousseau envisioned the people acting collectively because of their shared historical experience.

All Enlightenment thinkers were not radicals like Rousseau. There was never a uniform program for political and social reform, and the era's intellectuals often disagreed about principles and objectives. The Enlightenment is commonly associated with hostility toward religion and monarchy, but few European intellectuals openly expressed republican or atheist sentiments. The church was most commonly attacked when it attempted to censor ideas or ban books. Critics of monarchial authority were as likely to point out violations of ancient custom as to suggest democratic alternatives. Even Voltaire, one of the Enlightenment's most critical intel-

lects and one of the era's great celebrities, believed that Europe's monarchs were likely agents of political and economic reform, and he wrote favorably of China's Qing° emperors.

Indeed, sympathetic members of the nobility and reforming European monarchs such as Charles III of Spain (r. 1759–1788), Catherine the Great of Russia (r. 1762–1796), Joseph II of Austria (r. 1780–1790), and Frederick the Great of Prussia (r. 1740–1786) actively sponsored and promoted the dissemination of new ideas, providing patronage for many intellectuals. They recognized that elements of the Enlightenment critique of the ancien régime buttressed their own efforts to expand royal authority at the expense of religious institutions, the nobility, and regional autonomy. Goals such as the development of national bureaucracies staffed by civil servants selected on merit, the creation of national legal systems, and the modernization of tax systems united many of Europe's monarchs and intellectuals. Monarchs also understood that the era's passion for science and technology held the potential of fattening national treasuries and improving economic performance (see Environment and Technology: The Pencil). Periodicals disseminating new technologies often gained the patronage of these reforming monarchs.

Jean-Jacques Rosseau (zhahn-zhock roo-SOE)

Qing (ching)

The Pencil

From early times, Europeans had used sharp points, lead, and other implements to sketch, make marks, and write brief notes. At the end of the seventeenth century, a source of high-quality graphite was discovered at Borrowdale in northwestern England. Borrowdale graphite gained acceptance among artists, artisans, and merchants. At first, pure graphite was simply wrapped in string. By the eighteenth century, pieces of graphite were being encased in wooden sheaths and resembled modern pencils. Widespread use of this useful tool was retarded by the limited supply of high-quality graphite from the English mines.

The English crown periodically closed the Borrowdale mines or restricted production to keep prices high and maintain adequate supplies for future needs. As a result, artisans in other European nations developed alternatives that used lower-quality graphite or, most commonly, graphite mixed with sulfur and glues.

The major breakthrough occurred in 1793 in France when war with England ruptured trade links. The government of revolutionary France responded to the shortage of graphite by assigning a thirty-nine-year-old scientist, Nicolas-Jacques Conté, to find an alternative. Conté had earlier promoted the military use of balloons and conducted experiments with hydrogen. He also had had experience using graphite alloys in the development of crucibles for melting metal.

Within a short period, Conté produced a graphite that is the basis for most lead pencils today. He succeeded by mixing finely ground graphite with potter's clay and water. The resulting paste was dried in a long mold, sealed in a ceramic box, and fired in an oven. The graphite strips were then placed in a wooden case. Although some believed the Conté pencils were inferior to the pencils made from Borrowdale

Pencils   Wartime necessity led to invention of the modern pencil in France.   (Drawing by Fred Avent for Henry Petroski. Reproduced by permission)

graphite, Conté produced a very serviceable pencil that could be produced in uniform quality and unlimited amounts.

Henry Petroski, summarizing the achievement of Conté in his *The Pencil*, wrote: "The laboratory is really the modern workshop. And modern engineering results when the scientific method is united with experience with the tools and products of craftsmen. . . . Modern engineering, in spirit if not in name, would come to play a more and more active role in turning the craft tradition into modern technology, with its base of research and development."

Source: This discussion depends on Henry Petroski, *The Pencil: A History of Design and Circumstance* (New York: Knopf, 1990); the quotation is from pp. 50–78. Drawing by Fred Avent for Henry Petroski. Reproduced by permission.

Though willing to embrace reform proposals when they served royal interests, Europe's monarchs moved quickly to suppress or ban radical ideas that promoted republicanism or directly attacked religion. However, too many channels of communication were open to permit a thoroughgoing suppression of these ideas. In fact, censorship tended to enhance intellectual reputations, and persecuted intellectuals generally found patronage in the courts of foreign rivals.

Many of the major intellectuals of the Enlightenment maintained an extensive correspondence with each other as well as with political leaders. This communication led to numerous firsthand contacts among the intellectuals of different nations and helped to create a coherent assault on what was typically called ignorance—beliefs and values associated with the ancien régime. Rousseau, for example, briefly sought refuge in Britain, where the Scottish philosopher David Hume befriended him. Similarly, Voltaire sought patronage and protection in England and later Prussia.

Women were instrumental in the dissemination of the new ideas. In England educated middle-class women purchased and discussed the books and pamphlets of the era. Some were important contributors to intellectual life as writers and commentators, raising by example and in argument the issue of the rights of women. In Paris wealthy women made their homes centers of debate, intellectual speculation, and free inquiry. Their salons brought together philosophers, social critics, artists, and members of the aristocracy and commercial elite. Unlike their contemporaries in England, the women of the Parisian salons used their social standing more to direct the conversations of men rather than to give vent to their own opinions.

The intellectual ferment of the era deeply influenced the expanding middle class in Europe and the Western Hemisphere. Members of this class were eager consumers of books and the inexpensive newspapers and journals that were widely available in the eighteenth century. This broadening of the intellectual audience overwhelmed traditional institutions of censorship. Scientific discoveries, new technologies, and controversial work on human nature and politics also were discussed in the thousands of coffeehouses and teashops opening in major cities and market towns.

Many European intellectuals were interested in the Americas. Some Europeans continued to dismiss the New World as barbaric and inferior, but others used idealized accounts of the New World to support their critiques of European society. These thinkers looked to Britain's North American colonies for confirmation of their belief that human nature unconstrained by the corrupted practices of Europe's old order would quickly produce material abundance and social justice. More than any other American, the writer and inventor **Benjamin Franklin** came to symbolize both the natural genius and the vast potential of America.

Born in 1706 in Boston, the young Franklin was apprenticed to his older brother, a printer. At seventeen he ran away to Philadelphia, where he succeeded as a printer and publisher, best known for his *Poor Richard's Almanac*. By age forty-two he was a wealthy man. He retired from active business to pursue writing, science, and public affairs. In Philadelphia, Franklin was instrumental in the creation of the organizations that later became the Philadelphia Free Library, the American Philosophical Society, and the University of Pennsylvania.

His contributions were both practical and theoretical. He was the inventor of bifocal glasses, the lightning rod, and an efficient wood-burning stove. In 1751 he published a scientific work on electricity, *Experiments and Observations on Electricity*, that established his intellectual reputation in Europe. Intellectuals heralded the book as proof that the simple and unsophisticated world of America was a particularly hospitable environment for genius.

Franklin was also an important political figure. He served Pennsylvania as a delegate to the Albany (New York) Congress in 1754, which sought to coordinate colonial defense against attacks by the French and their Amerindian allies. Later he was a Pennsylvania delegate to the Continental Congress that issued the Declaration of Independence in 1776. His service in England as colonial lobbyist and later as the Continental Congress's ambassador to Paris allowed him to cultivate his European reputation. Franklin's wide achievement, witty conversation, and careful self-promotion make him a symbol of the era. In him the Enlightenment's most radical project, the freeing of human potential from the inhibitions of inherited privilege, found its most agreeable confirmation.

As Franklin's career demonstrates, the Western Hemisphere shared in the debates of Europe. New ideas penetrated the curricula of many colonial universities and appeared in periodicals and books published in the New World. As scientific method was applied to economic and political questions, colonial writers, scholars, and artists on both sides of the Atlantic were drawn into a debate that eventually was to lead to the rejection of colonialism itself. This radicalization of the colonial intellectual community was provoked by the European monarchies' efforts to reform colonial policies. As European authorities swept away colonial institutions and long-established political practices without consultation, colonial residents had to acknowledge that their status as colonies meant perpetual subordination to European rulers. Among people compelled to recognize this structural dependence and inferiority, the idea that government authority ultimately rested on the consent of the governed was potentially explosive.

Folk Cultures and Popular Protest

While intellectuals and the reforming royal courts of Europe were embracing the rational and secular enthusiasms of the Enlightenment, most people in Western society remained loyal to competing cultural values grounded in the preindustrial past. These regionally distinct folk cultures were framed by the memory of shared local historical experience and nourished by religious practices encouraging emotional release. They emphasized the obligations that people had to each other and local, rather than national, loyalties. Though never formally articulated, these cultural traditions composed a coherent expression of the mutual rights and obligations connecting the people and their rulers. Rulers who violated the constraints of these understandings were likely to face violent opposition.

In the eighteenth century, European monarchs sought to increase their authority and to centralize power by reforming tax collection, judicial practice, and public administration. Although monarchs viewed these changes as reforms, the common people often saw them as violations of sacred customs and sometimes expressed their outrage in bread riots, tax protests, and attacks on royal officials. These violent actions were not efforts to overturn traditional authority. They were efforts to preserve custom and precedent. In Spain and the Spanish colonies, for example, protesting mobs commonly asserted the apparently contradictory slogan

"Long live the King. Death to bad government." They expressed loyalty and love of their monarch while at the same time assaulting his officials and preventing the implementation of changes to long-established customs.

Folk cultures were threatened by other kinds of reform as well. Rationalist reformers of the Enlightenment sought to bring order and discipline to the citizenry by banning or by altering in form the numerous popular cultural traditions—such as harvest festivals, religious holidays, and country fairs—that enlivened the drudgery of everyday life. These events were popular celebrations of sexuality and individuality as well as occasions where masked and costumed celebrants mocked the greed, pretension, and foolishness of government officials, the wealthy, and the clergy. Hard drinking, gambling, and blood sports like cockfighting and bearbaiting were all popular activities in this preindustrial mass culture. Because these customs were viewed as corrupt and decadent by reformers influenced by the Enlightenment,

Beer Street (1751) This engraving by William Hogarth shows an idealized London street scene where beer drinking is associated with manly strength, good humor, and prosperity. The self-satisfied corpulent figure in the left foreground has been reading a copy of the king's speech to Parliament. We can imagine him offering a running commentary to his drinking companions as he reads. (The Art Archive Limited)

governments undertook efforts to substitute civic rituals, patriotic anniversaries, and institutions of self-improvement. These challenges to custom—like the efforts at political reform—often provoked protests, rebellions, and riots.

The efforts of ordinary men and women to resist the growth of government power and the imposition of new cultural forms provide an important political undercurrent to much of the revolutionary agitation and conflict from 1750 to 1850. Spontaneous popular uprisings and protests punctuated nearly every effort at reform in the eighteenth century. But these popular actions gained revolutionary potential only when they coincided with ideological divisions and conflicts within the governing class itself. In America and France the old order was swept away when the protests and rebellions of the rural and urban poor coincided with the appearance of revolutionary leaders who followed Enlightenment ideals in the effort to create secular republican states. Likewise, a slave rebellion in Saint Domingue (Haiti) achieved revolutionary potential when it attracted the support of black freedmen and disaffected poor whites who had been radicalized by news of the French Revolution.

THE AMERICAN REVOLUTION, 1775–1800

In British North America, clumsy efforts to reform colonial tax policy to cover rising defense expenditures and to diminish the power of elected colonial legislatures outraged a populace accustomed to greater local autonomy. Once begun, the American Revolution ushered in a century-long process of political and cultural transformation in Europe and the Americas. By the end of this revolutionary century, the authority of monarchs had been swept away or limited by constitutions, and religion had lost its dominating place in Western intellectual life. Moreover, the medieval idea of a social order determined by birth had been replaced by a capitalist vision that emphasized competition and social mobility.

Frontiers and Taxes

After defeating the French in 1763, the British government faced two related problems in its North American colonies. As settlers quickly pushed into Amerindian lands west of the Appalachian Mountains and across the Ohio River, the British government saw the likelihood of armed conflict with Amerindian peoples. Already burdened with debts from the French and Indian War, Britain desperately wanted to avoid additional expenditures for frontier defense. Because of the possibility of frontier conflict and the need to hold down defense costs, Britain tried to get the colonists to shoulder more of the costs of imperial defense and colonial administration.

Every effort to impose new taxes or prevent the settlement of the trans-Appalachian frontier provoked angry protests in the colonies. The situation was made politically explosive by the confrontational and impolitic way in which a succession of weak British governments responded. Because George III (r. 1760–1820) relied upon cabinet ministers selected from among court favorites without regard to parliamentary support, the common response to colonial protests was incendiary bluster and weak enforcement. British government in the period after 1763 was a dangerous combination of qualities: both overbearing and weak.

When the British replaced the French in the Great Lakes region, they angered indigenous peoples by refusing to follow the French practice of paying rent for frontier forts and giving gifts to Amerindian allies. They also reduced the prices paid for furs. Amerindians had become accustomed to the goods they received in exchange for furs, especially firearms, gunpowder, textiles, and alcohol. To get these commodities, they had greatly intensified their hunting practices, endangering some species. Relations deteriorated quickly as settlers and white fur traders pushed across the Appalachians, adding new pressures to the natural environment.

Britain soon demonstrated that it was unable to negotiate the diplomatic and military challenges inherent in the relationship between Amerindians and settlers. Led by Pontiac, an Ottawa chief, a broad alliance of native peoples successfully drove the British military from frontier outposts and then raided deep into the settled areas of Virginia and Pennsylvania. Although this Amerindian alliance was defeated decisively within a year, the potential for renewed violence existed all along the frontier.

The British government's panicked reaction to Pontiac's challenge was the Proclamation of 1763. It sought to establish an effective western limit for settlement. The proposed boundary threw into question the claims of thousands of already established farmers without effectively protecting Amerindian land. No one was satisfied. A decade later the British government irritated the colonists even more when it attempted to slow settlement in contested regions east of the Mississippi and north of the Ohio. The Quebec Act of 1774 annexed disputed lands to the province of Quebec, thus denying eastern colonies the authority to distribute lands claimed as a result of original charters. Colonists saw the Quebec Act as punitive and tyrannical, and Amerindian peoples received no relief from the continuous assault on their land.

Frontier wars were costly and destructive but did not threaten British authority directly. The British government's campaign of fiscal reforms and new taxes, however, sparked a political confrontation that ultimately led to rebellion. New commercial regulations that increased the cost of foreign molasses and endangered colonial exports cut into New England's profitable trade with Spanish and French Caribbean sugar colonies. Britain also outlawed the colonial practice of issuing paper money, a custom made necessary by the colonies' chronic balance-of-payments deficits. These actions, which restricted trade and limited the money supply, provoked widespread anger. Colonial legislatures formally protested, and angry colonists organized boycotts of British goods.

The Stamp Act of 1765 imposed a tax, to be paid in scarce coin, on all legal documents, newspapers, pamphlets, and nearly all other types of printed material. Propertied colonists, including holders of high office and members of the colonial elite, took leading roles in the resulting protests. They used fiery political language, even calling Britain's rulers "parricides" and "tyrants." In 1765 representatives from the colonies met in New York City to protest, and women from many of the most prominent colonial families organized boycotts of British goods. Organizations such as the Sons of Liberty held public meetings, intimidated royal officials, and developed committees to enforce the boycotts. The combination of violent protest and trade boycott forced the repeal of the Stamp Act in 1766. But new taxes and duties were soon imposed, and parliament granted colonial governors new powers, even sending British troops to quell urban riots.

The result was a new round of boycotts, which cut colonial imports of British goods by two-thirds. Angry colonists also destroyed property and bullied or attacked royal officials. The mob practice of covering despised British functionaries with hot tar and feathers became a symbol of American lawlessness for the British public. Unable to control the streets, British authorities reacted by threatening traditional liberties, even dissolving the colonial legislature of Massachusetts.

The cycle of confrontation in Boston prompted the British government to dispatch a warship and two regiments of soldiers to reestablish control of Boston's streets. Conflicts soon occurred when off-duty British soldiers sought part-time employment, further enraging Boston's working class, which was suffering through a

The Tarring and Feathering of a British Official, 1774   This illustration from a British periodical shows the unfortunate John Malcomb, commissioner of customs at Boston. By the mid-1770s, British periodicals were focusing public opinion on mob violence and the breakdown of public order in the colonies. British critics of colonial political protests viewed the demand for liberty as little more than an excuse for mob violence.   (The Granger Collection, New York)

period of low wages and high unemployment. Support for a complete break with Britain grew after March 5, 1770, when a British force fired on an angry Boston crowd, killing five civilians. This "Boston Massacre," which seemed to expose the naked force on which colonial rule rested, radicalized public opinion throughout the colonies.

Parliament attempted to calm public opinion by repealing some of the taxes and duties, then stumbled into another crisis by granting the British East India Company a monopoly for importing tea to the colonies. This monopoly raised anew the constitutional issue of Parliament's right to tax the colonies. It also offended wealthy colonial merchants, who were excluded from this profitable commerce. The crisis came to a head in the already politically overheated port of Boston when tea worth £10,000 was dumped into the harbor by protesters disguised as Amerindians. Britain responded by appointing a military man, Thomas Gage, as governor of Massachusetts and by closing the port of Boston. Public order in Boston now depended on British troops, and public administration was in the hands of a general. This militarization of colonial government in Boston undermined Britain's constitutional authority and made a military test of strength inevitable.

The Course of Revolution, 1775–1783

As the crisis mounted, new governing bodies created by patriot leaders effectively deposed many British governors, judges, and customs officers. The new institutions of colonial government created laws, appointed justices, and even took control of colonial militias. Simultaneously, radical leaders organized crowds to intimidate loyalists—people who were pro-British—and to enforce the boycott of British goods.

By the time elected representatives met in Philadelphia as the Continental Congress in 1775, blood had already been shed when patriot militia met British troops at Lexington and Concord, Massachusetts (see Map 23.1). Events were propelling the colonies toward revolution. Congress assumed the powers of government, creating a currency and organizing an army. **George Washington** (1732–1799), a Virginia planter who had served in the French and Indian War, was named commander.

Popular support for independence was given a hard edge by the angry rhetoric of thousands of street-corner speakers and the inflammatory pamphlet *Common Sense*, written by Thomas Paine, a recent immigrant from England. Paine's pamphlet alone sold 120,000 copies. On July 4, 1776, Congress approved the Declaration of Independence, the document that proved to be the most enduring statement of the revolutionary era's ideology:

> We hold these truths to be self evident: That all men are created equal; that they are endowed by their creator with certain unalienable rights; that among these are life, liberty and the pursuit of happiness; that, to secure these rights, governments are instituted among men, deriving their just powers from the consent of the governed.

The Declaration's affirmation of popular sovereignty and individual rights influenced the language of revolution and popular protest around the world.

Hoping to shore up British authority, Great Britain sent an expeditionary force of 32,000 soldiers and an armada of more than 400 ships to pacify the colonies. By 1778, British land forces numbered 50,000 supported by 30,000 German mercenaries. But this military commitment proved futile. Despite the existence of a large loyalist community in the colonies, the British army found it difficult to control the countryside. Although British forces won most of the battles, Washington slowly built a competent Continental army and civilian support networks that provided supplies and financial resources.

The real problem for the British government was its inability to discover a compromise solution that would satisfy colonial grievances. Half-hearted efforts to resolve the bitter conflict over taxes failed, and a later offer to roll back the clock and reestablish the administrative arrangements of 1763 made little headway. Independence had been declared, and blood had been shed. Overconfidence and poor leadership prevented the British from finding a political solution before revolutionary institutions were in place and the armies engaged. By allowing confrontation to occur, the British government lost the opportunity to mobilize and give direction to the large numbers of loyalists and pacifists in the colonies.

Along the Canadian border, both sides solicited Amerindians as potential allies and feared them as potential enemies. For over a hundred years, members of the powerful Iroquois Confederacy—Mohawk, Oneida, Onondaga, Cayuga, Seneca, and (after 1722) Tuscarora—had protected their traditional lands with a combination of diplomacy and warfare, playing a role in all the colonial wars of the eighteenth century. Just as the American Revolution forced neighbors and families to join the rebels or remain loyal, it divided the Iroquois, who fought on both sides. The Mohawk proved to be the most valuable of British allies among the Iroquois.

The Mohawk loyalist leader **Joseph Brant** (Thayendanegea°) organized Britain's most potent fighting force along the Canadian border. Portrayed in the propaganda of the revolutionaries as a symbol of Amerindian savagery, Brant organized raids along the northern frontier that earned him the title "Monster" Brant. Actually, he was a man who moved easily between European and Amerindian cultures. Educated by missionaries, he was fluent in English and helped to translate Protestant religious tracts into Mohawk. He was tied to many of the wealthiest loyalist families through his sister, formerly the mistress of Sir William Johnson, Britain's superintendent of Indian affairs for North America. Brant had traveled to London and had had an audience with George III. He

---

Thayendanegea (ta YEHN dah NEY geh ah)

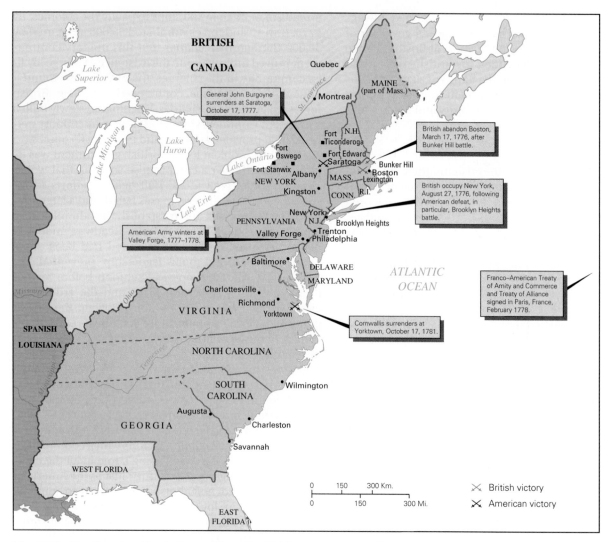

Map 23.1   The American Revolutionary War   The British army won most of the major battles, and British troops held most of the major cities. Even so, the American revolutionaries eventually won a comprehensive military and political victory.

had been embraced by London's aristocratic society and initiated into one of the most exclusive secret clubs.

The defeat in late 1777 of Britain's general John Burgoyne by General Horatio Gates at Saratoga, New York, put the future of the Mohawk at risk. This victory gave heart to patriot forces that had recently suffered a string of defeats, and it led to destructive attacks on Iroquois villages. Brant's supporters fought on to the end of the war, but patriot victories along the frontier curtailed Iroquois political and military power. Brant eventually joined the loyalist exodus to Canada and led an effort to integrate the Iroquois into the market economy of the settlers. For these Americans the revolution did not mean the protection of life and property.

The British defeat at Saratoga convinced France, in 1778, to enter the war as an ally of the United States. French military help proved crucial, supplying American forces and forcing the British to defend their colonies in the Caribbean. The French contribution was most clear in the final decisive battle, fought at Yorktown, Virginia (see Map 23.1). An American army, supported by French soldiers, besieged a British army led by General Charles Cornwallis. With escape cut off by a French fleet, Cornwallis surrendered to Washington as the British military band played "The World Turned Upside-Down."

This victory effectively ended the war. The Continental Congress sent representatives to the peace conference that followed with instructions to work in tandem with the French. Believing that France was more concerned with containing British power than with guaranteeing a strong United States, America's peace delegation negotiated directly with Britain and gained a generous settlement. The Treaty of Paris (1783) granted unconditional independence and established generous boundaries for the former colonies. The United States, in return, promised to repay prewar debts due to British merchants and to allow loyalists to recover property confiscated by patriot forces. In the end, loyalists were poorly treated and thousands of them, including Brant and other Mohawk, decided to leave for Canada.

The Construction of Republican Institutions, to 1800

Even before the Declaration of Independence, most of the colonies had created new governments. After independence, ignoring the British example of an unwritten constitution, leaders in each of the new states (as the former colonies were called) summoned constitutional conventions to draft formal charters and submitted the results to voters for ratification. Europeans were fascinated by the drafting of written constitutions and by the formal ratification of these constitutions by a vote of the people. Many of these documents were quickly translated and published in Europe. Here was the social contract of Locke and Rousseau made manifest. Remembering conflicts between royal governors and colonial legislatures, the authors of state constitutions placed severe limits on executive authority but granted legislatures greater powers than in colonial times. Many states also inserted in their constitutions a bill of rights to provide further protection against government tyranny.

An effective constitution for the new national government was developed more slowly and hesitantly. The Second Continental Congress sent the Articles of Confederation—the first constitution of the United States—to the states for approval in 1777, but it was not accepted by all the states until 1781. It created a one-house legislature in which each state was granted a single vote. A simple majority of the thirteen states was sufficient to pass minor legislation, but nine votes were necessary for declaring war, imposing taxes, and coining or borrowing money. Executive power was to be exercised by committees, not by a president. Given the intended weakness of this government, it is remarkable that it successfully organized the human and material resources to defeat Great Britain.

With the coming of peace, many of the most powerful political figures in the United States began an effort to fashion a new constitution. The Confederation government proved unable to enforce unpopular requirements of the peace treaty such as the recognition of loyalist property claims, the payment of prewar debts, and even the payment of military salaries and pensions. In September 1786 Virginia invited the other states to discuss the government's failure to deal with trade issues. This led to a call for a new convention to meet in Philadelphia nine months later. A rebellion led by Revolutionary War veterans in western Massachusetts gave the assembling delegates a sense of urgency.

The **Constitutional Convention,** which began meeting in May 1787, achieved a nonviolent second American Revolution. The delegates pushed aside the announced purpose of the convention—"to render the constitution of the federal government adequate to the exigencies of the union"—and in secret undertook to write a new constitution. George Washington was elected presiding officer. His reputation and popularity provided the solid foundation on which the delegates could contemplate an alternative political model. The real leader of the convention was James Madison of Virginia.

Debate focused on several issues: representation, electoral procedures, executive powers, and the relationship between the federal government and the states. Compromise solutions included distribution of political power among the executive, legislative, and judicial branches and the division of authority between the federal government and the states. The final compromise provided for a two-house legislature: the lower house (the House of Representatives) to be elected directly by voters and the upper house (the Senate) to be elected by state legislatures. The chief executive—the president—was to be elected indirectly by "electors" selected by ballot in the states (each state had a number of electors equal to the number of its representatives and senators).

Although the U.S. Constitution created the most democratic government of the era, only a minority of the adult population was given full rights. In some northern states where large numbers of free blacks had fought with patriot forces, there was hostility to the continuation of slavery, but southern leaders were able to protect it. Slaves were denied any participation in the political process. Slave states, however, were permitted to count three-fifths of the slave population in the calculations that determined number of congressional representatives, thus multiplying the political power of the slave-owning class in the national government. Southern delegates also gained a twenty-year continuation of the slave trade to 1808 and a fugitive slave clause that required all states to return runaway slaves to their masters.

Women were powerfully affected by their participation in revolutionary politics and by the changes in the economy brought on by the break with Britain. Women had led prewar boycotts and during the war had organized relief and charitable organizations. Nevertheless, they were denied political rights in the new republic. New Jersey briefly stood as an exception. Without specifically excluding women, the framers of that state's constitution had granted the right to vote to free residents who met modest property-holding requirements. As a result, women and African-Americans who met property requirements were able to vote in New Jersey until 1807, when lawmakers eliminated this right.

THE FRENCH REVOLUTION, 1789–1815

The French Revolution undermined traditional monarchy as well as the power of the Catholic Church and the hereditary aristocracy but, unlike the American Revolution, did not create an enduring form of representative democracy. The colonial revolution in North America, however, did not confront so directly the entrenched privileges of an established church, monarchy, and aristocracy, and the American Revolution produced no symbolic drama comparable to the public beheading of the French king Louis XVI in early 1793. Among its achievements, the French Revolution expanded mass participation in political life and radicalized the democratic tradition inherited from the English and American experiences. But in the end, the passions unleashed in France by revolutionary events could not be sustained, and popular demagogues and the dictatorship of Napoleon stalled democratic reform.

French Society and Fiscal Crisis

French society was divided into three groups. The clergy, called the First Estate, numbered about 130,000 in a nation of 28 million. The Catholic Church owned about 10 percent of the nation's land and extracted substantial amounts of wealth from the economy in the form of tithes and ecclesiastical fees. Despite its substantial wealth, the church was exempted from nearly all taxes. The clergy was organized hierarchically, and members of the hereditary nobility held almost all the upper positions in the church.

The 300,000 members of the nobility, the Second Estate, controlled about 30 percent of the land and re-

tained ancient rights on much of the rest. Nobles held the vast majority of high administrative, judicial, military, and church positions. Though traditionally barred from some types of commercial activity, nobles were important participants in wholesale trade, banking, manufacturing, and mining. Like the clergy, this estate was hierarchical: important differences in wealth, power, and outlook separated the higher from the lower nobility. The nobility was also a highly permeable class: the Second Estate in the eighteenth century saw an enormous infusion of wealthy commoners who purchased administrative and judicial offices that conferred noble status.

The Third Estate included everyone else, from wealthy financier to homeless beggar. The bourgeoisie°, or middle class, grew rapidly in the eighteenth century. There were three times as many members of this class in 1774, when Louis XVI took the throne, as there had been in 1715, at the end of Louis XIV's reign. Commerce, finance, and manufacturing accounted for much of the wealth of the Third Estate. Wealthy commoners also owned nearly a third of the nation's land. This literate and socially ambitious class supported an expanding publishing industry, subsidized the fine arts, and purchased many of the extravagant new homes being built in Paris and other cities.

Peasants accounted for 80 percent of the French population. Artisans and other skilled workers, small shopkeepers and peddlers, and small landowners held a more privileged position in society. They owned some property and lived decently when crops were good and prices stable. By 1780 poor harvests had increased their cost of living and led to a decline in consumer demand for their products. They were rich enough to fear the loss of their property and status, well educated enough to be aware of the growing criticism of the king, but too poor and marginalized to influence policy.

The nation's poor were a large, growing, and troublesome sector. The poverty and vulnerability of peasant families forced younger children to seek seasonal work away from home and led many to crime and beggary. That raids by roving vagabonds threatened isolated farms was one measure of this social dislocation. In Paris and other French cities, the vile living conditions and unhealthy diet of the working poor were startling to visitors from other European nations. Urban streets swarmed with beggars and prostitutes. Paris alone had 25,000 prostitutes in 1760. The wretchedness of the French poor is perhaps best indicated by the growing

bourgeoisie (boor-zwah-ZEE)

problem of child abandonment. On the eve of the French Revolution at least forty thousand children a year were given up by their parents. The convenient fiction was that these children would be adopted; in reality the majority died of neglect.

Unable to afford decent housing, obtain steady employment, or protect their children, the poor periodically erupted in violent protest and rage. In the countryside violence was often the reaction when the nobility or clergy increased dues and fees. In towns and cities an increase in the price of bread often provided the spark, for bread prices largely determined the quality of life of the poor. These explosive episodes, however, were not revolutionary in character. The remedies sought were conventional and immediate rather than structural and long-term. That was to change when the Crown tried to solve its fiscal crisis.

The expenses of the War of the Austrian Succession began the crisis. Louis XV (r. 1715–1774) first tried to impose new taxes on the nobility and on other groups that in the past had enjoyed exemptions. But this effort failed in the face of widespread protest and the refusal of the Parlement of Paris, a court of appeal that heard appeals from local courts throughout France, to register the new tax. The crisis deepened when debts from the Seven Years War compelled the king to impose emergency fiscal measures. Again, the king met resistance from the Parlement of Paris. In 1768 frustrated authorities exiled the members of that Parlement and pushed through a series of unpopular fiscal measures. When the twenty-two-year-old Louis XVI assumed the throne in 1774, he attempted to gain popular support by recalling the exiled members of the Parlement of Paris, but he soon learned that provincial parlements had also come to see themselves as having a constitutional power to check any growth in monarchial authority.

In 1774 Louis's chief financial adviser warned that the government could barely afford to operate; as he put it, "the first gunshot [act of war] will drive the state to bankruptcy." Despite this warning, the French took on the heavy burden of supporting the American Revolution, delaying collapse by borrowing enormous sums and disguising the growing debt in misleading fiscal accounts. By the end of the war with Britain, more than half of France's national budget was required to service the debt alone. It soon became clear that fiscal reforms and new taxes, not new loans, were necessary.

In 1787 the desperate king called an Assembly of Notables to approve a radical and comprehensive reform of the economy and fiscal policy. Despite the fact that the members of this assembly were selected by the king's advisers from the high nobility, the judiciary, and the

clergy, it proved unwilling to act as a rubber stamp for the proposed reforms or new taxes. Instead, these representatives of France's most privileged classes sought to protect their interests by questioning the competence of the king and his ministers to supervise the nation's affairs.

Protest Turns to Revolution, 1789–1792

In frustration, the king dismissed the Notables and attempted to implement some reforms on his own, but his effort was met by an increasingly hostile judiciary and by popular demonstrations. Because the king was unable to extract needed tax concessions from the French elite, he was forced to call the **Estates General,** the French national legislature, which had not met since 1614. The narrow self-interest and greed of the rich—who would not tolerate an increase in their taxes—rather than the grinding poverty of the common people, had created the conditions for political revolution.

In late 1788 and early 1789 members of the three estates came together throughout the nation to discuss grievances and elect representatives who would meet at Versailles°. The Third Estate's representatives were mostly men of property, but there was anger directed against the king's ministers and an inclination to move France toward constitutional monarchy with an elected legislature. Many nobles and members of the clergy sympathized with the reform agenda of the Third Estate, but deep internal divisions over procedural and policy issues limited the power of the First and the Second Estates.

Traditionally the three estates met separately, and a positive vote by two of the three was required for action. Tradition, however, was quickly overturned when the Third Estate refused to conduct business until the king ordered the other two estates to sit with it in a single body. During a six-week period of stalemate many parish priests from the First Estate began to meet with the commoners. When this expanded Third Estate declared itself the **National Assembly,** the king and his advisers recognized that the reformers intended to force them to accept a constitutional monarchy.

After being locked out of their meeting place, the Third Estate appropriated an indoor tennis court and pledged to write a constitution. The Oath of the Tennis Court ended Louis's vain hope that he could limit the agenda to fiscal reform. The king's effort to solve the

---

Versailles (vuhr-SIGH)

nation's fiscal crisis was being connected in unpredictable ways to the central ideas of the era: the people were sovereign, and the legitimacy of political institutions and individual rulers ultimately depended on their carrying out the people's will. Louis prepared for a confrontation with the National Assembly by moving military forces to Versailles. But before he could act, the people of Paris intervened.

A succession of bad harvests beginning in 1785 had propelled bread prices upward throughout France and provoked an economic depression as demand for nonessential goods collapsed. By the time the Estates General met, nearly a third of the Parisian work force was unemployed. Hunger and anger marched hand in hand through working-class neighborhoods.

When the people of Paris heard that the king was massing troops in Versailles to arrest the representatives, crowds of common people began to seize arms and mobilize. On July 14, 1789, a crowd searching for military supplies attacked the Bastille°, a medieval fortress used as a prison. The futile defense of the Bastille cost ninety-eight lives before its garrison surrendered. Enraged, the attackers hacked the commander to death and then paraded through the city with his head and that of Paris's chief magistrate stuck on pikes.

These events coincided with uprisings by peasants in the country. Peasants sacked manor houses and destroyed documents that recorded their traditional obligations. They refused to pay taxes and dues to landowners and seized common lands. Forced to recognize the fury raging through rural areas, the National Assembly voted to end traditional obligations and to reform the tax system. Having forced acceptance of their narrow agenda, the peasants ceased their revolt.

These popular uprisings strengthened the hand of the National Assembly in its dealings with the king. One manifestation of this altered relationship was passage of the **Declaration of the Rights of Man.** There were clear similarities between the language of this declaration and the U.S. Declaration of Independence. Indeed, Thomas Jefferson, who had written the American document, was U.S. ambassador to Paris and offered his opinion to those involved in the drafting of the French statement. The French declaration, however, was more sweeping in its language than the American one. Among the enumerated natural rights were "liberty, property, security, and resistance to oppression." The Declaration of the Rights of Man also guaranteed free expression of ideas, equality before the law, and representative government.

Bastille (bass-TEEL)

Parisian Stocking Mender The poor lived very difficult lives. This woman uses a discarded wine barrel as a shop where she mends socks. (Private collection)

While delegates debated political issues in Versailles, the economic crisis worsened in Paris. Women employed in the garment industry and in small-scale retail businesses were particularly hard hit. Because the working women of Paris faced high food prices every day as they struggled to feed their families, their anger had a hard edge. Public markets became political arenas where the urban poor met daily in angry assembly. Here the revolutionary link between the material deprivation of the French poor and the political aspirations of the French bourgeoisie was forged.

On October 5, market women organized a crowd of thousands to march the 12 miles (19 kilometers) to Versailles (see Society and Culture: The March to Versailles on page 588). Once there, they forced their way into the National Assembly to demand action from the frightened representatives: "the point is that we want bread."

Parisian Women Marching on Versailles   When the market women of Paris marched to Versailles and forced the royal family to return to Paris with them, they altered the course of the French Revolution. In this drawing the women are armed with pikes and swords and drag a cannon. Only the woman on the far left is clearly middle class, and she is pictured hesitating or turning away from the resolute actions of the poor women around her.   (Bibliothèque nationale de France)

The crowd then entered the royal apartments, killed some of the king's guards, and searched for Queen Marie Antoinette°, whom they loathed as a symbol of extravagance. Eventually, the crowd demanded that the royal family return to Paris. Preceded by the heads of two aristocrats carried on pikes and hauling away the palace's supply of flour, the triumphant crowd escorted the royal family to Paris.

With the king's ability to resist democratic change overcome by the Paris crowd, the National Assembly achieved a radically restructured French society in the next two years. It passed a new constitution that dramatically limited monarchial power and abolished the nobility as a hereditary class. Economic reforms swept away monopolies and trade barriers within France. The Legislative Assembly (the new constitution's name for the National Assembly) seized church lands to use as collateral for a new paper currency, and priests—who were to be elected—were put on the state payroll. When the government tried to force priests to take a loyalty

Antoinette (ann twah-NET)

oath, however, many Catholics joined a growing counterrevolutionary movement.

At first, many European monarchs had welcomed the weakening of the French king, but by 1791 Austria and Prussia threatened to intervene in support of the monarchy. The Legislative Assembly responded by declaring war. Although the war went badly at first for French forces, people across France responded patriotically to foreign invasions, forming huge new volunteer armies and mobilizing national resources to meet the challenge. By the end of 1792 French armies had gained the upper hand everywhere.

The Terror, 1793–1794

In this period of national crisis and foreign threat, the French Revolution entered its most radical phase. A failed effort by the king and queen to escape from Paris and find foreign allies cost the king any remaining popular support. As foreign armies crossed into France, his behavior was increasingly viewed as treasonous. On August 10, 1792, a crowd similar to the one that had marched on Versailles

The March to Versailles

Marie-Rose Barré, a 20-year old lace worker, participated in one of the most dramatic events of the French Revolution, the march of Parisian market women to Versailles in October 1789. The initial object of the march was to protest the high cost of bread. Once in Versailles, the crowd forced King Louis XVI and his family to return to Paris. In her testimony given shortly afterward to the Paris municipal council, Barré avoided any suggestion that she had been a leader of the march or that she had threatened the royal family.

. . . on October 5 last, at about eight o'clock in the morning, going to take back some work, she was stopped at the Pônt Notre Dame by about a hundred women who told her that it was necessary to go with them to Versailles to ask for bread there. Not being able to resist this great number of women, she decided to go with them. At the hamlet at the Point-du-Jour, two young men, unknown to her, who were on foot and going their way, told them that they were running a great risk, that there were cannon mounted at the bridge at Saint-Cloud. This did not prevent them from continuing on their way. . . . At Versailles they found the King's Guards lined up in three ranks before the palace. A gentleman dressed in the uniform of the King's Guard . . . came to ask them what they wanted of the King, recommending peaceful behavior on their part. They answered that they were coming to ask him for bread. This gen-

tleman was absent for a few minutes and then returned to take four of them to introduce them to the King. The deponent was one of the four. . . .

They spoke first to M. de Saint-Priest, and then to His Majesty, whom they asked for bread. His Majesty answered them that he was suffering at least as much as they were, to see them lacking it, and that so far as he was able he had taken care to prevent them from experiencing a dearth. . . . The King promised them to have the flour escorted and said that if it depended on him, they would have bread then and there. They took leave of His Majesty and were led, by a gentleman in a blue uniform with red piping, into the apartments and courts of the palace to the ranks of the Flanders regiment, to which they called out. "Vive Le Roi!" It was then about nine o'clock. After this, they retired into a house on Rue Satory and went to bed in a stable.

Is it likely that someone pressured to join this march would have been selected to meet with the king to present the protestors' grievances? Does the king's concern for the plight of the poor ring true?

Source: Philip Dawson, ed., *The French Revolution* (Englewood Cliffs, N.J.: Prentice-Hall, Inc., 1967), pp. 66-67. Reprinted with permission of Simon & Schuster. Copyright © 1967 by Prentice-Hall, Inc., renewed 1995 by Philip Dawson.

---

invaded his palace in Paris and forced the king to seek protection in the Legislative Assembly. The Assembly suspended the king, ordered his imprisonment, and called for the formation of a new National Convention to be elected by the vote of all men.

Rumors of counterrevolutionary plots kept working-class neighborhoods in an uproar. In September mobs surged through the city's prisons, killing nearly half of the prisoners. Swept along by popular passion, the newly elected National Convention convicted Louis XVI of treason, sentencing him to death and proclaiming France a republic. The guillotine ended the king's life in January 1793. Invented in the spirit of the era as a more humane way to execute the condemned, this machine was to become the bloody symbol of the revolution.

The National Convention—the new legislature of the new First Republic of France—convened in September. Almost all of its members were from the middle class, and nearly all were **Jacobins**°—the most uncompromising democrats. Deep political differences, however, separated moderate Jacobins—called "Girondists°," after a region in southern France—and radicals known as "the Mountain." Members of the Mountain—so named because their seats were on the highest level in the assembly hall—were more sympathetic than the Girondists to the demands of the Parisian working class and more impatient with parliamentary procedure and constitutional constraints on government action. The Mountain

---

Jacobin (JAK-uh-bin)   **Girondist** (juh-RON-dist)

Playing Cards from the French Revolution Even playing cards could be used to attack the aristocracy and Catholic Church. In this pack of cards, "Equality" and "Liberty" replaced kings and queens. (Jean-Loup Charmet)

came to be dominated by **Maximilien Robespierre°**, a young, little-known lawyer from the provinces who had been influenced by Rousseau's ideas.

With the French economy still in crisis and Paris suffering from inflation, high unemployment, and scarcity, Robespierre used the popular press and political clubs to forge an alliance with the volatile Parisian working class. His growing strength in the streets allowed him to purge the National Convention of his enemies and to restructure the government. Executive power was placed in the hands of the newly formed Committee of Public Safety, which created special courts to seek out and punish domestic enemies.

Among the groups that lost ground were the active feminists of the Parisian middle class and the working-class women who had sought the right to bear arms in defense of the Revolution. These women had provided decisive leadership at crucial times, helping propel the Revolution toward a widened suffrage and a more democratic structure. Armed women had actively participated in every confrontation with conservative forces. It is ironic that the National Convention—the revolutionary era's most radical legislative body, one elected by universal male suffrage—chose to repress the militant feminist forces that had prepared the ground for its creation.

Faced with rebellion in the provinces and foreign invasion, Robespierre and his allies unleashed a period of repression called the Reign of Terror (1793–1794). During the Terror, approximately 40,000 people were executed or died in prison, and another 300,000 were thrown into prison. New actions against the clergy were also approved, including the provocative measure of

Robespierre (ROBES-pee-air)

forcing priests to marry. Even time was subject to revolutionary change. A new republican calendar created twelve thirty-day months divided into ten-day weeks. Sunday, with its Christian meanings, disappeared from the calendar.

By the spring of 1794 the Revolution was secure from foreign and domestic enemies, but repression, now institutionalized, continued. Among the victims were some who had been Robespierre's closest political collaborators during the early stage of the Terror. The execution of these former allies prepared the way for Robespierre's own fall by undermining the sense of invulnerability that had secured the loyalty of his remaining partisans in the National Convention. After French victories eliminated the immediate foreign threat, conservatives in the Convention felt secure enough to vote for the arrest of Robespierre on July 27, 1794. Over the next two days, Robespierre and nearly a hundred of his remaining allies were executed by guillotine.

Reaction and Dictatorship, 1795–1815

Purged of Robespierre's collaborators, the Convention began to undo the radical reforms. It removed many of the emergency economic controls that had been holding down prices and protecting the working class. Gone also was toleration for violent popular demonstrations. When the Paris working class rose in protest in 1795, the Convention approved the use of overwhelming military force. Another retreat from radical objectives was signaled when the Catholic Church was permitted to regain much of its former influence. The church's confiscated wealth, however, was not returned.

Map 23.2   Napoleon's Europe, 1810   By 1810, Great Britain was the only remaining European power at war with Napoleon. Because of the loss of the French fleet at the Battle of Trafalgar in 1805, Napoleon was unable to threaten Britain with invasion, and Britain was able to actively assist the resistance movements in Spain and Portugal, thereby helping to weaken French power.

A more conservative constitution was also ratified. It protected property, established a voting process that reduced the power of the masses, and created a new executive authority, the Directory. Once installed in power, however, the Directory proved unable to end the foreign wars or solve domestic economic problems.

After losing the election of 1797, the Directory suspended the results. The republican phase of the Revolution was clearly dead. Legitimacy was now based on coercive power rather than on elections. Two years later, **Napoleon Bonaparte** (1769–1821), a brilliant young general in the French army, seized power. Just as the American and French Revolutions had been the start of the modern democratic tradition, the military intervention that brought Napoleon to power in 1799 marked the advent of another modern form of government: popular authoritarianism.

The American and French Revolutions had resulted in part from conflicts over representation. If the people were sovereign, what institutions best expressed popular will? In the United States, the answer was to expand the electorate and institute representative government. The French Revolution had taken a different direction with the Reign of Terror. Interventions on the floor of the National Convention by market women and soldiers, the presence of common people at revolutionary tribunals and at public executions, and expanded military service were all forms of political communication that satisfied, temporarily, the French people's desire to influence their government. Napoleon tamed these forms of political expression to organize Europe's first popular dictatorship. He succeeded because his military reputation promised order to a society exhausted by a decade of crisis, turmoil, and bloodshed.

In contrast to the National Convention, Napoleon proved capable of realizing France's dream of dominating Europe and providing effective protection for persons and property at home. Negotiations with the Catholic Church led to the Concordat of 1801. This agreement gave French Catholics the right to freely practice their religion, and it recognized the French government's authority to nominate bishops and retain priests on the state payroll. In his comprehensive rewriting of French law, the Civil Code of 1804, Napoleon won the support of the peasantry and of the middle class by asserting two basic principles inherited from the moderate first stage of the French Revolution: equality in law and protection of property. Even some members of the nobility became supporters after Napoleon declared himself emperor and France an empire in 1804. However, the discrimination against women that had begun during the Terror was extended by the Napoleonic Civil Code. Women were denied basic political rights and were able to participate in the economy only with the guidance and supervision of their fathers and husbands.

While providing personal security, the Napoleonic system denied or restricted many individual rights. Free speech and free expression were limited. Criticism of the government, viewed as subversive, was proscribed, and most opposition newspapers disappeared. Spies and informers directed by the minister of police enforced these limits to political freedom. Thousands of the regime's enemies and critics were questioned or detained in the name of domestic tranquillity.

Ultimately, the Napoleonic system depended on the success of French arms and French diplomacy (see Map 23.2). From Napoleon's assumption of power until his fall, no single European state could defeat the French military. Even powerful alliances like that of Austria and Prussia were brushed aside with humiliating defeats and forced to become allies of France. Only Britain, protected by its powerful navy, remained able to thwart Napoleon's plans to dominate Europe. His effort to mobilize forces for an invasion of Britain failed in late 1805 when the British navy defeated the French and allied Spanish fleets off the coast of Spain at the Battle of Trafalgar.

Desiring to extend French power again to the Americas, Napoleon invaded Portugal in 1807 and Spain in 1808. French armies soon became tied down in a costly conflict with Spanish and Portuguese patriots who had forged an alliance with the only available European power, Great Britain. Frustrated by events on the Iberian Peninsula and faced with a faltering economy, Napoleon made the fateful decision to invade Russia. In June 1812 Napoleon began his campaign with the largest army ever assembled in Europe, approximately 600,000 men. After fighting an inconclusive battle at Borodino, Napoleon pressed on to Moscow. Five weeks after occupying Moscow, he was forced to retreat by Russian patriots who set the city on fire and by approaching armies. He ordered a retreat, but the brutal Russian winter and attacks by Russian forces destroyed his army. A broken and battered fragment of 30,000 men returned home to France.

After the debacle in Russia, Austria and Prussia deserted Napoleon and entered an alliance with England and Russia. Unable to defend Paris, Napoleon was forced to abdicate the French throne in April 1814. The allies exiled Napoleon to the island of Elba off the coast of Italy and restored the French monarchy. The next year Napoleon escaped from Elba and returned to France. But his moment had passed. He was defeated by an allied army at Waterloo, in Belgium, after only one hundred days in power. His final exile was on the distant island of St. Helena in the South Atlantic, where he died in 1821.

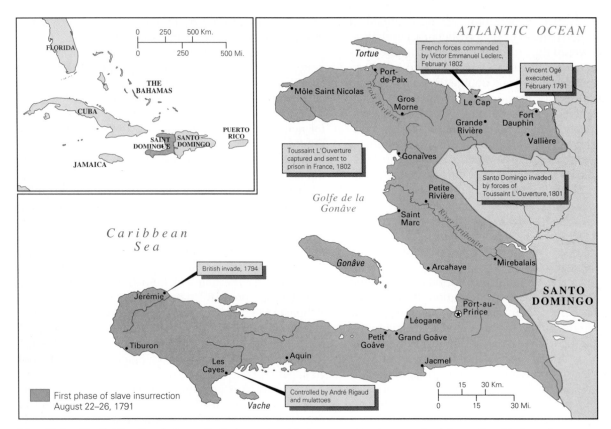

Map 23.3 **The Haitian Revolution** On their way to achieving an end to slavery and gaining national independence, the Haitian revolutionaries were forced to defeat British and French military interventions as well as the local authority of the slave masters.

REVOLUTION SPREADS, CONSERVATIVES RESPOND, 1789–1850

Even as the dictatorship of Napoleon eliminated the democratic legacy of the French Revolution, revolutionary ideology was spreading and taking hold in Europe and the Americas. In Europe, the French Revolution promoted nationalism and republicanism. In the Americas, the legacies of the American and French Revolutions led to a new round of struggles for independence. News of revolutionary events in France destabilized the colonial regime in Saint Domingue (present-day Haiti), a small French colony on the western half of the island of Hispaniola, and resulted in the first successful slave rebellion. In Europe, however, the spread of revolutionary fervor was checked by reaction as monarchs formed an alliance to protect themselves from further revolutionary outbreaks.

The Haitian Revolution, 1789–1804

In 1789 the French colony of Saint Domingue was among the richest European colonies in the Americas. Its plantations produced sugar, cotton, indigo, and coffee. The colony produced two-thirds of France's tropical imports and generated nearly one-third of all French foreign trade. This impressive wealth depended on a brutal slave regime. Saint Domingue's harsh punishments and poor living conditions were notorious throughout the Caribbean. The colony's high mortality and low fertility rates created an insatiable demand for African slaves. As a result the majority of the colony's 500,000 slaves in 1790 were African-born.

In 1789, when news of the calling of France's Estates General arrived on the island, wealthy white planters sent a delegation to Paris charged with seeking more home rule and greater economic freedom for Saint Domingue. The free mixed-race population, the ***gens de couleur°,*** also sent representatives. These delegates were mostly drawn from the large class of slave-owning small planters and urban merchants. They focused on gaining the end to race discrimination and the achievement of political equality with whites. They did not seek freedom for slaves, because the most prosperous gens de couleur were slave owners themselves. As the French Revolution became more radical, the gens de couleur forged an alliance with sympathetic French radicals, who came to identify the colony's wealthy planters as royalists and aristocrats.

The political turmoil in France weakened the ability of colonial administrators to maintain order. The authority of colonial officials was no longer clear, and the very legitimacy of slavery was being challenged in France. In the vacuum that resulted, rich planters, poor whites, and the gens de couleur each pursued their narrow interests, engendering an increasingly bitter and confrontational struggle. Given the slaves' hatred of the brutal regime that oppressed them and the accumulated grievances of the free people of color, there was no way to limit the violence once the control of the slave owners slipped. When Vincent Ogé°, leader of the gens de couleur mission to France, returned to Saint Domingue to organize a military force, planter forces captured, tortured, and executed him. This cruelty was soon repaid in kind.

By 1791 whites, led by the planter elite, and the gens de couleur were engaged in open warfare. This breach between the two groups of slave owners gave the slaves an opening. A slave rebellion began on the plantations of the north and spread throughout the colony (see Map 23.3). Plantations were destroyed, masters and overseers killed, and crops burned. An emerging rebel leadership that combined elements of African political culture with revolutionary ideology from France mobilized and directed the rebelling slaves.

The rebellious slaves eventually gained the upper hand under the leadership of **François Dominique Toussaint L'Ouverture,** a former domestic slave, who created a more disciplined military force. Toussaint was politically strengthened in 1794 when the radical National Convention in Paris abolished slavery in all French possessions. He overcame his rivals in Saint Domingue, defeated a British expeditionary force in 1798, and then

gens de couleur (zhahn deh koo-LUHR)   Ogé (oh-ZHAY)

Toussaint L'Ouverture Negotiating with the British   The former slave Toussaint L'Ouverture led the successful slave rebellion in Saint Domingue (Haiti). He then defended the revolution against British and French military intervention. Notice that in this print Toussaint seems to command the scene, directing the attention of the British officers to the document that he holds in his hand. (Bibliothèque nationale de France)

led an invasion of neighboring Santo Domingo, freeing the slaves there. Toussaint continued to assert his loyalty to France but gave the French government no effective role in local affairs.

As reaction overtook revolution in France, both the abolition of slavery and Toussaint's political position were threatened. When the Directory contemplated the reestablishment of slavery, Toussaint protested,

> Do they think that men who have been able to enjoy the blessing of liberty will calmly see it snatched away? They supported their chains only so long as they did not know any condition of life more happy than slavery. But today when they have left it, if they had a thousand lives they would sacrifice them all rather than be forced into slavery again.[1]

In 1802 Napoleon sent a large military force to Saint Domingue to reestablish both French authority and slavery (see Map 24.3). At first the French forces were successful. Toussaint was captured and sent to France, where he died in prison. Eventually, however, the loss of thousands of lives to yellow fever and the resistance of the revolutionaries turned the tide. Visible in the resistance to the French were small numbers of armed women. During the early stages of the Haitian Revolution very few slave women had taken up arms, although many had aided Toussaint's forces in support roles. But after a decade of struggle and violence, more Haitian women were politically aware and willing to join the armed resistance. In 1804 Toussaint's successors declared independence, and the free republic of Haiti joined the United States as the second independent nation in the Western Hemisphere. But independence and emancipation were achieved at a terrible price. Tens of thousands had died, the economy was destroyed, and public administration was corrupted by more than a decade of violence. Political violence and economic stagnation were to trouble Haiti throughout the nineteenth century.

The Congress of Vienna and Conservative Retrenchment, 1815–1820

From 1814 to 1815 representatives of Britain, Russia, Austria, and Prussia met as the **Congress of Vienna** to reestablish political order in Europe. While they were meeting, Napoleon escaped from Elba, then was defeated at Waterloo. The French Revolution and Napoleon's imperial ambitions had threatened the very survival of the European old order. Ancient monarchies had been overturned and dynasties replaced with interlopers. Long-established political institutions had been tossed aside, and long-recognized international borders had been ignored. The very existence of the nobility and church had been put at risk. Under the leadership of the Austrian foreign minister, Prince Klemens von Metternich° (1773–1859), the allies worked together in Vienna to create a comprehensive peace settlement that they hoped would safeguard the conservative order.

The central objective of the Congress of Vienna was to roll back the clock in France. Because the participants believed that a strong and stable France was the best guarantee of future peace, the French monarchy was reestablished and France's 1792 borders were recognized. Most of the continental European powers received some territorial gains, for Metternich sought to offset French strength with a balance of power. In addi-

tion, Austria, Russia, and Prussia formed a separate alliance to confront more actively the revolutionary and nationalist energies that the French Revolution had unleashed. In 1820 this "Holy Alliance" acted decisively to defeat liberal revolutions in Spain and Italy. By repressing republican and nationalist ideas in universities and the press, the Holy Alliance also attempted to meet the potential challenge posed by subversive ideas. Metternich's program of conservative retrenchment succeeded in the short term, but powerful ideas associated with liberalism and nationalism remained a vital part of European political life throughout the nineteenth century.

Nationalism, Reform, and Revolution, 1821–1850

Despite the power of the conservative monarchs, popular support for national self-determination and democratic reform grew throughout Europe. Greece had been under Ottoman control since the fifteenth century. In 1821, Greek patriots launched an independence movement. Metternich and other conservatives opposed Greek independence, but European artists and writers enamored with the cultural legacy of ancient Greece rallied political support for intervention. After years of struggle, Russia, France, and Great Britain forced the Ottoman Empire to recognize Greek independence in 1830.

Louis XVIII, brother of the executed Louis XVI, had been placed on the throne of France by the victorious allies in 1814. He ruled as a constitutional monarch until his death in 1824 and was followed to the throne by his brother, Charles X. Charles attempted to rule in the pre-revolutionary style of his ancestors, repudiating the constitution in 1830. Unwilling to accept this reactionary challenge, the people of Paris rose up and forced Charles to abdicate. His successor was his cousin Louis Philippe° (r. 1830–1848), who accepted the reestablished constitution and extended voting privileges.

At the same time, in both the United States and Great Britain, democratic reform movements appeared. In the United States after 1790, new states with constitutions granting voting rights to most free males joined the original thirteen states. After the War of 1812, the right to vote was expanded in the older states as well. This broadening of the franchise led in 1828 to the election of the populist president Andrew Jackson (see Chapter 25).

However, revolutionary violence in France made the British aristocracy and the conservative Tory Party fearful of expanded democracy and mass movements of any kind. In 1815 the British government passed the Corn

---

Metternich (MET-uhr-nik)

Louis Philippe (loo-EE-fee-LEEP)

The Revolution of 1830 in Belgium   After the 1830 uprising that overturned the restored monarchy in France, Belgians rose up to declare their independence from Holland. In Poland and Italy, similar uprisings, combining nationalism and a desire for self-governance, failed. This painting by Baron Gustaf Wappers romantically illustrates the popular nature of the Belgian uprising by bringing to the barricades men, women, and children drawn from both the middle and the working classes.   (Musées royaux des Beaux-Arts de Belgique, Brussels)

Laws, which limited the importation of foreign grains. This law favored the profits of wealthy landowners that produced grain at the expense of the poor who were forced to pay more for their bread. When poor consumers organized to overturn these laws, the government outlawed most public meetings, using troops to crush protest in Manchester. Reacting against these policies, reformers gained the passage of laws that increased the power of the House of Commons, redistributed votes from agricultural to industrial districts, and increased the number of voters by nearly 50 percent. Although the most radical demands of these reformers, called Chartists, were defeated, new labor and economic reforms addressing the grievances of workers were passed (see Chapter 24).

Despite the achievement of Greek independence and limited political reform in France and Great Britain, conservatives continued to hold the upper hand in Europe. Finally, in 1848, the desire for democratic reform and national self-determination and the frustrations of urban workers led to upheavals across Europe. The **Revolutions of 1848** began in Paris, where members of the middle class and workers united to overthrow the regime of Louis Philippe and create the Second French Republic. Adult men were given voting rights, slavery was abolished in French colonies, the death penalty was ended, and a ten-hour workday was legislated for Paris. But Parisian workers' demand for programs to reduce unemployment and lower prices provoked conflicts with the middle class, which wanted to protect property rights. When workers rose up against the government, French troops were called out to crush them. Desiring the reestablishment of order, the French elected Louis Napoleon, nephew of the former emperor, president in December 1848. Three years later, he overturned the constitution as a result of popular plebiscite and, after ruling briefly as dictator, became Emperor Napoleon III. He remained in power until 1871.

Reformers in Hungary, Italy, Bohemia, and elsewhere pressed for greater national self-determination in 1848. When the Austrian monarchy hesitated to meet such demands, students and workers in Vienna took to the streets to force political reforms similar to those sought in Paris. With revolution spreading throughout the Austrian Empire, Metternich, the symbol of reaction, fled Vienna in disguise. Little lasting change occurred, however, because the new Austrian emperor, Franz Joseph (r. 1848–1916) was able to use Russian military assistance and loyal Austrian troops to reestablish central authority.

Middle-class reformers and workers in Berlin joined forces in an attempt to compel the Prussian king to accept a liberal constitution and seek unification of the German states. But the Constituent Assembly called to write a constitution and arrange for national integration became entangled in diplomatic conflicts with Austria and Denmark. As a result, Frederick William IV (r. 1840–1861) was able to reassert his authority, thwarting both constitutional reform and unification.

Despite their heroism on the barricades of Paris, Vienna, Rome, and Berlin, the revolutionaries of 1848 failed to gain either their nationalist or their republican objectives. Monarchs retained the support not only of aristocrats but also of professional militaries, largely recruited from among peasants who had little sympathy for urban workers. Revolutionary coalitions, in contrast, were fragile and lacked clear objectives. Workers' demands for higher wages, lower prices, and labor reform often drove their middle-class allies into the arms of the reactionaries.

part in the American Revolution helped ignite the French Revolution. Black freemen from Haiti traveled to France to seek their rights and returned to spread revolutionary passions. Each revolution had its own character. The revolutions in France and Haiti proved to be more violent and destructive than the American Revolution. Revolutionaries in France and Haiti, facing a more strongly entrenched and more powerful opposition and greater social inequalities, responded with greater violence.

The conservative retrenchment that followed the defeat of Napoleon succeeded in the short term. Monarchy, multinational empires, and the established church retained their hold on the loyalty of millions of Europeans and could count on the support of many of Europe's wealthiest and most powerful individuals. But liberalism and nationalism continued to stir revolutionary sentiment. The contest between adherents of the old order and partisans of change was to continue well into the nineteenth century. In the end, the nation-state, the Enlightenment legacy of rational inquiry, broadened political participation, and secular intellectual culture were to prevail. This outcome was determined in large measure by the old order's inability to satisfy the new social classes that appeared with the emerging industrial economy. The material transformation produced by industrial capitalism could not be contained in the narrow confines of a hereditary social system, nor could the rapid expansion of scientific learning be contained within the doctrines of traditional religion.

The revolutions of the late eighteenth century began the transformation of Western society, but they did not complete it. Only a minority gained full political rights. Women achieved full political rights only in the twentieth century. Democratic institutions, as in revolutionary France, often failed. Moreover, as Chapter 25 will discuss, slavery endured in the Americas past the mid-1800s, despite the revolutionary era's enthusiasm for individual liberty.

CONCLUSION

This era of revolution was, in large measure, the product of a long period of costly warfare among the imperial nations of Europe. Using taxes and institutions inherited from the past, England and France found it increasingly difficult to fund distant wars in the Americas or in Asia. Royal governments attempting to impose new taxes met with angry resistance. The spread of literacy and the greater availability of books helped create a European culture more open to reform or revolutionary change of existing institutions. The ideas of Locke and Rousseau guided critics of monarchy toward a new political culture of elections and representative institutions. Each new development served as example and provocation for new revolutionary acts. French officers who took

■ Key Terms

Enlightenment	Jacobins
Benjamin Franklin	Maximilien Robespierre
George Washington	Napoleon Bonaparte
Joseph Brant	*gens de couleur*
Constitutional Convention	François Dominique
Estates General	Toussaint L'Ouverture
National Assembly	Congress of Vienna
Declaration of the Rights of Man	Revolutions of 1848

Suggested Reading

The American Revolution has received a great amount of attention from scholars. Colin Bonwick, *The American Revolution* (1991), and Edward Countryman, *The American Revolution* (1985), provide excellent introductions. Edmund S. Morgan, *The Challenge of the American Revolution* (1976), remains a major work of interpretation. Gordon S. Wood, *The Radicalism of the American Revolution* (1992), is a brilliant examination of the ideological and cultural meanings of the Revolution. See also William Howard Adams, *The Paris Years of Thomas Jefferson* (1997). Lance Banning, *The Sacred Fire of Liberty: James Madison and the Founding of the Federal Republic* (1995), is a convincing revision of the story of Madison and his era. For the role of women in the American Revolution see Linda K. Kerber, *Women of the Republic: Intellect and Ideology in Revolutionary America* (1980), and Mary Beth Norton, *Liberty's Daughters: The Revolutionary Experience of American Women, 1750–1800* (1980). Also recommended is Norton's *Founding Mothers and Fathers: Gendered Power and the Forming of American Society* (1996). Among the many works that deal with African-Americans and Amerindians during the era, see Sylvia Frey, *Water from Rock: Black Resistance in a Revolutionary Age* (1991); Barbara Graymont, *The Iroquois in the American Revolution* (1972); and William N. Fenton, *The Great Law and the Longhouse: A Political History of the Iroquois Confederacy* (1998).

For intellectual life in the era of the French Revolution see Anne Goldgar, *Impolite Learning: Conduct and Community in the Republic of Letters, 1680–1750* (1995), and Dena Goodman, *The Republic of Letters: A Cultural History of the Enlightenment* (1994). For the "underside" of this era see *Shaping History: Ordinary People in European Politics, 1500–1700* (1998), by Wayne Te Brake, for a discussion of "folk culture." François Furet, *Interpreting the French Revolution* (1981), breaks with interpretations that emphasize class and ideological interpretations. Georges Lefebvre, *The Coming of the French Revolution*, trans. R. R. Palmer (1947), presents the classic class-based analysis. George Rudé, *The Crowd in History: Popular Disturbances in France and England* (1981), remains the best introduction to the role of mass protest in the period. Lynn Hunt, *The Family Romance of the French Revolution* (1992), examines the gender content of revolutionary politics. For the role of women see Joan Landes, *Women and the Public Sphere in the Age of the French Revolution* (1988), and the recently published *The Women of Paris and Their French Revolution* (1998) by Dominique Godineau. Felix Markham, *Napoleon* (1963), and Robert B. Holtman, *The Napoleonic Revolution* (1967), provide reliable summaries of the period.

The Haitian Revolution has received less extensive coverage than the revolutions in the United States and France. C. L. R. James, *The Black Jacobins*, 2d ed. (1963), is the classic study. Anna J. Cooper, *Slavery and the French Revolutionists, 1788–1805* (1988), also provides an overview of this important topic. Carolyn E. Fick, *The Making of Haiti: The Saint Domingue Revolution from Below* (1990), is the best recent synthesis. David P. Geggus, *Slavery, War, and Revolution* (1982), examines the British role in the revolutionary period. See also David Barry Gaspar and David Patrick Geggus, eds., *A Turbulent Time: The French Revolution and the Greater Caribbean* (1997).

For the revolutions of 1830 and 1848 see Arthur J. May, *The Age of Metternich, 1814–48*, rev. ed. (1963), for a brief survey. Henry Kissinger's *A World Restored* (1957) remains among the most interesting discussions of the Congress of Vienna. Eric Hobsbawm's *The Age of Revolution* (1962) provides a clear analysis of the class issues that appeared during this era. Paul Robertson's *Revolutions of 1848: A Social History* (1960) remains a valuable introduction. See also Peter Stearns and Herrick Chapman, *European Society in Upheaval* (1991). For the development of European social reform movements see Albert Lindemann, *History of European Socialism* (1983).

For national events in Hungary see István Deák's examination of Hungary, *The Lawful Revolution: Louis Kossuth and the Hungarians, 1848–49* (1979). For Germany, see Theodore S. Hamerow, *Restoration, Revolution, and Reaction, 1815–1871* (1966), For French events see Roger Price, *A Social History of Nineteenth-Century France* (1987). Barbara Taylor, *Eve and the New Jerusalem: Socialism and Feminism in the Nineteenth Century* (1983), analyzes connections between workers' and women's rights issues in England.

Note

1. Quoted in C. L. R. James, *The Black Jacobins*, 2d ed., rev. (New York: Vintage Books, 1963), 196.

24

THE EARLY INDUSTRIAL REVOLUTION,

1760–1851

Causes of the Industrial Revolution • The Technological Revolution •
The Impact of the Industrial Revolution • Ideological and Political Responses
to Industrialization • Industrialization and the Nonindustrial World

ENVIRONMENT AND TECHNOLOGY: "The Annihilation of Time and Space"

SOCIETY AND CULTURE: Charles Babbage, Ada Lovelace, and the "Analytical Engine"

Opening of the Saltash Bridge over the Tamar River in England in 1859 During the celebrations,
a steam locomotive pulled a train over the bridge while a steam-powered paddle wheeler passed underneath.

On January 1840, a shipyard in Britain launched a radically new ship. The *Nemesis* had an iron hull, a flat bottom so it could navigate in shallow waters, and a steam engine to power it upriver and against the wind. The ship was heavily armed. In November it arrived off the coast of China. Though ships from Europe had been sailing to China for three hundred years, the *Nemesis* was the first steam-powered iron gunboat seen in Asian waters. A Chinese observer noted: "Iron is employed to make it strong. The hull is painted black, weaver's shuttle fashion. On each side is a wheel, which by the use of coal fire is made to revolve as fast as a running horse. . . . At the vessel's head is a Marine God, and at the head, stern, and sides are cannon, which give it a terrific appearance. Steam vessels are a wonderful invention of foreigners, and are calculated to offer delight to many."[1]

Instead of offering delight, the *Nemesis* and other steam-powered warships that soon joined it steamed up the Chinese rivers, bombarded forts and cities, and brought in troops and supplies. With this new weapon, Britain, a small island nation half a world away, was able to defeat the largest and most populated country in the world in its own heartland.

The *Nemesis* was no isolated invention. Its outstanding features—steam power and cheap iron—were part of a larger phenomenon, the **Industrial Revolution,** that involved dramatic innovations in manufacturing, mining, transportation, and communications and equally rapid changes in society and commerce. New technologies and new social and economic arrangements allowed the industrializing countries—first Britain, followed by western Europe and the United States—to unleash massive increases in production and productivity, exploit the world's natural resources as never before, and transform the environment and human life in unprecedented ways.

The distribution of this power and wealth was very uneven. The people who owned and controlled these innovations amassed wealth and power over nature and over other people. Workers and their children were harmed, for industrialization widened the gap between rich and poor.

The effect of the Industrial Revolution around the world was also very uneven. The first countries to industrialize grew in wealth and power. But in Russia and eastern Europe, we cannot speak of an industrial revolution until the end of the nineteenth century. In Egypt, India, and a few other non-Western countries, the economic and military power of the European countries soon stifled the tentative beginnings of industrialization. China and other regions without industry were easily taken advantage of. The disparity between the industrial and the nonindustrial countries that exists today dates from the early nineteenth century.

As you read this chapter, ask yourself the following questions:

- What caused the Industrial Revolution?
- What were the key innovations that increased productivity and drove industrialization?
- What was the impact of these changes on the society and environment of the industrializing countries?
- How did the Industrial Revolution affect the relations between the industrialized and the nonindustrialized parts of the world?

CAUSES OF THE INDUSTRIAL REVOLUTION

What caused the Industrial Revolution, and why did it begin in England in the late eighteenth century? These are two of the great questions of history. The basic precondition of this momentous event seems to have been economic development propelled by population growth, an agricultural revolution, the expansion of trade, and an openness to innovation.

Population

The population of Europe rose in the eighteenth century—slowly at first, faster after 1780, then even faster in the early nineteenth century. The fastest growth took place in England and Wales. Population there rose from 5.5 million in 1688 to 9 million in 1801 and to 18 million by 1851—increases never before experienced in history.

The growth of population resulted from more reliable food supplies and more widespread resistance to disease. We know that industrialization was not the cause, for the populations of China and eastern and southern Europe were also growing. We also know that the population boom did not cause industrialization. But when economic growth and population growth occurred together, they reinforced each other.

More dependable food supplies and job opportunities led people to marry at an earlier age and have more children. A high birthrate meant a large percentage of children in the general population. In the early nineteenth century some 40 percent of the population of Britain was under fifteen years of age. This high proportion of youths explains both the vitality of the British people in that period and the widespread use of child labor. People also migrated at an unprecedented rate—from the countryside to the cities, from Ireland to England, and, more generally, from Europe to the Americas. Thanks to immigration, the population of the United States rose from 4 million in 1791 to 9.6 million in 1820 to 31.5 million in 1860—faster growth than in any other part of the world at the time.

The Agricultural Revolution

Innovations in manufacturing, energy, transportation, and communications could only have taken place alongside a simultaneous revolution in farming that provided food for city dwellers and forced poorer peasants off the land. This **agricultural revolution** began long before the eighteenth century. One important aspect was the acceptance of the potato, introduced from South America centuries earlier. In the cool and humid regions of Europe, from Ireland to Russia, potatoes yielded two or three times more food per acre than grain. Maize (American corn) was grown across Europe from southwestern France to the Balkans. Turnips, legumes, and clover did not deplete the soil and could be fed to cattle, sources of milk and meat. Additional manure from cattle in turn fertilized the soil for other crops.

Only prosperous landowners with secure titles to their land could afford the risks of new methods and new crops. Rich landowners therefore "enclosed" the land—that is, consolidated their holdings—and took over the commons that in the past had been open to all. Once in control of the land, they could make their tenants drain and improve the soil, breed better livestock, and introduce crop rotation. The security of small-scale tenant farmers and sharecroppers depended on traditional methods and rural customs such as gleaning in others' fields after the harvest, pasturing their animals on common village lands, and gathering firewood in common woods. This "enclosure movement" turned tenants and sharecroppers into landless farm laborers. Many moved to the cities to seek work; others became homeless migrants and vagrants; others emigrated.

In eastern Europe, as in Britain, large estates predominated and aristocratic landowners used such improvements to increase their wealth and political influence. In western Europe, enclosure was hampered by the fact that the law gave secure property rights to numerous small farmers.

Trade and Inventiveness

In most of Europe, the increasing demand that accompanied economic growth was met by increasing production in traditional ways. Roads were improved, so stagecoaches could travel faster. Royal manufacturers trained additional craftsmen to produce fine china, silks, and carpets by hand. In rural areas much production was carried out through the putting-out system. Merchants delivered fibers, leather, and other raw materials to craftspeople (often farmers in the off-season), and picked up the finished products.

The growth of the population and food supply was accompanied by the growth of trade. Most of it was local trade in traditional goods and services. But a growing share consisted of simple goods that even middle-class people could afford: sugar, tea, cotton textiles, iron hardware, pottery. Products from other parts of the world like tea and sugar, required extensive networks of shipping and finance.

In the late eighteenth century, technology and innovation fascinated educated people throughout Europe and eastern North America. The French *Encyclopédie* contained thousands of articles and illustrations of handicrafts. The American Benjamin Franklin, like many others, experimented with electricity. The Montgolfier brothers invented a hot-air balloon. Claude Chappe created the first semaphore telegraph. French artillery officers and the American Eli Whitney proposed making guns with interchangeable parts.

Britain and Continental Europe

Economic growth was evident everywhere in the North Atlantic area, yet industrialization did not take place everywhere at once. To understand why, we must look at the peculiar role of Great Britain.

Britain enjoyed a rising standard of living during the eighteenth century, thanks to good harvests, a growing

CHRONOLOGY

	Technology	Economy, Society, and Politics
1750		
	1759 Josiah Wedgwood opens pottery factory	
	1764 Spinning jenny	
	1769 Richard Arkwright's water frame; James Watt patents steam engine	**1776** Adam Smith's *Wealth of Nations*
	1779 First iron bridge	**1776–1783** American Revolution
	1785 Boulton and Watt sell steam engines; Samuel Crompton's mule	**1789–1799** French Revolution
	1793 Eli Whitney's cotton gin	
1800	**1800** Alessandro Volta's battery	
	1807 Robert Fulton's *Clermont*	**1804–1815** Napoleonic Wars
	1820s Construction of Erie Canal	**1820s** U.S. cotton industry begins
	1829 *Rocket,* first steam-powered locomotive	**1833** Factory Act in Britain
	1837 Wheatstone & Cooke's telegraph	**1834** German Zollverein; Robert Owen's Grand National Consolidated Trade Union
	1838 First ships steam across the Atlantic	
	1840 *Nemesis* sails to China	
	1843 Samuel Morse's Baltimore–to–Washington telegraph	**1846** Repeal of British Corn Laws
		1847–1848 Irish famine
1850	**1851** Crystal Palace opens in London	**1848** Collapse of Chartist movement; Revolutions in Europe
		1854 First cotton mill in India

population, and a booming overseas trade. Until the mid-eighteenth century, the British were better known for their cheap imitations than for their innovations or quality products. But they put inventions into practice more quickly than other people, as the engineer John Farey told a parliamentary committee in 1829: "The prevailing talent of English and Scotch people is to apply new ideas to use and to bring such applications to perfection, but they do not imagine as much as foreigners."

Britain was the world's leading exporter of tools, guns, hardware, and other craft goods (see Map 24.1). Its mining and metal industries employed engineers willing to experiment with new ideas. It had the largest merchant marine and produced more ships, naval supplies, and navigation instruments than other countries.

Before 1790, Britain had a more fluid society than the rest of Europe. The English royal court was less ostentatious than the courts of France, Spain, or Austria. Its aristocracy was less powerful, and the lines separating the social classes were less sharply drawn. Political power was not as centralized as on the European continent, and the government employed fewer bureaucrats and officials. Members of the gentry, and even some aris-

tocrats, married into merchant families. Intermarriage among the families of petty merchants, yeoman farmers, and town craftsmen was common. Guilds, which resisted innovation, were relatively weak. Ancestry remained important, but wealth also commanded respect. A businessman with enough money could buy a landed estate, a seat in Parliament, and the social status that accompanied them.

At a time when transportation by land was very costly, Great Britain had good water transportation, thanks to its indented coastline, navigable rivers, and growing network of canals. It had a unified internal market, with none of the duties and tolls that goods had to pay every few miles in France. This encouraged specialization and trade.

Britain was highly commercial. More people there were involved in production for export and in trade and finance than in any other major country. It was especially active in overseas trade with the Americas, West Africa, the Middle East, and India. It had financial and insurance institutions able to support growing business enterprises and a patent system that offered inventors the hope of rich rewards. The example of men who be-

Map 24.1 The Industrial Revolution in Britain, ca. 1850
The first industries arose in northern and western England.
These regions had abundant coal and iron-ore deposits for
the iron industry and a moist climate and fast-flowing rivers,
factors important for the cotton-textile industry.

forms, metal goods, food, and horses. The insecurity of
the times and the interruption of trade with Britain
weakened the incentive to invest in new technologies.

The political revolutions swept away the restrictions
of the old regimes. After 1815, when peace returned, the
economies of western Europe were ready to begin industrializing. Industrialization first took hold in Belgium
and northern France, as their businessmen visited
Britain to observe the changes and to spy out industrial
secrets. In spite of British laws forbidding the emigration
of skilled workers and the export of textile machinery,
many slipped through. By the 1820s, several thousand
Britons were at work on the continent of Europe setting
up machines, training workers in the new methods, and
even starting their own businesses.

Acutely aware of Britain's head start and of the need
to stimulate their own industrialization, European governments took action. They created technical schools.
They eliminated internal tariff barriers, tolls, and other
hindrances to trade. They encouraged the formation of
joint-stock companies and banks to channel private savings into industrial investments. On the European continent, as in Britain, cotton was the first industry. The mills
of France, Belgium, and Germany served local markets
but could not compete abroad with the more advanced
British industry. By 1830, the political climate in western
Europe was as favorable to business as Britain's had been
a half-century earlier.

THE TECHNOLOGICAL REVOLUTION

Five revolutionary innovations spurred industrialization: (1) mass production through the division of labor, (2) new machines and mechanization, (3) a great
increase in the supply of iron, (4) the steam engine and
the changes it made possible in industry and transportation, and (5) the electric telegraph.

Mass Production: Pottery

The pottery industry offers a
good example of **mass production,** the making of many identical items by breaking the
process into simple repetitive tasks. East Asian potters
had long known how to make fine glazed porcelain, or
"china." In Europe before the mid-eighteenth century
only the wealthy could afford fine porcelain imported

came wealthy and respected for their inventions—such
as Richard Arkwright, the cotton magnate, and James
Watt, the steam engine designer—stimulated others.

In the eighteenth century, the economies of continental Europe underwent a dynamic expansion, thanks
to the efforts of individual entrepreneurs and investors.
Yet growth was still hampered by high transportation
costs, misguided government regulations, and rigid social structures. The Low Countries were laced with
canals, but the terrain elsewhere in Europe made canal
building costly and difficult. The ruling monarchies
made some attempts to import British techniques and
organize factory production, but they all floundered for
lack of markets or management skills. From 1789 to
1815, Europe was the scene of revolutions and wars. War
created opportunities for suppliers of weapons, uni-

from Asia. Middle-class people used pewter tableware, and the poor ate from wooden or earthenware bowls. Several royal manufactures—Meissen in Saxony, Delft in Holland, and Sèvres in France—were founded to produce exquisite handmade products for the courts and aristocracy, but their products were much too expensive for mass consumption. Meanwhile, more and more Europeans acquired a taste for tea, cocoa, and coffee, and wanted porcelain that would not spoil the flavor of hot beverages. This demand created opportunities for inventive entrepreneurs.

Britain, like other countries, had many small pottery workshops where craftsmen made a few plates and cups at a time. Much of this activity took place in a part of the Midlands that possessed good clay, coal for firing, and lead for glazing. There **Josiah Wedgwood** opened a pottery business in 1759. Today, the name Wedgwood is associated with expensive, highly decorated china. But Wedgwood's most important contribution lay in producing ordinary porcelain cheaply, by means of the **division of labor.**

To do so, he subdivided the work into highly specialized and repetitive tasks, such as unloading the clay, mixing it, pressing flat pieces, dipping the pieces in glaze, putting handles on cups, packing kilns, and carrying things from one part of his plant to another. He substituted the use of molds for the potter's wheel wherever possible, a change that not only saved labor but created identical plates and bowls that could be stacked. Wedgwood was also interested in new technologies. He invested in toll roads and canals so that clay could be shipped economically from southwestern England to his factories in the Midlands. In 1782, to mix clay and grind flint, he purchased one of the first steam engines to be used in industry.

These were radical departures from the age-old methods of craftsmanship. But the division of labor, strict discipline, and new machinery allowed Wedgwood to lower the cost of his products while improving their quality, and to offer his wares for sale at lower prices. His factory grew far larger than his competitors' factories and employed several hundred workers. His own salesmen traveled throughout England touting his goods.

Wedgwood's interest in applying technology to manufacturing was connected with his membership in the Birmingham Lunar Society, a group of manufacturers, scientists, and inventors who met when the moon was full so they could see their way home after dark. This critical mass of creative thinkers willing to exchange ideas and discoveries encouraged the atmosphere of experimentation and innovation that characterized late-eighteenth-century England. Similar societies through-

Wedgwood's Potteries In Staffordshire, England, Josiah Wedgwood established a factory to mass-produce beautiful and inexpensive china. The bottle-shape buildings are kilns in which thousands of pieces of china could be fired at one time. Kilns, factories, and housing were all mixed together in pottery towns, and smoke from burning coal filled the air. (Mary Evans Picture Library)

out Britain were creating a vogue for science and giving the word *progress* a new meaning: "change for the better."

Mechanization: The Cotton Industry

The cotton industry, the largest industry in this period, illustrates the role of **mechanization,** the use of machines to do work previously done by hand. Cotton cloth had long been the most common fabric in China, India, and the Middle East, where it was spun and woven by hand. The cotton plant did not grow in Europe, but the cloth was so much cooler, softer, and cleaner than wool that wealthy Europeans developed a liking for this costly import. When the powerful English woolen industry persuaded Parliament to forbid the import of cotton cloth into England, it stimulated attempts to import cotton fiber and make the cloth locally. Here was an opportunity for enterprising inventors to reduce costs with labor-saving machinery.

To turn inventions into successful businesses, inventors had to link up with entrepreneurs or become businessmen themselves. Making a working prototype often took years, even decades, and many inventions led to dead ends. History remembers the successful, but even they struggled against great odds (see Society and Culture: Charles Babbage, Ada Lovelace, and the "Analytical Engine").

Beginning in the 1760s, a series of inventions revolutionized the spinning of cotton thread. The first was the spinning jenny, invented in 1764, which drew out the cotton fibers and twisted them into thread. The jenny was simple, cheap to build, and easy for one person to operate. Early models spun six or seven threads at once, later ones up to eighty. The thread, however, was soft and irregular and could be used only in combination with linen.

In 1769 **Richard Arkwright** invented another spinning machine, the water frame, which produced thread strong enough to be used without linen. Arkwright was both a gifted inventor and a successful businessman. His machine was larger and more complex than the jenny and required a source of power such as a water wheel, hence the name "water frame." To obtain the necessary energy, he installed many machines in one building, next to a fast-flowing river. The resemblance to a flour mill gave such enterprises the name cotton mill.

In 1785 Samuel Crompton patented a machine that combined the best features of the jenny and the water frame. This device, called a mule, produced a thread that was both strong and fine enough to be used in the finer qualities of cotton called muslin. The mule could make a finer, more even thread than any human, and at a lower cost. Now British industry could undersell high-quality handmade cotton cloth from India. As a result, British cotton output increased tenfold between 1770 and 1790.

The boom in thread production and the soaring demand for cloth created bottlenecks in weaving. Inventors in England rose to the challenge. The first power loom was introduced in 1784 but was not perfected until after 1815. Other inventions of that period included carding machines, chlorine bleach, and cylindrical printing presses. By the 1830s large English textile mills powered by steam engines were turning raw cotton into printed cloth. This was a far cry from the cottage industries of the previous century.

Mechanization offered two advantages: (1) productivity for the manufacturer and (2) price for the consumer. Whereas in India it took 500 hours to spin a pound of cotton, the mule of 1790 could do so in 3 person-hours, and the self-acting mule—an improved version introduced in 1830—required only 80 minutes. Cotton mills needed very few skilled workers, and managers often hired children to tend the spinning machines. The same was true of power looms, which gradually replaced handloom weaving: the number of power looms rose from 2,400 in 1813 to 500,000 by 1850. Meanwhile, the price of cloth fell by 90 percent from 1782 to 1812 and kept on dropping.

The industrialization of Britain made cotton into America's most valuable crop. In the 1790s, most of Britain's cotton came from India, as the United States produced a mere 750 tons, mostly long-staple cotton from South Carolina. In 1793, the American Eli Whitney patented his cotton gin, a simple device that separated the bolls from the fiber and made the growing of short-staple cotton economical. This invention permitted the spread of cotton farming into Georgia, then into Alabama, Mississippi, and Louisiana, and finally as far west as Texas. By the late 1850s the southern states were producing a million tons of cotton a year, five-sixths of the world's total.

With the help of British craftsmen who introduced jennies, mules, and power looms, Americans developed a cotton industry in the 1820s. By 1840, the United States had 1,200 cotton mills, two-thirds of them in New England, powered by water rather than steam.

The Iron Industry

Iron making also was transformed during the Industrial Revolution. Throughout Eurasia and Africa, iron had been in use for thousands of years for tools, swords and other weapons, and household items such as knives, pots, hinges, and locks. In the eleventh century, during the Song period, Chinese forges had produced cast iron in large quantities. Production declined after the Song, but iron continued to be common and inexpensive in China. Wherever iron was produced, however, deforestation eventually drove up the cost of charcoal (used for smelting) and restricted output. Furthermore, iron had to be repeatedly heated and hammered to drive out impurities, a difficult and costly process. Because of limited wood supplies and the high cost of skilled labor, iron was a rare and valuable metal outside China before the eighteenth century.

A major breakthrough occurred in 1709 when Abraham Darby discovered that coke (coal from which the impurities have been cooked out) could be used in place of charcoal. The resulting metal was of lower quality than charcoal-iron but much cheaper to produce, for coal was

Charles Babbage, Ada Lovelace, and the "Analytical Engine"

In the early nineteenth century, many professions relied on tables of numbers such as logarithms, astronomical positions, and actuarial data. Calculated by hand, these tables were full of arithmetic and typographical errors. In 1820, while correcting such a table, the English mathematician Charles Babbage exclaimed: "I wish to God these calculations had been executed by steam." Babbage went on to devise a machine—he called it the "Difference Engine"—to perform calculations and print out the results as flawlessly as a power loom produced cloth. While a prototype was being built, he designed the "Analytical Engine," which could interpret instructions inserted on punched cards and could alter its calculations in response to the results of previous calculations.

One of Babbage's assistants, Ada, the countess of Lovelace, translated an article by the Italian military engineer, L. F. Menabrea, about the Analytical Engine for the magazine Taylor's Scientific Memoirs. *In his autobiography, published in 1864, Babbage recalled: "The late Countess of Lovelace informed me that she had translated the memoir of Menabrea. I asked why she had not herself written an original paper on a subject with which she was so intimately acquainted? To this Lady Lovelace replied that the thought had not occurred to her. I then suggested that she should add some notes to Menabrea's memoir; an idea which was immediately adopted. . . . The notes of the Countess of Lovelace extend to about three times the length of the original memoir. Their author has entered fully into almost all the very difficult and abstract questions concerned with the subject.*

In the notes that she added to Menabrea's article, Ada Lovelace wrote the following:

The distinctive characteristic of the Analytical Engine, and that which has rendered it possible to endow mechanism with such extensive faculties as bid fair to make this engine the executive right-hand of abstract algebra, is the introduction into it of the principle which Jacquard devised for regulating, by means of punched cards, the most complicated patterns in the fabrication of brocaded stuffs [fabrics]. . . .

The bounds of *arithmetic* were outstepped the moment the idea of applying the cards had occurred; and the Analytical Engine does not occupy common ground with mere "calculating machines." It holds a position wholly its own; and the considerations it suggests are most interesting in their nature. . . . A new, a vast, and a powerful language is developed for the future use of analysis, in which to wield its truths so that these may become of more speedy and accurate practical application for the purposes of mankind than the means hitherto in our possession have rendered possible. Thus not only the mental and the material, but the theoretical and the practical in the mathematical world, are brought into more intimate and effective connexion with each other. We are not aware of its being on record that anything partaking in the nature of what is so well designated the *Analytical Engine* has been hitherto proposed, or even thought of, as a practical possibility, any more than the idea of a thinking or of a reasoning machine.

In short, Babbage invented the computer.

The first working computers were not built until a hundred years later, but Babbage is honored as the first person to imagine such a machine. And the widely used programming language Ada is named after his friend, the countess of Lovelace.

Is "a thinking or . . . a reasoning machine" a good description of a computer? Because Babbage's Analytical Engine did not use electricity, can it really be called a computer?

Crystal Palace Interior The Crystal Palace, built for the Universal Exposition of 1851, was the largest structure in England. It was made entirely prefabricated of iron and glass and was a forerunner of the great railroad stations of the late nineteenth century and the skyscrapers of the twentieth. (Guildhall Library, Corporation of London, The Bridgeman Art Library, London and New York)

plentiful. In 1784 Henry Cort found a way to remove some of the impurities in coke-iron by puddling—stirring the molten iron with long rods. By 1790 four-fifths of Britain's iron was made with coke; other countries still used charcoal. Coke-iron was cheaper and less destructive of forests, and it allowed a great expansion in the size of individual blast furnaces, substantially reducing the cost of iron. There seemed almost no limit to the quantity of iron that could be produced with coke. Britain's iron production began rising fast, from 17,000 tons in 1740 to 3 million tons in 1844, as much as in the rest of the world put together.

In turn, there seemed no limit to the amount of iron that an industrializing society would purchase or to the novel applications for this cheap and useful material. In 1779 the iron manufacturer Abraham Darby III (grand-

son of the first Abraham Darby) built a bridge of iron across the Severn River. In 1851 Londoners marveled at the **Crystal Palace,** a huge greenhouse made entirely of iron and glass and large enough to enclose the tallest trees.

The idea of interchangeable parts originated in the eighteenth century, when French army officers attempted, without success, to persuade gun makers to produce precisely identical parts. The craftsmen continued to use traditional methods to make gun parts that had to be fitted together by hand. By the mid-nineteenth century, however, interchangeable-parts manufacturing had been adopted in the manufacture of firearms, farm equipment, and sewing machines. At the Crystal Palace exhibition of 1851, Europeans called it the "American system of manufactures." In the next hundred years, the use of machinery to mass-produce consumer items was to become the hallmark of American industry.

The Steam Engine

Although the mechanization of manufacturing was very important, the most revolutionary invention of the Industrial Revolution was surely the **steam engine,** a mechanical substitute for human and animal power as well as wind and water power. By the late seventeenth century many activities were experiencing serious bottlenecks for lack of energy. In particular, deep mines filled with water faster than horses could pump it out.

Scientists understood the concept of atmospheric pressure and had created experimental devices to turn heat into motion, but they had not found a way to put those devices to practical use. Then, between 1702 and 1712, Thomas Newcomen developed the first practical steam engine, a crude and inefficient device. Its voracious appetite for fuel mattered little in coal mines, where fuel was cheap, but it was too costly for other uses.

James Watt, an instrument maker at Glasgow University in Scotland, was asked to repair the university's model Newcomen engine. Watt realized that the engine wasted fuel because the cylinder had to be alternately heated and cooled. He developed a separate condenser—a vessel into which the steam was allowed to escape after it had done its work, leaving the cylinder always hot and the condenser always cold. Watt patented his idea in 1769. He enlisted the help of the iron manufacturer Matthew Boulton to turn his invention into a commercial product. In 1785, Boulton and Watt began selling steam engines to manufacturers of iron, pottery, and cotton.

Watt's steam engine was the most celebrated invention of the eighteenth century. Because there seemed almost no limit to the amount of coal in the ground, steam-generated energy seemed an inexhaustible source of power, and steam engines could be used where animal, wind, and water power were lacking. Without the steam engine, industrialization would have been a limited phenomenon.

Inspired by the success of Watt's engine, inventors in France in 1783, in the United States in 1787, and in England in 1788 put steam engines on boats. The need to overcome great distances in the United States explains why the first commercially successful steamboat was Robert Fulton's *Clermont*, which steamed between New York City and Albany in 1807.

Soon steamboats were launched on other American rivers, especially the Ohio and the Mississippi, gateways to the midwest. In the 1820s, the Erie Canal linked the Atlantic seaboard with the Great Lakes and opened Ohio, Indiana, and Illinois to European settlement. Steamboats proliferated west of the Appalachian Mountains; by 1830 some three hundred plied the Mississippi and its tributaries. To counter the competition from New York State, Pennsylvania built a thousand miles of canals by 1840. The United States was fast becoming a nation that moved by water.

Oceangoing steam-powered ships were much more difficult to build than riverboats, for the first steam engines used so much coal that no ship could carry more than a few days' worth. The *Savannah*, which crossed the Atlantic in 1819, was a sailing ship with an auxiliary steam engine that was used for only 90 hours of its 29-day trip. But engineers soon developed more efficient engines, and in 1838 two steamers, the *Great Western* and the *Sirius*, crossed the Atlantic on steam power alone. Elsewhere, sailing ships held their own until late in the century, for world trade was growing so fast that there was enough business for ships of every kind.

On land as on water, the problem was not imagining uses for steam-powered vehicles but building ones that worked, for steam engines were too heavy and weak to pull any weight. After Watt's patent expired in 1800, inventors experimented with lighter, more powerful high-pressure engines—an idea Watt had rejected as too dangerous. In 1804, the engineer Richard Trevithick built an engine that consumed twelve times less than Newcomen's and three times less than Watt's. With it, he built several steam-powered vehicles able to travel on roads or rails.

Horses could pull heavier wagons on wooden or iron rails than on cobblestone roads. By the 1820s England had many horse-powered railways. On one of them, the Stockton and Darlington Railway, the chief engineer, George Stephenson, began using steam locomotives in 1825. Four years later, the owners of the Liverpool and Manchester Railway organized a contest between steam-powered locomotives and horse-drawn wagons. Stephenson and his son Robert easily won the contest with their locomotive *Rocket*, which pulled a 20-ton train at up to 30 miles (48 kilometers) per hour. After that triumph, a railroad-building mania that lasted for twenty years swept Britain. The first lines linked towns and mines with the nearest harbor or waterway. In the late 1830s, passenger traffic soared, and entrepreneurs built lines between the major cities and then to small towns as well. Railroads were far cheaper, faster, and more comfortable than stagecoaches, and millions of people got in the habit of traveling.

The De Witt Clinton Locomotive, 1835–1840   The De Witt Clinton was the first steam locomotive built in the United States. The high smokestack let the hot cinders cool so they would not set fire to nearby trees, an important consideration at a time when eastern North America was still covered with forests. The three passenger cars are clearly horse-carriages fitted with railroad wheels.   (Corbis)

In the United States, entrepreneurs built railroads as fast and cheaply as possible with an eye to quick profits, not long-term durability. By the 1840s, 6,000 miles (10,000 kilometers) of track radiated westward from Boston, New York, Philadelphia, and Baltimore and connected these cities to one another. The boom of the 1840s was dwarfed by the mania of the 1850s, when 21,000 miles (34,000 kilometers) of new track were laid, much of it westward across the Appalachians to Memphis, St. Louis, and Chicago. After 1856, the trip from New York to Chicago, which once took three weeks by boat and on horseback, could be made in forty-eight hours. More than anything else, it was the railroads that opened up the midwest, turning the vast prairie into wheat fields and pasture for cattle to feed the industrial cities of the eastern United States.

Railways triggered the industrialization of Europe (see Map 24.2). Belgium, independent since 1830, quickly copied the British. In France and Prussia, the state planned and supervised railroad construction from the start. This delayed construction until the mid-1840s. When it began, however, it had a greater impact than in Britain, for it not only satisfied the long-standing need for transportation, but also stimulated the iron, machinery, and construction industries.

Abundant coal and iron-ore deposits determined the concentration of industries in a swath of territories running from northern France through Belgium and the Ruhr district of western Germany to Silesia in Prussia (now part of Poland). In the 1850s and 1860s, the states of Germany experienced an industrial boom, as did France and Belgium.

Borsig Ironworks in Germany in the 1840s   This foundry was built to supply rails, locomotives, and other iron products to the German railroads, then under construction. (Deutsches Technikmuseum Berlin. Photo: Hans-Joachim Bartsch. Bildarchiv Preussischer Kulturbesitz)

Map 24.2   Industrialization in Europe, ca. 1850   In 1850 industrialization was in its early stages on the European continent. The first industrial regions were comparatively close to England and possessed rich coal deposits: Belgium and the Ruhr district of Germany. Politics determined the location of railroads. Notice the star-shaped French network of rail lines emanating from Paris and the lines linking the different parts of the German Confederation.

Communication over Wires

The advent of railroads coincided with the development of the **electric telegraph.** After the Italian scientist Alessandro Volta invented the battery in 1800, making it possible to produce an electric current, many inventors tried to apply electricity to communication. The first practical telegraphy systems were developed almost simultaneously in England and America. In England, Wheatstone and Cooke introduced a five-needle telegraph in 1837; it remained in use until the early twentieth century. That same year, the American Samuel Morse introduced a code of dots and dashes that could be transmitted with a single wire; in 1843, he erected a line between Washington and Baltimore.

By the late 1840s, telegraph wires were being strung throughout the eastern United States and western Europe. In 1851, the first submarine telegraph cable was laid across the English Channel from England to France; it was the beginning of a network that eventually enclosed the entire globe. The world was rapidly shrinking, to the applause of Europeans and Americans for whom speed was a clear measure of progress (see Environmental and Technology: "The Annihilation of Time and Space"). No longer were communications limited to the speed of which a ship could sail or a horse could gallop.

"The Annihilation of Time and Space"

In the 1780s it took from five to eight months to sail from England to India, and a European writing a letter to someone in India usually had to wait two years for an answer. Fifty years later, when the first steamships and telegraph lines appeared, telegraph pioneer William O'Shaughnessy, serving with the British army in India, wrote:

The progress of science is hourly adding to the catalogue of triumphs effected by the sagacity of man over the seeming impossibilities of nature. . . . A conquest still greater than all which I have quoted would be the annihilation of time and space in the accomplishment of correspondence.

By 1870, the voyage to India had been shortened to three weeks, and correspondents could expect answers to their letters in less than two months. What O'Shaughnessy called "the annihilation of time and space" had begun.

The telegraph had an even more astonishing impact on global communications. Beginning in the 1860s, cables laid on the ocean floor allowed telegrams to be sent across oceans as readily as on land. When the first cable to India was completed in June 1870, the chairman of the Eastern Telegraph Company, John Pender, sent a telegram to Bombay and received an answer 4 minutes and 22 seconds later. The *Daily Telegraph* of London reported this astonishing news:

Aladdin . . . must have dropped his wonderful lamp in sheer amazement and neglect, and sold his magic ring for old gold. Time itself is telegraphed out of existence. Today communicates on one hand with Yesterday, on the other, with tomorrow.

The easy, almost instantaneously communication with any country in the world that we take for granted today began in the mid-nineteenth century. Since that time, communications technologies have made the world a much smaller and more intimate place—for those who can afford them.

Source: Sir William Brooke O'Shaughnessy, "Memoranda Relative to Experiments on the Communication of Telegraphic Signals by Induced Electricity," *Journal of the Asiatic Society of Bengal* (September 1839): 720–721. Quoted in G. R. M. Garatt, *One Hundred Years of Submarine Cables* (London: HMSO, 1950), 29.

Transatlantic Steamship Race   In 1838, two ships equipped with steam engines, the *Sirius* and the *Great Western*, steamed from England to New York. Although the *Sirius* left a few days earlier, the *Great Western*—shown here arriving in New York harbor—almost caught up with it, arriving just four hours after the *Sirius*. This race inaugurated regular transatlantic steamship service.   (Courtesy of the Mariner's Museum, Newport News, VA)

Overcrowded London   The French artist Gustave Doré depicted the tenements of industrial London where workers and their families lived. This drawing shows crowded and unsanitary row houses, each one room wide, with tiny back yards, and a train steaming across a viaduct overhead.   (Prints Division, New York Public Library, Astor, Lenox, and Tilden Foundations)

THE IMPACT OF THE INDUSTRIAL REVOLUTION

Although inventions were the most visible aspect of the Industrial Revolution, many other changes in society, politics, and the economy took place, interacting with one another. At first, the changes were quite local: smoky cities, slum neighborhoods, polluted water, child labor in mines and textile mills. By the mid-nineteenth century, the worst local effects were being alleviated. Replacing them on a national or even international scale were more complex problems: business cycles, labor conflicts, and the transformation of entire regions into industrial landscapes.

The New Industrial Cities

The most dramatic environmental changes brought about by industrialization occurred in the towns. Never before had towns grown so fast. London, one of the largest cities in Europe in 1700 with 500,000 inhabitants, grew to 959,000 by 1800, and to 2,363,000 by 1850; it was then the largest city the world had ever known. Smaller towns grew even faster. Manchester, a small town of 20,000 in 1758, reached 400,000 a century later, an eightfold increase. Liverpool grew sixfold in sixty years, from 82,000 in 1801 to 472,000 in 1861. New York City, already 100,000 strong in 1815, reached 600,000 (including Brooklyn) in 1850. These were not isolated instances. In some areas, towns merged and formed megalopolises, such as Greater London, the English Midlands, central Belgium, and the Ruhr district of Germany.

Industrialization made some people very prosperous. A great deal of this new wealth went into the building of fine homes, churches, museums, and theaters in wealthy neighborhoods in London, Berlin, and New York. Much of the beauty of London dates from the time of the Industrial Revolution. Yet, by all accounts, the industrial cities grew much too fast, and much of the growth occurred in the poorest neighborhoods.

As poor migrants streamed in from the countryside, developers built cheap, shoddy row houses for them to rent. These tenements were dangerously overcrowded. Often, several families had to live in one small room.

Sudden population growth, overcrowding, and inadequate municipal services conspired to make urban problems more serious than in earlier times. Town dwellers recently arrived from the country brought country ways with them. People threw their sewage and trash out the windows to be washed down the gutters in the streets. The poor kept pigs and chickens, the rich kept horses, and pedestrians stepped into the street at their own risk. Factories and workers' housing were mixed together. Air pollution from burning coal, a problem since the sixteenth century, got steadily worse. Londoners in particular breathed dense and noxious coal smoke. Although humans tolerated the burning of coal, it was too polluting for smelting iron or baking bread. People drank water drawn from wells and rivers contaminated by sewage and industrial runoff. The River Irwell, which ran through Manchester, was, in the words of one visitor, "considerably less a river than a flood of liquid manure."

"Every day that I live," wrote an American visitor to Manchester, "I thank Heaven that I am not a poor man with a family in England." In his poem "Milton," William Blake (1757–1827) expressed the revulsion of sensitive people at the spoliation of England's "mountains green" and "pleasant pastures":

> And did the Countenance Divine
> Shine forth upon our clouded hills?
> And was Jerusalem builded here
> Among these dark Satanic Mills?

Railroads invaded the towns. Railroad companies built their stations as close to the heart of cities as they could. On the outskirts of cities, railroad yards, sidings, and repair shops covered acres of land, surrounded by miles of warehouses and workers' housing. Farther out, far from the dangerous and polluted cities where their factories were located, newly rich industrialists created an environment halfway between country homes and townhouses: the first suburbs.

Under these conditions, diseases proliferated. To the long list of preindustrial urban diseases such as smallpox, dysentery, and tuberculosis, industrialization added new ailments. Rickets, a bone disease caused by lack of sunshine, became endemic in dark and smoky industrial cities. Steamships brought cholera from India, causing great epidemics that struck the poor neighborhoods especially hard. In the 1850s, when the average life expectancy in England was forty years, it was only twenty-four years in Manchester, and around seventeen years in Manchester's poorest neighborhoods, because of the high infant mortality. Observers of nineteenth-century industrial cities documented the horrors of slum life in vivid detail. Their shocking reports led to municipal reforms, such as garbage removal, water and sewage systems, and parks and schools. These measures began to alleviate the ills of urban life after the mid-nineteenth century.

Rural Environments

Long before the Industrial Revolution began, practically no wilderness areas were left in Britain and very few in western Europe. Almost every piece of land was covered with fields, forests, or pastures shaped by human activity, or by towns; yet humans continued to alter the environment. The most serious problem was deforestation. People cut timber to build ships and houses, to heat homes, and to manufacture bricks, iron, glass, beer, bread, and many other items.

Americans transformed their environment even faster than Europeans. Land in North America seemed practically free for the taking, and, east of the Appalachian Mountains, settlers viewed forests not as a valuable resource but as a hindrance to development. In their haste to "open up the West," pioneers felled trees and burned them, built houses and abandoned them, and then moved on. The cultivation of cotton was especially harmful. Planters cut down forests, grew cotton for a few years until it depleted the soil, then moved west, abandoning the land to scrub pines. This was slash-and-burn agriculture on an industrial scale.

At that time, America seemed immune to human depredations. Americans thought of nature as an obstacle to be overcome and dominated. This mindset persisted long after the entire continent was occupied and the environment truly endangered.

Paradoxically, in some ways industrialization actually relieved pressures on the environment in Britain. Raw materials once grown on British soil (for example, wood, hay, and wool) were replaced by materials found underground (iron ore and coal) or obtained overseas (cotton). While Russia, Sweden, the United States, and other forested countries continued to smelt iron with charcoal, the British substituted coke made from coal. As the British population increased, and land grew scarcer, the cost of growing feed for horses rose, creating incentives to find new, less land-hungry means of transportation. Likewise, as iron became cheaper and wood more expensive, ships and many other things formerly made of wood began to be made of iron.

To contemporaries, the most obvious changes in rural life were brought about by the new transportation systems. In the eighteenth century, France had a national network of quality roads, which Napoleon extended into Italy and Germany. In Britain, local governments' neglect of the roads that served long-distance traffic led to the formation of private enterprises—"Turnpike Trusts"—that built numerous toll roads. For heavy goods, horse-drawn wagons were too costly even on good roads. The growing volume of heavy freight triggered canal-building booms in Britain, France, and the Low Countries in the late eighteenth century. Some canals, like the duke of Bridgewater's canal in England, connected coal mines to towns or navigable rivers. Others linked navigable rivers and created national transportation networks.

Canals were marvels of construction, with deep cuts, tunnels, and even aqueducts that carried barges over rivers. They also were a sort of school where engineers learned skills they were able to apply to the next great transportation system: the railroads. They laid track across rolling country by cutting deeply into hillsides and erecting daringly long bridges of stone and iron across valleys. Lesser lines snaked their way to small towns hidden in remote valleys. Soon, clanking trains pulled by puffing, smoke-belching locomotives were invading long-isolated districts.

Thus, in the century after industrialization began, the landscape of industrializing countries was transformed more rapidly than ever before. But the ecological changes, like the technological and economic changes that caused them, were only beginning.

Working Conditions

Industrialization offered new opportunities to the enterprising. Carpenters, metalworkers, and machinists were in great demand. Since industrial machines were fairly simple, some workers became engineers or went into business for themselves. The boldest in England moved to the European Continent, the Americas, or India, taking their skills with them to establish new industries.

The successful, however, were a minority. Most industrial jobs were unskilled, repetitive, and boring. Factory work did not vary with the seasons or the time of day but began and ended by the clock. Workdays were long, there were few breaks, and foremen watched constantly. Workers who performed one simple task over and over had little sense of achievement or connection to the final product. Industrial accidents were common and could ruin a family. Unlike even the poorest preindustrial farmer or artisan, factory workers had no control over their tools, jobs, or working hours.

Industrial work, by definition, was physically removed from the home. This had a major impact on women and on family life. Women workers were concentrated in textile mills, partly because of ancient traditions, partly because textile work required less strength than metalworking, construction, or hauling. On average, women earned one-third to one-half as much as men. Young unmarried women worked to support themselves or to save for marriage. Married women took factory jobs when their husbands were unable to support the family. Mothers of infants faced a hard choice: whether to leave their babies with wet-nurses at great expense and danger or to bring them to the factory and keep them quiet with opiates. Rather than working together as family units, husbands and wives increasingly worked in different places.

Even where factory work was available, it was never the main occupation of working women in the early years of industrialization. Most young women who sought paid employment became domestic servants in spite of the low pay, drudgery, and risk of sexual abuse by male employers. Women with small children tried hard to find work they could do at home, such as laundry, sewing, embroidery, millinery, or taking in lodgers.

Even with both parents working, poor families found it hard to make ends meet. As in preindustrial societies, parents thought children should contribute to their upkeep as soon as they were able to. The first generation of workers brought their children with them to the factories and mines as early as age five or six; they had little choice, since there were no public schools or day-care centers. Employers encouraged the practice and even hired orphans. They preferred children because they were cheaper and more docile than adults and were better able to tie broken threads or crawl under machines to sweep the dust.

In Arkwright's cotton mills, two-thirds of the workers were children. In another mill, 17 percent were under ten years of age and 53 percent were between ten and seventeen; they worked 14 to 16 hours a day and were beaten if they made a mistake or fell asleep. Mine operators used children to pull coal carts along the low passageways from the coal face to the mine shaft. In the mid-nineteenth century, when the British government began restricting child labor, mill owners increasingly recruited Irish immigrants.

Cotton Mill in Early-Nineteenth-Century New England   These machines, called self-acting mules, could spin hundreds of threads at once. Most of the workers tending the mules were women and children.   (The Granger Collection, New York)

American industry began on a somewhat different note than the British. In the early nineteenth century, Americans still remembered their revolutionary ideals. When Francis Cabot Lowell built a cotton mill in Massachusetts, he deliberately hired the unmarried daughters of New England farmers, promising them decent wages and housing in dormitories under careful moral supervision. Other manufacturers eager to combine profits with morality followed his example. But soon the profit motive won out and manufacturers imposed longer hours, harsher working conditions, and lower wages. The young women protested: "As our fathers resisted with blood the lordly avarice of the British ministry, so we, their daughters, never will wear the yoke which has been prepared for us." When they went on strike, the factory owners replaced them with Irish immigrant women willing to accept lower pay and worse conditions.

While the cotton boom enriched planters, merchants, and manufacturers, African-Americans paid for it with their freedom. In the 1790s, 700,000 slaves of African descent lived in the United States, but their numbers were diminishing and the founders of the American republic did not consider slavery a serious problem. The rising demand for cotton and the abolition of the African slave trade in 1808 caused an increase in the price of slaves. As the "Cotton Kingdom" expanded, the number of slaves rose through natural increase and the reluctance of slaveowners to free their slaves. By 1850 the United States had 3,200,000 slaves, 60 percent of whom grew cotton. Similarly, Europe's and North America's surging demand for tea and coffee prolonged slavery in the sugar plantations of the West Indies and caused it to spread to the coffee-growing regions of southern Brazil.

Slavery was not, as white American southerners maintained, a "peculiar institution"—a consequence of biological differences, biblical injunctions, or African traditions. Slavery was part and parcel of the Industrial Revolution, just as much as child labor in Britain, the clothes that people wore, and the beverages they drank.

Changes in Society

Industrialization accentuated the polarization of society and disparities of income. In his novel *Sybil; or, The Two Nations*, the British politician Benjamin Disraeli° (1804–1881) spoke of "Two nations between whom there is no intercourse and no sympathy, who are as ignorant of each other's habits, thoughts, and feelings as if they were dwellers in different zones, or inhabitants of different planets . . . the rich and the poor."

Disraeli (diz-RAY-lee)

In Britain, the worst-off were those who clung to an obsolete skill or craft. The cotton-spinning boom of the 1790s briefly brought prosperity to weavers. Their high wages and low productivity, however, induced inventors to develop power looms. As a result, by 1811 the wages of handloom weavers had fallen by a third; by 1832, by two-thirds. Even by working more hours, they could not escape destitution.

The wages and standard of living of factory workers did not decline steadily like those of handloom weavers; they fluctuated wildly. During the war years 1792 to 1815, the price of food, on which the poor spent most of their income, rose faster than wages. The result was widespread hardship. Then, in the 1820s, real wages and public health began to improve. Industrial production grew at over 3 percent a year, pulling the rest of the economy along. Prices fell and wages rose. Even the poor could afford comfortable, washable cotton clothes and underwear.

Improvement, however, was not steady. One reason was the effect of **business cycles**—recurrent swings from economic hard times to recovery and growth, then back to hard times and a repetition of the sequence. When demand fell, businesses contracted or closed, and workers found themselves unemployed without any savings or insurance. Hard times returned in the "hungry forties." In 1847–1848 the potato crop failed in Ireland. One-quarter of the Irish population died in the resulting famine, and another quarter emigrated to England and America. On the European continent, the negative effects of economic downturns were tempered by the existence of small family farms to which urban workers could return when they were laid off.

Overall, the benefits of industrialization—cheaper food, clothing, and utensils—did not improve workers' standard of living until the 1850s. The real beneficiaries of the Industrial Revolution were the middle class. In Britain, landowning gentry and merchants had long shared wealth and influence. In the late eighteenth century, a new group arose: entrepreneurs whose money came from manufacturing. Most, like Arkwright and Wedgwood, were the sons of middling shopkeepers, craftsmen, or farmers. Their enterprises were usually self-financed, for little capital was needed to start a cotton-spinning or machine-building business. Many tried and some succeeded, largely by plowing their profits back into the business. A generation later, in the nineteenth century, some newly rich industrialists bought their way into high society.

Before the Industrial Revolution, wives of merchants had often participated in the family business; occasionally, widows managed sizable businesses on their own.

With industrialization came a "cult of domesticity" to justify removing middle-class women from contact with the business world. Instead, they became responsible for the home, the servants, the education of children, and the family's social life.

Middle-class people who attributed their success, often correctly, to their own efforts and virtues believed in individual responsibility: if some people could succeed through hard work, thrift, and temperance, then those who did not succeed had no one but themselves to blame for their failure. Many workers, however, newly arrived from rural districts, earned too little to save for the long stretches of unemployment they periodically experienced, and the squalor and misery of life in factory towns led to a noticeable increase in drunkenness on paydays. While the life of the poor remained brutal, the well-to-do—with no hypocrisy—espoused sobriety, thrift, industriousness, and responsibility. This moral position was a middle-class expression of sincere concern coupled with feelings of helplessness in the face of terrible social problems.

IDEOLOGICAL AND POLITICAL RESPONSES TO INDUSTRIALIZATION

Changes as profound as the Industrial Revolution could not occur without political ferment and ideological conflict. So many other momentous events took place during those years—the American Revolution (1776–1783), the French Revolution (1789–1799), the Napoleonic Wars (1804–1815), the reactions and revolts that periodically swept over Europe after 1815—that we cannot neatly separate out the consequences of industrialization from the rest. But it is clear that the Industrial Revolution strengthened the ideas of laissez faire° and socialism and sparked workers' protests.

Laissez Faire and Its Critics

The most celebrated exponent of **laissez faire** ("let them do") was Adam Smith (1723–1790), a Scottish economist. In *The Wealth of Nations* (1776) Smith argued that if individuals

---

laissez faire (lay-say fair)

were allowed to seek their personal gain, the effect, as though guided by an "invisible hand," would be to increase the general welfare. Except to protect private property, the government should refrain from interfering in business; it should even allow duty-free trade with foreign countries.

Although it was true that governments at the time were incompetent at regulating their national economies, it was becoming obvious that industrialization was not improving the general welfare but was for some causing great misery. Two other thinkers, Thomas Malthus (1766–1834) and David Ricardo (1772–1832), attempted to explain the poverty they saw without changing the basic premises of laissez faire. The cause of the workers' plight, Malthus and Ricardo said, was the population boom, which outstripped the food supply and led to falling wages. The workers' poverty, they claimed, was as much a result of "natural law" as the wealth of successful businessmen, and the only way the working class could avoid mass famine was to delay marriage and practice self-restraint and sexual abstinence.

Laissez-faire provided an ideological justification for a special kind of capitalism: banks, stock markets, and chartered companies allowed investors to obtain profits with reasonable risks but with much less government control and interference than in the past. In particular, removing guild and other restrictions allowed businesses to employ women and children and keep wages low.

Business people in Britain eagerly adopted laissez-faire ideas that justified their activities and kept the government at bay. But not everyone accepted the grim conclusions of the "dismal science," as economics was then known. Jeremy Bentham (1748–1832) believed that it was possible to maximize "the greatest happiness of the greatest number," if only a Parliament of enlightened reformers would study the social problems of the day and pass appropriate legislation; his philosophy became known as utilitarianism.

The German economist Friedrich List (1789–1846) rejected laissez faire and free trade as a British trick "to make the rest of the world, like the Hindus, its serfs in all industrial and commercial relations." To protect their "infant" industries from British competition, he argued, countries like Germany had to erect high tariff barriers. On the European continent, List's ideas were as influential as those of Smith and Ricardo and led to the formation of the Zollverein°, a customs union of most of the German states in 1834.

Positivists and Utopian Socialists

Bentham optimistically advocated gradual improvements. In contrast, some French social thinkers, moved by sincere concern for the poor, offered a radically new vision of a just civilization. Espousing a philosophy called **positivism,** the count of Saint-Simon (1760–1825) argued that the scientific method could solve social as well as technical problems. He recommended that the poor, guided by scientists and artists, form workers' communities under the protection of benevolent business leaders. These ideas found no following among workers, but they attracted the enthusiastic support of bankers and entrepreneurs, inspired by visions of railroads, canals, and other symbols of progress.

Meanwhile, the **utopian° socialism** of Charles Fourier (1768–1837), who loathed capitalists, imagined an ideal society in which groups of sixteen hundred workers would live in dormitories and work together on the land and in workshops where music, wine, and pastries would soften the hardships of labor. For this idea, critics called him "utopian"—a dreamer, after the Greek word *utopia* meaning "nowhere."

The person who came closest to creating a utopian community was the Englishman Robert Owen (1771–1858), a successful cotton manufacturer who believed that industry could provide prosperity for all. Conscience-stricken by the appalling plight of the workers, Owen took over the management of New Lanark, a mill town south of Glasgow. He improved the housing and added schools, a church, and other amenities. He also testified before Parliament against child labor and for government inspection of working conditions, thereby angering his fellow industrialists.

Protests and Reforms

Workers benefited little from the ideas of these middle-class philosophers. Instead, they resisted the harsh working conditions in their own ways. They changed jobs frequently. They often were absent, especially on Mondays. And when they were not closely watched, the quality of their work was likely to be poor.

Periodically, workers rioted or went on strike. Protests coincided with periods of high food prices and with downturns in the business cycle that left many unemployed. In some places, craftsmen broke into factories and destroyed the machines that threatened their livelihoods. Such acts of resistance did nothing, however, to change the nature of industrial work. Not until

---

Zollverein (TSOLL-feh-rine)

utopian (you-TOE-pee-uhn)

workers learned to act together could they hope to have much influence.

Gradually they formed benevolent societies and organizations to demand universal male suffrage and shorter workdays. In 1834 Robert Owen organized the Grand National Consolidated Trade Union to lobby for an eight-hour workday; it gained half a million members but failed a few months later in the face of government prosecution of trade-union activities. The Chartist movement had more success, gathering petitions by the thousands to present to Parliament. Although Chartism collapsed in 1848, it left a legacy of labor organizing.

Eventually, mass movements persuaded political leaders to look into the abuses of industrial life, despite the prevailing laissez-faire philosophy. In the 1820s and 1830s, the British Parliament began investigating conditions in the factories and mines. The Factory Act of 1833 prohibited the employment of children under age nine in textile mills. It also limited the working hours of children between the ages of nine and thirteen to eight hours a day and the daily working hours of fourteen- to eighteen-year-olds to twelve. The Mines Act of 1842 prohibited the employment of all women and of boys under age ten underground. Several decades passed before the government appointed enough inspectors to enforce the new laws.

Most important was the struggle over the Corn Laws—tariffs on imported grain. Their repeal in 1846, in the name of "free trade," was designed to lower the cost of food for workers and thereby allow employers to pay lower wages. A victory for laissez-faire, the repeal also represented a victory for the rising class of manufacturers, merchants, and investors over the conservative landowners who had long dominated politics.

The British learned to seek reform through accommodation. On the European continent, in contrast, the revolutions of 1848 revealed widespread discontent with repressive governments but failed to soften the hardships of industrialization.

INDUSTRIALIZATION AND THE NONINDUSTRIAL WORLD

The spread of the Industrial Revolution to western Europe and North America in the early nineteenth century delayed industrialization elsewhere. In most places, trade with the industrial countries meant exporting raw materials, not locally made handicraft products. In the few countries whose governments were tempted to imitate the West, cheap Western imports, backed by the power of Great Britain, thwarted the spread of industry for a century or more.

We will consider three places where industrialization did *not* occur in this period: Russia, whose society and institutions delayed industrialization by a century, and Egypt and India, where industrialization was stifled at the outset. In these three cases, we can discern the outlines of the Western domination that has characterized the history of the world since the late nineteenth century.

Russia

Russia had been in close contact with western Europe since the seventeenth century. Its aristocrats spoke French, its army was modeled on the armies of western Europe, and it participated in European wars and diplomacy. Yet Russia differed from western Europe in one important aspect: it had almost no middle class. Thus industrialization there arose not from the initiative of local entrepreneurs but by government decree and through the work of foreign engineers.

Tsar Nicholas I (r. 1825–1855) built the first railroad in Russia from St. Petersburg, the capital, to his summer palace in 1837. A few years later, he insisted that the trunk line from St. Petersburg to Moscow run in a perfectly straight line. American engineers built locomotive workshops in Russia, and British engineers set up textile mills. These projects, though well publicized, were oddities in a society where most people were serfs tied to the estates of powerful noble landowners and towns were few and far apart.

Until the late nineteenth century, the Russian government's interest in industry was limited and hesitant. An industrial revolution, to be successful, required large numbers of educated and independent-minded artisans and entrepreneurs. Suspicious of Western ideas, especially anything smacking of liberalism, socialism, or revolution, the Russian government feared the spread of literacy and of modern education beyond the minimum needed to train the officer corps and the bureaucracy. Rather than run the risk of allowing a middle class and a working class to arise that might challenge its control, the regime of Nicholas I kept the peasants in serfdom and preferred to import most industrial goods and pay for them with exports of grain and timber.

Russia aspired to Western-style economic development. But fear of political change caused the country to fall further behind western Europe, economically and technologically, than it had been a half-century before. When France and Britain went to war against Russia in 1854, they faced a Russian army equipped with obsolete weapons and bogged down for lack of transportation.

Steam Tractor in India Power machinery was introduced slowly into India because of the abundance of skilled low-cost labor. In this scene, a steam tractor fords a shallow stream, to the delight of onlookers. The towerlike construction on the right is probably a pier for a railroad bridge. (Billie Love Historical Collection)

Egypt

Like Russia, Egypt began to industrialize in the early nineteenth century. The driving force was its ruler, Muhammad Ali (1769–1849), a man who was to play a major role not only in the history of Egypt but in the Middle East and East Africa as well (see Chapter 26). He wanted to build up the Egyptian economy and military in order to become less dependent on the Ottoman sultan, his nominal overlord. To do so, he imported advisers and technicians from Europe and built cotton mills, foundries, shipyards, weapons factories, and other industrial enterprises. To pay for all this, he made the peasants grow wheat and cotton, which the government bought at a low price and exported at a profit. He also imposed high tariffs on imported goods in order to force the pace of industrialization.

Muhammad Ali's efforts, however, fell afoul of the British, who did not want a powerful country threatening to interrupt the flow of travelers and mail cross Egypt, the shortest route between Europe and India. When Egypt went to war against the Ottoman Empire in 1839, Britain intervened and forced Muhammad Ali to eliminate all import duties in the name of free trade. Unprotected, Egypt's fledgling industries could not compete with the flood of cheap British products. Thereafter, Egypt exported raw cotton and imported manufactured goods and became, in effect, an economic dependency of Britain.

India

Until the late eighteenth century, India had been the world's largest producer and exporter of cotton textiles, handmade by skilled spinners and weavers. The British East India Company took over large parts of India just as the Industrial Revolution was beginning in Britain. Thus cheap British factory-made textiles began flooding into India duty-free, putting first spinners and then handloom weavers out of work. Unlike Britain, India had no factories to which displaced handicraft workers could turn for work. Most of them became landless peasants, eking out a precarious living.

Like other tropical regions, India became an exporter of raw materials and an importer of British industrial goods. To hasten the process, British entrepreneurs and colonial officials introduced railroads into the subcontinent. The construction of India's railroad network began in the mid-1850s, along with coal mining to fuel the locomotives and the installation of telegraph lines to connect the major cities.

Some Indian entrepreneurs saw opportunities in the atmosphere of change that the British created. In 1854 the Bombay merchant Cowasjee Nanabhoy Davar imported an engineer, four skilled workers, and several textile machines from Britain and started India's first textile mill. This was the beginning of India's cotton industry. But, despite many gifted entrepreneurs, India's industrialization proceeded at a snail's pace, for the government was in British hands and the British did nothing to encourage Indian industry.

CONCLUSION

In the period from 1760 to 1851, the new technologies of the Industrial Revolution greatly increased humans' power over nature. Goods could be manufactured in vast quantities at low cost. People and messages could travel at unprecedented speeds. In addition to utilizing the energy produced by muscle power, wind, and water, humans gained access to the energy stored in coal. Faster than ever before, humans turned woodland into farmland, dug canals and laid tracks, bridged rivers and cut through mountains, and covered the countryside with towns and cities.

This newfound power over nature, far from benefiting everyone, increased the disparities between individuals and societies. Industrialization brought forth entrepreneurs—whether in the mills of England or on plantations in the American south—with enormous power over their employees or slaves, a power that they found easy and profitable to abuse. Some people acquired great wealth while others lived in poverty and squalor. Middle-class women were restricted to the care of their homes and children. Many working-class women had to leave home to earn wages in factories or as domestic servants. These changes in work and family life provoked intense debates among intellectuals. Some defended the disparities in the name of laissez faire; others criticized the injustices that industrialization brought. Society was slow to bring these abuses under control.

By the 1850s, the Industrial Revolution had spread from Britain to western Europe and the United States, and its impact was being felt around the world. To make a product that was sold on every continent, the British cotton industry used African slaves, American land, British machines, and Irish workers. Iron ships and steam engines shifted the historic balance between Europe and China. After the 1850s—as we shall see in Chapter 29—no part of the world remained untouched by the power of industry.

■ Key Terms

Industrial Revolution
agricultural revolution
   (eighteenth century)
mass production
Josiah Wedgwood
division of labor
mechanization
Richard Arkwright

Crystal Palace
steam engine
James Watt
electric telegraph
business cycle
laissez faire
positivism
utopian socialism

■ Suggested Readings

General works on the history of technology give pride of place to industrialization. For an optimistic overview see Joel Mokyr, *The Lever of Riches: Technological Creativity and Economic Progress* (1990). Other important recent works include James McClellan III and Harold Dorn, *Science and Technology in World History* (1999); David Landes, *The Wealth and Poverty of Nations* (1998); and Ian Inkster, *Technology and Industrialization: Historical Case Studies and International Perspectives* (1998).

There is a rich literature on the British industrial revolution, beginning with T. S. Ashton's classic *The Industrial Revolution, 1760–1830*, published in 1948 and often reprinted.

The impact of industrialization on workers is the theme of E. P. Thompson's classic work *The Making of the English Working Class* (1963), but see also E. R. Pike, *"Hard Times": Human Documents of the Industrial Revolution* (1966). The role of women is most ably revealed in Lynn Y. Weiner, *From Working Girl to Working Mother: The Female Labor Force in the United States, 1820–1980* (1985), and in Louise Tilly and Joan Scott, *Women, Work, and Family* (1978).

European industrialization is the subject of J. Goodman and K. Honeyman, *Gainful Pursuits: The Making of Industrial Europe: 1600–1914* (1988); John Harris, *Industrial Espionage and Technology Transfer: Britain and France in the Eighteenth Century* (1998); and David Landes, *The Unbound Prometheus: Technological Change and Industrial Development in Western Europe from 1750 to the Present* (1972). On the beginnings of American industrialization see David Jeremy, *Artisans, Entrepreneurs and Machines: Essays on the Early Anglo-American Textile Industry, 1770–1840* (1998).

On the environmental impact of industrialization see Richard Wilkinson, *Poverty and Progress: An Ecological Perspective on Economic Development* (1973), and Richard Tucker and John Richards, *Global Deforestation in the Nineteenth-Century World Economy* (1983).

The first book to treat industrialization as a global phenomenon is Peter Stearns, *The Industrial Revolution in World History* (1993); see also Louise Tilly's important article "Connections" in *American Historical Review* (February 1994).

■ Note

1. *Nautical Magazine* 12 (1843): 346.

25

NATION BUILDING AND ECONOMIC TRANSFORMATION IN THE AMERICAS, 1800–1890

Independence in Latin America, 1800–1830 • The Problem of Order, 1825–1890 • The Challenge of Economic and Social Change

ENVIRONMENT AND TECHNOLOGY: The McCormick Reaper

SOCIETY AND CULTURE: Villages in New England and Mexico

The Train Station in Orizaba, Mexico, 1877   In the last decades of the nineteenth century, Mexico's political leaders actively promoted economic development. The railroad became the symbol of this ideal.

n 1862, seeing Mexico divided by violent factional conflicts and the United States convulsed by the Civil War, Napoleon III seized the opportunity to project French power into the Americas by sending a large military force to Mexico. Mexican conservatives who resented their government's efforts to introduce democratic reforms and limit the power of the Catholic Church supported the invasion. After driving the liberal president, Benito Juárez°, from Mexico City, Napoleon III and a group of Mexican conservatives in 1864 convinced Archduke Maximilian of Habsburg, brother of Emperor Franz Joseph of Austria, to accept the throne of Mexico.

Although Maximilian embraced Mexican patriotic symbols and accepted some of Juárez's reforms, he failed to win popular support. Armed resistance by Mexican liberals and diplomatic pressure by the United States after the conclusion of the Civil War led to a French pullout. Then, on the morning of June 19, 1867, a Mexican firing squad executed Maximilian. His young wife Charlotte, daughter of King Leopold of Belgium, was in Europe trying to convince the emperor of France or the pope to intervene to save her husband when news of his death swept her into madness. For Mexicans, the defeat and execution of Maximilian signaled an end to intervention and the triumph of republicanism.

The independence of Britain's thirteen North American colonies set in motion a radical transformation of the New World. Spurred by the revolutionary examples of the United States and France (see Chapter 23) and buttressed by Enlightenment ideology, which exalted political freedom, most of the Spanish and Portuguese colonies in the New World gained independence in the early decades of the nineteenth century. As the French intervention in Mexico illustrates, however, European powers were ready to challenge the sovereignty of many of the new American nations.

Through the nineteenth century, the new nations in the Western Hemisphere wrestled with the difficult questions that independence raised. If colonies could reject submission to imperial powers, could not regions with distinct cultures, social structures, and economies refuse to accept the political authority of the newly formed nation-states? How could nations born in revolution accept the political strictures of written constitutions—even those they wrote themselves? How could the ideals of liberty and freedom expressed in those constitutions be reconciled with the denial of rights to Amerindians, slaves, recent immigrants, and women?

While trying to resolve these political questions, the new nations also attempted to promote economic growth. But just as the legacy of class and racial division thwarted the realization of political ideals, colonial economic development, with its emphasis on agricultural and mining exports, inhibited efforts to promote diversification and industrialization.

As you read this chapter, ask yourself the following questions:

- What were the causes of the revolutions for independence in Latin America?
- What major political challenges did Western Hemisphere nations face in the nineteenth century?
- How did abolitionism, the movement for women's rights, and immigration change the nations of the Western Hemisphere?
- How did industrialization and new agricultural technologies affect the environment?

INDEPENDENCE IN LATIN AMERICA, 1800–1830

As the eighteenth century drew to a close, Spain and Portugal held vast colonial possessions in the Western Hemisphere, although their power had declined relative to that of their British and French rivals. Both Iberian empires had reformed colonial administration and strengthened their military forces in the eighteenth century. Despite these efforts, the same economic and political forces that had undermined British rule in the

---

Benito Juárez (beh-NEE-toh WAH-rez)

colonies that became the United States were present in Spanish America and Brazil.

Roots of Revolution, to 1810

Wealthy colonial residents of Latin America were frustrated by the political and economic power of colonial officials and angered by high taxes and imperial monopolies. By 1800, the examples of the American and French Revolutions had stirred enthusiasm for self-government (see Chapter 23). The great works of the Enlightenment as well as revolutionary documents like the Declaration of Independence and the Declaration of the Rights of Man circulated widely in Latin America. But it was Napoleon's decision to invade Portugal (1807) and Spain (1808), not revolutionary ideas, that ignited Latin America's struggle for independence.

In 1808 the royal family of Portugal fled to Brazil. King John VI maintained his court there for over a decade. In Spain, in contrast, Napoleon forced King Ferdinand VII to abdicate and placed his own brother, Joseph Bonaparte, on the throne. Spanish patriots fighting against the French created a new political body, the Junta° Central, to administer the areas they controlled. Most Spaniards viewed the Junta as a temporary patriotic institution created to govern Spain while the king remained a French prisoner. The Junta, however, claimed the right to exercise the king's powers over Spain's colonies, and this claim provoked a crisis.

Large numbers of colonists in Spanish America, perhaps a majority, favored obedience to the Junta Central. A vocal minority, which included many wealthy and powerful individuals, objected. The dissenters argued that they were subjects of the king, not dependents of the Spanish nation. They wanted to create local juntas and govern their own affairs until Ferdinand regained the throne. Spanish loyalists in the colonies resisted this tentative assertion of local autonomy and thus provoked armed uprisings. In late 1808 and 1809, popular movements overthrew Spanish colonial officials in Venezuela, Mexico, and Bolivia and created local juntas. In each case, Spanish officials quickly reasserted control and punished the leaders. Their harsh repression, however, further polarized public opinion in the colonies and gave rise to a greater sense of a separate American nationality. By 1810 Spanish colonial authorities were facing a new round of revolutions more clearly focused on the achievement of independence.

Junta (HUN-tah)

Simón Bolívar   Simón Bolívar was the greatest of Latin America's independence-era leaders. There are many portraits of Bolívar, each suggesting distinct elements of his political legacy. This portrait shows him in uniform and cape mounted on a white horse. His gaze is focused on the horizon, suggesting his unique ability to foresee the future's challenges.   (Organization of American States)

Spanish South America, 1810–1825

In Caracas (the capital city of modern Venezuela), a revolutionary Junta led by creoles (colonial-born whites) declared independence in 1811. Although this group espoused popular sovereignty and representative democracy, its leaders were large landowners who defended slavery and opposed full citizenship for the black and mixed-race majority. Their aim was to expand their own privileges by eliminating Spaniards from the upper levels of Venezuela's government and from the church. The junta's narrow agenda spurred loyalists in the colonial administration and church hierarchy to rally thousands of free blacks and

CHRONOLOGY

	United States and Canada	Mexico and Central America	South America
1800	**1789** U.S. Constitution ratified **1803** Louisiana Purchase		**1808** Portuguese royal family arrives in Brazil
1825	**1812–1815** War of 1812	**1810–21** Mexican movement for independence	**1808–1809** Revolutions for independence begin in Spanish South America
	1837 Texas gains independence from Mexico **1845** Texas admitted as a state		**1822** Brazil gains independence
1850	**1848** Women's Rights Convention in Seneca Falls, New York **1861–1865** Civil War **1867** Creation of Dominion of Canada	**1846–1848** War between Mexico and the United States **1847–1870** Caste War **1862–1867** French invade Mexico	
1875	**1876** Sioux and allies defeat United States Army in Battle of Little Bighorn		**1865–1870** Argentina, Uruguay, and Brazil wage war against Paraguay **1870s** Governments of Argentina and Chile begin final campaigns against indigenous peoples **1879–1881** Chile wages war against Peru and Bolivia **1888** Abolition of slavery in Brazil

slaves to defend the Spanish Empire. Faced with this determined resistance, the revolutionary movement placed overwhelming political authority in the hands of its military leader **Simón Bolívar°** (1783–1830), who later became the preeminent leader of the independence movement in Spanish South America.

The son of wealthy Venezuelan planters, Bolívar had studied both the classics and the works of the Enlightenment. He used the force of his personality to mobilize political support and to hold the loyalty of his troops. Defeated on many occasions, Bolívar successfully adapted his objectives and policies to attract new allies and build coalitions. Although initially opposed to the abolition of slavery, for example, he agreed to support emancipation in order to draw slaves and freemen to his cause and to gain supplies from Haiti. Bolívar was also capable of

using harsh methods to ensure victory. Attempting to force resident Spaniards to join the rebellion in 1813, he proclaimed: "Any Spaniard who does not . . . work against tyranny in behalf of this just cause will be considered an enemy and punished; as a traitor to the nation, he will inevitably be shot by a firing squad."[1]

Between 1813 and 1817 military advantage shifted back and forth between the patriots and loyalists. Bolívar's ultimate success was aided by his decision to enlist demobilized English veterans of the Napoleonic Wars and by a military revolt in Spain in 1820. The English veterans, hardened by combat, helped improve the battlefield performance of Bolívar's army. The revolt in Spain forced Ferdinand VII—he was restored to the throne in 1814 after the defeat of Napoleon—to accept a constitution that limited the powers of both the monarch and the church. Colonial loyalists who for a decade had fought to maintain the authority of monarch and church viewed those reforms as unacceptably liberal.

Simón Bolívar (see-MOAN bow-LEE-varh)

OREGON COUNTRY (Joint U.S.-British occupation)

BRITISH NORTH AMERICA (Gr. Br.)

Mississippi

UNITED STATES

Colorado

Rio Grande

MEXICO 1821

San Antonio•

Gulf of Mexico

Mexico City• •Veracruz

BAHAMA IS. (Gr. Br.)

Havana•

CUBA (Spain)

HAITI 1804

PUERTO RICO (Spain)

BRITISH HONDURAS (Gr. Br.)

JAMAICA (Gr. Br.)

GUATEMALA Guatemala

Caribbean Sea

UNITED PROVINCES OF CENTRAL AMERICA 1823–1839

Panama•

Caracas•

TRINIDAD (Gr. Br.)

VENEZUELA

BR. GUIANA (Gr. Br.)

DUTCH GUIANA (Neth.)

FRENCH GUIANA (France)

Magdalena

•Socorro

Bogotá•

GRAN COLOMBIA 1819–1830

Galápagos Islands

•Quito

ECUADOR

Amazon

ATLANTIC OCEAN

EMPIRE OF BRAZIL 1822

PERU 1824

Lima•

PACIFIC OCEAN

BOLIVIA 1825

La Paz•

•Sucre

•Bahia

Paraná

PARAGUAY 1811

São Paulo•

Rio de Janeiro•

CHILE 1817

UNITED PROVINCES OF THE RÍO DE LA PLATA 1816

Valparaíso• Santiago•

URUGUAY 1828

ARGENTINA Buenos Aires• Bahía Blanca•

Montevideo•

1811 Year independence gained

Colony

0 500 1000 Km.

0 500 1000 Mi.

PATAGONIA (Disputed between Argentina and Chile)

Islas Malvinas (Falkland Islands)

With the king's supporters divided, momentum swung irreversibly to the patriots. After liberating present-day Venezuela, Colombia, and Ecuador, Bolívar's army occupied the area that is now Peru and Bolivia (named for Bolívar). Finally defeating the last Spanish armies in 1824, Bolívar and his closest supporters attempted to draw the former Spanish colonies into a formal confederation. The first step was to forge Venezuela, Colombia, and Ecuador into a single nation: Gran Colombia (see Map 25.1). With Bolívar's encouragement, Peru and Bolivia also experimented with unification. Despite his prestige, however, all of these initiatives had failed by 1830.

Buenos Aires (the capital city of modern Argentina) was the second important center of revolutionary activity in Spanish South America. In Buenos Aires, news of Ferdinand VII's abdication led to the creation of a junta, organized by militia commanders, merchants, and ranchers, which overthrew the viceroy in 1810. To deflect the opposition of loyalists and Spanish colonial officials, the junta claimed loyalty to the imprisoned king. After Ferdinand regained the Spanish throne, however, junta leaders dropped this pretense. In 1816 they declared independence as the United Provinces of the Río de la Plata.

Patriot leaders in Buenos Aires at first sought to retain control over the territory of the Viceroyalty of Río de la Plata, which had been created in 1776 and included modern Argentina, Uruguay, Paraguay, and Bolivia. But Spanish loyalists in Uruguay and Bolivia and a separatist movement in Paraguay defeated these ambitions. Even within the territory of Argentina, the government in Buenos Aires was unable to control regional rivalries and political differences. As a result, the region rapidly descended into political chaos.

A weak succession of juntas, collective presidencies, and dictators soon lost control over much of the interior of Argentina. However, in 1817 the government in Buenos Aires did manage to support a mixed force of Chileans and Argentines led by José de San Martín° (1778–1850), who crossed the Andes Mountains to attack Spanish military forces in Chile and Peru. During this campaign, San Martín's most effective troops were former slaves, who had gained their freedom by enlisting in the army, and gauchos, the cowboys of the Argentine

pampas (prairies). After gaining victory in Chile, San Martín pushed on to Peru in 1820 but failed to gain a clear victory there. The violent and destructive uprising of Tupac Amaru II in 1780 had traumatized the Andean region and colonists fearful that support for independence might unleash another Amerindian uprising. Unable to make progress, San Martín surrendered command of patriot forces in Peru to Simón Bolívar, who overcame final Spanish resistance in 1824.

Mexico, 1810–1823

In 1810, Mexico was Spain's richest and most populous colony. Its silver mines were the richest in the world, and the colony's capital, Mexico City, was larger than any city in Spain. Mexico also had the largest population of Spanish immigrants among the colonies. Spaniards dominated the government, church, and economy of Mexico. When news of Napoleon's invasion of Spain reached the colony, conservative Spaniards in Mexico City overthrew the local viceroy because he was too sympathetic to the Creoles. This action by Spanish loyalists underlined the new reality: with the king of Spain in a French prison, colonial authority now rested on brute force.

The first stage of the revolution against Spain occurred in central Mexico. In this region wealthy ranchers and farmers had aggressively forced many Amerindian communities from their traditional agricultural lands. A series of crop failures and epidemics further afflicted the region's rural poor. At the same time, miners and the urban poor faced higher food prices and rising unemployment. With the power of colonial authorities weakened by events in Spain, anger and fear spread through towns and villages in central Mexico.

On September 16, 1810, **Miguel Hidalgo y Costilla°**, parish priest of the small town of Dolores, rang the church bells, attracting thousands. In a fiery speech he urged the crowd to rise up against the oppression of Spanish officials. Tens of thousands of the rural and urban poor joined his movement. They lacked military discipline and adequate weapons but knew who their oppressors were, spontaneously attacking the ranches and mines that had been exploiting them. Many Spaniards and colonial-born whites were murdered or assaulted. At first, wealthy Mexicans were sympathetic to Hidalgo's objectives, but they eventually supported Spanish authorities when they recognized the threat that the angry masses following Hidalgo posed to them. The military

Map 25.1   Latin America by 1830   By 1830, patriot forces had overturned the Spanish and Portuguese Empires of the Western Hemisphere. Regional conflicts, local wars, and foreign interventions challenged the survival of many of these new nations following independence.

José de San Martín (hoe-SAY deh san mar-TEEN)
Miguel Hidalgo y Costilla (mee-GEHL ee-DAHL-go ee cos-TEA-ah)

tide quickly turned against Hidalgo, and he was captured, tried, and executed in 1811.

The revolution continued under the leadership of another priest, **José María Morelos°,** a former student of Hidalgo. A more adept military and political leader than his mentor, Morelos created a formidable fighting force and, in 1813, convened a congress that declared independence and drafted a constitution. Despite these achievements, loyalist forces also proved too strong for Morelos. He was defeated and executed in 1815.

Although small numbers of insurgents continued to wage war against Spanish forces, colonial rule seemed secure in 1820. However, news of the military revolt in Spain unsettled the conservative groups and church officials who had defended Spanish rule against Hidalgo and Morelos. In 1821 Colonel Agustín de Iturbide° and other loyalist commanders forged an alliance with remaining insurgents and declared Mexico's independence. The conservative origins of Mexico's transition to independence were highlighted by the decision to create a monarchial form of government and crown Iturbide as emperor. In early 1823, however, the army overthrew Iturbide and Mexico became a republic.

Brazil, to 1831

The arrival of the Portuguese royal family in Brazil in 1808 helped to maintain the loyalty of the colonial elite and to stimulate the local economy. After the defeat of Napoleon in Europe, the Portuguese government called for King John VI to return to Portugal. He at first resisted this pressure. Then in 1820 the military uprising in Spain provoked a sympathetic liberal revolt in Portugal, and the Portuguese military garrison in Rio de Janeiro forced the king to permit the creation of juntas. John recognized that he needed to take dramatic action to protect his throne. In 1821, he returned to Portugal. Hoping to protect his claims to Brazil, he left his son Pedro in Brazil as regent.

By 1820, the Spanish colonies along Brazil's borders had experienced ten years of revolution and civil war, and some, like Argentina and Paraguay, had gained independence. Unable to ignore these struggles, some Brazilians began to reevaluate Brazil's relationship with Portugal. Many Brazilians resented their homeland's economic subordination to Portugal. The arrogance of Portuguese soldiers and bureaucrats led others to talk openly of independence. Rumors circulated that Portuguese troops were being sent to discipline Brazil and force the regent Pedro to join his father in Lisbon.

José María Morelos (hoe-SAY mah-REE-ah moh-RAY-los)
Agustín de Iturbide (ah-goos-TEEN deh ee-tur-BEE-deh)

Unwilling to return to Portugal and committed to maintaining his family's hold on Brazil, Pedro aligned himself with the rising tide of independence sentiment. In 1822, he declared Brazilian independence. Pedro's decision launched Brazil into a unique political trajectory. Unlike its neighbors, which became constitutional republics, Brazil gained independence as a constitutional monarchy with Pedro I, heir to the throne of Portugal, as emperor.

Pedro I was committed both to monarchy and to many liberal principles. He directed the writing of the constitution of 1824, which provided for an elected assembly and granted numerous protections for political opposition. But he made powerful enemies by attempting to protect the Portuguese who remained in Brazil from arbitrary arrest and seizure of their property. More dangerously still, he opposed slavery in a nation dominated by the slave-owning class. In 1823 Pedro I anonymously published an article that characterized slavery as a "cancer eating away at Brazil." Despite opposition, he then concluded a treaty with Great Britain to end Brazilian participation in the slave trade in 1830. The political elite of Brazil's slave-owning regions opposed the treaty and for nearly two decades worked tirelessly to prevent enforcement. Pedro also continued his father's costly commitment of military forces to control neighboring Uruguay. As military losses and costs rose, the Brazilian public grew impatient. A small but vocal minority that opposed the monarchy and sought the creation of a democracy used these issues to rally public opinion against the emperor.

Confronted by street demonstrations and violence between Brazilians and Portuguese, Pedro I abdicated the throne in 1831 in favor of his five-year-old son Pedro II. After a nine-year regency, Pedro II assumed full powers as emperor of Brazil. He reigned until he was overthrown by republicans in 1889.

THE PROBLEM OF ORDER, 1825–1890

All the newly independent nations of the Western Hemisphere had difficulties establishing stable political institutions. The idea of popular sovereignty found broad support across the hemisphere. As a result, written constitutions and elected assemblies were put in place, often before the actual achievement of independence. Even in the hemisphere's two monarchies, Mexico and Brazil, the emperors sought to legitimize their rule by accepting constitutional limits on their authority and by the creation of representative assemblies. Nevertheless, widespread support for constitutional order and for representative government failed to prevent bitter factional conflict, regionalism, and the appearance of charismatic political leaders and military uprisings.

Constitutional Experiments

In reaction to the arbitrary and tyrannical authority of colonial rulers, revolutionary leaders in both the United States and Latin America espoused constitutionalism. They believed that the careful description of political powers in written constitutions offered the best protection for individual rights and liberties. In practice, however, many new constitutions proved unworkable. In the United States, George Washington, James Madison, and other leaders became dissatisfied with the nation's first constitution, the Articles of Confederation. They led the effort to write a new constitution, which was put into effect in 1789. In Latin America, few constitutions survived the rough-and-tumble of national politics. Between 1811 and 1833 Venezuela and Chile alone ratified and then rejected a combined total of nine constitutions.

Important differences in colonial political experience influenced later political developments in the Americas. The ratification of a new constitution in the United States was the culmination of a long historical process that had begun with the development of English constitutional law and continued under colonial charters. Many more residents of the British North American colonies had had the experience of voting and holding political office than was true in the colonial societies of Portuguese or Spanish America. The British colonies provided opportunities for holding elective offices in town governments and colonial legislatures, and, by the time of independence, citizens had grown accustomed to elections, political parties, and factions. In contrast, constitutional government and elections were only briefly experienced in Spanish America between 1812 and 1814—while Ferdinand VII was a prisoner of Napoleon—and this short period was disrupted by the early stages of the revolutions for independence. Brazil had almost no experience with popular politics before independence. Despite these differences in experience and constitutional forms, every new republic in the Americas initially limited the right to vote to free men of property.

Democratic passions and the desire for effective self-rule led to significant political reform in the Americas, even in some of the region's remaining colonies. British Canada was divided into separate colonies and territories each with a separate and distinct government. Political life in each colony was dominated by a provincial governor and appointed advisory councils drawn from the local elite. Elected assemblies existed within each province, but they exercised limited power. Agitation to end oligarchic rule and make government responsive to the will of the assemblies led to armed rebellion in 1837. In the 1840s Britain responded by establishing responsible government in each of the Canadian provinces, allowing limited self-rule. By the 1860s regional political leaders interested in promoting economic development realized that railroads and other internal improvements required a government with a "national" character. Moreover, civil war in the U.S. and raids from U.S. territory into Canada by Irish nationalists focused attention on the need to protect the border. Negotiations led to the **Confederation of 1867,** which included the provinces of Ontario, Quebec, New Brunswick, and Nova Scotia. The Confederation that created the new Dominion of Canada with a central government in Ottawa (see Map 25.2) was hailed by one observer as the "birthday of a new nationality." [2]

The path to effective constitutional government was rockier to the south. Because neither Spain nor Portugal had permitted anything like the elected legislatures and municipal governments of colonial North America, the drafters of Latin American constitutions were less constrained by practical political experience. As a result, many of the new Latin American nations experimented with untested political institutions. For example, Simón Bolívar, who wrote the first constitutions of five South American republics, included in Bolivia's constitution a fourth branch of government that had "jurisdiction over the youth, the hearts of men, public spirit, good customs, and republican ethics."

Most Latin American nations found it difficult to define the political role of the Catholic Church after independence. In the colonial period the Catholic Church was a religious monopoly that controlled all levels of education, and dominated intellectual life. Many early constitutions aimed to reduce this power by making education secular and by permitting the practice of other religions. The church reacted by organizing its allies and financing conservative political movements. In Mexico, Colombia, Chile, and Argentina conflicts between liberals who sought the separation of church and state and supporters of the church's traditional powers dominated political life until late in the nineteenth century.

Limiting the power of the military proved to be another significant stumbling block to the creation of constitutional governments in Latin America. The wars for independence elevated the prestige of military leaders. When the wars were over, Bolívar and other military commanders seldom proved willing to subordinate themselves to civilian authorities. At the same time, frustrated

Map 25.2 Dominion of Canada, 1873 Although independence was not yet achieved and settlement remained concentrated along the U.S. border, Canada had established effective political and economic control over its western territories by 1873.

by the often-chaotic workings of constitutional democracy, few citizens were willing to support civilian politicians in any contest with the military. As a result, many Latin American militaries successfully resisted civilian control. Brazil, ruled by Emperor Pedro I, was the principal exception to this pattern.

Personalist Leaders

Successful patriot leaders in both the United States and Latin America gained mass followings during the wars for independence. They recruited and mobilized popular support by using patriotic symbols and by carefully associating their actions with national objectives. After independence, many patriot military leaders were able to use their personal followings to gain national political leadership. George Washington's ability to dominate the political scene in the early republican United States anticipated the later political ascendancy of revolution-

ary heroes such as Iturbide in Mexico and Bolívar in Gran Colombia. In each case, military reputation provided the foundation for personal political power. These **personalist leaders** relied on their ability to mobilize and direct the masses of these new nations rather than on the authority of constitutions and laws. Their model was Napoleon, who rose from the French army to become emperor, not John Madison, the primary author of the U.S. Constitution. In Latin America, a personalist leader who gained and held political power without constitutional sanction was called a *caudillo°*.

Latin America's slow development of stable political institutions made personalist politics more influential than was the case in the United States (see Society and Culture: Villages in New England and Mexico). Nevertheless, charismatic politicians in the United States such as Andrew Jackson did sometimes challenge constitutional limits to their authority, as did the caudillos of Latin

caudillo (kouh-DEE-yoh)

Villages in New England and Mexico

Born in Scotland, Fanny Calderón de la Barca lived briefly in Boston. She married a Spanish diplomat who later became ambassador to Mexico. She was a very critical observer of Mexican customs and culture. In this brief selection from Life in Mexico, *published in 1843, she compares village life in Mexico and New England. We can see clearly Calderón de la Barca's obvious affection for her native land and prejudice against Mexico. Historians often deal with biased or prejudiced sources and develop strategies to overcome these weaknesses to order to illuminate the past. This source challenges us to overcome the author's prejudice in order to undertake a comparative analysis of why Mexico and the United States developed so differently in response to the opportunities and challenges of the nineteenth century.*

If anyone wishes to try the effect of strong contrast, let him come direct from the United States to this country; but it is in the villages especially that the contrast is most striking. Travelling in New England, for example, we arrive at a small village. We see four new churches, proclaiming four different sects; religion suited to all customers. These wooden churches or meeting houses are all new, all painted white. . . . Houses, churches, stores, and taverns, all are of a piece. They are suited to the present emergency, whatever that may be, though they will never make fine ruins. Everything proclaims prosperity, equality, consistency; the past forgotten, the present all and all, and the future taking care of itself. . . . No beggars.

Transport yourself in imagination [to] Mexico. The Indian huts, with their half-naked inhabitants, and little gardens full of flowers; the huts themselves built either of clay or the [stones of a ruined building]. . . . [T]he church, gray and ancient, but strong as if designed for eternity; with its saints and virgins, and martyrs and relics, its gold and silver and precious stones, whose value could buy up all the spare lots in the New England village; the [beggar] with scarce a rag to cover him, kneeling on the marble pavement. . . . Here, everything reminds us of the past; of the conquering Spaniards, who seemed to build for eternity; impressing each work with their own solid, grave, and religious character; of the triumphs of Catholicism. . . . It is the present that seems like a dream, a pale reflection of the past. All is decaying and growing fainter, and men seem trusting to some unknown future which they may never see. One government has been abandoned, and there is none in its place. One revolution follows another, yet the remedy is not found. Let them beware lest half a century later, they be awakened from their delusion.

How does Fanny Calderón de la Barca attempt to connect the visual differences between New England and Mexican villages to differences in culture? What does she say about how these two societies regarded their pasts and futures? What threat does the author seem to see in Mexico's future? Find one example of bias in her comparison.

Source: Fanny Calderón de la Barca, *Life in Mexico* (1843), reprinted in an abridged form in Lewis Hanke, ed., *Latin America: A Historical Reader* (Boston: Little, Brown, 1974), 440–441.

America. Unlike Latin America, however, the United States never experienced an armed rebellion that overturned the results of an election.

Throughout the Western Hemisphere, charismatic military men played key roles in attracting mass support for independence movements that were commonly dominated by colonial elites. Although this popular support was often decisive in the struggle for independence, the first constitutions of nearly all the American republics excluded large numbers of poor citizens from full political participation. But nearly everywhere in the Americas marginalized groups found populist leaders to articulate their concerns and challenge these limits on their political participation. Using informal means, these leaders sought to influence the selection of officeholders and to place their concerns in the public arena. Despite their success in overturning the deference-based politics of the colonial past, this populist political style at times threatened constitutional order and led to dictatorship.

Andrew Jackson of the United States and **José Antonio Páez°** of Venezuela were political leaders whose powerful personal followings allowed them to challenge constitutional limits to their authority. During the independence

---

José Antonio Páez (hoe-SAY an-TOE-nee-oh PAH-eez)

wars in Venezuela and Colombia, Páez (1790–1873) organized and led Bolívar's most successful cavalry force. Like most of his followers, Páez was uneducated and poor, but his physical strength, courage, and guile made him a natural guerrilla leader and helped him build a powerful political base in Venezuela. Páez described his authority in the following manner: "[the soldiers] resolved to confer on me the supreme command and blindly to obey my will, confidant . . . that I was the only one who could save them."[3] Able to count on the personal loyalty of his followers, Páez was seldom willing to accept the constitutional authority of a distant president.

After defeating the Spanish armies, Bolívar pursued his dream of forging a permanent union of former Spanish colonies modeled on the federal system of the United States. But he underestimated the strength of nationalist sentiment unleashed during the independence wars. Páez and other Venezuelan leaders resisted the surrender of their hard-won power to Bolívar's Gran Colombia government in distant Bogotá (the capital city of modern Colombia). When Bolívar's authority was challenged by political opponents in 1829, Páez declared Venezuela's independence. Merciless to his enemies and indulgent with his followers, Páez ruled the country as president or dictator for the next eighteen years. Despite implementing an economic program favorable to the elite, Páez remained popular with the masses by skillfully manipulating popular political symbols. Even as his personal wealth grew through land acquisitions and commerce, Páez took care to present himself as a common man.

Andrew Jackson (1767–1845) was the first president of the United States born in humble circumstances. A self-made man who eventually acquired substantial property and owned over a hundred slaves, Jackson was extremely popular among frontier residents, urban workers, and small farmers. Although he was notorious for his untidy personal life as well as for dueling, his courage, individualism, and willingness to challenge authority helped him lead a successful political career as judge, general, congressman, senator, and president.

During his military career, Jackson proved to be impatient with civilian authorities. Widely known because of his victories over the Creek and Seminole peoples, he was elevated to the pinnacle of American politics by his celebrated defeat of the British at the Battle of New Orleans in 1815 and by his seizure of Florida from the Spanish in 1818. In 1824 he received a plurality of the popular votes cast for the presidency, but he failed to win a majority of the electoral votes and was denied the presidency when the House of Representatives chose John Quincy Adams.

Jackson's followers viewed his landslide election victory in 1828 and reelection in 1832 as the triumph of democracy over the entrenched aristocracy. In office Jackson challenged constitutional limits on his authority, substantially increasing presidential power at the expense of Congress and the Supreme Court. Like Páez, Jackson was able to dominate national politics by blending a populist political style that celebrated the virtues and cultural enthusiasms of common people with support for policies that promoted the economic interests of some of the nation's most powerful propertied groups.

Personalist leaders were common in both Latin America and the United States, but Latin America's weaker constitutional tradition, more limited protection of property rights, lower literacy levels, and less-developed communications systems provided fewer checks on the ambitions of popular politicians. The Constitution of the United States was never suspended, and no national election result in the United States was ever successfully overturned by violence. Latin America's personalist leaders, however, often ignored constitutional restraints on their authority, and election results seldom determined access to presidential power. As a result, by 1900, every Latin American nation had experienced periods of dictatorship.

The Threat of Regionalism

After independence, new national governments were generally weaker than the colonial governments they replaced. In debates over tariffs, tax and monetary policies, and, in many nations, slavery and the slave trade, regional elites often were willing to lead secessionist movements or to provoke civil war rather than accept laws that threatened their interests. Some of the hemisphere's newly independent nations did not survive these struggles; others lost territories to aggressive neighbors.

In Spanish America, all of the postindependence efforts to forge large multistate federations failed. Central America and Mexico maintained their colonial-era administrative association following independence in 1821. After the overthrow of Iturbide's imperial rule in Mexico in 1823, however, regional politicians split with Mexico and created the independent Republic of Central America. Regional rivalries and civil wars during the 1820s and 1830s forced the breakup of that entity as well and led to the creation of five separate nations. Bolívar attempted to maintain the colonial unity of Venezuela, Colombia, and Ecuador by creating the nation of Gran Colombia with its capital in Bogotá. But even before his death in 1830, not only Venezuela but also Ecuador had become independent states.

During colonial times, Argentina, Uruguay, Paraguay, and Bolivia had been united in a single viceroyalty with its capital in Buenos Aires. With the defeat of Spain, political leaders in Paraguay, Uruguay, and Bolivia declared their independence from Buenos Aires. Argentina, the area that remained after this breakup, was itself nearly overwhelmed by these powerful centrifugal forces. After independence, Argentina's liberals took power in Buenos Aires. They sought a strong central government to promote secular education, free trade, and immigration from Europe. Conservatives dominated the interior provinces. They supported the Catholic Church's traditional control of education as well as the protection of local textile and winemaking industries from European imports. When, in 1819, political leaders in Buenos Aires imposed a national constitution that ignored these concerns, the conservatives of the interior rose in rebellion.

After a decade of civil war and rebellions, a powerful local caudillo, Juan Manuel de Rosas°, came to power. For more than two decades he dominated Argentina, running the nation as if it were his private domain. The economy expanded under Rosas, but his use of intimidation, mob violence, and assassination created many enemies. In 1852 an alliance of foreign and domestic enemies overthrew him, but a new cycle of provincial rivalry and civil war prevented the creation of a strong central government until 1861.

Regionalism threatened the United States as well. The defense of state and regional interests played an important role in the framing of the U.S. Constitution. Many important constitutional provisions represented compromises forged among competing state and regional leaders. The creation of a Senate with equal representation from each state, for example, was an attempt to calm small states, which feared they might be dominated by larger states. The formula for representation in the House of Representatives was also an effort to compromise the divisions between slave and free states. Yet, despite these constitutional compromises, the nation was still threatened by regional rivalries.

Slavery increasingly divided the nation into two separate and competitive societies. A rising tide of immigration to the northern states in the 1830s and 1840s began to move the center of political power in the House of Representatives away from the south. Many southern leaders sought to protect slavery by expanding it to new territories. They supported the Louisiana Purchase in 1803 (see Map 25.3). This agreement with France transferred to the United States a vast territory extending from the Gulf of Mexico to Canada. Southern leaders also supported statehood for Texas and war with Mexico (discussed later in the chapter).

Juan Manuel de Rosas (huan man-WELL deh ROH-sas)

The territorial acquisitions proved a mixed blessing to the defenders of slavery because they forced a national debate about slavery itself. Should slavery be allowed to expand into new territories? Could slavery be protected if new territories eligible for statehood were overwhelmingly free?

In 1860 Abraham Lincoln (1809–1865), who was committed to checking the spread of slavery, was elected president of the United States. In response, the planter elite in the southern states chose the dangerous course of secession from the federal Union. The seceding states formed a new government, the Confederate States of America, known as the Confederacy. Lincoln was able to preserve the Union, but his victory was purchased at an enormous cost. The U.S. Civil War (1861–1865), waged by southern Confederate forces and northern Union (U.S.) forces, was the most destructive conflict in the history of the Western Hemisphere. More than 600,000 lives were lost before the Confederacy surrendered in 1865. The Union victory led to the abolition of slavery. It also transferred national political power to a northern elite committed to industrial expansion and federal support for the construction of railroads and other internal improvements.

The Confederate States of America was better prepared politically and economically for independence than were the successful secessionist movements that broke up Gran Colombia and other Spanish American federations. Nevertheless, the Confederacy failed, in part because of poor timing. The new nations of the Western Hemisphere were most vulnerable during the early years of their existence; indeed, all the successful secessions occurred within the first decades following independence. In the case of the United States, southern secession was defeated by an experienced national government legitimated and strengthened by more than seventy-five years of stability and reinforced by economic and population growth.

Foreign Interventions and Regional Wars

With the exception of the U.S. Civil War, in the nineteenth century the scale of military conflict was far smaller in the Western Hemisphere than in Europe. Nevertheless, wars often determined national borders, access to natural resources, and control of markets in the hemisphere. Even after independence, some Western Hemisphere nations had to defend themselves against Europe's great powers. Contested national borders and regional rivalries also led to wars between Western Hemisphere nations. By the end of the nineteenth century, the United States, Brazil, Argentina, and Chile

Map 25.3 Territorial Growth of the United States, 1783–1853 The rapid western expansion of the United States resulted from aggressive diplomacy and warfare against Mexico and Amerindian peoples. Railroad development helped integrate the trans-Mississippi west and promote economic expansion.

Benito Juárez's Triumph over the French   Benito Juárez overcame humble origins to lead the overthrow of Emperor Maximilian and the defeat of French imperialism. He remains a powerful symbol of secularism and republican virtue in Mexico. In this 1948 mural by José Clemente Orozco, Juárez's face dominates a scene of struggle that pits Mexican patriots against the allied forces of the Catholic Church, Mexican conservatives, and foreign invaders.   (Museo Nacional de Historia/CENIDIAP-INBA)

had successfully waged wars against their neighbors and established themselves as regional powers.

Within thirty years of independence, the United States fought a second war with England—the War of 1812 (1812–1815). The weakness of the new republic was symbolized by the burning of the White House and Capitol by British troops in 1814. This humiliation was soon overcome, however, and by the end of the nineteenth century the United States was the hemisphere's greatest military power. Its war against Spain in 1898–1899 created an American empire that reached from the Philippines in the Pacific Ocean to Puerto Rico in the Caribbean Sea.

Europe also challenged the sovereignty of Latin American nations. During the first decades after independence, Argentina faced British and French naval blockades, and British naval forces systematically violated Brazil's territorial waters to stop the importation of slaves. Mexico faced graver threats to its sovereignty, defeating a weak Spanish invasion in 1829 and then a French assault on the city of Veracruz in 1838.

The French used Mexico's inability to repay a loan as an excuse for an invasion in 1862. Mexico had been weakened by a destructive war between conservatives and liberals (1858–1862), and the conservatives allied themselves with the French invaders. The French army quickly forced the president of Mexico, **Benito Juárez,** to flee Mexico City. The French then installed the Austrian Habsburg Maximilian as emperor of Mexico. Juárez, the orphaned child of Amerindian parents, organized an effective military resistance and after years of warfare drove the French army out of Mexico in 1867. After capturing Maximilian, Juárez ordered his execution.

Wars between Western Hemisphere nations commonly produced more enduring results. The United States greatly expanded its land area through military conflicts. In the 1820s Mexico had encouraged Americans to immigrate to Texas, which at that time was part of Mexico. By the early 1830s Americans outnumbered Mexican nationals in Texas by four to one and were aggressively challenging Mexican laws such as the prohibition of slavery. In 1835 political turmoil in Mexico led to a rebellion in Texas by an alliance of Mexican liberals and American settlers. Mexico was defeated in a brief war, and in 1837 Texas became an independent nation. In

1845 the United States made Texas a state, provoking war with Mexico a year later. Mexican forces fought well, but U.S. forces captured Mexico City, and the United States imposed a punitive peace treaty in 1848. Compounding the loss of Texas in 1837, the treaty of 1848 forced Mexico to cede vast territories to the United States, including present-day Texas, New Mexico, Arizona, and California. In return Mexico received $15 million. When gold was discovered in California in 1848, the magnitude of Mexico's loss became clear.

In two wars with neighbors, Chile established itself as the leading military and economic power on the west coast of South America. Between 1836 and 1839, Chile defeated the Confederation of Peru and Bolivia. In 1879 Chilean and British investors in nitrate mines located in the Atacama Desert, a disputed border region, provoked a new war with Peru and Bolivia. The Chilean army and navy won a crushing victory in 1881, forcing Bolivia to cede its only outlet to the sea and Peru to yield the mining districts.

Argentina and Brazil fought over control of Uruguay in the 1820s, but a military stalemate eventually forced them to recognize Uruguayan independence. In 1865 Argentina and Uruguay joined Brazil to wage war against Paraguay. After five years of warfare, the Paraguayan dictator Francisco Solano López° and more than 20 percent of the population of Paraguay were dead. Paraguay suffered military occupation, lost territory to the victors, and was forced to open its markets to foreign trade.

Native Peoples and the Nation-State

Both diplomacy and military action shaped relations between the Western Hemisphere's new nation-states and the indigenous peoples living within them. During late colonial times, to avoid armed conflict and to limit the costs of frontier defense, Spanish, Portuguese, and British imperial governments attempted to limit the expansion of settlements into territories already occupied by Amerindians. With independence, the colonial powers' role as mediator for and protector of native peoples ended.

Still-independent Amerindian peoples posed a significant military challenge to many Western Hemisphere republics. Weakened by civil wars and constitutional crises, many of the new nations were less able to maintain frontier peace than the colonial governments had been. After independence, Amerindian peoples in Argentina, the United States, Chile, and Mexico succeeded in pushing back some frontier settlements. But despite these early victories, native military resistance was finally overcome by the end of the 1880s in both North and South America.

After the American Revolution, the rapid expansion of agricultural settlements threatened native peoples in North America. Between 1790 and 1810 tens of thousands of settlers entered territories guaranteed to Amerindians in treaties with the United States. In Ohio alone more than 200,000 white settlers were present by 1810. Indigenous leaders responded by seeking the support of British officials in Canada and by forging broad indigenous alliances. American forces decisively defeated one such Amerindian alliance in 1794 at the Battle of Fallen Timbers in Ohio. After 1800 two Shawnee leaders, the brothers **Tecumseh**° and Prophet (Tenskwatawa), created a larger and better-organized alliance among southern and western Amerindian peoples and gained some support from Great Britain. In 1811 American military forces attacked and destroyed the ritual center of the alliance, Prophet Town. The final blow came during the War of 1812 when Tecumseh, fighting alongside his British allies, was killed in battle.

In the 1820s white settlers forced native peoples living in Ohio, southern Indiana and Illinois, southwestern Michigan, most of Missouri, central Alabama, and southern Mississippi to cede their land. The 1828 presidential election of Andrew Jackson, a veteran of wars against native peoples, brought matters to a head. In 1830 Congress passed the Indian Removal Act, forcing the resettlement of the Cherokee, Creek, Choctaw, and other eastern peoples to land west of the Mississippi River. The removal was carried out in the 1830s, and nearly half of the forced migrants died on this journey, known as the Trail of Tears.

Amerindians living on the Great Plains offered formidable resistance to the expansion of while settlement. By the time substantial numbers of white buffalo hunters, cattlemen, and settlers reached the American west indigenous peoples were skilled users of horses and firearms. These technologies had transformed the cultures of the Sioux, Comanche, Pawnee, Kiowa, and other Plains peoples. The improved efficiency of the buffalo hunt reduced their dependence on agriculture. As a result, women, whose primary responsibility had been raising crops, lost prestige and social power to male hunters. Living arrangements also changed as the single-family tepees of migratory buffalo hunters replaced the multigenerational lodges of the traditional farming economy.

During the U.S. Civil War, native peoples experienced a disruption of their trade with Eastern merchants and the suspension of treaty indemnities. After the war,

---

Francisco Solano López (fran-CEES-co so-LAN-oh LOH-pez)

Tecumseh (teh-CUM-sah)

Navajo Leaders Gathered in Washington to Negotiate As settlers, ranchers, and miners pushed west in the nineteenth century, leaders of Amerindian peoples were forced to negotiate territorial concessions with representatives of the U.S. government. In order to impress Amerindian peoples with the wealth and power of the United States, many of their leaders were invited to Washington, D.C. This photo shows Navajo leaders and their Anglo translators in Washington, D.C., in 1874. (#5851 Frank McNill Collection, State Records Center & Archives, Sante Fe, NM)

ever more settlers pushed onto the plains. Buffalo herds were hunted to near extinction for their hides, and land was lost to farmers and ranchers. During nearly four decades of armed conflict with the United States Army, Amerindian peoples were forced to give up their land and their traditional ways. The Comanche, who had dominated the southern plains during the period of Spanish and Mexican rule, were forced by the U.S. government to cede most of their land in Texas in 1865. The Sioux and their allies resisted. In 1876 they overwhelmed General George Armstrong Custer and the Seventh Cavalry in the Battle of Little Bighorn (in the southern part of the present-day state of Montana). But finally the Sioux also were forced to accept reservation life. Military campaigns in the 1870s and 1880s then broke the resistance of the Apache.

The indigenous peoples of Argentina and Chile experienced a similar trajectory of adaptation, resistance, and defeat. Herds of wild cattle provided indigenous peoples with a limitless food supply, and horses and metal weapons increased their military capacities. Thus, for a while, the native peoples of Argentina and Chile effectively checked the southern expansion of agriculture and ranching. Amerindian raiders operated within 100 miles (160 kilometers) of Buenos Aires into the 1860s. Unable to defeat these resourceful enemies, the governments of Argentina and Chile relied on an elaborate system of gift giving and prisoner exchanges to maintain peace on the frontier. By the 1860s, however, population increase, political stability, and military modernization allowed Argentina and Chile to take the offensive.

In the 1870s the government of Argentina used overwhelming military force to crush native resistance. Thousands of Amerindians were killed, and survivors were driven onto marginal land. In Chile the story was the same. When civil war and an economic depression weakened the Chilean government at the end of the 1850s, the Mapuches° (called "Araucanians" by the Spanish) attempted to push back frontier settlements. Despite early successes, the Mapuches were defeated in the 1870s by modern weaponry. In Chile, as in Argentina and the United States, military campaigns against native peoples were justified by demonizing the Amerindians. Newspaper editorials and the speeches of politicians portrayed Amerindians as brutal and cruel, and as obstacles to progress. In April 1859, a Chilean newspaper commented:

> The necessity, not only to punish the Araucanian race, but also to make it impotent to harm us, is well recognized . . . as the only way to rid the country of a million evils. It is well understood that they are odious and prejudicial guests in Chile . . . conciliatory measures have accomplished nothing with this stupid race—the infamy and disgrace of the Chilean nation.[4]

Political divisions and civil wars within the new nations sometimes provided an opportunity for long-pacified native peoples to rebel. In the Yucatán region of Mexico, the owners of henequen (the agave plant that produces fiber used for twine) and sugar plantations had forced

Mapuches (mah-POO-chez)

many Maya° communities off their traditional agricultural lands, reducing thousands of them to peonage. This same regional elite declared itself independent of the government in Mexico City that was convulsed by civil war in the late 1830s. The Mexican government was unable to reestablish control because it faced the greater threat of invasion by the United States. Seeing their oppressors divided, the Maya rebelled in 1847. This well-organized and popular uprising, known as the **Caste War,** nearly returned the Yucatán to Maya rule. Grievances accumulated over more than three hundred years led to great violence and property destruction. The Maya were not defeated until the war with the United States ended. Even then Maya rebels retreated to unoccupied territories and created an independent state, which they called the "Empire of the Cross." Organized around a mix of traditional beliefs and Christian symbols, this indigenous state resisted Mexican forces to 1870. A few defiant Maya strongholds survived until 1901.

THE CHALLENGE OF ECONOMIC AND SOCIAL CHANGE

During the nineteenth century, the newly independent nations of the Western Hemisphere struggled to realize the Enlightenment ideals of freedom and individual liberty that had helped to ignite the revolutions for independence. The achievement of these objectives was slowed by the persistence of slavery and other oppressive colonial-era institutions. Cultural and racial diversity also presented obstacles to reform. Nevertheless, by century's end reform movements in many of the hemisphere's nations had succeeded in ending the slave trade, abolishing slavery, expanding voting rights, and assimilating immigrants from Asia and Europe.

The consequences of increased industrialization and greater involvement in the evolving world economy challenged the region's political stability and social arrangements. A small number of nations embraced industrialization, but most Western Hemisphere economies became increasingly dependent on the export of agricultural goods and minerals during the nineteenth century. While the industrializing nations of the hemisphere became richer than the nations that remained

exporters of raw materials, all the region's economies became more vulnerable and volatile as a result of greater participation in international markets. Like contemporary movements for social reform, efforts to assert national economic control produced powerful new political forces.

The Abolition of Slavery

In both the United States and Latin America, strong antislavery sentiments were expressed during the struggles for independence. In nearly all the new nations of the Western Hemisphere, revolutionary leaders asserted universal ideals of freedom and citizenship that contrasted sharply with the reality of slavery. Men and women who wanted to outlaw slavery were called **abolitionists.** Despite the efforts of abolitionists, slavery survived in much of the hemisphere until the 1850s. In regions where the export of plantation products was most important—such as the United States, Brazil, and Cuba—the abolition of slavery was achieved with great difficulty.

In the United States, slavery was weakened by abolition in some northern states and by the termination of the African slave trade in 1808. But this progress was stalled by the profitable expansion of cotton agriculture after the War of 1812. In Spanish America, tens of thousands of slaves gained freedom by joining revolutionary armies during the wars for independence. After independence, most Spanish American republics prohibited the slave trade. Counteracting that trend was the growing international demand for sugar and coffee, products traditionally produced on plantations by slaves. As prices rose for plantation products in the first half of the nineteenth century, Brazil and Cuba (the island remained a Spanish colony until 1899) increased their imports of slaves.

During the long struggle to end slavery in the United States, American abolitionists argued that slavery offended both morality and the universal rights asserted in the Declaration of Independence. Abolitionist Theodore Weld articulated the religious objection to slavery in 1834:

> No condition of birth, no shade of color, no mere misfortune of circumstance, can annul the birth-right charter, which God has bequeathed to every being upon whom he has stamped his own image, by making him a free *moral agent* [emphasis in original], and that he who robs his fellow man of this tramples upon right, subverts justice, outrages humanity . . . and sacrilegiously assumes the prerogative of God.[5]

Maya (MY-ah)

Two groups denied full rights of citizenship under the Constitution, women and free African-Americans, played important roles in the abolition of slavery. Women served on the executive committee of the American Anti-Slavery Society and produced some of the most effective propaganda against slavery. Eventually, thousands of women joined the abolitionist cause, where they provided leadership and were effective speakers and propagandists. When social conservatives attacked this highly visible public role, many women abolitionists responded by becoming public advocates of female suffrage as well.

Frederick Douglass, a former slave, became one of the most effective abolitionist speakers and writers. Other more radical black leaders pushed the abolitionist movement to accept the inevitability of violence. They saw civil war or slave insurrection as necessary for the ending of slavery. One argued passionately that slaves should "RISE AT ONCE, en masse, and THROW OFF THEIR FETTERS" (capitalization in original).

In the 1850s the growing electoral strength of the newly formed Republican Party forced a confrontation between slave and free states. After the election of Abraham Lincoln in 1860, the first of the thirteen southern states that formed the Condeferacy seceded from the Union. During the Civil War, pressure for emancipation rose as tens of thousands of black freemen and escaped slaves joined the Union army. Hundreds of thousands of other slaves fled their masters' plantations and farms for the protection of advancing northern armies. In 1863, in the midst of the Civil War and two years after the abolition of serfdom in Russia (see Chapter 27), President Lincoln began the abolition of slavery by issuing the Emancipation Proclamation, which ended slavery in rebel states not occupied by the Union army. Final abolition was accomplished after the war, in 1865, by the Thirteenth Amendment to the Constitution.

In Brazil slavery survived more than two decades after it was abolished in the United States. Progress toward abolition was not only slower in Brazil but also depended on foreign pressure. In 1830 Brazil signed a treaty with the British ending the slave trade. Despite this agreement, Brazil illegally imported over a half-million more African slaves before the British navy finally forced compliance in the 1850s. In the 1850s and 1860s the Brazilian emperor, Pedro II, and many liberals worked to abolish slavery, but their desire to find a form of gradual emancipation acceptable to slave owners slowed progress.

During the war with Paraguay (1865–1870), large numbers of slaves joined the Brazilian army in exchange for freedom. Their loyalty and heroism undermined the military's support for slavery. Educated Brazilians in-

A Former Brazilian Slave Returns from Military Service   The heroic participation of black freemen and slaves in the Paraguayan War (1885–1870) led many Brazilians to advocate the abolition of slavery. The original caption for this drawing reads: "On his return from the war in Paraguay: Full of glory, covered with laurels, after having spilled his blood in defense of the fatherland and to free a people from slavery, the volunteer sees his own mother bound and whipped! Awful reality!"   (Courtesy, Fundacao Biblioteca Nacional, Brazil)

creasingly viewed slavery as an obstacle to economic development and an impediment to democratic reform. In the 1870s, as abolitionist sentiment grew, reformers forced the passage of laws providing for the gradual emancipation of slaves. When political support for slavery weakened in the 1880s, growing numbers of slaves forced the issue by fleeing from bondage. By the 1880s, however, army leaders were resisting demands that they capture and return runaway slaves. Legislation abolishing slavery finally was passed by the Brazilian parliament and accepted by the emperor in 1888.

The plantations of the Caribbean region received almost 40 percent of all African slaves shipped to the New World. As a result, throughout the region tiny white minorities lived surrounded by slave and free colored majorities. At the end of the eighteenth century, the slave rebellion in Saint Domingue (see Chapter 23) spread terror across the Caribbean. Because of fear that any effort to overthrow colonial rule might unleash new slave rebellions, there was little enthusiasm among free settlers in Caribbean colonies for independence. Nor did local support for abolition appear among white settlers or free colored populations. Thus abolition in most Caribbean colonies commonly resulted from political decisions made in Europe by colonial powers.

Nevertheless, like slaves in Brazil, the United States, and Spanish America, slaves in the Caribbean helped propel the movement toward abolition by rebelling, running away, and resisting in more subtle ways. Although initially unsuccessful, the rebellions that threatened other French Caribbean colonies after the Haitian Revolution (1789–1804)) weakened France's support for slavery. Jamaica and other British colonies also experienced rebellions and saw the spread of communities of runaways. In Spanish Cuba as well, slave resistance forced increases in expenditures for police forces in the nineteenth century.

After 1800, the profitability of sugar plantations in the British West Indian colonies declined, and a coalition of labor groups, Protestant dissenters, and free traders in Britain pushed for the abolition of slavery. Britain, the major participant in the eighteenth-century expansion of slavery in the Americas, ended its participation in the slave trade in 1807. It then negotiated a series of treaties with Spain, Brazil, and other importers of slaves to eliminate the slave trade to the Americas. Once these treaties were in place, British naval forces acted to force compliance.

Slavery in British colonies was abolished in 1834. However, the law compelled "freed" slaves to remain with former masters as "apprentices." Abuses by planters and resistance to apprenticeship by former slaves led to complete abolition in 1838. A decade later slavery in the French Caribbean was abolished after upheavals in France led to the overthrow of the government of Louis Philippe (see Chapter 23).

Slavery lasted longest in Cuba and Puerto Rico, Spain's remaining colonies. Britain's use of diplomatic pressure and naval force to limit the arrival of African slaves weakened slavery after 1820. More important, however, was the growth of support for abolition in these colonies. Both Cuba and Puerto Rico had larger white and free colored populations than did the Caribbean colonies of Britain and France. As a result, there was less fear in Cuba and Puerto Rico that abolition would lead to the political ascendancy of former slaves (as had occurred in Haiti). In Puerto Rico, where slaves numbered approximately thirty thousand, local reformers sought and gained the abolition of slavery in 1873. In the midst of a decade-long war to defeat forces seeking the independence of Cuba, the Spanish government moved gradually toward abolition. Initially, slave children born after September 18, 1868, were freed but obligated to work for their former masters for eighteen years. In 1880 all other slaves were freed on the condition that they serve their masters for eight additional years. Finally, in 1886, these conditions were eliminated, slavery was abolished, and Cuban patriots forged the multiracial alliance that was to initiate a war for Cuban independence in 1895 (See Chapter 29).

Immigration

During the colonial period, free Europeans were a minority among immigrants to the Western Hemisphere. Between 1500 and 1760, African slaves entering the Western Hemisphere outnumbered European immigrants by nearly two to one. Another 4 million or so African slaves were imported before the effective end of the slave trade at the end of the 1850s. As the African slave trade came to an end, the arrival of millions of immigrants from Europe and Asia in the nineteenth century contributed to the further transformation of the Western Hemisphere. This new wave of immigration fostered rapid economic growth and the occupation of frontier regions in the United States, Canada, Argentina, Chile, and Brazil. It also promoted urbanization. By century's end, nearly all of the hemisphere's fastest-growing cities (Buenos Aires, Chicago, New York, and São Paulo, for example) had large immigrant populations.

During the nineteenth century, Europe provided the majority of immigrants to the Western Hemisphere. For much of the century, these people came primarily from western Europe, but after 1870 most came from southern and eastern Europe. The scale of immigration increased dramatically in the second half of the century. The United States received approximately 600,000 European immigrants in the 1830s, 1.5 million in the 1840s, and then 2.5 million per decade until 1880. In the 1890s an astonishing total of 5.2 million immigrants arrived. European immigration to Latin America also increased dramatically after 1880. Combined immigration to Argentina and Brazil rose from just under 130,000 in the 1860s to 1.7 million in the 1890s. By 1910, 30 percent of the Argentine population was foreign-born, more than twice the proportion in the U.S. population. Argentina was an extremely attractive destination for European immigrants, receiving more than twice as many immigrants as Canada between 1870 and 1930. Even so, immigration to Canada increased tenfold during this period.

Asian immigration to the Western Hemisphere increased after 1850. Between 1849 and 1875, approximately 100,000 Chinese immigrants arrived in Peru and another 120,000 entered Cuba. Canada attracted about 50,000 Chinese in the second half of the century. The United States, however, was the primary North American destination for Chinese immigrants, receiving 300,000 between 1854 and 1882. India also contributed to the social transformation of the Western Hemisphere, sending more than a half-million immigrants to the Caribbean region. British Guiana alone received 238,000 immigrants from the Asian subcontinent.

Despite the obvious economic benefits that accompanied this inflow of people, hostility to immigration mounted in many nations. Nativist political movements argued that large numbers of foreigners could not be successfully integrated into national political cultures. By the end of the century, fear and prejudice led many governments in the Western Hemisphere to limit immigration or to distinguish between "desirable" and "undesirable" immigrants, commonly favoring Europeans over Asians.

Asians faced more obstacles to immigration than did Europeans and were more often victims of violence and extreme forms of discrimination in the New World. In the 1870s and 1880s anti-Chinese riots erupted in many western cities in the United States. Congress responded to this wave of racism by passing the Chinese Exclusion Act in 1882, which eliminated most Chinese immigration. In 1886 fears that Canada was being threatened by "inferior races" led to the imposition of a head tax that made immigration to Canada more difficult for Chinese families. During this same period, strong anti-Chinese prejudice surfaced in Peru, Mexico, and Cuba. Japanese immigrants in Brazil and East Indians in the English-speaking Caribbean faced similar prejudice.

Immigrants from Europe also faced prejudice and discrimination. In the United States, Italians were commonly portrayed as criminals or anarchists. In Argentina, social scientists attempted to prove that Italian immigrants were more violent and less honest than the native-born population. Immigrants from Spain were widely stereotyped in Argentina as miserly and dishonest. Eastern European Jews seeking to escape pogroms and discrimination at home found themselves barred from many educational institutions and professional careers in both the United States and Latin America. Negative stereotypes were invented for German, Swedish, Polish, and Middle Eastern immigrants as well. The perceived grievances used to justify these common prejudices were remarkably similar from Canada to Argentina. Immigrants, it was argued, threatened the well-being of native-born workers by accepting low wages, and they threatened national culture by resisting assimilation.

Many intellectuals and political leaders wondered if the evolving mix of culturally diverse populations could sustain a common citizenship. As a result, efforts were directed toward compelling immigrants to assimilate.

Arrest of Labor Activist in Buenos Aires
The labor movement in Buenos Aires grew in numbers and became more radical with the arrival of tens of thousands of Italian and Spanish immigrants. Fearful of socialist and anarchist unions, the government of Argentina used an expanded police force to break strikes by arresting labor leaders. (Archivo General de la Nacion, Buenos Aires)

Schools became cultural battlegrounds where language, cultural values, and patriotic feelings were transmitted to the children of immigrants. Across the hemisphere, school curricula were revised to promote national culture. Ignoring Canada's large French-speaking population, an English-speaking Canadian reformer commented on recent immigration: "If Canada is to become in a real sense a nation, if our people are to become one people, we must have one language."[6] Fear and prejudice led to the singing of patriotic songs, the veneration of national flags and other symbols, and the writing of national histories that emphasized patriotism and civic virtue. Nearly everywhere in the Americas schools worked to create homogeneous national cultures.

American Cultures

Despite discrimination, immigrants continued to stream into the Western Hemisphere, introducing new languages, living arrangements, technologies, and work customs. Immigrants altered the politics of many of the hemisphere's nations as they sought to influence government policies. Where immigrants arrived in the greatest numbers, they put enormous pressure on housing, schools, and social welfare services. To compensate for their isolation from home, language, and culture, immigrants often created ethnically based mutual aid societies, sports and leisure clubs, and neighborhoods. Ethnic organizations and districts provided valuable social and economic support for recent arrivals while sometimes worsening the fears of the native-born that immigration posed a threat to national culture.

Immigrants were changed by their experiences in their adopted nations and by programs that forced them to accept new cultural values through education or, in some cases, service in the military. The modification of the language, customs, values, and behaviors of a group as a result of contact with people from another culture is called **acculturation.** Immigrants and their children, in turn, made their mark on the cultures of their adopted nations. They learned the language spoken in their adopted countries as fast as possible in order to improve their earning capacity. At the same time, words and phrases from their languages entered the language of the host nations. Languages as diverse as Yiddish and Italian strongly influenced American English, Argentine Spanish, and Brazilian Portuguese. Dietary practices introduced from Europe and Asia altered the cuisine of nearly every American nation. In turn, immigrants commonly added native foods to their diets, especially the hemisphere's abundant and relatively cheap meats.

American popular music changed as well. For example, the Argentine tango, based on African-Argentine rhythms, was transformed by new instrumentation and orchestral arrangements brought by Italian immigrants. Mexican ballads blended with English folk music in the U.S. southwest, and Italian operas played to packed houses in Buenos Aires. Sports, games of chance, and fashion also experienced this process of borrowing and exchange.

Union movements and electoral politics in the hemisphere also felt the influence of new arrivals who aggressively sought to influence government and improve working conditions. The labor movements of Mexico, Argentina, and the United States, in particular, were influenced by the anarchist and socialist beliefs of European immigrants. Mutual benevolent societies and less formal ethnic associations pooled resources to help immigrants open businesses, aid the immigration of their relatives, or bury their family members. They also established links with political movements, sometimes exchanging votes for favors.

Women's Rights and the Struggle for Social Justice

The abolition of slavery in the Western Hemisphere did not end racial discrimination or provide full political rights for every citizen. Not only blacks but also women, new immigrants, and native peoples in nearly every Western Hemisphere nation suffered the effects of political and economic discrimination. During the second half of the nineteenth century, reformers struggled to remove these limits on citizenship while also addressing the welfare needs of workers and the poor.

In 1848 a group of women angered by their exclusion from an international antislavery meeting issued a call for a meeting to discuss women's rights. The **Women's Rights Convention** at Seneca Falls, New York, issued a statement that said in part, "We hold these truths to be self-evident: that all men and women are equal." While moderates focused on the issues of greater economic independence and full legal rights, increasing numbers of women demanded the right to vote. Others lobbied to provide better conditions for women working outside the home, especially in textile factories. Sarah Grimké responded to criticism of women's activism:

This has been the language of man since he laid aside the whip as a means to keep woman in subjection. He spares her body, but the war he has waged against her mind, her heart, and her soul, has been no less destructive to her as a moral being. How monstrous is the doctrine that woman is to be dependent on man![7]

Progress toward equality between men and women was equally slow in Canada and Latin America. Canada's first women doctors received their training in the United States because no woman was able to receive a medical degree in Canada until 1895. Full enfranchisement occurred in Canada in the twentieth century, but Canadian women did gain the right to vote in some provincial and municipal elections before 1900. Like women in the United States, Canadian women provided leadership in temperance, child welfare, and labor reform movements. Argentina and Uruguay were among the first Latin American nations to provide public education for women. Both nations introduced coeducation in the 1870s. Chilean women gained access to some careers in medicine and law in the 1870s. In Argentina, the first woman doctor graduated from medical school in 1899. In Brazil, where many women were active in the abolitionist movement, four women graduated in medicine by 1882. Throughout the hemisphere, more rapid progress was achieved in lower status careers that threatened male economic power less directly, and by the end of the century, women dominated elementary school teaching throughout the Western Hemisphere.

From Canada to Argentina and Chile, the majority of working-class women had no direct involvement in these reform movements, but in their daily lives they succeeded in transforming gender relations. By the end of the nineteenth century, large numbers of poor women worked outside the home on farms, in markets, and, increasingly, in factories. Many bore full responsibility for providing for their children. Whether men thought women should remain in the home or not, by the end of the century women were unambiguously present in the economy (see also Chapter 28).

Throughout the hemisphere there was little progress toward eliminating racial discrimination. Blacks were denied the vote throughout the southern United States. They also were subjected to the indignity of segregation— consigned to separate schools, hotels, restaurants, seats in public transportation, and even water fountains. Racial discrimination against men and women of African descent was also common in Latin America, though seldom spelled out in legal codes. Unlike the southern states of the United States, Latin American nations did not insist on formal racial segregation or permit lynching. Nor did they enforce a strict color line. Many men and women of mixed background were able to enter the skilled working class or middle class. Latin Americans tended to view racial identity across a continuum of physical characteristics rather than in the narrow terms of black and white that defined race relations in the United States.

The Children's Aid Society of Toronto   Throughout the Western Hemisphere, women led the effort to develop social welfare institutions. Their leadership was most clearly evident in providing protection for poor and abandoned children. This photo shows a social worker and children sitting on the front step of the Children's Aid Society of Toronto in 1895.   (City of Toronto Archives, #SC1-3)

The successful movements to abolish slavery in Latin America did not lead to an end to racial discrimination. But some of the participants in the abolition struggles later organized to promote racial integration in their societies. They demanded access to education, the right to vote, and greater economic opportunity, pointing out the economic and political costs paid by poor countries that denied full rights to all citizens. Their success depended on political organization and the forging of alliances with sympathetic white politicians. Black intellectuals also struggled to overturn racist stereotypes. In Brazil, Argentina, and Cuba, as in the United States, political and literary magazines celebrating black cultural achievement became powerful weapons in the struggle against racial discrimination. Despite these efforts, men and women of African descent continued to suffer discrimination everywhere in the Americas at century's end.

Development and Underdevelopment

Although the Atlantic economy experienced three periods of economic contraction during the nineteenth century, nearly all the nations of the Western Hemisphere were richer in 1900 than in 1800. The Industrial Revolution, worldwide population growth, and an increasingly integrated world market stimulated economic expansion (see Environment and Technology: The McCormick Reaper). Wheat, corn, wool, meats, and nonprecious minerals joined the region's earlier exports of silver, sugar, dyes, coffee, and cotton. During the nineteenth century, the United States was the only Western Hemisphere nation to industrialize, but nearly every government promoted new economic activities. Throughout the hemisphere investments were made in roads, railroads, canals, and telegraphs to better serve distant markets. In addition, tariff and monetary policies helped to foster economic diversification and growth. Yet only three Western Hemisphere nations—the United States, Canada, and Argentina—achieved individual income levels similar to those in western Europe by 1900.

New demands for copper, zinc, lead, coal, and tin unleashed by the Industrial Revolution led to mining booms in the western United States and in Mexico and Chile. Unlike the small-scale and often short-term gold- and silver-mining operations of the colonial era, the mining companies of the late nineteenth century were heavily capitalized international corporations that could bully governments and buy political favors. During this period, European or North American corporations owned most new mining enterprises in Latin America. Petroleum development, which occurred at the end of the century, followed this pattern as well.

New technology accelerated economic integration, but the high cost of this technology often increased dependence on foreign capital. Many of the hemisphere's governments promoted railroads by granting tax benefits, free land, and monopoly rights to both domestic and foreign investors. By 1890 vast areas of the Great Plains in the United States and Canada, the Argentine pampas, and the northern part of Mexico were producing grain and livestock for foreign markets opened by the development of railroads. Steamships also lowered the cost of transportation to distant markets, and the telegraph stimulated expansion by speeding the spread of information about the demand for and availability of products.

The acquisition of bundles of new technologies at the same time often multiplied the cumulative effects of individual technologies. In Argentina, for example, the railroad, telegraph, barbed wire, and refrigeration all appeared within a single generation in the 1870s and 1880s. Although Argentina had had abundant livestock herds since the colonial period, the great distance separating Argentina from Europe's markets prevented Argentine cattle raisers from efficiently exporting either fresh meat or live animals. Technology changed this situation. The combination of railroads and the telegraph lowered freight costs and improved information about markets. Steamships shortened trans-Atlantic crossings. Refrigerated ships made it possible to sell meat from Argentina's pampas in the markets of Europe. As land values rose and livestock breeding improved, new investments were protected by barbed wire, the first inexpensive fencing available on the nearly treeless plains.

Despite these shared experiences, growing interdependence and increased competition produced deep structural differences among Western Hemisphere economies by 1900. Two distinct economic tracks became clearly visible. One led to industrialization and prosperity, what is now called **development.** The other continued colonial dependence on the export of raw materials and low-wage industries, now commonly called **underdevelopment.** By the end of the nineteenth century, material prosperity was greater and economic development was more diversified in English-speaking North America than in the nations of Latin America. With a temperate climate, vast fertile prairies, and an influx of European immigrants, Argentina was the only Latin American nation to imitate the prosperity of the United States and Canada in the nineteenth century.

These important differences in regional economic development were due in part to cyclical swings in international markets. When the United States gained independence in 1783, the world capitalist economy was in the first years of a four-decade period of rapid growth. With a large merchant fleet, a diversified economy that included some manufacturing, and adequate banking and insurance services, the United States benefited from the expansion of the world economy. Rapid population growth due in large measure to immigration, high levels of individual wealth, widespread landownership, and relatively high literacy rates also fostered rapid economic development in the United States.

Canada's struggle for greater political autonomy, which culminated in the Confederation of 1867, coincided with a second period of global economic expansion. Canada also benefited from its special trading relationship with Britain, the world's preeminent industrial nation, and from a rising tide of immigrants after 1850.

The McCormick Reaper

The McCormick reaper was one of the great industrial success stories of the nineteenth century. McCormick reapers and other agricultural implements dominated agriculture and gained export markets throughout the Western Hemisphere and Europe. By leading the mechanization of agriculture, the McCormick Havesting Machine Company reduced labor costs and promoted the development of large-scale commercial farming in the midwestern United States and Canada. Aided by mechanization, wheat production grew by 70 percent in the 1850s alone.

Cyrus McCormick and his family began building reapers in their blacksmith shop in Rockbridge County, Virginia, in 1840. In the early years, slaves owned by the family helped handcraft the reapers from raw materials found locally. Although McCormick faced competition from other manufacturers, the business grew quickly, in part because McCormick was a great promoter who effectively used advertising to develop his business. As demand rose, he increased production by adding new skilled workers and by licensing other manufacturers to produce the company's reapers.

These licensing agreements caused problems of quality control that led McCormick to move all the company's production to a custom-built factory in Chicago in 1848. Production in the new factory quickly reached 1,500 units per year, far outstripping the 200 units per year produced in the Virginia operation. Nearly all this increase came from adding skilled workers and from the closer supervision of subcontractors who supplied blades and other parts. By 1876, 14,000 reapers were produced.

At the end of the 1870s, Cyrus broke with his brother, Leander, and brought in a factory manager who had worked at Colt firearms and the Wilson Sewing Machine Company. Under this new leadership, the company introduced a new industrial process that emphasized standardization and the use of special-purpose machine tools for fabrication. Production reached 48,000 units in 1885 and then soared to 100,000 in 1889. These changes in technology and production methods, however, changed the work force from skilled to unskilled labor and contributed to increased numbers of strikes and work stoppages.

Source: This discussion follows the analysis in David A. Hounshell, *From the American System to Mass Production, 1800–1932: The Development of Manufacturing Technology in the United States* (Baltimore: Johns Hopkins University Press, 1984), 153–189.

The McCormick Reaper In the nineteenth century, the machine age arrived in the countryside. The McCormick reaper increased productivity and also promoted the concentration of land in grain producing regions of the United States. (Navistar International Harvester Archives)

The Introduction of New Technologies Changes the Mining Industry Powerful hydraulic technologies were introduced in western mining sites in the United States. This early photo shows how high power water jets could transform the natural environment. (Colorado Historical Society)

Nevertheless, some regions within each of these prosperous North American nations—Canada's Maritime Provinces and the southern part of the United States, for example—demonstrated the same patterns of underdevelopment found in Latin America.

Latin American nations gained independence in the 1820s, when the global economy was contracting due to the end of the Napoleonic Wars and market saturation provoked by the early stages of European industrialization. During the colonial period the region's economic resources had been concentrated on the production of agricultural and mining exports. After independence those raw-material exports faced increased competition. Although these sectors experienced periods of great prosperity in the nineteenth century, their markets experienced sharp moves not only up but down. The history of these specialized Latin American economies, subject to periodic problems of oversupply and low prices, was one of boom and bust. The efforts of Latin American

governments to gain competitive market advantages by defeating union activity, holding down wages, and opening markets to foreign manufactures further complicated the movement toward industrialization.

Weak governments, political instability, and, in some cases, civil war also slowed Latin American economic development. A comparative examination of Western Hemisphere economic history makes clear that stable and reliable public administration is a necessary part of the development process. Because Latin America was dependent on capital and technology obtained from abroad, Great Britain and, by the end of the century, the United States often were able to impose unfavorable trade conditions or even intervene militarily to protect investments. The combined impact of these domestic and international impediments to development became clear when Mexico, Chile, and Argentina failed to achieve high levels of domestic investment in manufacturing late in the nineteenth century, despite a rapid accumulation of wealth induced by a rising tide of income derived from traditional exports.

Altered Environments

Population growth, economic expansion, new technologies, and the introduction of plants and animals to new regions dramatically altered the Western Hemisphere's environment. Many of Cuba's forests were cut in the early nineteenth century to expand sugar production. The expansion of livestock raising put heavy pressure on fragile environments in Argentina, Uruguay, southern Brazil, and the southwestern United States. Other forms of commercial agriculture also threatened the environment. Farmers in South Carolina and Georgia gained a short-term increase in cotton production by abandoning crop rotation after 1870, but this practice quickly led to soil exhaustion and erosion. The use of plows on the North American prairies and the Argentine pampa eliminated many native grasses and increased the threat of soil erosion. Coffee planters in Brazil exhausted soil fertility with a destructive cycle of overplanting followed by expansion onto forest reserves cleared by cutting and burning.

Rapid urbanization also put heavy pressure on the environment. New York, Chicago, Rio de Janeiro, Buenos Aires, and Mexico City were among the world's fastest-growing cities in the nineteenth century. Governments strained to keep up with the need for sewers, clean water, and garbage disposal. A rising demand for building materials led to the rapid spread of the timber industry in many countries. Under the Timber and Stone Act of

1878, more than 3.5 million acres (1.4 million hectares) of public land in the United States had been claimed at low cost by 1900. Similar transfers of land from public to private ownership occurred in Argentina and Brazil.

As the mining frontier advanced into Nevada, Montana, and California after 1860, erosion and pollution resulted. Similar results occurred in other mining areas. The expansion of nitrate mining and, later, open-pit copper mining in Chile scarred and polluted the environment. The state of Minas Gerais in Brazil experienced a series of mining booms that began with gold in the late seventeenth century and continued with iron ore in the nineteenth. By the end of the century, its red soil was ripped open, its forests were depleted, and the resulting erosion was uncontrolled. Similar devastation afflicted parts of Bolivia and Mexico.

Efforts to meet increasing domestic demand for food and housing and to satisfy foreign demands for exports led to environmental degradation but also contributed significantly to the growth of the world economy and to regional prosperity. By the end of the nineteenth century, small-scale conservation efforts were under way in many nations, and the first national parks and nature reserves had been created. But when confronted by a choice between economic growth and environmental protection, all of the hemisphere's nations embraced growth.

CONCLUSION

The nineteenth century witnessed enormous changes in the Western Hemisphere. With the exception of Canada and many Caribbean islands, colonial controls were removed by century's end. The powerful new political ideas of the Enlightenment and an increased sense of national identity contributed to the desire for independence and self-rule. The success of the American and Haitian revolutions began the assault on the colonial order, transforming the hemisphere's politics. Napoleon's invasion of Portugal and Spain then helped initiate the movement toward independence in Latin America.

Once colonial rule was overturned, the creation of stable and effective governments proved difficult. Powerful personalist leaders resisted the constraints imposed by constitutions. National governments often confronted divisive regional political movements. From Argentina in the south to the United States in the north regional political rivalries provoked civil wars that challenged the very survival of the new nations. Foreign military interven-

tions and wars with native peoples also consumed resources and determined national boundaries. The effort to fulfill the promise of universal citizenship led to struggles to end slavery, extend civil and political rights to women and minorities, and to absorb new immigrants. These objectives were only partially achieved.

Industrialization had a transforming effect on the hemisphere as well. Wealth, political power, and population were increasingly concentrated in urban areas. Bankers and manufacturers, not farmers and plantation owners, directed national destinies. The United States, the most industrialized nation in the Americas, played an aggressive economic role in the region's affairs and used its growing military power as well. Industrialization altered the natural environment in dramatic ways. Modern factories consumed huge amounts of raw materials and energy. Copper mines in Chile and Mexico, Cuban sugar plantations, Brazilian coffee plantations, and Canadian lumber companies all left their mark on the natural environment, and all had ties to markets in the United States. The concentration of people in cities in the United States and Latin America put pressure on water supplies, sewage treatment, and food supplies.

By 1900, however, the hemisphere's national governments were much stronger than they had been at independence. Latin America lagged behind the United States and Canada in institutionalizing democratic political reforms, but Latin American nations in 1900 were stronger and more open than they had been in 1850. By 1900, all of the hemisphere's nations also were better able to meet the threats of foreign intervention and regionalism. Among the benefits resulting from the increased strength of national governments were the abolition of slavery and the extension of political rights to formerly excluded citizens.

Serious challenges remained. Amerindian peoples were forced to resettle on reservations, were excluded from national political life, and, in some countries, remained burdened with special tribute and tax obligations. Women began to enter occupations previously reserved to men but still lacked full citizenship rights. The baneful legacy of slavery and colonial racial stratification remained a barrier to many men and women. The benefits of economic growth were not equitably distributed among the nations of the Western Hemisphere or within individual nations. In 1900 nearly every American nation was wealthier, better educated, more democratic, and more populous than at independence. But they also were generally more vulnerable to distant economic forces, more profoundly split between haves and have-nots, and more clearly divided into a rich North and a poorer South.

◼ Key Terms

Simón Bolívar	Tecumseh
Miguel Hidalgo y Costilla	Caste War
José María Morelos	abolitionists
Confederation of 1867	acculturation
personalist leaders	Women's Rights Convention
Andrew Jackson	development
José Antonio Páez	underdevelopment
Benito Juárez	

◼ Suggested Reading

For the independence era in Latin America see John Lynch, *The Spanish American Revolutions, 1808–1826,* 2d ed. (1986); Jay Kinsbruner, *Independence in Spanish America* (1994); and A. J. R. Russell-Wood, ed., *From Colony to Nation: Essays on the Independence of Brazil* (1976).

The postindependence political and economic struggles in Latin America can be traced in David Bushnell and Neil Macaulay, *The Emergence of Latin America in the Nineteenth Century* (1988). Tulio Halperin-Donghi, *The Contemporary History of Latin America* (1993), and E. Bradford Burns, *The Poverty of Progress: Latin America in the Nineteenth Century* (1980), argue in different ways that Latin America's economic and social problems originated in unfavorable trade relationships with more-developed nations. See also an excellent collection of essays, Leslie Bethell, ed., *The Cambridge History of Latin America,* vol. 3, *From Independence to c. 1870* (1985).

There is an enormous literature on politics and nation building in the United States and Canada. Among the many worthy studies of the United States are William J. Cooper, *The South and the Politics of Slavery, 1828–1856* (1978); Kenneth M. Stampp, *America in 1857* (1991); and Lawrence Frederick Kohl, *The Politics of Individualism: Parties and the American Character in the Jacksonian Era* (1989). For Canada see J. M. S. Careless, *The Union of the Canadas: The Growth of Canadian Institutions, 1841–1857* (1967); Ged Martin, ed., *The Causes of Canadian Confederation* (1990); and Arthur I. Silver, *The French-Canadian Idea of Confederation, 1864–1900* (1982).

The social and cultural issues raised in this chapter are also the subject of a vast literature. For an excellent history of the immigration era see Walter Nugent, *Crossing: The Great Transatlantic Migrations, 1870–1914* (1992). See also Gunther Barth, *Bitter Strength: A History of Chinese in the United States, 1850–1870* (1964), and Nicolás Sánchez-Albornoz, *The Population of Latin America: A History* (1974).

On the issue of slavery see David Brion Davis, *Slavery and Human Progress* (1984); George M. Frederickson, *The Black Image in the White Mind: The Debate on Afro-American Character and Destiny, 1817–1914* (1971); and Benjamin Quarles, *Black Abolitionists* (1969). For the women's rights movement see Ellen C. Du Bois, *Feminism and Suffrage: The Emergence of an Indepen-*dent Woman's Movement in the Nineteenth Century* (1984), and Lori D. Ginzberg, *Women and the Work of Benevolence: Morality, Politics, and Class in the Nineteenth-Century United States* (1990). Among numerous excellent studies of Indian policies see Robert M. Utley, *The Indian Frontier of the American West, 1846–1890* (1984). On those topics for Canada see J. R. Miller, *Skyscrapers Hide the Heavens: A History of Indian White Relations in Canada* (1989); Olive Patricia Dickason, *Canada's First Nations* (1993); and Alison Prentice, *Canadian Women: A History* (1988).

For abolition in Latin America and the Caribbean see Rebecca Scott, *Slave Emancipation in Cuba: The Transition to Free Labor, 1860–1899* (1985); Robert Conrad, *The Destruction of Brazilian Slavery, 1850–1888* (1973); and William A. Green, *British Slave Emancipation: The Sugar Colonies and the Great Experiment, 1830–1865*. An introduction to the place of women in Latin American society is found in Francesca Miller, *Latin American Women and the Search for Social Justice* (1991), and Jane Jaquette, ed., *The Women's Movement in Latin America* (1989). See also David Barry Gaspar and Darlene Clark Hine, eds., *More Than Chattel: Black Women and Slavery in the Americas* (1996).

An introduction to environmental consequence of North American development is provided by William Cronon, *Nature's Metropolis: Chicago and the Great West* (1991); Joseph M. Petulla, *American Environmental History* (1973); and Donald Worster, *Rivers of Empire: Water, Aridity, and the Growth of the American West* (1985). For Brazil see Warren Dean, *With Broadax and Firebrand: The Destruction of the Brazilian Atlantic Forest* (1995); and for Argentina, Uruguay, and Chile, Alfred Crosby, *Ecological Imperialism: The Biological Expansion of Europe, 900–1900* (1986).

◼ Notes

1. Quoted in Lyman L. Johnson, "Spanish American Independence and Its Consequences," in *Problems in Modern Latin American History: A Reader,* ed. John Charles Chasteen and Joseph S. Tulchin (Wilmington, DE: Scholarly Resources, 1994), 21.

2. Quoted in Margaret Conrad, Alvin Finkel, and Cornelius Jaenen, *History of the Canadian Peoples,* vol. 1 (Toronto: Copp Clark Pittman Ltd., 1993), 606–607.

3. José Antonio Páez, *Autobiografía del General José Antonio Páez,* vol. 1 (Nueva York: Hallety Breen, 1869), 83.

4. Quoted in Brian Loveman, *Chile: The Legacy of Hispanic Capitalism* (New York: Oxford University Press, 1979), 170.

5. Quoted in Bernard Bailyn, David Brion Davis, David Herbert Donald, John L. Thomas, Robert H. Wiebe, and Gordon S. Wood, *The Great Republic: A History of the American People* (Lexington, MA: D. C. Heath, 1981), 398.

6. J. S. Woodsworth in 1909, quoted in R. Douglas Francis, Richard Jones, and Donald B. Smith, *Destinies: Canadian History Since Confederation,* 2d ed. (Toronto: Holt, Rinehart and Winston, 1992), 141.

7. Sarah Grimké, "Reply to the Massachusetts Clergy," in Nancy Woloch, ed., *Early American Women: A Documentary History, 1600–1900* (Belmont, CA: Wadsworth, 1992), 343.

26

AFRICA, INDIA, AND THE NEW BRITISH EMPIRE,

1750–1870

Changes and Exchanges in Africa • India Under Company Rule •
Britain's Eastern Empire
ENVIRONMENT AND TECHNOLOGY: Whaling
SOCIETY AND CULTURE: Ceremonials of Imperial Domination

Indian Railroad Station, 1866   British India built the largest network
of railroads in Asia. People of every social class traveled by train.

n 1782 Tipu Sultan inherited the throne of the state of Mysore°, which his father had made the most powerful state in South India. The ambitious and talented new ruler also inherited a healthy distrust of the British East India Company's territorial ambitions. Before the company could invade Mysore, Tipu Sultan launched his own attack in 1785. He then sent an embassy to France in 1788 seeking an alliance against Britain. Neither of these ventures was immediately successful.

Not until a decade later did the French agree to a loose alliance with Tipu Sultan as part of their plan to challenge Britain's colonial and commercial supremacy in the Indian Ocean. General Napoleon Bonaparte invaded Egypt in 1798 to threaten British trade routes to India and hoped to use the alliance with Tipu Sultan to drive the British out of India. The French invasion of Egypt went well enough at first, but a British naval blockade and the ravages of disease crippled the French force. When the French withdrew, another military adventurer, Muhammad Ali, commander of the Ottoman army in Egypt, took advantage of the situation to revitalize Egypt and expand its rule.

Meanwhile, Tipu's struggle with the East India Company was going badly. A military defeat in 1792 forced him to surrender most of his coastal lands. Despite the loose alliance with France, he was unable to stop further British advances. Tipu lost his life in 1799 while defending his capital against a British assault. Mysore was divided between the British and their Indian allies.

As these events illustrate, talented local leaders and European powers were both vying to expand their influence in South Asia and Africa between 1750 and 1870. Midway through that period, it was by no means clear who would gain the upper hand. Britain and France were as likely to fight each other as they were to fight any Asian or African state. In 1800, the two nations were engaged in their third major war for overseas supremacy since 1750. By 1870, however, Britain had gained a decisive advantage over France.

The new British empire in the East included the subcontinent of India, settler colonies in Australia and New Zealand, and a growing network of trading outposts. By 1870 Britain had completed the campaign to replace the overseas slave trade from Africa with "legitimate" trade and had spearheaded new Asian and South Pacific labor migrations into a rejuvenated string of tropical colonies.

As you read this chapter, ask yourself the following questions:

- Why were the British able to gain decisive advantages in distant lands?
- Why were Asians and Africans so divided, some choosing to cooperate with the Europeans while others resisted their advances?
- How important an advantage were Britain's weapons, ships, and economic motives?
- How much of the outcome was the result of advance planning, and how much was due to particular individuals or to chance?
- By 1870, how much had the British and the different peoples of Africa and Asia gained or lost?

CHANGES AND EXCHANGES IN AFRICA

During the century before 1870, Africa underwent dynamic political changes and a great expansion of foreign trade. Indigenous African leaders as well as Middle Eastern and European imperialists built powerful new states or expanded old ones. As the continent's external slave trades to the Americas and to Islamic lands died slowly under British pressure, trade in goods such as palm oil, ivory, timber, and gold grew sharply. In return Africans imported large quantities of machine-made textiles and firearms. These complex changes are best understood by looking at African regions separately.

Mysore (my-SORE)

CHRONOLOGY

	Empire	Africa	India
1750	1763 End of Seven Years War 1769–1778 Captain James Cook explores New Zealand and eastern Australia 1795 End of Dutch East India Company		1756 Black Hole of Calcutta 1765 East India Company (EIC) rule of Bengal begins
1800		1795 Britain takes Cape Colony 1798 Napoleon invades Egypt	1798 Britain annexes Ceylon 1799 EIC defeats Mysore
	1808 Britain outlaws slave trade	1805 Muhammad Ali seizes Egypt 1808 Britain takes over Sierra Leone 1809 Sokoto Caliphate founded 1818 Shaka founds Zulu kingdom 1821 Foundation of Republic of Liberia; Egypt takes control of Sudan	1818 EIC creates Bombay Presidency 1826 EIC annexes Assam and northern Burma 1828 Brahmo Samaj founded
	1834 Britain abolishes slavery	1831–1847 Algerians resist French takeover 1836–1839 Afrikaners' Great Trek 1840 Omani sultan moves capital to Zanzibar	1834 Indentured labor migrations begin
1850	1867 End of Atlantic slave trade 1877 Queen Victoria becomes Empress of India	1869 Jaja founds Opobo 1889 Menelik unites modern Ethiopia	1857–1858 Sepoy Rebellion leads to end of EIC rule and Mughal rule 1885 First Indian National Congress

New States in Southern and Inland West Africa

Internal forces produced clusters of new states in two parts of sub-Saharan Africa between 1750 and 1870. In southern Africa changes in warfare gave rise to a powerful Zulu kingdom and other new states. In inland West Africa Islamic reformers created the gigantic Sokoto° Caliphate and companion states (see Map 26.1).

In the fertile coastlands of southeastern Africa (in modern South Africa), the Nguni° peoples for many centuries had pursued a life based on cattle and agriculture. Small independent chiefdoms suited their political needs until a serious drought hit the region at the beginning of the nineteenth century. Out of the conflict for grazing and farming lands an upstart military genius named Shaka (r. 1818–1828) in 1818 created the **Zulu** kingdom. Strict military drill and close-combat warfare featuring oxhide shields and lethal stabbing spears made the Zulu the most powerful and most feared fighters in southern Africa.

Shaka expanded his kingdom by raiding his African neighbors, seizing their cattle, and capturing their women and children. Breakaway military bands spread this system of warfare and state building inland to the high plateau country, across the Limpopo River (in modern Zimbabwe°), and as far north as Lake Victoria. As the power and population of these new kingdoms increased, so too did the number of displaced and demoralized refugees around them.

To protect themselves from the Zulu, some neighboring Africans created their own states. The Swazi kingdom consolidated north of the Zulu, and the kingdom of Lesotho° grew by attracting refugees to strongholds in

---

Sokoto (SOH-kuh-toh)   **Nguni** (ng-GOO-nee)

Zimbabwe (zim-BAH-bway)   **Lesotho** (luh-SOO-too)

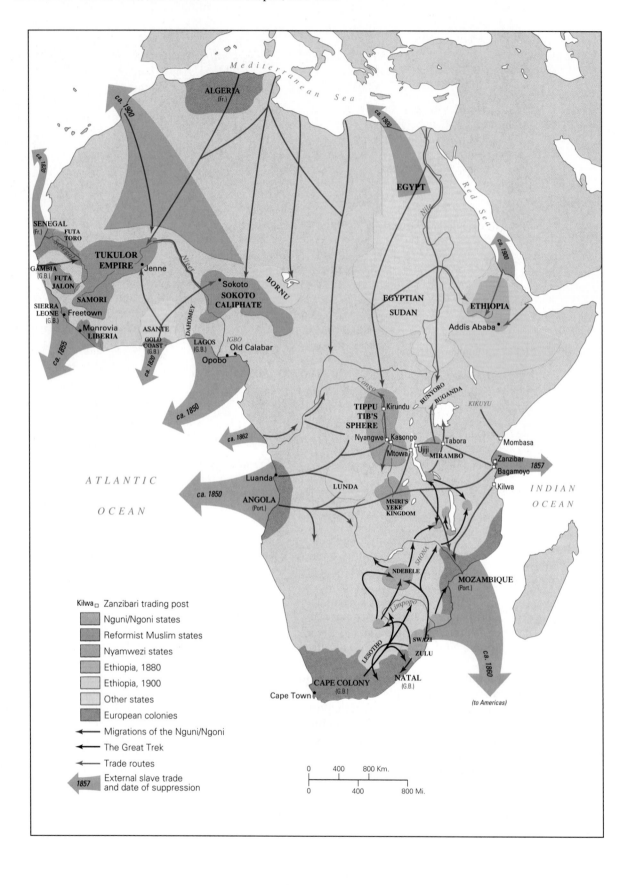

Mediterranean Sea

ALGERIA
(Fr.)

ca. 1900

ca. 1900

ca. 1820

EGYPT

Red Sea

Nile

SENEGAL
(Fr.)
FUTA
TORO

Senegal

TUKULOR
EMPIRE • Jenne

Niger

EGYPTIAN
SUDAN

ca. 1900

ETHIOPIA

GAMBIA
(G.B.)
FUTA
JALON

• Sokoto
SOKOTO
CALIPHATE

BORNU

Addis Ababa •

SAMORI

SIERRA
LEONE
(G.B.) • Freetown

• Monrovia
LIBERIA

ASANTE

DAHOMEY

GOLD
COAST
(G.B.)

ca. 1820

LAGOS
(G.B.)

IGBO

Old Calabar

Opobo

ca. 1855

ca. 1850

Congo

BUNYORO
BUGANDA

KIKUYU

TIPPU
TIB'S
SPHERE • Kirundu

ca. 1862

Nyangwe • Kasongo
Mtowa •
Ujiji

• Tabora

Mombasa

ATLANTIC

OCEAN

ca. 1850

LUNDA

MIRAMBO

Zanzibar
Bagamoyo

1857

INDIAN

• Luanda

ANGOLA
(Port.)

MSIRI'S
YEKE
KINGDOM

• Kilwa

OCEAN

SHONA

NDEBELE

MOZAMBIQUE
(Port.)

Limpopo

Kilwa □ Zanzibari trading post

Nguni/Ngoni states

Reformist Muslim states

Nyamwezi states

Ethiopia, 1880

Ethiopia, 1900

Other states

European colonies

Migrations of the Nguni/Ngoni

The Great Trek

Trade routes

1857 External slave trade
and date of suppression

LESOTHO

SWAZI
ZULU

ca. 1860

CAPE COLONY

Cape Town •

NATAL
(G.B.)

(to Americas)

0   400   800 Km.

0   400   800 Mi.

Map 26.1   Africa in the Nineteenth Century   Expanding internal and overseas trade drew much of Africa into global networks, but foreign colonies in 1870 were largely confined to Algeria and southern Africa. Growing trade, Islamic reform movements, and other internal forces created important new states throughout the continent.

southern Africa's highest mountains. Both Lesotho and Swaziland survive as independent states to this day.

Although Shaka ruled for little more than a decade, he succeeded in creating a new national identity as well as a new kingdom. He grouped all the young people in his domains by age into regiments. Regiment members lived together and immersed themselves in learning Zulu lore and customs, including fighting methods for the males. A British trader named Henry Francis Fynn expressed his "astonishment at the order and discipline" he found everywhere in the Zulu kingdom. He witnessed public festivals of loyalty to Shaka at which regiments of young men and women numbering in the tens of thousands danced around the king for hours. Parades showed off the king's enormous herds of cattle, a Zulu measure of wealth.

Meanwhile, Islamic reform movements were creating another cluster of powerful states in the savannas of West Africa. Islam had been a force in the politics and cities of this region for centuries, but it had made only slow progress among most rural people. As a consequence, most Muslim rulers had found it prudent to tolerate the older religious practices of their rural subjects. In the 1770s, local Muslim scholars began preaching the need for a vigorous reform of Islamic practices. They condemned the accommodations Muslim rulers had made with older traditions and called for a forcible conquest of rural "pagans." The reformers followed a classic Muslim pattern: a *jihad* (holy war) added new lands, where governments enforced Islamic laws and promoted the religion's spread among conquered people.

The largest of the new Muslim reform movements occurred in the Hausa° states (in what is now northern Nigeria) under the leadership of Usuman dan Fodio° (1745–1817), a Muslim cleric of the Fulani° people. He charged that the Hausa kings, despite their official profession of Islam, were "undoubtedly unbelievers . . . because they practice polytheistic rituals and turn people away from the path of God." Distressed by the lapses of a former pupil, the king of Gobir, Usuman issued a call in

Hausa (HOW-suh)
Usuman dan Fodio (OO-soo-mahn dahn FOH-dee-oh)
Fulani (foo-LAH-nee)

Zulu in Battle Dress, 1838   Elaborate costumes helped impress opponents with the Zulu's strength. Shown here are long-handled spears and thick leather shields. The stabbing spear is not shown. (Killie Campbell Africana Library. Photo: Jane Taylor/Sonia Halliday)

1804 for a jihad to overthrow him. Muslims unhappy with their social or religious position spread the movement to other Hausa states. The successful armies united the conquered Hausa states and neighboring areas under a caliph (sultan) who ruled from the city of Sokoto. The **Sokoto Caliphate** (1809–1906) was the largest state in West Africa since the fall of Songhai in the sixteenth century.

As in earlier centuries, these new Muslim states became centers of Islamic learning and reform. Schools for training boys in Quranic subjects spread rapidly, and the great library at Sokoto attracted many scholars. Although officials permitted non-Muslims within the empire to follow their religions in exchange for paying a special tax, they suppressed public performances of dances and ceremonies associated with traditional religions. During the jihads, many who resisted the expansion of Muslim rule were killed, enslaved, or forced to convert.

Sokoto's leaders sold some captives into the Atlantic slave trade and many more into the trans-Saharan slave trade, which carried ten thousand slaves a year, mostly women and children, across the desert to North Africa and the Middle East. Slavery also increased greatly within the Sokoto Caliphate and other new Muslim states. It is estimated that by 1865 there were more slaves in the Sokoto Caliphate than in any remaining slaveholding state in the Americas.[1] Most of the enslaved persons raised food, making possible the seclusion of free women in their homes in accordance with reformed Muslim practice.

Modernization and Expansion in Egypt and Ethiopia

While new states were arising elsewhere, the ancient African states of Egypt and Ethiopia in northeastern Africa were undergoing a period of growth and **modernization.** Napoleon's invading army had withdrawn from Egypt by 1801, but the shock of this display of European strength and Egyptian weakness was long lasting. The successor to Napoleon's rule was **Muhammad Ali** (1769–1849), who eliminated his rivals and ruled Egypt from 1805 to 1848. He began the political, social, and economic reforms that created modern Egypt.

Muhammad Ali's central aim was to give Egypt sufficient military strength to prevent another European conquest, but he was pragmatic enough to make use of European experts and techniques to achieve that goal. His reforms transformed Egyptian landholding, increased agricultural production, and created a modern administration and army. To train candidates for the army and administration, Muhammad Ali set up a European-style state school system and opened a military college at Aswan°. To pay for these ventures and for the European experts and equipment that he imported, he required Egyptian peasants to cultivate cotton and other crops for export.

In the 1830s Muhammad Ali headed the strongest state in the Islamic world and the first to employ Western methods and technology for modernization. The process was far from a blind imitation of the West. Rather, the technical expertise of the West was combined with Islamic religious and cultural traditions. For example, the Egyptian printing industry, begun to provide Arabic translations of technical manuals, turned out critical editions of Islamic classics and promoted a revival of Arabic writing and literature later in the century.

By the end of Muhammad Ali's reign in 1848, the modernization of Egypt was well under way. The population had nearly doubled, trade with Europe had expanded by almost 600 percent, and a new class of educated Egyptians had begun to replace the old ruling aristocracy. Egyptians were replacing many of the foreign experts, and the fledgling program of industrialization was providing the country with its own textiles, paper, weapons, and military uniforms. The demands on peasant families for labor and military service, however, were acutely disruptive.

Ali's grandson Ismail° (r. 1863–1879) placed even more emphasis on westernizing Egypt. "My country is no longer in Africa," Ismail declared, "it is in Europe."[2] His efforts increased the number of European advisers in Egypt—and Egypt's debts to French and British banks. In the first decade of his reign, revenues increased thirty-fold and exports doubled (largely because of a huge increase in cotton exports during the American Civil War). By 1870 there was a network of new irrigation canals, 800 miles (1,300 kilometers) of railroads, a modern postal service, and the dazzling new capital city of Cairo. When the market for Egyptian cotton collapsed after the American Civil War, however, Egypt's debts to British and French investors led to the country's partial occupation.

From the middle of the century, state building and reform also were under way in the ancient kingdom of Ethiopia, whose rulers had been Christian for fifteen hundred years. Weakened by internal divisions and the pressures of its Muslim neighbors, Ethiopia was a shadow of what it had been in the sixteenth century, but under Emperor Téwodros° II (r. 1833–1868) and his successor Yohannes° IV (r. 1872–1889) most highland regions were brought back under imperial rule. The only large part of ancient Ethiopia that remained outside Emperor Yohannes's rule was the Shoa kingdom, ruled by King Menelik° from 1865. When Menelik succeeded Yohannes as emperor in 1889, the merger of their separate realms created the modern boundaries of Ethiopia.

Beginning in the 1840s, Ethiopian rulers purchased modern weapons from European sources and created strong armies loyal to the ruler. Emperor Téwodros also encouraged the manufacture of weapons locally. With the aid of Protestant missionaries his craftsmen even constructed a giant cannon capable of firing a half-ton shell. However, his efforts to coerce more technical aid by holding some British officials captive backfired when the British invaded instead. As the British forces advanced, Téwodros committed suicide to avoid being taken prisoner. Satisfied that their honor was avenged, the British withdrew. Later Ethiopian emperors kept up the program of reform and modernization.

Aswan (AS-wahn)

Ismail (is-MAH-eel)   Téwodros (tay-WOH-druhs)
Yohannes (yoh-HAHN-nehs)   Menelik (MEN-uh-lik)

Téwodros's Mighty Cannon   Like other modernizers in the nineteenth century, Emperor Téwodros of Ethiopia sought to reform his military forces. In 1861 he forced resident European missionaries and craftsmen to build guns and cannon, including this 7-ton behemoth nicknamed "Sebastapol" after the Black Sea port that had been the center of the Crimean War. It took five hundred men to haul the cannon across Ethiopia's hilly terrain.   (From Hormuzd Rassam, *Narrative of the British Mission to Theodore, King of Abyssinia, II*, London 1869, John Murray)

European Invaders and Explorers

More lasting than Britain's punitive invasion of Ethiopia was France's conquest of Algeria, a move that anticipated the general European "Scramble for Africa" after 1870. Equally pregnant with future meaning was the Europeans' exploration of the inland parts of Africa in the middle decades of the century.

Long an exporter of grain and olive oil to France, the North African state of Algeria had even supplied Napoleon with grain for his 1798 invasion of Egypt. The failure of French governments to repay this debt led to many disputes between Algeria and France and eventually to a serving of diplomatic relations in 1827, after the ruler of Algeria, annoyed with the French ambassador, allegedly struck him with a fly whisk. Three years later an unpopular French government, hoping to stir French nationalism with an easy overseas victory, attacked Algeria on the pretext of avenging this insult.

The invasion of 1830 proved a costly mistake. The French government was soon overthrown, but the war in Algeria dragged on for eighteen years. The attack by an alien Christian power united the Algerians behind 'Abd al-Qadir°, a gifted and resourceful Muslim holy man. To achieve victory, the French built up an army of over 100,000 that broke Algerian resistance by destroying farm animals and crops and massacring villagers by the tens of thousands. After 'Abd al-Qadir was captured and exiled in 1847, the resistance movement fragmented, but the French occupiers faced resistance in the mountains for another thirty years. Poor European settlers, who rushed in to take possession of Algeria's rich coastlands, numbered 130,000 by 1871.

Meanwhile, a more peaceful European intrusion was penetrating Africa's geographical secrets. Small expeditions of adventurous explorers, using their own funds or financed by private geographical societies, were seeking to uncover the mysteries of inner Africa that had eluded Europeans for four centuries. Besides discovering more about the course of Africa's mighty rivers, these explorers wished to assess the continent's mineral wealth or convert the African millions to Christianity.

'Abd al-Qadir (AHB-dahl-KAH-deer)

Many of the explorers were concerned with tracing the course of Africa's great rivers. Explorers learned in 1795 that the Niger River in West Africa flowed from west to east (not the other way as had often been supposed) and in 1830 that the great morass of small streams entering the Gulf of Guinea was in fact the Niger Delta.

The north-flowing Nile, whose annual floods made Egypt bloom, similarly attracted explorers bent on finding the headwaters of the world's longest river. In 1770 Lake Tana in Ethiopia was established as a major source, and in 1861–1862 Lake Victoria (named for the British sovereign) was found to be the other main source.

In contrast to the heavily financed expeditions with hundreds of African porters that searched the Nile, the Scottish missionary David Livingstone (1813–1873) organized modest treks through southern and Central Africa. The missionary doctor's primary goal was to scout out locations for Christian missions, but he was also highly influential in tracing the course of the Zambezi River, between 1853 and 1856. He named its greatest waterfall for the British monarch Queen Victoria. Livingstone also traced the course of the upper Congo River, where in 1871 he was met by the Welsh-American journalist Henry Morton Stanley (1841–1904) on a publicity-motivated search for the "lost" missionary doctor. On an expedition from 1874 to 1877, Stanley descended the Congo River to its mouth.

One of the most remarkable features of the explorers' experiences in Africa was their ability to move unmolested from place to place. The strangers were seldom harmed without provocation. Stanley preferred large expeditions that fought their way across the continent, but Livingstone's modest expeditions, which posed no threat to anyone, regularly received warm hospitality.

Abolition and Legitimate Trade in Coastal West Africa

No sooner was the mouth of the Niger River discovered than eager entrepreneurs began to send expeditions up the river to scout out its potential for trade. Along much of coastal West Africa, commercial relations with Europeans remained dominant between 1750 and 1870. The value of trade between Africa and the other Atlantic continents more than doubled between the 1730s and the 1780s, then doubled again by 1870.[3] Before about 1825 the slave trade accounted for most of that increase, but thereafter African exports of vegetable oils, gold, ivory, and other goods drove overseas trade to new heights.

Europeans played a critical role in these changes in Africa's overseas trade. The Atlantic trade had arisen to serve the needs of the first European empires, and its transformation was linked to the ideas and industrial needs of Britain's new economy and empire.

One step in the Atlantic slave trade's extinction was the successful slave revolt in Saint Domingue in the 1790s (see Chapter 23). It ended slavery in the largest plantation colony in the West Indies, and elsewhere in the Americas it inspired slave revolts that were brutally repressed. As news of the slave revolts and their repression spread, humanitarians and religious reformers called for an end to the slave trade. Since it was widely believed that African-born slaves were more likely to rebel than were persons born into slavery, support for abolition of the slave trade was found even among Americans wanting to preserve slavery. In 1808 both Great Britain and the United States made carrying and importing slaves from Africa illegal for their citizens. Most other Western countries followed suit by 1850, but few enforced abolition with the vigor of the British.

Once the world's greatest slave traders, the British became the most aggressive abolitionists. Britain sent a naval patrol to enforce the ban along the African coast and negotiated treaties allowing the patrol to search other nations' vessels suspected of carrying slaves. During the half-century after 1815, Britain spent some $60 million (£12 million) in its efforts to end the slave trade, a sum equal to the profits British slave traders had made in the fifty years before 1808.

Although British patrols captured 1,635 slave ships and liberated over 160,000 enslaved Africans, the trade proved difficult to stop, for Cuba and Brazil continued to import huge numbers of slaves. Such demand drove prices up and persuaded some African rulers and merchants to continue to sell slaves and to help foreign slavers evade the British patrols. After British patrols quashed the slave trade along the Gold Coast, the powerful king of Asante° even tried to persuade a British official in 1820 that reopening the trade would be to their mutual profit. Because the slave trade moved to other parts of Africa, the trans-Atlantic slave trade did not end until 1867.

The demand for slaves in the Americas claimed the lives and endangered the safety of untold numbers of Africans, but the trade also satisfied other Africans' desires for the cloth, metals, and other goods that European traders brought in return. To continue their access to those imports, Africans expanded their **"legitimate" trade** (exports other than slaves). They revived old trades or developed new exports as the Atlantic slave trade was shut down. On the Gold Coast, for example, annual exports of gold climbed to nearly 25,000 ounces (750 kilograms) in the 1840s and 1850s, compared to 10,000 ounces (300 kilograms) in the 1790s.

Asante (uh-SHAHN-tee)

The most successful of the new exports from West Africa was palm oil, a vegetable oil used by British manufacturers for soap, candles, and lubricants. Though still a major source of slaves until the mid-1830s, the trading states of the Niger Delta simultaneously emerged as the premier exporters of palm oil. In inland forests men climbed tall oil palms and cut down large palm-nut clusters, which women pounded to extract the thick oil. Coastal African traders bought the palm oil at inland markets and delivered it to European ships at the coast.

The dramatic increase in palm-oil exports—from a few hundred tons at the beginning of the century to tens of thousands of tons by midcentury—did not require any new technology, but it did alter the social structure of the coastal trading communities. Coastal traders grew rich and used their wealth to buy large numbers of male slaves to paddle the giant dugout canoes that transported palm oil from inland markets along the narrow delta creeks to the trading ports. Niger Delta slavery could be as harsh and brutal as slavery on New World plantations, but it offered some male and female slaves a chance to gain wealth and power. Some female slaves who married big traders exercised great authority over junior members of trading households. Male slaves who supervised canoe fleets were well compensated, and a few even became wealthy enough to take over the leadership of the coastal "canoe houses" (companies). The most famous, known as "Jaja" (ca. 1821–1891), rose from being a canoe slave to the head of a major canoe house. To escape discrimination by free-born Africans, in 1869 he founded the new port of Opobo, which he ruled as king. In the 1870s Jaja of Opobo was the greatest palm-oil trader in the Niger Delta.

Another effect of the suppression of the slave trade was the spread of Western cultural influences in West Africa. To serve as a base for their anti-slave-trade naval squadron, in 1808 the British had taken over the small colony of Sierra Leone°. Over the next several years, 130,000 men, women, and children taken from "captured" vessels were liberated in Sierra Leone. Christian missionaries helped settle these impoverished and dispirited **recaptives** in and around Freetown, the capital. In time the mission churches and schools made many willing converts among such men and women.

Sierra Leone's schools also produced a number of distinguished graduates. For example, Samuel Adjai Crowther (1808–1891), freed as a youth from a slave ship in 1821 by the British squadron, became the first Anglican bishop in West Africa in 1864, administering a pioneering diocese along the lower Niger River. James

---

Sierra Leone (see-ER-uh lee-OWN)

King Jaja of Opobo   This talented man rose from slavery in the Niger Delta port of Bonny to head one of the town's major palm-oil trading firms, the Anna Pepple House, in 1863. Six years later, Jaja founded and ruled his own trading port of Opobo. (Reproduced from *West Africa: An Introduction to Its History,* by Michael Crowder, by courtesy of the publishers, Addison Wesley Longman)

Africanus Horton (1835–1882), the son of a slave liberated in Sierra Leone, became a doctor and the author of many studies of West Africa.

Other Western cultural influences came from people of African birth or descent returning to their ancestral homeland in this era. In 1821, to the south of Sierra Leone, free black Americans began a settlement that grew into the Republic of Liberia, a place of liberty at a time when slavery was illegal and flourishing in the

United States. After their emancipation in 1865 other African-Americans moved to Liberia. Emma White, a literate black woman from Kentucky, moved from Liberia to Opobo in 1875, where King Jaja employed her to write his commercial correspondence and run a school for his children. Edward Wilmot Blyden (1832–1912), born in the Danish West Indies and proud of his West African parentage, emigrated to Liberia in 1851 and became a professor of Greek and Latin (and later Arabic) at the fledgling Liberia College. Free blacks from Brazil and Cuba chartered ships to return to their West African homelands, bringing with them Roman Catholicism, architectural motifs, and clothing fashions from the New World. Although the number of Africans exposed to Western culture in 1870 was still small, this influence grew rapidly.

Slaves and Secondary Empires in Eastern Africa

When British patrols hampered the slave trade in West Africa, slavers moved southward and then around the tip of southern Africa to eastern Africa. There the Atlantic slave trade joined an existing trade in slaves to the Islamic world that also was expanding. Two-thirds of the 1.2 million slaves exported from eastern Africa in the nineteenth century went to markets in North Africa and the Middle East; the other third went to plantations in the Americas and to European-controlled Indian Ocean islands.

Slavery also became more prominent within eastern Africa itself. Between 1800 and 1873, Arab and Swahili owners of clove plantations along the coast purchased some 700,000 slaves from inland eastern Africa to do the labor-intensive work of harvesting this spice. The plantations were on Zanzibar Island and in neighboring territories belonging to the Sultanate of Oman, an Arabian kingdom on the Persian Gulf that had been expanding its control over the East African coast since 1698. The sultan had even moved his court to Zanzibar in 1840 to take better advantage of the burgeoning trade in cloves. Zanzibar also was an important center of slaves and ivory. Most of the ivory was shipped to India, where much of it was carved into decorative objects for European markets.

Ivory caravans came to the coast from hundreds of miles inland under the direction of African and Arab merchants. Some of these merchants brought large personal empires under their control by using capital they had borrowed from Indian bankers and modern firearms they had bought from Europeans and Americans. Some trading empires were created by inland

Nyamwezi° traders, who worked closely with the indigenous Swahili° and Arabs in Zanzibar to develop the long-distance caravan routes.

The largest of these personal empires, along the upper Congo River, was created by Tippu Tip (ca. 1830–1905), a trader from Zanzibar, who was Swahili and Nyamwezi on his father's side and Omani Arab on his mother's. Livingstone, Stanley, and other explorers who received Tippu Tip's gracious hospitality in the remote center of the continent praised their host's intelligence and refinement. On an 1876 visit, for example, Stanley recorded in his journal that Tippu Tip was "a remarkable man," a "picture of energy and strength" with "a fine intelligent face: almost courtier-like in his manner."

Tippu Tip also composed a detailed memoir of his adventures in the heart of Africa, written in the Swahili language of the coast. In it he mocked innocent African villagers for believing that his gunshots were thunder. As the memoir and other sources make clear, these modern rifles not only felled countless elephants for their ivory tusks but also inflicted widespread devastation and misery on the people of this isolated area.

One can blame Tippu Tip and other Zanzibari traders for the pillage and havoc in the once-peaceful center of Africa, along with their master, the sultan of Oman. However, the circle of responsibility was still broader. Europeans supplied the weapons used by the invaders and were major consumers of ivory and cloves. For this reason histories have referred to the states carved out of eastern Africa by the sultans of Oman, Tippu Tip, and others as "secondary empires," in contrast to the empire that Britain was establishing directly. At the same time, Britain was working to bring the Indian Ocean slave trade to an end in eastern Africa. British officials pressured the sultan of Oman into halting the Indian Ocean slave trade from Zanzibar in 1857 and ending the import of slaves into Zanzibar in 1873.

Egypt's expansion southward during the nineteenth century can also be considered a secondary empire. Muhammad Ali had pioneered the conquest of the upper Nile, in 1821 establishing at Khartoum° a major base that became the capital of the Egyptian Sudan. A major reason for his invasion of Sudan was to secure slaves for his army so that more Egyptian peasants could be left free to grow cotton for export. From the 1840s unscrupulous traders of many origins, leading forces armed with European weapons, pushed south to the modern frontiers of Uganda and Zaire in search of cattle, ivory, and slaves. They set one African community against another and reaped profit from the devastation they sowed.

Nyamwezi (nn-nyahm-WAY-zee) **Swahili** (swah-HEE-lee)
Khartoum (khar-TOOM)

British Mem–Sahib, ca. 1782   This charming painting by a Bengali artist shows Lady Impey, wife of the British East India Company's chief justice of Bengal, surrounded by her Indian servants in a room that mixes Indian and European decor. The Hindi word *sahib* was an honorific title; *mem-sahib* was the Anglo-Indian feminine form reserved for European women.   (The Art Archive Ltd.)

INDIA UNDER BRITISH RULE

The people of South Asia felt the impact of European commercial, cultural, and colonial expansion more immediately and profoundly than did the people of Africa. While Europeans were laying claim to only small parts of Africa between 1750 and 1870, nearly all of India (with three times the population of all of Africa) came under Britain's direct or indirect rule. During the 250 years after the founding of East India Company in 1600, British interests commandeered the colonies and trade of the Dutch, fought off French and Indian challenges, and picked up the pieces of the decaying Mughal° Empire. By 1763 the French were stymied, in 1795 the Dutch East India Company was dissolved, and in 1858 the last Mughal emperor was dethroned, leaving the vast subcontinent in British hands.

Company Men   As Mughal power weakened in the eighteenth century, Europeans were not the first outsiders to make a move. In 1739, Iranian armies defeated the Mughal forces, sacked Delhi, and returned home with vast amounts of booty. Indian states also took advantage of Mughal weakness to assert their independence. By midcentury, the Maratha° Confederation, a coalition of states in central India, controlled more land than the Mughals did (see Map 26.2). Also ruling their own powerful states were the **nawabs**° (a term used for Muslim princes who were deputies of the Mughal emperor, though in name only): the nawab of Bengal in the northeast; the nawab of Arcot in the southeast, Haidar Ali (1722–1782)—the father of Tipu Sultan and ruler of the southwestern state of Mysore; and many others.

British, Dutch, and French companies were also eager to expand their profitable trade into India in the eighteenth century. Such far-flung European trading

---

Mughal (MOO-guhl

Maratha (muh-RAH-tuh)   **nawab** (NAH-wab)

Map 26.2 India, 1707–1805 As Mughal power weakened during the eighteenth century, other Indian states and the British East India Company expanded their territories.

companies were speculative and risky ventures in 1750. Their success depended on hard-drinking and ambitious young "Company Men," who used hard bargaining, and hard fighting when necessary, to persuade Indian rulers to allow them to establish trading posts at strategic points along the coast. To protect their fortified warehouses from attack by other Europeans or by native states, the companies hired and trained Indian troops known as **sepoys°**. In divided India these private armies came to hold the balance of power.

In 1691 the East India Company (EIC) had convinced the nawab of the large state of Bengal in northeast India to let the company establish a fortified outpost at the fishing port of Calcutta. A new nawab, pressing claims

---

sepoy (SEE-poy)

for additional tribute from the prospering port, overran the fort in 1756 and imprisoned a group of EIC men in a cell so small that many died of suffocation. To avenge their deaths in this "Black Hole of Calcutta," a large EIC force from Madras, led by the young Robert Clive, overthrew the nawab. The weak Mughal emperor was persuaded to acknowledge the East India Company's right to rule Bengal in 1765. Fed by the tax revenues of Bengal as well as by profits from trade, the EIC was on its way. Calcutta grew into a city of 250,000 by 1788.

In southern India, Clive had used EIC forces from Madras to secure victory for the British Indian candidate for nawab of Arcot during the Seven Years War (1756–1763), thereby gaining an advantage over French traders who had supported the loser. The defeat of Tipu Sultan of Mysore at the end of the century (described at the start of the chapter) secured south India for the company and prevented a French resurgence.

Along with Calcutta and Madras, the third major center of British power in India was Bombay, on the western coast. There, after a long series of contests with the Maratha Confederation rulers, the East India Company gained a decisive advantage in 1818, annexing large territories to form the core of what was called the "Bombay Presidency." Some states were taken over completely, as Bengal had been, but very many others remained in the hands of local princes who accepted the political control of the company.

The Raj and the Rebellion, 1818–1857

In 1818 the East India Company controlled an Empire with more people than in all of western Europe and fifty times the population of the colonies the British had lost in North America. One thrust of **British raj** (reign) was to remake India on a British model through administrative and social reform, economic development, and the introduction of new technology. But at the same time the company men—like the Mughals before them—had to temper their interference with Indian social and religious customs lest they provoke rebellion or lose the support of their Indian princely allies. For this reason and because of the complexity of the task of ruling such a vast empire, there were many inconsistencies in Britain's policies toward India.

The main policy was to create a powerful and efficient system of government. British rule before 1850 relied heavily on military power—170 sepoy regiments and 16 European regiments. Another policy very much in the interests of India's new rulers was to disarm approximately 2 million warriors who had served India's many states and turn them to civilian tasks, mostly cultivation. A third policy was to give freer rein to Christian missionaries eager to convert and uplift India's masses. Few converts were made, but the missionaries kept up steady pressure for social reforms.

Another key British policy was to substitute ownership of private property for India's complex and overlapping patterns of landholding. In Bengal this reform worked to the advantage of large landowners, but in Mysore the peasantry gained. Private ownership made it easier for the state to collect the taxes that were needed to pay for the costs of administration, the army, and economic reform.

Such policies of "westernization, Anglicization, and modernization," as they have been called, were only one side of British rule. The other side was the bolstering of "traditions"—both real and newly invented. In the name of tradition the Indian princes who ruled nearly half of British India were frequently endowed by their British overlords with greater power and splendor and longer tenure than their predecessors had ever had. Hindu and Muslim holy men were able to expand their "traditional" power over property and people far beyond what had ever been the case in earlier times. Princes, holy men, and other Indians frequently used claims of tradition to resist British rule as well as to turn it to their advantage. The British rulers themselves invented many "traditions"—including elaborate parades and displays—half borrowed from European royal pomp, half freely improvised from Mughal ceremonies (see Society and Culture: Ceremonials of Imperial Domination).

The British and Indian elites danced sometimes in close partnership, sometimes in apparent opposition. But the ordinary people of India suffered. Women of every status, members of subordinate Hindu castes, the "untouchables" and "tribals" outside the caste system, and the poor generally found less benefit in the British reforms and much new oppression in the taxes and "traditions" that exalted their superiors' status.

The transformation of British India's economy was also doubled-edged. On the one hand, British raj created many new jobs as a result of the growth of internal and external trade and the expansion of agricultural production, such as in opium in Bengal—largely for export to China (see Chapter 27)—coffee in Ceylon (an island off the tip of India), and tea in Assam (a state in northeastern India). On the other hand, competition from cheap cotton goods produced in Britain's industrial mills drove many Indians out of the handicraft textile industry. In the eighteenth century India had been the world's greatest exporter of cotton textiles; in the nineteenth century India increasingly shipped raw cotton fiber to Britain.

Ceremonials of Imperial Domination

These excerpts from a letter written to Queen Victoria by the viceroy of India, Lord Lytton, describe the elaborate ceremonies the colony staged in 1876 in anticipation of her being named "Empress of India" and the effects they had on the Indian princes who governed many parts of India. Although British India's power still rested on the threat of military force, its leaders grew increasingly skilled at using symbolic displays of authority and material rewards to win the support of Indian allies.

The day before yesterday (December 23), I arrived, with Lady Lytton and all my staff at Delhi. . . . I was received at the [railroad] station by all the native chiefs and princes, and, . . . after shaking hands . . . , I immediately mounted my elephant, accompanied by Lady Lytton, our two little girls following us on another elephant. The procession through Delhi to the camp . . . lasted upwards of three hours. . . . The streets were lined for many miles with troops; those of the native princes being brigaded with those of your Majesty. The crowd along the way, behind the troops, was dense, and apparently enthusiastic; the windows, walls, and housetops being thronged with natives, who salaamed, and Europeans, who cheered as we passed along. . . .

My reception by the native princes at the station was most cordial. The Maharaja of Jeypore (who has lighted the Viceroy's camp with gas of his own manufacture) informed Sir John Strachey that India had never seen such a gathering as this, in which not only all the great native princes (many of whom have never met before), but also chiefs and envoys from Khelat, Burmah, Siam, and the remotest parts of the East, are assembled to do homage to your Majesty. . . .

On Tuesday (December 26) from 10 A.M. till past 7 P.M., I was, without a moment's intermission, occupied in receiving visits from native chiefs, and bestowing on those entitled to them the banners, medals, and other honours given by your Majesty. The durbar, which lasted all day and long after dark, was most successful. . . . Your Majesty's portrait, which was placed over the Viceregal throne in the great durbar tent, was thought by all to be an excellent likeness of your Majesty. The native chiefs examined it with special interest.

On Wednesday, the 27th, I received visits from native chiefs, as before, from 10 A.M. til 1 P.M., and from 1:30 P.M. to 7:30 P.M., was passed in returning visits. I forgot to mention that on Tuesday and Wednesday evenings I gave great State dinners to the Governors of Bombay and Madras. Every subsequent evening of my stay at Delhi was similarly occupied by state banquets and receptions [for officials, foreign dignitaries, and] many distinguished natives. After dinner on Thursday, I held a levee [reception], which lasted till one o'clock at night, and is said to have been attended by 2,500 persons—the largest, I believe, ever held by any Viceroy or Governor-General in India.

. . . your Majesty will, perhaps, allow me to mention, in connection with [the ruler of Kashmir], one little circumstance which appears to me very illustrative of the effect which the assemblage has had on him and others. In the first interviews which took place months ago between myself and Kashmir, . . . I noticed that, though perfectly courteous, he was extremely mistrustful of the British Government and myself. . . . On the day following the Imperial assemblage, I had another private interview with Kashmir for the settlement of some further details. His whole manner and language on this last occasion were strikingly different. [He said:] "I am now convinced that you mean nothing that is not for the good of me and mine. Our interests are identical with those of the empire. Give me your orders and they shall be obeyed."

What is significant about the fact that Lord Lytton and his family arrived in Delhi by train and then chose to move through the city on elephants? What impression did the viceroy intend to create in the minds of the Indian dignitaries by assembling so many of them together and bestowing banners, medals, and honors on them? What might account for the Indian ruler of Kashmir's remarkable change of attitude toward the viceroy and the empire? How differently might a member of the Indian middle class or an unemployed weaver have reacted?

Source: Lady Betty Balfour, *The History of Lord Lytton's Indian Administration, 1876 to 1880* (London: Longmans, Green, and Co., 1899), 116–121, 132.

Even the beneficial economic changes introduced under Britain rule were disruptive, and there were no safety nets for the needy. Thus local rebellions by displaced ruling elites, disgruntled religious traditionalists, and the economically dispossessed were almost constant during the first half of the nineteenth century. Officials' greatest concern was over the continuing loyalty of Indian sepoys in the East India Company's army. Their numbers had increased to 200,000 in 1857, along with 38,000 British officers. Armed with the latest rifles and disciplined in fighting methods, the sepoys had a potential for successful rebellion that other groups lacked.

In fact, discontent was growing among Indian soldiers. In the early decades of EIC rule, most sepoys came from Bengal, one of the first states the company had annexed. The Bengali sepoys resented the active recruitment of other ethnic groups into the army after 1848, such as Sikhs° from Punjab and Gurkhas from Nepal. Many high-caste Hindus objected to a new law in 1856 requiring new recruits to be available for service overseas in the growing Indian Ocean empire, for their religion prohibited ocean travel. The replacement of the standard military musket by the far more accurate Enfield rifle in 1857 also caused problems. Soldiers were ordered to use their teeth to tear open the ammunition cartridges, which were greased with animal fat. Hindus were offended by this order if the fat came from cattle, which they considered sacred. Muslims were offended if the fat came from pigs, which they considered unclean.

Although the cartridge-opening procedure was quickly changed, the initial discontent grew into rebellion by Hindu sepoys in May 1857. British troubles mushroomed when Muslim sepoys, peasants, and discontented elites joined in. The rebels asserted old traditions to challenge British authority: sepoy officers in Delhi proclaimed their loyalty to the Mughal emperor; others rallied behind the Maratha leader Nana Sahib. The rebellion was put down by March 1858, but it shook this piecemeal empire to its core.

Historians have attached different names and meanings to the events of 1857 and 1858. Concentrating on the technical fact that the uprising was an unlawful action by soldiers, nineteenth-century British historians labeled it the **"Sepoy Rebellion"** or the "Mutiny," and these names are still commonly used. Seeing in these events the beginnings of the later movement for independence, some modern Indian historians have termed it the "Revolution of 1857." In reality, it was much more than a simple mutiny, because it involved more than soldiers, but it was not yet a nationalist revolution, for the rebels' sense of a common Indian national identity was weak.

Sikh (seek)

Political Reform and Industrial Impact, 1858–1900

Whatever it is called, the rebellion of 1857–1858 was a turning point in the history of modern India. Some say it marks the beginning of modern India. In its wake Indians gained a new centralized government, entered a period of rapid economic growth, and began to develop a new national consciousness.

The changes in government were immediate. In 1858 Britain eliminated the last traces of Mughal and Company rule. In their place, a new secretary of state for India in London oversaw Indian policy, and a new government-general in Delhi acted as the British monarch's viceroy on the spot. A proclamation by Queen Victoria in November 1858 guaranteed all Indians equal protection of the law and the freedom to practice their religions and social customs; it also assured Indian princes that so long as they were loyal to the queen British India would respect their control of territories and "their rights, dignity and honour."[4]

British rule continued to emphasize both tradition and reform after 1857. At the top, the British viceroys lived in enormous palaces amid hundreds of servants and gaudy displays of luxury meant to convince Indians that the British viceroys were legitimate successors to the Mughal emperors. They treated the quasi-independent Indian princes with elaborate ceremonial courtesy and maintained them in splendor. When Queen Victoria was proclaimed "Empress of India" in 1877 and periodically thereafter, the viceroys put on great pageants known as **durbars.** The most elaborate of all was the durbar at Delhi in 1902 to celebrate the coronation of King Edward VII, at which Viceroy Lord Curzon honored himself with a 101-gun salute and a parade of 34,000 troops in front of 50 princes and 173,000 lesser visitors.

Behind the pomp and glitter, a powerful and efficient bureaucracy controlled the Indian masses. Members of the elite **Indian Civil Service** (ICS), mostly graduates of Oxford and Cambridge Universities, held the senior administrative and judicial posts. Numbering only a thousand at the end of the nineteenth century, these men visited the villages in their districts, heard lawsuits and complaints, and passed judgments. Beneath them were a far greater number of Indian officials and employees. Recruitment into the ICS was by open examinations. In theory any British subject could take these exams. But they were given in England, so in practice the system worked to exclude Indians. In 1870 only one Indian was a member of the ICS. Subsequent reforms by Viceroy Lord Lytton led to fifty-seven Indian appointments by 1887, but there the process stalled.

The key reason blocking qualified Indians' entry into the upper administration of their country was the racist contempt most British officials felt for the people they ruled. When he became commander-in-chief of the Indian army in 1892, Lord Kitchener declared:

> It is this consciousness of the inherent superiority of the European which had won for us India. However well educated and clever a native may be, and however brave he may have proved himself, I believe that no rank we can bestow on him would cause him to be considered an equal of the British officer.

A second transformation of India after 1857 resulted from involvement with industrial Britain. The government invested millions of pounds sterling in harbors, cities, irrigation canals, and other public works. British interests felled forests to make way for tea plantations, persuaded Indian farmers to grow cotton and jute for export, and created great irrigation systems to alleviate the famines that periodically decimated whole provinces. As a result, India's trade expanded rapidly.

Most of the exports were agricultural commodities for processing elsewhere: cotton fiber, opium, tea, silk, and sugar. In return India imported manufactured goods from Britain, including the flood of machine-made cotton textiles that severely undercut Indian hand-loom weavers. The effects on individual Indians varied enormously. Some women found new jobs, though at very low pay, on plantations or in the growing cities, where prostitution flourished. Others struggled to hold families together or ran away from abusive husbands. Everywhere in India poverty remained the norm.

The Indian government also promoted the introduction of new technologies into India not long after their appearance in Britain. Earlier in the century there were steamboats on the rivers and a massive program of canal building for irrigation. Beginning in the 1840s, a railroad boom (paid for out of government revenues) gave India its first national transportation network, followed shortly by telegraph lines. Indeed, in 1870 India had the greatest rail network in Asia and the fifth largest in the world. Originally designed to serve British commerce, the railroads were owned by British companies, constructed with British rails and equipment, and paid dividends to British investors. Ninety-nine percent of the railroad employees were Indians, but Europeans occupied all the top positions—"like a thin film of oil on top of a glass of water, resting upon but hardly mixing with [those] below," as one official report put it.

Although some Indians opposed the railroads at first because the trains mixed people of different castes, faiths, and sexes, the Indian people took to rail travel with great enthusiasm. Indians rode trains on business, on pilgrimage, and in search of work. In 1870 over 18 million passengers traveled along the network's 4,775 miles (7,685 kilometers) of track, and more than a half-million messages were sent up and down the 14,000 miles (22,500 kilometers) of telegraph wire. By 1900 India's trains were carrying 188 million passengers a year.

But the freer movement of Indian pilgrims and the flood of poor Indians into the cities also promoted the spread of cholera°, a disease transmitted through water contaminated by human feces. Cholera deaths rose rapidly during the nineteenth century, and eventually the disease spread to Europe. In many Indian minds *kala mari* ("the black death") was a divine punishment for failing to prevent the British takeover. This chastisement also fell heavily on British residents, who died in large numbers. In 1867 officials demonstrated the close connection between cholera and pilgrims who bathed in and drank from sacred pools and rivers. The installation of a new sewerage system (1865) and a filtered water supply (1869) in Calcutta dramatically reduced cholera deaths there. Similar measures in Bombay and Madras also led to great reductions, but most Indians lived in small villages where famine and lack of sanitation kept cholera deaths high. In 1900 an extraordinary four out of every thousand residents of British India died of cholera. Sanitary improvements lowered the rate later in the twentieth century.

Rising Indian Nationalism, 1828–1900

Ironically, both the successes and the failures of British India stimulated the development of Indian nationalism. Stung by the inability of the rebellion of 1857 to overthrow British rule, some thoughtful Indians began to argue that the only way for Indians to regain control of their destiny was to reduce their country's social and ethnic divisions and promote Pan-Indian nationalism.

Individuals such as Rammohun Roy (1772–1833) had promoted development along these lines a generation earlier. A Western-educated Bengali from a Brahmin family, Roy was a successful administrator for the British East India Company and a thoughtful student of comparative religion. His Brahmo Samaj° (Divine Society), founded in 1828, attracted Indians who sought to reconcile the values they found in the West with the ancient religious traditions of India. They supported efforts to reform some Hindu customs, including the restrictions on widows and the practice of child marriage. They

cholera (KAHL-uhr-uh)   **Bramo Samaj** (BRAH-moh suh-MAHJ) advocated reforming the caste system, encouraged a monotheistic form of Hinduism, and urged a return to the founding principles found in the Upanishads, ancient sacred writings of Hinduism.

Roy and his supporters had backed earlier British efforts to reform or ban some practices they found repugnant. Widow burning (*sati°*) was outlawed in 1829 and slavery in 1843. Reformers sought to correct other abuses of women: prohibitions against widows remarrying were revoked in 1856, and female infanticide was made a crime in 1870.

Although Brahmo Samaj remained an influential movement after the rebellion of 1857, many Indian intellectuals turned to Western secular values and nationalism as the way to reclaim India for its people. In this process the spread of Western education played an important role. Roy had studied both Indian and Western subjects, mastering ten languages in the process, and helped found the Hindu College in Calcutta in 1816. Other Western-curriculum schools quickly followed, including Bethune College in Calcutta, the first secular school for Indian women, in 1849. European and American missionaries played a prominent role in the spread of Western education. In 1870 there were 790,000 Indians in over 24,000 elementary and secondary schools, and India's three universities (established in 1857) awarded 345 degrees. Graduates of these schools articulated a new Pan-Indian nationalism that transcended regional and religious differences.

Many of the new nationalists came from the Indian middle class, which had prospered from the increase of trade and manufacturing. Such educated and ambitious people were angered by the obstacles that British rules and prejudices put in the way of their advancement. Hoping to increase their influence and improve their employment opportunities in the Indian government, they convened the first **Indian National Congress** in 1885. The members sought a larger role for Indians in the Civil Service. They also called for reductions in military expenditures, which consumed 40 percent of the government's budget, so that more could be spent on alleviating the poverty of the Indian masses. The Indian National Congress promoted unity among the country's many religions and social groups, but most early members were upper-caste Western-educated Hindus and Parsis (members of a Zoroastrian religious sect descended from Persians). The Congress effectively voiced the opinions of elite Indians, but until it attracted the support of the masses, it could not hope to challenge British rule.

BRITAIN'S EASTERN EMPIRE

In 1750 Britain's empire was centered on slave-based plantation and settler colonies in the Americas. A century later its main focus was on commercial networks and colonies in the East. In 1750 the French and Dutch were also serious contenders for global dominion. A century later they had been eclipsed by the British colossus straddling the world. Several distinct changes facilitated this expansion and transformation of Britain's overseas empire: a string of military victories pushed aside other rivals for overseas trade and colonies; new policies favored free trade over mercantilism; and changes in shipbuilding techniques increased the speed and volume of maritime commerce. Linked to these changes were new European settlements in southern Africa, Australia, and New Zealand and the growth of a new long-distance trade in indentured labor.

| **Colonial Rivalries and Trading Networks** | As the story of Tipu Sultan told at the beginning of this chapter illustrates, France was still a serious rival to Britain for dominion in the Indian Ocean at |

the end of the eighteenth century. However, France's defeats in the wars of French Revolution (see Chapter 23) ended Napoleon's dream of restoring French dominance overseas. The wars also dismantled much of the Netherlands' Indian Ocean empire. When French armies occupied the Netherlands, the Dutch ruler, who had fled to Britain in January 1795, authorized the British to take over Dutch possessions overseas, to keep them out of French hands. During 1795 and 1796 British forces quickly occupied the Cape Colony at the tip of southern Africa, the strategic Dutch port of Malacca on the strait between the Indian Ocean and the South China Sea, and the island of Ceylon (see Map 26.3).

Then the British occupied Dutch Guiana° and Trinidad in the southern Caribbean. In 1811 they even seized the island of Java, the center of the Netherlands' East Indian empire. British forces had also attacked French possessions, gaining control of the islands of Mauritius° and Réunion in the southwestern Indian Ocean. At the end of the Napoleonic Wars in 1814, Britain returned Java to the Dutch and Réunion to the French but kept the Cape Colony, British Guiana (once

---

sati (suh-TEE)

Guiana (ghee-AH-nuh)   **Mauritius** (moh-RIH-uhs)

Map 26.3   European Possessions in the Indian Ocean and South Pacific, 1870   After 1750, French and British competition for new territories generally expanded the European presence established earlier by the Portuguese, Spanish, and Dutch. By 1870 the British controlled much of India, were settling Australia and New Zealand, and possessed important trading enclaves throughout the region.

part of Dutch Guiana), Trinidad, Ceylon, Malacca, and Mauritius.

The Cape Colony was valuable because of Cape Town's strategic importance as a supply station for ships making the long voyages between Britain and India. With the port city came some twenty thousand descendants of earlier Dutch and French settlers who occupied far-flung farms and ranches in its hinterland. Despite their European origins, these people thought of themselves as permanent residents of Africa and were beginning to refer to themselves as "Afrikaners°" ("Africans" in their dialect of Dutch). British governors prohibited any expansion of the white settler frontier because such expansion invariably led to wars with indigenous Africans. This decision, along with the imposition of laws protecting African rights within Cape Colony (including the emancipation of slaves in 1834), alienated many Afrikaners.

Between 1836 and 1839, parties of Afrikaners embarked on a "Great Trek," leaving British-ruled Cape Colony for the fertile high *veld* (plateau) to the north that two decades of Zulu wars had depopulated. The Great Trek led to the foundation of three new settler colonies in southern Africa by 1850: the Afrikaners' Orange Free State and Transvaal on the high veld and the British colony of Natal on the Indian Ocean coast. Although firearms enabled the settlers to win some important battles against the Zulu and other Africans, they were still a tiny minority surrounded by the populous and powerful independent African kingdoms that had grown up at the beginning of the century. A few thousand British settlers came to Natal and the Cape Colony by midcentury, but these colonies' strategic importance to Britain was only as stopovers for shipping between Britain and British India.

Meanwhile, another strategic British outpost was being established in Southeast Asia. One prong of the advance was led by Thomas Stamford Raffles, who had governed Java during the period of British occupation from 1811 to 1814. After Java's return to the Dutch, Raffles helped the British East India Company establish a new free port at Singapore in 1824, on the site of a small Malay fishing village with a superb harbor. By attracting British merchants and Chinese businessmen and laborers, Singapore soon became the center of trade and shipping between the Indian Ocean and China. Along with Malacca and other possessions on the strait, Singapore formed the "Straits Settlements," which British India administered until 1867.

Further British expansion in Malaya (now Malaysia) did not occur until after 1874, but in neighboring Burma

---

Afrikaner (af-rih-KAHN-uhr)

Great Trek Aided by African Servants   The ox-drawn wagons of the Afrikaners struggled over the Drakensberg Mountains to the high plains in an effort to escape British control.   (Hulton Getty/Liaison)

it came more quickly. Burma had emerged as a powerful kingdom by 1750, with plans for expansion. In 1785 Burma tried to annex neighboring territories of Siam (now Thailand) to the east, but a coalition of Thai leaders thwarted Burmese advances by 1802. Burma next attacked Assam to the west, but this action led to war with British India, which was concerned for the security of its own frontier with Assam. After a two-year war, India annexed Assam in 1826 and occupied two coastal provinces of northern Burma. As rice and timber trade from these provinces grew important, the occupation became permanent, and in 1852 British India annexed the port of Rangoon and the rest of coastal Burma.

Imperial Policies and Shipping

Through such piecemeal acquisitions, by 1870 Britain had added several dozen colonies to the twenty-six colonies it had in 1792, after the loss of the thirteen in North America (see Chapter 23). Nevertheless, historians usually portray Britain in this period as a reluctant empire builder, its leaders unwilling to acquire new outposts that could prove difficult and expensive to administer. This apparent contradiction is resolved when one recognizes that the underlying goal of most British imperial expansion during these decades was trade rather than territory. Most of the new colonies were meant to serve as ports in the growing network of shipping that encircled the globe or as centers of production and distribution for those networks.

This new commercial expansion was closely tied to the needs of Britain's growing industrial economy and reflected a new philosophy of overseas trade. Rather than rebuilding the closed, mercantilist network of trade with its colonies, Britain sought to trade freely with all parts of the world. Free trade was also a wise policy in light of the independence of so many former colonies in the Americas (see Chapter 25).

Whether colonized or not, more and more African, Asian, and Pacific lands were being drawn into the commercial networks created by British expansion and industrialization. As was pointed out earlier, uncolonized parts of West Asia became major exporters to Britain of vegetable oils for industrial and domestic use and forest products for dyes and construction, while areas of eastern Africa free of European control exported ivory that ended up as piano keys and decorations for the elegant homes of the industrial middle class. From the far corners of the world came coffee, cocoa, and tea for the tables of the new industrial classes in Britain and other parts of Europe (along with sugar to sweeten these beverages), and indigo dyes and cotton fibers for their expanding textile factories.

In return, the factories of the industrialized nations supplied manufactured goods at very attractive prices. By the mid-nineteenth century a major part of their textile production was destined for overseas markets. Sales of cotton cloth to Africa increased 950 percent from the 1820s to the 1860s. British trade to India grew 350 percent between 1841 and 1870 while India's exports increased 400 percent. Trade with other regions also expanded rapidly. In most cases such trade benefited both sides, but there is no question that the industrial nations were the dominant partners.

A second impetus to global commercial expansion was the technological revolution in the construction of oceangoing ships under way in the nineteenth century. The middle decades of the century were the golden age of the sailing ship. Using iron to fasten timbers together permitted shipbuilders to construct much larger vessels. Merchant ships in the eighteenth century rarely exceeded 300 tons, but after 1850 swift American-built **clipper ships** of 2,000 tons were commonplace in the British merchant fleet. Huge canvas sails hung from tall masts made the streamlined clippers faster than earlier vessels. Ships from the East Indies or India had taken six months to reach Europe in the seventeenth century; after 1850 the new ships could complete the voyage in half that time.

This increase in size and speed lowered shipping costs and further stimulated maritime trade. The growth in size and numbers of ships increased by the tonnage of British merchant shipping by 400 percent between 1778 and 1860. To extend the life of such ships in tropical lands, clippers intended for Eastern service generally were built of teak and other tropical hardwoods from new British colonies in South and Southeast Asia. Although tropical forests began to be cleared for rice and sugar plantations as well as for timbers, the effects on the environment and people of Southeast Asia came primarily after 1870.

Colonization of Australia and New Zealand

The development of new ships and shipping contributed to a third form of British rule in the once-remote South Pacific. In contrast to the rule over an indigenous population in India or the commercial empire overseen from Singapore and Cape Town, in the new British colonies of Australia and New Zealand British settlers displaced indigenous populations, just as they had done in North America.

Portuguese mariners had sighted the continent of Australia in the early seventeenth century, but its remoteness made the land of little interest to Europeans. However, after the English adventurer Captain James Cook made the first systematic European exploration of New Zealand and the fertile eastern coast of Australia between 1769 and 1778, expanding shipping networks brought in growing numbers of visitors and settlers.

At the time of Cook's visits Australia was the home of about 650,000 hunting and gathering people, whose Melanesian° ancestors had settled there some 40,000 years earlier. The two islands of New Zealand, lying 1,000 miles (1,600 kilometers) southeast of Australia, were inhabited by about 250,000 Maori°, who practiced hunting, fishing, and simple forms of agriculture, which their Polynesian ancestors had introduced around 1200 C.E. Because of their long isolation from the rest of humanity, the populations of Australia and New Zealand were as vulnerable as the Amerindians had been to unfamiliar

---

Melanesian (mel-uh-NEE-zhuhn)
Maori (MOW-ree [*ow* as in *cow*])

diseases introduced by new overseas contacts. By the late nineteenth century only 93,000 aboriginal Australians and 42,000 Maori survived. By then they were outnumbered and dominated by British settler populations.

The first permanent British settlers in Australia were 736 convicts, of whom 188 were women, sent into exile from British prisons in 1788. For the next few decades Australian penal colonies grew slowly and had only slight contact with the indigenous population, whom the British called "Aborigines." However, the discovery of gold in 1851 brought a flood of free European settlers (and some Chinese) and hastened the end of the penal colonies. After 1850 tens of thousands of British settlers received government-subsidized passages "down under" on the improved sailing ships of that era, although the voyage still took more than three months. By 1860 the settler population had reached 1 million, and it doubled over the next fifteen years.

British settlers were drawn more slowly to New Zealand. Some of the first were temporary residents along the coast who slaughtered seals and exported seal pelts to Western countries to be made into men's felt hats. A single ship in 1806 took away sixty thousand sealskins. By the early 1820s overhunting had nearly exterminated the seal population. Sperm whales were also hunted extensively near New Zealand for their oil, used for lubrication, soap, and lamps; ambergris°, an ingredient in perfume; and bone, used in women's corsets (see Environment and Technology: Whaling). Military action that overcame Maori resistance, a brief gold rush, and the availability of faster ships and subsidized passages attracted more British immigrants after 1860. The colony especially courted women immigrants to offset the preponderance of single men. By the early 1880s, fertile agricultural lands of this farthest frontier of the British Empire had a settler population of 500,000.

The model that in 1867 had formed the giant Dominion of Canada out of the very diverse and thinly settled colonies of British North America was applied to the newer colonies in Australia and New Zealand. In 1901 Australia emerged from the federation of six separate colonies. New Zealand became a separate colony in 1840 and a self-governing dominion in 1907.

Britain's policies toward its settler colonies in Canada and the South Pacific were shaped by a desire to avoid the conflicts that had led to the American Revolution in the eighteenth century. By gradually turning over governing power to the colonies' inhabitants, Britain accomplished three things. It satisfied the settlers' desire

---

ambergris (AM-ber-grees)

British Proclamation to the Australian Aborigines, ca. 1830
Affixed to trees in rural areas, this poster was intended to convey to the indigenous population the message that the European settlers wanted to be their friends and the settler government would punish murders of either race with equal severity. The poster failed to produce mutual trust.   (Tasmanian Museum & Art Gallery)

for greater control over their own territories, it muted demands for independence, and it made the colonial governments responsible for most of their own expenses. Indigenous peoples were outvoted by the settlers or even excluded from voting. An 1897 Australian law segregated the remaining Aborigines onto reservations, where they lacked the rights of Australian citizenship. The requirement that voters had to be able to read and write English kept Maori from voting in early New Zealand elections, but four seats in the lower house of the legislature were reserved for Maori from 1867.

Whaling

The rapid expansion of whaling aptly illustrates the growing power of technology over nature in this period. Many contemporaries, like many people today, were sickened by the killing of the planet's largest living mammals. American novelist Herman Melville captured the conflicting sentiments in his epic whaling story, *Moby Dick* (1851). One of his characters enthusiastically explains why the grisly and dangerous business existed:

> But, though the world scorns us as whale hunters, yet does it unwittingly pay us the profoundest homage; yea, an all abounding adoration! for almost all the tapers, lamps, and candles that burn around the globe, burn, as before so many shrines, to our glory!

Melville's character overstates the degree to which whale oil dominated illumination and does not mention its many other industrial uses. Neither does he describe the commercial importance of whalebone (baleen). For a time its use in corsets allowed fashionable women to achieve the hourglass shape that fashion dictated. Whalebone's use for umbrella stays, carriage springs, fishing rods, suitcase frames, combs, brushes, and many other items made it the plastic of its day.

New manufacturing technologies went hand in hand with new hunting technologies. The revolution in ship design enabled whalers from Europe and North America to extend the hunt into the southern oceans off New Zealand. By the nineteenth century whaling ships were armed with guns that shot a steel harpoon armed with vicious barbs deep into the whale. In the 1840s explosive charges on harpoon heads ensured the whale's immediate death. Yet, as this engraving of an expedition off New Zealand shows, flinging small harpoons from rowboats in the open sea continued to be part of the dangerous work.

Another century of extensive hunting devastated many whale species before international agreements finally limited the killing of these giant sea creatures.

South Pacific Whaling   One boat was swamped, but the hunters killed the huge whale.   (The Granger Collection, New York)

Asian Laborers in British Guiana The manager of the sugar estate reposes on the near end of the gallery of his house with the proprietor's attorney. At the other end of the gallery European overseers review the plantation's record books. In the yard, cups of lifeblood are being drained from bound Chinese and Indian laborers. This allegorical drawing by a Chinese laborer represents the exploitation of Asian laborers by Europeans. (Boston Athenaeum)

In other ways the new settler colonies were more progressive. Australia developed very powerful trade unions, which improved the welfare of skilled and semi-skilled urban white male workers, promoted democratic values, and exercised considerable political clout. In New Zealand, where sheep raising was the main occupation, populist and progressive sentiments promoted the availability of land for the common person. Australia and New Zealand were also among the first states in the world to grant women the right to vote, beginning in 1894.

New Labor Migrations

Europeans were not the only people to transplant themselves overseas in the mid-nineteenth century. Between 1834 and 1870 large numbers of Indians, Chinese, and Africans responded to labor recruiters, especially to work overseas on sugar plantations. In the half-century after 1870 tens of thousands of Asians and Pacific Islanders made similar voyages. The scale of such population movements and fact that many of these migrants traveled halfway around the world show the capacities of the new sailing ships. The power and interdependence of the British Empire are revealed in the fact that British India was the greatest source of such laborers and other British colonies were their principal destinations.

After Britain's emancipation of slaves in 1834, the freed Africans were no longer willing to work the long hours they had been forced to work as slaves. When given full freedom of movement in 1839, many men and women left the plantations. British colonies had to find other laborers if they were to compete successfully with sugar plantations in Cuba, Brazil, and the French Caribbean that were still using slave labor.

India's impoverished people seemed one obvious alternative. After planters on Mauritius successfully introduced Indian laborers, the Indian labor trade was extended to the British Caribbean in 1838. Free Africans were another possibility. In 1841, the British government allowed Caribbean planters to recruit Africans whom British patrols had rescued from slave ships and brought to liberation depots in Sierra Leone and elsewhere. By 1870, over a half-million Indians had left their homes for Mauritius or the British Caribbean along with nearly 40,000 Africans and over 18,000 Chinese for the British Caribbean colonies. After the French abolished slavery in 1848, their colonies also recruited 19,000 laborers from Africa and nearly 80,000 from India. Also ending slavery in 1848, Dutch Guiana recruited 57,000 new Asian workers for its plantations.

Although African slave labor was not abolished in Cuba until 1886, the rising cost of slaves led the burgeoning sugar plantations to recruit 138,000 new laborers from China between 1847 and 1873. Such labor recruitment also became the mainstay of new sugar plantations in places that had never known slave labor: after 1850 American planters in Hawaii recruited labor from China and Japan; British planters in Natal recruited from India; and those in Queensland (in northeastern Australia) relied on laborers from neighboring South Pacific islands.

Larger, faster ships made transporting laborers halfway around the world affordable, though voyages from Asia to the Caribbean still took an average of three months. Despite close regulation and supervision of shipboard conditions, the crowded accommodations on the long voyages encouraged the spread of cholera and other contagious diseases that took many migrants' lives.

All of these laborers served under **contracts of indenture,** which bound them to work for a specified period (usually from five to seven years) in return for free passage to their overseas destination. They were also paid a small salary and were provided with housing, clothing, and medical care. Indian indentured laborers also received the right to a free passage home if they worked a second five-year contract. British Caribbean colonies required that forty women be recruited for every hundred men as a way to promote family life. So many Indians chose to stay on in Mauritius, Trinidad, British Guiana, and Fiji that they constituted a third or more of the total population of these colonies by the early twentieth century.

Although many early recruits from China and the Pacific Islands were kidnapped or otherwise coerced into leaving their homes, in most cases the new indentured migrants had much in common with contemporary emigrants from Europe (described in Chapter 24). Both groups chose to leave their homelands in hopes of improving their economic and social conditions. Both earned modest salaries. Many saved to bring money back with them when they returned home, or they used their earnings to buy land or to start a business in their new countries, where large numbers chose to remain. One major difference was that people recruited as indentured laborers were generally so much poorer than emigrants from Europe that they had to accept lower-paying jobs in less desirable areas because they could not pay their own way. However, it is also true that many European immigrants into distant places like Australia and New Zealand had their passages subsidized but did not have to sign a contract of indenture. This shows that racial and cultural preferences, not just economics, shaped the flow of labor into European colonies.

A person's decision to accept an indentured labor contract could also be shaped by political circumstances. In India, disruption brought by British colonial policies and the suppression of the 1857 rebellion contributed significantly to people's desire to emigrate. Poverty, famine, and warfare had not been strangers in precolonial India. Nor were these causes of emigration absent in China and Japan (see Chapter 27).

Not simply the creation of Western imperialism, the indentured labor trade both allured and repelled the Asians and Africans. The commercial and industrial expansion of the West created an unequal relationship but not an entirely one-sided one. Most men and women who signed indentured contracts were trying to improve their lives by emigrating, and many succeeded in manipulating the system to their own advantage. Whether for good or ill, more and more of the world's peoples saw their lives being influenced by the existence of Western colonies, Western ships, and Western markets.

CONCLUSION

What is the global significance of these complex political and economic changes in southern Asia, Africa, and the South Pacific? One perspective stresses the continuing exploitation of the weak by the strong, of African, Asian, and Pacific peoples by aggressive Europeans. In this view, the emergence of Britain as a dominant power in the Indian Ocean basin and South Pacific continues the European expansion that the Portuguese and the Spanish pioneered and the Dutch continued. Likewise, Britain's control over the densely populated lands of South and Southeast Asia and over the less populated lands of Australia and New Zealand can be seen as a continuation of the conquest and colonization of the Americas.

From another perspective what was most important about this period was not the political and military strength of the Europeans but their growing dominance of the world's commerce, especially through long-distance ocean shipping. In this view, like other Europeans, the British were drawn to Africa and southern Asia by a desire to obtain new materials.

Britain's commercial expansion in the nineteenth century, however, was increasingly the product of

Easterners' demand for industrial manufactures. The growing exchanges could be mutually beneficial. African and Asian consumers found industrially produced goods far cheaper and sometimes better than the handicrafts they replaced or supplemented. Industrialization created new markets for African and Asian goods, as in the case of the vegetable-oil trade in West Africa or cotton in Egypt and India. There also was a negative impact, in the case of the weavers of India and the damage to species of seals and whales.

The emphasis on Europeans' military and commercial strength did not mean that African, Asian, and Pacific peoples were reduced to appendages of Europe. The balance of power was shifting in the Europeans' favor between 1750 and 1870, but local cultures were still vibrant and local initiatives often dominant. Islamic reform movements and the rise of the Zulu nation had greater significance for their respective regions of Africa than did Western forces. Despite some ominous concessions to European power, Southeast Asians were still largely in control of their own destinies. Even in India, most people's lives and beliefs showed more continuity with the past than the change due to British rule.

Finally, it must not be imagined that Asians and Africans were powerless in dealing with European expansion. The Indian princes who extracted concessions from the British in return for their cooperation and the Indians who rebelled against the raj both forced the system to accommodate their needs. Moreover, some Asians and Africans were beginning to use European education, technology, and methods to transform their own societies. Leaders in Egypt, India, and other lands, like those in Russia, the Ottoman Empire, China, and Japan—the subject of Chapter 27—were learning to challenge the power of the West on its own terms. In 1870 no one could say how long and how difficult that learning process would be, but Africans and Asians would continue to shape their own futures.

■ Key Terms

Zulu	British raj
Sokoto Caliphate	Sepoy Rebellion
modernization	durbar
Muhammad Ali	Indian Civil Service
"legitimate" trade	Indian National Congress
recaptives	clipper ship
nawab	contract of indenture
sepoy	

■ Suggested Reading

Volumes 2 and 3 of *The Oxford History of the British Empire*, ed. William Roger Louis, (1998, 1999), are the most up-to-date global surveys of this period. Less Anglocentric in their interpretations are Immanuel Wallerstein's *The Modern World-System III: The Second Era of Great Expansion of the Capitalist World-Economy, 1730–1840s* (1989) and William Wodruff's *Impact of Western Man: A Study of Europe's Role in the World Economy, 1750–1960* (1982). Atlantic relations are well handled by David Eltis, *Economic Growth and the Ending of the Transatlantic Slave Trade* (1987). For the Indian Ocean basin see Sugata Bose, ed., *South Asia and World Capitalism* (1990).

Roland Oliver and Anthony Atmore provide a brief introduction to Africa in *Africa Since 1800*, 4th ed. (1994). More advanced works are J. F. Ade Ajayi, ed., *UNESCO General History of Africa*, vol. 6, *Africa in the Nineteenth Century until the 1880s* (1989), and John E. Flint, ed., *The Cambridge History of Africa*, vol. 5, *From c. 1790 to c. 1870* (1976). Although specialized literature has refined some of their interpretations, the following are excellent introductions to their subjects: J. D. Omer-Cooper, *The Zulu Aftermath* (1966); Murray Last, *The Sokoto Caliphate* (1967); A. G. Hopkins, *An Economic History of West Africa* (1973); Robert W. July, *The Origins of Modern African Thought* (1967); and Robert I. Rotberg, ed., *Africa and Its Explorers: Motives, Methods, and Impact* (1970). For eastern and northeastern Africa see Norman R. Bennett, *Arab Versus European: War and Diplomacy in Nineteenth Century East Central Africa* (1985); P. J. Vatikiotis, *The History of Modern Egypt: From Muhammad Ali to Mubarak,* 4th ed. (1991); and, for the negative social impact of Egyptian modernization, Judith Tucker, "Decline of the Family Economy in Mid-Nineteenth-Century Egypt," *Arab Studies Quarterly 1* (1979): 245–271.

Very readable introductions to India in this period are Sugata Bose and Ayeshia Jalal, *Modern South India* (1998); Burton Stein, *A History of India* (1998); and Stanley Wolpert, *A New History of India,* 6th ed. (1999). More advanced treatments in the "New Cambridge History of India" series are P. J. Marshall, *Bengal: The British Bridgehead: Eastern India, 1740–1828* (1988); C. A. Bayly, *Indian Society and the Making of the British Empire* (1988); Sugata Bose, *Peasant Labour and Colonial Capital: Rural Bengal Since 1700* (1993); and Kenneth W. Jones, *Socio-Religious Reform Movements in British India* (1989). Environmental and technological perspectives on India are offered in the appropriate parts of Daniel Headrick, *The Tentacles of Progress: Technology Transfer in the Age of Imperialism, 1850–1940* (1988); Mashav Gadgil and Ramachandra Guha, *This Fissured Land: An Ecological History of India* (1992); and David Arnold, *Colonizing the Body: State Medicine and Epidemic Disease in Nineteenth-Century India* (1993).

A good introduction to the complexities of Southeast Asian history is D. R. SarDesai, *Southeast Asia: Past and Present,* 2d ed. (1989). More detail can be found in the appropriate chapters of Nicholas Tarling, ed., *The Cambridge History of South East Asia,* 2 vols. (1992). The second and third volumes of *The Oxford History of Australia,* ed. Geoffrey Bolton (1992, 1988), deal with the period covered by this chapter. A very readable multicultural and gendered perspective is provided by *Images of Australia*, ed. Gillian Whitlock and David Carter (1992). *The Oxford Illustrated History of New Zealand*, ed. Keith Sinclair (1990), provides a wide-ranging introduction to that nation.

For summaries of recent scholarship on the indentured labor trade see David Northrup, *Indentured Labor in the Age of Imperialism, 1834–1922* (1995), and Robin Cohen, ed., *The Cambridge Survey of World Migration*, part 3, "Asian Indentured and Colonial Migration" (1995).

An outstanding analysis of British whaling is Gordon Jackson's *The British Whaling Trade* (1978). Edouard A. Stackpole's *Whales & Destiny: The Rivalry Between America, France, and Britain for Control of the Southern Whale Fishery, 1785–1825* (1972) is more anecdotal.

■ Notes

1. Paul E. Lovejoy and Jan S. Hogendorn, *Slow Death for Slavery: The Course of Abolition in Northern Nigeria, 1897–1936* (New York: Cambridge University Press, 1993).
2. Quoted in P. J. Vatikiotis, *The History of Modern Egypt: From Muhammad Ali to Mubarak*, 4th ed. (Baltimore: Johns Hopkins University Press, 1991), 74.
3. David Eltis, "Precolonial Western Africa and the Atlantic Economy," in *Slavery and the Rise of the Atlantic Economy*, ed. Barbara Solow (New York: Cambridge University Press, 1991), table 1.
4. Quoted by Bernard S. Cohn, "Representing Authority in Victorian India," in *The Invention of Tradition*, ed. Eric Hobsbawm and Terence Ranger (Cambridge, England: Cambridge University Press, 1983), 165.

27

THE OTTOMAN EMPIRE AND EAST ASIA,

1800–1870

The Ottoman Empire and the European Model • The Qing Empire and Foreign Coercion • Japan from Shogunate to Empire

ENVIRONMENT AND TECHNOLOGY: The Web of War

SOCIETY AND CULTURE: Fighting the Opium Trade

Netting Whales   During the Tokugawa, the Japanese began using nets to catch large numbers of whales, and many provinces became dependent on the new industry.

When the emperor of the Qing° (the last empire to rule China) died in 1799, the imperial court received a shock. For decades officials had known that the emperor was indulging his handsome young favorite, Heshen°, allowing him extraordinary privileges and power. Senior bureaucrats hated Heshen, suspecting him of overseeing a widespread network of corruption. They believed he had been scheming to prolong the inconclusive wars against the native Miao° peoples of southwest China in the late 1700s. Glowing reports of successes against the rebels had poured into the capital, and enormous sums of government money had flowed to the battlefields. But there was no adequate accounting for the funds, and the war persisted.

After the emperor's death, Heshen's enemies ordered his arrest. When they searched his mansion, they discovered a magnificent hoard of silk, furs, porcelain, furniture, and gold and silver. His personal cash alone exceeded what remained in the imperial treasury. The new emperor ordered Heshen to commit suicide with a rope of gold silk. The government seized Heshen's fortune, but the financial damage could not be undone. The expenses of the government were so great that it was permanently bankrupt. The declining agricultural base could not replenish the state coffers, and pressures for internal police and military action rose after 1800. Repeated investigations of the bureaucracy revealed growing corruption. Thus, in the 1800s, the Qing Empire faced increasing challenges from Europe and the United States with an empty treasury, a stagnant economy, and a troubled society.

The Qing Empire's problems were not unique. They were common to all of the land-based empires of Eurasia. During the early 1800s, rapid population growth and slow agricultural growth affected much of Eurasia. Earlier military expansion had overstretched the resources of the imperial treasuries. As these traditional regimes were experiencing economic and social crises in the 1800s, the militarily advanced sea-based powers of western Europe were pressing them for economic concessions. The result was general indebtedness—either through direct loans or failure to pay indemnities after losing military conflicts—to France, Britain, and other Western powers.

This chapter concentrates on the experiences of the Ottoman and Qing Empires. To understand the significance of the similarities between them, it is necessary to examine a dramatic contrasting case: Japan. Like the Ottoman and Qing Empires, Japan in the 1800s was in the late decades of a long-lived political system—the Tokugawa Shogunate. Also like the imperial Ottomans and Qing, the Tokugawa government saw revenues steeply declining, the agricultural base stagnating, and the central government engulfed in corruption. And finally, Japan like other East Asian countries experienced the shock of military and economic confrontation with a foreign power in the mid-1800s. But the decentralized system of rule under the Tokugawa made it impossible for Japan to attempt the top-down reforms tried by the Ottomans and Qing. Instead, Japan's first direct contact with a foreign sea power led to the destruction, not reform, of the traditional state. It was replaced by a centralized and relatively efficient order whose leaders were determined to avoid becoming victims of European expansion and to participate in the evolving colonial order in Asia.

As you read this chapter, ask yourself the following questions:

- Why did the Ottoman and Qing Empires find themselves at a disadvantage during their encounters with Europeans in the 1800s?

- What were the best options for the land-based empires facing military challenges from Europe?

- Why was Japan's experience so different from that of China?

Qing (ching)   Heshen (huh-shun)   Miao (mee-ow)

CHRONOLOGY

	Ottoman Empire	Qing Empire	Japan
			Since 1600 Decentralized rule of Tokugawa Shogunate
1800	**1789–1807** Rule of Selim III	**1794–1804** White Lotus Rebellion	
	1826 Janissary corps dissolved **1829** Greek independence **1839** Abdul Mejid begins Tanzimat reforms	**1839–1842** Opium War	
1850	**1853–1856** Crimean War	**1850–1864** Taiping Rebellion	**1853** First visit by Commodore Matthew Perry **1854** Perry returns **1858** Treaty of Kanagawa
		1856–1860 Arrow War **1860** Sack of Beijing **1862–1875** Reign of Tongzhi	**1867** Civil war **1868** Meiji Restoration
	1876 First constitution by an Islamic government		

THE OTTOMAN EMPIRE AND THE EUROPEAN MODEL

Though the Ottoman Empire experienced the problems and challenges sketched above, its position close to Europe gave it relatively early exposure to European ambitions and capabilities. The Ottoman rulers were earlier than the rulers of other Eurasian empires to experiment with financial and military modernization. Not until the mid-1800s, however, did the Ottoman government overcome entrenched opposition to change and put into place a series of reforms designed to remove the influence of religious elites from many areas of the state and economy. The reforms could not move rapidly enough to preserve the empire's independence from western Europe, but they created momentum for centralization, helped promote nationalism in the late nineteenth century, and created a practical base for the creation of a Turkish republic in the twentieth century.

Early Struggles for Reform, 1793–1807

At the end of the eighteenth century Sultan Selim° III (r. 1789–1807) introduced reforms to strengthen the military, bring provincial governors under the control of the central government, and standardize taxation and land tenure. The rise in government expenditures to implement the reforms was supposed to be offset by taxes on selected items, primarily tobacco and coffee.

These reforms failed for political reasons, more than economic. The most violent and persistent opposition came from the **Janissaries°,** the traditional corps of Ottoman military slaves. The Janissaries were originally Christian boys required to convert to Islam and serve for life in the Ottoman army. Over the years, the Janissaries became a significant political force, and their conservative attitudes dissuaded many Ottoman rulers and officials from pursuing reform.

At times the disapproval of the Janissaries produced military uprisings. An early example occurred in the

Selim (seh-LEEM)   **Janissaries** (JAN-nih-say-rees)

Change with Tradition   Change in the Ottoman armies was gradual, beginning with the introduction of European guns and artillery. To use the new weapons efficiently and safely, the Janissaries were required to modify their dress and their beards. Beards were trimmed, and elaborate headgear was reserved for ritual occasions. Traditional military units attempted to retain distinctive dress whenever possible, and one compromise was the brimless cap, the fez (shown here), adapted from the high hats that some Janissaries had traditionally worn.   (Courtesy, Turkish Ministry of Culture and Tourism. Photo: Necmettin Kulahci)

The Janissaries were not the only opponents of reform. In some parts of the empire, including Anatolia, revolts by the Janissaries were encouraged by noblemen who had been supporters of earlier imperial reforms but now feared that further reform would result in new taxes. Also opposed to reform were the congregations of Muslim councilors, the *ulama*, who distrusted the secularization of law and taxation that Selim proposed. In the face of widespread rejection of his reforms, Selim suspended his program in 1806. Nevertheless, a massive military uprising occurred at Istanbul, and the sultan was deposed and imprisoned. Reform forces rallied and recaptured the capital, but not before Selim had been executed.

Army and Society in the Early Tanzimat, 1826–1853

In 1826 Selim's cousin Sultan Mahmud° II (r.1808–1839) revived the reform movement. The fate of Selim III had taught the Ottoman court that reform needed to be more systematic and imposed more forcefully. Mahmud II was able to use the loss of Greece, formerly an Ottoman colony, as a sign of the weakness of the empire and the pressing need for reform.

Greek independence in 1829 was a complex event that had dramatic international significance. Earlier Ottoman rulers had pointed to the shattering of Byzantine rule over Greece and Anatolia as a triumph of Islamic civilization and proof of God's favor. Europeans and Russians, however, saw the capture of the former Byzantine capital, Constantinople—now the Ottoman capital, Istanbul—as justification for a new holy war to be waged

Balkans, in the Ottoman territory of **Serbia,** where Janissaries acted as provincial governors. Their control in Serbia was intensely resented by the local residents, particularly Orthodox Christians who claimed that the Janissaries abused them. In response to the charges, Selim threatened to reassign the Janissaries to the Ottoman capital at Istanbul. Suspecting that the sultan's threat signaled the beginning of the end of their political power, the Janissaries in 1805 revolted against Selim, and massacred Christians in Serbia. Selim was unable to reestablish central Ottoman rule over Serbia. Instead, the Ottoman court had to rely on the ruler of Bosnia, another Balkan province, who joined his troops with the peasants of Serbia to suppress the Janissary uprising. The threat of Russian intervention prevented the Ottomans from disarming the victorious Serbians, so Serbia became effectively independent.

Mahmud (MACH-mood)

Map 27.1   Disintegration of the Ottoman Empire, 1829–1914   At its height the Ottoman Empire controlled most of the perimeter of the Mediterranean Sea. But in the 1800s Ottoman territory shrank as many countries gained their independence—frequently with the aid of France or Russia. The Black Sea, which left the Turkish coast vulnerable to assault by the Russian navy, was a weak spot that intensely contested in the Crimean dispute.

by Christian countries against the Ottoman Empire. By the early nineteenth century, interest in the classical age of Greece and Rome had intensified Europeans' desire to encourage and if possible aid the Greeks' struggle for independence from Ottoman rule. Europeans considered the war for Greek independence a campaign to recapture the classical roots of their civilization from Muslim despots, and many—including the "mad, bad and dangerous to know" English poet Lord Byron, who lost his life in the war—went to Greece to fight as volunteers. The Ottomans depended on Ibrahim Pasha° of Egypt (son of Muhammad Ali°) to preserve their rule in Greece, but the combined squadrons of the British, French, and Russian

Ibrahim Pasha (EEB-RAH-heem PAH-shah)
Muhammad Ali (moo-HAM-mad AH-lee)

fleets handily defeated him. Not only did Ottoman control of Greece end, but the Ottoman's tenuous rule in Egypt was further damaged (see Map 27.1).

Europeans trumpeted the victory of the Greeks as a triumph of European civilization over the Ottoman Empire, and Mahmud II agreed that the loss of Greece indicated a profound weakness—he considered it backwardness—in Ottoman military and financial organization. Like his predecessors, Mahmud believed that the Janissaries should be destroyed, and with popular outrage over the loss of Greece strong, he made his move in 1826. First he announced the creation of a new army corps, which would be open to the Janissaries. Then, when the Janissaries rose in revolt, he ordered loyal troops to attack the Janissary barracks and obliterate the force.

Mahmud also reduced the political power of the religious elite. To accomplish this reform, he had to restructure the bureaucracy, because education and law were to be under the authority of the civil government. Property laws too were amended, to make the charitable trusts by which religious communities and families managed their wealth subject to civil review and regulation. Even the public judgments of the ulama were to be bureaucratically regulated.

In attempting to secularize the state, Mahmud relied heavily on establishing a uniform code of civil law. Many of his ideas received their widest expression in the **Tanzimat°** ("restructuring"), a series of reforms announced by his sixteen-year-old son and successor, Abdul Mejid°, in 1839. One proclamation guaranteeing basic political rights has been compared to England's Magna Carta (1215). It called for public trials and equal protection under the law for all, whether Muslim, Christian, or Jew. It also guaranteed some rights of privacy, equalized the eligibility of men for conscription into the army, and provided for a new, formalized method of tax collecting that legally ended tax farming in the Ottoman Empire. No Islamic country had ever produced anything so nearly approaching a constitution, and the Ottoman Empire enjoyed a renewed reputation as a progressive influence in the Middle East.

The successors to Mahmud II and Abdul Mejid were less zealous in their legal ideologies and later created a mixed court system that permitted *qadi°* (religious judges) to decide certain matters. Nevertheless, the distinction between religious and secular law continued to be observed. In the mid-1800s, the commercial code was remodeled along the lines of the French system, and the rulers affirmed that trade and finance were outside the jurisdiction of religious law.

Military cadets were sent to France and the German states for training, and military uniforms were modeled on those of France. In the 1830s an Ottoman imperial school of military sciences was established at Istanbul. Instructors imported from western Europe taught chemistry, engineering, mathematics, and physics in addition to military history. Reforms in military education became the model for more general educational reforms. In 1838 the first medical school was established, for army doctors and surgeons. Later, a national system of preparatory schools was created. The subjects that were taught and many of the teachers were foreign, so the issue of whether Turkish would be a language of instruction in the new schools was a serious one. Because it was easier to import and use foreign textbooks than to write

European Exposure Increasing exposure to French and British influence stimulated the programs of the Ottoman rulers to modernize their armies. By the time of the Crimean War, the Janissaries had been replaced by a professional military, trained in special schools, adept in the use of modern artillery, and dressed in the fashion of the European infantry and cavalry. (Hulton Getty Liaison)

new ones in Turkish, French became the preferred language in all advanced professional and scientific training. The translation of fundamental works into Turkish was still not completed by the end of the 1800s.

The importance of educational institutions in the early reforms accelerated the growth in wealth and influence of the urban elites. At Istanbul, the capital, a cosmopolitan milieu embracing European language and culture, as well as military professionalism and an interest in progressive political reform, thrived. Newspapers—most of them in French—were founded at Istanbul, and travel to Europe—particularly to England and France—by wealthy Turks became more common. Interest in importing European military, industrial, and communications technology remained strong through the 1800s.

The Ottoman rulers quickly learned that limited improvements in military technology had unforeseen cultural and social effects. The introduction of modern weapons and drill required a change in traditional mili-

---

Tanzimat (TAHNZ-ee-MAT)   **Abdul Mejid** (ab-dul MAY-jeed)
qadi (KAW-dee)

tary dress. Beards were deemed unhygienic and, in artillery units, a fire hazard. They were restricted, along with the wearing of loose trousers and turbans. Military headgear also became controversial. European military caps, which had leather bills on the front to protect against the glare of the sun, were not acceptable because they interfered with Muslim soldiers' touching their foreheads to the ground during daily prayers. The compromise was the brimless cap now called the *fez*, which was adopted by the military and then by Ottoman civil officials in the early years of Mahmud II's reign.

Military castes had been important in traditional Ottoman society, and the changes in military dress—so soon after the suppression of the Janissaries—were recognized as an indication of the change in the social meaning of military service. A conscript army was created, and with it came educational reforms that attempted to promote secular, international, urban cultural attitudes. Among self-consciously progressive men, European dress became the fashion in the Ottoman cities of the later 1800s. Traditional dress became a symbol of the religious, the rural, and the parochial.

Secularization of the legal code had profound implications for the non-Muslim subjects of the Ottomans. Non-Muslims frequently had been required to pay extra taxes and had been excluded from certain professions, including the military, unless they converted to Islam. In addition, the role of Islamic judges in the legal process had limited non-Muslim's access to the law courts. Secularization of the law, however, gave all male subjects access to the courts. It also resulted in equalization of taxation.

The public rights and political participation granted during the Tanzimat were explicitly restricted to men. Private life, including everything connected to marriage and divorce, was left within the sphere of religious law, and at no time was there a question of political participation or reformed education for women. Indeed, the reforms actually decreased the influence of women. The political changes ran parallel to economic changes that also narrowed women's opportunities.

The influx of silver from the Americas that began in the 1600s increased the monetarization of some sectors of the Ottoman economy, particularly in the cities. Workers were increasingly paid in cash rather than goods, and businesses associated with banking, finance, and law developed. Competition drove women from the work force. Early industrial labor and the professions were not open to women, and traditional "woman's work" such as weaving was increasingly mechanized and done by men.

Nevertheless, well into the 1800s some women retained considerable power in the management and disposal of their own property. After marriage a woman was often pressured to convert her landholdings to cash in order to transfer her personal wealth to her husband's family, with whom she and her husband would reside. Until the 1820s, many women retained their say in the distribution of property through the creation of charitable trusts for their sons. Because these trusts were set up in the religious courts, they could be designed to conform to the wishes of family members, and they gave women of wealthy families an opportunity to exercise significant indirect control over property. Then, in the 1820s and 1830s, the secularizing reforms of Mahmud II transferred jurisdiction over the charitable trusts from religious courts to the state and ended women's control over their own and their families' property. In addition, reforms in the military, higher education, the professions, and commerce all bypassed women. By the late 1800s, the seclusion of women had become a highly valued symbol of Turkish nativism and Muslim traditionalism.

The Crimean War, 1853–1856

Since the reign of Peter the Great (r. 1689–1725) the Russian Empire had been attempting to expand southward at the Otttomans' expense. By 1815 Russia had pried the Georgian region of the Caucasus away from the Ottomans, and the threat of Russian intervention in Serbia had prevented the Ottomans from crushing Serbian independence. Russia seemed poised to exploit Ottoman weakness and seize key territories in the Balkans, Central Asia, and possibly the Middle East.

Between 1853 and 1856 the **Crimean° War** raged on the Black Sea and its northern shore. This extremely destructive conflict was nominally a war between the Russian and Ottoman Empires about whether Russia could claim to protect Christians in the Ottoman domains. But also involved in the dispute were Austria, Britain, France, and the Italian kingdom of Sardinia-Piedmont, all of whom sided—actively or passively—with the Ottoman Empire. These European nations feared Russia's power and influence, which they suspected would increase because of the Ottomans' weakness. The war was fought at sea as well as on land. During the prolonged sea conflict, Britain and France trapped the Russian fleet in the Black Sea. The lack of railways hampered Russian attempts to supply both its land and its sea forces. Tsar Alexander II (r. 1855–1881) abandoned the key fortress of Sevastopol in 1855 and sued for peace.

A formal alliance among Britain, France, and the Ottoman Empire blocked Russian expansion into eastern Europe and the Middle East. The terms of peace also

Crimean (cry-ME-uhn)

The Web of War

The lethal military technologies of the mid-nineteenth century used on battlefields in the United States, Russia, India, and China were rapidly transmitted from one conflict to the next. This dissemination was due not only to the rapid development of communications but also to the existence of a new international network of soldiers who moved from one trouble spot to another, bringing with them expertise in the use of new techniques.

General Charles Gordon (1833–1885), for instance, was commissioned in the British army in 1852, then served in the Crimean War after Britain entered on the side of the Ottomans. In 1860 he was dispatched to China. He served British forces during the Arrow War and took part in the sack of Beijing. Afterward, he stayed in China and was seconded to the Qing imperial government until the suppression of the Taipings in 1864, earning himself the nickname "Chinese" Gordon. Gordon later served the Ottoman rulers of Egypt as governor of territory along the Nile. He was killed in Egypt in 1885 while attempting to lead his Egyptian troops in defense of the city of Khartoum against an uprising by the local religious leader, the Mahdi.

Journalism played an important part in the developing web of telegraph communications that speeded orders to and from the battlefields. Readers in London could learn details of the drama occurring in the Crimea or in China within a week—or in some cases days—after they occurred. Print and, later, photographic journalism created new "stars" from these war experiences. Charles Gordon was one. Florence Nightingale was another.

In the great wars of the 1800s, the vast majority of deaths resulted from infection or excessive bleeding, not from the wounds themselves. Florence Nightingale (1820–1910), while still a young woman, became interested in hospital management and nursing. She went to Prussia and France to study advanced techniques and before the outbreak of the Crimean War was credited with bringing about marked improvement in British health care. When the public reacted to news reports of the suffering in the Crimea, the British government sent Nightingale to the region. Within a year of her arrival the death rate in the military hospitals there dropped from 45 percent to under 5 percent. Her techniques for preventing septicemia and dysentery and for promoting healing therapies were quickly adopted by those working for and with her. On her return to London, Nightingale established institutes for nursing that soon were recognized around the world as leaders. She herself was lionized by the British public and received the Order of Merit in 1907, three years before her death.

The importance of Nightingale's innovations in public hygiene is underscored by the life of her contemporary, Mary Seacole (1805–1881). A Jamaican woman who volunteered to nurse British troops in the Crimean War, Seacole was excluded repeatedly from nursing service by British authorities. She eventually went to Crimea and used her own funds to run a hospital there, bankrupting herself in the process. The drama of the Crimean War moved the British public to support Seacole after her sacrifices were publicized. She was awarded medals by the British, French, and Turkish governments and today is recognized with her contemporary Florence Nightingale as an innovative field nurse and a champion of public hygiene in peacetime.

With Florence Nightingale in Crimea Readers could see as well as read about war dramas with vivid illustrations and telegraphed copy.
(The Granger Collection, New York)

We Have Got the Maxim Gun   These two representatives of the Qing Empire visited northern England after the Taiping Rebellion to examine and, if possible, purchase new weapons. They posed for a photograph after watching the famous Maxim gun shoot a tree in half.   (Peter Newark's Military Pictures)

gave Britain and France a means of checking each other's colonial ambitions in the Middle East: neither, according to the agreement that ended the war, was entitled to take Ottoman territory for its exclusive use.

The Crimean War brought significant changes to all the combatants. The tsar and his government, already beset by demands for the reform of serfdom, education, and the military, were further discredited. They plunged into reforms that slightly improved Russia's economy but profoundly destabilized its political system. In Britain and France the conflict was accompanied by massive propaganda campaigns. For the first time newspapers were an important force mobilizing public support for a war. Press accounts of British participation in the war were often so glamorized that ever since the false impression has lingered that Ottoman and Egyptian troops played a negligible role in the conflict. At the time, however, British and French military commanders noted the massive losses among Turkish troops in particular. The French press, dominant in Istanbul, promoted a sense of unity between Turkish and French society that continued to influence many aspects of Turkish urban culture.

The larger significance of the Crimean War was that it marked the transition from traditional to modern warfare (see Environment and Technology: The Web of War). The high casualty count of the war resulted in part from the clash of mechanized and unmechanized means of killing. All the combatant nations in the Crimean War once prided themselves on their effective use of highly trained cavalry to smash through the front lines of infantry. Cavalry coexisted with firearms until the early 1800s, primarily because early rifles were awkward to load, vulnerable to explosion, and not very accurate. Swift and expert cavalry could storm infantry lines during the intervals between volleys and even penetrate artillery barrages. Then in the 1830s and 1840s, **percussion caps** were widely adopted in Europe. In Crimean War battles, many cavalry units were destroyed by the rapid and relatively accurate fire of **breech-loading rifles.** That was the fate of the British "Light Brigade," which was sent to relieve an Ottoman unit surrounded by Russian troops. Cavalry were not the only victims of the new speed of the guns. Many traditional infantry units came to grief attempting to use ranks of marching, brightly coated soldiers to overwhelm lines of rapidly firing riflemen.

In the great conflicts that followed the Crimean War—the Indian Uprising, the Taiping° Rebellion in China, and the American Civil War—percussion-cap technology in combination with new designs of repeating guns led to

---

Taiping (tie-PING)

the creation of machine guns. Originally called Agar guns, then Gatling guns, machine guns resulted in a new scale of battlefield fatalities, mounting into many hundreds of thousands over only a few years. New manufacturing techniques allowed unprecedented precision in the fitting of caps and bullets within the firing chambers, creating propulsive force never before encountered so widely. Railways permitted the rapid transfer of heavy weaponry toward the front, as well as the transport of the wounded to hospitals, and also aided in the conveyance of iron and coal to manufacturing centers.

The transformation of decisive weaponry meant a change in the general ways of war. Cavalry did not immediately disappear, but the emphasis on speed and the use of light, accurate firearms by riders created more and more deadly conditions for mounted soldiers. Heavily armed infantry units pinned each other down in trenches for weeks, waiting for the enemy to be wiped out by disease or despair. Long-range artillery took on greater strategic significance and was combined with mines, early hand grenades, and mustard gas. Soldiers were reorganized, taught to scatter and shoot from trenches or from behind natural barriers, and dressed in inconspicuous colors. In such circumstances, the military began to lose its traditional connection with the aristocracy, with horses, and with ceremonial uniforms. Conscript armies took on new importance, and warfare became a political issue. Though the transformation of traditional warfare was not completed in the cycle of regional conflicts that began with the Crimean War, the process began that led toward the patterns of warfare that were to become familiar in the twentieth century.

European Patronage and Economic Decline, to 1878

After the Crimean War, declining state revenues and increasing integration with European commercial networks created hazardous economic conditions in the Ottoman Empire. Mahmud II's successors continued to secularize Ottoman financial and commercial institutions, modeling them closely on European counterparts. The Ottoman imperial bank was founded in 1840, and a few years later currency reform pegged the value of Ottoman gold coins to the British pound. Sweeping changes in the 1850s expedited the creation of banks, insurance companies, and legal firms throughout the empire. These and other reforms facilitating trade contributed to a strong demographic shift in the Ottoman Empire between about 1850 and 1880, as many people from the countryside headed for the cities Within this period many of the major cities of the empire—Istanbul, Ankara, Damascus, Cairo—doubled in size. A strong urban professional class emerged, as well as a considerable class of wage laborers. This shift was magnified by an influx into the northern Ottoman territories of refugees from Poland and Hungary, where rivalry between the European powers and the Russian Empire caused political tension and sporadic warfare.

The Ottoman reforms stimulated commerce and urbanization, but no reform could repair the chronic insolvency of the imperial government. Ottoman finances were damaged by declining revenues from agricultural yields and by widespread corruption. Some of the corruption received spectacular exposure in the early 1840s. From the conclusion of the Crimean War in 1856 on, the Ottoman government became heavily dependent on foreign loans. In return for loans, Ottoman tariffs were lowered to favor European imports, and European banks opened for business in Ottoman cities. The Ottoman currency was changed to allow more systematic conversion to European currencies. Europeans were allowed to live in Istanbul and other commercial centers in their own enclaves, subject to their own laws and exempt from Ottoman jurisdiction. This status was known as **extraterritoriality.**

As the cities prospered, they became attractive to laborers, and still more people moved from the countryside. But opportunities for wage workers reached a plateau in the bloated cities. Foreign trade brought in large numbers of imports, but—apart from the Turkish opium that American traders took to China to compete against the Indian opium of the British—few exports were sent abroad. Together with the growing national debt, these factors in the mid-1800s aggravated inflationary trends that left urban populations in a precarious position.

In the 1860s and 1870s, reform groups demanded a constitution, the possibility of a law permitting all men to vote was discussed, the prospect of the Muslims' loss of all political privilege arose. The Muslim majority was disturbed by the apparent signal that the Ottoman Empire was no longer a Muslim society. Muslims also were suspicious of the motives of Christians, many of whom were not of Turkish descent. Many Ottoman Muslims remembered attempts by Russia and France to interfere in Ottoman affairs in order to benefit Christians. Hostilities against Christians in Ottoman territories in Europe, Armenia, and the Middle East could be rationalized on the grounds of Turkish patriotism.

The decline of Ottoman power and prosperity had a strong impact on a group of urban and well-educated young men who aspired to wealth and influence. They believed that the Ottoman rulers would be forced to—or would be willing to—allow the continued domination of the empire's political, economic, and cultural life by Europeans. Inspired by the European nationalist movements of 1848 (see Chapter 23), they began to band together in the 1860s as the "Young Turks." The granting of a constitution in 1876 was regarded abroad as a great achievement because it was the first constitution to be adopted by an Islamic government. The apparent triumph of liberal reform was short lived. A *coup d'état* resulted in the enthroning of a new ruler who was hostile to democratization. A threat of war over the Balkans arose, and the imperial government used the crisis to disable the new Parliament and suspend the Constitution in 1877. But it did not quash the movement by Turks for greater independence from foreign interference. To the Young Turks, freedom from European domination required the destruction of the Ottoman Empire from within. They proposed to replace it with a Turkish national state, their "Fatherland." Though nationalism continued to be fostered by the leaders of the Young Turks—who exploited the new institutions of newspapers and private schools to spread their message—the Ottoman Empire continued its weakened existence under the sponsorship of Western powers until 1922.

THE QING EMPIRE AND FOREIGN COERCION

In 1800 the Qing Empire faced many of the crises the Ottomans had encountered, but no early reform movement of the kind initiated by Selim III emerged in China. The reasons are not difficult to understand. The Qing Empire, created by the Manchus, had distinguished itself in the 1600s for its adept maneuverings against Russia, both strategic and diplomatic. The Qing rulers had earned the admiration of the Jesuits, who transmitted to Europe a very appealing image of the emperors in China as enlightened philosopher-kings. But the failure in 1793 of the British attempt to establish diplomatic and trade relations with the Qing—the Macartney mission—turned European opinion against China, and in the very early 1800s few Europeans apart from traders based in Canton had much contact with or interest in China. For their part, the Qing rulers and bureaucrats were embroiled in some serious crises and had neither the time nor the inclination to explore new contacts with far-off Europeans. Complaints from European merchants at Canton, who

chafed against the restrictions of the "Canton system" by which the Qing limited and controlled foreign trade, were brushed off.

The empire's troubles were primarily domestic and seemed depressingly familiar to Chinese historians and officials: rebellions by displaced indigenous peoples and the poor, and protests against the injustice of the local magistrates. These troubles, it was thought, could be dealt with in the usual way, by suppressing rebels and dismissing incompetent or untrustworthy officials. Unlike the Ottoman rulers of the same period, the Qing rulers of 1800 had no compelling reason to think that cataclysmic challenges were headed their way.

Economic and Social Disorder

Early Qing successes gave rise to much of the domestic and political chaos of the later period. The Qing conquest in the 1600s brought stability to central China, previously subjected to decades of rebellion and agricultural shortages. The Qing emperors encouraged the recovery of farmland, the opening of previously uncultivated areas, and the restoration and expansion of the road and canal systems. The result was a great expansion of the agricultural base together with a doubling of the population between about 1650 and about 1800. Enormous numbers of farmers, merchants, and day laborers migrated across the Qing Empire in search of less crowded conditions, and a permanent floating population of the unemployed and homeless emerged. By 1800, population strain on the land had caused serious environmental damage in some parts of central and western China. Deforestation, erosion, and soil exhaustion left swollen populations stranded on rapidly deteriorating land.

Many groups had serious grievances against the government. Minority peoples in central and southwestern China resented having been driven off their lands during the boom of the 1700s. Mongols resisted the appropriation of their grazing lands and the displacement of their traditional elites. Village vigilante organizations had grown used to policing and practically governing regions that the Qing government had become too weak to manage. And growing numbers of people mistrusted the government, suspecting that all officials were corrupt. Discontent was aggravated by the growing presence of foreign merchants and missionaries in Canton and in the Portuguese colony of Macao.

In some parts of China the Qing were hated because they themselves were a foreign conquest regime and were suspected of having sympathies with the Europeans. Indeed as the nineteenth century opened, the

White Lotus Rebellion (1794–1804)—partly inspired by a mystical ideology that predicted the restoration of the Chinese Ming dynasty and the coming of the Buddha—was raging across central China and could not be suppressed until 1804.

The White Lotus was the first large rebellion in a series of internal conflicts that continued through the 1800s. Ignited by deepening social instabilities, these movements were sometimes intensified by local ethnic conflicts and by unapproved religions. The magnitude of the conflicts was increased by the improving ability of some village militias to defend themselves (and attack others). Some of these techniques were effectively utilized by southern coastal populations attempting to fend off British invasion.

The Opium War, 1839–1842

Unlike the Ottomans, the Qing believed that the Europeans were remote and only casually interested in trade. They knew little of the enormous fortunes being made in the early 1800s by European and American merchants smuggling opium into China. They did not know that silver gained in this illegal trade was helping to finance the industrial transformation of England and the United States. But Qing officials slowly learned that Britain was not really so far away. It had colonies in India, where opium was grown. And it had a major naval base at Singapore, through which it could transport opium to East Asia.

For more than a century, British officials had been frustrated by the enormous trade deficit caused by the British demand for tea and the Qing refusal to facilitate the importation to China of any British product. In the early 1700s, a few European merchants and their Chinese partners were importing small quantities of opium, and in 1729 the first Qing law making it illegal to import opium was promulgated. By 1800, however, smuggling had increased the quantity of annual imports of opium to as many as four thousand chests. British merchants had discovered an extremely profitable trade, and a large Chinese commerce had arisen around the distribution of the drugs that foreigners brought to shore. British importers were competing with Americans, and in the early 1820s a price war raised demand so sharply that by the 1830s as many as thirty thousand chests were being imported. Addiction spread to people at all levels of Qing society, including a large number of very high-ranking officials. For a time the Qing emperor and his officials debated whether to legalize and tax opium or to more strictly enforce the existing ban on the drug. They decided to root out the use and the importation of opium,

and in 1839 they sent Lin Zexu° to Canton to deal with the matter (see Society and Culture: Fighting the Opium Trade).

Britain considered the Qing ban on the importation of opium an intolerable restraint of trade, a direct threat to Britain's economic health, and indirectly a cause for war. British naval and marine forces arrived at the south China coast in late 1839. The significance of naval power, which the Ottomans had understood but not learned to master in the Mediterranean and Black Seas, dawned on the Qing slowly. Indeed, the difference between a naval invasion and piracy was not clear to Qing strategists until the Opium War was nearly ended.

The **Opium War** (1839–1842) broke out when negotiations between the Qing and British representatives became stalemated. The war exposed the fact that the traditional, hereditary soldiers of the Qing Empire—the **Bannermen**—were, like the Janissaries of the Ottoman Empire, hopelessly obsolete. As in the Crimean War, the British attempted to keep most confrontations on the sea, where they had a distinct technological advantage. British ships landed marines who pillaged coastal cities and then returned to their ships and sailed to new destinations (see Map 27.2). The Qing had no imperial navy, and until they were able to engage the British in prolonged fighting on land, they were unable to defend themselves against British attacks. Even in the land engagements, Qing resources proved woefully inadequate. The British could quickly transport their forces by sea along the coast. Qing troops, in contrast, moved primarily on foot. Moving Qing reinforcements from central to eastern China took more than three months, and when the defense forces arrived, they were exhausted and basically without weapons.

Against the British invaders, the Bannermen used the few muskets the Qing had imported during the 1700s. The weapons were matchlocks, which required the soldiers to ignite the load of gunpowder in them by hand. Firing the weapons was dangerous, and the canisters of gunpowder that each musketeer carried on his belt was likely to explode if a fire broke out nearby—a frequent occurrence in encounters with the British artillery. A majority of the Bannermen, however, had no guns and fought with swords, knives, spears, and clubs. Soldiers under British command—many of them were Indians—carried percussion-cap rifles, which were far quicker, safer, and more accurate than the matchlocks. In addition, the long-range artillery of the British could be moved from place to place and proved deadly in the cities and villages of eastern China.

Lin Zexu (lin zuh-SHOO)

Fighting the Opium Trade

In early 1839, Lin Zexu resigned his post as a provincial governor in order to act as a special imperial commissioner at Canton. The Qing court suspected that local officials were partial to the interests of the Canton merchants, and that enforcement of an anti-opium policy would be impossible without an agent as determined and honest as Lin Zexu. Shortly after his imperial appointment, Lin wrote to Queen Victoria, hoping to persuade her to prevent British merchants from continuing the opium trade.

We find that your country is [very far] from China. Yet there are barbarian ships that strive to come here for trade for the purpose of making a great profit. . . . That is to say, the great profit made by barbarians is all taken from the rightful share of China. By what right do they in return use the poisonous drug to injure the Chinese people? Even though the barbarians may not necessarily intend to do us harm, yet in coveting profit to an extreme, they have no regard for injuring others. Let us ask, where is your conscience? I have heard that the smoking of opium is very strictly forbidden by your country; that is because the harm caused by opium is clearly understood. Since it is not permitted to do harm to your own country, then even less should you let it be passed on to the harm of other countries—how much less to China! Of all that China exports to foreign countries, there is not a single thing which is not beneficial to people: they are of benefit when eaten, or of benefit when used, or of benefit when resold: all are beneficial. Is there a single article from China that has done harm to other countries?

When open warfare broke out between the Qing and British Empires, the governments of both countries blamed Lin for the conflict. The Qing court banished him to remote Xinjiang province. In a letter to a friend he reflected on the consequences of Qing technology gap with Britain.

When I was in office in [Canton] I had made plans regarding the problems of ships and cannon and a water force. Afraid that there was not enough time to build ships, I at first rented them. Afraid that there was not enough time to cast cannon and that it would not be done according to the regulations, I at first bought foreign ones. The most painful thing was that when the [harbor] was broken into, a large number of good cannon fell into the hands of the rebellious barbarians. I recall that after I had been punished two years ago, I still took the risk of calling the Emperor's attention to two things: ships and guns.

Though Lin's analysis of the predicament that the empire found itself in because of its neglect of technology was penetrating, it came too late. By the time Lin arrived at this conclusion, the Qing Empire was under such pressure from European powers and the United States that systematic, centralized reforms were very difficult to accomplish.

How do the attitudes expressed in these two passages from Lin's writings contrast with each other? How do they compare with the attitudes of Ottoman elites in the 1830s and 1840s?

Source: Adapted from Ssu-Yu Teng, Ssu-Tu-Teng, and John King Fairbank, *China's Response to the West: A Documentary Survey, 1839–1923* (Cambridge, MA: Harvard University Press, 1979), 24–29. Reprinted by permission of the publisher. Copyright © 1979 by the President and Fellows of Harvard College.

Qing commanders thought that British gunboats would ride so low in the water that they would not be able to sail up Chinese rivers, and that evacuating the coasts would protect the country from the British threat. But the British deployed new gunboats able to proceed in shallow water and moved without difficulty up the Yangzi River.

When the invaders approached Nanjing, the revered former Ming capital, the Qing decided to negotiate an end to the war. In 1842 the terms of the **Treaty of Nanking** (the British name for Nanjing) were concluded. The old Canton system was broken. The number of **treaty ports**—cities opened to foreign residents—was increased from one (Canton) to five (Canton, Xiamen,

Map 27.2 Conflicts in the Qing Empire, 1839–1870 In both the Opium War of 1839–1842 and the Arrow War of 1856–1860, the sea coasts saw most of the action. Since the Qing had no imperial navy, the well-armed British ships encountered little resistance as they shelled the southern coasts. In inland conflicts, such as the Taiping Rebellion, the opposing armies were massive and slow moving. Battles on land were often prolonged attempts by one side to starve out the other side before making a major assault.

Fuzhou, Ningbo, and Shanghai°), and the island of Hong Kong became a permanent British colony. British residents in China were granted the rights of extraterritoriality. The Qing government had to agree to a low tariff of 5 percent on imports and to pay an indemnity of 21 million ounces of silver to Britain as a penalty for having started the war. A supplementary treaty the following year guaranteed **most-favored nation status** to Britain: any privileges that China granted to another country would be automatically extended to Britain as well. This

provision effectively prevented the colonization of China, because giving land to one country would have necessitated giving it to all.

With each round of treaties came a new round of privileges for foreigners. In 1860 a new treaty legalized the right of foreigners to import opium. Later, French treaties established the rights of foreign missionaries to travel extensively in the Chinese countryside and preach their religion. The number of treaty ports grew, too; by 1900 they numbered more than ninety.

The treaty system in China resulted in the colonization of small pockets of Qing territory, where foreign

---

Shanghai (shahng-hie)

merchants enjoyed the rights of extraterritoriality (the same system existed in the Ottoman Empire and elsewhere in Asia). As in the case of the Ottoman Empire, the greatest territorial losses for the Qing resulted from the actual or nominal independence of outlying regions it had dominated. In the early 1800s, Britain and Russia were both active in attempts to erase the last traces of Qing sovereignty in Central Asia. In the late 1800s France forced the court of Vietnam to end its vassalage to the Qing, while Britain encouraged Tibetan independence.

In Canton, Shanghai, and other coastal cities, Europeans and Americans maintained offices and factories in which all but a few of the local Chinese were assigned to menial labor. The foreigners built comfortable housing in zones where Chinese were not permitted to live, and they entertained themselves in exclusive restaurants and bars. Around the foreign establishments, gambling and prostitution offered employment to some of the local urban population.

Often, the work of Christian missionaries both in the cities and in the countryside was regarded as benevolent, as when the congregations sponsored hospitals, shelters, and soup kitchens or gave stipends to Chinese who attended church. But just as often the missionaries themselves were regarded as another evil. They seemed to subvert Confucian beliefs, whether by condemning ancestor worship, pressuring poor families to put their children into orphanages, or fulminating against footbinding. The growing numbers of foreigners, and their growing privileges, quickly became a target of resentment for a deeply dissatisfied, daily more impoverished, and increasingly militarized society.

The Taiping Rebellion, 1850–1864

The most startling demonstration of the inflammatory mixture of social unhappiness and foreign intrusion was the great civil war usually called the **Taiping Rebellion.** In Guangxi, where the Taiping movement originated, entrenched social problems had been generating disorders for half a century. Agriculture in the region was unstable, and many people made their living from arduous and despised trades such as disposing of human waste, making charcoal, and mining. Ethnic divisions complicated economic distress. A minority group, the Hakkas, were frequently to be found in the lowliest trades, and tensions between them and the majority were rising. It is possible that the local economy had been affected by the sharp rises and falls in the trade of opium, which after 1842 flooded the coastal and riverine portions of China, then collapsed as domestically grown opium began to dominate the market. Also, the area was close enough to Canton to feel the cultural and economic impact of the growing number of Europeans and Americans.

All these factors were significant in the experience of Hong Xiuquan°, the founder of the Taiping movement. Hong came from a humble Hakka background. After years of study, he competed in the provincial Confucian examinations, hoping for a post in government. He failed the examinations repeatedly, and it appears that in his late thirties he suffered a nervous breakdown. Afterward he spent some time in Canton, where he met both Chinese and American Protestant missionaries, who inspired him with their teachings. Hong had his own interpretation of the Christian message. He saw himself as the younger brother of Jesus, commissioned by God to found a new kingdom on earth and drive the Manchu conquerors, the Qing, out of China. The result would be universal peace. Hong called his new religious movement the "Heavenly Kingdom of Great Peace."

Hong quickly attracted a community of believers, primarily Hakkas like himself. They believed in the prophecy of dreams and claimed they could walk on air. Hong and his rivals for leadership in the movement went in and out of ecstatic trances. They denounced the Manchus as creatures of Satan. News of the heresy reached the government, and Qing troops were sent to arrest the Taiping leaders. But the Taipings soundly repelled the imperial troops. Local loyalty to the Taipings spread quickly, their numbers multiplied, and they began to enlarge their domain.

It appears that at first the Taipings relied on Hakka sympathy and the charismatic appeal of their religious doctrine to attract followers. But as their numbers and power grew, they altered their methods of preaching and governing. They stopped enlisting Hakkas with anti-Chinese appeals and began to enlist Chinese with anti-Manchu rhetoric. They forced the populations of captured villages to join their movement, and once people were absorbed, the Taipings strictly monitored their activities. They segregated men and women and organized them into work and military teams. Women were forbidden to bind their feet (the Hakkas had never practiced footbinding), and they participated fully in farming and laboring. Brigades of women soldiers took to the field against Qing forces.

As the movement grew, it began to move toward eastern and northern China (see Map 27.2). Panic preceded the Taipings. Villagers feared being forced into Taiping units, and Confucian elites recoiled in horror from the bizarre ideology of foreign gods, totalitarian rule, and walking, working, warring women. But the

---

Hong Xiuquan (hoong shee-OH-chew-an)

Nanjing Encircled   For a decade the Taipings held the city of Nanjing as their capital. For years Qing and international troops attempted to break the Taiping hold. By the summer of 1864, Qing forces had built tunnels leading to the foundations of Nanjing's city walls and had planted explosives. The detonation of the explosives signaled the final Qing assault on the rebel capital. As shown here, the common people of the city, along with their starving livestock, were caught in the cross-fire. Many of the Taiping leaders escaped the debacle at Nanjing, but nearly all were hunted down and executed.   (Roger-Viollet)

huge numbers the Taipings were able to muster over-whelmed attempts at local defense. The tremendous growth in the number of Taiping followers required the movement to establish a permanent base. When the rebel army conquered Nanjing in 1853, the Taiping leaders decided to settle there and make it the capital of the new "Heavenly Kingdom of Great Peace."

At the time the Taipings were brought to a halt by the growth of their population and their organization, Qing forces attempting to defend north China against them were becoming more successful. Increasing Qing military success was due mainly to the flexibility of the imperial military commanders in the face of an unprecedented challenge. In addition, the military commanders received

strong backing from a group of civilian provincial governors who had studied the techniques developed by local militia forces for self-defense. In essence, certain of the provincial governors, especially Zeng Guofan°, combined their knowledge of civilian self-defense and local terrain with more efficient organization and the use of modern weaponry. The result was the formation of new military units, in which many of the Bannermen voluntarily served under civilian governors. The Qing court agreed to special taxes to fund the new armies and acknowledged the new combined leadership of the civilian and professional force.

Zeng Guofan (zung gwoh-FAN)

When the Taipings settled into Nanjing, the new Qing armies surrounded the city, hoping to starve out the rebels. The Taipings, however, had provisioned and fortified themselves well. They also had the services of several brilliant young military commanders, who mobilized enormous campaigns in nearby parts of eastern China, scavenging supplies and attempting to break the encirclement of Nanjing. For more than a decade the Taiping leadership remained ensconced at Nanjing, and the "Heavenly Kingdom" endured.

In 1856, Britain and France, freed from their preoccupation with the Crimean War, turned their attention to China. European and American missionaries had visited Nanjing, curious to see what their fellow Christians were up to. The reports they sent home were discouraging. Hong Xiuquan and the other leaders appeared to lead lives of indulgence and abandon, and more than one missionary accused them of homosexual practices. Now having no fear of being accused of quashing an appealing Christian movement, the British and French considered the situation. Though the Taipings were not going to topple the Qing, the outbreak of a rebellion by the Nian in northern China in the 1850s was ominous. A series of simultaneous large insurrections might indeed destroy the empire. Perhaps more important, Britain and France were now considering making war on the Qing again themselves. The Qing had not observed the provisions of the treaties signed after the Opium War, and European patience was exhausted.

In 1856 the British and French launched a series of swift, brutal coastal attacks—a second opium war, called the Arrow War (1856–1860)—which culminated in a British and French invasion of Beijing and the sacking of the Summer Palace in 1860. A new round of treaties punished the Qing for not enacting all the provisions of the Treaty of Nanking. Having secured their principal objective, the British and French forces now joined the Qing in the campaign against the Taipings. Attempts to coordinate the international forces were sometimes riotous and sometimes tragic, but the injection of European weaponry and money aided in the quelling of both the Taiping and the Nian Rebellions during the 1860s.

The Taiping Rebellion ranks as the world's bloodiest civil war and the greatest armed conflict before the twentieth century. Estimates of deaths range from 20 million to 30 million. The loss of life was due primarily to starvation and disease, for most engagements consisted of surrounding the enemy holed up in fortified cities and waiting until they died, surrendered, or were so weakened that they could be easily defeated. Many sieges continued for months, and people within some cities found that after starving for a year under the occupation of the rebels they had to starve for another year under the occupation of the imperial forces. Reports of people eating grass, leather, hemp, and human flesh were widespread. The dead were rarely buried properly, and epidemic disease was common.

The area of early Taiping fighting was close to the regions of southwest China where bubonic plague had been lingering for centuries. When the rebellion was suppressed, many Taiping followers sought safety in the highlands of Laos and Vietnam, which soon showed infestation by plague. Within a few years the disease reached Hong Kong. From there it spread to Singapore, San Francisco, Calcutta, and London. In the late 1800s there was intense apprehension over the possibility of a worldwide outbreak, and Chinese immigrants were regarded as likely carriers. This fear became a contributing factor in the passage of discriminatory immigration bans on Chinese in the United States in 1882.

The Taiping Rebellion devastated the agricultural centers of China. Many of the most intensely cultivated regions of central and eastern China were depopulated and laid barren. Decades later, some were still uninhabited, and provincial population figures show that major portions of the country did not recover until the twentieth century. Cities, too, were hard hit. Shanghai, a treaty port of modest size before the rebellion, saw its population multiplied many times by the arrival of refugees from the war-blasted neighboring provinces. The city then endured months of siege by the Taipings. Major cultural centers in eastern China lost masterpieces of art and architecture, imperial libraries were burned or their collections exposed to the weather, and the printing blocks used to make books were destroyed. While the empire faced the mountainous challenge of dealing with the material and cultural destruction from the war, it also was burdened by a major ecological disaster in the north: the Yellow River changed course in 1855, destroying the south part of impoverished Shandong province with flood and leaving the former riverbed in northern Shandong to decades of drought.

Decentralization at the End of the Qing Empire

The Qing government emerged from the 1850s with no hope of achieving solvency. The treasury had been bankrupted by the corruption of the 1700s, the attempts in the very early 1800s to restore waterworks and roads, and declining yields from land taxes. By 1850, before the Taiping Rebellion had begun, the Qing government already was spending ten times more than it took in. The burden of indemnities demanded by Europeans after the Opium and Arrow Wars foreclosed any hope that the Qing would get out of debt. Vast stretches of formerly productive rice land were devastated, the population was dispersed, immediate relief for refugees was demanded, and the imperial, volunteer, foreign, and mercenary troops that had suppressed the Taipings were demanding their unpaid wages.

With the Qing government so deeply in their debt, Britain and France became active participants in the period of recovery in China that followed the rebellion. This period is sometimes called the "Tongzhi Restoration," since it occurred during the reign of Tongzhi (r. 1862–1875). To ensure that the Qing government began repaying its debt to Britain, Robert Hart was installed as inspector-general of a newly created Imperial Maritime Customs Service. The revenues he collected were split between Britain and the Qing. Britons and Americans put themselves in the employ of the Qing government as advisers and ambassadors, attempting to smooth communications between the Qing, Europe, and the United States while the imperial government started up the diplomatic machinery demanded by Europe in its latest treaties.

The real work of the recovery, however, was managed by the provincial governors who had come to the forefront in the struggle against the Taipings. To prosecute the war, they had won the right to levy their own taxes, raise their own troops, and run their own bureaucracies. These special powers were not entirely canceled

when the war ended. Chief among these governors was Zeng Guofan, who oversaw programs to restore agriculture, communications, education, and publishing, as well as efforts to reform the military and industrialize armaments manufacture.

Like many provincial governors, Zeng preferred to look to the United States rather than to Britain for models and aid. He hired American advisers to run his weapons factories, shipyards, and military academies. He sponsored a daring program in which promising Chinese boys were sent to Hartford, Connecticut, to learn English, science, mathematics, engineering, and history. They returned to China to assume some of the positions previously held by foreign advisers. Though Zeng was never an advocate of participation in public life by women, he was a firm adherent of the Confucian elite view that educated mothers were a necessity, perhaps now more than ever. He not only encouraged but partly oversaw the advanced classical education of his own daughters. Zeng's death in 1872 deprived the empire of a major force for reform.

The period of recovery marked a fundamental structural change in the Qing Empire. Although the emperors after 1850 were ineffective rulers, a coalition of aristocrats supported the reform and recovery programs. If they had been unwilling to legitimate the new powers of provincial governors such as Zeng Guofan, the empire

Cixi's Allies In the 1860s and 1870s, Cixi was a supporter of reform. In later years she was widely regarded as corrupt and self-centered and as an obstacle to reform. Her greatest allies were the court eunuchs. Introduced to palace life in early China as managers of the imperial harems, enuchs became powerful political parties at court. The first Qing emperors refused to allow the eunuchs any political influence, but by Cixi's time the eunuchs once again were a political factor. (Freer Gallery, Smithsonian Institution)

Japan from Shogunate to Empire

might have evaporated within a generation. A crucial member of this alliance was Cixi°, after the 1880s known as the "Empress Dowager." Later observers, both Chinese and foreign, reviled her as a monster of corruption and arrogance. But in the 1860s and 1870s Cixi was a supporter of the provincial governors, some of whom became so powerful that they were managing Qing foreign policy as well as domestic affairs.

No longer a conquest regime dominated by a Manchu military caste and its Chinese civilian appointees, the empire came under the control of a group of reformist aristocrats and military men, independently powerful civilian governors, and a small number of foreign advisers. The Qing lacked strong, central, unified leadership, and could not recover their powers of taxation, legislation, and military command once they had been granted to the provincial governors. From the 1860s forward, the Qing Empire disintegrated into a set of large power zones in which provincial governors handed over leadership to their protégés in a pattern that the Qing court eventually could only ritually legitimate.

JAPAN FROM SHOGUNATE TO EMPIRE

The Qing Empire in the 1600s and 1700s had worked systematically to establish centralized control over China and its neighboring regions. In Japan, a completely different political organization was in place. For a thousand years Japan had had a ruler who in English is called an "emperor," but this ruler had no political power. Instead, since the twelfth century Japan had been governed by shogunates—decentralized secular government under a military leader (*shogun*) who was loyal to the emperor. This was an effective solution to the civil wars that on occasion afflicted Japan. Local lords were permitted to control their lands and populations with very little interference from the shogunate, and enough of the lords remained loyal to the shogun to prevent very frequent changes of regime.

In times of threat from outside, this system showed many weaknesses. It did not permit the coordination of resources and communications on a national scale that would be necessary to resist a major invasion from abroad. Shoguns and their advisers understood the basic weakness of the system and attempted to minimize exposure to and possible threat from foreign powers. In the early 1600s they prohibited foreigners from entering Japan and Japanese from going abroad.

The penalties for breaking these laws was death, but many Japanese ignored them anyway. The most flagrant violations were by powerful local lords in southern Japan, who ran large and very successful pirate operations or black-market trade in stolen or faked passes granting entry into the carefully regulated Qing trading ports. In their entrepreneurial activities these local lords benefited from the decentralization of the shogunal political system. But when a genuine foreign threat was suggested—as when, in 1792, Russian and British ships were spotted off the Japanese coast in separate incidents—the local lords realized that their relative independence would be no help if there was a foreign invasion.

For a time, the Tokugawa Shogunate responded to the threat of foreign invasion by attempting to strengthen its finances and its military forces, much as the more centralized Ottoman and Qing Empires had done. But unlike those empires, the Tokugawa government was limited in the measures it could decree to improve national preparedness, and it was not able to carry out a single policy to resist European and American encroachment. Instead, some of the regional lords of Japan, who did not believe the Tokugawa Shogunate had the ability or the will to protect the islands, developed their own reformed armies, arsenals, and shipyards. In 1853 the arrival of a small U.S. fleet with demands for an opening of Japan to trade with the United States started a process that ended with the destruction of the Tokugawa Shogunate by leaders of the more powerful provinces.

Collapse of the Shogunate

By the 1800s, several of the regional provinces had emerged as much wealthier and more ambitious than others. This was particularly true of Satsuma° and Choshu°, two large domains in southern Japan (see Map 27.3). Because the ancestors of their ruling houses had not been supporters of the Tokugawa lineage, they were punished by being given sparsely settled lands far from the shogunal court. Over time, this location proved to offer a distinct advantage. These regions could rapidly expand their agricultural base when more central regions had reached their limits, and Satsuma and Choshu enjoyed high rates of growth in revenue and population during the early 1800s. The remoteness and the economic vigor of these provinces also fostered a strong sense of local self-reliance.

Cixi (tsuh-shee)

Satsuma (SAT-soo-mah)   **Choshu** (CHOE-shoo)

Map 27.3 Tokugawa Japan, to 1867 The Tokugawa Shogunate was the last of the decentralized governments of Japan that put primary power into the hands of a military leader and protector of the emperor. Under the Tokugawa regime, provincial leaders at the western extreme of Honshu Island—regarded as an undesirable site in the early Tokugawa period—experienced higher rates of economic growth and managerial innovation than did provincial leaders in the central provinces.

The economic and political weakness of the shogunate prompted some leaders in the Tokugawa government to attempt a restrengthening, primarily by placing new burdens on the hereditary provincial governors. Some provincial academies for aspiring soldiers, scholars, and bureaucrats became centers for the development and dissemination of a new ideology of loyalty to the shoguns, who depended on the politically weak emperors of Japan for their legitimacy. But the arrival of the American Commodore Matthew C. Perry and his fleet of what the Japanese called "black ships" in 1853 shattered the shogunate's attempts to restore its influence across the provinces. While the Japanese, like other East Asians, had been focused on intruders from their west such as the Dutch, British, French, and Russians, the Americans'

search for a route to bring pelts from northwest America across the Pacific had led them to surprise Japan with an approach from the east. Perry demanded that Japan open its ports to U.S. ships for refueling and for trade when he returned in 1854.

Perry's terms sparked a crisis in the shogunate. Consultation among the provincial governors and the shogunal officials was extensive. In the end, the shogunal advisers advocated capitulation to Perry. They pointed to China's humiliating defeats in the Opium and Arrow Wars and expressed doubt that the treaty powers in China would be discouraged from seeking other ports in East Asia. Leaders of the provincial governors opposed this view. They pointed out that the United States was not a formidable power like Britain and predicted that a

Arrivals from the East   In 1853 Commodore Matthew Perry's ships surprised the Tokugawa Shogunate by appearing not in Kyushu or southern Honshu, where European ships previously had been spotted, but at Uraga on the coast of eastern Honshu. The Japanese soon learned that Perry had come not from the south but across the Pacific from the east. The novelty of the threat unsettled the provincial leaders, who were largely responsible for their own defense. In this print done after the Meiji Restoration, the traditionally dressed local samurai go out to confront the mysterious "black ships."   (Courtesy of the Trustees of the British Museum)

refusal by Japan would result only in the Americans seeking an easier refueling location elsewhere.

In 1854, Perry's fleet returned, and representatives of the Tokugawa shogun indicated their willingness to sign the Treaty of Kanagawa°—modeled on the unequal treaties between China and the Western powers. Before provincial leaders considered the discussion closed, shogunal representatives signed the treaty in 1858. Angry and disappointed, some provincial governors began to encourage an underground movement calling for the destruction of the Tokugawa regime and the banning of foreigners from Japan.

Kanagawa (KAH-nah-GAH-wah)

Tensions between the shogunate and some provincial leaders, particularly in Choshu and Satsuma, increased in the early 1860s. British and French shelling of the southwestern coasts in 1864 further enraged provincial samurai who rejected the Treaty of Kanagawa and resented the Shogunate's inability to protect the country. Young, ambitious, educated men who faced mediocre prospects under the rigid Tokugawa class system emerged as provincial leaders. Among them, the Choshu leaders Yamagata Aritomo and Ito Hitobumi were outstanding. They realized in 1867 that they should stop warring with their rival province, Satsuma, and instead join forces to lead a rebellion against the shogunate. The civil war was intense but brief. In 1868, a new government was founded, and the young emperor Mutsuhito (r. 1868–1912) was declared "restored."

The Meiji Restoration

To destroy the old state was one thing; to create a new state with the resources and will to deal with economic and military problems was quite another. Though Japan is smaller than the landmass of either the Qing or the Ottoman Empire, its many islands are far-flung and its natural resources extremely limited. Thus the size of Japan was not necessarily a major explanation for the apparent ease with which it was reformed. Perhaps more important was the fact that, unlike the Qing and Ottoman Empires, Japan was of no great strategic importance to Europe or the United States.

American merchants expected that Japan, like China, would be a rich market for their goods, and American naval planners wanted a reprovisioning station in Japan to facilitate the movement of U.S. ships along the China coast. But neither of these considerations would have propelled the United States to initiate war with Japan in the 1850s. Also, the European powers showed only a casual interest in Japan. Thus there was no foreign effort to economically or strategically sustain the Tokugawa Shogunate, and when it was destroyed, the small group who controlled the new government—often called the Meiji° oligarchs—were unimpeded in their plans for a centralized, industrialized national state.

The ideology of the new state, known by Mutsuhito's reign name, *Meiji*, ("enlightened rule"), was one source of its power. By "restoring" the emperor, the new leaders claimed to have ended centuries of imperial seclusion and disempowerment by the shoguns. The mysticism of the emperors, nationalism, and anxiety over the foreign threat were all combined to create a decade of focused effort on the transformation of Japan from a decentralized, traditional military government to a centralized, civil, industrializing state. The nationalistic ideology of the Meiji Restoration coexisted with intense interest in European practices in government, education, industry, dress, and even popular culture.

The achievements of the **Meiji Restoration** were remarkable. The oligarchs were extraordinarily talented and far-sighted men. They overcame regional resistance to political and social reform, and gradually but systematically they effected the dissolution of the traditional provincial governorships and of the samurai class. Though the Tokugawa government had been poor, there was

Meiji (MAY-gee)

wealth in some of the provinces. The literacy rate may have been as high as 35 percent—certainly the highest in Asia at the time—and the oligarchs shrewdly exploited it in their introduction of new educational systems, a conscript army, and new communications. The government was able to establish heavy industry through the use of judicious deficit financing without extensive foreign debt, thanks to decades of experimentation with industrial development and financing in the provinces in the earlier 1800s. With a conscript army and a revamped educational system the oligarchs attempted to create a new citizenry that was literate and competent but also loyal and obedient.

CONCLUSION

The response of Japan to the challenge of the industrializing nations was a striking contrast to the responses of the Ottoman and Qing Empires. An important point of comparison is the relationship between financial resources and reform from the elite levels downward. In the Ottoman and Qing (as well as the Russian) Empires, the imperial courts attempted to mandate reforms in the military. To meet the cost, these revenue-starved empires debased their currencies, thereby stimulating inflation. To continue the reforms, they became dependent on foreign loans, which ultimately led to control of their finances, commercial strategies, and in some cases revenue-producing organs by European powers. Japan, in contrast, experienced comparatively few top-down major reforms under the Tokugawa shoguns. Instead, the decentralized provinces provided their own means of experimenting with local military improvement, new educational programs, and deficit financing before the Meiji Restoration of 1868. Afterward, they could compare their experiences and apply what they had learned.

Japan's exposure to the military and economic pressure of the sea powers was much more limited than that of the Ottoman and Qing Empires. One reason for this difference was that Japan was not an empire in the same sense. It did not control extensive trade networks and urban centers to which Britain and France wished to gain privileged access. Nor was its position, on the far eastern of the Eurasian continent, regarded as strategically significant in the West. The treaty that the United States forced on Japan was practically Japan's only experience with unequal treaties. In contrast, the Treaty of Nanking of 1842 ushered in the period of unequal treaties that resulted in the installation of a vast system of foreign privilege in China. European and American pressure on the Qing Empire became so intense that the Chinese could neither learn to finance the industries necessary for a strong military nor find a period of peace in which to develop the educational institutions that would have produced a new generation of leaders.

The Meiji oligarchs hoped that Japan's relatively remote location and relatively insignificant political status would permit it breathing space to make the revolutionary changes they envisaged. The Qing and the Ottoman rulers could only hope that mutual distrust by the European powers would limit the ambitions of any individual European state. This strategy—in China known as "using the barbarians against the barbarians"—continually embroiled the Qing Empire in short, localized wars or threatened wars with aspiring signatories in the unequal treaty system.

In the Qing territories and in the Ottoman Empire, Europeans and Americans did not need to establish colonies in order to enjoy privileged status. Neither Ottoman nor Qing lands were in need of "development" by colonial forces. Pockets of wealth—primarily in the cities—could be exploited, and this maneuvering was best done through strategic alliances or diplomacy, not by the expensive and risky methods of colonization. It is not a coincidence that both of the empires whose territorial integrity the European powers—and, in the case of China, the United States—swore to defend were ultimately derided as the "sick men" of Eurasia, unable to defend themselves against their defenders, and kept in a state of low-grade survival to provide markets, raw materials, and strategic advantages to smaller, more dynamic nations.

The Crimean War and Taiping Rebellion were watershed events in the loss of centralization and autonomy for, respectively, the Ottoman and Qing Empires. In each conflict the Eurasian empire in question emerged as nominally victorious. But both land-based empires were overextended. They suffered from declining revenues and social dislocation. Ironically, within these empires were enclaves of merchants and artisans who were enriched by the trade with Europe and America, but the imperial governments never found a way to tax these new incomes.

Much domestic wealth flowed from the Ottoman and Qing Empires to foreign countries in payment for legal as well as illegal commodities, and state resources for arms and education could not be found. Increasing pressure from Britain and France deepened the financial woes and political tensions of both empires and heightened the elite's awareness of the necessity for military reform. During the Crimean War and the Taiping Rebellion, the financial obligations of each empire and the strategic advantages of its existence led to the formation of alliances with Britain and France. And in the aftermath of the conflicts, each empire experienced serious problems with decentralization, loss of control over its borders, permanent indebtedness and inflation, a progressive loss of international and domestic credibility, and new dependence on foreign protection.

The differences between the Ottoman and Qing also are illuminating. The Ottomans made an attempt to modernize their military and make their government more efficient before the end of the 1700s. Their proximity to Europe gave them direct experience with the Napoleonic era and the rising nationalism of the 1800s. The intense struggle between France and Russia, in particular, gave the Ottomans a strategic position that made it distinctly to the advantage of France to side with the Ottomans in their territorial struggles. For their part, the Ottomans were comparatively swift in their adaptation of aspects of French culture, military practices, and commercial institutions. This adaptability sustained Ottoman political credibility in Europe through the critical period of the war for Greek independence, and later it allowed design and implementation of the reform program under Mahmud II. On the strength of that recentralization, the secular programs that defined a civil sphere and a Turkish identity gave strength to the very nationalist movement that eventually helped destroy the empire.

Unlike the Ottomans, the Qing were not able to achieve even a modest degree of recentralization. Suppression of the Taiping Rebellion required the dissolution of the traditional military structures, the regionalization of command and support, and finally the use of foreign troops. The alliance formed by Britain and France at this time was to become more active in the very late 1800s, as the European powers and the United States attempted repeatedly to prevent the colonization of Qing territory by Japan.

■ Key Terms

Janissaries	Opium War
Serbia	Bannermen
Tanzimat	Treaty of Nanking
Crimean War	treaty ports
percussion cap	most-favored-nation status
breech-loading rifle	Taiping Rebellion
extraterritoriality	Meiji Restoration

■ Suggested Reading

For the Ottoman Empire there is a large and interesting literature, much of it based on original documents, some in translation, relating to Ottoman administration throughout Europe and the Middle East. For widely available general histories see Stanford Shaw, *History of the Ottoman Empire and Modern Turkey* (1976–1977), and J.P.D.B. Kinross, *The Ottoman Centuries: The Rise and Fall of the Turkish Empire* (1977).

On the economy and society of the nineteenth-century Ottoman Empire see Huri Islamoglu-Inan, ed., *The Ottoman Empire and the World-Economy* (1987); Resat Kasaba, *The Ottoman Empire and the World Economy: The Nineteenth Century* (1988); Sevket Pamuk, *The Ottoman Empire and European Capitalism, 1820–1913: Trade, Investment, and Production* (1987); Kemal H. Karpat, *Ottoman Population, 1830–1914: Demographic and Social Characteristics* (1985); and Carter V. Findley, *Bureaucratic Reform in the Ottoman Empire: The Sublime Porte, 1789–1922* (1980). On the reform program and the emergence of national concepts see also Selim Deringil, *The Well-Protected Domains: Ideology and the Legitimation of Power in the Ottoman Empire, 1876–1909* (1998).

On the Qing Empire of the nineteenth century see Pamela Kyle Crossley, *Orphan Warriors: Three Manchu Generations and the End of the Qing World* (1990), and for a more detailed political history see Mary C. Wright, *The Last Stand of Chinese Conservatism: The T'ung-chih Restoration, 1862–1874* (1971). There is a very large literature on both the Opium War and the Taiping Rebellion, including reprinted editions of contemporary observers. For general histories of the Opium War see Peter Ward Fay, *The Opium War, 1840–1842: Barbarians in the Celestial Empire in the Early Part of the Nineteenth Century and the War by Which They Forced Her Gates Ajar* (1975); Christopher Hibbert, *The Dragon Wakes: China and the West, 1793–1911* (1970); and the classic study by Chang Hsin-pao, *Commissioner Lin and the Opium War* (1964). For a recent, more monographic study on Qing political thought in the period of the Opium War see James M. Polachek, *The Inner Opium War* (1992). On the Taiping Rebellion, enduring sources are S. Y. Têng, *The Taiping Rebellion and the Western Powers: A Comprehensive Survey* (1971), and C. A. Curwen, *Taiping Rebel: the Deposition of Li Hsiu-ch'eng* (1976); see also Caleb Carr, *The Devil Soldier: the Story of Frederick Townsend Ward* (1992). The most recent study is Jonathan D. Spence, *God's Chinese Son: The Taiping Heavenly Kingdom of Hong Xiuquan* (1996).

The classic work on the period leading to the Meiji Restoration in Japan is Albert M. Craig, *Choshu in the Meiji Restoration* (1961). See also Conrad Totman, *The Collapse of the Tokugawa Bakufu, 1862–1868* (1980), Bob Tadashi Wakabayashi, *Anti-Foreignism and Western Learning in Early-Modern Japan: The New Theses of 1825* (1986); Peter Booth Wiley with Korogi Ichiro, *Yankees in the Land of the Gods: Commodore Perry and the Opening of Japan* (1990); and George M. Wilson, *Patriots and Redeemers in Japan : Motives in the Meiji Restoration* (1992).

PART SEVEN

GLOBAL DOMINANCE AND DIVERSITY, 1850–1945

etween 1850 and 1950, Europe, the United States, and Japan industrialized and became powerful. One cause of the power of Europe, the United States, and Japan was nationalism, a bond uniting people on the basis of a common culture or shared historical experiences. In some nations, public participation resulted in basic freedoms and strong parliamentary institutions. In others, authoritarian leaders used nationalist feelings to mobilize mass support.

Another cause of Western and Japanese power in this period was industrialization itself. New technologies and economic arrangements transformed the lives of people of all classes and professions. Work in-creasingly took place in factories and offices, separating employment from home life, husbands from wives, children from parents. A growing proportion of married women became housewives, and compulsory education systems took over the care of children. Intensifying industrial activities transformed the natural environment. Pollution from manufacturing, long a local problem, began to affect entire regions.

Industrialization led to the creation of increasingly destructive weapons that enabled the Western powers to extend their commercial and political influence over Africa, most of Asia, and Latin America. By 1914, Britain, France, and the United States dominated over half of the area and peoples of the world.

697

By the time Germany and Japan entered the competition for overseas colonial empires, few unconquered territories remained.

Germany's desire to become a global power was a major cause of the First World War. The defeat of Germany did not restore the prewar equilibrium, as the victorious Allied nations had hoped. The Russian Revolution of 1917 led to the establishment of the world's first communist state. The collapse of the Ottoman Empire sparked changes in Middle Eastern societies, most dramatically in Turkey itself.

When the world economy collapsed in the 1930s, social disruption in Germany and Japan brought to power extremist politicians who sought to solve their countries' economic woes by seizing neighboring territories. Nationalism assumed its most hideous form in World War II. The war led to the massacre of millions of innocent people and the destruction of countless cities.

Domination by the great powers inspired a new generation of leaders to embrace the politics of national liberation. After decades of struggle India achieved independence in 1947. Two years later Communists led by Mao Zedong overthrew a Chinese government they denounced as too subservient to the West. In Latin America leaders turned to nationalist economic and social politics.

The year 1945 marked the end of western European dominance. Only the United States and the Soviet Union remained to compete for global influence. Meanwhile, nationalism was rapidly spreading to the rest of the world, bringing with it the urge to acquire the benefits and power of industrial technology.

	1850	1870	1890
Americas	U.S. Civil War **1861–1865** Creation of Dominion of Canada **1867** •	British build railroads in Brazil and Argentina **1880s** •	• **1890** U.S. is leading steel producer Spanish-American War **1898** • **1880–1914** Immigration from southern and eastern Europe surges
Europe	• **1851** Majority of British population living in cities • **1856** Transformation of steel and chemical industries begins	**1870–1914** Era of the New Imperialism • **1871** Unification of Germany, Italy	**1894–1906** Dreyfus affair in France
Africa	**1853–1877** Livingstone, Stanley expeditions in central Africa End of transatlantic slave trade **1867** • Gold discovered in southern Africa **1884–1886**	• **1880s** West Africa conquered by France and Britain **1884–1885** Berlin Africa Conference	• **1896** Ethiopians defeat Italian army at Adowa Nigeria becomes British protectorate **1899** •
Middle East	**1863–1879** Ismail westernizes Egypt Suez Canal opens **1869** •	• **1882** British occupy Egypt • **1878** Ottoman Empire loses most of its European territories	• **1904** Young Turk reforms in Ottoman Empire
Asia and Oceania	Direct British rule in India **1858** • Meiji Restoration in Japan **1868** •	• **1862** French conquer Indochina First Indian National Congress **1885** • Russia conquers Central Asia **1884–1887**	Boxer Rebellion in China **1900** • Sino-Japanese War **1894** • **1904–1905** Russo-Japanese War

ARCTIC OCEAN

Russia

(Union of Soviet Socialist Republics)

Britain
Germany
EUROPE
France
Italy
Ottoman
Empire
(Turkey)
Mediterranean Sea
Israel

ASIA

Pakistan
Korea
Japan
China

Algeria
Egypt
MIDDLE EAST
India
French Indochina

French West Africa
AFRICA
Nigeria
Ethiopia
Nile River
Congo River
Congo
Zambezi River

Philippines

PACIFIC OCEAN

INDIAN OCEAN

SOUTH ATLANTIC OCEAN

South Africa

AUSTRALIA

0   1000   2000   3000 Km.

0   1000   2000   3000 Mi.

1910   **1930**   **1950**

1906–1914 • **1913** First automobile assembly line   • **1929** U.S. stock market crash leads to Great Depression
U.S. builds Panama Canal   • **1917** U.S. enters World War I   • **1938** Mexico nationalizes oil industry
        • **1911–1920** Mexican Revolution   • **1946** Juan Perón becomes president of Argentina

• **1905** Revolution of 1905 in Russia   **1922–1940** Rise of fascism
        • **1917** Russian Revolutions
        1914–1918 World War I   **1939–1945** World War II

• **1908** Congo annexed by Belgium   **1939–1945** A million Africans
• **1909** African National Congress founded   serve in World War II
1900–1930 Railroads built from ports to interior

Balfour Declaration **1917** •   **1922–1938** Atatürk secularizes Turkey   • **1948** State of Israel founded
        • **1918** Breakup of Ottoman Empire
        1915–1918 Arab Revolt against Ottomans

• **1910** Korea annexed by Japan   • **1931** Japanese invasion   • **1949** Communists take power in China
• **1911** Overthrow of Qing dynasty in China   of Manchuria   • **1945** U.S. atomic bombs force Japanese surrender
                • **1947** India and Pakistan win independence

28

THE NEW POWER BALANCE,

1850–1900

New Technologies and the World Economy • Social Transformations •
Nationalism and the Unification of Germany • The Great Powers of Europe,
1871–1900 • New Great Powers: The United States and Japan

ENVIRONMENT AND TECHNOLOGY: Railroads and Immigration
SOCIETY AND CULTURE: Demonstrating for Women's Rights

Silk Factory in Japan　Silk manufacture, Japan's best-known industry, began to be mechanized in the 1870s. In this factory, as in most textile mills, the workers were women.

*O*n January 18, 1871, in the Hall of Mirrors of the palace of Versailles, King Wilhelm I of Prussia was proclaimed emperor of Germany before a crowd of officers and other German rulers. This ceremony marked the unification of many small German states into one nation. Off to one side stood Prussian chancellor Otto von Bismarck°, the man most responsible for the creation of a united Germany. A few years earlier, he had declared: "The great issues of the day will be decided not by speeches and votes of the majority—that was the great mistake of 1848 and 1849—but by iron and blood." Indeed it was "blood"—that is, victories on the battlefield—rather than popular participation that had led to the unification of Germany; among the dignitaries in the Hall of Mirrors that day, only two or three were civilians. As for "iron," it meant not only weapons but, more important, the industries required to produce weapons. Thus, after 1871, nationalism, once a dream of revolutionaries and romantics, became ever more closely associated with military force and with industry.

This chapter deals with a small group of countries—Germany, France, Britain, Russia, the United States, and Japan—that we call "great powers." In the next chapter, which deals with the era of the "New Imperialism" (1870–1914), we will see how these nations used their power to conquer colonial empires in Asia and Africa and to control Latin America. Together, Chapters 28 and 29 describe an era in which a handful of wealthy industrialized nations—all but one of them of European culture—imposed on the other peoples of the world a domination more powerful than any experienced before or since.

As you read this chapter, ask yourself the following questions:

- What new technologies and industries appeared between 1850 and 1900, and how did they affect the world economy?

- How did the societies of the industrial countries change during this period?

- Why do we call certain countries "great powers" but not others?

Otto von Bismark (UTT-oh fun BIS-mark)

NEW TECHNOLOGIES AND THE WORLD ECONOMY

After 1850, industrialization took off in new directions. It spread to new countries, especially Germany and the United States, which surpassed Great Britain as the world's leading industrial powers by 1890. Small companies, like those that had flourished in Britain in the late nineteenth century, were overshadowed by large corporations, some owned by wealthy capitalists, others (especially in Russia and Japan) by governments.

New technologies based on advances in physics and chemistry revolutionized everyday life and transformed the world economy. Some of the inventions of this period—the automobile, airplane, and radio in particular—aroused tremendous excitement but did not make an impact on people's lives until after World War I (see Chapter 30). Other advances, such as the steel and chemical industries, electricity, and the spreading networks of steamships, telegraphs, and railroads, were already important by 1900.

The Steel and Chemical Industries

Steel is a special form of iron, both hard and elastic. Until the eighteenth century, it could be made only by skilled blacksmiths in very small quantities at a very high cost and thus was reserved for swords, knives, axes, and watch springs. The invention of the crucible (a container in which molten iron was stirred until it turned to steel) in the 1740s made steel cheap enough for tools, weapons, and machines. By 1850 Britain was producing some 60,000 tons a year.

Then came a series of inventions that made steel the cheapest and most versatile metal ever known. In the 1850s, William Kelly, a Kentucky iron master, discovered that air forced through molten pig iron turned it into steel without additional fuel. In 1856 the Englishman Henry Bessemer improved Kelly's method. The Bessemer converter produced steel at one-tenth the cost of the crucible method. Other new processes permitted steel to be made from scrap iron, an increasingly important raw material, and from the phosphoric iron ores common in western Europe. As a result, world steel production rose from a half-million tons in 1870 to 28 million in 1900, of which the United States produced 10 million, Germany 8, and Britain 4.9. Steel became cheap and abundant enough to make rails, bridges, ships, and even "tin" cans meant to be used once and thrown away.

Paris Lit Up by Electricity, 1900 The electric light bulb was invented in the United States and Britain, but Paris made such extensive use of the new technology that it was nicknamed "City of Lights." To mark the Paris Exposition of 1900, the Eiffel Tower and all the surrounding buildings were illuminated with strings of light bulbs while powerful spotlights swept the sky. (Courtesy, Civiche Raccolte d'Art Applicata ed Incisioni (Raccolte Bertarelli) Photo: Foto Saporetti)

The new steel mills were hungry consumers of coal, iron ore, limestone, and other raw materials. They took up as much space as whole towns, belched smoke and particulate night and day, and left behind huge hills of slag and other waste products. Environmental degradation, long familiar in certain communities, affected entire regions such as the English Midlands, the German Ruhr, and parts of Pennsylvania.

The chemical industry followed a similar pattern. Until the late eighteenth century, chemicals were produced by trial and error in small workshops. By the early nineteenth century, soda, sulfuric acid, and chlorine bleach (used in the cotton industry) were manufactured on a large scale, especially in Britain. In 1856 the Englishman William Perkin created the first synthetic dye, aniline purple, from coal tar; the next few years were known in Europe as the "mauve decade" from the fashionable color for most women's clothes. Industry began mass-producing other organic chemicals—compounds containing carbon atoms. Toward the end of the century, German chemists synthesized red, violet, blue, brown, and black dyes as well. These bright, long-lasting colors delighted consumers but damaged the natural-dye exports of many tropical countries, especially hurting plantations in India that produced indigo, a blue vegetable dye.

Chemistry also made important advances in the manufacture of explosives. The first of these were nitrocellulose and nitroglycerin, a liquid so dangerous that it

explodes when shaken. In 1866 the Swedish scientist Alfred Nobel found a way to turn nitroglycerin into a stable solid—dynamite. This and other new explosives were very useful in mining and the construction of railroads and canals. They also enabled the armies and navies of the great powers to arm themselves with increasingly accurate and powerful rifles and cannon.

The growing complexity of industrial chemistry made it one of the first fields where science and technology interacted on a daily basis. This development gave a great advantage to Germany, which had the most advanced engineering schools and scientific institutes of its time. While the British government paid little attention to science and engineering, the German government funded research and encouraged cooperation between universities and industries. By the end of the nineteenth century, Germany was the world's leading producer of dyes, drugs, synthetic fertilizers, ammonia, and nitrates used in making explosives.

Electricity

The third innovation that transformed the world of the late nineteenth century was **electricity.** At first, producing electric current was so costly that it was used only for electroplating and telegraphy. In 1831 the Englishman Michael Faraday showed that the motion of a copper wire through a magnetic field induced an electric current in the wire. Based on his

CHRONOLOGY

	Europe	United States	East Asia
1850	**1851** Majority of British population living in cities **1856** Bessemer converter; first synthetic dye **1859** Charles Darwin, *On the Origin of Species* **1861** Emancipation of serfs (Russia) **1866** Alfred Nobel develops dynamite **1867** Karl Marx, *Das Kapital*		
		1865 Civil War ends; economic expansion begins **1865–1914** Surge of immigration from southern and eastern Europe	**1862–1908** Rule of Dowager Empress Cixi (China)
1870	**1871** Unification of Germany; unification of Italy **1875** Social Democratic Party founded in Germany **1882** Married Women's Property Act (Britain)	**1879** Thomas Edison develops incandescent lamp	**1868** Meiji Restoration begins modernization drive in Japan
1890	**1894–1906** Dreyfus affair (France)	**1890** United States is the world's leading producer of steel **1890s** "Jim Crow" laws enforce segregation in southern states **1899** United States acquires Puerto Rico and the Philippines	**1894** Sino-Japanese War
	1905 Revolution of 1905 (Russia)		**1900** Boxer Uprising (China) **1904–1905** Russo-Japanese War **1910** Japan annexes Korea

discovery, in the 1870s inventors devised efficient generators that turned mechanical energy into electric current and opened the way to a host of new applications.

Arc lamps lit up public squares, theaters, and stores. For a while, homes continued to rely on gas lamps, which produced a softer light. Then in 1879 **Thomas Edison** in the United States developed an incandescent lamp well suited to lighting small rooms. In 1882 Edison created the world's first electrical distribution network, in New York. By the turn of the century, electric lighting was rapidly replacing dim and smelly gas lamps in the cities of Europe and North America.

Other uses of electricity quickly appeared. Electric streetcars and, later, subways helped reduce the traffic jams that clogged the large cities of Europe and North America. Electric motors replaced steam engines and power belts, increasing productivity and improving workers' safety. As demand for electricity grew, engineers learned to use waterpower to produce electricity, and hydroelectric plants were built. The plant at Niagara Falls, on the border between Ontario, Canada, and New

York State, opened in 1895 and produced an incredible 11,000 horsepower.

Electricity helped alleviate some environmental problems. Electric motors and lamps did not pollute the air. Power plants were built at a distance from cities. As electric trains and streetcars replaced horse-drawn trolleys and coal-burning locomotives, cities became noticeably cleaner and healthier. At the same time, electricity created a huge demand for copper, bringing Chile, Montana, and southern Africa into the world economy as never before.

Shipping and Telegraph Cables

The late nineteenth century saw a tremendous expansion of railroads and shipping, linked to growth in world trade and to technological innovations. Steam-powered ships dated back to the 1830s but were too costly at first for anything but first-class passenger traffic. Then, midcentury, a series of developments radically transformed ocean shipping. First iron, then steel, replaced the wood that had been used for hulls since shipbuilding began. Propellers replaced paddle wheels. Engineers built more powerful and fuel-efficient engines. By the turn of the century a marine engine could convert the heat produced by burning a single sheet of paper into the power to move one ton over half a mile. The average size of freighters increased from 200 tons in 1850 to 7,500 tons in 1900. Coaling stations and ports able to handle large ships were built around the world. Most of all, the Suez Canal, constructed in 1869, shortened the distance between Europe and Asia and triggered a massive switch from sail power to steam (see Chapter 29).

The steamers of the turn of the century were so costly they had to be used as efficiently as possible. As the world's fleet of merchant ships grew from 9 million to 35 million tons between 1850 and 1910, new organizations developed to make the best use of ships. One such organization was the shipping line, a company that offered fast, punctual, and reliable service on a fixed schedule. Passengers, mail, and perishable freight traveled on scheduled liners. Most ships, however, were tramp freighters that voyaged from one port to another under orders from their company headquarters in Europe or North America.

To control their ships around the globe, shipping companies used a new medium of communications: **submarine telegraph cables** laid on the ocean floor linking the continents. Cables were laid across the Atlantic in 1866, to India in 1870, to China, Japan, and Australia in 1871 and 1872, to Latin America in 1872 and 1873, to East and South Africa in 1879, and to West Africa in 1886. By the turn of the century, cables connected every country and almost every inhabited island. As the public and the press extolled the "annihilation of time and space" (see the Environment and Technology feature in Chapter 24), cables became the indispensable tools of modern shipping and business.

Railroads

By 1850 the first **railroads** had proved so successful that every industrializing country, and many that aspired to become industrial, began to build lines. The next fifty years saw a tremendous expansion of the world's rail networks. After a rapid spurt of building new lines, British railroad mileage leveled off at around 20,000 miles (over 32,000 kilometers) in the 1870s. France and Germany built networks longer than Britain's, as did Canada and Russia. When Japan began building its railway network in the 1870s, it imported several hundred engineers from the United States and

Britain. In the 1880s, it replaced them with newly trained Japanese engineers. By the early twentieth century, rail lines reached every city and province in Japan (see Map 28.1).

The largest rail network by far was the rail network of the United States. At the end of its Civil War in 1865, the United States already had 35,000 miles (over 56,000 kilometers) of track, three times as much as Britain. By 1915, the American network reached 390,000 miles (around 628,000 kilometers), more than the next seven longest networks combined.

Railroads were not confined to the industrialized nations; they could be constructed almost anywhere they would be of value to business or government. That included regions with abundant raw materials or agricultural products, like South Africa, Mexico, or Argentina, and densely populated countries like Egypt. The British built the fourth largest rail network in the world in India in order to reinforce their presence and develop trade with their largest colony (see Chapter 26).

Railroads consumed huge amounts of land. Many old cities doubled in size to accommodate railroad stations, sidings, tracks, warehouses, and repair shops. In the countryside, railroads required bridges, tunnels, and embankments. Railroads also consumed vast quantities of timber for ties to hold the rails and for bridges, often using up whole forests for miles on either side of the tracks. Throughout the world, they opened new land to agriculture, mining, and other human exploitation of natural resources, whether for the benefit of the local inhabitants, as in Europe and North America, or for a distant power, as in the colonial empires.

World Trade and Finance

Between 1850 and 1913 world trade expanded tenfold. Because steamships were much more efficient than sailing ships, the cost of freight dropped between 50 and 95 percent, making it worthwhile to ship even cheap and heavy products halfway around the world. Europe imported wheat from the United States and India, wool from Australia, and beef from Argentina, and exported coal, railroad equipment, textiles, and machinery.

The growth of world trade transformed the economies of different parts of the world in different ways. The economics of western Europe and North America, the first to industrialize, grew more prosperous and diversified. Their capitalist economies, however, were prey to sudden swings in the business cycle—booms followed by deep depressions in which workers lost their jobs and investors their fortunes. For example, because of the close

Map 28.1   Expansion and Modernization of Japan, 1868–1918   As Japan acquired modern industry, it followed the example of the European powers in seeking overseas colonies. Its colonial empire grew at the expense of its neighbors: Taiwan was taken from China in 1895. Karafutu (now Sakhalin) from Russia in 1905, and all of Korea became a colony in 1910.

connections among the industrial economies, the collapse of a bank in Austria in 1873 triggered a depression that spread to the United States, causing mass unemployment. Worldwide recessions occurred in the mid-1880s and mid-1890s as well.

In the late 1870s and early 1880s, Germany, the United States, and other late-industrializing Western nations raised tariffs to protect their industries from British

competition. Yet trade barriers could not insulate them from the business cycle, for money continued to flow almost unhindered around the world. One of the main causes of the growing interdependence of the global economy was the financial power of Great Britain. Long after German and American industries surpassed the British, Britain continued to dominate the flow of trade, finance, and information. In 1900 two-thirds of the world's submarine cables were British or passed through Britain. Over half of the world's shipping was British owned. Britain invested one-fourth of its national wealth overseas, much of it in the United States and Argentina. British money financed many of the railroads, harbors, mines, and other big projects outside Europe. While other currencies fluctuated, the pound sterling was as good as gold, and nine-tenths of international transactions used sterling.

Nonindustrial areas also were tied to the world economy as never before. They were more vulnerable to changes in price and demand than were the industrialized nations, for many of them produced raw materials that could be replaced by synthetic substitutes or alternative sources of supply. Even products in constant demand, like Cuban sugar or Bolivian tin, were subject to wild swings in price on the world market. Nevertheless, until World War I, the value of exports from the tropical countries generally remained high, and the size of their populations remained moderate.

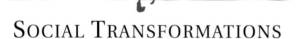

SOCIAL TRANSFORMATIONS

The technological and economic changes of the late nineteenth century sparked profound social changes in the industrial nations. A fast-growing population swelled cities to unprecedented size, and millions of Europeans emigrated to the Americas. Strained relations between industrial employers and workers spawned labor movements and new forms of radical policies. And women found their lives dramatically altered.

Population and Migrations

The population of Europe grew faster from 1850 to 1914 than ever before or since, almost doubling from 265 million to 468 million. In non-European countries with predominantly white populations—the United States, Canada, Australia, New Zealand, and Argentina—the increase was even greater because of the inflow of Europeans. There were many reasons for the mass migrations of this period: the Irish famine of 1847–1848; the persecution of Jews in Russia; poverty and population growth in Italy, Spain, Poland, and Scandinavia; and the cultural ties between Great Britain and English-speaking countries overseas. Equally important was the availability of cheap and rapid steamships and railroads serving travelers at

both ends (see Environment and Technology: Railroads and Immigration). Between 1850 and 1900, on average, 400,000 Europeans migrated overseas every year; between 1900 and 1914 the flood rose to over 1 million a year. From 1850 to 1910 the population of the United States and Canada rose from 25 million to 98 million, nearly a fourfold increase. The proportion of people of European ancestry in the world's population rose from one-fifth to one-third.

Why did the number of Europeans and their descendants overseas jump so dramatically? Much of the increase came from a drop in the death rate, as epidemics and starvation became less common. The Irish famine was the last peacetime famine in European history. As farmers plowed up the plains of North America and planted wheat, much of which was shipped to Europe, food supplies increased faster than the population. Fertilizers boosted crop yields, and canning and refrigeration made food abundant year-round. The diet of Europeans and North Americans improved as meat, fruit, vegetables, and oils became part of the daily fare of city dwellers, in winter as well as summer.

Asians also migrated in large numbers during this period, often as indentured laborers recruited to work on plantations, in mines, and on railroads. Indians went mainly to Africa, Southeast Asia, and other tropical colonies of Great Britain. Chinese emigrated to Southeast Asia and the East Indies. Many Chinese, as well as Japanese and Filipinos, went to Hawaii and California, where they encountered growing hostility from Europeans.

Urbanization and Social Structures

In 1851 Britain became the first nation to have a majority of its population living in towns and cities. By 1914, 80 percent of its population was urban, as were 60 percent of the German and 45 percent of the French populations. Cities grew to unprecedented size. London grew from 2.7 million in 1850 and to 6.6 million in 1900. New York, a small town of 64,000 people in 1800, reached 3.4 million by 1900, a fiftyfold increase. Population growth and the building of railroads and industries allowed cities to invade the countryside, swallowing nearby towns and villages. In 1800 New York had covered only the southernmost quarter of Manhattan Island, some 3 miles (nearly 8 square kilometers); by 1900 it covered 150 square miles (390 square kilometers). London in 1800 measured about 4 square miles (about 10 square kilometers); by 1900 it covered twenty times more area. In the English Midlands, in the German Ruhr, and around Tokyo Bay, towns

Urban Growth: Vienna in 1873   During the nineteenth century, European cities grew with unprecedented speed. This bird's-eye view of the Austro-Hungarian capital shows the transformation. The densely populated inner city surrounded the cathedral. In 1857 high walls that once had protected the old city from attack were torn down to make room for the Ringstrasse, a broad, tree-shaded boulevard lined with public buildings, museums, churches, and a university. Beyond the Ring, the newly wealthy bourgeoisie built new neighborhoods of large houses and apartment buildings.   (Museen der Stadt, Vienna)

fused into one another, filling in the fields and woods that once had separated them.

As cities grew, they changed in character. Newly built railroads not only brought goods into the cities on a predictable schedule but also allowed people to live farther apart. At first, only the well-to-do could afford to commute by train; by the end of the century, electric streetcars and subways allowed working-class people to live miles from their workplaces.

In preindustrial and early industrial cities, the poor crowded together in tenements, sanitation was bad, water often was contaminated with sewage, and darkness made life dangerous. New urban technologies transformed city life for all but the poorest residents. The most important change was the installation of pipes to bring in clean water and to carry away sewage. First gas lighting and then electric lighting made cities safer and more pleasant at night. By the turn of the century, municipal governments provided police and fire depart-

ments, sanitation and garbage removal, building and health inspection, schools, parks, and other amenities unheard of a century earlier.

As sanitation improved, epidemics became rare. For the first time, urban death rates fell below birthrates. The decline in infant mortality was especially significant. Confident that their children would survive infancy, couples began to limit the number of children they had, and ancient scourges like infanticide and child abandonment became less frequent. By the beginning of the twentieth century, middle- and even working-class couples began using contraceptives.

To accommodate the growing population, builders created new neighborhoods, from crowded tenements for the poor to opulent mansions for the newly rich. In the United States, planners laid out new cities, such as Chicago, on a rectangular grid, and middle-class families moved to new developments on the edges of cities. In Paris, older neighborhoods with narrow crooked streets

Railroads and Immigration

Why did so many Europeans emigrate to North America in the late nineteenth and early twentieth centuries? The quick answer is, They wanted to. Millions of people longed to escape the poverty or tyranny of their home countries and start a new life in a land of freedom and opportunity. Personal desire alone, however, does not account for the migrations. After all, poverty and tyranny existed long before the late nineteenth century. Two other factors helped determine when and where people migrated: whether they were allowed to migrate and whether they were able to.

In the nineteenth century, Asians were recruited to build railroads and work on farms. But from the 1890s on, the United States and Canada closed their doors to non-Europeans, so regardless of what they wanted, they could not move to North America. In contrast, emigrants from Europe were admitted until after the First World War.

The ability to travel was a result of improvements in transportation. Until the 1890s, most immigrants came from Ireland, England, or Germany—countries with good rail transportation to their own harbors and low steamship fares to North America. As rail lines were extended into eastern and southern Europe, more and more immigrants came from Italy, Austria-Hungary, and Russia.

Similarly, until the 1870s most European immigrants to North America settled on the east coast. Then, as the railroads pushed west, more of them settled on farms in the central and western parts of the continent. The power of railroads moved people as much as their desires did.

Emigrant Waiting Room   The opening of the western region of the United States attracted settlers from the east coast and from Europe. These migrants are waiting for a train to take them to the Black Hills of Dakota during one of the gold rushes of the late nineteenth century.   (Library of Congress)

and rickety tenements were replaced with broad boulevards and modern apartment buildings. Brilliantly lit by gas and electricity, Paris became the "city of lights," a model for city planners from New Delhi to Buenos Aires. The rich continued to live in inner cities that contained the monuments, churches, and palaces of preindustrial times, while workers moved to the outskirts.

Lower population densities and better transportation divided cities into industrial, commercial, and residential zones occupied by different social classes. Improvements such as water and sewerage, electricity, and streetcars always benefited the wealthy first, then the middle class, and finally the working class. In the complex of urban life, businesses of all kinds arose, and the professions—engineering, accounting, research, journalism, the law, among others—took on increased importance. The new middle class exhibited its wealth in fine houses, servants, and elegant entertainment.

In fast-growing cities such as London, New York, or Chicago, newcomers arrived so quickly that housing construction and municipal services could not keep up. Immigrants who saved their money to reunite their families could not afford costly municipal services. As a result, the poorest neighborhoods remained as overcrowded, unhealthy, and dangerous as they had been since the early decades of industrialization.

While urban environments improved in many ways, air quality worsened. Coal, burned to power steam engines and heat buildings, polluted the air, creating unpleasant and sometimes dangerous "pea-soup" fog and coating everything with a film of grimy dust. And the thousands of horses that pulled the carts and carriages covered the streets with their wastes, causing a terrible stench.

Labor Movements and Socialist Politics

Industrialization combined with the revolutionary ideas of the late eighteenth century to produce two kinds of movements —socialism and labor movements—calling for further changes. **Socialism** was an ideology developed by radical thinkers who questioned the sanctity of private property and argued in support of industrial workers against their employers. **Labor unions** were organizations formed by industrial workers to defend their interests in negotiations with employers. The socialist and labor movements were never identical. Most of the time they were allies; occasionally they were rivals.

Since the beginning of the nineteenth century, workers had united to create "friendly societies" for mutual assistance in times of illness, unemployment, or

disability. Anticombination laws, however, forbade workers to strike. These laws were abolished in Britain in the 1850s and in the rest of Europe in subsequent decades. Labor unions sought not only better wages but also improved working conditions and insurance against illness, accidents, disability, and old age. They grew slowly because they required a permanent staff and a great deal of money to sustain their members during strikes. By the end of the century, British labor unions counted 2 million members, and German and American unions had a million members each.

Socialism began as an intellectual movement. By far the best-known socialist was **Karl Marx** (1818–1883), a German journalist and writer who lived most of his life in England. He combined German philosophy, French revolutionary ideas, and knowledge of British industrial conditions. He expressed his ideas succinctly in the *Communist Manifesto* (1848) and in great detail in *Das Kapital*° (1867). He argued that the capitalist system allowed the bourgeoisie (the owners of businesses and factories) to extract the "surplus value" of workers' labor—that is, the difference between workers' wages and the value of the goods they manufactured. He saw business enterprises becoming larger and more monopolistic and workers growing more numerous and impoverished with every downturn in the business cycle.

Marx provided an intellectual framework for the growing dissatisfaction with raw industrial capitalism. In the late nineteenth century, business tycoons spent money lavishly on mansions, yachts, private railroad cars, and other displays of wealth that contrasted sharply with the poverty of the workers. Even though industrial workers were not becoming poorer as Marx believed, the class struggle between workers and employers was brutally real. What Marx did was to offer a persuasive explanation of the causes of this contrast and the antagonisms it bred.

Marx was not just a philosopher; he also made a direct impact on politics. In 1864 he helped found the International Working Man's Association (later known as the First International), a movement he hoped would bring about the overthrow of the bourgeoisie. However, it attracted more intellectuals than workers. Workers found other means of redressing their grievances, such as the vote and labor unions.

Just as labor unions strove to enable workers to share in the benefits of a capitalist economy, so did electoral politics persuade workers to become part of the existing political system instead of seeking to overthrow it. The nineteenth century saw a gradual extension of the

Das Kapital (DUSS cop-ee-TALL)

right to vote throughout Europe and North America. Universal male suffrage became law in the United States in 1870, in France and Germany in 1871, in Britain in 1885, and in the rest of Europe soon thereafter. With universal male suffrage, socialist politicians could expect to capture many seats in their nations' parliaments, because the newly enfranchised working class was so numerous. The goal of the socialists was to use their voting power to gain concessions from government and eventually even to win elections.

The classic case of socialist electoral politics is the Social Democratic Party of Germany. Founded in 1875 with a revolutionary socialist program, within two years it won a half-million votes and several seats in the Reichstag° (the lower house of the German parliament). Through superb organizing efforts and important concessions wrung from the government, the party grew fast, by 1912 garnering 4.2 million votes and winning more seats in the Reichstag than any other party. In pursuit of electoral success, the Social Democrats became more reformist and less radical. By joining the electoral process, they abandoned the idea of violent revolution.

Working-class women, burdened with both job and family responsibilities, found little time for politics and were not welcome in the male-dominated trade unions or radical political parties. A few radical women, such as the anarchist Emma Goldman in the United States and the German socialist Rosa Luxemburg, became famous but never had a large following. It was never easy to reconcile the demands of workers and those of women. In 1889 the German socialist Clara Zetkin wrote: "Just as the male worker is subjected by the capitalist, so is the woman by the man, and she will always remain in subjugation until she is economically independent. Work is the indispensable condition for economic independence." Six years later, she added: "The proletarian woman cannot attain her highest ideal through a movement for the equality of the female sex, she attains salvation only through the fight for the emancipation of labor".[1]

Working-Class Women and Men

The lives of middle-class women in the Victorian Age were a mixture of luxury and discrimination, but working-class women led lives of toil and pain, considerably harder than the lives of their menfolk. Although the worst abuses of child labor had been banned in most European countries by 1850, parents expected girls as young as ten to contribute to the household. Many be-

came domestic servants, commonly working sixteen or more hours a day, six and a half days a week, for little more than room and board. Their living quarters, usually in the attic or basement, contrasted with the luxurious quarters of their masters. Without appliances, much of their work was physically hard: hauling coal and water up stairs, washing laundry by hand.

Female servants were vulnerable to sexual abuse by their masters or their masters' sons. A well-known case is that of Helene Demuth, who worked for Karl and Jenny Marx all her life. At age thirty-one she bore a son by Karl Marx and put him with foster parents rather than leave the family. She was more fortunate than most, for most families fired a servant who got pregnant, rather than embarrass the master of the house.

Young women often preferred work in a factory to domestic service. Here, too, Victorian society practiced a strict division of labor by gender. Men worked in construction, iron and steel, heavy machinery, or on railroads; women worked in textiles and the clothing trades, two extensions of traditional women's household work. Appalled by the abuses of women and children in the early years of industrialization, most industrial countries passed protective legislation limiting the hours or forbidding the employment of women in the hardest and most dangerous occupations, such as mining and foundry work. Such legislation limited abuses but also reinforced gender divisions in industry, keeping women in low-paid, subordinate positions. Denied access to the better-paid jobs of foremen or machine repairmen, female factory workers earned, on average, between one-third and two-thirds of men's wages.

Married women with children were expected to stay home, even if their husbands did not make enough to support the family. Most married women of the working class had double responsibilities within the home: not only the work of child rearing and housework but also that of contributing to the family's income. Families who had room to spare, even a bed or a corner in the kitchen, took in boarders. Many women did piecework such as sewing dresses, making lace, hats, or gloves, or weaving baskets. The hardest and worst-paid work was washing other people's clothes. Often women worked at home ten to twelve hours a day and enlisted the help of their small children, perpetuating practices long outlawed in factories. Since electric lighting and indoor plumbing cost more than most working-class families could afford, even ordinary household duties like cooking and washing remained heavy burdens.

The poorest of the poor were orphans and single women with children. Unable to find jobs or support themselves at home, many turned to prostitution. The

Reichstag (RIKES-tog)

wealth of middle-class men made it easy for them to take advantage of the poverty of working-class women.

The Victorian Age and Women's "Separate Sphere"

In English-speaking countries, the period from about 1850 to 1914 is known as the **"Victorian Age."** The expression refers not only to the reign of Queen Victoria of England (r. 1837–1901) but to rules of behavior and to an ideology surrounding the family and the relations between men and women. The Victorians emphasized the differences between people more than their common humanity: white skin versus dark skin, rich versus poor, male versus female. They stressed the romantic aspects of love and marriage and both partners' duty to family and religious values. They contrasted the masculine ideals of strength and courage with the feminine virtues of beauty and kindness, and they idealized the home as a peaceful and loving refuge from the dog-eat-dog world of competitive capitalism. Although Victorian ideas contained elements of racism, sexism, and class discrimination, they were widely and sincerely felt at the time and have had an enormous impact on Western gender relations ever since.

Victorian morality claimed to be universal, yet it best fit the European upper- and middle-class family. Men and women were thought to belong in **"separate spheres."** Successful businessmen spent their time at work or relaxing in men's clubs. They put their wives in charge of rearing the children, running the household, and spending the family money to enhance the family's social status.

The word *lady*, once the feminine equivalent of *lord*, came to mean the wife of a *gentleman*, a member of the genteel bourgeoisie. As the Englishwoman Margaretta Greg explained in 1853: "A lady, to be such, must be a mere lady. She must not work for profit, or engage in any occupation that money can command, lest she invade the rights of the working classes, who live by their labour."

Before electric appliances, however, a middle-class home demanded enormous amounts of work. Not only were families larger, but middle-class couples entertained often and lavishly. To carry out all these tasks required servants. A family's status and the activities and lifestyle of the "mistress of the house" depended on the availability of servants to help her with the household tasks. Only families that employed at least one full-time servant were considered middle class.

Toward the turn of the century, modern technology began to transform middle-class homes. Plumbing eliminated the pump and the outhouse. Central heating replaced fireplaces, stoves, trips to the basement for coal, and endless dusting. Gas and electricity lit houses and cooked food without soot, smoke, and ashes. By the early twentieth century, a few wealthy families acquired the first vacuum cleaners and washing machines. Did these technological advances mean less housework for women? Not right away. As families acquired new household technologies, they raised their standards of cleanliness, thus demanding just as much labor as before.

The most important duty of middle-class women was rearing children. Unlike the rich of previous eras, who handed their children over to wet nurses and tutors, Victorian mothers nursed their own babies and showered their children with love and attention. Even those who could afford nannies and governesses remained personally involved in their children's education. However, girls received an education very different from that of boys. While boys were being prepared for the business world or the professions, girls were taught such skills as embroidery, drawing, and music, which offered no monetary reward or professional preparation but enhanced their social graces and marriage prospects.

Governments enforced legal discrimination against women. Until the end of the century, most European countries considered women minors for life—that is, subject to their fathers before marriage and to their husbands after. Even Britain, among the most progressive countries, did not give women the right to control their own property until 1882, with passage of the Married Women's Property Act.

Victorian morality frowned on careers for middle-class women. Young women could work until they got married, but only in genteel occupations such as retail and office work, never in factories. When the typewriter and telephone were introduced into the business world in the 1880s, only men could use these "high-technology" devices. Soon, however, businessmen found they could get better work at lower wages from educated young women, and operating these machines was typecast as women's work.

Jobs that required higher education, especially jobs in the professions, were closed to women. Until late in the century, few universities granted degrees to women. In the United States women's higher education was restricted to elite colleges like Smith, Wellesley, and Radcliffe in the east and to teachers' colleges in the midwest. European women had fewer opportunities. Before 1914 very few women became doctors, lawyers, or professional musicians.

The first profession open to women was teaching, as more and more countries passed laws calling for

Demonstrating for Women's Rights

Before the First World War, no country allowed all women to vote. In Britain, women who demonstrated for voting rights were known as "suffragettes." When petitions to Parliament and peaceful demonstrations had no effect, Emmeline Pankhurst, the leader of the movement, concluded that more forceful measures were required. In the following passage, she describes the tactics she devised to call attention to the cause of women's suffrage.

Whatever preparations the police department were making to prevent the demonstration, they failed because, while as usual, we were able to calculate exactly what the police department were going to do, they were utterly unable to calculate what we were able to do. We had planned a demonstration for March 4th, and this one we announced. We planned another demonstration for March 1st, but this one we did not announce. Late on the afternoon of Friday, March 1st, I drove in a taxicab, accompanied by the Hon. Secretary of the Union, Mrs. Tuke and another of our members, to No. 10 Downing Street, the official residence of the Prime Minister. It was exactly half past five when we alighted from the cab and threw our stones, four of them, through the window panes. As we expected we were promptly arrested and taken to Cannon Row police station. The hour that followed will long be remembered in London. At intervals of fifteen minutes relays of women who had volunteered for the demonstration did their work. The first smashing of glass occurred in the Haymarket and Picadilly, and greatly startled and alarmed both pedestrians and police. A large number of women were arrested, and everybody thought that this ended the affair. But before the excited populace and the frustrated shop owners' first exclamation had died down, before the police had reached the station with their prisoners, the ominous crashing and splintering of plate glass began again, this time along both sides of Regent Street and the Strand. A furious rush of police and people toward the second scene of action ensued. While their attention was taken up with occurrences in this quarter, the third relay of women began breaking the windows in Oxford Circus and Bond Street. The demonstration ended for the day at half past six with the breaking of many windows in the Strand. . . .

The demonstration had taken place in the morning, when a hundred or more women had walked quietly into Knightsbridge and walking singly along the streets demolished nearly every pane of glass they passed. Taken by surprise the police arrested as many as they would reach, but most of the women escaped.

For that two days' work something like two hundred suffragettes were taken to the various police stations, and for days the long procession of women streamed through the courts.

If the goal was to obtain the right to vote, why did the demonstrators break store windows? And why did they do so at fifteen-minute intervals?

Source: Emmeline Pankhurst, *My Own Story* (London, 1914), 211–219.

---

universal compulsory education. By 1911, for instance, 73 percent of all teachers in England were women. They were considered well suited to teaching young children and girls—an extension of the duties of Victorian mothers. Teaching, however, was judged suitable only for single women. Married women were expected to get pregnant right away and stay home taking care of their own children rather than the children of other people. In 1901, Mary Murphy, a teacher with ten years' experience, was charged with misconduct and fired from her teaching job in a Brooklyn school when she got married. After a three-year legal battle, a judge ruled that marriage was not misconduct, and she was reinstated with back pay.

A home life, no matter how busy, did not satisfy all middle-class women. Some became volunteer nurses or social workers, receiving little or no pay. Others organized to fight prostitution, alcohol, and child labor. By the turn of the century, a few were challenging male domination of politics and the law. Women suffragists, let in Britain by Emmeline Pankhurst and in the United States by Elizabeth Cady Stanton and Susan B. Anthony, demanded the right to vote. The more radical used violent tactics such as breaking windows, setting fire to

Emmeline Pankhurst Under Arrest   The leader of the British woman suffrage movement frequently called attention to her cause by breaking the law to protest discrimination against women. Here she is being arrested and carried off to jail by the police.   (Mary Evans Picture Library)

houses, or throwing themselves under horses' hoofs. (See Society and Culture: Demonstrating for Women's Rights). By 1914, women had won the right to vote in twelve states of the United States. British women did not vote until 1918.

NATIONALISM AND THE UNIFICATION OF GERMANY

The most influential idea of the nineteenth century was **nationalism**. The French revolutionaries had defined people, previously considered the subjects of a sovereign, as the citizens of a *nation*—a concept identified with a territory, the state that ruled it, and the culture of its people. Because the most widely spoken language in nineteenth-century Europe was German, the unification of most German-speaking people into a single state in 1871 had momentous consequences for the world.

Language and National Identity Before 1871

Language was usually the crucial element in creating a feeling of national unity. It was important both as a way to unite the people of a nation and as the means of persuasion by which political leaders could inspire their followers. Language was the tool of the new generation of political activists, most of them lawyers, teachers, students, and journalists. Yet language and citizenship seldom coincided.

The fit between France and the French language was exceptional. The Italian- and German-speaking peoples were divided among many small states. Living in the Austrian Empire were peoples who spoke German, Czech, Slovak, Hungarian, Polish, and other languages. Even where people spoke a common language, they could be divided by religion or institutions. The Irish, though English-speaking, were mostly Catholic, whereas the English were primarily Protestant; and in the United States, the issue of slavery divided the south from the north, creating a southern identity.

The idea of redrawing the boundaries of states to accommodate linguistic, religious, or cultural differences was revolutionary. In Italy and Germany, in 1871, it led to the forging of large new states out of many small ones. In central and eastern Europe, nationalism threatened to break up large states into smaller ones.

Until the 1860s, nationalism was associated with **liberalism,** the revolutionary middle-class ideology that emerged from the French Revolution (see Chapter 23) and asserted the sovereignty of the people and demanded constitutional government, a national parliament, and freedom of expression. The most famous nationalist of the early nineteenth century was the Italian liberal Giuseppe Mazzini° (1805–1872), the leader of the failed revolution of 1848 in Italy. Mazzini not only sought to unify the Italian peninsula into one nation but associated with like-minded revolutionaries elsewhere to bring nationhood and liberty to all peoples oppressed by tyrants and foreigners. Although the governments of Russia, Prussia, and Austria censored the new ideas, they could not be quashed. To staff bureaucracies and police forces to maintain law and order, even conservative regimes required educated personnel, and education

Giuseppe Mazzini (jew-SEP-pay mots-EE-nee)

meant universities, the seedbed of new ideas transmitted by a national language.

Although the revolutions of 1848 failed except in France (see Chapter 23), the strength of the revolutionary movements convinced conservatives that governments could not forever keep their citizens out of politics, and that mass politics, if properly managed, could strengthen rather than weaken the state. A new generation of conservative political leaders learned how to preserve the social status quo through public education, universal military service, and colonial conquests, all of which built a sense of national unity.

The Unification of Germany

Until the 1860s, the region of Central Europe where people spoke German (the former Holy Roman Empire) consisted of Prussia, the western half of the Austrian Empire, and numerous smaller states. Some German nationalists wanted to unite all Germans under the Austrian throne.

Others wanted to exclude Austria with its many non-Germanic peoples and unite all other German-speaking areas under Prussia. The divisions were also religious: Austria and southwestern Germany were Catholic; Prussia and the northeast were Lutheran. The Prussian state had two advantages: (1) the newly developed industries of the Rhineland and (2) the first European army to make use of railroads, telegraphs, breechloading rifles, steel artillery, and other products of modern industry.

The king of Prussia, Wilhelm I (r. 1861–1888), had entrusted the running of his government to his chancellor, the brilliant and authoritarian aristocrat **Otto von Bismarck** (1815–1898). Bismarck was determined to use Prussian industry and German nationalism to advance the interests of the Prussian state. In 1864, after a quick victory against Denmark, he set his sights higher.

In 1866 Prussia defeated Austria. To everyone's surprise, Prussia took no Austrian territory. Instead, Prussia and some smaller states formed the North German Confederation, the nucleus of a future Germany. Then in 1870, confident that Austria would not hinder him,

Wilhelm I Proclaimed Emperor of Germany   On January 18, 1871, Prussia and the smaller states of Germany united to form the German Reich (empire). King Wilhelm I of Prussia was proclaimed kaiser (emperor) as his chancellor, Otto von Bismarck (in a white jacket), and dozens of generals and lesser princes cheered. The ceremony took place in the Great Hall of Mirrors in the palace of Versailles, near Paris, to mark Prussia's stunning victory over France.   (Bismarck Museum, Friedrichsruh)

Bismarck provoked with France the war known as the "Franco-Prussian War." Prussian armies, joined by troops from southern as well as northern Germany, used their superior firepower and tactics to achieve a quick victory.

The spoils of victory included a large indemnity and two provinces of France bordering on Germany: Alsace and Lorraine. The French paid the indemnity easily enough but resented the loss of their provinces. To the Germans, this region was German because a majority of its inhabitants spoke German. To the French, it was French because it had been so when the nation of France was forged in the Revolution and because most of its inhabitants considered themselves French. These two conflicting definitions of nationalism kept enmity between France and Germany smoldering for decades. In this case, nationalism turned out to be a divisive rather than a unifying force.

Nationalism After 1871

The Franco-Prussian War of 1870–1871 changed the political climate of Europe. France became wholeheartedly liberal. The Italian peninsula became unified as the kingdom of Italy. Germany, Austria-Hungary (as the Austrian Empire had renamed itself in 1867), and Russia remained conservative and used nationalism to maintain the status quo.

All politicians tried to manipulate public opinion to bolster their governments. They were greatly aided by the press, especially cheap daily newspapers that sought to increase their circulation by publishing sensational articles about overseas conquests and foreign threats. As governments increasingly came to recognize the advantages of an educated population in the competition between states, they opened public schools in every town, opening public service jobs to women for the first time. The spread of literacy allowed politicians and journalists to appeal to the emotions of the poor, diverting their anger from their employers to foreigners and their votes from socialist to nationalist parties.

In many countries, the dominant group used nationalism to justify the imposing of its language, religion, or customs on minority populations. The Russian Empire attempted to "Russify" its diverse ethnic populations. The Spanish government made the Spanish language compulsory in the schools, newspapers, and courts of its Basque- and Catalan-speaking provinces. Immigrants to the United States were expected to learn English, to safeguard national unity.

Nationalism soon spread to other continents (see Chapters 26, 27, and 32). By the 1880s signs of national consciousness appeared in Egypt, Japan, India, and other non-Western countries, inspiring anti-Western and anti-colonial movements.

Western culture in the late nineteenth century exalted the powerful over the weak, men over women, rich over poor, Europeans over other races, and humans over nature. Some people looked to science for support of political dominance. One of the most influential scientists of the century, and the one whose ideas were most widely cited and misinterpreted, was the English biologist **Charles Darwin** (1809–1882).

As a young man, Darwin spent several years traveling through South America and the South Pacific studying plant and animal life. On his return to England, he published his explanation for the great variety of natural life forms he had seen. In *On the Origin of Species by Means of Natural Selection* (1859), he showed that the earth was extremely old and that over hundreds of thousands of years living beings had either evolved in the struggle for survival or become extinct.

The philosopher Herbert Spencer (1820–1903) and others took up Darwin's ideas of "natural selection" and "survival of the fittest" and applied them to human society. Extreme Social Darwinists developed elaborate pseudo-scientific theories of racial differences, claiming that they were the result not of history but of biology. If Europeans had conquered empires in Asia and Africa, if men had more political power than women, if workers earned less than the well-to-do, they argued, these differences must have "natural" causes. Although not based on any research, these ideas became very popular at the turn of the century, for they gave a scientific-sounding justification for the power of the privileged.

THE GREAT POWERS OF EUROPE, 1871–1900

After 1871, politicians and journalists discovered how easily they could whip up popular frenzy against neighboring countries. Military officers, impressed by the awesome power of the weapons that industry provided, began to think these weapons were invincible. Rivalries over colonial territories, ideological differences between liberal and conservative governments, and even minor border incidents or trade disagreements contributed to a growing atmosphere of international tension.

Germany at the Center of Europe

International relations revolved around a united Germany, because Germany was located in the center of Europe and had the most powerful army on the European continent. After creating a unified Germany in 1871, Bismarck declared that his country had no further territorial ambitions and put his effort into maintaining the peace in Europe. It isolate France, the only country with a grudge against Germany, he forged a loose coalition with Austria-Hungary and Russia, the other two conservative powers. Despite the competing ambitions of Austria and Russia in the Balkans, he was able to keep his coalition together for twenty years.

Bismarck proved equally adept at manipulating mass politics at home. To weaken the influence of middle-class liberals, he extended the vote to all adult men. By imposing high tariffs on manufactured goods and wheat, he gained the support of both the wealthy industrialists of the Rhineland and the great landowners of eastern Germany, traditional rivals for power. He stole the thunder of the socialists by introducing social legislation—medical, unemployment, and disability insurance and old-age pensions—long before other industrial countries. Under his leadership, the German people developed a strong sense of national unity and pride in their industrial and military power.

In 1888 Wilhelm I was succeeded by his grandson Wilhelm II (r. 1888–1918), a vulgar, insecure, and arrogant man who tried to gain respect by using bullying tactics. Within two years he had dismissed Chancellor Bismarck and surrounded himself with yes men and flatterers. Whereas Bismarck had shown little interest in acquiring colonies overseas, Wilhelm II talked about his "global policy" and demanded a colonial empire. Ruler of the nation with the mightiest army and the largest industrial economy in Europe, he felt that Germany deserved "a place in the sun."

The Liberal Powers: France and Great Britain

France, once the dominant nation in Europe, had difficulty reconciling itself to being in second place. Though a prosperous country with flourishing agriculture and a large colonial empire, the French republic had some serious weaknesses. Its population was scarcely growing; in 1911 France had only 39 million people compared to Germany's 64 million. In an age when the power of nations was roughly proportional to the size of their army, France could field an army only two-thirds the size of Germany's. Another weakness was the slow growth of French industry compared to Germany's, due to the loss of the iron and coal mines of Lorraine.

The French people were deeply divided over the very nature of the state: some were monarchists and Catholic; a growing number held republican and anticlerical views. These divisions came to a head at the turn of the century over the case of Captain Alfred Dreyfus, a Jewish officer falsely convicted of spying for the Germans in 1894. French society, even families, split between those who felt that reopening the case would only dishonor the army and those who believed that letting injustice go unchallenged dishonored the nation. The case reawakened the dormant anti-Semitism in French society. Not until 1906, after twelve painful years, was Dreyfus exonerated. Yet if French political life seemed fragile and frequently in crisis, a long tradition of popular participation in politics and a strong sense of nationhood, reinforced by a fine system of universal public education, gave the French people a deeper cohesion than appeared on the surface.

Great Britain was the only other country in Europe with a democratic tradition. The British government alternated smoothly between the Liberal and Conservative Parties, and the income gap between rich and poor gradually narrowed. Nevertheless, Britain had problems that grew more apparent as time went on.

One problem was Irish resentment of English rule. Nationalism had strengthened the allegiance of the English, Scots, and Welsh to the British crown and state. But the Irish, excluded because they were Catholic and predominantly poor, felt the British were a foreign occupying force.

Another problem was the British economy. Once the workshop of the world, Great Britain had fallen behind the United States and Germany in such important industries as iron and steel, chemicals, electricity, and textiles. Even in shipbuilding and shipping, Britain's traditional specialties, Germany was catching up.

Also, Britain was preoccupied with its enormous and fast-growing empire. A source of wealth for investors and the envy of other imperialist nations, the empire was also a constant drain on Britain's finances. The revolt of 1857 against British rule in India (see Chapter 26) was crushed with difficulty and kept British politicians worried thereafter. The empire required Britain to maintain several costly fleets of warships stationed throughout the world.

For most of the nineteenth century, Britain turned its back on Europe and pursued a policy of "splendid isolation." Only once, in 1854, did it intervene militarily in Europe, joining France in the Crimean War of 1854–1856 against Russia (see Chapter 27). Britain's preoccupation with India and the shipping routes through the

The Doss House   Late-nineteenth-century cities showed more physical than social improvements. This painting by Makovsky of a street in St. Petersburg contrasts the broad avenue and impressive new buildings with the poverty of the crowd.   (The State Russian Museum/Smithsonian Institution Traveling Exhibit)

Mediterranean led British statesmen to exaggerate the Russian threat to the Ottoman Empire and to the Central Asian approaches to India. Periodic "Russian scares" and Britain's age-old rivalry with France for overseas colonies diverted the attention of British politicians away from the rise of a large, powerful, united Germany.

The Conservative Powers: Russia and Austria-Hungary

The forces of nationalism weakened rather than strengthened Russia and Austria-Hungary. The reason for this effect was that their populations were far more divided, socially and ethnically, than were the German, French, or British peoples.

Nationalism was most divisive in south-central Europe, where many different language groups lived in close proximity. In 1867 the Austrian Empire's decision to rename itself the Austro-Hungarian Empire appeased its Hungarian critics but alienated its Slavic-speaking mi-

norities. The Austro-Hungarian Empire still thought of itself as a great power, but instead of seeking conquests in Asia or Africa, it attempted to dominate the Balkans. This strategy irritated Russia, which thought of itself as the protector of Slavic peoples everywhere. The Austrian annexation of the former Turkish province of Bosnia-Herzegovina in 1908 worsened relations between the Austro-Hungarian and Russian Empires. Festering quarrels over the Balkans—the "tinderbox of Europe"—eventually pushed Europe into war (see Chapter 30).

Ethnic diversity also contributed to the instability of imperial Russia. The Polish people, never reconciled to being annexed by Russia in the eighteenth century, rebelled in 1830 and 1863–1864. The tsarist empire also included Finland, Estonia, Lavia, Lithuania, and Ukraine, the very mixed peoples of the Caucasus, and the Muslim population of Central Asia conquered between 1865 and 1881. Furthermore, Russia had the largest Jewish population in Europe, despite the harshness of its anti-Semitic laws and periodic *pogroms* (massacres), which prompted many Jews to flee to America. All in all, only 45 percent of the peoples of the tsarist empire spoke Russian. This meant that Russian nationalism and the state's attempts to impose the Russian language on its subjects were divisive instead of unifying forces in the empire.

Russia was the most misunderstood country in Europe. Its enormous size and population led many Europeans to exaggerate its military potential, but France and Britain had easily defeated Russia in the Crimean War.

In 1861, the moderate conservative Tsar Alexander II (r. 1855–1881) emancipated the peasants from serfdom. He did so partly out of a genuine desire to strengthen the bonds between the monarchy and the Russian people, and partly to promote industrialization by enlarging the labor pool. That half-hearted measure, however, did not create a modern society on the western European model. It only turned serfs into communal farmers with few skills and little capital. Though technically "emancipated," the great majority of Russians had little education, few legal rights, and no say in their government. After Alexander's assassination in 1881, his successors Alexander III (r. 1881–1894) and Nicholas II (r. 1894–1917) opposed all forms of social change. Although the Russian government employed many bureaucrats and policemen, its commercial middle class was small and had little influence. Industrialization consisted largely of state-sponsored projects, such as railroads, iron foundries, and armament factories, and led to social unrest among urban workers. Wealthy landowning aristocrats continued to dominate the Russian court and administration and succeeded in blocking most reforms.

The weaknesses in Russia's society and government became glaringly obvious during a war with Japan in 1904 and 1905. The fighting in the Russo-Japanese War took place in Manchuria, a province in northern China far from European Russia. The Russian army, which received all its supplies by means of the inefficient Trans-Siberian Railway, was soon defeated by the better trained and equipped Japanese. The Russian navy, after a long journey around Europe, Africa, and Asia, was met and sunk by the Japanese fleet at the Battle of Tsushima Strait in 1905.

The shock of defeat caused a popular uprising, the Revolution of 1905, that forced Tsar Nicholas II to grant a constitution and an elected Duma (parliament). But as soon as he was able to rebuild the army and the police, he reverted to the traditional despotism of his forefathers. Small groups of radical intellectuals, angered by the contrast between the wealth of the elite and the poverty of the common people, began plotting the violent overthrow of the tsarist autocracy.

NEW GREAT POWERS: THE UNITED STATES AND JAPAN

Since the sixteenth century, Europeans had come to regard their continent as the center of the universe and their states as the only great powers in the world. The rest of the world was either ignored or used as bargaining chips in the game of power politics. The late nineteenth century marked the high point of European power and arrogance, as the nations of Europe, in a frenzy known as the "New Imperialism," rushed to gobble up the last remaining unclaimed pieces of the world (see Chapter 29).

Yet at that very moment two nations outside Europe were becoming great powers. One of them, the United States, was inhabited mainly by people of European origin, and its rise to great-power status had been predicted early in the nineteenth century by astute observers like the French statesman Alexis de Tocqueville. The other one, Japan, seemed so distant and exotic in 1850 that no European had guessed it would join the ranks of the great powers.

The United States, 1865–1900

After the Civil War ended in 1865, the United States entered a period of vigorous growth (see Chapter 25). Hundreds of thousands of immigrants arrived every year, mainly from Russia, Italy, and Central Europe, raising the population from 39 million in 1871 to 63 million in 1891, an increase of 62 percent. Although many settled on the newly opened lands west of the Mississippi (see Map 28.2), most of the migrants moved to the towns, which mushroomed into cities in a few years. Chicago, for example, grew fourfold, from 444,000 in 1870 to 1,700,000 in 1900. In the process, the nation became an industrial giant. The rail network, already the world's longest in 1865, multiplied eleven-fold by 1915, creating the largest single integrated market in the world. To make the rails, locomotives, bridges, and other material, industry produced 20 million tons of steel annually in 1900. By then the United States had overtaken Britain and Germany as the world's leading industrial power.

This explosive growth was accomplished with few government restrictions. In fact, in the last years of the nineteenth century, the federal state, and local governments seemed to be influenced by (if not in the pay of)

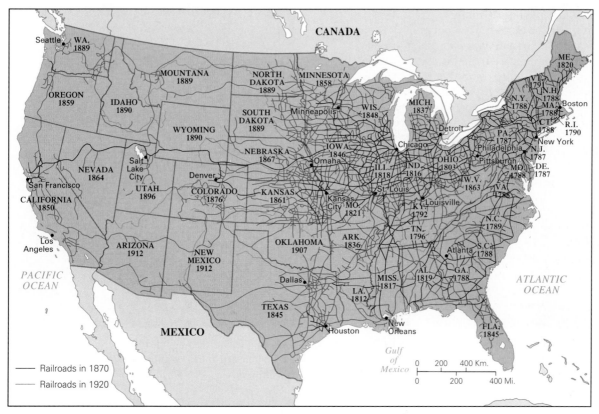

Map 28.2   The United States, 1850–1920   This map shows the expansion of the United States from the coasts into the interior of the continent. In the western half of the continent, only California and Texas were states in 1850; territories located further from the coasts became states later. The economic development, shown by the railroad lines, followed much the same pattern, radiating west and south from the northeastern states and—to a lesser extent—eastward from California.

the business sector, on which they lavished free land, tariffs, and other benefits. Giant monopolies, like John D. Rockefeller's Standard Oil Company, and steel and railroad trusts dominated American life. In this atmosphere of unfettered free enterprise, the nation got rich fast, as did its upper and middle classes.

Expansion created many victims. First among them were the American Indians. When the railroads penetrated the west after the Civil War, they brought white colonists eager to start farming, ranching, or mining. The indigenous Indians whose lands they invaded fought back with great courage but were outnumbered and outgunned. In Canada, the government tried to protect the Indians from the whites. The United States Army, however, always sided with the settlers. The U.S. government had signed numerous treaties with the Indians but tore them up when settlers demanded land. After decades of warfare, massacres, and starvation, the gov-

ernment confined the remaining Indians to reservations on the poorest lands.

The U.S. government also abandoned African-Americans in 1877, after the end of Reconstruction, especially in the defeated southern states. Though freed from slavery in 1865, most of them became sharecroppers who were at the mercy of their landowners. In the 1890s, the southern states instituted "Jim Crow" laws segregating blacks in public transportation, jobs, and schools. Not only did southern judges apply harsh laws in a biased manner, but black Americans were also subject to the lawless violence of mobs, which lynched an average of fifty blacks a year until well into the twentieth century.

Racism also affected Asian immigrants, many of whom had come to the United States to build railroads in the western states. In 1882 the U.S. government barred the Chinese from immigrating by enacting the first of many racial exclusion laws.

Deforestation   As European settlers moved into the forest regions of North America, they cut the trees for timber and to clear the land for farming. Much of Michigan, Wisconsin, and Ontario were deforested in this way. This picture shows a farmer contemplating his newly cleared land.   (State Historical Society of Wisconsin)

Working-class whites benefited little from the booming economy. Economic depressions in 1873 and 1893 caused more distress in the United States than in Europe, because the United States had few labor laws and no unemployment compensation to soften the hardships. Police or the army repressed strikes and unions. The courts consistently supported employers against their employees, capital against labor, and business against government.

Working-class women bore the brunt of repressive labor practices because they earned less than men, had more responsibilities, and seldom were members of labor unions. As in Britain, activist middle-class women organized to demand female suffrage and to fight against alcohol, prostitution, and other social evils.

The booming economy and the waves of immigrants radically transformed the environment. Timber companies clear-cut large areas of Michigan, Wisconsin, and the Appalachian Mountains to provide lumber for railroad ties and frame houses, pulp for paper, and fuel for locomotives and iron foundries. Farmers cleared the forests and plowed the prairies. Buffalo, the dominant animals of the western territories, were massacred by the hundreds of thousands to starve out the Indians and clear the land for cattle. In the west, the government be-

gan massive irrigation projects. In the industrial northeast, iron foundries, steel mills, and steam engines caused severe local air pollution.

In spite of all the assaults, the North American continent was so huge that large parts of it remained unspoiled. A few especially beautiful areas were declared national parks, beginning with Yellowstone in Wyoming in 1872, thereby marking a new state in Americans' attitude toward nature. Thanks to the efforts of naturalist John Muir and President Theodore Roosevelt (1901–1909), large parts of the western states were set aside as national forests.

Most citizens showed little interest in foreign affairs. Patriots tended to celebrate American freedom and democracy, the conquest of a huge continent, and the country's remarkable technological achievements. In this period, the inventor Thomas Edison was probably the most admired man in America.

The expansionism of the United States and its businesses did not stop at the borders but exerted a strong influence on Mexico and the Caribbean. Naval officers, bankers, and politicians urged active intervention in the Western Hemisphere. In 1899 the United States defeated Spain, annexed Puerto Rico and the Philippines, and turned Cuba into an American protectorate (see Chapter

29). Long recognized as the leading power in the Americas, the United States found itself involved in Asian affairs as well. Nevertheless, although their country was fast becoming a global power, most Americans still preferred George Washington's policy of "no European entanglements."

The Rise of Japan, 1868–1900

In the late nineteenth century, China and Japan—the two largest countries in East Asia—both felt the influence of the Western powers as never before, but their responses were completely opposite. China resisted Western influence and became weaker. Japan transformed itself into a major industrial and military power. One reason for this difference was the Western powers' heavy involvement in China and lack of strategic interest in Japan, the nation most remote from Europe by ship. But the contrast can mainly be attributed to the difference between the Chinese and Japanese elites and attitudes toward foreign cultures.

In the 1860s, China had not yet recovered from the Taiping° Rebellion (see Chapter 27), and the French and British took advantage of China's troubles to demand treaty ports where they could trade at will. The British took over China's customs and allowed the free import of opium until 1917. Foreign influence penetrated inland as well. By 1894, some two thousand Christian missionaries (many of them Americans) were founding churches, hospitals, and schools throughout the country, taking over the traditional role of the Chinese gentry. Though Christians had little success in gaining converts, the gentry resented their special privileges.

A Chinese "self-strengthening movement" tried in vain to bring about significant reforms by reducing government expenditures and eliminating corruption. The **Empress Dowager Cixi**° (r. 1862–1908) had once encouraged the construction of shipyards, arsenals, and telegraph lines. But now she opposed railways and other foreign technologies that could carry foreign influences to the interior. Government officials, who did not dare resist the Westerners outright, secretly encouraged crowds to attack and destroy the intrusive devices. They were able to slow the foreign intrusion, but in doing so, they denied themselves the best means of defense against foreign pressure.

In 1868, as we saw in Chapter 27, provincial rebels overthrew the Tokugawa Shogunate and proclaimed the "Meiji° Restoration," after the reign name (*Meiji* means

"enlightened rule") of the young Emperor Mutsuhito° (r. 1868–1912). From then until the early twentieth century, Japan was led by a remarkable group of men known as the Meiji oligarchs. Determined to protect their country from Western imperialism, they encouraged its transformation into a world-class industrial and military power. Although they claimed to be restoring the emperor to his rightful place at the head of the government, they used him as a figurehead, the embodiment of the nation in the national Shinto religion. Though imposed by an elite, the Meiji Restoration marked as profound a change as the French Revolution.

The new Japanese rulers, unlike the Chinese, were under no illusion that they could fend off the Westerners without changing their institutions or their society. In the Charter Oath issued in 1868, the young emperor included the prophetic phrase: "Knowledge shall be sought throughout the world and thus shall be strengthened the foundation of the imperial polity." It was to be the motto of a new Japan, which embraced all foreign ideas, institutions, and techniques that could strengthen the nation.

Japan had a long history of adopting ideas and patterns of culture from China and Korea; in the same spirit, the Japanese eagerly sought to learn the secrets of Western strength. To do so, the Japanese people had to acquire foreign knowledge. In the 1870s and 1880s, the government sent hundreds of students to Britain, Germany, and the United States and hired foreign experts to teach Japanese how to build railroads, organize a modern army and navy, and operate a bureaucracy.

The Meiji leaders created a government structure similar to that of imperial Germany. They introduced Western-style posts and telegraphs, railroads and harbors, banking, clocks, and calendars. They modeled the new Japanese navy on the British and the army on the Prussian. They even encouraged foreign clothing styles and pastimes.

The government was especially interested in Western technology. It opened vocational, technical, and agricultural schools and founded four imperial universities. It brought in foreign experts to advise on medicine, science, and engineering. At the newly created Imperial College of Engineering, an Englishman, William Ayrton, became the first professor of electrical engineering anywhere in the world. His students later went on to found major corporations and government research institutes.

The Japanese government also encouraged industrialization. It taxed farmers heavily to pay for the purchase of ships, machines, and other capital goods. It set up

---

Taiping (tie-PING) **Cixi** (TSEE-she) **Meiji** (MAY-gee)   **Mutsuhito** (moo-tsoo-HE-toe)

Yamagata Aritomo　As a young man, Yamagata had joined with other provincial leaders to overthrow the Tokugawa Shogunate in 1867–1868 and form a new government. He modernized Japan's army and remained a formidable force in Japanese policymaking until his death in 1922.　(Asahi Shimbun Photo)

state-owned enterprises to manufacture cloth and inexpensive consumer goods for sale abroad. The first Japanese industries, some of which had been founded in the early nineteenth century, exploited their workers ruthlessly, just as the first industries in Europe and America had done. Peasant families, squeezed by rising taxes and rents, often had to send their daughters to work in textile mills in a form of indentured servitude. In 1881, to pay off its debts, the government sold these enterprises to private investors, mainly large *zaibatsu°*, or conglomerates. But there was room for individual technological innovation as well. Thus the carpenter Toyoda Sakichi founded the Toyoda Loom Works (now Toyota Motor

Company) in 1906; ten years later, he patented the world's most advanced automatic loom.

In 1889 Japan promulgated a new and authoritarian constitution modeled on that of Germany, with a bicameral legislature and a cabinet led by a prime minister. But the army and navy remained free of civilian control, only wealthy men were allowed to vote, and important decisions were made without popular input or even knowledge.

By 1900 Japan was sufficiently westernized that the Western powers rescinded the unequal treaties they had imposed forty years earlier. The motive for the transformation of Japan was defensive—to protect the nation from the Western powers—but the methods that strengthened Japan against the imperial ambitions of others could also be used to carry out its own conquests. In 1876, having purchased some modern warships from Britain, Japan sent them to Korea to extort the same privileges the Westerners had obtained in Japan. This action provoked the intervention of China, which had long claimed suzerainty over Korea.

Japan's path to imperialism and independence was pointed out more vigorously by **Yamagata Aritomo.** As a young man he had been a leader of the anti-Tokugawa warriors who had effected the Meiji Restoration. In 1910 Yamagata was still leading the government. He believed that to be independent Japan had to define a "sphere of influence," to include Korea, Manchuria, and part of China. If Japan controlled this sphere, it would be secure. If other countries controlled it, Japan would be at risk. Yamagata insisted that in order to protect this sphere of influence Japan must sustain a vigorous program of military industrialization, culminating in the building of battleships. Yamagata was opposed to placing policy in the hands of a voting public, for he believed military budgets had to be protected from unpredictable political trends. He also feared popular nationalism, which could push the government into premature confrontation with dangerous imperialist powers.

Meanwhile, China was growing weaker as Japan grew stronger. In 1894, the two nations went to war. The Japanese defeated China in less than six months, forcing it to evacuate Korea, cede Taiwan and the Liaodong Peninsula, and pay a heavy indemnity. France, Germany, Britain, Russia, and the United States, upset at seeing a newcomer join the ranks of the imperialists, made Japan give up Liaodong in the name of the "territorial integrity" of China. In exchange for their "protection," the Western powers then made China grant them territorial and trade concessions, including ninety treaty ports.

In China, the humiliations suffered at the hands of Japan and the European powers led reformers around

zaibatsu (zye-BOT-soo)

Emperor Guangxu to press for changes inspired by the Meiji Restoration. The changes they introduced during the "Hundred Days of Reform" threatened the power and position of the Empress Dowager Cixi and the officials around her, however. In September 1898, Cixi had the emperor put under house arrest and the reforms rescinded.

In 1900, the officials who had seized power encouraged a series of antiforeign riots known as the Boxer Uprising. Military forces from the European powers, Japan, and the United States put down the riots and occupied Beijing. Emboldened by China's obvious weakness, Japan and Russia competed for possession of the mineral-rich Chinese province of Manchuria.

Japan's participation in the suppression of the Boxer Uprising demonstrated its military power in East Asia. In 1905 Japan surprised the world by defeating Russia in the Russo-Japanese War. In spite of Western attempts to restrict it to the role of junior partner, Japan continued to increase its influence. It gained control of southern Manchuria, with its industries and railroads, and established a protectorate over Korea. In 1910 it finally annexed Korea, joining the ranks of the world's colonial powers.

CONCLUSION

After World War I broke out in 1914, many people, especially in Europe, looked back on the period from 1850 to 1914 as a golden age. For some, and in certain ways, it was. Industrialization was a powerful torrent changing Europe, North America, and East Asia. While other technologies like shipping and railroads increased their global reach, new ones—electricity, the steel and chemical industries, and the global telegraph network—contributed to the enrichment and empowerment of the industrial nations. Memories of the great scourges—famines, wars, and epidemics—faded. Clean water, electric lights, and railways began to improve the lives of city dwellers, even the poor. Goods from distant lands, even travel to other continents, came within the reach of millions.

European and American society seemed to be heading toward better organization and greater security. Municipal services made city life less dangerous and chaotic. Through labor unions, workers achieved some measure of recognition and security. By the turn of the century, liberal political reforms had taken hold in western Europe and the United States and seemed about to triumph in Russia as well. Morality and legislation aimed at providing security for women and families, though equality between the sexes was still beyond reach.

The framework for all these changes was the nation-state. The world economy, international politics, even cultural and social issues revolved around a handful of countries—the great powers—that believed themselves in control of the destiny of the world. These included the most powerful European nations of the previous century, as well as two newcomers—the United States and Japan—that were to play important roles in the future. Seldom in history had there been such a concentration of wealth, power, and self-confidence.

The success of the great powers rested on their ability to extract resources from nature and from other societies, especially in Asia, Africa, and Latin America. In a global context, the counterpart of the rise of the great powers is the story of imperialism and colonialism. To complete our understanding of the period before 1914, let us turn now to the relations between the great powers and the rest of the world.

■ Key Terms

steel	Victorian Age
electricity	"separate spheres"
Thomas Edison	nationalism
submarine telegraph cables	liberalism
railroads	Otto von Bismarck
socialism	Charles Darwin
labor unions	Empress Dowager Cixi
Karl Marx	Yamagata Aritomo

■ Suggested Reading

More has been written on the great powers in the late nineteenth century than on any previous period in their histories. The following are some interesting recent works and a few classics.

Industrialization is the subject of Peter Stearns, *The Industrial Revolution in World History* (1993), and David Landes, *The Unbound Prometheus: Technological Change and Industrial Development in Western Europe from 1750 to the Present* (1969). Two interesting works on nationalism are E. J. Hobsbawm, *Nation and Nationalism Since 1780* (1990), and Benedict Anderson, *Imagined Communities: Reflections on the Origin and Spread of Nationalism* (1991).

Barrington Moore, *The Social Origins of Dictatorship and Democracy* (1966), is a classic essay on European society. On European women see Renate Bridenthal, Claudia Koonz, and Susan Stuard, eds., *Becoming Visible: Women in European History* (1987); Patricia Branca, *Silent Sisterhood: Middle-Class Women in the Victorian Home* (1975); Louise Tilly and Joan Scott, *Women, Work, and Family* (1987); and Theresa McBride, *The Domestic Revolution: The Modernization of Household Service in England and France, 1820–1920* (1976). The history of family life is told in Beatrice Gottlieb, *The Family in the Western World from the Black Death to the Industrial Age* (1993). Albert Lindemann, *A History of European Socialism* (1983), covers the labor movements as well.

There are many excellent histories of individual countries. Germany in the late nineteenth century is well treated in Erich Eyck, *Bismarck and the German Empire* (1964). On Britain see Donald Read, *The Age of Urban Democracy: England, 1868–1914* (1994), and David Thomson, *England in the Nineteenth Century, 1815–1914* (1978). On France, Eugen Weber, *Peasants into Frenchmen* (1976), and Roger Price, *A Social History of Nineteenth-Century France* (1987), are especially recommended. A good introduction to Russian history is Hans Rogger, *Russia in the Age of Modernization and Revolution, 1881–1917* (1983).

Three very different aspects of American life are described in Carl Degler, *Out of Our Past: The Forces That Shaped Modern America* (1970); Thomas Hughes, *American Genesis: A Century of Invention and Technological Enthusiasm* (1989); and John Opie, *Nature's Nation: An Environmental History of the United States* (1998).

There are several interesting books on Japan, in particular Peter Duus, *The Rise of Modern Japan*, 2d ed. (1998), and Tessa Morris-Suzuki, *The Technological Transformation of Japan* (1994). Two fine books cover the history of modern China: John King Fairbank, *The Great Chinese Revolution, 1800–1985* (1987), and Jonathan D. Spence, *The Search for Modern China* (1990).

■ Note

1. Quoted in Bonnie S. Anderson and Judith P. Zinsser, *A History of Their Own: Women in Europe from Prehistory to the Present*, vol. 2 (New York: Harper & Row, 1988), 372, 387.

THE NEW IMPERIALISM,
1869–1914

Opening of the Suez Canal When the canal opened in 1869, thousands
of dignitaries and ordinary people gathered to watch the ships go by.

n November 1869, Empress Eugénie of France, Emperor Francis Joseph of Austria-Hungary, and sixteen hundred other dignitaries from the Middle East and Europe assembled at Port Said° in Egypt to celebrate the inauguration of the greatest construction project of the century: the **Suez Canal**. Ismail°, the khedive° (ruler) of Egypt, had invited all the Christian princes of Europe and all the Muslim princes of Asia and Africa, except the Ottoman sultan, his nominal overlord. He wanted to show that Egypt was not only independent but an equal of the great powers.

Ismail used this occasion to emphasize the harmony and cooperation between the peoples of Africa, Asia, and Europe. A French journalist wrote:

> This multitude, coming from all parts of the world, presented the most varied and singular spectacle. All races were represented. . . . We saw, coming to attend this festival of civilization, men of the Orient wearing clothes of dazzling colors, chiefs of African tribes wrapped in their great coats, Circassians in war costumes, officers of the British army of India with their shakos [hats] wrapped in muslin, Hungarian magnates wearing their national costumes.[1]

To bless the inauguration, Ismail also had invited clergy of the Muslim, Orthodox, and Catholic faiths. A reporter noted: "The Khedive . . . wished to symbolize thereby the unity of men and their brotherhood before God, without distinction of religion; it was the first time that the Orient had seen such a meeting of faiths to celebrate and bless together a great event and a great work."[2]

The canal was a great success, but not in the way Ismail intended it to be. Ships using it could travel between Europe and India in less than two weeks—much less time than the month or longer consumed by sailing around Africa and into the Indian Ocean. By lowering freight costs, the canal stimulated shipping and the construction of steamships, giving an advantage to nations that had heavy industry and a large maritime trade over land-based empires and countries that had few merchant ships. Great Britain, which long opposed construction of the canal for fear that it might fall into enemy hands, benefited more than any other nation. France, which provided half of the capital and most of the engineers, came in a distant second, for it had less trade with Asia than Britain did. Egypt, which contributed the other half of the money and most of the labor, was the loser in this affair. Instead of making Egypt powerful and independent, the Suez Canal provided the excuse for a British invasion and occupation of Egypt. Far from inaugurating an era of harmony among the peoples of three continents and three faiths, the canal triggered a wave of European domination over Africa and Asia.

Between 1869 and 1914 Germany, France, Britain, Russia, and the United States used industrial technology to impose their will on the nonindustrial parts of the world. Historians use the expression **New Imperialism** to describe this exercise of power.

As you read this chapter, ask yourself the following questions:

- What motivated the industrial nations to conquer new territories, and what means did they use?
- Which parts of the world were annexed to the new empires, and which ones became their economic dependencies?
- How did the environment change in the lands subjected to the New Imperialism?

THE NEW IMPERIALISM: MOTIVES AND METHODS

Europe had a long tradition of imperialism reaching back to the twelfth-century Crusades against the Arabs, and the United States greatly expanded its territory after achieving independence in 1783 (see Map 25.3). During the first two-thirds of the nineteenth century, the European powers continued to increase their influence overseas (see Chapter 26). The New Imperialism was characterized by an explosion of territorial conquests even more rapid than the Spanish conquests of

---

Port Said (port sah-EED)   **Ismail** (is-mah-EEL)
khedive (kuh-DEEV)

CHRONOLOGY

	The Scramble for Africa	Asia and Western Dominance	Imperialism in Latin America
1870	**1869** Opening of the Suez Canal **1874** Warfare between the British and the Asante (Gold Coast) **1877–1879** Warfare between the British and the Xhosa and between the British and the Zulu (South Africa) **1882** British forces occupy Egypt **1884–1885** Berlin Conference; Leopold II obtains Congo Free State	**1862–1895** French conquer Indochina **1865–1876** Russian forces advance into Central Asia **1878** United States obtains Pago Pago Harbor (Samoa) **1885** Britain completes conquest of Burma **1887** United States obtains Pearl Harbor (Hawaii)	**1870–1910** Railroad building boom: British companies in Argentina and Brazil; U.S. companies in Mexico.
1890		**1894–1895** China defeated in Sino-Japanese War	
	1896 Ethiopians defeat Italian army at Adowa; warfare between the British and the Asante **1898** Battle of Omdurman	**1895** France completes conquest of Indochina **1898** United States annexes Hawaii and purchases Philippines from Spain	**1895–1898** Cubans revolt against Spanish rule **1898** Spanish-American War; United States annexes Puerto Rico and Guam
	1899–1902 South African War between Afrikaners and the British **1902** First Aswan Dam completed (Egypt)	**1899–1902** U.S. forces conquer and occupy Philippines **1903** Russia completes Trans-Siberian Railway **1904–1905** Russia defeated in Russo-Japanese War	**1901** United States imposes Platt Amendment on Cuba **1903** United States backs secession of Panama from Colombia **1904–1907, 1916** U.S. troops occupy Dominican Republic **1904–1914** United States builds Panama Canal
1910	**1908** Belgium annexes Congo		**1912** U.S. troops occupy Nicaragua and Honduras

the sixteenth century. Between 1869 and 1914, in a land grab of unprecedented speed, Europeans seized territories in Africa and Central Asia, and both Europeans and Americans took territories in Southeast Asia and the Pacific. Approximately 10 million square miles (26 million square kilometers) and 150 million people fell under the rule of Europe and the United States in this period.

The New Imperialism, however, was more than a land grab. The imperial powers used economic and technological means to reorganize dependent regions and bring them into the world economy as suppliers of food-stuffs and raw materials and as consumers of industrial products. In Africa and other parts of the world, this was done by conquest and colonial administration. In the Latin American republics, the same result was achieved indirectly. Those republics became economic dependencies of the United States and Europe even though they remained politically independent.

What inspired Europeans and Americans to venture overseas and impose their will on other societies? There is no simple answer to this question. Economic, cultural, and political motives were involved in each case.

Religion and Imperialism European penetration into Africa was accompanied by enthusiastic efforts to convert the Africans to Christianity. European missionaries built schools and clinics as well as churches. Here African schoolchildren are shown a picture of the Virgin Mary holding the baby Jesus, an image designed to replace traditional African religious objects. Mary and Jesus are represented as Europeans. (USGP)

Political Motives

The great powers of the late nineteenth century, as well as less powerful countries like Italy, Portugal, and Belgium, were competitive and hypersensitive about their status. French leaders, humiliated by their defeat by Prussia in 1871 (see Chapter 28), sought to reestablish their nation's prestige through territorial acquisitions overseas. Great Britain, already in possession of the world's largest and richest empire, felt the need to protect India, its "jewel in the crown," by acquiring colonies in East Africa and Southeast Asia. Chancellor Otto von Bismarck had little interest in acquiring colonies, but many Germans believed that a country as important as theirs required an impressive empire overseas.

Political motives were not limited to statesmen in the capital cities. Colonial governors, even officers posted to the farthest colonial outposts, practiced their own diplomacy. They often decided on their own to claim a piece of land before some rival got it. Armies fighting frontier wars found it easier to defeat their neighbors than to make peace with them. In response to border skirmishes with neighboring states, colonial agents were likely to send in troops, take over their neighbors' territories, and then inform their home governments. Governments felt obligated to back up their men-on-the-spot in order not to lose face. The great powers of Europe acquired much of West Africa, Southeast Asia, and the Pacific islands in this manner.

Cultural Motives

The late nineteenth century saw a Christian revival in Europe and North America, as both Catholics and Protestants founded new missionary societies. Their purpose was not only religious—to convert nonbelievers, whom they regarded as "heathen"—but also cultural in a broader sense. They sought to export their own norms of "civilized" behavior: they were determined to abolish slavery in Africa and bring Western education, medicine, hygiene, and monogamous marriage to all the world's peoples.

Among those attracted by religious work overseas were many women who joined missionary societies to become teachers and nurses, positions of greater authority than they could hope to find at home. Although they did not challenge colonialism directly, their influence often helped soften the harshness of colonial rule—for example, by calling attention to issues of maternity and women's health. Mary Slessor, a British missionary who lived for forty years among the people of southeastern Nigeria, campaigned against slavery, human sacrifice, and the killing of twins and, generally, for women's rights. In India, missionaries denounced the customs of child marriages and *sati* (the burning of widows on their husbands' funeral pyres). Such views often clashed with the customs of the people among whom they settled.

The sense of moral duty and cultural superiority was not limited to missionaries. Many Europeans and Americans equated technological innovations with "progress" and "change for the better." They believed that Western technology proved the superiority of Western ideas, customs, and culture. This attitude at least included the idea that non-Western peoples could achieve, through education, the same cultural level as Europeans and Americans. More harmful were racist ideas that relegated non-Europeans to a status of permanent inferiority. Social Darwinists (see Chapter 28) assigned different stages of biological development to peoples of different races and cultures. They divided humankind into several races based on physical appearance and ranked these races in a hierarchy that ranged from "civilized" at the highest level down through "semibarbarous," "barbarian," and finally, at the bottom, "savage." Caucasians—whites—were always at the top of this ranking. Such ideas were often presented as an excuse for permanent rule over Africans and Asians.

Imperialism first interested small groups of explorers, clergy, and businessmen but soon attracted people from other walks of life. Young men, finding few opportunities for adventure and glory at home in an era of peace, sought them overseas as the Spanish *conquistadores* had done over three centuries earlier. At first, the European public and parliaments were indifferent or hostile to overseas adventures, but a few easy victories in the 1880s helped to overcome their reluctance. The United States was fully preoccupied with its westward expansion until the 1880s, but in the 1890s popular attention shifted to lands outside U.S. borders. Newspapers, which achieved a wide readership in the second half of the nineteenth century, discovered they could boost circulation with reports of wars and conquests. By the 1890s, imperialism was a popular cause; it was the overseas extension of the nationalism propelling the power politics of the time.

Economic Motives

The industrialization of Europe and North America stimulated the demand for minerals—copper for electrical wiring, tin for canning, chrome and manganese for the steel industry, coal for steam engines, and, most of all, gold and diamonds. The demand for such industrial crops as cotton and rubber and for stimulants such as sugar, coffee, tea, and tobacco also grew. These products were found in the tropics, but never in sufficient quantities. An economic depression lasting from the mid-1870s to the mid-1890s caused European merchants, manufacturers, and shippers to seek protection against foreign competition (see below). They argued that their respective countries needed secure sources of tropical raw materials and protected markets for their industries. Declining business opportunities at home prompted entrepreneurs and investors to look for profits from mines, plantations, and railroads in Asia, Africa, and Latin America. Since investment in countries so different from their own was extremely risky, businessmen sought the backing of their governments, preferably with soldiers.

These reasons explain why Europeans and Americans wished to expand their influence over other societies in the late nineteenth and early twentieth centuries. Yet motives alone are not enough to explain the events of that time. What made it possible to conquer a piece of Africa, to convert the "heathen," or to start a plantation was the sudden increase in the power that industrial

peoples could wield over nonindustrial peoples and over the forces of nature. Technological advances explain both the motives and the outcome of the New Imperialism.

The Tools of the Imperialists

To succeed, empire builders needed the means to achieve their objectives at a reasonable cost. These means were provided by the Industrial Revolution (see Chapter 24). In the early part of the nineteenth century, technological innovations began to tip the balance of power in favor of Europe. Europeans had dominated the oceans since about 1500, and their naval power increased still more with the introduction of steamships. The first steamer reached India in 1825 and was soon followed by regular mail service in the 1830s. The long voyage around Africa was at first too costly for cargo steamers, for coal had to be shipped from England. The building of the Suez Canal and the development of increasingly efficient engines solved this problem and led to a boom in shipping to the Indian Ocean and East Asia. Whenever fighting broke out, passenger liners were requisitioned as troopships, giving European forces greater mobility than Asians and Africans. Their advantage was enhanced even more by the development of a global network of submarine telegraph cables connecting Europe with North America in the 1860s, with Latin America and Asia in the 1870s, with Africa in the 1880s, and finally across the Pacific in 1904 (see Environment and Technology: "The Annihilation of Time and Space," in Chapter 24).

Until the middle of the nineteenth century, western Europeans were much weaker on land than at sea. Thereafter, Europeans used gunboats with considerable success in China, Burma, Indochina, and the Congo Basin. Although gunboats opened the major river basins to European penetration, the invaders often found themselves hampered by other natural obstacles. *Falciparum* malaria, found only in Africa, was so deadly to Europeans that few explorers survived before the 1850s. In 1854 a British doctor discovered that the drug quinine, taken regularly during one's stay in Africa, could prevent the disease. This and a few sanitary precautions reduced the annual death rate among whites in West Africa from between 250 and 750 per thousand in the early nineteenth century to between 50 and 100 per thousand after 1850. This reduction was sufficient to open the continent to merchants, officials, and missionaries.

Muzzleloading smoothbore muskets had been used in Europe, Asia, and the Americas since the late seventeenth century, and by the early nineteenth century they were also common in much of Africa. The development

The Battle of Omdurman   In the late nineteenth century, most battles between European (or European-led) troops and African forces were one-sided encounters because of the disparity in the opponents' firearms and tactics. The Battle of Omdurman in Sudan in 1898 is a dramatic example. The forces of the Mahdi, some on horseback, were armed with spears and single-shot muskets. The British troops and their Egyptian allies, lined up in the foreground, used repeating rifles and machine guns able to shoot much farther than the Sudanese weapons. As a result, there were many Sudanese casualties but very few British or Egyptian.   (The Art Archive Limited)

of new and much deadlier firearms in the 1860s and 1870s shifted the balance of power on land between Westerners and other peoples. One of these was the breechloader, which could be fired accurately ten times as fast as, and five or six times farther than, a musket. By the 1870s armies in Europe and the United States had all switched to these new rifles. Two more innovations appeared in the 1880s: smokeless powder, which did not foul the gun or reveal the soldier's position, and repeating rifles, which could shoot fifteen rounds in fifteen seconds. In the 1890s, European and American armies began using machine guns, which could fire eleven bullets per second.

In the course of the century, Asians and Africans also acquired better firearms, mostly old weapons that Euro-

pean armies had discarded. As European firearms improved, the firepower gap widened, making colonial conquests easier than ever before. By the 1880s and 1890s, European-led forces of a few hundred could defeat non-European armies of thousands. Against the latest weapons, African and Asian soldiers armed with muskets or, in some cases, with spears did not stand a chance, no matter how numerous and courageous they were.

A classic example is the **Battle of Omdurman** in the Sudan. On September 2, 1898, 40,000 Sudanese attacked an Anglo-Egyptian expedition that had come up the Nile on six steamers and four other boats. General Horatio Kitchener's troops had twenty machine guns and four artillery pieces; the Sudanese were equipped with muskets and spears. Within a few hours, 11,000 Sudanese and 48 British lay dead. Winston Churchill, the future British prime minister, witnessed the battle and called it

> The most signal triumph ever gained by the arms of science over barbarians. Within the space of five hours the strongest and best-armed savage army yet arrayed against a modern European Power had been destroyed and dispersed, with hardly any difficulty, comparatively small risk, and insignificant loss to the victors.[3]

Colonial Agents and Administration

Once colonial agents took over a territory, their home government expected them to cover their own costs and, if possible, return some profit to the home country. The system of administering and exploiting colonies for the benefit of the home country is known as **colonialism.** In some cases, such as along the West African coast or in Indochina, there was already a considerable trade that could be taxed. In other places, profits could come only from investments and a thorough reorganization of the indigenous societies. In applying modern scientific and industrial methods to their colonies, colonialists started the transformation of Asian and African societies and landscapes that has continued to our day.

Legal experts and academics placed a great emphasis on the differences between various systems of colonial government and debated whether colonies eventually should be assimilated into the ruling nation, associated in a federation, or allowed to rule themselves. Colonies that were protectorates retained their traditional governments, even their monarchs, but had a European "resident" or "consul-general" to "advise" them. Other colonies were directly administered by a European governor. In fact, the impact of colonial rule depended much more on economic and social conditions than on narrow legal distinctions.

One important factor was the presence or absence of European settlers. In Canada, Australia, and New Zealand, whites were already in the majority by 1869, and their colonial "mother-country," Britain, encouraged them to elect parliaments and rule themselves. Where European settlers were numerous but still a minority of the population, as in Algeria and South Africa, settlers and the home country struggled for control over the indigenous population. In colonies with few white settlers, the European governors ruled autocratically.

In the early years of the New Imperialism, colonial administrations consisted of a governor and his staff, a few troops to keep order, and a small number of tax collectors and magistrates. Nowhere could colonialism operate without the cooperation of indigenous elites, because no colony was wealthy enough to pay the salaries of more than a handful of European officials. In most cases, the colonial governors exercised power through traditional rulers willing to cooperate, as in the Princely States of India (see Chapter 26). In addition, colonial governments educated a few local youths for "modern" jobs as clerks, nurses, policemen, customs inspectors, and the like. Thus colonialism relied on two rival indigenous elites.

European and American women seldom took part in the early stages of colonial expansion. As conquest gave way to peaceful colonialism and as steamships and railroads made travel less difficult, colonial officials and settlers began bringing their wives to the colonies. By the 1880s, the British Women's Emigration Association was recruiting single women to go out to the colonies to marry British settlers. As one of its founders, Ellen Joyce, explained, "The possibility of the settler marrying his own countrywoman is of imperial as well as family importance."

The arrival of white women in Asia and Africa led to increasing racial segregation. As Sylvia Leith-Ross, wife of a colonial officer in Nigeria, explained, "When you are alone, among thousands of unknown, unpredictable people, dazed by unaccustomed sights and sounds, bemused by strange ways of life and thought, you need to remember who you are, where you come from, what your standards are." Many colonial wives found themselves in command of numerous servants and expected to follow the complex etiquette of colonial entertainment in support of their husbands' official positions. Occasionally they found opportunities to exercise personal initiatives, usually charitable work involving indigenous women and children. However well meaning, their efforts were always subordinate to the work of men.

THE SCRAMBLE FOR AFRICA

Until the 1870s, African history was largely shaped by internal forces and local initiatives (see Chapter 26). Outside Algeria and southern Africa, only a handful of Europeans had ever visited the interior of Africa, and European countries possessed only small enclaves on the coasts. As late as 1879, Africans ruled more than 90 percent of the continent. Then within a decade Africa was invaded and divided among the European powers in a movement often referred to as the **"scramble" for Africa**

(See Map 29.1). This invasion affected all regions of the continent. Let us look at the most significant cases, beginning with Egypt, the wealthiest and most populated part of the continent.

Egypt

Ironically, European involvement in Egypt resulted from Egypt's attempt to free itself from Ottoman Turkish rule. Throughout the mid-nineteenth century, the khedives of Egypt had tried to modernize their armed forces; build canals, harbors, railroads, and other public works; and reorient agriculture toward export crops, especially cotton (see Chapters 24 and 26). Their interest in the Suez Canal was also part of this policy. Khedive Ismail even tried to make Egypt the center of an empire reaching south into the Sudan and Ethiopia.

These ambitions cost vast sums of money, which the khedives borrowed from European creditors at high interest rates. By 1876, Egypt's foreign debt had risen to £100 million sterling, and the interest payments alone consumed one-third of its foreign export earnings. To avoid bankruptcy, the Egyptian government sold its shares in the Suez Canal to Great Britain and accepted four foreign "commissioners of the debt" to oversee its finances. French and British bankers, still not satisfied, lobbied their governments to secure the loans by stronger measures. In 1878 the two governments obliged Ismail to appoint a Frenchman as minister of public works and a Briton as minister of finance. When high taxes caused hardship and popular discontent, the French and British persuaded the Ottoman sultan to depose Ismail. This foreign intervention provoked a military uprising under Egyptian army colonel Arabi Pasha, which threatened the Suez Canal.

Fearing for their investments, the British sent an army into Egypt in 1882. They intended to occupy Egypt for only a year or two. But theirs was a seaborne empire that depended on secure communications between Britain and India. So important was the Suez Canal to their maritime supremacy that they stayed for seventy years. During those years the British ruled Egypt "indirectly"—that is, they maintained the Egyptian government and the fiction of Egyptian sovereignty but retained real power in their own hands.

Eager to develop Egyptian agriculture, especially cotton production, the British brought in engineers and contractors to build the first dam across the Nile, at Aswan in upper Egypt. When it was completed in 1902, it was one of the largest dams in the world. It captured the annual Nile flood and released its waters throughout the year, allowing farmers to grow two, sometimes three, crops a year. This doubled the effective acreage compared with the basin system of irrigation practiced since the time of the pharaohs, in which the annual floodwaters of the Nile were retained by low dikes around the fields.

The economic development of Egypt by the British enriched a small elite of landowners and merchants, many of them foreigners. Egyptian peasants got little relief from the heavy taxes collected to pay for their country's crushing foreign debt and the expenses of the British army of occupation. Western ways that conflicted with the teachings of Islam—such as the drinking of alcohol and the relative freedom of women—offended Muslim religious leaders. Most Egyptians found British rule more onerous than that of the Ottomans. By the 1890s, Egyptian politicians and intellectuals were demanding that the British leave, but to no avail.

Western and Equatorial Africa

While the British were taking over Egypt, the French were planning to extend their empire into the interior of West Africa. Starting from the coast of Senegal, which had been in French hands for centuries, they hoped to build a railroad from the upper Senegal River to the upper Niger, to open the interior to French merchants. This in turn led the French military to undertake the conquest of the western Sudan.

Meanwhile, it was the actions of three individuals, rather than a government, that brought about the occupation of the Congo Basin, an enormous forested region in the heart of equatorial Africa (see Map 29.1). In 1879 the American journalist **Henry Morton Stanley,** who had explored the area, persuaded **King Leopold II** of Belgium to invest his personal fortune in "opening up" equatorial Africa. With Leopold's money, Stanley returned to Africa from 1879 to 1884 to establish trading posts along the southern bank of the Congo River. At the same time, an Italian explorer obtained from an African ruler living on the opposite bank, a treaty that placed the area under the "protection" of France. These events sparked a flurry of diplomatic activity.

German chancellor Bismarck called the **Berlin Conference** on Africa of 1884 and 1885. There the major powers agreed that henceforth "effective occupation"

Map 29.1 Africa in 1878 and 1914 In 1878 the European colonial presence was limited to a few coastal enclaves, plus portions of Algeria and South Africa. By 1914, Europeans had taken over all of Africa except Ethiopia and Liberia.

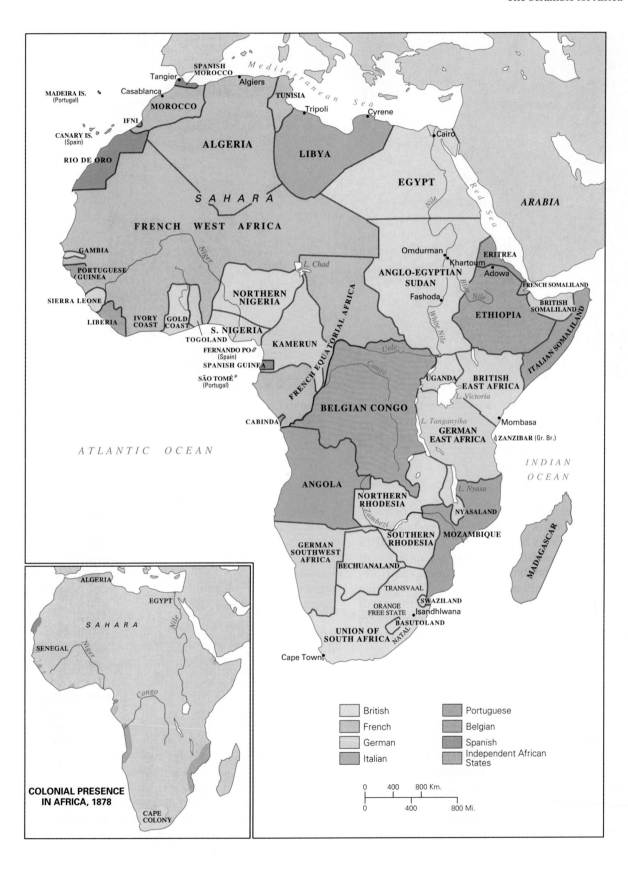

SPANISH MOROCCO

Tangier
Casablanca
MADEIRA IS.
(Portugal)
IFNI
CANARY IS.
(Spain)
RIO DE ORO

ALGIERS

TUNISIA
Tripoli
Cyrene

Mediterranean Sea

MOROCCO

ALGERIA

LIBYA

EGYPT

Cairo

Red Sea

ARABIA

S A H A R A

Nile

FRENCH   WEST   AFRICA

GAMBIA

PORTUGUESE
GUINEA

SIERRA LEONE

LIBERIA

IVORY
COAST
GOLD
COAST

S. NIGERIA

TOGOLAND

FERNANDO PO
(Spain)
SPANISH GUINEA

SÃO TOMÉ
(Portugal)

Niger

L. Chad

NORTHERN
NIGERIA

KAMERUN

FRENCH EQUATORIAL AFRICA

Uele

Congo

Omdurman
Khartoum

ANGLO-EGYPTIAN
SUDAN

Fashoda

Blue Nile

White Nile

ERITREA

Adowa

FRENCH SOMALILAND
BRITISH
SOMALILAND

ETHIOPIA

ITALIAN SOMALILAND

UGANDA

BRITISH
EAST
AFRICA

L. Victoria

L. Tanganyika

Mombasa

ZANZIBAR (Gr. Br.)

BELGIAN CONGO

CABINDA

GERMAN
EAST AFRICA

ATLANTIC   OCEAN

*INDIAN
OCEAN*

ANGOLA

NORTHERN
RHODESIA

L. Nyasa

NYASALAND

MOZAMBIQUE

GERMAN
SOUTHWEST
AFRICA

SOUTHERN
RHODESIA

Zambezi

BECHUANALAND

TRANSVAAL

SWAZILAND
Isandhlwana

ORANGE
FREE STATE
BASUTOLAND

UNION OF
SOUTH AFRICA

NATAL

Cape Town

MADAGASCAR

**COLONIAL PRESENCE
IN AFRICA, 1878**

ALGERIA

EGYPT

SAHARA

Nile

SENEGAL

Niger

Congo

CAPE
COLONY

British
French
German
Italian

Portuguese
Belgian
Spanish
Independent African
States

0   400   800 Km.

0   400   800 Mi.

A Steamboat for the Congo River   Soon after the Congo Basin was occupied by Europeans, the new colonial rulers realized they needed to improve transportation. Since access from the sea was blocked by rapids on the lower Congo River, steamboats had to be brought in sections, hauled from the coast by thousands of Congolese over very difficult terrain. This picture shows the pieces arriving at Stanley Pool, ready to be reassembled. (From H. M. Stanley, *The Congo*, vol. 2, London, 1885)

would replace the former trading relations between Africans and Europeans. This meant that every country with colonial ambitions had to send troops into Africa and participate in the division of the spoils. As a reward for triggering the "scramble" for Africa, Leopold II acquired a personal domain under the name "Congo Free State," while France and Portugal took most of the rest of equatorial Africa. In this manner, the European powers and King Leopold managed to divide Africa among themselves, at least on paper.

"Effective occupation," required many years of effort. In the interior of West Africa, French troops encountered the determined opposition of Muslim rulers who resisted the French invasion for up to thirty years. The French advance encouraged the Germans to stake claims to parts of the region and the British to move north from their coastal enclaves, until the entire region was occupied by Britain, France, and Germany.

Because West Africa had long had a flourishing trade, the new rulers took advantage of existing trade networks, taxing merchants and farmers, investing the profits in railroads and harbors, and paying dividends to European stockholders. In the Gold Coast (now Ghana), British trading companies bought the cocoa grown by African farmers at low prices and resold it for large profits. The interior of French West Africa lagged behind. Although the region could produce cotton, peanuts, and other crops, the difficulties of transportation limited its development before 1914.

Compared to West Africa, equatorial Africa had few inhabitants and little trade. Rather than try to govern these vast territories directly, authorities in the Congo Free State, the French Congo, and the Portuguese colonies of Angola and Mozambique farmed out huge pieces of land to private concession companies, offering them a monopoly on the natural resources and trade of their territories and the right to employ soldiers and tax the inhabitants. The inhabitants, however, had no cash crops that they could sell to raise the money they needed to pay their taxes.

Freed from outside supervision, the companies forced the African inhabitants at gunpoint to produce cash crops and carry them, on their heads or backs, to the nearest railroad or navigable river. The worst abuses

Founding of South Africa   In May 1910, the *Cape Times* celebrated the founding of the Union of South Africa with a picture of Britannia releasing the dove of peace while the ship *Union* is towed out to sea.   (South African Library, Capetown)

took place in the Congo Free State, where a rubber boom lasting from 1895 to 1905 made it profitable for private companies to coerce Africans to collect latex from vines that grew in the forests. One Congolese refugee told the British consul Roger Casement who investigated the atrocities:

> We begged the white men to leave us alone, saying we could get no more rubber, but the white men and their soldiers said: 'Go. You are only beasts yourselves, you are only *nyama* (meat).' We tried, always going further into the forest, and when we failed and our rubber was short, the soldiers came to our towns and killed us. Many were shot, some had their ears cut off; others were tied up with ropes around their necks and bodies and taken away.[4]

After 1906 the British press began publicizing the horrors. The public outcry that followed, coinciding with the end of the rubber boom, convinced the Belgian government to take over Leopold's private empire in 1908.

Southern Africa

The history of southern Africa between 1869 and 1914 differs from that of the rest of the continent in several important respects. One was that the land had long attracted settlers. African pastoralists and farmers had inhabited the region for centuries. **Afrikaners,** descendants of Dutch settlers on the Cape of Good Hope, moved inland throughout the nineteenth century; British prospectors and settlers arrived later in the century; and, finally, Indians were brought over by the British and stayed.

Southern Africa attracted European settlers because of its good pastures and farmland and its phenomenal deposits of diamonds, gold, and copper, as well as coal and iron ore. This was the new El Dorado that imperialists had dreamed of since the heyday of the Spanish Empire in Peru and Mexico in the sixteenth century.

The discovery of diamonds at Kimberley in 1868 lured thousands of European prospectors as well as Africans looking for work. It also attracted the interest of Great Britain, colonial ruler of the Cape Colony, which annexed the diamond area in 1871, thereby angering the Afrikaners. Once in the interior, the British defeated the Xhosa° people in 1877 and 1878. Then in 1879 they confronted the Zulu, militarily the most powerful of the African peoples in the region.

The Zulu, led by their king Cetshwayo°, resented their encirclement by Afrikaners and British. A growing sense of nationalism and their proud military tradition led them into a war with the British in 1879. At first they

---

Xhosa (KOH-sah)   **Cetshwayo** (set-SHWAH-yo)

held their own, defeating the British at Isandhlwana°, but a few months later they were in turn defeated. Cetshwayo was captured and sent into exile, and the Zulu lands were given to white ranchers. Yet throughout those bitter times, the Zulu's sense of nationhood remained strong.

Relations between the British and the Afrikaners, already tense as a result of British encroachment, took a turn for the worse when gold was discovered in the Afrikaner republic of Transvaal° in 1886. In the gold rush that ensued, the British soon outnumbered the Afrikaners.

Britain's invasion of southern Africa was driven in part by the ambition of **Cecil Rhodes** (1853–1902), who once declared that he would "annex the stars" if he could. Rhodes made his fortune in the Kimberley diamond fields, founding De Beers Consolidated, a company that has dominated the world's diamond trade ever since. He then turned to politics. He led a concession company, the British South Africa Company, to push north into Central Africa, where he named two new colonies after himself: Southern Rhodesia (now Zimbabwe) and Northern Rhodesia (now Zambia). The Ndebele° and Shona peoples, who inhabited the region, resisted this invasion, but the machine guns of the British finally defeated them.

British attempts to annex the two Afrikaner republics, Transvaal and Orange Free State, and the inflow of English-speaking whites into the gold- and diamond-mining areas led to the South African War, which lasted from 1899 to 1902. At first the Afrikaners had the upper hand, for they were highly motivated, possessed modern rifles, and knew the land. In 1901, however, Great Britain brought in 450,000 troops and crushed the Afrikaner armies. Ironically, the Afrikaners' defeat in 1902 led to their ultimate victory. Wary of costly commitments overseas, the British government expected European settlers in Africa to manage their own affairs, as they were doing in Canada, Australia, and New Zealand. Thus in 1910 the European settlers created the Union of South Africa, in which the Afrikaners eventually emerged as the ruling element.

Unlike Canada, Austria, and New Zealand, South Africa had a majority of indigenous inhabitants and substantial numbers of Indians and "Cape Coloureds" (people of mixed ancestry). Yet the Europeans were both numerous enough to demand self-rule and powerful enough to deny the vote and other civil rights to the majority. In 1913 the South African parliament passed the Natives Land Act, assigning Africans to reservations and forbidding them to own land elsewhere. This and other racial policies turned South Africa into land of segregation, oppression, and bitter divisions.

Political and Social Consequences

Africa at the time of the European invasion contained a wide variety of societies. Some parts of the continent had long-established kingdoms with aristocracies or commercial towns dominated by a merchant class. In other places, agricultural peoples lived in villages without any outside government. Still elsewhere, pastoral nomads were organized along military lines. In some remote areas, people lived from hunting and gathering. It is not surprising that these societies responded in very different ways to the European invasion.

Some peoples welcomed the invaders as allies against local enemies. Under colonial rule, they sought a Western education and work in government service or in European firms. In exchange, they were often the first to receive benefits such as schools and roads.

Others, especially peoples with a pastoral or a warrior tradition, fought tenaciously. Examples abound, from the Zulu and Ndebele of southern Africa to the followers of charismatic leaders such as the Mahdi° in the eastern Sudan or Samori in the western Sudan (now Mali). In Southwest Africa (now Namibia), the pastoral Herero° people rose up against German invaders in 1904; in repressing the uprising, the Germans exterminated two-thirds of them.

Some commercial states with a long history of contact with Europeans also fought back. The kingdom of **Asante°** in Gold Coast rose up three times (in 1874, 1896, and 1900) before it was finally overwhelmed. In the Niger Delta, the ancient city of Benin, rich with artistic treasures, resisted colonial control until 1897, when a British "punitive expedition" set it on fire and carted its works of art off to Europe.

One resistance movement succeeded, to the astonishment of Europeans and Africans alike. When **Menelik** became emperor of Ethiopia in 1889 (see Chapter 26), his country was threatened by Sudanese Muslims to the west and by France and Italy, which controlled the Red Sea coast to the east. For many years, Ethiopia had been purchasing weapons. By the Treaty of Wichelle (1889), Italy agreed to sell more weapons to Ethiopia. Six years later, when Italians attempted to establish a protectorate over Ethiopia, they found the Ethiopians armed with thousands of rifles and even a few machine guns and ar-

---

Isandhlwana (ee-sawn-dull-WAH-nah) Transvaal (trans-VAHL)
Ndebele (en-duh-BELL-ay)

Mahdi (MAH-dee) Herero (hair-AIR-oh) Asante (uh-SAWN-tay)

Victorious Ethiopians   Among the states of Africa, Ethiopia alone was able to defend itself against European imperialism. In the 1880s, hemmed in by Italian advances to its east and north and by British advances to its south and west, Ethiopia purchased modern weapons and trained its army to use them. Thus prepared, the Ethiopians defeated an Italian invasion at Adowa in 1896. These Ethiopian army officers wore their most elaborate finery to pose for a photograph after their victory.   (National Archives)

tillery pieces. Although Italy sent twenty thousand troops to attack Ethiopia, they were defeated at Adowa° in 1896 by a larger and better-trained Ethiopian army.

Most Africans neither joined nor fought the European invaders but tried to continue living as before. They found this increasingly difficult because colonial rule disrupted every traditional society. The presence of colonial officials meant that rights to land, commercial transactions, and legal disputes were handled very differently, and that traditional rulers lost all authority, except where Europeans used them as local administrators.

Changes in landholding were especially disruptive, for most Africans were farmers or herders for whom access to land was a necessity of life. In areas with a high population density, such as Egypt and West Africa, colonial rulers left peasants in place but encouraged them to grow cash crops and collected taxes on the product of their labor. Elsewhere, the new rulers declared any land that was not farmed to be "waste" or "vacant" and gave it to private concession companies or to European planters and ranchers. Africans found themselves squatters, sharecroppers, or ranch hands on land they had farmed for generations. In the worst cases, as in South Africa,

---

Adowa (AH-doe-ah)

many were forced off their lands and onto "reserves," like the Indians of North America (see Chapter 25).

Although the colonial rulers harbored designs on the land, they were even more interested in African labor. They did not want to pay wages high enough to attract workers voluntarily. Instead, they imposed various taxes, such as the hut tax or the head tax, which Africans had to pay regardless of their income. To find the money, Africans had little choice but to accept whatever work the Europeans offered. In this way, Africans were recruited to work on plantations, railroads, and other modern enterprises. In the South African mines, Africans were paid, on average, one-tenth as much as Europeans.

Some Africans came to the cities and mining camps seeking a better life than they had on the land. Many migrated great distances and stayed away for years at a time. Most migrants workers were men who left their wives and children behind in villages and on reserves. In some cases, the authorities did not allow them to bring their families and settle permanently in the towns. This caused great hardship for African women, who had to grow food for their families during the men's absences and care for sick and aged workers. Long separations between spouses also led to an increase in prostitution and to the spread of sexually transmitted diseases.

A Nigerian Woman
Remembers Her Childhood

First-person accounts of the period from 1869 to 1914 by African women are extremely rare, for few African women knew how to write and almost none wrote their memoirs. One exception is Baba of Karo, a woman from Zarewa in the Sokoto Caliphate (now northern Nigeria), who told her life story to a visiting American anthropologist. This is her recollection of the arrival of the British who conquered Sokoto between 1901 and 1903, when she was a young girl.

When I was a maiden the Europeans first arrived. Ever since we were quite small the *malams* [Quranic scholars] had been saying that the Europeans would come with a thing called a train, they would come with a thing called a motor-car, in them you would go and come back in a trice. They would stop wars, they would repair the world, they would stop oppression and lawlessness, we should live at peace with them. We used to go and sit quietly and listen to the prophecies. They would come, fine handsome people, they would not kill anyone, they would not oppress anyone, they would bring all their strange things. We were young girls when a European came with his attendants—"See, there's a white man, what has brought him?" He was asking the way to some town, we ran away and shut the door and he passed by and went on his way. . . .

I remember when a European came to Karo on a horse, and some of his foot soldiers went into the town. Everyone came out to look at them, but in Zarewa they didn't see the European. Everyone at Karo ran away—"There's a European! There's a European!" He came from Zaria with a few black men, two on horses and four on foot. We were inside the town. Later on we heard that they were there in Zaria in crowds, clearing spaces and building houses. One of my younger "sisters" was at Karo, she was pregnant, and when she saw the European she ran away and shut the door.

At that time Yusufu was the king of Karo. He did not like the Europeans, he did not wish them, he would sign their treaty. When he saw that perforce he would have to agree, so he did. We Habe [Hausa] wanted them to come, it was the Fulani [ruling class of Sokoto] who did not like it. When the Europeans came the Habe saw that if you worked for them they paid you for it, they didn't say, like the Fulani, "Commoner, give me this! Commoner, bring me that!" Yes, the Habe wanted them; they saw no harm in them. From Zaria they came to Rogo, they were building their big road to Karo City. They called out the people and said they were to come and make the road, if there were trees in the way they cut them down. The Europeans paid them with goods, they collected the villagers together and each man brought his large hoe. Money was not much use to them, so the Europeans paid them with food and other things.

The Europeans said that there were to be no more slaves; if someone said "Slave!" you could complain to the *alkali* [judge] who would punish the master who said it, the judge said "That is what the Europeans have decreed." The first order said that any slave, if he was younger than you, was your younger brother, if he was older than you he was your elder brother—they were all brothers of their master's family. No one used the world "slave" any more. When slavery was stopped, nothing much happened at our *rinji* [slave quarters] except that some slaves whom we had bought in the market ran away. Our own father went to his farm and worked, he and his son took up their large hoes; they loaned out their spare farms. Tsoho our father and Kadiri my brother with whom I live now and Balambo worked, they farmed guinea-corn and millet and groundnuts and everything; before this they had supervised the slaves' work—now they did their own. . . .

In the old days if the chief liked the look of your daughter he would take her and put her in his house; you could do nothing about it. Now they don't do that.

How did people in this part of Africa anticipate the arrival of the Europeans? Who favored their coming, and who did not? Why? What impact did the Europeans have on slavery and on labor in this area? Overall, did Baba of Karo approve or disapprove of their coming? Why?

Source: From M. F. Smith, ed., *Baba of Karo: A Woman of the Muslim Hausa* (New York: Philosophical Library, 1955), 66–68. Copyright © 1955. Reprinted by permission of Regeen Najor.

Some African women welcomed colonial rule, for it brought an end to fighting and slave raiding (see Society and Culture: A Nigerian Woman Remembers Her Childhood). A few succeeded in becoming wealthy traders or owners of livestock. On the whole, however, African women benefited less than men from the economic changes that colonialism introduced. In areas where the colonial rulers replaced communal property (traditional in most of Africa) with private property, property rights were assigned to the head of the household—that is, to the man. Almost all the jobs open to Africans, even those considered "women's work" in Europe such as nursing or domestic service, were reserved for men.

Cultural Responses

More Africans came into contact with missionaries than with any other Europeans. Missionaries, both men and women, opened schools to teach reading, writing, and arithmetic to village children. Boys were taught crafts such as carpentry and blacksmithing, while girls learned domestic skills such as cooking, laundry, and child care.

Along with basic skills, the first generation of Africans educated in mission schools acquired Western ideas of justice and progress. Samuel Ajayi Crowther, a Yoruba rescued from slavery as a boy and educated in mission schools in Sierra Leone, went on to become an Anglican minister and, in 1864, the first African bishop. Crowther thought that Africa needed European assistance in achieving both spiritual and economic development:

> Africa has neither knowledge nor skill . . . to bring out her vast resources for her own improvement. . . . Therefore to claim Africa for the Africans alone, is to claim for her the right of a continued ignorance. . . . For it is certain, unless help [comes] from without, a nation can never rise above its present state.[5]

After the first generation, many of the teachers in mission schools were African, themselves the products of a mission education. They discovered that Christian ideals clashed with the reality of colonial exploitation. As one convert wrote in 1911:

> There is too much failure among all Europeans in Nyasaland. The three combined bodies—Missionaries, Government and Companies or gainers of money—do form the same rule to look upon the native with mockery eyes. . . . If we had enough power to communicate ourselves to Europe, we would advise them not to call themselves Christendom, but Europeandom. Therefore the life of the three combined bodies is altogether too cheaty, too thefty, too mockery. Instead of "Give," they say "Take away from." There is too much breakage of God's pure law.[6]

Christian missionaries from Europe and America were not the only ones to bring religious change to Africa. In southern and Central Africa, indigenous preachers adapted Christianity to African values and customs and founded new denominations known as "Ethiopian" churches.

Christianity proved successful in converting followers of traditional religions but made no inroads among Muslims. Instead, Islam, long predominant in northern and eastern Africa, spread southward as Muslim teachers established Quranic schools in the villages and founded Muslim brotherhoods. European colonialism unwittingly helped the diffusion of Islam. By building cities and increasing trade, colonial rule permitted Muslims to settle in new areas. As Islam—a universal religion without the taint of colonialism—became increasingly relevant to Africans, the number of Muslims in sub-Saharan Africa probably doubled between 1869 and 1914.

ASIA AND WESTERN DOMINANCE

During the period from 1869 to 1914, the pressure of the industrial powers was felt throughout Asia, the East Indies, and the Pacific islands. As trade with these regions grew in the late nineteenth century, so did their attractiveness to imperialists eager for economic benefits and national prestige.

Europeans had traded along the coasts of Asia and the East Indies since the early sixteenth century. By 1869, Britain already controlled most of India and Burma, Spain occupied the Philippines, and the Netherlands held large parts of the East Indies (now Indonesia). Between 1862 and 1895, France conquered Indochina (now Vietnam, Kampuchea, and Laos). It was the existence of these Asian colonial possessions that had inspired the building of the Suez Canal.

We have already seen the special cases of British imperialism in India (Chapter 26) and of Japanese imperialism in China and Korea (Chapter 28). Here let us look at the impact of the New Imperialism on Central and Southeast Asia, Indonesia, the Philippines, and Hawaii (see Map 29.2)

Map 29.2   Asia in 1914   By 1914, much of Asia was claimed by the colonial powers. The southern rim, from the Persian Gulf to the Pacific, was occupied by Great Britain, France, the Netherlands, and the United States. Central Asia had been incorporated into the Russian Empire. Japan, now industrialized, had joined the Western imperialist powers in expanding its territory and influence at the expense of China.

Central Asia

For over seven centuries, Russians had been at the mercy of the nomads of the Eurasian steppe extending from the Black Sea to Manchuria. When the nomadic tribesmen were united, as they were under the Mongol ruler Genghis Khan (r. 1206–1227), they could defeat the Russians; when they were not, the Russians moved into the steppe. This age-old ebb and flow ended when Russia acquired modern rifles and artillery.

Between 1865 and 1876, Russian forces advanced into Central Asia. Nomads like the Kazakhs, who lived east of the Caspian Sea, fought bravely but in vain. The fertile agricultural land of Kazakhstan attracted 200,000 Russian settlers. Although the governments of Tsar Alexander II (r. 1855–1881) and Tsar Alexander III (r. 1881–1894) claimed not to interfere in indigenous customs, they declared communally owned grazing lands "waste" or "vacant" and turned them over to farmers from Russia. By the end of the nineteenth century, the nomads were fenced out and reduced to starvation. Echoing the beliefs of other European imperialists, an eminent Russian jurist declared: "International rights cannot be taken into account when dealing with semibarbarous peoples."

South of the Kazakh steppe land were deserts dotted with oases where the fabled cities of Tashkent, Bukhara, and Samarkand served the caravan trade between China and the Middle East. For centuries the peoples of the region had lived under the protection of the Mongols and later the Qing Empire. But by the 1860s and 1870s, the Qing Empire was losing control over Central Asia (see Chapter 27), so it was fairly easy for Russian expeditions to conquer the indigenous peoples. Russia thereby acquired land suitable for cotton, along with a large and growing Muslim population.

Russian rule brought few benefits to the peoples of the Central Asian oases and few real changes. The Russians abolished slavery, built railroads to link the region with Europe, and planted hundreds of thousands of acres of cotton. Unlike the British in India, however, they did not attempt to change the customs, languages, or religious beliefs of their subjects.

Southeast Asia and Indonesia

The peoples of the Southeast Asian peninsula and the Indonesian archipelago had been in contact with outsiders—Chinese, Indians, Arabs, Europeans—for centuries. Java and the smaller islands—the fabled Spice Islands (the Moluccas)—had long been subject to Portuguese and later to Dutch domination. Until the mid-nineteenth century, however, most of the region was made up of independent kingdoms.

As in Africa, there is considerable variation in the history of different parts of the region, yet they all came under intense imperialist pressure during the nineteenth century. Burma (now Myanmar), nearest India, was gradually taken over by the British in the course of the century, until the last piece was annexed in 1885. Indochina fell piece by piece under French control until it was finally subdued in 1895. Similarly, Malaya (now Malaysia) came under British rule in stages during the 1870s and 1880s. By the early 1900s the Dutch had subdued northern Sumatra, the last part of the Dutch East Indies to be conquered. Only Siam (now Thailand) remained independent, although it lost several border provinces.

Despite their varied political histories, all these regions had features in common. They all had fertile soil, constant warmth, and heavy rains. Furthermore, the peoples of the region had a long tradition of intensive gardening, irrigation, and terracing. In those parts of the region where the population was not very dense, Europeans found it easy to import landless laborers from China and India seeking better opportunities overseas. Another reason for the region's wealth was the transfer of commercially valuable plants from other parts of the world. Tobacco, cinchona° (an antimalarial drug), manioc (an edible root crop), maize (corn), and natural rubber were brought from the Americas; sugar from India; tea from China; and coffee and oil palms from Africa. By 1914, much of the world's supply of these valuable products—in the case of rubber, almost all—came from Southeast Asia and Indonesia (see Environment and Technology: Imperialism and Tropical Ecology).

Most of the wealth of Southeast Asia and Indonesia was exported to Europe and North America. In exchange, the inhabitants of the region received two benefits from colonial rule: peace and a reliable food supply. As a result, their numbers increased at an unprecedented rate. For instance, the population of Java (an island the size of Pennsylvania) doubled from 16 million in 1870 to over 30 million in 1914.

Colonialism and the growth of population brought many social changes. The more numerous agricultural and commercial peoples gradually moved into mountainous and forest areas, displacing the earlier inhabitants who practiced hunting and gathering or shifting agriculture. The migrations of the Javanese to Borneo and Sumatra are but one example. Immigrants from China and India (see Chapter 26) changed the ethnic composition and culture of every country in the region. Thus the population of the Malay Peninsula became one-third Malay, one-third Chinese, and one-third Indian.

cinchona (sin-CHO-nah)

Imperialism and Tropical Ecology

Like all conquerors before them, the European imperialists of the nineteenth century exacted taxes and rents from the peoples they conquered. But they also sent botanists and agricultural experts to their tropical colonies to increase the production of commercial crops. In doing so, they radically changed the landscapes of their tropical dependencies.

The most dramatic effects were brought about by the deliberate introduction of new crops—an acceleration of the Columbian Exchange that had begun in the fifteenth century. In the early nineteenth century, tea was transferred from China to India and Ceylon. In the 1850s, British and Dutch botanists smuggled seeds of the cinchona tree from the Andes in South America to India and Java. They had to operate in secret, because the South American republics, knowing the value of this crop, prohibited the export of seeds. With the seeds, the British and Dutch established cinchona plantations in Ceylon and Java, respectively, to produce quinine, which was essential as an antimalarial drug and a flavoring for tonic water. Similarly, in the 1870s, British agents stole seeds of the rubber tree from the Amazon rain forest and transferred them to Malaya and Sumatra.

Before these transfers, vast forests covered the highlands of India, Southeast Asia, and Indonesia, precisely the lands where the new plants grew best. So European planters had the forests cut down and replaced with thousands of acres of commercially profitable trees and bushes, all lined up in perfect rows and tended by thousands of indigenous laborers to satisfy the demands of customers in faraway lands. The crops that poured forth from the transformed environments brought great wealth to the European planters and the imperial powers. In 1909 the British botanist John Willis justified the transformation in these terms:

> Whether planting in the tropics will always continue to be under European management is another question, but the northern powers will not permit that the rich and as yet comparatively undeveloped countries of the tropics should be entirely wasted by being devoted merely to the supply of the food and clothing wants of their own people, when they can also supply the wants of the colder zones in so many indispensable products.

This quotation raises important questions about trade versus self-sufficiency. If a region's economy supplies the food and clothing wants of its own people, is its output "entirely wasted"? What is the advantage of trading the prod-

Branch of a Cinchona Tree The bark of the cinchona tree was the source of quinine, the only antimalarial drug known before 1940. Quinine made it much safer for Europeans to live in the tropics. (From Bentley & Trimen's *Medicinal Plants*. Hunt Institute for Botanical Documentation, Carnegie Mellon University)

ucts of one region (such as the tropics) for those of another (such as the colder zones)? Is this trade an obligation? Should one part of the world (such as the "northern powers") let another refuse to develop and sell its "indispensable products"? Can you think of a case where a powerful country forced a weaker one to trade?

Source: The quotation is from John Christopher Willis, *Agriculture in the Tropics: An Elementary Treatise* (Cambridge: Cambridge University Press, 1909), 38–39.

As in Africa, European missionaries attempted to spread Christianity under the colonial umbrella. Islam, however, was much more successful in gaining new converts, for it had been established in the region for centuries and people did not consider it a religion imposed on them by foreigners.

Education and European ideas had an impact on the political perceptions of the peoples of Southeast Asia and Indonesia. Just as important was their awareness of events in neighboring Asian countries: India, where a nationalist movement arose in the 1880s (see Chapter 26); China, where modernizers were undermining the authority of the Qing (Chapter 27); and especially Japan, whose rapid industrialization culminated in its brilliant victory over Russia in the Russo-Japanese War (1904–1905) (Chapter 28). The spirit of a rising generation was expressed by a young Vietnamese writing soon after the Russo-Japanese War.

> I, . . . an obscure student, having had occasion to study new books and new doctrines, have discovered in a recent history of Japan how they have been able to conquer the impotent Europeans. This is the reason why we have formed an organization. . . . We have selected from young Annamites [Vietnamese] the most energetic, with great capacities for courage, and are sending them to Japan for study. . . . Several years have passed without the French being aware of the movement. . . . Our only aim is to prepare the population for the future.[7]

Hawaii and the Philippines, 1878–1902

By the 1890s, the United States had a fast-growing population and industries that produced more manufactured goods than they could sell at home. Merchants and bankers began to look for export markets. The political mood was also expansionist, and many echoed the feelings of the naval strategist Alfred T. Mahan°: "Whether they will or no, Americans must now begin to look outward. The growing production of the country requires it."

Some Americans had been looking outward for quite some time, especially across the Pacific to China and Japan. In 1878 the United States obtained the harbor of Pago Pago in Samoa as a coaling and naval station, and in 1887 it secured the use of Pearl Harbor in Hawaii for the same purpose. Six years later, American settlers in Hawaii deposed Queen Liliuokalani (1838–1917) and of-

fered the Hawaiian Islands to the United States. At the time President Grover Cleveland (1893–1897) was opposed to annexation, and the settlers had to content themselves with an informal protectorate. By 1898, however, the United States under President William McKinley (1897–1901) had become openly imperialistic. It annexed Hawaii for strategic reasons as a steppingstone to Asia. As the United States became ever more involved in Asian affairs, Hawaii's strategic location brought an inflow of U.S. military personnel, and its fertile land caused planters to import farm laborers from Japan, China, and the Philippines. These immigrants soon outnumbered the native Hawaiians.

While large parts of Asia were falling under colonial domination, the people of the Philippines were chafing under their Spanish rulers. The movement for independence began among young Filipinos studying in Europe. José Rizal, a young doctor working in Spain, was arrested and executed in 1896 for writing patriotic and anticlerical novels. Thereafter, the center of resistance shifted to the Philippines, where **Emilio Aguinaldo,** leader of a secret society, rose in revolt and proclaimed a republic in 1898. The revolutionaries had a good chance of winning independence, for Spain had its hands full with a revolution in Cuba (see below).

Unfortunately for Aguinaldo and his followers, the United States went to war against Spain in April 1898 and quickly overcame Spanish forces in the Philippines and in Cuba. President McKinley had not originally intended to acquire the Philippines. But after the Spanish defeat, he realized that a weakened Spain might lose the islands to another imperialist power. Japan, having recently defeated China in the Sino-Japanese War (1894–1895) and annexed Taiwan (see Chapter 28), was eager to expand its empire. So was Germany, which had taken over parts of New Guinea and Samoa and several Pacific archipelagoes during the 1880s. To forestall them, McKinley purchased the Philippines from Spain for $20 million.

The Filipinos were not eager to trade one master for another. For a while, Aguinaldo cooperated with the Americans in the hope of achieving full independence. When his plan was rejected, in 1899 he rose up again and proclaimed the independence of his country. In spite of protests by anti-imperialists in the United States, the U.S. government decided that its global interests outweighed the interests of the Filipino people. In rebel areas, a U.S. army of occupation tortured prisoners, burned villages and crops, and forced the inhabitants into "reconcentration camps." Many American soldiers tended to look on Filipinos with the same racial contempt with which Europeans viewed their colonial subjects. By the end of the insurrection in 1902, the war had cost the lives of 5,000 Americans and 200,000 Filipinos.

Mahan (mah-HAHN)

Emilio Aguinaldo   In 1896, a revolt led by Emilio Aguinaldo attempted to expel Spaniards from the Philippines. When the United States purchased the Philippines from Spain two years later, the Filipino people were not consulted. Aguinaldo continued his campaign, this time against the American occupation forces, until his capture in 1901. In this picture, he appears on horseback, surrounded by some of his troops.   (Corbis)

After the end of the insurrection, the United States attempted to soften its rule with public works and economic development projects. New buildings went up in the city of Manila; roads, harbors, and railroads were built; and the Philippine economy was tied ever more closely to that of the United States. In 1907 Filipinos were allowed to elect representatives to a legislative assembly; however, ultimate authority remained in the hands of a governor appointed by the president of the United States. In 1916 the Philippines were the first U.S. colony to be promised independence, a promise fulfilled thirty years later.

IMPERIALISM IN LATIN AMERICA

Nations in the Americas followed two divergent paths (see Chapter 25). In Canada and the United States there arose manufacturing industries, powerful corporations, and wealthy financial institutions. Latin America and the Caribbean exported raw materials and foodstuffs and imported manufactured goods. The poverty of their people, the preferences of their elites, and the pressures of the world economy made them increasingly dependent on the industrialized countries. Their political systems saved them from outright annexation by the colonial empires. But their natural resources made them attractive targets for manipulation by the industrial powers, including the United States, in a form of economic dependence called **free-trade imperialism.**

In the Western Hemisphere, therefore, the New Imperialism manifested itself not by a "scramble" for territories but in two other ways. In the larger republics of South America, the pressure was mostly financial and economic. In Central America and the Caribbean, it also included military intervention by the United States.

Railroads and the Imperialism of Free Trade

Latin America's economic potential was huge, for the region could produce many agricultural and mineral products in demand in the industrial countries. What was needed was a means of opening the interior to development. Railroads seemed the perfect answer.

Foreign merchants and bankers as well as Latin American landowners and politicians embraced the new technology. Starting in the 1870s, almost every country

Railroads Penetrate South America   The late nineteenth century saw the construction of several railroad networks in South America, often through rugged and dangerous terrain. This photograph shows the opening of a bridge on the Transandine Railroad in Peru. Flags were raised in honor of American construction and British ownership of the railroad.   (Tony Morrison/South American Pictures)

in Latin America acquired railroads, usually connecting mines or agricultural regions with the nearest port rather than linking up the different parts of the interior. Since Latin America did not have any steel or mechanical industries, all the equipment and building material came from Britain or the United States. So did the money to build the networks, the engineers who designed and maintained them, and the managers who ran them.

Argentina, a land of rich soil that produced wheat, beef, and hides, gained the longest and best-developed rail network south of the United States. By 1914, 86 percent of the railroads in Argentina were owned by British firms, 40 percent of the employees were British, and the official language of the railroads was not Spanish but English. The same was true of mining and industrial enterprises and public utilities throughout Latin America.

In many ways, the situation resembled that of India or Ireland, which also obtained a rail network in exchange for raw materials and agricultural products. The Argentine nationalist Juan Justo saw the parallel:

> English capital has done what English armies could not do. Today our country is tributary to England . . . the gold that the English capitalists take out of Argentina or carry off in the form of products does us no more good than the Irish get from the revenues that the English lords take out of Ireland.[8]

The difference was that the Indians and Irish had little say in the matter because they were under British rule. But in Latin America the political elites encouraged foreign companies with generous concessions as the most rapid way to modernize their countries and enrich the property owners. In countries where the majority of the poor were Indians (as in Mexico and Peru) or of African origin (as in Brazil), they were neither consulted nor allowed to benefit from the railroad boom.

American Expansionism and the Spanish-American War, 1898

After 1865, the European powers used their financial power to penetrate Latin America. But they avoided territorial acquisitions, for four reasons: (1) they were overextended in Africa and Asia; (2) there was no need, because the Latin American governments provided the political backing for the economic arrangements; (3) the Latin Americans had shown themselves capable of resisting invasions, most recently when Mexico fought off the French in the 1860s (see Chapter 25); and (4) the United States, itself a former colony, claimed to defend the entire Western Hemisphere against all outside intervention. This claim, made in the Monroe Doctrine (1823), did not prevent the United States itself from intervening in Latin American affairs.

The United States had long had interests in Cuba, the closest and richest of the Caribbean islands and a Spanish colony. American businesses had invested great sums of money in Cuba's sugar and tobacco industries, and tens of thousands of Cubans had migrated to the United States. In 1895 the Cuban nationalist José Martí started a revolution against Spanish rule. American newspapers thrilled readers with lurid stories of Spanish atrocities, businessmen worried about their investments, and politicians demanded that the U.S. government help liberate Cuba.

On February 15, 1898, the U.S. battleship *Maine* accidentally blew up in Havana harbor, killing 266 American sailors. The U.S. government immediately blamed Spain and issued an ultimatum that the Spanish evacuate Cuba. Spain agreed to the ultimatum, but the American press and Congress were eager for war, and President McKinley did not restrain them.

The Spanish-American War was over quickly. On May 1, 1898 U.S. warships destroyed the Spanish fleet at Manila in the Philippines. Two months later, the United States Navy sank the Spanish Atlantic fleet off Santiago, Cuba. By mid-August, Spain was suing for peace. U.S. Secretary of State John Hay called it "a splendid little war." The United States purchased the Philippines from Spain but took over Puerto Rico and Guam as war booty. The two islands remain American possessions to this day. Cuba became an independent republic, subject, however, to intense interference by the United States.

American Intervention in the Caribbean and Central America, 1901–1914

The nations of the Caribbean and Central America were small and poor, and their governments were corrupt, unstable, and often bankrupt. They seemed to offer an open invitation to foreign interference. A government would borrow money to pay for railroads, harbors, electric power, and other symbols of modernity. When it could not repay the loan, the lending banks in Europe or the United States would ask for assistance from their home governments, which sometimes threatened to intervene. To ward off European intervention, the United States sent in the marines on more than one occasion.

Presidents Theodore Roosevelt (1901–1909), William Taft (1909–1913), and Woodrow Wilson (1913–1921) differed sharply on the proper policy the United States should follow toward the small nations to the south. But all three felt impelled to intervene in the region. Having "liberated" Cuba from Spain, the United States forced the Cuban government to accept the Platt Amendment in 1901. The amendment gave the United States the "right to intervene" to maintain order on the island. The United States used this excuse to occupy Cuba militarily from 1906 to 1909, in 1912, and again from 1917 to 1922. In all but name, Cuba became an American protectorate. U.S. troops also occupied the Dominican Republic from 1904 to 1907 and again in 1916, Nicaragua and Honduras in 1912, and Haiti in 1915. They brought sanitation and material progress but no political improvements.

The United States was especially forceful in Panama, which was a province of Colombia. Here the issue was not corruption or debts but a more vital interest: the construction of a canal across the isthmus of Panama to speed shipping between the east and west coasts of the United States. In 1878 the Frenchman Ferdinand de Lesseps, builder of the Suez Canal, had obtained a concession from Colombia to construct a canal across the isthmus, which lay in Colombian territory. Financial scandals and yellow fever, however, doomed his project.

When the United States acquired Hawaii and the Philippines, it recognized the strategic value of a canal that would allow warships to move quickly between the Atlantic and Pacific Oceans. The main obstacle was Colombia, whose senate refused to give the United States a piece of its territory. In 1903 the U.S. government supported a Panamanian rebellion against Colombia and quickly recognized the independence of Panama. In exchange, it obtained the right to build a canal and to occupy a zone 5 miles (8 kilometers) wide on either side of it. Work began in 1904, and the **Panama Canal** opened on August 15, 1914.

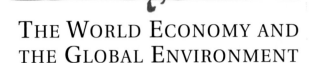

THE WORLD ECONOMY AND THE GLOBAL ENVIRONMENT

The New Imperialists were not traditional conquerors or empire builders like the Spanish conquistadors. Although their conquests were much larger (see Map 29.3), their aim was not only to extend their power over new territories and peoples but to control both the natural world and indigenous societies and put them to work more efficiently than had ever been done before. Both their goals and their methods were industrial. A railroad, for example, was an act of faith as well as a means of transportation. They expressed their belief in progress and their good intentions in the clichés of the time: "the conquest of nature," "the annihilation of time and space," "the taming of the wilderness," and "our civilizing mission."

Expansion of the World Economy

For centuries, spices, sugar, silk and other exotic or tropical products had found a ready market in Europe. The Industrial Revolution vastly expanded this demand. Imports of foods and stimulants such as tea, coffee, and cocoa increased substantially during the nineteenth century. The trade in industrial raw materials grew even faster. Some were the products of agriculture, such as cotton, jute for bags, and palm oil for soap and lubricants. Others were minerals such as diamonds, gold, and copper. There also were wild forest products that only later came to be cultivated: timber for buildings and railroad ties, cinchona bark, rubber for rainwear and tires, and gutta-percha° to insulate electric cables.

The growing needs of the industrial world could not be met by the traditional methods of production and transportation of the nonindustrial world. When the U.S. Civil War interrupted the export of cotton to England in the 1860s, the British turned to India. But they found that Indian cotton was ruined by exposure to rain and dust during the long trip on open carts from the interior of the country to the harbors. To prevent the expansion of their industry from being stifled by the technological backwardness of their newly conquered territories, the imperialists made every effort to bring those territories into the mainstream of the world market.

One great change was in transportation. The Suez and Panama Canals cut travel time and lowered freight costs dramatically. Steamships became more numerous, and as their size increased, new, deeper harbors were needed. The Europeans also built railroads throughout the world; India alone had 37,000 miles (nearly 60,000 kilometers) of track by 1915, almost as much as Germany or Russia. Railroads reached into the interior of Latin America, Canada, China, and Australia. In 1903 the Russians completed the Trans-Siberian Railway from Moscow to Vladivostok on the Pacific. Visionaries even made plans for railroads from Europe to India and from Egypt to South Africa.

Transformation of the Global Environment

The economic changes brought by Europeans and Americans also altered environments around the world. The British, whose craving for tea could not be satisfied with the limited exports available from China, introduced tea into the warm, rainy hill country of Ceylon and northeastern India. In those areas and in Java, thousands of square miles of tropical rain forests were felled to make way for tea plantations.

Economic botany and agricultural science were applied to every promising plant species. European botanists had long collected and classified exotic plants from around the world. In the nineteenth century, they founded botanical gardens in Java, India, Mauritius°, Ceylon, Jamaica, and other tropical colonies. These gardens not only collected local plants but also exchanged plants with other gardens. They were especially active in systematically transferring commercially valuable plant species from one tropical region to another. Cinchona, tobacco, sugar, and other crops were introduced, improved, and vastly expanded in the colonies of Southeast Asia and Indonesia (see Environment and Technology: Imperialism and Tropical Ecology). Cocoa and coffee growing spread over large areas of Brazil and Africa; oil-palm plantations were established in Nigeria and the Congo Basin. Rubber, used to make waterproof garments and bicycle tires, originally came from the latex of *Hevea* trees growing wild in the Brazilian rain forest. Then in the 1870s, British agents smuggled seedlings from Brazil to the Royal Botanic Gardens at Kew near London, and from there to the Botanic Garden of Singapore. These plants formed the nucleus of the enormous rubber economy of Southeast Asia.

Throughout the tropics, land once covered with forests or devoted to shifting slash-and-burn agriculture were transformed into permanent farms and plantations. Even in areas not developed to export crops, growing

---

gutta-percha (gut-tah–PER-cha)

Mauritius (maw-REE-shuss)

Map 29.3 The Great Powers and Their Colonial Possessions in 1913 By 1913, a small handful of countries claimed sovereignty over more than half the land area of the earth. Global power was closely connected with industries and a merchant marine, rather than with a large territory. This explains why Great Britain, the smallest of the great powers, possessed the largest empire.

The colonial powers and their possessions

- Germany
- France
- Great Britain
- Russia
- United States
- Japan
- Belgium
- Netherlands
- Portugal
- Italy
- Spain
- Major shipping routes

populations put pressure on the land. In Java and India, farmers felled trees to obtain arable land and firewood. They terraced hillsides, drained swamps, and dug wells.

Irrigation and water control transformed the dry parts of the tropics as well. In the 1830s, British engineers in India had restored ancient canals that had fallen into disrepair. Their success led them to build new irrigation canals, turning thousands of previously barren acres into well-watered, densely populated farmland. The migration of European experts spread the newest techniques of irrigation engineering around the world. By the turn of the century, irrigation projects were under way wherever rivers flowed through dry lands. In Egypt and Central Asia, irrigation brought more acres under cultivation in one forty-year span than in all previous history.

Railroads had voracious appetites for land and resources. They cut into mountains, spanned rivers and canyons with trestles, and covered as much land with their freight yards as whole cities had needed in previous centuries. They also consumed vast quantities of iron, timber for ties, and coal or wood for fuel. Most important of all, railroads brought people and their cities, farms, and industries to areas previously occupied by small, scattered populations.

Prospectors looking for valuable minerals opened the earth to reveal its riches: gold in South Africa, Australia, and Canada; tin in Nigeria, Malaya, and Bolivia; copper in Chile and Central Africa; iron ore in northern India; and much else. Where mines were dug deep inside the earth, the dirt and rocks brought up with the ores formed huge mounds near mine entrances. Open mines dug to obtain ores lying close to the surface created a landscape of lunar craters, and runoff from the minerals poisoned the water for miles around. Refineries that processed the ores fouled the environment with slag heaps and more toxic runoff.

The transformation of the land by human beings, a constant throughout history, accelerated sharply. Only the changes occurring since 1914 can compare with the transformation of the global environment that took place between 1869 and 1914.

CONCLUSION

The industrialization of the late nineteenth century increased the power of Europeans and North Americans over nature and over the peoples of other continents. They used their new-found power to conquer empires.

The opening of the Suez Canal in 1869 was the symbolic beginning of the New Imperialism. It demonstrated the power of modern industry to subdue nature by carving the land. It stimulated shipping and trade between the industrial countries and the tropics. It deepened the involvement of Europeans in the affairs of the Middle East, Africa, and Asia. From that year until 1914, not only the great powers but smaller countries too—even, in some cases, individual Europeans or Americans—had the power to decide the fate of whole countries. The motivation to conquer or control other lands surely helps explain the New Imperialism. But the means at the disposal of the imperialists—that is, the gap that opened between their technologies and forms of organization and those available to Asians, Africans, and Latin Americans—is equally important.

The new technological means and the enhanced motivations of the imperialists resulted in the most rapid conquest of territories in the history of the world. In less than half a century, almost all of Africa and large parts of Asia and Oceania were added to the colonial empires, while Latin America, nominally independent, was turned into an economic colony of the industrial powers. In the process of developing the economic potential of their empires, the colonial powers transformed natural environments around the world.

The opening of the Panama Canal in August 1914 confirmed the new powers of the industrializing nations—but with a twist, for it was the United States, a latecomer to the game of imperialism, that created the canal. In that same month, the other imperialist nations turned their weapons against one another and began a life-or-death struggle for supremacy in Europe. That conflict is the subject of the next chapter.

■ Key Terms

Suez Canal	Afrikaners
New Imperialism	Cecil Rhodes Asante
Battle of Omdurman	Asante
colonialism	Emperor Menelik
"scramble" for Africa	Emilio Aguinaldo
Henry Morton Stanley	free-trade imperialism
King Leopold II (Belgium)	Panama Canal
Berlin Conference	

■ Suggested Readings

Two good introductions to imperialism are D. K. Fieldhouse, *Colonialism, 1870–1945* (1981), and Scott B. Cook, *Colonial Encounters in the Age of High Imperialism* (1996). The debate on the theories of imperialism is presented in Roger Owen and Robert Sutcliffe, *Studies in the Theory of Imperialism* (1972), and in Winfried Baumgart, *Imperialism* (1982). The British Empire is the subject of Bernard Porter, *The Lion's Share: A Short History of British Imperialism, 1850–1970* (1976).

On Africa in this period see Roland Oliver and Anthony Atmore, *Africa Since 1800*, new ed. (1994); Roland Oliver and G. N. Sanderson, eds., *From 1870 to 1905* (1985), and A. D. Roberts, ed., *From 1905 to 1940* (1986), in *The Cambridge History of Africa*; and A. Adu Boahen, ed., *Africa Under Colonial Domination, 1880–1935* (1985), in *UNESCO General History of Africa*. The European conquest of Africa is recounted in Thomas Pakenham, *The Scramble for Africa* (1991); Bruce Vandervort, *Wars of Imperial Conquest in Africa, 1830–1914* (1998); and Ronald Robinson and John Gallagher, *Africa and the Victorians: The Climax of Imperialism* (1961). Adam Hochschild's *King Leopold's Ghost: A Story of Greed, Terror, and Heroism in Colonial Africa* (1998) is a very readable account of imperialism in the Belgian Congo. The classic novel about the impact of colonial rule on African society is Chinua Achebe's *Things Fall Apart* (1958).

Imperial rivalries in Asia are the subject of Akira Iriye, *Across the Pacific: An Inner History of American-East Asian Relations*, rev. ed. (1992); David Gillard, *The Struggle for Asia, 1828–1914: A Study in British and Russian Imperialism* (1977); and Peter Hopkirk, *The Great Game: The Struggle for Empire in Central Asia* (1994). On other aspects of imperialism in Asia see Clifford Geertz, *Agricultural Involution: The Process of Ecological Change in Indonesia* (1963), especially chapters 4 and 5, and Stanley Karnow, *In Our Image: America's Empire in the Philippines* (1989).

On Latin America in this period see David Bushnell and Neill Macauley, *The Emergence of Latin America in the Nineteenth Century* (1994). Free-trade imperialism is the subject of D. C. M. Platt, *Latin America and British Trade, 1806–1914* (1973). On American expansionism see David Healy, *Drive to Hegemony: The United States in the Caribbean, 1898–1917* (1989), and Walter LaFeber, *The Panama Canal*, rev. ed. (1990).

On race relations in the colonial world see Noel Mostert, *Frontiers: The Epic of South Africa's Creation and the Tragedy of the Xhosa People* (1992), and Robert Huttenback, *Racism and Empire: White Settlers and Colored Immigrants in the British Self-Governing Colonies, 1830–1910* (1976). Gender relations are the subject of Caroline Oliver, *Western Women in Colonial Africa* (1982), and Cheryl Walker, ed., *Women and Gender in Southern Africa to 1945* (1990). David Northrup's *Indentured Labor in the Age of Imperialism, 1834–1922* (1995), discusses migrations and

labor. Franz Fanon, *The Wretched of the Earth* (1966), and Albert Memmi, *The Colonizer and the Colonized* (1967), examine colonialism from the point of view of the colonized.

The impact of technology on the New Imperialism is the subject of Daniel R. Headrick, *The Tools of Empire: Technology and European Imperialism in the Nineteenth Century* (1981) and *The Tentacles of Progress: Technology Transfer in the Age of Imperialism, 1850–1940* (1988), and Clarence B. Davis and Kenneth E. Wilburn, Jr., eds., *Railway Imperialism* (1991).

On the economic and demographic transformation of Africa and Asia see Eric Wolf, *Europe and the People Without History* (1982), especially chapters 11 and 12. The impact on the environment is the subject of R. P. Tucker and J. F. Richards, *Deforestation and the Nineteenth-Century World Economy* (1983); Donal McCracken, *Gardens of Empire: Botanical Institutions of the Victorian British Empire* (1997); Lucile H. Brockway, *Science and Colonial Expansion: The Role of the British Royal Botanic Gardens* (1979); and David Arnold and Ramchandra Guha, eds., *Nature, Culture, Imperialism: Essays on the Environmental History of South Asia* (1995).

▪ Notes

1. *Journal officiel* (November 29, 1869), quoted in Georges Douin, *Histoire du règne du khédive Ismaïl* (Rome: Reale Societá di geografia d'Egitto, 1933), 453.

2. E. Desplaces in *Journal de l'Union des Deux Mers* (December 15, 1869), quoted ibid., 453.

3. Winston Churchill, *The River War: An Account of the Reconquest of the Soudan* (New York: Charles Scribner's Sons, 1933), 300.

4. "Correspondence and Report from His Majesty's Consul at Boma respecting the Administration of the Independent State of the Congo," *British Parliamentary Papers, Accounts and Papers*, 1904 (Cd. 1933), lxii, 357.

5. Robert W. July, *A History of the Africa People*, 3d ed. (New York: Charles Scribner's Sons, 1980), 323.

6. George Shepperson and Thomas Price, *Independent African* (Edinburgh: University Press, 1958), 163–164, quoted in Roland Oliver and Anthony Atmore, *Africa Since 1800*, 4th ed. (Cambridge: Cambridge University Press, 1994), 150.

7. Thomas Edson Ennis, *French Policy and Development in Indochina* (Chicago: University of Chicago Press, 1936), 178, quoted in K. M. Panikkar, *Asia and Western Dominance* (New York: Collier, 1969), 167.

8. Quoted in Stanley J. Stein and Barbara H. Stein, *The Colonial Heritage of Latin America* (New York: Oxford University Press, 1970), 151.

30

THE CRISIS OF THE IMPERIAL ORDER,

1900–1929

Origins of the Crisis in Europe and the Middle East • The "Great War" and the
Russian Revolutions, 1914–1918 • Peace and Dislocation in Europe, 1919–1929 •
China and Japan: Contrasting Destinies • The New Middle East •
Society, Culture, and Technology in the Industrialized World

ENVIRONMENT AND TECHNOLOGY: Cities Old and New

SOCIETY AND CULTURE: The Experience of Battle

The Western Front in World War I   In a landscape ravaged by artillery fire,
two soldiers dash for cover amid shell holes and the charred remains of a forest.

On June 28, 1914, Archduke Franz Ferdinand, heir to the throne of Austria-Hungary, was riding in an open carriage through Sarajevo, capital of the province of Bosnia-Herzegovina, which Austria had annexed six years before. When the carriage stopped momentarily, Gavrilo Princip, member of a pro-Serbian conspiracy, fired his pistol twice, killing the archduke and his wife.

Those shots ignited a war that spread throughout Europe, then turned into a global war as the Ottoman Empire fought against Britain in the Middle East and Japan attacked German positions in China. France and Britain involved their empires in the war and brought Africans, Indians, Australians, and Canadians to Europe to fight and labor on the front lines. Finally, in 1917, the United States entered the fray.

The next three chapters tell a story of violence and hope. In this chapter, we will look at the causes of war between the great powers, the consequences of that conflict in Europe, the Middle East, and Russia, and the upheavals in China and Japan. At the same time, we will review the accelerating rate of technological change, which made the first half of the twentieth century so violent and so hopeful. Industrialization continued apace. Entirely new technologies, and the organizations that produced and applied them, made war more dangerous yet also allowed far more people to live healthier, more comfortable, and more interesting lives than ever before.

As you read this chapter, ask yourself the following questions:

- How did the First World War lead to revolution in Russia and the disintegration of several once-powerful empires?
- What role did the war play in eroding European dominance in the world?
- Why did China and Japan follow such divergent paths in this period?
- How did European and North American society and technology change in the aftermath of the war?

ORIGINS OF THE CRISIS IN EUROPE AND THE MIDDLE EAST

When the twentieth century opened, the world seemed firmly under the control of the great powers that you read about in Chapter 28. The first decade of the twentieth century was a period of relative peace and economic growth in most of the world. Trade boomed. Several new technologies—airplanes, automobiles, radio, and cinema—aroused much excitement. The great powers consolidated their colonial conquests of the previous decades. Their alliances were so evenly matched that they seemed, to observers at the time, likely to maintain peace. The only international war of the period, the Russo-Japanese War (1904–1905), ended quickly with a decisive Japanese victory.

However, two major changes were undermining the apparent stability of the world. In Europe, tensions mounted as Germany, with its growing industrial and military might, challenged Britain at sea and France in Morocco. The Ottoman Empire grew weaker, leaving a dangerous power vacuum. The resulting chaos in the Balkans, the unstable borderlands between a predominantly Christian Europe and a predominantly Muslim Middle East, gradually draw the European powers into a web of hostilities.

| **The Ottoman Empire and the Balkans** | From the fifteenth to the nineteenth century, the Ottoman Empire was one of the world's richest and most powerful |

states. By the late nineteenth century, however, it had fallen behind economically, technologically, and militarily, and Europeans referred to it as the "sick man of Europe."

As the Ottoman Empire weakened, it began losing those outlying provinces situated closest to Europe. Macedonia rebelled in 1902–1903. In 1908 Austria-Hungary annexed Bosnia. Crete, occupied by European "peacekeepers" since 1898, merged with Greece in 1909. A year later, Albania became independent. In 1912 Italy conquered Libya, the Ottomans' last foothold in Africa. In 1912–1913 in rapid succession came two Balkan Wars in which Serbia, Bulgaria, Romania, and Greece chased the Turks out of Europe, except for a small enclave around Constantinople.

CHRONOLOGY

	Europe and North America	Middle East	East Asia
1900			**1900** Boxer Rebellion in China
	1904 British-French Entente		**1904–1905** Russo-Japanese War
	1907 British-Russian Entente		
1910		**1909** Young Turks overthrow Sultan Abdul Hamid	**1911** Chinese revolutionaries led by Sun Yat-sen overthrow Qing dynasty
	1912–1913 Balkan Wars	**1912** Italy conquers Libya, last Ottoman territory in Africa	
	1914 Assassination of Archduke Franz Ferdinand sparks World War I	**1915** British defeat at Gallipoli	**1915** Japan presents Twenty-One Demands to China
	1916 Battles of Verdun and the Somme	**1916** Arab Revolt in Arabia	
	1917 Russian Revolutions; United States enters the war	**1917** Balfour Declaration	
	1918 Armistice ends World War I		
	1918–1921 Civil war in Russia		
	1919 Treaty of Versailles	**1919–1922** War between Turkey and Greece	**1919** May Fourth Movement in China
1920	**1920** First commercial radio broadcast (United States)		
	1921 New Economic Policy in Russia	**1922** Egypt nominally independent	
		1923 Mustafa Kemal proclaims Turkey a republic	
	1927 Charles Lindbergh flies alone across the Atlantic		**1927** Guomindang forces occupy Shanghai and expel Communists

The European powers meddled in the internal affairs of the Ottoman Empire, sometimes cooperatively but often as rivals. Russia saw itself as the protector of the Slavic peoples of the Balkans. France and Britain, posing as protectors of Christian minorities, controlled Ottoman finances, taxes, railroads, mines, and public utilities. Austria-Hungary coveted Ottoman lands inhabited by Slavs, thereby angering the Russians.

In reaction, the Turks began to assert themselves against rebellious minorities and meddling foreigners. Many officers in the army, the most Europeanized segment of Turkish society, blamed Sultan Abdul Hamid II (r. 1876–1909) for the decline of the empire. The group known as "Young Turks" began conspiring to force a constitution on the Sultan. They alienated other anti-Ottoman groups by advocating centralized rule and the Turkification of ethnic minorities.

In 1909 the parliament, dominated by Young Turks, overthrew Abdul Hamid and replaced him with his brother. The new regime began to reform the police, the bureaucracy, and the education system. At the same time, it cracked down on Greek and Armenian minori-

ties. Galvanized by their defeat in the Balkan Wars, the Turks turned to Germany, the European country that had meddled least in Ottoman affairs, and hired a German general to modernize Turkey's armed forces.

Nationalism, Alliances, and Military Strategy

The assassination of the Archduke Franz Ferdinand triggered a chain of events over which military and political leaders lost control. The escalation from assassination to global war had causes that went back many years. One was nationalism, which bound citizens to their ethnic group and led them, when called upon, to kill people they viewed as enemies. Another was the system of alliances and military plans that the great powers had devised to protect themselves from their rivals. A third was Germany's yearning to dominate Europe.

Nationalism was deeply rooted in European culture. As we saw in Chapter 28, it united the citizens of France, Britain, and Germany behind their respective

Map 30.1 Europe in 1913 On the eve of World War I, Europe was divided between two great alliance systems—the Central Powers (Germany, Austria-Hungary, and Italy) and the Entente (France, Great Britain, and Russia)—and their respective colonial empires. These alliances were not stable. When war broke out, the Central Powers lost Italy but gained the Ottoman Empire.

governments and gave them tremendous cohesion and strength of purpose. Only the most powerful feelings could inspire millions of men to march obediently into battle and sustain civilian populations through years of hardship.

Nationalism could also be a dividing rather than a unifying force. The large but fragile multinational Russian, Austro-Hungarian, and Ottoman Empires contained numerous ethnic and religious minorities. Having repressed them for centuries, the governments could never count on their full support. The very existence of an independent Serbia threatened Austria-Hungary by stirring up the hopes and resentments of its Slavic populations.

Because of the spread of nationalism, most people viewed war as a crusade for liberty or as long-overdue revenge for past injustices. In the course of the nineteenth century, as memories of the misery and carnage caused by the Napoleonic Wars faded, revulsion against war gradually weakened. The few wars fought in Europe after 1815, such as the Crimean War of 1853–1856 and the Franco-Prussian War of 1871, had been short and caused few casualties or long-term consequences. And in the wars of the New Imperialism (see Chapter 29), Europeans almost always had been victorious at a small cost in money and manpower. The well-to-do began to believe that only war could heal the class divisions in their societies and make workers unite behind their "natural" leaders.

What turned an incident in a small town in the Balkans into a conflict involving all the great powers was the system of alliances that had grown up over the previous decades. At the center of Europe stood Germany, the most heavily industrialized country in Europe. Its army was the best trained and equipped. Germany was challenging Great Britain's naval supremacy by building a series of "dreadnoughts"—heavily armed battleships. It joined Austria-Hungary and Italy in the Triple Alliance in 1882, while France allied itself with Russia. In 1904 Britain joined France in an Entente° ("understanding"), and in 1907 Britain and Russia buried their differences and formed an Entente. Europe was thus divided into two blocs of roughly equal power (see Map 30.1).

The alliance system was cursed by inflexible military planning. In 1914 western and central Europe had highly developed railroad networks but very few motor vehicles. European armies had grown to include millions of soldiers and more millions of reservists. To mobilize these forces and transport them to battle would be an enormous project requiring thousands of trains running on precise schedules. As a result, once under way, a country's mobilization could not be canceled or postponed without creating chaos.

In the years before World War I, military planners in France and Germany had worked out elaborate railroad timetables to mobilize their respective armies in a few days. Other countries were less well prepared. Russia, a large country with an underdeveloped rail system, needed several weeks to mobilize its forces. Britain, with only a tiny volunteer army, had no mobilization plans, and German planners believed that the British would stay out of a war on the European continent. So that Germany could avoid having to fight France and Russia at the same time, German war plans called for German generals to defeat France in a matter of days, then transport their entire army by train across Germany to the Russian border before Russia could fully mobilize.

On July 28, emboldened by the backing of Germany, Austria-Hungary declared war on Serbia. Diplomats, statesmen, and monarchs sent one another frantic telegrams, but they had lost control of events, for the declaration of war triggered the general mobilization plans of Russia, France, and Germany. On July 29, the Russian government ordered general mobilization to force Austria to back down. On August 1, France honored its treaty obligation to Russia and ordered general mobilization. Minutes later Germany did likewise. Because of the rigid railroad timetables, war was now automatic.

The German plan was to wheel around through neutral Belgium and into northwestern France. The German General Staff expected France to capitulate before the British could get involved. But on August 3, when German troops entered Belgium, Britain demanded their withdrawal. When Germany refused, Britain declared war on Germany.

THE "GREAT WAR" AND THE RUSSIAN REVOLUTIONS, 1914–1918

Throughout Europe, people greeted the outbreak of war with parades and flags and hopes for a quick victory. German troops marched off to the front shouting "To Paris!" Spectators in France encouraged marching French troops with shouts of "Send me the Kaiser's moustache!" The British poet Rupert Brooke began a poem with the line: "Now God be thanked Who has matched us with His hour." The German sociologist Max

---

Entente (on-TONT)

Weber wrote: "This war, with all its ghastliness, is nevertheless grand and wonderful. It is worth experiencing." When the war began, very few imagined that their side might not win, and no one foresaw that everyone would lose.

In Russia the effect of the war was especially devastating, for it destroyed the old society, opened the door to revolution and civil war, and introduced a radical new political system. By clearing away the old, the upheaval of war prepared Russia to industrialize under the leadership of professional revolutionaries.

Stalemate, 1914–1917

The war that erupted in 1914 was known as the "Great War" until the 1940s, when a far greater one overshadowed it. Its form came as a surprise to all belligerents, from the generals on down. In the classic battles—from the time of Alexander the Great to Napoleon—that every officer studied, the advantage always went to the fastest-moving army led by the boldest general. In 1914 the generals' carefully drawn-up plans went awry from the start. Believing that a spirited attack would always prevail, French generals hurled their troops, dressed in bright blue-and-red uniforms, against the well-defended German border and suffered a crushing defeat. In battle after battle the much larger German armies defeated the French and the British. By early September they held Belgium and northern France and were fast approaching Paris.

German victory seemed assured. But German troops, who had marched and fought for a month, were exhausted, and their generals wavered. When Russia attacked eastern Germany, troops needed for the final push into France were shifted to the Russian front. A gap opened between two German armies along the Marne River, into which General Joseph Joffre moved France's last reserves. At the Battle of the Marne (September 5–12, 1914), the Germans were thrown back several miles.

During the next month, both sides spread out until they formed an unbroken line extending over 300 miles

Trench Warfare in World War I German and Allied soldiers on the Western Front faced each other from elaborate networks of trenches. Attacking meant jumping out of the trenches and racing across a no-man's land of mud and barbed wire. Here we see Princess Patricia's Canadian Light Infantry repelling a German attack near Ypres, in northern France, in March 1915, using machine guns, rifles, and hand grenades. (Courtesy, The Princess Patricia's Canadian Light Infantry, Regimental Museum and Archives)

SOCIETY & CULTURE

The Experience of Battle

What is it like to be a soldier in the midst of a battle? Here is how the German writer Erich Maria Remarque, a veteran of World War I, described a battle from a soldier's point of view in his classic war novel All Quiet on the Western Front *(1928).*

Night again. We are deadened by the strain—a deadly tension that scrapes along one's spine like a gapped knife. Our legs refuse to move, our hands tremble, our bodies are a thin skin stretched painfully over repressed madness, over an almost irresistible, bursting roar. We have neither flesh nor muscles any longer, we dare not look at one another for fear of some incalculable thing. So we shut our teeth—it will end—it will end—perhaps we will come through.

Suddenly the nearer explosions cease. The shelling continues but it has lifted and falls behind us, our trench is free. We seize the hand-grenades, pitch them out in front of the dug-out and jump after them. The bombardment has stopped and a heavy barrage now falls behind us. The attack has come.

No one would believe that in this howling waste there could still be men; but steel helmets now appear on all sides of the trench, and fifty yards from us a machine-gun is already in position and barking.

The wire entanglements are torn to pieces. Yet they offer some obstacle. We see the storm-troops coming. Our artillery opens fire. Machine-guns rattle, rifles crack. The charge works its way across. Haie and Kropp begin with the hand-grenades. They throw as fast as they can, others pass them the handles with the strings already pulled. . . .

We recognize the smooth distorted faces, the helmets: they are French. They have already suffered heavily when they reach the remnants of the barbed wire entanglements. A whole line has gone down before our machine-guns; then we have a lot of stoppages and they come nearer.

I see one of them, his face upturned, fall into a wire cradle. His body collapses, his hands remain suspended as though he were praying. Then his body drops clean away and only his hands with the stumps of his arms, shot off, now hang in the wire.

How successful is Remarque in conveying a soldier's experiences to readers who have never been to war? How do you explain what makes men willing to fight such battles?

Source: Erich Maria Remarque, *All Quiet on the Western Front,* trans. A. W. Wheen (Boston: Little, Brown, 1958), 98–99. *Im Westen Nichts Neues,* copyright 1928 by Ullstein A. G. Copyright renewed © 1956, 1957, 1958 by Erich Maria Remarque. *All Quiet on the Western Front,* copyright © 1929, 1930 by Little, Brown and Company. All rights reserved.

(some 500 kilometers) from the North Sea to the border of Switzerland. All along this line, the **Western Front,** the opposing troops prepared their defenses. Their most potent weapons were machine guns, which provided an almost impenetrable defense against advancing infantry but were useless for the offensive because they were too heavy for one man to carry and took too much time to set up. To escape the deadly streams of bullets, soldiers dug holes for themselves in the ground, connected the holes to form shallow trenches, then dug communications trenches to the rear. Within weeks, the battlefields were scarred up with lines of trenches several feet deep, their tops protected by sandbags and their floors covered with planks. Despite all the work they put into them, the soldiers spent much of the year soaked and covered with mud (see Society and Culture: The Experience of Battle). Trenches were nothing new. What was extraordinary about this war was that the trenches along

the entire Western Front were connected, leaving no gaps through which armies could advance (see Map 30.2). How, then, could either side ever hope to win?

For four years, generals on each side again and again ordered their troops to attack. They knew the casualties would be enormous, but they expected the enemy to run out of young men before their side did. In battle after battle, thousands of young men on one side climbed out of their trenches, raced across the open fields, and were mowed down by enemy machine-gun fire. Hoping to destroy the machine guns, the attacking force would saturate the entrenched enemy lines with artillery barrages. But this tactic would alert the defenders to an impending attack and allow them to rush in reinforcements and set up new machine guns. Attacking troops released poison gas to kill or blind the defenders, only to find that gas also immobilized the onrushing attackers themselves, adding to the horror of battle.

Map 30.2 **The First World War in Europe** Most of the fighting in World War I took place on two fronts. After an initial surge through Belgium into northern France, the German offensive bogged down for four years along the Western Front. To the east, the German armies conquered a large part of Russia during 1917 and early 1918. Despite spectacular victories in the east, Germany lost the war because its armies collapsed along the strategically important Western Front.

The year 1916 saw the bloodiest and most futile battles of the war. The Germans attacked French forts at Verdun, losing 281,000 men and causing 315,000 French casualties. In retaliation, the British attacked the Germans at the Somme River and suffered 420,000 casualties—60,000 on the first day alone—while the Germans lost 450,000 and the French 200,000.

This was not warfare as it had ever been waged before; it was mass slaughter in a moonscape of mud, steel, and flesh. Both sides attacked and defended, but neither side could win, for the armies were stalemated by trenches and machine guns. During four years of the bloodiest fighting the world had ever seen, the Western Front moved no more than a few miles one way or another.

At sea, the war was just as inconclusive. As soon as the war broke out, the British cut the German overseas telegraph cables, blockaded the coasts of Germany and Austria-Hungary, and set out to capture or sink all enemy ships still at sea. The German High Seas Fleet, built at enormous cost, seldom left port. Only once, in May 1916, did it confront the British Grand Fleet. At the Battle of Jutland, off the coast of Denmark, the two fleets lost roughly equal numbers of ships, and the Germans escaped back to their harbors.

Britain ruled the waves but not the ocean below the surface. In early 1915, in retaliation for the British naval blockade, Germany announced a blockade of Britain by submarines. Unlike surface ships, submarines could not rescue the passengers of a sinking ship or distinguish between neutral and enemy ships. German submarines attacked every vessel they could. One of their victims was British ocean liner *Lusitania*. The death toll from that attack was 1,198 people, 139 of them Americans. When the United States protested, Germany ceased its submarine campaign, hoping to keep America neutral.

The Home Front and the War Economy

Trench-bound armies demanded ever more weapons, ammunition, and food, so civilians had to work harder, eat less, and pay higher taxes. Textiles, coal, meat, fats, and imported products such as tea and sugar were strictly rationed. Governments gradually imposed stringent controls over all aspects of their economies. Socialists and labor unions participated actively in the war effort, for they found government regulation more to their liking than unfettered free enterprise.

The war economy transformed civilian life. In France and Britain, food rations were allocated according to need, improving nutrition among the poor. Unemployment vanished. Thousands of Africans, Indians, and

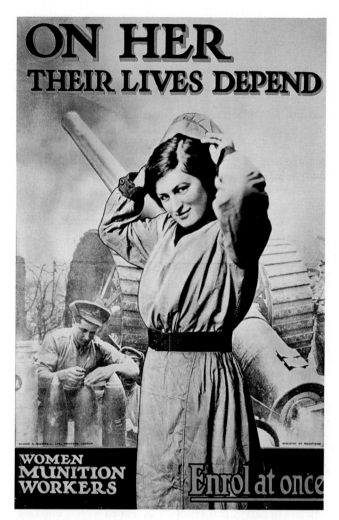

Women in World War I Women played a more important role in World War I than in previous wars. As the armies drafted millions of men, employers hired women for essential war work. This poster extolling the importance of women workers in supplying munitions was probably designed to recruit women for factory jobs. (The Art Archive Limited)

Chinese were recruited for heavy labor in Europe. Employers hired women to fill jobs in steel mills, mines, and munitions plants vacated by men off to war. Some women became streetcar drivers, mail carriers, and police. Others found work in the burgeoning government bureaucracies. Many joined auxiliary military services as doctors, nurses, mechanics, and ambulance drivers; after 1917, as the war took its toll of young men, the British government established women's auxiliary units for the army, navy, and air force. Though clearly intended "for the duration only," these positions gave thousands of women a sense of participation in the war effort and a taste of personal and financial independence.

German civilians paid an especially high price for the war, for the British naval blockade severed their overseas trade. The German chemical industry developed synthetic explosives and fuel, but synthetic food was not an option. Wheat flour disappeared, replaced first by rye, then by potatoes and turnips, then by acorns and chestnuts, and finally by sawdust. After the failure of the potato crop in 1916 came the "turnip winter," when people had to survive on 1,000 calories per day, half of the normal amount that an active adult needed. Women, children, and the elderly were especially hard hit. Soldiers at the front went hungry and raided enemy lines to scavenge food.

When the war began, the British and French overran German Togo on the West African coast. The much larger German colonies of Southwest Africa and German Cameroon were conquered in 1915. In Tanganyika, the Germans remained undefeated until the end of the war.

The war also brought hardships to Europe's African colonies. The Europeans requisitioned foodstuffs, imposed heavy taxes, and forced Africans to grow export crops and sell them at low prices. Many Europeans stationed in Africa left to join the war, leaving large areas with little or no European presence. In Nigeria, Libya, Nyasaland (now Malawi), and other colonies, the combination of increased demands on Africans and fewer European officials led to uprisings that lasted for several years.

Over a million Africans served in the various armies, and perhaps three times that number were drafted as porters to carry army equipment. Faced with a shortage of young Frenchmen, France drafted Africans into its army, where many fought side by side with Europeans. The Senegalese Blaise Diagne°, the first African elected to France's Chamber of Deputies in 1914, campaigned for African support of the war effort. Put in charge of recruiting African soldiers, he insisted on equal rights for African and European soldiers and an extension of the franchise to educated Africans. These demands were only partially met.

One country grew rich during the war: the United States. For two and a half years, the United States stayed technically neutral—that is, it did not fight but did a roaring business supplying France and Britain. When the United States entered the war in 1917, businesses engaging in war production made spectacular profits. Civilians were exhorted to help the war effort by investing their savings in war bonds and growing food in backyard "victory gardens." Facing labor shortages, employers hired women and African-Americans. Employment opportunities created by the war played a major role in the migration of black Americans from the rural south to the cities of the north.

The Ottoman Empire at War

On August 2, 1914, the Turks signed a secret alliance with Germany. In November they joined the fighting, hoping to gain land at Russia's expense. But the campaign in the Caucasus proved disastrous for both armies and for the civilian populations as well. The Turks deported the Armenians, whom they suspected of being pro-Russian, from their homelands in eastern Anatolia to Syria and other parts of the Ottoman Empire. During the forced march across the mountains in the winter, hundreds of thousands of Armenians died of hunger and exposure; this massacre was a precedent for even ghastlier tragedies still to come.

The Turks also closed the Dardanelles, the strait between the Mediterranean and Black Seas (see Map 30.2). British officials, seeing little hope of victory on the Western Front, tried to force open the Dardanelles by landing troops on the nearby Gallipoli Peninsula in 1915. Turkish troops pushed the invaders back into the sea.

Having failed at the Dardanelles, the British tried to subvert the Ottoman Empire from within by promising the emir (prince) of Mecca, Hussein ibn Ali, a kingdom of his own if he would lead an Arab revolt against the Turks. In 1916 Hussein rose up and was proclaimed king of Hejaz° (western Arabia). His son **Faisal**° led an Arab army in support of the British advance from Egypt into Palestine and Syria. The Arab Revolt of 1916 did not affect the struggle in Europe, but it did contribute to the defeat of the Ottoman Empire.

The British made promises to Jews as well as Arabs. For centuries, Jewish minorities had lived in eastern and Central Europe, where they developed a thriving culture despite frequent persecutions. By the early twentieth century a nationalist movement called Zionism, led by **Theodore Herzl,** arose among those who wanted to return to their ancestral homeland in Palestine. The concept of a Jewish homeland appealed to many Europeans, Jews and gentiles alike, as a humanitarian solution to the problem of anti-Semitism.

By 1917, Chaim Weizmann°, leader of the British Zionists, had persuaded several British politicians that a

---

Blaise Diagne (blez dee-AHN-yuh)

Hejaz (HEE-jaz)   **Faisal** (fie-SAHL)
Chaim Weizmann (hi-um VITES-mun)

Jewish homeland in Palestine should be carved out of the Ottoman Empire and placed under British protection, thereby strengthening the Allied cause (as the Entente was now called). In November, as British armies were advancing on Jerusalem, Foreign Secretary Sir Arthur Balfour wrote that "His Majesty's Government view with favor the establishment in Palestine of a national home for the Jewish people and will use their best endeavours to facilitate the achievement of that object, it being clearly understood that nothing shall be done which may prejudice the civil and religious rights of existing non-Jewish communities in Palestine." The British did not foresee that this statement, known as the **Balfour Declaration,** would lead to conflicts between Palestinians and Jewish settlers.

Britain also sent troops to southern Mesopotamia to secure the oil pipeline from Iran. Then they moved north, taking Baghdad in early 1917. The officers for the Mesopotamian campaign were British, but most of the troops and equipment came from India. Most Indians, like other colonial subjects of Britain, supported the war effort despite the hardships it caused. Their involvement in the war bolstered the movement for Indian independence (see Chapter 32).

Double Revolution in Russia, 1917

At the beginning of the war, Russia had the largest army in the world, but its generals were incompetent, supplies were lacking, and soldiers were poorly trained and equipped. In August 1914, two Russian armies invaded eastern Germany but were thrown back. Several times the Russians defeated the Austro-Hungarian army, only to be defeated in turn by the Germans.

In 1916, after a string of defeats, the Russian army ran out of ammunition and other essential supplies. Soldiers were ordered into battle unarmed and told to pick up the rifles of fallen comrades. With so many men in the army, railroads broke down for lack of fuel and parts, and crops rotted in the fields. Civilians faced shortages and widespread hunger. In the cities food and fuel became scarce. During the bitterly cold winter of 1916–1917, factory workers and housewives had to line up in front of grocery stores before dawn in order to get something to eat. The court of Tsar° Nicholas II, however, remained as extravagant and corrupt as ever.

In early March 1917 (February by the old Russian calendar), food ran out in Petrograd (formerly called St. Petersburg), the capital. Housewives and women factory

workers staged mass demonstrations. Soldiers mutinied and joined striking workers to form soviets (councils) to take over factories and barracks. A few days later, the tsar abdicated, and leaders of the parliamentary parties, led by Alexander Kerensky, formed a Provisional Government. Thus began what Russians called the "February Revolution."

Revolutionary groups formerly hunted by the tsar's police came out of hiding. Most numerous were the Social Revolutionaries, who advocated the redistribution of land to the peasants. The Social Democrats, a Marxist party, were divided into two factions: Mensheviks and Bolsheviks. The Mensheviks advocated electoral politics and reform in the tradition of European Socialists and had a large following among intellectuals and factory workers. The **Bolsheviks,** their rivals, were a small but tightly disciplined group of radicals obedient to the will of their leader, **Vladimir Lenin** (1870–1924).

Lenin, the son of a government official, became a revolutionary in his teens when his older brother was executed for plotting to kill the tsar. He spent years in exile, first in Siberia and later in Switzerland, where he devoted his full attention to organizing his followers. He professed Marx's ideas concerning class conflict (see Chapter 28), but he never visited a factory or a farm. His goal was to create a party that would lead the revolution rather than wait for it. He explained: "Classes are led by parties and parties are led by individuals. . . . The will of a class is sometimes fulfilled by a dictator."

In early April 1917, the German government, hoping to destabilize Russia, allowed Lenin to travel from Switzerland to Russia in a sealed railway car. As soon as he arrived in Petrograd, he announced his program: immediate peace, all power to the soviets, and transfers of land to the peasants and factories to the workers. This plan proved immensely popular among soldiers and workers exhausted by the war.

The next few months witnessed a tug-of-war between the Provisional Government and the various revolutionary factions in Petrograd. When Kerensky ordered another offensive against the Germans, Russian soldiers began to desert by the hundreds of thousands, throwing away their rifles and walking back to their villages. As the Germans advanced, Russian resistance melted and the government lost what little support it had.

The Bolsheviks meanwhile were gaining support among the workers of Petrograd and the soldiers and sailors stationed there. On November 6, 1917 (October 24 in the Russian calendar), they rose up and took over the city, calling their action the "October Revolution." Their sudden move surprised rival revolutionary groups that believed that a "socialist" revolution could happen

---

tsar (zahr)

only after many years of "bourgeois" rule. Lenin, however, was more interested in power than in the fine points of Marxist doctrine. He overthrew the Provisional Government and arrested Mensheviks, Social Revolutionaries, and other rivals.

Seizing Petrograd was only the first step, for the rest of Russia was in chaos. The Bolsheviks nationalized all private land and ordered the peasants to hand over their crops without compensation. The peasants, having seized their landlords' estates, resisted. In the cities, the Bolsheviks took over the factories and drafted the workers into compulsory labor brigades. To enforce his rule, Lenin created the Cheka, a secret police force with powers to arrest and execute opponents.

The Bolsheviks also sued for peace with Germany and Austria-Hungary. By the Treaty of Brest-Litovsk, signed on March 3, 1918, Russia lost territories containing a third of its population and wealth. Poland, Finland, and the Baltic states (Estonia, Latvia, and Lithuania) became independent republics. Russian colonies in Central Asia and the Caucasus broke away temporarily.

The End of the War in Western Europe, 1917–1918

Like many other Americans, President **Woodrow Wilson** wanted to stay out of the European conflict. For nearly three years he kept the United States neutral and tried to persuade the belligerents to compromise. But in late 1916, German leaders decided to starve the British into submission by using submarines to sink merchant ships carrying food supplies to Great Britain. The Germans knew that unrestricted submarine warfare was likely to bring the United States into the war, but they were willing to gamble that Britain and France would collapse before the United States could send enough troops to help them.

The submarine campaign resumed on February 1, 1917, but the German gamble failed. The British organized their merchant ships into convoys protected by destroyers, and on April 6, President Wilson asked the United States Congress to declare war on Germany.

On the Western Front, the two sides were so evenly matched in 1917 that the war seemed unlikely to end until one side or the other ran out of young men. Losing hope of winning, soldiers began to mutiny. In May 1917, before the arrival of U.S. forces, fifty-four of one hundred French divisions along the Western Front refused to attack. During the summer, Italian troops also mutinied, panicked, or deserted.

Between March and August 1918, General Erich von Ludendorff launched a series of surprise attacks that broke through the front at several places and pushed to within 40 miles (64 kilometers) of Paris. But victory eluded him. Meanwhile, every month was bringing another 250,000 American troops to the front. In August, the Allies counterattacked, and the Germans began a retreat that could not be halted, for German soldiers, many of them sick with the flu, had lost the will to fight.

In late October, Ludendorff resigned and sailors in the German fleet mutinied. Two weeks later Kaiser Wilhelm fled to Holland as a new German government signed an armistice. On November 11 at 11 A.M., the guns on the Western Front went silent.

PEACE AND DISLOCATION IN EUROPE, 1919–1929

The Great War lasted four years. It took almost twice as long for Europe to recover. Millions of people had died or been disabled, political tensions and resentments lingered, and national economies remained depressed until the mid-1920s. In the late 1920s, peace and prosperity finally seemed assured, but this hope proved to be illusory.

The Impact of the War

The war left more dead and wounded and more physical destruction than any previous conflict. It is estimated that between 8 million and 10 million people died, almost all of them young men. Perhaps twice that many returned home wounded, gassed, or shell-shocked, many of them injured for life. Among the dead were about 2 million Germans, 1.7 million Russians, and 1.7 million Frenchmen. Austria-Hungary lost 1.5 million, the British Empire a million, Italy 460,000, and the United States 115,000.

Besides ending over 8 million lives, the war dislocated whole populations, creating millions of refugees. War and revolution forced almost 2 million Russians, 750,000 Germans, and 400,000 Hungarians to flee their homes. War led to the expulsion of hundreds of thousands of Greeks from Anatolia and Turks from Greece.

Many refugees found shelter in France, which welcomed 1.5 million people to bolster its declining population. The preferred destination, however, was the United States, the most prosperous country in the world. About 800,000 immigrants succeeded in reaching it before U.S. immigration laws passed in 1921 and 1924 closed the door to eastern and southern Europeans. Canada, Australia, and New Zealand adopted similar restrictions on immigration. The Latin American republics welcomed European refugees, but their economies were hard hit by the drop in the prices of their main exports and their poverty discouraged potential immigrants.

One unexpected byproduct of the war was the great influenza epidemic of 1918–1919, which started among soldiers heading for the Western Front. This was no ordinary flu but a virulent strain that infected almost everyone on earth and killed one person in every forty. It caused the largest number of deaths in so short a time in the history of the world. Half a million Americans perished in the epidemic—five times as many as died in the war. Worldwide, some 30 million people died, 20 million in India alone.

The war also caused serious damage to the environment. No place on earth was ever so completely devastated as the scar across France and Belgium known as the Western Front. The fighting ravaged forests and demolished towns. The earth was gouged by trenches, pitted with craters, and littered with ammunition, broken weapons, chunks of concrete, and the bones of countless soldiers. After the war, it took a decade to clear away the debris, rebuild the towns, and create dozens of military cemeteries with neat rows of crosses stretching for miles. To this day, farmers plow up fragments of old weapons and ammunition, and every so often, a long-buried shell explodes. The war also hastened the buildup of industry, with mines, factories, and railroad tracks.

The Peace Treaties

In early 1919, delegates of the victorious powers met in Paris. The defeated powers were kept out until the treaties were ready for signing. Russia, in the throes of civil war, was not invited.

From the start, three men dominated the Paris Peace Conference: United States president Wilson, British prime minister David Lloyd George, and French premier Georges Clemenceau°. They ignored the Italians, who had joined the Allies in 1915. They paid even less attention to the delegates of smaller European nations and none at all to non-European nationalities. They rejected the Japanese proposal that all races be treated equally. They ignored the Pan-African Congress organized by the African-American W. E. B. Du Bois to call attention to the concerns of African peoples around the world. They also ignored the ten thousand other delegates of various nationalities that did not represent sovereign states—the Arab leader Faisal, the Zionist Chaim Weizmann, and several Armenian delegations—who came to Paris to lobby for their causes. They were, in the words of Britain's Foreign Secretary Balfour, "three all-powerful, all-ignorant men, sitting there and carving up continents" (see Map 30.3).

Each one had his own agenda. Wilson, a high-minded idealist, wanted to apply the principle of self-determination to European affairs, by which he meant creating nations that reflected ethnic or linguistic divisions. He proposed a **League of Nations,** a world organization to safeguard the peace and foster international cooperation. His idealism clashed with the more hard-headed and self-serving nationalism of the Europeans. To satisfy his constituents, Lloyd George insisted that Germany pay a heavy indemnity. Clemenceau wanted Germany to give Alsace and Lorraine (a part of France before 1871) and the industrial Saar region to France and demanded that the Rhineland be detached from Germany to form a buffer state.

The result was a series of compromises that satisfied no one. The European powers formed a League of Nations, but the United States Congress, reflecting the isolationist feelings of the American people, refused to let the United States join. France recovered Alsace and Lorraine but was unable to detach the Rhineland and had to content itself with vague promises of British and American protection if Germany ever rebuilt its army. Britain acquired new territories in Africa and the Middle East but was greatly weakened by human losses and the disruption of its trade.

On June 28, 1919, the German delegates reluctantly signed the **Treaty of Versailles°.** Germany was forbidden to have an air force and was permitted only a token army and navy. It gave up large parts of its eastern territory to a newly reconstituted Poland. The Allies made Germany promise to pay reparations, but they did not set a figure or a period of time for payment. A "guilt clause," which was to rankle for years to come, obliged the Germans to accept "responsibility for causing all the loss and damage" of the war. The Treaty of Versailles left Germany humiliated but largely intact and potentially the most powerful nation in Europe. Establishing a peace neither of punishment nor of reconciliation, the treaty was one of the great failures in history.

Georges Clemenceau (zhorzh cluh-mon-SO)

Versailles (vuhr-SIGH)

Map 30.3   Territorial Changes in Europe After World War I   Although the heaviest fighting took place in western Europe, the territorial changes there were relatively minor; two provinces taken by Germany in 1871, Alsace and Lorraine, were returned to France. In eastern Europe, in contrast, the changes were enormous. The disintegration of the Austro-Hungarian Empire and the defeat of Russia allowed a belt of new countries to arise, stretching from Finland in the north to Yugoslavia in the south.

Meanwhile, the Austro-Hungarian Empire had fallen apart. In the Treaty of Saint-Germain° (1920) Austria and Hungary each lost three-quarters of their territory. New countries appeared in the lands lost by Russia, Germany, and Austria-Hungary: Poland, resurrected after over a century; Czechoslovakia, created from the northern third of Austria-Hungary; and Yugoslavia, combining Serbia and the former south Slav provinces of Austria-Hungary. The new boundaries coincided with the major linguistic groups of eastern Europe, but they all contained disaffected minorities. These small nations were safe only as long as Germany and Russia lay defeated and prostrate.

Saint-Germain (san–chur-MEN)

Lenin the Orator   The leader of the Bolshevik revolutionaries was a spellbinding orator. Here Lenin is addressing Red Army soldiers in Sverdlov Square, Moscow, in 1920. At the time, the Bolsheviks were mopping up the last of the anti-Bolshevik forces and were fully engaged in a war with Poland. The fate of the Revolution depended on the fighting spirit of the Red Army soldiers and on their loyalty to Lenin. (David King Collection)

Russian Civil War and the New Economic Policy

The end of the Great War did not bring peace to all of Europe. Fighting continued in Russia for another three years. The Bolshevik Revolution had provoked Allied intervention. French troops occupied Odessa in the south, the British and Americans landed in Archangel and Murmansk in the north, and the Japanese occupied Vladivostok in the far east. Liberated Czech prisoners of war briefly seized the Trans-Siberian Railway.

Also, in December 1918, civil war broke out in Russia. The Communists—as the Bolsheviks called themselves after March 1918—held central Russia, but all the surrounding provinces rose up against them. Counter-revolutionary armies led by former tsarist officers obtained weapons and supplies from the Allies. For three years the two sides fought each other. They burned farms and confiscated crops, causing a famine that claimed 3 million victims, more than had died in Russia in seven years of fighting. By 1921, the Communists had defeated most of their enemies, for the anti-Bolshevik forces were never united and the peasants feared that a tsarist victory would mean the return of their landlords. The Communists' victory was also due to the superior discipline of their Red Army, and the military genius of their army commander, Leon Trotsky.

Finland, the Baltic states, and Poland remained independent, but the Red Army reconquered other parts of the tsar's empire one by one. In December 1920 Ukrainian Communists declared the independence of a Soviet republic of Ukraine, then in 1922 it merged with Russia to create the Union of Soviet Socialist Republics (USSR), or Soviet Union. The provinces of the Russian Empire in the Caucasus and Central Asia had also declared their independence in 1918. Although the Bolsheviks staunchly supported anticolonialist movements in Africa and Asia, they opposed what they called "feudalism" in the former Russian colonies. Also, they were eager to control the oil fields in both regions. In 1920–1921 the Red Army reconquered the Caucasus and replaced the indigenous leaders with Russians. In 1922 the new Soviet republics of Georgia, Armenia, and Azerbaijan joined the USSR. In this way the Bolsheviks rid Russia of the taint of tsarist colonialism but retained control over lands and peoples that had been part of the tsar's empire.

Years of warfare, revolution, and mismanagement ruined the Russian economy. By 1921 it had declined to one-sixth of its prewar level. Factories and railroads had shut down for lack of fuel, raw materials, and parts. Farmland had been devastated and livestock killed, causing hunger in the cities. Finding himself master of a country in ruin, Lenin decided to release the economy from party and government control. In March 1921 he announced The **New Economic Policy** (N.E.P.) It allowed peasants to own land and sell their crops, private merchants to trade, and private workshops to produce goods and sell them on the free market. Only the biggest businesses, such as banks, railroads, and factories, remained under government ownership.

The relaxation of controls had an immediate effect. Production began to climb, and food and other goods became available. In the cities, food remained scarce because farmers used their crops to feed their livestock rather than sell them. But the N.E.P. reflected no change in the ultimate goals of the Communist Party. It merely provided breathing space, what Lenin called "two steps back to advance one step forward." The Communists had every intention of creating a modern industrial economy without private property, under party guidance. This meant investing in heavy industry and electrification and moving farmers to the cities to work in the new industries. It also meant providing food for the urban workers without spending scarce resources to purchase it from the peasants. In other words, it meant making the peasants, the great majority of the Soviet people, pay for the industrialization of Russia. This turned them into bitter enemies of the Communists.

When Lenin died in January 1924, his associates jockeyed for power. The leading contenders were Leon Trotsky, commander of the Red Army, and Joseph Stalin, general secretary of the Communist Party. Trotsky had the support of many "Old Bolsheviks" who had joined the party before the Revolution. Having spent years in exile, he saw the revolution as a spark that would ignite a world revolution of the working class. Stalin, the only leading Communist who had never lived abroad, insisted that socialism could survive "in one country."

Stalin filled the party bureaucracy with individuals loyal to himself. In 1926–1927 he had Trotsky expelled for "deviation from the party line." In January 1929 he forced Trotsky to flee the country. Then, as absolute master of the party, he prepared to industrialize the Soviet Union at breakneck speed.

An Ephemeral Peace

The 1920s were a decade of apparent progress hiding irreconcilable tensions. Conservatives in Britain and France longed for a return to the stability of the prewar era—the hierarchy of social classes, prosperous world trade, and European dominance over the rest of the world. Elsewhere, all over the world, people's hopes had been raised by the rhetoric of the war, then dashed by its outcome. In Europe, Germans felt cheated out of a victory that had seemed within their grasp, and Italians were disappointed that their sacrifices had not been rewarded at Versailles with large territorial gains. In the Middle East and Asia, Arabs and Indians longed for independence; the Chinese looked for social justice and a lessening of foreign intrusion; and the Japanese hoped to expand their influence in China. In Russia, the Communists were eager to consolidate their power and export their revolution to the rest of the world.

The decade after the end of the war can be divided into two distinct periods: five years of painful recovery and readjustment (1919–1923), followed by six years of growing peace and prosperity (1924–1929). In 1923, Germany suspended reparations payments. In retaliation for the French occupation of the Ruhr, the German government began printing money recklessly, causing the most severe inflation the world had ever seen. Soon German money was worth so little that it took a wheelbarrowful to buy a loaf of bread. As Germany teetered on the brink of civil war, radical nationalists called for revenge and tried to overthrow the government. Finally, the German government issued a new currency and promised to resume reparations payments, and the French agreed to withdraw their troops from the Ruhr.

Beginning in 1924, the world enjoyed a few years of calm and prosperity. After the end of the German crisis of 1923, the western European nations became less confrontational, and Germany joined the League of Nations. The vexed issue of reparations also seemed to vanish, as Germany borrowed money from New York banks to make its payments to France and Britain, which used the money to repay their wartime loans from the United States. This triangular flow of money, based on credit, stimulated the rapid recovery of the European economies. France began rebuilding its war-torn northern zone, Germany recovered from its hyperinflation, and in the United States a boom began that was to last over five years.

While their economies flourished, governments grew more cautious and businesslike. Even the Communists, after Lenin's death, seemed to give up their attempts to spread revolution abroad. Yet neither Germany nor the Soviet Union accepted their borders with the small nations that had arisen between them. In 1922 they signed a secret pact allowing the German army to conduct maneuvers in Russia (in violation of the Versailles treaty) in exchange for German help in building up Russian industry and military potential.

The League of Nations proved adept at resolving numerous technical issues pertaining to health, labor relations, and postal and telegraph communications. But the League could carry out its main function, preserving

Rice Paddies in China   After irrigating all the level land, Chinese farmers turned to the hillsides. To grow rice even on the steepest slopes, they terraced the land and controlled the flow of water so that each field received the optimum amount that the rice shoots required.   (Julia Waterlow/Eye Ubiquitous)

the peace, only when the great powers (Britain, France, and Italy) were in agreement. Without U.S. participation, sanctions against states that violated League rules carried little weight.

CHINA AND JAPAN: CONTRASTING DESTINIES

China and Japan share a common civilization, and both have been subject to Western pressures, but their modern histories have been completely opposite. China clung much longer than Japan to a traditional social structure and economy, then collapsed into chaos and revolution (see below). Japan experienced reform from above (see Chapter 28), acquiring industry and a powerful military, which it used to take advantage of China's weakness. Their different reactions to the pressures of the West put these two great nations on a collision course.

Social and Economic Change

China's population—about 400 million in 1900—was the largest of any country in the world and growing fast. But China had little new land to put into cultivation. In 1900, peasant plots averaged between 1 and 4 acres (less than 2 hectares) apiece, half as large as they had been two generations earlier. Farming methods had not changed in centuries. Landlords and tax collectors took more than half of the harvest. Most Chinese worked incessantly, survived on a diet of grain and vegetables, and spent their lives in fear of floods, bandits, and tax collectors.

Constant labor was needed to prevent the Yellow River from bursting its dikes and flooding the low-lying fields and villages on either side. In times of war and civil disorder, when flood-control precautions were neglected, disasters ensued. Between 1913 and 1938 the river burst its dikes seventeen times, each time killing thousands of people and making millions homeless.

Japan had few natural resources and very little arable land on which to grow food for its rising population. It did not suffer from devastating floods like China, but it was subject to other natural calamities. Typhoons regularly hit its southern regions. Earthquakes periodically shook the country, which lies on the great ring of tectonic fault lines that surround the Pacific Ocean. The Kanto earthquake of 1923 destroyed all of Yokohama and half of Tokyo and killed as many as 200,000 people.

Above the peasantry, Chinese society was divided into many groups and strata. Landowners lived off the rents of their tenants. Officials, chosen through an elaborate examination system, enriched themselves from taxes and the government's monopolies on salt, iron, and other products. Wealthy merchants handled China's growing import-export trade in collaboration with foreign companies. Shanghai, China's financial and commercial center, was famous for its wealthy foreigners and its opium addicts, prostitutes, and gangsters.

Although foreign trade represented only a small part of China's economy, contact with the outside world had a tremendous impact on Chinese politics. Young men living in the treaty ports saw no chance for advancement in the old system of examinations and official positions. Some learned foreign ideas in Christian mission schools or abroad. The contrast between the squalor in which most urban residents lived and the luxury of the foreigners' enclaves in the treaty ports sharpened the resentment of educated Chinese.

Japan's population reached 60 million in 1925 and was increasing by a million a year. The crash program of industrialization begun in 1868 by the Meiji oligarchs (see Chapter 28) accelerated during the First World War, when Japan exported textiles, consumer goods, and munitions. In the war years, its economy grew four times as fast as western Europe's, eight times faster than China's.

In the 1880s, electrification was still in its infancy, so Japan became competitive very early on. Blessed with a rainy climate and many fast-flowing rivers, Japan quickly expanded its hydroelectric capacity. By the mid-1930s, 89 percent of Japanese households had electric lights, compared with 68 percent of U.S. households and 44 percent of British.

Economic growth aggravated social tensions. The *narikin* ("new rich") affected Western ways and lifestyles that clashed with the austerity of earlier times. In the big cities, *mobos* (modern boys) and *mogas* (modern girls) shocked traditionalists with their foreign ways: dancing together, wearing short skirts and tight pants, behaving like Americans. Students who flirted with dangerous thoughts were called "Marx boys."

The main beneficiaries of prosperity were the *zaibatsu*°, four giant corporations—Mitsubishi, Sumitomo, Yasuda, and Mitsui—that controlled most of Japan's industry and commerce. Farmers, who constituted half of the population, remained poor; some, in desperation, sold their daughters to textile mills or into domestic service, where young women formed the bulk of the labor force. Labor unions were weak and repressed by the police.

Japanese prosperity depended on foreign trade and imperialism in Asia. The country exported silk and light manufactures and imported almost all its fuel, raw materials, and machine tools, and even some of its food. Though less at the mercy of the weather than China, Japan was much more vulnerable to swings in the world economy.

Revolution and War, 1900–1918

In 1900, China's Empress Dowager Cixi°, who had seized power in a palace coup two years earlier, encouraged a secret society, the Righteous Fists, or Boxers, to rise up and expel all the foreigners from China. When the Boxers threatened the foreign legation in Beijing, an international force from the Western powers and Japan captured the city and forced China to pay a huge indemnity. Shocked by these events, many Chinese students became convinced that China needed a revolution to get rid of the Qing dynasty and modernize their country. In Shanghai, dissidents published works that would have been forbidden elsewhere in China.

When Cixi died in 1908, the Revolutionary Alliance led by **Sun Yat-sen**° (Sun Zhongshan, 1867–1925) prepared to take over. Sun had spent much of his life in Japan, England, and the United States, plotting the overthrow of the Qing dynasty. His ideas were a mixture of nationalism, socialism, and Confucian philosophy. His patriotism, his powerful ambition, and his tenacious spirit attracted a large following.

The military thwarted Sun's plans. After China's defeat in the war with Japan in 1895, the government had agreed to equip the army with modern rifles and machine guns. The combination of traditional regional autonomy with modern tactics and equipment led to the creation of local armies beholden to local generals known as warlords, rather than to the central government. When a regional army mutinied in October 1911, **Yuan Shikai**°, the most powerful of the regional generals, refused to defend the Qing. A revolutionary assembly at Nanjing elected Sun president of China in December 1911, and the last Qing ruler, the boy-emperor Puyi,

---

zaibatsu (zie-BOT-soo)

Cixi (tsuh-shee)   **Sun Yat-sen** (soon yot-SEN)
Yuan Shikai (you-AHN she-KIE)

abdicated the throne. But Sun had no military forces at his command. To avoid a clash with the army, he resigned after a few weeks, and a new national assembly elected Yuan president of the new Chinese republic.

Yuan was an able military leader, but he had no political program. When Sun reorganized his followers into a political party called **Guomindang**° (National People's Party), Yuan quashed every attempt at creating a Western-style government and harassed Sun's followers. Victory in the first round of the struggle to create a new China went to the military.

The Japanese were quick to join the Allied side in World War I. They saw the war as a golden opportunity to advance their interests while the Europeans were occupied elsewhere. The war created an economic boom, as the Japanese suddenly found their products in greater demand than before. But it also created hardships for workers, who rioted when the cost of rice rose faster than their wages.

The Japanese soon conquered the German colonies in the northern Pacific and on the coast of China, then turned their attention to the rest of China. In 1915 Japan presented China with Twenty-One Demands, which would have turned it into a virtual protectorate. Britain and the United States persuaded Japan to soften the demands but could not prevent it from keeping the German coastal enclaves and extracting railroad and mining concessions at China's expense. In protest, anti-Japanese riots and boycotts broke out throughout China. Thus began a bitter struggle between the two countries that was to last for thirty years.

Chinese Warlords and the Guomindang, 1919–1929

At the Paris Peace Conference, the great powers went along with Japan's seizure of the German enclaves in China. To many educated Chinese, this decision was a cruel insult. On May 4, 1919, students demonstrated in front of the Forbidden City of Beijing. Despite a government ban, the May Fourth Movement spread to other parts of China. A new generation was growing up to challenge the old officials, the regional generals, and the foreigners.

China's regional generals—the warlords—still supported their armies through plunder and arbitrary taxation. They frightened off trade and investment in railroads, industry, and agricultural improvement. While neglecting the dikes and canals on which the livelihood of Chinese farmers depended, they fought one another

and protected the gangsters who ran the opium trade. During the warlord era, China grew poorer and only the treaty ports prospered.

Sun Yat-sen tried to make a comeback in Canton (Guangzhou) in the early 1920s. Though not a Communist, he was impressed with the efficiency of Lenin's revolutionary tactics and let a Soviet adviser reorganize the Guomindang along Leninist lines. He also welcomed members of the newly created Chinese Communist Party into the Guomindang.

When Sun died in 1925, the leadership of his party passed to Jiang Jieshi, known in the West as Chiang Kai-shek° (1887–1975). An officer and director of the military academy, Chiang trained several hundred young officers who remained loyal to him thereafter. In 1927 he determined to crush the regional warlords. As his army moved north from its base in Canton, he briefly formed an alliance with the Communists. Once his troops had occupied Shanghai, however, he allied himself with local gangsters to crush the labor unions and decimate the Communists, whom he considered a threat. He then defeated or co-opted most of the other warlords and established a dictatorship.

Chiang's government issued ambitious plans to build railroads, develop agriculture and industry, and modernize China from the top down. However, his followers were neither competent administrators like the Japanese officials of the Meiji Restoration nor ruthless modernizers like the Russian Bolsheviks. Instead, the government attracted thousands of opportunists whose goal was to "become an official and get rich" by taxing and plundering businesses. In the countryside, tax collectors and landowners squeezed the peasants ever harder, even at times of natural disasters. What little money reached the government's coffers went to the military. For twenty years after the fall of the Qing, China remained mired in poverty, subject to corrupt officials and the whims of nature.

THE NEW MIDDLE EAST

Having contributed to the Allied victory, the Arab peoples expected to have a say in the outcome of the Great War. But the victorious French and British planned to treat the Middle East like a territory open to colonial rule. The result was a legacy of instability that has persisted to this day.

Guomindang (gwo-min-dong)

Chiang Kai-shek (chang kie-shek)

Mustafa Kemal Atatürk   After World War I, Mustafa Kemal was determined to modernize Turkey on the western model. Here he is shown wearing a European-style suit and teaching the Latin alphabet.   (Stock Montage)

The Mandate System

At the Paris Peace Conference, France, Britain, Italy, and Japan proposed to divide the former German colonies and the territories of the Ottoman Empire among themselves, but their ambitions clashed with President Wilson's ideal of national self-determination. Eventually, the victors arrived at a compromise solution called the **mandate system:** colonial rulers would administer the territories but would be accountable to the League of Nations for "the material and moral well-being and the social progress of the inhabitants."

Class C Mandates—those with the smallest populations—were treated as colonies by their conquerors. South Africa replaced Germany in Southwest Africa (now Namibia). Britain, Australia, New Zealand, and Japan took over the German islands in the Pacific. Class B Mandates, larger than Class C but still underdeveloped, were to be ruled for the benefit of their inhabitants under League of Nations supervision. They were to receive autonomy at some unspecified time in the future. Most of Germany's African colonies fell into this category.

The Arab-speaking territories of the old Ottoman Empire were Class A Mandates. The League of Nations declared that they had "reached a state of development where their existence as independent nations can be provisionally recognized subject to the rendering of administrative advice and assistance by a Mandatory, until such time as they are able to stand alone." Arabs interpreted this ambiguous wording as a promise of independence. Britain and France sent troops into the region "for the benefit of its inhabitants." Palestine (now Israel), Transjordan (now Jordan), and Iraq (formerly Mesopotamia) became British mandates; France claimed Syria and Lebanon (see Map 30.4).

The Rise of Modern Turkey

At the end of the war, as the Ottoman Empire teetered on the brink of collapse, France, Britain, and Italy saw an opportunity to expand their empires, and Greece eyed those parts of Anatolia inhabited by Greeks. In 1919 French, British, Italian, and Greek forces occupied Constantinople and parts of Anatolia. By the Treaty of Sèvres (1920), the Allies made the sultan give up most of his lands.

In 1919, Mustafa Kemal, a hero of the Gallipoli campaign, had formed a nationalist government in central Anatolia with the backing of fellow army officers. After a short but fierce war against invading Greeks, his armies reconquered Anatolia and the area around Constantinople in 1922. The victorious Turks forced hundreds of thousands of Greeks from their ancestral homes in Anatolia. In response the Greek government expelled all Muslims from Greece. The ethnic diversity that had prevailed in the region for centuries ended.

As a war hero and proclaimed savior of his country, Kemal was able to impose wrenching changes on his people faster than any other reformer would have dared. An outspoken modernizer, he was eager to bring Turkey closer to Europe as quickly as possible. He abolished the

Map 30.4   Territorial Changes in the Middle East After World War I   The defeat and dismemberment of the Ottoman Empire at the end of World War I resulted in an entirely new political map of the region. The Turkish Republic inherited Anatolia and a small piece of the Balkans, while the Ottoman Empire's Arab provinces were divided between France and Great Britain as "Class A Mandates." The French acquired Syria and Lebanon and the British got Palestine (now Israel), Transjordan (now Jordan), and Iraq. Only Iran and Egypt remained as they had been.

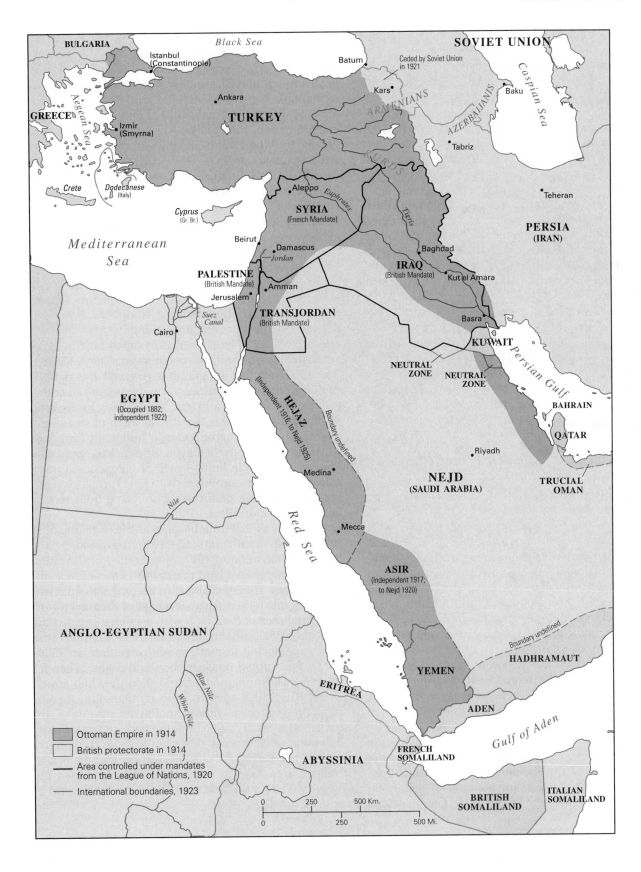

BULGARIA

Black Sea

SOVIET UNION

Istanbul
(Constantinople)

Batum

Ceded by Soviet Union
in 1921

*Caspian
Sea*

Kars

Baku

GREECE

*Aegean
Sea*

Izmir
(Smyrna)

Ankara

TURKEY

ARMENIANS

AZERBAIJANIS

Tabriz

KURDS

Teheran

Crete

Dodecanese
(Italy)

Cyprus
(Gr. Br.)

Aleppo

Euphrates

SYRIA
(French Mandate)

Tigris

Beirut

Damascus

Baghdad

PERSIA
(IRAN)

*Mediterranean
Sea*

Jordan

IRAQ
(British Mandate)

PALESTINE
(British Mandate)

Amman

Kut el Amara

Jerusalem

*Suez
Canal*

Cairo

TRANSJORDAN
(British Mandate)

Basra

KUWAIT

Persian Gulf

NEUTRAL
ZONE

NEUTRAL
ZONE

EGYPT
(Occupied 1882;
independent 1922)

(Independent 1916; to Nejd 1925)

HEJAZ

Boundary undefined

BAHRAIN

QATAR

Riyadh

Nile

Medina

NEJD
(SAUDI ARABIA)

TRUCIAL
OMAN

Red Sea

Mecca

ASIR
(Independent 1917;
to Nejd 1920)

ANGLO-EGYPTIAN SUDAN

Boundary undefined

HADHRAMAUT

Blue Nile

White Nile

YEMEN

ERITREA

ADEN

FRENCH
SOMALILAND

Gulf of Aden

ABYSSINIA

BRITISH
SOMALILAND

ITALIAN
SOMALILAND

Ottoman Empire in 1914

British protectorate in 1914

Area controlled under mandates
from the League of Nations, 1920

International boundaries, 1923

0   250   500 Km.

0   250   500 Mi.

sultanate, in 1923 declared Turkey a secular republic, and introduced European laws. In a radical break with Islamic tradition, he suppressed Muslim courts, schools, and religious orders and replaced the Arabic alphabet with the Latin alphabet.

Kemal attempted to westernize the traditional Turkish family. Women received civil equality, including the right to vote and be elected to the national assembly. Kemal forbade polygamy and instituted civil marriage and divorce. He even changed people's clothing, strongly discouraging women from veiling their faces and replacing the fez, until then the traditional Turkish men's hat, with the European brimmed hat. He ordered everyone to take a family name, choosing the name Atatürk ("father of the Turks") for himself. His reforms spread quickly in the cities; but in rural areas, where Islamic traditions remained strong, people resisted them for a long time.

Arab Lands and the Question of Palestine

Among the Arab people, the thinly disguised colonialism of the mandate system set off protests and rebellions, not only in the mandated territories, but even as far away as Morocco. Arabs viewed the European presence not as "liberation" from Ottoman "oppression" but as foreign occupation.

After World War I, Middle Eastern society underwent dramatic changes. Nomads disappeared from the deserts as trucks replaced camel caravans. The rural population grew fast, and many landless peasants migrated to the swelling cities. The population of the region is estimated to have increased by 50 percent between 1914 and 1939, while that of large cities such as Constantinople, Baghdad, and Cairo doubled.

The urban and mercantile middle class, encouraged by the transformation of Turkey, adopted Western ideas, customs, and styles of housing and clothing. Some families sent their sons to European secular or mission schools, then to Western colleges in Cairo and Beirut or universities abroad, to prepare for jobs in government and business. Among the educated elite were a few women who became schoolteachers or nurses. There were great variations, ranging from Lebanon, with its strong French influence, to Arabia and Iran, which retained their diverse cultural traditions.

The region in closest contact with Europe was the Maghrib—Algeria, Tunisia and Morocco—which the French army considered its private domain. Alongside the old native quarters, the French built modern neighborhoods inhabited mainly by Europeans (see Environment and Technology: Cities Old and New). France had occupied Algeria since 1830 and had encouraged European immigration. The settlers owned the best lands and monopolized government jobs and businesses while Arabs and Berbers remained poor and suffered intense discrimination. Nationalism was only beginning to appear before World War II, and the settlers quickly blocked any attempt at reform.

The British attempted to control the Middle East with a mixture of bribery and intimidation. They helped Faisal, leader of the Arab Revolt, become king of Syria. When the French ousted him, the British made him king of Iraq. They used bombers to quell rural insurrections in Iraq. In 1931 they reached an agreement with King Faisal's government: official independence for Iraq in exchange for the right to keep two air bases, a military alliance, and an assured flow of petroleum. France, meanwhile, sent thousands of troops to Syria and Lebanon to crush nationalist uprisings.

In Egypt as in Iraq, the British substituted a phony independence for official colonialism. They declared Egypt independent in 1922 but reserved the right to station troops along the Suez Canal to secure their link with India in the event of war. Most galling to the Wafd (Nationalist) Party was the British attempt to remove Egyptian troops from the Sudan, a land many Egyptians considered a colony of Egypt. Britain was successful in keeping Egypt in limbo—neither independent nor a colony—thanks to an alliance with King Farouk and conservative Egyptian politicians who feared both secular and religious radicalism.

As soon as Palestine became a British mandate in 1920, Jewish immigrants arrived, encouraged by the Balfour Declaration of 1917. Most settled in the cities, but some purchased land to establish *kibbutzim*, communal farms. Their goals were to become self-sufficient and reestablish their ties to the land of their ancestors. The purchases of land by Jewish agencies angered the indigenous Palestinians, especially tenant farmers who had been evicted to make room for settlers. In 1920–1921 riots erupted between Jews and Arabs. When far more Jewish immigrants arrived than they had anticipated, the British tried to limit immigration, thereby alienating the Jews without mollifying the Arabs. Increasingly, Jews arrived without papers, smuggled in by militant Zionist organizations. In the 1930s the country was torn by strikes and guerrilla warfare that the British could not control. In the process, Britain earned the hatred of both sides and of much of the Arab world as well.

Cities Old and New

Cities do not just grow larger; they change, sometimes radically, in response to culture and technology. The impact of cultural dominance and technological innovations on urban design is evident in these photographs of Cairo.

The European colonial presence was felt more strongly in cities than in the countryside. Cairo, the largest city in the Arab world before the British conquest, grew much larger after 1882. However, the construction of modern quarters for Europeans and wealthy Egyptians had little impact on the older quarters where most Cairenes lived. In the picture of the old quarter of Cairo in 1900 with its narrow streets and open stalls, men wear the burnoose and women cover their faces with a veil. The later picture, taken in 1904, shows Shepheard's hotel, one of the most luxurious hotels in the world, built on a broad avenue in the city's modern quarter.

The picture at left reflects the traditional architecture of hot desert countries: narrow streets, thick whitewashed walls, small windows, and heavy doors, all designed to keep out the heat of the day and protect privacy. The picture below shows the ideas Europeans brought with them about how a city should look. The wide streets and high airy buildings with windows and balconies mimic the urban design of late-nineteenth-century Paris, London, or Rome.

Cairo—Modern and Traditional The luxurious Shepheard's Hotel (below) was built in the European style on a broad avenue in the new quarter of Cairo. In stark contrast is the street (above) in the old quarter of the city: the street is narrow, the walls of the buildings are thick, and the windows small in order to protect the interiors from the heat of the sun. (Billie Love Historical Collection)

SOCIETY, CULTURE, AND TECHNOLOGY IN THE INDUSTRIALIZED WORLD

With the signing of the peace treaties, the countries that had fought for four years turned their efforts toward building a new future. The war had left a deep imprint on European society and culture. Advances in science offered astonishing new insights into the mysteries of nature and the universe. New technologies, many of them pioneered in the United States, promised to change the daily lives of millions of people.

Class and Gender

After the war, class distinctions began to fade. Many European aristocrats had died on the battlefields, and with them went their class's long domination of the army, the diplomatic corps, and other elite sectors of society. The United States and Canada had never had as rigidly defined a class structure as European societies or as elaborate a set of traditions and manners. During the war, displays of wealth and privilege seemed unpatriotic, and remained so afterward. On both sides of the Atlantic, engineers, businessmen, lawyers, and other professionals rose to prominence, increasing the relative importance of the middle class.

The activities of governments had expanded during the war and continued to grow. Governments provided housing, highways, schools, public health facilities, broadcasting, and other services. This growth of government influence created a need for thousands more bureaucrats. Department stores, banks, insurance companies, and other businesses also increased the white-collar work force.

In contrast with the middle class, the working class did not expand. The introduction of new machines and new ways of organizing work, such as the automobile assembly line that Henry Ford devised, increased workers' productivity so that greater outputs could be achieved without expanding the labor force.

Women's lives changed more rapidly in the 1920s than in any previous decade. Although the end of the war marked a retreat from wartime job opportunities, some women remained in the work force as wage earners and as salaried professionals. The young and wealthy enjoyed more personal freedoms than their mothers had before the war. They drove cars, played sports, traveled alone, and smoked in public. Emancipated from the corsets and long dresses of prewar fashion, they wore their skirts and their hair short and danced to jazz instead of waltzes, to the consternation of their elders. Others found that the upheavals of war brought more suffering than liberation. Millions of women had lost their fathers, brothers, sons, husbands, and fiancés in the war or in the great influenza epidemic. After the war, the shortage of young men caused many single women to lead lives of loneliness and destitution.

In Europe and North America advocates of women's rights—labeled "suffragettes" by their critics—had been demanding the vote for women since the 1890s. Only in New Zealand (in 1893) did women receive the vote before the twentieth century. Women in Norway were the first to obtain it in Europe, in 1915. Russian women followed in 1917, Canadian and German women in 1918. Britain gave women over age thirty the vote in 1918 and later extended it to younger women. The Nineteenth Amendment to the U.S. Constitution granted suffrage to American women in 1920. Women in Turkey began voting in 1934. Most other countries did not allow women to vote until after 1945.

In dictatorships, voting rights for women made no difference, and in democratic countries, women tended to vote like their male relatives. In the British elections of 1918—the first to include women—they overwhelmingly voted for the Conservative Party. Everywhere, their influence on politics was less radical than feminists had hoped and conservatives had feared. Even when it did not alter the political situation, however, the right to vote was a potent symbol.

Revolution in the Sciences

For two hundred years, scientists, following in Isaac Newton's footsteps, had applied the same laws and equations to astronomical observations and to laboratory experiments. At the end of the nineteenth century, however, a revolution in physics undermined all the old certainties about nature. Physicists discovered that atoms, the building blocks of matter, are not indivisible but consist of far smaller subatomic particles. In 1900 the German physicist **Max Planck** (1858–1947) found that light and energy do not flow in a continuous stream but travel in small units, which he called *quanta*. These findings seemed strange enough, but what really undermined Newtonian physics was the general theory of relativity developed by **Albert Einstein** (1879–1955), another German physicist. In 1916 Einstein announced that not only is matter made of insubstantial particles, but time, space, and mass are not fixed but are relative to one another. Other physicists said that light is made up of either waves or particles, depending on the observer, and that an experiment could determine either the speed or the position of a particle of light, but never both.

To nonscientists it seemed as though theories expressed in arcane mathematical formulas were replacing truth and common sense. Far from being mere speculation, however, the new physics promised to unlock the secrets of matter and provide humans with plentiful—and potentially dangerous—new sources of energy.

The new social sciences were even more unsettling than the new physics, for they challenged Victorian morality, middle-class values, and notions of Western superiority. Sigmund Freud (1856–1939), a Viennese physician, developed a technique—psychoanalysis—to probe the minds of his patients. He found not only rationality but also hidden layers of emotion and desire repressed by social restraints. "The primitive, savage and evil impulses have not vanished from any individual, but continue their existence, although in a repressed state," he warned. Meanwhile, sociologists and anthropologists had begun the empirical study of societies, both Western and non-Western. Before the war, the French sociologist Emile Durkheim (1858–1917) had come to the then-shocking conclusion that "there are no religions that are false. All are true in their own fashion."

If the words *primitive* and *savage* applied to Europeans as well as to other peoples, and if religions were all equally "true," then what remained of the superiority of Western civilization? Cultural relativism, as the new approach to human societies was called, was as unnerving as relativity in physics.

Although these ideas had been expressed before 1914, wartime experiences called into question the West's faith in reason and progress. Some people accepted the new ideas with enthusiasm. Others condemned and rejected them, clinging to the sense of order and faith in progress that had energized European and American culture before the war.

The New Technologies of Modernity

Some Europeans and Americans viewed the sciences with mixed feelings, but the new technologies aroused almost universal excitement. In North America, even working-class people could afford some of the new products of scientific research, inventors' ingenuity, and industrial production. Mass consumption lagged in Europe, but science and technology were just

as advanced, and public fascination with the latest inventions—the cult of the modern—was just as strong.

Of all the innovations of the time, none attracted public interest as much as airplanes. In 1903 two young American mechanics, Wilbur and Orville Wright, built the first aircraft that was heavier than air and could be maneuvered in flight. From that moment on, wherever they appeared, airplanes fascinated people. During the war, the exploits of air aces relieved the tedium of news from the front. In the 1920s aviation became a sport and a form of entertainment, and flying daredevils achieved extraordinary fame by pushing their planes to the very limit—and often beyond. Among the most celebrated pilots were three Americans. Amelia Earhart was the first woman to fly across the Atlantic Ocean, and her example encouraged other women to fly. Richard Byrd flew over the North Pole in 1926. The most admired of all was Charles Lindbergh, the first person to fly alone across the Atlantic, in 1927. The heroic age of flight lasted until the late 1930s, when aviation became a means of transportation, a business, and a male preserve.

Electricity, produced in industrial quantities since the 1890s (see Chapter 28), began to transform home life. The first home use of electricity was for lighting, thanks to the economical and long-lasting tungsten bulb. Then, having persuaded people to wire their homes, electrical utilities joined manufacturers in advertising electric irons, fans, washing machines, hot plates, and other electric appliances.

Radio—or wireless telegraphy, as it was called—had served ships and the military during the war as a means of point-to-point telecommunication. After the war, amateurs used surplus radio equipment to talk to one another. The first commercial station began broadcasting in Pittsburgh in 1920. By the end of 1923, six hundred stations were broadcasting news, sports, soap operas, and advertising to homes throughout North America. By 1930, 12 million families owned radio receivers. In Europe, radio spread more slowly because governments reserved the airwaves for cultural and official programs and taxed radio owners to pay for the service.

Another medium that spread explosively in the 1920s was film. Motion pictures had begun in France in 1895 and flourished there and elsewhere in Europe, where the dominant concern was to reproduce stage plays. In the United States, filmmaking started at almost the same time, but American filmmakers considered it their business to entertain audiences rather than preserve outstanding theatrical performances. In competing for audiences, they looked to cinematic innovation, broad humor, and exciting spectacles, in the process developing styles of filmmaking that became immensely popular.

Diversity was a hallmark of the early film industry. After World War I filmmaking took root and flourished in Japan, India, Turkey, Egypt, and a suburb of Los Angeles, California, called Hollywood. American and European movie studios were both successful in exporting films, since silent movies presented no language problems. In 1929, out of an estimated 2100 films produced worldwide, 510 were made in the United States and 750 in Japan. But by then the United States had introduced the first "talking" motion picture, *The Jazz Singer* (1927), which changed all the rules. The number of Americans who went to see their favorite stars in thrilling adventures and heart-breaking romances rose from 40 million in 1922 to 100 million in 1930, at a time when the population of the country was about 120 million. Europeans had the technology and the art but neither the wealth nor the huge market of the United States. Hollywood studios began the diffusion of American culture that has continued to this day.

Health and hygiene were also part of the cult of modernity. Advances in medicine—some learned in the war—saved many lives. Wounds were regularly disinfected, and x-ray machines helped diagnose fractures. Since the late nineteenth century, scientists had known that disease-causing bacteria could be transmitted through contaminated water, spoiled food, or fecal matter. After the war, cities built costly water supply and sewage treatment systems. By the 1920s, indoor plumbing and flush toilets were becoming common even in working-class neighborhoods.

Interest in cleanliness altered private life. Doctors and home economists bombarded women with warnings and advice on how to banish germs. Soap and appliance manufacturers filled women's magazines with advertisements for products to help housewives keep their family's homes and clothing spotless and their meals fresh and wholesome. The decline in infant mortality and improvements in general health and life expectancy in this period owe as much to the cult of cleanliness as to advances in medicine.

Technology and the Environment

Two new technologies—the skyscraper and the automobile—transformed the urban environment even more radically than the railroad had done in the nineteenth century. At the end of the nineteenth century, architects had begun to design ever-higher buildings using load-bearing steel frames and passenger elevators. Major corporations in Chicago and New York competed to build the most daring buildings in the world, such as New York's 55-story Woolworth Building (1912) and Chicago's 34-story Tribune Tower (1923). A building boom in the late 1920s produced dozens of skyscrapers, culminating with the 86-story, 1,239-foot (377-meter) Empire State Building in New York, completed in 1932.

European cities restricted the height of buildings to protect their architectural heritage; Paris forbade buildings over 56 feet (17 meters) high. In innovative designs, however, European architects led the way. In the 1920s the Swiss architect Charles Edouard Jeanneret (1887–1965), known as Le Corbusier°, outlined a new approach to architecture that featured simplicity of form, absence of surface ornamentation, easy manufacture, and inexpensive materials. Among his influential designs were the main buildings of Chandigarh, the new capital of the Indian state of Punjab. Other architects—including the Finn Ero Saarinen, the Germans Ludwig Mies van der Rhoe° and Walter Gropius, and the American Frank Lloyd Wright—advanced his lines of thought and added their own to create what became known as the International Style.

While central business districts were reaching for the sky, outlying areas were spreading far out into the countryside, thanks to the automobile. The assembly line pioneered by Henry Ford mass-produced vehicles in ever-greater volume and at falling prices. By 1929, the United States had one car for every five people, five-sixths of the world's automobiles. Far from being blamed for their exhaust emissions, automobiles were praised as the solution to urban pollution. As cars replaced carts and carriages, horses disappeared from city streets, as did tons of manure.

The most important environmental effect of automobiles was suburban sprawl. Middle-class families could now live in single-family homes too spread apart to be served by public transportation. By the late 1920s, paved roads rivaled rail networks both in length and in the surface they occupied. As middle- and working-class families bought cars, cities acquired rings of automobile suburbs. Los Angeles, the first true automobile city, consisted of suburbs spread over hundreds of square miles and linked together by broad avenues. In those sections of the city where streetcar lines went out of business, the automobile, at first a plaything for the wealthy, became a necessity for commuters. Many Americans saw Los Angeles as the portent of a glorious future when everyone would have a car; only a few foresaw the congestion and pollution that would ensue.

Technological advances also transformed rural environments. Automobile owners quickly developed an interest in "motoring"—driving their vehicles out into the

Le Corbusier (luh cor-booz-YEH)
Ludwig Mies van der Rohe (LOOD-vig MEES fon der ROW-uh)

The Archetypal Automobile City   As Los Angeles grew from a modest town into a sprawling metropolis, broad avenues, parking lots, and garages were built to accommodate automobiles. By 1929, most families owned a car and streetcar lines had closed for lack of passengers. This photograph shows a street in the downtown business district.   (Ralph Morris Archives/Los Angeles Public Library)

country on weekends or on holiday trips. Farmers began buying cars and light trucks, using them to transport produce as well as passengers. Governments obliged by building new roads and paving old ones to make automobile travel smoother and safer.

Until the 1920s, horses remained the predominant source of energy for pulling plows and reapers and powering threshing machines on American farms. Only the wealthiest farmers could afford the slow and costly steam tractors. In 1915, Ford introduced a gasoline-powered tractor, and by the mid-1920s, these versatile machines began replacing horses. Larger farms profited most from this innovation, while small farmers sold their land and moved to the cities. Tractors hastened the transformation of agriculture from family enterprises to the large agribusinesses of today.

In India, Australia, and the western United States, where there was little virgin rain-watered land left to cultivate, engineers built dams and canals to irrigate dry lands. Dams offered the added advantage of producing electricity, for which there was a booming demand. The immediate benefits of irrigation—land, food, and electricity—far outweighed such distant consequences as salt deposits on irrigated lands and harm to wildlife.

CONCLUSION

In the late 1920s, it seemed as though the victors in the Great War might reestablish the prewar prosperity and European dominance of the globe. But the spirit of the 1920s was an illusion—not real peace but the eye of a hurricane.

The Great War caused a major realignment among the nations of the world. France and Britain, the two leading colonial powers, emerged economically weakened despite their victory. The war brought defeat and humiliation to Germany but did not reduce its military or industrial potential. It destroyed the old regime and the aristocracy of Russia, leading to civil war and revolution from which the victorious powers sought to isolate themselves. Two other old empires—the Austro-Hungarian and the Ottoman—were divided into many smaller and weaker nations. For a while, the Middle East seemed ripe for a new wave of imperialism. But there and throughout Asia, the war unleashed revolutionary nationalist movements that challenged European influence.

Only two countries benefited from the war. Japan took advantage of the European conflict to develop its industries and press its demands on a China weakened by domestic turmoil and social unrest. The United States emerged as the most prosperous and potentially most powerful nation, restrained only by the isolationist sentiments expressed by many Americans.

Modern technology and industrial organization had long been praised in the name of "progress" for their ability to reduce toil and disease and improve living standards. The war showed that they possessed an equally awesome destructive potential. As we shall see in the next chapter, most survivors wanted no repeat of such a nightmare. But a small minority worshiped violence and saw in the new weaponry a means to dominate those who feared conflict and death.

■ Key Terms

Western Front	Treaty of Versailles
Faisal	New Economic Policy
Theodore Herzl	Sun Yat-sen
Balfour Declaration	Yuan Shikai
Bolsheviks	Guomindang
Vladimir Lenin	mandate system
Woodrow Wilson	Max Planck
League of Nations	Albert Einstein

■ Suggested Reading

Bernadotte Schmitt and Harold C. Bedeler, *The World in the Crucible, 1914–1918* (1984), and John Keegan, *The First World War* (1999), are two engaging overviews of World War I. Imanuel Geiss, *July 1914: The Outbreak of the First World War* (1967), argues that Germany caused the conflict. Barbara Tuchman's *The Guns of August* (1962) and Alexander Solzhenitsyn's *August 1914* (1972) recount the first month of the war in detail. Keegan's *The Face of Battle* (1976) vividly describes the Battle of the Somme from the soldiers' perspective. On the technology of warfare see William H. McNeill, *The Pursuit of Power: Technology, Armed Force, and Society* (1982), and John Ellis, *The Social History of the Machine Gun* (1975). The role of women and the home front is the subject of essays in Margaret Higonnet et al., eds., *Behind the Lines: Gender and the Two World Wars* (1987), and sections of Lynn Weiner, *From Working Girl to Working Mother* (1985). The definitive work on the flu epidemic is Alfred W. Crosby, *America's Forgotten Pandemic: The Influenza of 1918* (1989). Two famous novels about the war are Erich Maria Re-

marque's *All Quiet on the Western Front* (1928) and Robert Graves's *Goodbye to All That* (1929). The war in English literature is the subject of Paul Fussell, *The Great War and Modern Memory* (1975).

For the background to the Russian Revolution read Theodore von Laue's *Why Lenin? Why Stalin?* 2d ed. (1971); but see also Richard Pipes, *The Russian Revolution* (1990), and Orlando Figes, *A People's Tragedy: The Russian Revolution, 1891–1924* (1996). The classic eyewitness account of the Revolution is John Reed's *Ten Days That Shook the World* (1919). On gender issues see Wendy Goldman, *Women, the State, and Revolution: Soviet Family Policy and Social Life, 1917–1936* (1993). The best-known novel about the Revolution and civil war is Boris Pasternak's *Doctor Zhivago* (1958).

John Maynard Keynes's *The Economic Consequences of the Peace* (1920) is a classic critique of the Paris Peace Conference. Arno Mayer's *Political Origins of the New Diplomacy, 1917–1918* (1959) analyzes the tensions and failures of great-power politics. The 1920s are discussed in Raymond Sontag's *A Broken World, 1919–1939* (1971).

The best recent book on Japan in the twentieth century is Daikichi Irokawa's *The Age of Hirohito: In Search of Modern Japan* (1995). See also Richard Storry, *A History of Modern Japan* (1982), and Tessa Morris-Suzuki, *The Technological Transformation of Japan* (1994). In the large and fast-growing literature on twentieth-century China, two general introductions are especially useful: John K. Fairbank, *The Great Chinese Revolution, 1800–1985* (1986), and Jonathan Spence, *The Search for Modern China* (1990). On the warlord and Guomindang periods see Lucien Bianco, *Origins of the Chinese Revolution, 1915–1949* (1971).

On the war and its aftermath in the Middle East see David Fromkin, *A Peace to End All Peace* (1989), and M. E. Yapp, *The Near East Since the First World War* (1991). Bernard Lewis, *The Emergence of Modern Turkey* (1968), is a good introduction. On Africa in this period see A. Adu Boahen, ed., *Africa Under Colonial Domination, 1880-1935*, volume 7 of the *UNESCO General History of Africa* (1985), and A. D. Roberts, ed., *Cambridge History of Africa*, vol. 7, *1905–1940* (1986).

The cultural transformation of Europe is captured in H. Stuart Hughes, *Consciousness and Society: The Reorientation of European Social Thought, 1890–1930* (1958). The towering intellectuals of that era are the subject of Peter Gay, *Freud: A Life for Our Time* (1988), and Abraham Pais, *Subtle Is the Lord: The Science and Life of Albert Einstein* (1982). Three books capture the enthusiastic popular response to technological innovations: David E. Nye, *Electrifying America: Social Meanings of a New Technology* (1990); Peter Fritzsche, *A Nation of Fliers: German Aviation and the Popular Imagination* (1992); and the sweeping overview by Thomas Hughes, *American Genesis: A Century of Invention and Technological Enthusiasm, 1870–1970* (1989).

31

THE COLLAPSE OF THE OLD ORDER,

1929–1949

**The Stalin Revolution • The Depression • The Rise of Fascism •
East Asia, 1931–1945 • The Second World War • The Character of Warfare**
ENVIRONMENT AND TECHNOLOGY: Biomedical Technologies
SOCIETY AND CULTURE: Preparing for Combat

German Dive-Bomber over Eastern Europe   A German ME-100 fighter plane
attacks a Soviet troop convoy on the Eastern Front

efore the First World War, the Italian futurist poets exalted violence as a noble and manly idea. Filippo Marinetti defined their creed in these words: "We want to glorify war, the world's only hygiene—militarism, deed, destroyer of anarchisms, the beautiful ideas that are death-bringing, and the subordination of women." His friend Gabriele d'Annunzio said: "If it is a crime to incite citizens to violence, I shall boast of this crime."

The war taught most survivors to abhor violence. During the 1920s, the world seemed to return to what United States president Warren Harding called "normalcy": prosperity in Europe and America, European colonialism in Asia and Africa, paternalistic U.S. domination of Latin America, and peace almost everywhere. But that euphoria did not last, for its economic underpinnings were fragile, political contentment was superficial, and the yearning to solve social problems by violent means lay close to the surface. For a few, war and domination became a creed and a goal.

In 1929 the artificial normalcy of the 1920s began to come apart. The Great Depression caused governments to turn against one another in a desperate attempt to protect their people's livelihood. As the economic crisis spread around the world, businesses went bankrupt, prices fell, factories closed, and workers were laid off. Even wholly agricultural nations and colonies suffered as markets for their exports shriveled.

While some countries accepted poverty and unemployment, others chose to solve their problems by violent means. As some nations shut their doors to Japan's products, the Japanese military tried to save their country by conquering China, which erupted in revolution. In Germany, the Depression reawakened resentments against the victors of the Great War; people who feared communism or blamed Jews for their troubles turned to Hitler and the Nazis, who promised to save their society by dominating others. In the Soviet Union, Stalin used energetic and murderous means to force his country into a communist version of the Industrial Revolution.

The result was war. The Second World War engulfed more lands and peoples and caused far more deaths and destruction than any previous conflict. At the end of it, much of Europe and East Asia lay in ruins, and millions of destitute refugees sought safety in other lands. The European colonial powers were either defeated or so weakened that they could no longer hold onto their empires when Asian and African peoples asserted their desire for independence.

As you read this chapter, ask yourself the following questions:

- How did the Soviet Union change under Stalin, and at what cost?
- What were the main causes of the Second World War?
- How was the war fought, and why did Japan and Germany lose?

THE STALIN REVOLUTION

During the 1920s, other countries ostracized the Soviet Union as it recovered from the Revolutions of 1917 and the civil war that followed (see Chapter 30). After Stalin achieved total mastery over this huge nation in early 1929, he led it through another revolution—an economic and social transformation that turned it into a great industrial and military power and intensified both admiration for and fear of communism throughout the world.

Five-Year Plans

Joseph Stalin (1879–1953) was born Joseph Vissarionovich Dzhugashvili into the family of a poor shoemaker. Before becoming a revolutionary, he studied for the priesthood. Under the name "Stalin" (Russian for "man of steel"), he played a small part in the Revolutions of 1917. He was a hard-working and skillful administrator who rose within the party bureaucracy and filled its upper ranks with men loyal to himself. By 1925, he had ousted Leon Trotsky, the best-known revolutionary after Lenin, from the party. He then proceeded to squeeze all other rivals out of positions of power, make himself absolute dictator, and transform Soviet society.

Stalin's ambition was to turn the USSR into an industrial nation. Industrialization was to serve a different

CHRONOLOGY

	Europe and North Africa	Asia and the Pacific
1930	**1931** Great Depression reaches Europe **1933** Hitler comes to power in Germany	**1931** Japanese forces occupy Manchuria **1934–1935** Mao leads Communists on Long March
1935	**1936** Hitler invades the Rhineland	**1937** Japanese troops invade China, conquer coastal provinces; Chiang Kai-shek flees to Sichuan **1937–1938** Japanese troops take Nanjing
1940	**1939 (Sept. 1)** German forces invade Poland **1940 (March–April)** German forces conquer Denmark, Norway, the Netherlands, and Belgium **1940 (May–June)** German forces conquer France **1940 (June–Sept.)** Battle of Britain **1941 (June 21)** German forces invade USSR **1942–1943** Allies and Germany battle for control of North Africa; Soviet victory in Battle of Stalingrad (1943) **1943–1944** Red Army slowly pushes Wehrmacht back to Germany **1944 (June 6)** D-day: U.S., British, and Canadian troops land in Normandy	**1941 (Dec. 7)** Japanese aircraft bomb Pearl Harbor **1942 (Jan–March)** Japanese conquer Thailand, Philippines, Malaya **1942 (June)** United States Navy defeats Japan at Battle of Midway
1945	**1945 (May 7)** Germany surrenders	**1945 (Aug. 6)** United States drops atomic bomb on Hiroshima **1945 (Aug. 14)** Japan surrenders **1945–1949** Civil war in China **1949** Communists defeat Guomindang; Mao proclaims People's Republic (Oct. 1)

purpose in the USSR than in other countries, however. It was not expected to produce consumer goods for a mass market, as in Britain and the United States, or to enrich individuals. Instead, its aim was to increase the power of the Communist Party domestically and the power of the Soviet Union in relation to other countries.

By building up Russia's industry, Stalin was determined to prevent a repetition of the humiliating defeat Russia had suffered at the hands of Germany in 1917. His goal was to quintuple the output of electricity and double that of heavy industry—iron, steel, coal, and machinery—in five years. To do so, he devised the first of a series of **Five-Year Plans,** a system of centralized control copied from the German experience of World War I.

Beginning in October 1928, the Communist Party and government created whole industries and cities from scratch, then recruited millions of peasants and trained them to work in the new factories and mines and offices. In every way except actual fighting, Stalin's Russia resembled a nation at war.

Rapid industrialization hastened environmental changes. Hydroelectric dams turned rivers into strings of reservoirs. Roads, canals, and railroad tracks cut the landscape. Forests and grassland were turned into farmland. From an environmental perspective, the outcome of the Five-Year Plans resembled the transformation that had occurred in the United States and Canada a few decades earlier (see Chapter 25).

Collectivization of Agriculture

Since the Soviet Union was still a predominantly agrarian country, the only way to pay for these massive investments, provide the labor, and feed the millions of new industrial workers was to squeeze the peasantry. Stalin therefore proceeded with the most radical social experiment conceived up to that time: the collectivization of agriculture.

Collectivization meant consolidating small private farms into vast collectives and making the farmers work

The Collectivization of Soviet Agriculture   One of the goals of collectivization was to introduce modern farm machinery. This poster shows delighted farmers operating new tractors and threshers.   (David King Collection)

together in commonly owned fields. Each collective was expected to supply the government with a fixed amount of food and distribute what was left among its members. Machine Tractor Stations leased agricultural machinery to several farms in exchange for the government's share of the crop. Collectives were to become outdoor factories where food was manufactured through the techniques of mass production and the application of machinery. Collectivization was an attempt to replace what Lenin called the peasants' "petty bourgeois" attitudes with an industrial way of life, the only one Communists respected. Collectivization was expected to bring the peasants once and for all under government control so they never again could withhold food supplies as they had done during the period of Lenin's New Economic Policy (see Chapter 30).

When collectivization was announced, the government mounted a massive propaganda campaign and sent party members into the countryside to enlist the farmers' support. At first all seemed to go well, but soon *kulaks*° ("fists"), the better-off peasants, began to resist giving up all their property. When soldiers came to force them into collectives at gunpoint, the kulaks burned their own crops, smashed their own equipment, and slaughtered their own livestock. Within a few months, they slaughtered half of the Soviet Union's horses and cattle and two-thirds of its sheep and goats. In retaliation, Stalin ruthlessly ordered the "liquidation of kulaks as a class" and incited the poor peasants to attack their wealthier neighbors. Over 8 million kulaks were arrested. Many were executed. The rest were sent to slave labor camps, where most starved to death.

The peasants who were left had been the least successful before collectivization and proved to be the least competent after. Many were sent to work in factories. The rest were forbidden to leave their farms. With half of their draft animals gone, they could not plant or harvest enough to meet the swelling demands of the cities. Yet government agents took whatever they could find, leaving little or nothing for the farmers themselves. After bad harvests in 1933 and 1934, a famine swept through the countryside, killing some 5 million people, about one in every twenty farmers.

Stalin's second Five-Year Plan, designed to run from 1933 to 1937, was originally intended to increase the output of consumer goods. But when the Nazis took over Germany in 1933 (see below), Stalin changed the plan to emphasize heavy industries that could produce armaments. Between 1927 and 1937 the Soviet output of metals and machines increased fourteen-fold while consumer goods became scarce and food was rationed. After a decade of Stalinism, the Soviet people were more poorly clothed, fed, and housed than they had been during the years of the New Economic Policy.

Terror and Opportunities

The 1930s brought both terror and new opportunities to the Soviet people. The forced pace of industrialization, the collectivization of agriculture, and the uprooting of millions of people could be accomplished only under duress. To prevent any possible resistance or rebellion, the NKVD, Stalin's secret police force, created a climate of suspicion and fear. The terror that pervaded the country was a

kulaks (COO-lox)

reflection of Stalin's own paranoia, for he distrusted everyone and feared for his life.

As early as 1930, Stalin had hundreds of engineers and technicians arrested on trumped-up charges of counterrevolutionary ideas and sabotage. Three years later, he expelled a million members of the Communist Party—one-third of the membership—on similar charges. He then turned on his most trusted associates.

In December 1934 Sergei Kirov, the party boss of Leningrad (formerly called Petrograd), was assassinated, perhaps on Stalin's orders. Stalin made a public display of mourning Kirov while blaming others for the crime. He then ordered a series of spectacular purge trials in which he accused most of Lenin's associates of "antiparty activities," the worst form of treason. In 1937 he had his eight top generals and many lesser officers charged with treason and executed, leaving the Red Army dangerously weakened. He even executed the head of the dreaded NKVD, which was enforcing the terror. Under torture or psychological pressure, almost all the accused confessed to the "crimes" they were charged with.

While "Old Bolsheviks" and high officials were being put on trial, terror spread steadily downward. The government regularly made demands on people that they could not meet, so everyone was guilty of breaking some regulation or other. People from all walks of life were arrested, sometimes on a mere suspicion or because of a false accusation by a jealous coworker or neighbor, sometimes for expressing a doubt or working too hard or not hard enough, sometimes for being related to someone previously arrested, sometimes for no reason at all. Millions of people were sentenced without a trial. At the height of the terror, some 8 million were sent to *gulags*° (labor camps), where perhaps a million died each year of exposure or malnutrition. To its victims, the terror seemed capricious and random. Yet it turned a sullen and resentful people into docile hard-working subjects of the party.

In spite of the fear and hardships, Stalin's regime received the support of many Soviet citizens. Suddenly, with so many people gone and new industries and cities being built everywhere, there were opportunities for those who remained, especially the poor and the young. Women entered careers and jobs previously closed to them, such as steelworkers, physicians, and office managers; but they retained their household and child-rearing duties, receiving little help from men. People who moved to the cities, worked enthusiastically, and asked no questions could hope to rise into the upper ranks of the Communist Party, the military, the government, or the professions—where the privileges and rewards were many.

Stalin's brutal methods helped the Soviet Union industrialize faster than any country had ever done. By the late 1930s, the USSR was the world's third largest industrial power, after the United States and Germany. To foreign observers it seemed to be booming with construction projects, production increases, and labor shortages. Even anti-Communist observers admitted that only a planned economy subject to strict government control could avoid the Depression. To millions of Soviet citizens who took pride in the new strength of their country, and to many foreigners who contrasted conditions in the Soviet Union with the unemployment and despair in the West, Stalin's achievement seemed worth any price.

THE DEPRESSION

On October 24, 1929—"Black Thursday"—the New York stock market went into a dive. Within days, stocks lost half of their value, and their value continued to fall for three years. Millions of investors lost money, as did the banks and brokers who had lent them money. People with savings accounts rushed to make withdrawals, causing thousands of banks to collapse.

Economic Crisis What began as a stock-market crash soon turned into the deepest and most widespread depression in history. As consumers reduced their purchases, businesses cut production. General Motors, for example, saw its sales drop by half between 1929 and 1931. Companies laid off thousands of workers, throwing them onto public charity. Business and government agencies replaced their women workers with men, arguing that men had to support their families whereas women worked only for "pin money." Jobless men deserted their families. As farm prices fell, small farmers went bankrupt and lost their land. By mid-1932, the American economy had fallen by half, and unemployment had risen to an unprecedented 25 percent of the work force. Government spending on welfare and public works was unable to restore prosperity. Many observers thought the free-enterprise system would be replaced by bread lines, soup kitchens, men selling apples on street corners, and hoboes riding freight trains.

---

gulag (GOO-log)

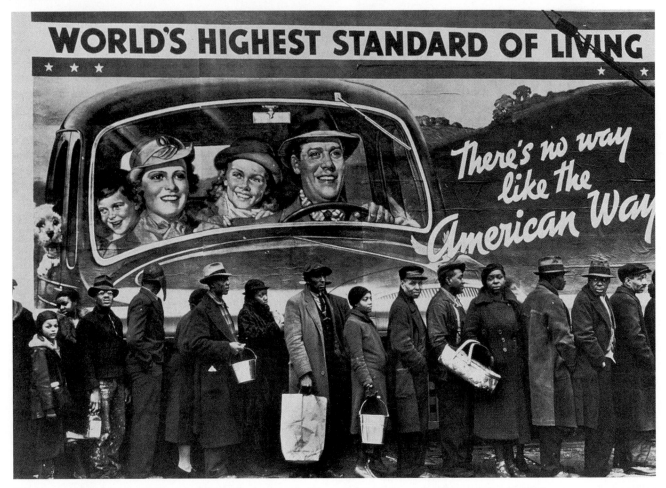

Two Views of the American Way   In this classic photograph, *Life* magazine photographer Margaret Bourke-White captured the contrast between advertisers' view of the ideal American family and the reality of mass poverty in a land of plenty.   (Margaret Bourke-White/LIFE Magazine © Time Inc.)

Frightened by the stock-market collapse, the New York banks called in their loans to Germany and Austria. Without American money, Germany and Austria stopped paying reparations to France and Britain, which then could not repay their war loans to America. Governments canceled both reparations payments and war loans, but it was too late to save the world economy.

In 1930 the U.S. government, hoping to protect domestic industries from foreign competition, imposed the Smoot-Hawley tariff, the highest import duty in American history. In retaliation, other countries raised their tariffs in a wave of "beggar thy neighbor" protectionism. The result was to cripple export industries and shrink world trade. By 1931 the Depression had spread to Europe. While global industrial production declined by 36 percent between 1929 and 1932, world trade dropped by a breathtaking 62 percent.

Depression in Industrial Nations

France and Britain escaped the worst of the Depression by making their colonial empires purchase their products rather than the products of other countries. Nations that relied on exports to pay for imported food and fuel, in particular Japan and Germany, suffered much more. In Germany, unemployment reached 6 million by 1932, twice as high as in Britain. Half of the German population lived in poverty. Thousands of teachers and engineers were laid off, and those who kept their jobs saw their salaries cut and their living standards fall. In Japan, the burden of the Depression fell on the farmers and fishermen, who saw their incomes drop sharply. Some, in desperation, revived the ancient practice of selling their daughters.

This massive economic upheaval had profound political repercussions. Many people in capitalist countries began calling for government intervention in the economy. In the United States, Franklin D. Roosevelt was elected president in 1932 on a "New Deal" platform of government programs to stimulate and revitalize the economy. Although the American, British, and French governments intervened in their economies, they remained democratic.

Even government control of a national economy could be jeopardized by the swings of the world market; hence nationalists everywhere yearned for autarchy, or independence from the world economy. Only two industrial nations—the United States and the Soviet Union—even came close to self-sufficiency; two others, Britain and France, survived by trading with their colonial empires. In Germany and Japan, as economic grievances worsened long-festering political resentments, radical politicians took over the economy and turned their nations into machines to make war, hoping to acquire, by war if necessary, empires large enough to support a self-sufficient economy.

Depression in Nonindustrial Regions

The Depression spread to Asia, Africa, and Latin America, but very unevenly. By 1930 India had erected a wall of import duties to protect its infant industries from foreign competition; its living standards stagnated but did not drop. Except for its coastal regions, China was little affected by trade with other countries; as we shall see, its problems were more political than economic.

Countries that depended on exports—sugar from the Caribbean, coffee from Brazil and Colombia, wheat and beef from Argentina, tea from Ceylon and Java, tin from Bolivia, and many other products—were hard hit by the Depression. Malaya, Indochina, and the Dutch East Indies produced most of the world's natural rubber. When automobile production dropped by half in the United States and Europe, so did imports of rubber, devastating the economies of Southeast Asia. During the 1920s, Cuba had been a playground for American tourists who basked in the sun and quaffed liquor forbidden at home by Prohibition. When the Depression hit, the tourists vanished and with them went Cuba's prosperity.

Throughout Latin America, unemployment and homelessness increased markedly. The industrialization of Argentina and Brazil was set back a decade or more. In response to the Depression, military officers seized power in several Latin American countries. Consciously imitating dictatorships emerging in Europe, they imposed authoritarian control over their economies, hoping to stimulate local industries and curb imports.

Outside of the USSR, only southern Africa boomed during the 1930s. As other prices dropped, gold became relatively more valuable. Copper deposits, found in Northern Rhodesia (now Zambia) and the Belgian Congo, proved to be cheaper to mine than Chilean copper. But this mining boom benefited only a small number of European and white South African mine owners. For Africans it was at best a mixed blessing, for mining offered jobs and cash wages to men while women stayed behind in the villages, farming, herding, and raising children without their husbands' help.

THE RISE OF FASCISM

The Russian Revolution and its Stalinist aftermath frightened property owners in Europe and North America. In the democracies of western Europe and North America, where there was little fear of Communist uprisings or electoral victories, middle- and upper-income voters took refuge in conservative politics. Political institutions in southern and Central Europe, in contrast, were frail and lacked popular legitimacy. The war had turned people's hopes of victory to bitter disappointment. Many were bewildered by modernity—with its cities, factories, and department stores—which they blamed on ethnic minorities, especially Jews. In their yearning for a mythical past of family farms and small shops, increasing numbers rejected representative government and sought more dramatic solutions.

Radical politicians quickly learned to use wartime propaganda techniques to appeal to a confused citizenry, especially young and unemployed men. They promised to use any means necessary to bring back full employment, stop the spread of communism, and achieve the territorial conquests that World War I had denied them. They borrowed their tactics from the Bolsheviks and their goals from the war.

Mussolini's Italy

The first country to seek radical answers was Italy. World War I, which had never been popular, left thousands of veterans who found neither pride in their victory nor jobs in the postwar economy. Unemployed veterans and violent youths banded together into *fasci di combattimento* (fighting units) to demand action and intimidate politicians. When workers threatened to strike, factory and property owners hired gangs of these *fascisti* to defend them.

Benito Mussolini (1883–1945) had once been a member of the Socialist Party, but he was expelled for supporting Italy's entry into the war. A spellbinding orator, he quickly became the leader of the **Fascist Party,** which glorified warfare and the Italian nation. By 1921 the party had 300,000 members, many of whom used violent methods to repress strikes, intimidate voters, and seize municipal governments. A year later, Mussolini threatened to march on Rome if he was not appointed prime minister. The government, composed of timid parliamentarians, gave in.

Mussolini proceeded to install Fascist Party members in all government jobs, crush all opposition parties, and jail anyone who criticized him. The party took over the press, public education, and youth activities and gave employers control over their workers. The Fascists lowered living standards but reduced unemployment and provided social security and public services. On the whole, they proved to be neither ruthless radicals nor competent administrators.

What Mussolini and the Fascist movement really excelled at was publicity: bombastic speeches, spectacular parades, news bulletins full of praise for *Il Duce*° ("the leader"), and signs everywhere proclaiming "Il Duce is always right!" Mussolini's genius was to apply the techniques of modern mass communications and advertisement to political life. Billboards, movie footage, and radio news bulletins galvanized the masses in ways never before seen in peacetime. Although his rhetoric was filled with words like *war, violence,* and *struggle,* his foreign policy was cautious. But his techniques of whipping up public enthusiasm were not lost on other radicals. By the 1930s, fascist movements had appeared in most European countries, as well as in Latin America, China, and Japan. Of all of Mussolini's imitators, none was as sinister as Adolf Hitler.

Hitler's Germany

Germany had lost the First World War after coming very close to winning. The hyperinflation of 1923 wiped out the savings of middle-class families. Less than ten years later, the Depression caused more unemployment and misery than in any other country. Millions of Germans blamed Socialists, Jews, and foreigners for their troubles. Few foresaw that they were about to get a dictatorship dedicated to war and mass murder.

Adolf Hitler (1889–1945) was born in Austria, the son of a minor government official. At the start of World War I, he joined the German army and was wounded at the front. He later looked back fondly on the clear lines of authority and the camaraderie he had experienced in battle. After the war, he used his gifts as an orator to lead a political splinter group called the National Socialist German Workers' Party—**Nazis** for short. In 1924 he led a small and unsuccessful uprising in Munich. While serving a brief jail sentence, he wrote *Mein Kampf*° (*My Struggle*), a book in which he outlined his goals and beliefs.

When it was published in 1925, *Mein Kampf* attracted little notice. Its ideas seemed so insane that almost no one took it, or its author, seriously. Hitler's ideas went far beyond ordinary nationalism. He believed that Germany should incorporate all German-speaking people, even those who lived in neighboring countries. He distinguished among a "master race" of Aryans (he meant Germans, Scandinavians, and Britons), a degenerate "Alpine" race of French and Italians, and an inferior race of Russian and eastern European Slavs, who he believed were fit only to be slaves of the master race. He reserved his most intense hatred for Jews, on whom he blamed every disaster that had befallen Germany, especially the defeat of 1918. He glorified violence, interpreting the Darwinian idea of "survival of the fittest" (see Chapter 28) to mean that in a future war the "master race" would defeat and subjugate all others.

His first goal was to repeal the humiliation and military restrictions of the Treaty of Versailles. Then he planned to annex all German-speaking territories to a greater Germany and then conquer *Lebensraum*° (room to live) at the expense of Poland and the USSR. Finally, he planned to eliminate all Jews from Europe.

From 1924 to 1930, Hitler's followers remained a tiny minority, for most Germans found his ideas too extreme. But when the Depression hit, the Nazis gained supporters among the unemployed who believed Nazi promises of jobs for all and among property owners frightened by the growing popularity of Communists. In March 1933, as leader of the largest party in Germany, Hitler became chancellor.

Once in office, he quickly assumed dictatorial power. From the Reichstag° (parliament) he obtained the power to govern by decree, legally ending democracy in Germany. He put Nazis in charge of all government agencies, educational institutions, and professional organizations. He banned all other political parties and threw their leaders into concentration camps. The Nazis deprived Jews of their citizenship and civil rights, prohibited them from marrying "Aryans," ousted them from the professions, and confiscated their property. In August 1934

Il Duce (eel DOO-chay)

Mein Kampf (mine compf)   *Lebensraum* (LAY-bens-rowm)
Reichstag (RIKES-tog)

Hitler the Orator   A masterful public speaker, Adolf Hitler often captivated mass audiences at Nazi Party rallies.   (Roger Viollet)

Hitler proclaimed himself *Führer*° ("leader") and called Germany the "Third Reich" (empire)—the third after the Holy Roman Empire of medieval times and the German Empire of 1871 to 1918.

The Nazis' economic and social policies were spectacularly effective. The government undertook massive public works projects. Businesses got contracts to manufacture weapons for the armed forces. Women, who had entered the work force during and after World War I, were urged to return to "Kinder, Kirche, Küche" (children,

---

Führer (FEW-rer)

church, kitchen), releasing jobs for men. By 1936 business was booming, unemployment was at its lowest level since the 1920s, and living standards were rising. Hitler's popularity soared because most Germans believed their economic well-being outweighed the loss of liberty.

The Road to War, 1933–1939

Hitler's goal was not prosperity or popularity but conquest. As soon as he came to office, he began to build up the armed forces. Meanwhile, he tested the reactions of the other powers through a series of surprise moves followed by protestations of peace.

In 1933 Hitler withdrew Germany from the League of Nations. France and Britain hesitated to retaliate by blockading or invading Germany. Two years later he announced that Germany was going to introduce conscription, build up its army, and create an air force—in violation of the Versailles treaty. Instead of protesting, Britain signed a naval agreement with Germany. The message was clear: neither Britain nor France was willing to risk war by standing up to Germany. The United States, absorbed in its domestic economic problems, reverted to isolationism.

In 1935, emboldened by the weakness of the democracies, Italy invaded Ethiopia, the last independent state in Africa and a member of the League of Nations. The League and the democracies protested but refused to close the Suez Canal to Italian ships or impose an oil embargo. The following year, when Hitler sent troops into the Rhineland on the borders of France and Belgium, the other powers merely protested.

By 1938 Hitler decided his rearmament plans were far enough advanced that he could afford to escalate his demands. In March, Germany invaded Austria. Most of its citizens were German-speakers and accepted the annexation of their country without protest. Then came the turn of Czechoslovakia, where a German-speaking minority lived along the German border. Hitler first demanded their autonomy from Czech rule, then their annexation to Germany. Throughout the summer he threatened to go to war. At the Munich Conference of September 1938, he met with the leaders of France, Britain, and Italy, who gave him everything he wanted without consulting Czechoslovakia. Once again, Hitler learned that aggression paid off and that the democracies would always give in.

The weakness of the democracies—now called "appeasement"—ran counter to the traditional European balance of power. It had three causes. The first was the deep-seated fear of war among all people who had lived through World War I. Unlike the dictators, politicians in the democracies could not ignore their constituents' yearnings for peace. Politicians and most other people believed that the threat of war might go away if they wished for peace fervently enough.

The second cause of appeasement was fear of communism among the conservative politicians who ruled France and Britain. Until very late in the day, they were more afraid of Stalin than of Hitler, for Hitler claimed to respect Christianity and private property. Distrust of the Soviet Union prevented them from recreating the only viable counterweight to Germany: the pre–World War I alliance of Britain, France, and Russia.

The third cause was the very novelty of fascist tactics. Britain's Prime Minister Neville Chamberlain assumed that political leaders (other than the Bolsheviks) were honorable men and that an agreement was as valid as a business contract. Thus, when Hitler promised to incorporate only German-speaking people into Germany and said he had "no further territorial demands," Chamberlain believed him.

After Munich it was too late to stop Hitler, short of war. Germany and Italy were now united in an alliance called the Axis. In March 1939 Germany invaded what was left of Czechoslovakia. Belatedly realizing that Hitler could not be trusted, France and Britain sought Soviet help. Stalin, however, distrusted the "capitalists" as much as they distrusted him. Hitler, meanwhile, offered to divide Poland between Germany and the Soviet Union. On August 23, Stalin accepted. The Nazi-Soviet Pact freed Hitler from the fear of a two-front war and gave Stalin two more years of peace to build up his armies. One week later, on September 1, 1939, German forces swept into Poland. The war was on.

EAST ASIA, 1931–1945

When the Depression hit, China and the United States erected barriers against Japanese imports. The collapse of demand for silk and rice ruined thousands of Japanese farmers; to survive, many sold their daughters into prostitution while their sons flocked to the military. Ultra-nationalists, including young army officers, resented their country's dependence on foreign trade. If only Japan had a colonial empire, they thought, it would not be beholden to the rest of the world. But Europeans and Americans had already taken most potential colonies in Asia. Japan had only Korea, Taiwan, and a railroad in Manchuria. China, however, had not yet been conquered. Japanese nationalists saw the conquest of China, with its vast population and resources, as the solution to their country's problems.

The Manchurian Incident of 1931

Meanwhile, in China the Guomindang° was becoming stronger and preparing to challenge the Japanese presence in Manchuria, a province rich in coal and iron ore. Junior officers in the Japanese army guarding the South Manchurian Railway, frustrated by the caution of their superiors, determined to take action. In September 1931, an explosion on a railroad track, probably staged, gave them an excuse to conquer the entire province. In Tokyo, weak civilian ministers were intimidated by the military. Informed after the fact, they acquiesced to the attack to avoid losing face but privately one said: "From beginning to end the government has been utterly fooled by the army."

When Chinese students, workers, and housewives boycotted Japanese goods, Japanese troops briefly took over Shanghai, China's major industrial city, and the area around Beijing. Japan thereupon recognized the "independence" of Manchuria under the name "Manchukuo°."

The U.S. government condemned the Japanese conquest. The League of Nations refused to recognize Manchukuo and urged the Japanese to remove their troops from China. Persuaded that the Western powers would not fight, Japan simply resigned from the League.

During the next few years, the Japanese built railways and heavy industries in Manchuria and northeastern China and sped up their rearmament. At home, production was diverted to the military, especially to building warships. The government grew more authoritarian, jailing thousands of dissidents. On several occasions, super-patriotic junior officers mutinied or assassinated leading political figures. The mutineers received mild punishments, and generals and admirals sympathetic to their views replaced more moderate civilian politicians.

The Chinese Communists and the Long March

Until the Japanese seized Manchuria, the Chinese government seemed to be consolidating its power and creating the conditions for a national recovery. The main challenge to the government of **Chiang Kai-shek°** came from the Communists. The Chinese Communist Party was founded in 1921 by a handful of intellectuals. For several years it lived in the shadow of the Guomindang, kept there by orders of Joseph Stalin, who expected it to subvert the government from within. All its efforts to manipulate the Guomindang and to recruit members among industrial workers came to nought in

---

Guomindang (gwo-min-dong)   **Manchukuo** (man-CHEW-coo-oh)
Chiang Kai-shek (chang kie-shek)

1927, when Chiang Kai-shek arrested and executed Communists and labor leaders alike. The few Communists who escaped the mass arrests fled to the remote mountains of Jiangxi°, in southeastern China.

Among them was **Mao Zedong°** (1893–1976), a farmer's son who had left home to study philosophy. He was not a contemplative thinker but a man of action whose first impulse was to call for violent effort: "To be able to leap on horseback and to shoot at the same time; to go from battle to battle; to shake the mountains by one's cries, and the colors of the sky by one's roars of anger." In the early 1920s Mao discovered the works of Karl Marx, joined the Communist Party, and soon became one of its leaders.

In Jiangxi, Mao began studying conditions among the peasants, in whom Communists had previously shown no interest. He planned to redistribute land from the wealthier to the poorer peasants, thereby gaining adherents for the coming struggle with the Guomindang army. In this, he was following the example of innumerable leaders of peasant rebellions over the centuries. His goal, however, was not just a nationalist revolution against the traditional government and foreign intervention, but a complete social revolution from the bottom up. Mao's reliance on the peasantry was a radical departure from Marxist-Leninist ideology, which stressed the backwardness of the peasants and pinned its hopes on the industrial workers. Mao therefore had to be careful to cloak his pragmatic tactics in Communist rhetoric in order to allay the suspicions of Stalin and his agents.

Mao was also an advocate of women's equality. Radical ideas such as those of Margaret Sanger, the American leader of the birth-control movement, and the feminist play *A Doll's House* by the Norwegian playwright Henrik Ibsen inspired veterans of the May Fourth Movement and young women attending universities and medical or nursing schools. Before 1927 the Communists had organized the women who worked in Shanghai's textile mills, the most exploited of all Chinese workers. Later, in their mountain stronghold in Jiangxi, they organized women farmers, allowed divorce, and banned arranged marriages and footbinding. But they did not admit women to leadership positions, for the party was still run by men whose primary task was warfare.

The Guomindang army pursued the Communists into the mountains, building small forts throughout the countryside. Rather than risk direct confrontations, Mao responded with guerrilla warfare. He harassed the army at its weak points with hit-and-run tactics, relying on the terrain and the support of the peasantry. Government

Mao on the Long March   In 1934–1935, Mao Zedong led his rag-tag army of guerrillas across the rugged mountains of southern and western China. In this romanticized painting, young Mao is speaking to a group of soldiers in spotless uniforms who look up at him with worshipful expressions.   (Library of Congress)

troops often mistreated civilians, but Mao insisted that his soldiers help the peasants, pay a fair price for food and supplies, and treat women with respect.

In spite of their good relations with the peasants of Jiangxi, the Communists gradually found themselves encircled by government forces. In 1934 Mao and his followers decided to break out of the southern mountains and trek to Shaanxi°, an even more remote province in northwestern China. The so-called **Long March** took them 6,000 miles (nearly 9,700 kilometers) in one year, 17 miles (27 kilometers) a day over desolate mountains and through swamps and deserts, pursued

Jiangxi (jang -she)   **Mao Zedong** (ma-oh zay-dong)

Shaanxi (SHAWN-she)

by the army and bombed by Chiang's aircraft. Of the 100,000 Communists who left Jiangxi in October 1934, only 4,000 reached Shaanxi a year later (see Map 31.1). Chiang's government thought it was finally rid of the Communists.

The Sino-Japanese War, 1937–1945

In Japan, politicians, senior officers, and business leaders disagreed on how to solve their country's economic problems. Some proposed a quick conquest of China; others advocated war with the Soviet Union. While their superiors hesitated, junior officers decided to take matters into their own hands.

On July 7, 1937, Japanese troops attacked Chinese forces near Beijing. As in 1931, the junior officers who ordered the attack quickly obtained the support of their commanders and then, reluctantly, of the government. Within weeks, Japanese troops seized Beijing, Tianjin, Shanghai, and other coastal cities, and the Japanese navy blockaded the entire coast of China.

Once again, the United States and the League of Nations denounced the Japanese atrocities. Yet the Western powers were too preoccupied with events in Europe and with their own economic problems to risk a military confrontation in Asia. When the Japanese sank a U.S. gunboat and shelled a British ship on the Yangzi River, the U.S. and British governments responded only with righteous indignation and pious resolutions.

The Chinese armies were large and fought bravely, but they were poorly led and armed and lost every battle. Japanese planes bombed Nanjing, Hankou, and Canton, while on the ground, soldiers broke dikes and burned villages, killing thousands of civilians. Within a year, Japan controlled the coastal provinces of China and the lower Yangzi and Yellow River Valleys, China's richest and most populated regions (see Map 31.1).

In spite of Japanese organizational and fighting skills, the attack on China did not bring the victory Japan had hoped for. The Chinese people continued to resist, either in the army or, increasingly, with the Communist guerrilla forces. Japan's periodic attempts to turn the tide by conquering one more piece of China only pushed Japan deeper into the quagmire. For the Japanese people, life became harsher and more repressive as taxes rose, food and fuel became scarce, and more and more young men were drafted. Japanese leaders belatedly realized that the war with China was a drain on the Japanese economy and manpower and that their war machine was becoming increasingly dependent on the United States for steel and machine tools and for nine-tenths of its oil.

Warfare between Chinese and Japanese was incredibly violent. In the winter of 1937–1938, Japanese troops took Nanjing, raped 20,000 women, killed 200,000 prisoners and civilians, and looted and burned the city. To slow them down, Chiang ordered the Yellow River dikes blasted open, causing a flood that destroyed 4,000 villages, killed 890,000 people, and made 12.5 million homeless. Two years later, when the Communists ordered a massive offensive, the Japanese retaliated with a "kill all, burn all, loot all" campaign, destroying hundreds of villages down to the last person, building, and farm animal.

The Chinese government, led by Chiang Kai-shek, escaped to the mountains of Sichuan in the center of the country. There he built up a huge army, not to fight Japan but to prepare for a future confrontation with the Communists. The army drafted over 3 million men, even though it had only a million rifles and could not provide food or clothing for all its soldiers. The Guomindang raised farmers' taxes, even when famine forced farmers to eat the bark of trees. Such taxes were not enough to support both a large army and the thousands of government officials and hangers-on who had fled to Sichuan. To avoid taxing its wealthy supporters, the government printed money, causing inflation, hoarding, and corruption.

From his capital of Yan'an in Shaanxi province, Mao also built up his army and formed a government. Until early 1941, he received a little aid from the Soviet Union; then, after Stalin signed a Soviet-Japanese Neutrality Pact, none at all. Unlike the Guomindang, the Communists listened to the grievances of the peasants, especially the poor, to whom they distributed land confiscated from wealthy landowners. They imposed rigid discipline on their officials and soldiers and tolerated no dissent or criticism from intellectuals. Though they had few weapons, the Communists obtained support and intelligence from farmers in Japanese-occupied territory. They turned military reversals into propaganda victories, presenting themselves as the only group in China that was serious about fighting the Japanese.

Map 31.1 Chinese Communist Movements and the Sino-Japanese War, to 1938 During the 1930s, China was the scene of a three-way war. The Nationalist government attacked and pursued the Communists, who escaped into the mountains of Shaanxi. Meanwhile, Japanese forces, having seized Manchuria in 1931, attacked China in 1937 and quickly conquered its eastern provinces.

THE SECOND WORLD WAR

Many people feared the Second World War would be a repetition of the First. Instead, it was much bigger in every way. It was fought around the world, from Norway to New Guinea, from Hawaii to Egypt, and on every ocean. It killed far more people than World War I. It was a total war involving all productive forces and all civilians, and it showed how effectively industry, science, and nationalism could be channeled into mass destruction.

The War of Movement

Defensive maneuvers had dominated in World War I. In World War II, motorized weapons gave back the advantage to the offensive. Opposing forces moved fast, their victories hinging as much on the aggressive spirit of their commanders and the military intelligence they obtained as on numbers of troops or firepower.

The Wehrmacht°, or German armed forces, was the first to learn this lesson. It not only had tanks, trucks, and fighter planes but perfected their combined use in a tactic called *blitzkrieg*° (lightning war): fighter planes scattered enemy troops and disrupted communications, and tanks punctured the enemy's defenses and then, with the help of the infantry, encircled and captured enemy troops. At sea, the navies of both Japan and the United States had developed aircraft carriers that could launch planes against targets hundreds of miles away.

Yet the very size and mobility of the opposing forces made the fighting far different from any the world had ever seen. Instead of engaging in localized battles, armies ranged over vast theaters of operation. Countries were conquered in a matter of days or weeks. The belligerents mobilized the economies of entire continents, squeezing them for every possible resource. They tried not only to defeat their enemies' armed forces but—by means of blockades, submarine attacks on shipping, and bombing raids on industrial areas—to damage the economies that supported those armed forces. They thought of civilians not as innocent bystanders but as legitimate targets and, later, as vermin to be exterminated.

Wehrmacht (VAIR-mokt)
blitzkrieg (BLITS-creeg)

War in Europe and North Africa

It took less than a month for the Wehrmacht to conquer Poland. Britain and France declared war on Germany but took no military action. Meanwhile, the Soviet Union invaded eastern Poland and the Baltic republics of Lithuania, Latvia, and Estonia. Although the Poles fought bravely, the Polish infantry and cavalry were no match for German or Russian tanks. During the winter of 1939–1940, Germany and the Western democracies faced each other in what soldiers called a "phony war" and watched as the Soviet Union attacked Finland, which resisted for many months.

In March 1940, Hitler went on the offensive again, conquering Denmark, Norway, the Netherlands, and Belgium in less than two months. In May, he attacked France. Although the French army had as many soldiers, tanks, and aircraft as the Wehrmacht, its morale was low and it quickly collapsed. By the end of June, Hitler was master of all of Europe between Russia and Spain.

Germany still had to face one enemy: Britain. The British had no army to speak of, but they had other assets: the English Channel, the Royal Navy and Air Force, and a tough new prime minister, Winston Churchill. The Germans knew they could invade Britain only by gaining control of the airspace over the Channel, so they launched a massive air attack—the Battle of Britain—lasting from June through September. They failed, however, because the Royal Air Force had better fighters and used radar and code-breaking to detect approaching German planes.

Frustrated in the west, Hitler turned his attention eastward. So far he had gotten the utmost cooperation from Stalin, who supplied Germany with grain, oil, and strategic raw materials. Yet he had always wanted to conquer lebensraum in the east and enslave the Slavic peoples who lived there, and he feared that if he waited, Stalin would build up a dangerously strong army. In June 1941 he launched the largest attack in history, with 3 million soldiers and thousands of planes and tanks. Within five months the Wehrmacht conquered the Baltic states, Ukraine, and half of European Russia, captured a million prisoners of war, and stood at the very gates of Moscow and Leningrad (now St. Petersburg). The USSR seemed on the verge of collapse when suddenly the weather turned cold, machines froze, and the fighting came to a halt. Like Napoleon, Hitler had ignored the environment of Russia to his peril.

The next spring the Wehrmacht renewed its offensive. It surrounded Leningrad in a siege that was to cost a million lives. Leaving Moscow aside, it turned toward the Caucasus and its oil wells. In August, the Germans at-

The Enigma Machine   During World War II, German armed forces used Enigma machines like the one seen here in the vehicle of a German tank commander. With Enigmas, they could encrypt and decode radio messages, keeping them secret (they believed) from enemy code-breakers.   (Brian Johnson)

brought the Germans to their rescue. During 1942 the German army and the forces of the British Empire (now known as the Commonwealth) seesawed back and forth across the deserts of Libya and Egypt. At **El Alamein** in northern Egypt the British prevailed because they had more weapons and supplies. Thanks to their success at breaking German codes, they also were better informed about their enemies' plans. The Germans were finally expelled from Africa in May 1943.

War in Asia and the Pacific

The fall of France and the involvement of Britain and the USSR against Germany presented Japan with the opportunity it had been looking for. Suddenly the European colonies in Southeast Asia, with their abundant oil, rubber, and other strategic materials, seemed ripe for the taking. In July 1941, the French government allowed Japanese forces to occupy Indochina. Instead of merely complaining, the United States and Britain stopped shipments of steel, scrap iron, oil, and other products that Japan desperately needed. This left Japan with three alternatives: accept the shame and humiliation of giving up its conquests, as the Americans insisted; face economic ruin; or widen the war. Japan chose war (see Society and Culture: Preparing for Combat).

Admiral Isoroku Yamamoto, commander of the Japanese fleet, told Prime Minister Fumimaro Konoye: "If I am told to fight regardless of the consequences, I shall run wild for the first six months or a year, but I have utterly no confidence for the second or third year. . . . I hope that you will endeavor to avoid a Japanese-American war." Finally they agreed on a plan for a surprise attack on the United States Navy, followed by an invasion of Southeast Asia. They knew they could not hope to defeat the United States, but they calculated that the shock of the attack would be so great that isolationist Americans would accept the Japanese conquest of Southeast Asia as readily as they had acquiesced to Hitler's conquests in Europe.

On December 7, 1941, Japanese planes bombed the U.S. naval base at **Pearl Harbor,** Hawaii, sinking or damaging scores of warships but missing the aircraft carriers, which were at sea. Then, between January and March 1942, the Japanese bombed Hong Kong and Singapore and invaded Thailand, the Philippines, and Malaya. Within a few months they occupied all of Southeast Asia and the Dutch East Indies. The Japanese claimed to be liberating the inhabitants of these lands from European colonialism. But they soon began to confiscate food and raw materials and demand heavy labor from the

tacked **Stalingrad** (now Volgagrad), the key to the Volga River and the supply of oil. For months, German and Soviet soldiers fought over every street and every house. When winter came, the Red Army counterattacked and encircled the city. In February 1943 the remnants of the German army in Stalingrad surrendered. Hitler had lost his greatest gamble (see Map 31.2).

From Europe, the war spread to Africa. When France fell in 1940, Mussolini began imagining himself a latter-day Roman emperor and decided the time had come to realize his imperial ambitions. Italian forces quickly overran British Somaliland, then invaded Egypt. Their victories were ephemeral, however, for when the British counterattacked, Italian resistance crumbled. During 1941, British forces conquered Italian East Africa and invaded Libya as well. The Italian rout in North Africa

Map 31.2 World War II in Europe and North Africa In a series of quick and decisive campaigns from September 1939 to December 1941, German forces overran much of Europe and North Africa. There followed three years of bitter fighting as the Allies slowly pushed the Germans back. This map shows the maximum extent of Germany's conquests and alliances, as well as the key battles and the front lines at various times.

Preparing for Combat

All armies train their recruits to face the violence of battle. Tominaga Shozo, a young officer in the Japanese army, describes his training in brutality. As you read this passage, compare it to the experience of battle in the First World War, as described by Erich Maria Remarque in the Society and Culture feature in Chapter 30.

It was July 30, 1941, when I reported in. They took me to the infantry company where I had been assigned as a second lieutenant. I was fresh from officer school. "These men are the members of the second platoon" was my only introduction to those who would be under my command. I'll never forget meeting them.... When I looked at the men of my platoon I was stunned—they had evil eyes. They weren't human eyes but the eyes of leopards or tigers....

The next-to-last day of the exercise, Second Lieutenant Tanaka took us to the detention center. Pointing at the people in a room, all Chinese, he announced, "These are the raw materials for your trial of courage." We were astonished at how thin and emaciated they looked. Tanaka told us, "They haven't been fed for several days, so they'll be ready for their part in tomorrow's plan." He said that it was to be a test to see if we were qualified to be platoon leaders. He said we wouldn't be qualified if we couldn't chop off a head.

On the final day, we were taken out to the site of our trial. Twenty-four prisoners were squatting there with their hands tied behind their backs. They were blindfolded. A big hole had been dug—ten meters long, and more than three meters deep. The regimental commander, the battalion commanders, and the company commanders all took the seats arranged for them. Second Lieutenant Tanaka bowed to the regimental commander and reported, "We shall now begin." He ordered a soldier on fatigue duty to haul one of the prisoners to the edge of the pit; the prisoner was kicked when he resisted. The soldier finally dragged him over and forced him to his knees. Tanaka turned toward us and looked into each of our faces in turn. "Heads should be cut off like this," he said, unsheathing his army sword. He scooped water from a bucket with a dipper. Then poured it over both sides of the blade. Swishing off the water, he raised his sword in a long arc. Standing behind the prisoners, Tanaka steadied himself, legs spread apart, and cut off the man's head with a shout, "Yo!" The head flew more than a meter away. Blood spurted up in two fountains from the body and sprayed the hole.

After witnessing this demonstration, Lieutenant Tominaga Shozo is required to do the same to another prisoner. He writes:

At that moment I felt something change inside me. I don't know how to put it, but I gained strength somewhere in my gut.... We returned to our companies. Until that day I had been overwhelmed by the sharp eyes of my men when I called the roll each night. That night I realized I was not self-conscious at all in front of them. I didn't even find their eyes evil anymore.

Why did Tominaga Shozo first think the soldiers had "evil eyes," then change his mind? What was the purpose of training officers to kill prisoners?

Source: Tominaga Shozo, "Qualifying as a Leader," in Haruko Taya Cook and Theodore F. Cook, *Japan at War: An Oral History* (New York: New Press, 1992), 40–41. Copyright © 1992. Reprinted by permission of The New Press.

inhabitants, whom they treated with contempt. Those who protested were brutally punished.

Japan's dream of an East Asian empire seemed within reach, for its victories surpassed even Hitler's in Europe. Yamamoto's fears were justified, however, because the United States, far from being cowed into submission, joined Britain and the Soviet Union in an alliance called the United Nations (or the Allies) and began preparing for war. In April 1942, American planes bombed Tokyo. In May the United States Navy defeated a Japanese fleet in the Coral Sea, ending Japanese plans to conquer Australia. A month later, at the **Battle of Midway,** Japan lost four of its six largest aircraft carriers. Japan did not have enough industry to replace them, for its war production was only one-tenth that of the United States. In the vastness of the Pacific Ocean, aircraft carriers held the key to victory, and without them, Japan faced a long and hopeless war (see Map 31.3).

Map 31.3   World War II in Asia and the Pacific   After having conquered much of China between 1937 and 1941, Japanese forces launched a sudden attack on Southeast Asia, Indonesia, and the Pacific in late 1941 and early 1942. American forces slowly reconquered the Pacific islands and the Philippines until August 1945, when the atomic bombing of Hiroshima and Nagasaki forced Japan's surrender.

The End of the War   After the Battle of Stalingrad, the advantage on the Eastern Front shifted to the Soviet Union. By 1943 the Red Army was receiving a growing stream of supplies from factories in Russia and the United States. Slowly at first and then with increasing vigor, it pushed the Wehrmacht back toward Germany.

The Western powers, meanwhile, staged two invasions of Europe. Beginning in July 1943, they captured Sicily and invaded Italy. Mussolini resigned and Italy

signed an armistice, but German troops held off the Allied advance for two years. Then on June 6, 1944—forever after known as D-day—156,000 British, American, and Canadian troops landed on the coast of Normandy in western France—the largest shipborne assault ever staged. Within a week, the Allies had more troops in France than Germany did, and by September Germany faced an Allied army of over 2 million men with half a million vehicles of all sorts. Although the Red Army was on the eastern border of Germany, ready for the final

Hiroshima After the Atomic Bomb   On August 6, 1945, an atomic bomb destroyed the city, killing over fifty thousand people. This photo shows the devastation of the city center, where only a few concrete buildings remained standing.   (Wide World Photos)

push, Hitler transferred part of the Wehrmacht westward. Despite overwhelming odds, Germany held out for almost a year, a result of the fighting qualities of its soldiers and the terror inspired by the Nazi regime, which commanded obedience to the end. On May 7, 1945, a week after Hitler committed suicide, German military leaders surrendered.

Japan fought on a while longer, in large part because the United States had aimed most of its war effort at Germany. In the Pacific, U.S. forces "leap-frogged" some heavily fortified Japanese island bases in order to capture others closer to Japan itself. By June 1944, U.S. bombers were able to attack Japan. Meanwhile, U.S. submarines sank ever larger numbers of Japanese merchant ships, gradually cutting Japan off from its sources of oil and other raw materials. In 1944 a terrible earthquake devastated the city of Nagoya, compounding the misery of war and bombing raids. After May 1945, with the Japanese air force grounded for lack of fuel, U.S. planes began destroying Japanese shipping, industries, and cities at will.

Even as their homeland was being pounded, the Japanese still held strong positions in Asia. At first, Asian nationalists such as the Indonesian Achmed Sukarno were glad to get rid of the white colonialists and welcomed the Japanese. Yet despite its name, "Greater East Asian Co-Prosperity Sphere," the Japanese occupation was harsh and brutal. By 1945 Asians were eager to see the Japanese leave but not to welcome back the Europeans; instead, they looked forward to independence (see Chapters 32 and 33).

On August 6, 1945, the United States dropped an atomic bomb on **Hiroshima,** killing some 80,000 people in a flash and leaving about 120,000 more to die an agonizing death from burns and radiation. Three days later, another atomic bomb destroyed Nagasaki. Were these atomic weapons necessary? At the time, Americans believed that the conquest of the Japanese homeland would take more than a year and cost the lives of hundreds of thousands of American soldiers. Although some Japanese were determined to fight to the bitter end, others were willing to surrender if they could retain their emperor. Had the Allies agreed sooner to keep the monarchy, Japan might have surrendered without the nuclear devastation. On August 14, Japan offered to surrender and Emperor Hirohito himself gave the order to lay down arms. Two weeks later, Japanese leaders signed the terms of surrender. The war was officially over.

Chinese Civil War and Communist Victory

The formal Japanese surrender in September 1945 came as a surprise to the Guomindang. American transport planes flew Guomindang officials and troops to all the cities of China. The United States gave millions of dollars of aid and weapons to the Guomindang, all the while urging "national unity" and a "coalition government" with the Communists. But Chiang used American aid and all other means available to prepare for a civil war. By late 1945 he had an army of 2.7 million, more than twice the size of the Communist forces.

From 1945 to 1949 the contest between the Guomindang and the Communists intensified. Guomindang forces started with many advantages: more troops and weapons, U.S. support, and control of China's cities. But their behavior eroded whatever popular support they had. As they moved into formerly Japanese-held territory, they acted like an occupation force. They taxed the people they "liberated" more heavily than the Japanese had, looted businesses, confiscated supplies, and enriched themselves at the expense of the population. To pay its bills, Chiang's government printed money so fast that it soon lost all its value, ruining merchants and causing hoarding and shortages. In the countryside, the Guomindang's brutality alienated the peasants.

Meanwhile, the Communists obtained Japanese equipment seized by the Soviets in the last weeks of the war and American weapons brought over by deserting Guomindang soldiers. In Manchuria, where they were strongest, they pushed through a radical land reform program, distributing the properties of wealthy landowners among the poorest peasants. In battles against government forces, the higher morale and popular support they enjoyed outweighed the heavy equipment of the Guomindang, whose soldiers began deserting by the thousands.

In April 1947, as Chinese Communist forces surrounded Nanjing, the British frigate *Amethyst* sailed up the Yangzi River to evacuate British civilians. Dozens of times since the Opium War of 1839–1842, foreign powers had dispatched warships up the rivers of China to rescue their citizens, enforce their treaty rights, or intimidate the Chinese. Foreign warships deep in the heart of China were the very symbols of its weakness. This time, however, Chinese Communist artillery damaged the *Amethyst* and beat back other British warships sent to its rescue.

By 1949 the Guomindang armies were collapsing everywhere, defeated more by their own greed and ineptness than by the Communists. As the Communists advanced, high-ranking members of the Guomindang fled to Taiwan, protected from the mainland by the United States Navy. On October 1, 1949, Mao Zedong announced the founding of the People's Republic of China.

THE CHARACTER OF WARFARE

The war left an enormous death toll. Recent estimates place the figure at close to 60 million deaths, six to eight times more than in World War I. Over half of the dead were civilian victims of massacres, famines, or bombs. The Soviet Union lost between 20 million and 25 million people, more than any other country. China suffered 15 million deaths; Poland lost some 6 million, of whom half were Jewish; the Jewish people lost another 3 million outside Poland. Over 4 million Germans and over 2 million Japanese died. In much of the world, almost every family mourned one or more of its members. In contrast, Great Britain lost 400,000 people, the United States only 300,000.

Many parts of the world were flooded with refugees. Some 90 million Chinese fled the Japanese advance. In Europe, millions fled from the Nazis or the Red Army or were herded back and forth on government orders. Many refugees never returned to their homes, creating new ethnic mixtures more reminiscent of the New World than of the Old.

One reason for the terrible toll in human lives and suffering was a change in moral values, as belligerents identified not just soldiers but entire peoples as enemies. Some belligerents even labeled their own ethnic minorities as "enemies." Another reason for the devastation was the appearance of new technologies that carried destruction deep into enemy territory far beyond the traditional battlefields. Let us consider the new technologies of warfare, the changes in morality, and their lethal combination.

The War of Science

As fighting spread around the world, the features that had characterized the early years of the war—the mobilization of manpower and economies and the mobility of the armed forces—grew increasingly powerful. Meanwhile, new aspects of war took on a growing importance. One of these was the impact of science on the technology of warfare. Chemists found ways to make synthetic rubber from coal or oil. Physicists perfected radar, which warned of approaching enemy aircraft and submarines. Cryptanalysts broke enemy codes and were able to penetrate secret military communications. Pharmacologists developed antibiotics that saved the lives of countless wounded soldiers, who in any earlier war would have died of infections (see Environment and Technology: Biomedical Technologies).

Biomedical Technologies

Life expectancy at birth has nearly doubled in the past 150 years. Even in the poorest countries, life expectancy has risen from forty to sixty or seventy years. The cause of this remarkable change is threefold: clean water, immunizations, and antibiotics.

The realization that drinking water can spread disease came first to Dr. Charles Snow, who noticed the correlation between deaths from cholera and the water from a particular pump in London during an epidemic in 1854. Since then, public health officials have been very conscious of the quality of drinking water, although only wealthy cities can afford to purify and chlorinate water for all their inhabitants.

The practice of immunization goes back to the eighteenth century, when physicians in Turkey and in Europe applied infected pus from a person with smallpox (variolation) or an animal with cowpox (vaccination) to healthy persons to build up their resistance to smallpox. By the end of the nineteenth century, it became clear that immunity to many diseases could be conferred by injections of weakened bacteria. Immunizations offer the single most effective way to prevent childhood diseases and thereby increase life expectancy.

Antibiotics are more recent. In 1928 Dr. Alexander Fleming discovered that a certain mold, *Penicillin notatum*, could kill bacteria. Antibiotics were first used in large quantities in the Second World War. Along with two other innovations—synthetic antimalarial drugs and blood transfusions—antibiotics helped cut the fatality of battlefield wounds from 11 percent in World War I to 3 percent in World War II.

The remarkable success of these technologies has led people to consider good health their natural birthright. Unfortunately, the victory over disease is temporary at best. The abuse of antibiotics and of antibacterial products encourages the growth of new strains of old diseases, such as tuberculosis, which can resist all known antibiotics. And although bacterial diseases are no longer as prevalent as they once were, humans are still susceptible to viral afflictions such as influenza and AIDS.

Biotechnology in Action   Campaigns to immunize children against diseases reached even remote villages, as here in Thailand. (Peter Charlesworth/Saba)

Aircraft development was especially striking. As war approached, German, British, and Japanese aircraft manufacturers developed fast, maneuverable fighter planes. U.S. industry produced aircraft of every sort but was especially noted for its heavy bombers designed to fly in huge formations and drop tons of bombs on enemy cities. The Japanese developed the Mitsubishi "Zero" fighter plane—light, fast, and agile but dangerous to fly. Unable to produce heavy planes in large numbers, Germany responded with radically new designs, including the first jet fighters, low-flying buzz bombs, and, finally, V-2 missiles, against which there was no warning or defense.

Military planners no longer dismissed the creations of civilian inventors, as they had done before World War I. Now they expected scientists to furnish secret weapons that could doom the enemy. In October 1939, President Roosevelt received a letter from physicist Albert Einstein, a Jewish refugee from Nazism, warning of the dangers of nuclear power: "There is no doubt that sub-atomic energy is available all around us, and that one day man will release and control its almost infinite power. We cannot prevent him from doing so and can only hope that he will not use it exclusively in blowing up his next door neighbor." Fearing that Germany might develop a nuclear bomb first, Roosevelt placed the vast resources of the U.S. government at the disposal of physicists and engineers, both Americans and refugees from Europe. By 1945 they had built two atomic bombs, each one powerful enough to annihilate an entire city.

Bombing Raids

German bombers damaged Warsaw in 1939 and Rotterdam and London in 1940. Yet Germany lacked a strategic bomber force capable of destroying whole cities. In this area, the British and Americans excelled. Since it was very hard to pinpoint individual buildings, especially at night, the British Air Staff under British Air Chief Marshal Arthur "Bomber" Harris decided that "operations should now be focused on the morale of the enemy civilian population and in particular the industrial workers."

In May 1942, 1,000 British planes dropped incendiary bombs on Cologne, setting fire to most of the old city. Between July 24 and August 2, 1943, 3,330 British and Americans bombers set fire to Hamburg, killing 50,000 people, mostly women and children. Later raids destroyed Berlin, Dresden, and other German cities. All in all, the bombing raids against Germany killed 600,000 people—more than half of them women and children—and injured 800,000. If the air strategists had hoped thereby to break the morale of the German people, they failed. German armament production continued to increase until late 1944, and the population remained obedient and hard working. The only effective bombing raids were those directed against oil depots and synthetic fuel plants; by early 1945, they had almost brought the German war effort to a standstill.

Japanese cities were also the targets of American bombing raids. As early as April 1942, sixteen planes launched from an aircraft carrier bombed Tokyo. Later, as American forces captured islands close to Japan, the raids intensified. Their effect was even more devastating than the fire-bombing of German cities, for Japanese cities were made of wood. In March 1945, bombs set Tokyo ablaze, killing 80,000 people and leaving a million homeless. It was a portent of worse destruction to come.

The Holocaust

In World War II, for the first time, more civilians than soldiers were deliberately put to death. The champions in the art of killing defenseless civilians were the Nazis. Their murders were not the accidental byproducts of some military goal but a calculated policy of exterminating whole races of people.

Their first targets were Jews. Soon after Hitler came to power, he deprived German Jews of their citizenship and legal rights. When eastern Europe fell under Nazi rule, the Nazis herded its large Jewish population into ghettos in the major cities, where many died of starvation and disease. Then, in early 1942, the Nazis decided to carry out Hitler's "final solution to the Jewish problem" by applying modern industrial methods to the slaughter of human beings. German companies built huge extermination camps in eastern Europe. Every day, trainloads of cattle cars arrived at the camps and disgorged thousands of captives and the corpses of those who had died of starvation or asphyxiation along the way. The strongest survivors were put to work and fed almost nothing until they died. Women, children, the elderly, and the sick were shoved into gas chambers and asphyxiated with poison gas. **Auschwitz,** the biggest camp, was a giant industrial complex designed to kill up to twelve thousand people a day. Most horrifying of all were the tortures inflicted on prisoners selected by Nazi doctors for "medical experiments." This mass extermination, now called the **Holocaust** ("burning") claimed some 6 million Jewish lives.

Besides the Jews, the Nazis also killed 3 million Polish Catholics—especially professionals, army officers, and the educated—in an effort to reduce the Polish people to slavery. They also exterminated homosexuals, Jehovah's Witnesses, Gypsies, the disabled, and the mentally ill—all in the interests of "racial purity." Whenever a German was killed in an occupied country, the Nazis retaliated by burning a village with all its inhabitants. After the invasion of Russia, the Wehrmacht was given orders to execute all captured communists, government employees, and officers. They also worked millions of prisoners of war to death or let them die of starvation.

The Holocaust   When Allied forces entered Germany, they found not only camp guards and their prisoners but also enormous numbers of corpses. This picture shows female guards at Bergen-Belsen dumping the bodies of Holocaust victims into a mass grave.   (Wide World Photos)

The Home Front in Europe and Asia

In the First World War, there had been a clear distinction between the "front" and the "home front." Not so in World War II, where rapid military movements and air power carried the war into people's homes. For the civilian populations of China, Japan, Southeast Asia, and Europe, the war was far more terrifying than their worst nightmares. Armies swept through the land, confiscating food, fuel, and anything else of value. Bombers and heavy artillery pounded cities into rubble, leaving only the skeletons of buildings, while survivors cowered in cellars and scurried like rats. Even when a city was not targeted, air-raid sirens awakened people throughout the night. In countries occupied by the Germans, the police arrested civilians, deporting many to die in concentration camps or to work as slave laborers in armaments factories. Millions fled their homes in terror, losing their families and friends. Even in Britain, which was never invaded, chil-dren and the elderly were taken from their families for their own safety and sent to live in the countryside.

The war demanded an enormous and sustained effort from all civilians, but more so in some countries than in others. In 1941, even as the Wehrmacht was routing the Red Army, the Soviets dismantled over fifteen hundred factories and rebuilt them in the Ural Mountains and Siberia, where they soon turned out more tanks and artillery than the Axis.

Half of the ships afloat in 1939 were sunk during the war, but the Allied losses were more than made up for by American shipyards, while Axis shipping was reduced to nothing by 1945. The production of aircraft, trucks, tanks, and other materiel showed a similar imbalance. Although the Axis Powers made strenuous efforts to increase their production, they could not compete with the vast outpouring of Soviet tanks and American materiel.

The Red Army eventually mobilized 22 million men; Soviet women took over half of all industrial and three-quarters of all agricultural jobs. In the other belligerent countries, women also played a major role in the war effort, replacing men in fields, factories, and offices. The Nazis, in contrast, believed that German women should stay home and bear children, and they imported 7 million "guest workers"—a euphemism for war prisoners and captured foreigners.

The Home Front in the United States

Unlike the other belligerents, the United States flourished during the war. Safe behind their oceans, Americans felt no bombs, saw no enemy soldiers, and suffered few military casualties and almost no civilian ones. The economy, still depressed in 1939, went into a prolonged boom after 1940. By 1944 the United States alone was producing twice as much as all the Axis Powers combined. Thanks to huge military orders, jobs were plentiful and opportunities beckoned. Bread lines disappeared, and nutrition and health improved. Consumer goods ranging from automobiles to nylon stockings were in short supply, and most Americans saved part of their paychecks, laying the basis for a phenomenal postwar consumer boom. Many Americans later looked back on that conflict as the "good war."

War always exalts such supposedly masculine qualities as physical courage, violence, and domination. These were the official virtues of the Axis Powers, but they were highly valued in America as well. Yet World War II also did much to weaken the hold of traditional ideas. On a much larger scale than in World War I, employers recruited women and members of racial minorities to work in jobs once reserved for white men. For example, 6 million women entered the labor force during the war, 2.5 million of them in manufacturing jobs previously considered "men's work." In a book entitled *Shipyard Diary of a Woman Welder* (1944), Augusta Clawson recalled her experiences in a shipyard in Oregon:

> The job confirmed my strong conviction—I have stated it before—what exhausts the woman welder is not the work, not the heat, nor the demands upon physical strength. It is the apprehension that arises from inadequate skill and consequent lack of confidence; and this *can* be overcome by the right kind of training. . . . I know I can do it if my machine is correctly set, and I have learned enough of the vagaries of machines to be able to set them. And so, in spite of the discomforts of climbing, heavy equipment, and heat, I enjoyed the work today because *I could do it.*

The expansion of job opportunities did not take place without friction. At the beginning, many men resisted the idea that women, especially mothers of young children, should take jobs that would take them away from their families. As the labor shortage got worse, however, employers and politicians grudgingly admitted that the government ought to help provide day care for the children of working mothers. The entry of women into the labor force proved to be one of the most significant consequences of the war. As one woman put it: "War jobs have uncovered unsuspected abilities in American women. Why lose all these abilities because of a belief that 'a women's place is in the home?' For some it is, for others not."

The war loosened racial bonds as well, bringing hardships for some and benefits for others. Seeking work in war industries, 1.2 million African-Americans migrated to the north and west. In the southwest, Mexican immigrants took jobs in agriculture and war industries. But no new housing was built to accommodate the influx of migrants to the industrial cities, and as a result many suffered from overcrowding and discrimination. Much worse was the fate of 112,000 Japanese-Americans living on the west coast of the United States; they were rounded up and herded into internment camps in the desert until the war was over, ostensibly for fear of spying and sabotage but actually because of their race.

War and the Environment

During the Depression, construction and industry had slowed to a crawl, reducing environmental stress. The war reversed this trend, sharply accelerating pressures on the environment.

One reason for the change was the fighting itself. Battles scarred the landscape, leaving behind spent ammunition and damaged equipment. Retreating armies flooded large areas of China and the Netherlands. The bombing of cities left ruins that remained visible for a generation or more. Much of the damage eventually was repaired, although the rusted hulls of ships still darken the lagoons of once-pristine coral islands in the Pacific.

The main cause of environmental stress, however, was not the fighting but the economic development that sustained it. The war's half-million aircraft required thousands of air bases, many of them in the Pacific, China, Africa, and other parts of the world that had seldom seen an airplane before. Barracks, shipyards, docks, warehouses, and other military construction sprouted on every continent.

As war industries boomed—the United States increased its industrial production fourfold during the war—so did the demand for raw materials. Mining companies opened new mines and towns in Central Africa to supply strategic minerals. Brazil, Argentina, and other Latin American countries deprived of manufactured imports began building their own steel mills, factories, and shipyards. In India, China, and Europe, timber felling accelerated far beyond the reproduction rate of trees, replacing forests with denuded land. In a few instances, the war was good for the environment. For example, submarine warfare made fishing and whaling so dangerous that fish and whale populations had a few years in which to increase.

We must keep the environmental effects of the war in perspective. Except for the destruction of cities, much of the war's impact was simply the result of industrial development only temporarily slowed by the Depression. During the war, the damage that military demand caused was tempered by restraints on civilian consumption. From the vantage point of the present, the environmental impact of the war seems quite modest in comparison with the damage inflicted on the earth by the long consumer boom that began in the post–World War II years.

CONCLUSION

Between 1929 and 1949 the old global order—conservative, colonialist, and dominated by Great Britain and France—was shattered by the Depression, the politics of violence, and the most devastating war in history. Stalin transformed the Soviet Union into an industrial giant at enormous human cost. Reacting to the Depression, which weakened the Western democracies, Hitler in Germany and military leaders in Japan prepared for a war of conquest. Though Germany and Japan achieved stunning victories at first, their forces soon faltered in the face of the greater industrial production of the United States and the Soviet Union.

The war was so destructive and spread to so much of the globe because rapidly advancing technology was readily converted from civilian to military production. Machines that had made cars could also manufacture bombers or tanks. Engineers could design factories to kill people with maximum efficiency. The accelerating technology of missiles and nuclear bombs made the entire planet vulnerable to human destruction for the first time in history.

Into the power vacuum left by the collapse of Germany and Japan stepped the two superpowers: the United States and the USSR. When the war ended, U.S. soldiers were stationed in Australia, Japan, and western Europe, and the Red Army occupied all of eastern Europe and parts of northern China. Within months of their victory, these one-time allies became ideological enemies hovering on the brink of war.

World War I had rearranged the colonial empires. In contrast, the global impact of World War II was drastic and almost immediate, because the war weakened the European colonial powers and because so much of the fighting took place in North Africa, Southeast Asia, and other colonial areas. Within fifteen years of the end of the war, almost every European colonial empire had disappeared. As the long era of European domination receded, Asians and Africans began reclaiming their independence.

■ Key Terms

Joseph Stalin	Long March
Five-Year Plans	Stalingrad
Benito Mussolini	El Alamein
Fascist Party	Pearl Harbor
Adolf Hitler	Battle of Midway
Nazis	Hiroshima
Chiang Kai-shek	Auschwitz
Mao Zedong	Holocaust

■ Suggested Reading

The literature on the period from 1929–1945 is enormous and growing fast. The following list is but a very summary introduction.

Charles Kindelberger's *The World in Depression, 1929–39* (1973) and Robert McElvaine's *The Great Depression: America, 1929–1941* (1984) provide a sophisticated economic analysis of the Depression. A. J. H. Latham's *The Depression and the Developing World, 1914–1939* (1981) gives a global perspective.

The best recent book on Japan in the twentieth century is Daikichi Irokawa's *The Age of Hirohito: In Search of Modern Japan* (1995). On Japanese expansion see W. G. Beasley, *Japanese Imperialism, 1894–1945* (1987). The race to war is covered in Akira Iriye, *The Origins of the Second World War in Asia and the Pacific* (1987); Michael Barnhart, *Japan Prepares for Total War* (1987), is short and well written.

In the large and fast-growing literature on twentieth-century China, two general introductions are especially useful: John K. Fairbank, *The Great Chinese Revolution, 1800–1985* (1986), and Jonathan Spence, *The Search for Modern China* (1990). On the warlord and Guomindang periods see Lucien Bianco, *Origins of the Chinese Revolution, 1915–1949* (1971). The Japanese invasion of China is the subject of Iris Chang, *The Rape of Nanking: The Forgotten Holocaust of World War II* (1997), and of James Hsiung and Steven Levine, eds., *China's Bitter Victory: The War with Japan, 1937–1945* (1992). Jung Chang, *Wild Swans: Three Daughters of China* (1991), is a fascinating account of women's experiences during the Revolution and the Mao era by the daughter of two Communist officials.

Among recent biographies of Stalin, see Dmitrii Volkogonov's *Stalin: Triumph and Tragedy* (1991) and Robert Tucker's *Stalin as Revolutionary, 1879–1929* (1973) and *Stalin in Power: The Revolution from Above, 1928–1941* (1990). On the transformation of the USSR, see Roy Medvedev's *Let History Judge: The Origins and Consequences of Stalinism* (1989) and Stephen Kotkin's *Magnetic Mountain: Stalinism as Civilization* (1995). Stalin's collectivization of agriculture is vividly portrayed in Robert Conquest's *Harvest of Sorrow* (1986); see also Sheila Fitzpatrick's *Stalin's Peasants: Resistance and Survival in the Russian Village After Collectivization* (1994). Conquest's *The Great Terror: A Reassessment* (1990) describes the purges of the 1930s. Alexander Solzhenitsyn, a veteran of Stalin's prisons, explores them in a detailed history, *The Gulag Archipelago, 1918–1956* (3 vols. 1974–1978), and in a short but brilliant novel *One Day in the Life of Ivan Denisovich* (1978).

Alexander De Grand provides an excellent interpretation of fascism in *Italian Fascism: Its Origins and Development*, 2d ed. (1989). William Shirer's *The Rise and Fall of the Third Reich* (1960) is a long but very dramatic eyewitness description of Nazi Germany by a journalist. The dictators are the subject of two fine biographies: Denis Mack Smith's *Mussolini* (1982) and Alan Bullock's *Hitler: A Study in Tyranny* (1965). See also A. J. P. Taylor's controversial classic *The Origins of the Second World War* (1966).

Two very detailed books on World War II are John Keegan, *The Second World War* (1990), and Gerhard Weinberg, *A World at Arms: A Global History of World War II* (1994). Particular aspects of the war in Europe are covered in Alexander Werth, *Russia at War, 1941–1945* (1965), and Conrad Crane, *Bombs, Cities, and Civilians* (1993). One of the most readable accounts of the war in Asia and the Pacific is Ronald Spector's *Eagle Against the Sun* (1988). Also see Akira Iriye, *Power and Culture: The Japanese-American War, 1941–1945* (1981), and James Hsiung and Steven Levine, eds., *China's Bitter Victory: The War with Japan, 1937–1945* (1992).

The terror of life under Nazi rule is the subject of two powerful memoirs: Anne Frank's *The Diary of a Young Girl* and Eli Wiesel's *Night* (1960). On the Holocaust see Lucy Dawidowicz, *The War Against the Jews, 1933–1945*, 2d ed. (1986); Leni Yahil, *The Holocaust: The Fate of European Jewry* (1990); and a controversial book by Daniel Goldhagen, *Hitler's Willing Executioners: Ordinary Germans and the Holocaust* (1996).

Among the many books that capture the scientific side of warfare, two are especially recommended: Richard Rhodes's long but fascinating *The Making of the Atomic Bomb* (1986), and F. H. Hinsley and Alan Stripp, eds., *Code Breakers* (1993).

Among the many books on the home front in the United States, the most vivid is Studs Terkel, *"The Good War": An Oral History of World War Two* (1984). Margaret Higonnet et al., eds., *Behind the Lines: Gender and the Two World Wars* (1987), discusses the role of women in the war.

32

STRIVING FOR INDEPENDENCE:
AFRICA, INDIA, AND LATIN AMERICA,
1900–1949

**Sub-Saharan Africa, 1900–1945 • The Indian Independence
Movement, 1905–1947 • The Mexican Revolution, 1910–1940 •
Argentina and Brazil, 1900–1949**

ENVIRONMENT AND TECHNOLOGY: Gandhi and Technology

SOCIETY AND CULTURE: Self-Government in Africa

African Farmers in the Gold Coast African farmers in the Gold Coast (now Ghana) sold their
cocoa beans to government agents. The government kept the price artifically low in order to profit on the transactions.

miliano Zapata°, leader of a peasant rebellion in the Mexican Revolution, liked to be photographed on horseback, carrying a sword and a rifle and draped with bandoliers of bullets. Mahatma Gandhi°, who led the independence movement in India, preferred to be seen sitting at a spinning wheel, dressed in a *dhoti*°, the simple loincloth worn by Indian farmers. The images they liked to project and the methods they used could not have been more opposed. Yet their goals were similar: each wanted social justice and a better life for the poor in a country free of foreign domination.

The previous two chapters focused on a world convulsed by war and revolution. The world wars involved Europe, East Asia, the Middle East, and the United States, and they sparked violent revolutions in Russia and China. They accelerated the development of aviation, electronics, nuclear power, and other technologies. Although these momentous events dominate the history of the first half of the twentieth century, parts of the world that were little touched by war also underwent profound changes in this period, partly for internal reasons and partly because of the influence of warfare and revolution in other parts of the world.

In this chapter we examine the changes that took place in three regions: in sub-Saharan Africa, in India, and in three major countries of Latin America—Mexico, Brazil, and Argentina. These three regions represent three very distinct cultures, yet they had much in common. Africa and India were colonies of Europe, both politically and economically. Though politically independent, the Latin American republics were dependent on Europe and the United States for the sale of raw materials and commodities and for imports of manufactured goods, technology, and capital. In all three regions, independence movements tried to wrest control from distant foreigners and improve the livelihood of their peoples. Their success was partial at best.

As you read this chapter, ask yourself the following questions:

- How did wars and revolutions in Europe and East Asia affect the countries of the Southern Hemisphere?
- Why did educated Indians and Africans want independence?
- What could Latin Americans do to achieve social justice and economic development? Were these two goals compatible?

SUB-SAHARAN AFRICA, 1900–1945

Of all the continents, Africa was the last to come under European rule (see Chapter 29). The first half of the twentieth century, when nationalist movements threatened European rule in Asia, was Africa's period of classic colonialism. After World War I, Britain, France, Belgium, and South Africa divided Germany's African colonies among themselves. In the 1930s, Italy invaded Ethiopia. The colonial empires reached their peak shortly before World War II.

Colonial Africa: Economic and Social Changes

Outside of Algeria, Kenya, and South Africa, few Europeans lived in Africa. In 1930, Nigeria, with a population of 20 million, was ruled by 386 British officials and by 8,000 policemen and military, of whom 150 were European. Yet even such a small presence stimulated deep social and economic changes.

Since the turn of the century, the colonial powers had built railroads from coastal cities to mines and plantations in the interior, in order to provide raw materials to the industrial world. The economic boom of the interwar years benefited few Africans. Colonial governments took lands that Africans owned communally and sold or leased them to European companies or, in eastern and southern Africa, to white settlers. Large European companies dominated wholesale commerce, while immigrants from various countries—Indians in East Africa, Greeks and Syrians in West Africa—handled much of the retail trade. Airplanes and automobiles were even more alien to the experience of Africans than railroads had been to an earlier generation.

Zapata (zeh-PAH-teh)   Gandhi (GAHN-dee)   *dhoti* (DOE-tee)

CHRONOLOGY

	Africa	India	Latin America
1900	**1900s** Railroads connect ports to the interior **1909** African National Congress founded	**1905** Viceroy Curzon splits Bengal; mass demonstrations **1906** Muslims found All-India Muslim League **1911** British transfer capital from Calcutta to Delhi	**1876–1910** Porfirio Díaz, dictator of Mexico **1911–1919** Mexican Revolution; Emiliano Zapata and Pancho Villa against the Constitutionalists
1920	**1920s** J. E. Casely Hayford organizes political movement in British West Africa	**1919** Amritsar Massacre **1929** Gandhi leads March to the Sea **1930s** Gandhi calls for independence; he is repeatedly arrested	**1917** New constitution proclaimed in Mexico **1928** Plutarco Elías Calles founds Mexico's National Revolutionary Party **1930–1945** Getulio Vargas, dictator of Brazil **1934–1940** Lázaro Cárdenas, president of Mexico
1940	**1939–1945** A million Africans serve in World War II	**1939** British bring India into World War II **1940** Muhammad Ali Jinnah demands a separate nation for Muslims **1947** Partition and independence of India and Pakistan	**1938** Cárdenas nationalizes Mexican oil industry; Vargas proclaims Estado Novo in Brazil **1943** Juan Perón leads military coup in Argentina **1946** Perón elected president of Argentina

Where land was divided into small farms, some Africans benefited from the boom. Farmers in the Gold Coast (now Ghana°) profited from the high prices of cocoa, as did palm-oil producers in Nigeria and coffee growers in East Africa. In most of Africa, women played a major role in the retail trades, selling pots and pans and other hardware, toys, cloth, and food in the markets. Many maintained their economic independence and kept their household finances separate from those of their husbands, following a custom that predated the colonial period.

For many Africans, economic development meant working in European-owned mines and plantations, often under compulsion. Colonial governments were eager to develop the resources of the territories under their control but could not afford to pay high enough wages to attract workers. Instead, they used their police powers to force Africans to work under harsh conditions for little or no pay. In the 1920s, when the government of French Equatorial Africa decided to build a railroad from Brazzaville to the Atlantic coast, a distance of 312 miles (502 kilometers), it drafted 127,000 men to carve a roadbed across mountains and through rain forests. For lack of food, clothing, and medical care, 20,000 of them died, an average of 64 deaths per mile of track.

Europeans prided themselves on bringing modern health care to Africa; yet before the 1930s, there was too little of it to help the majority of Africans, and other aspects of colonialism actually worsened public health. Migrants to cities, mines, and plantations and soldiers moving from post to post spread syphilis, gonorrhea, tuberculosis, and malaria. Sleeping sickness and smallpox epidemics raged throughout Central Africa. In recruiting men to work, colonial governments depleted rural areas of farmers needed to plant and harvest crops. Forced requisitions of food taken to feed the workers left the remaining populations undernourished and vulnerable to

---

Ghana (GAH-nuh)

Diamond Mining in Southern Africa   The discovery of diamonds in the Transvaal in 1867 attracted prospectors to the area around Kimberley. The first wave of prospectors consisted of individual "diggers," including a few Africans. By the late 1870s, surface deposits had been exhausted and further mining required complex and costly machinery. After 1889, one company, De Beers Consolidated, owned all the diamond mines. This photograph shows the entrance to a mine shaft and mine workers surrounded by heavy equipment.   (Royal Commonwealth Society. By permission of the Syndics of Cambridge University Library.)

diseases. Not until the 1930s did colonial governments realize the negative consequences of their labor policies and begin to invest in agricultural development and in health care for Africans.

In 1900 Ibadan° in Nigeria was the only city in sub-Saharan Africa with more than 100,000 inhabitants; fifty years later, dozens of cities had reached that size, including Nairobi° in Kenya, Johannesburg in South Africa, Lagos in Nigeria, Accra in Gold Coast, and Dakar in Senegal. Africans migrated to cities because they offered hope of jobs and excitement and, for a few, the chance to become wealthy.

However, migrations damaged the family life of those involved, for almost all the migrants were men

leaving women in the countryside to farm and raise children. Cities built during the colonial period reflected the colonialists' attitudes with their racially segregated housing, clubs, restaurants, hospitals, and other institutions. Patterns of racial discrimination were most rigid in the white-settler colonies of eastern and southern Africa.

Religious and Political Changes

Traditional religious belief could not explain the dislocations that foreign rule, migrations, and sudden economic changes brought to the lives of Africans. Many therefore turned to one of the two universal religions, Christianity and Islam, for guidance. A major attraction of the Christian denominations was their mission schools, which taught

---

Ibadan (ee-BAH-dahn)   **Nairobi** (nie-ROE-bee)

Self-Government in Africa

Colonialism rested on the presumption of European superiority. Nowhere was that presumption more evident than in Africa, where colonialists argued that Africans had not evolved politically and therefore would not be ready for self-rule for a long time. Here is an expression of such thinking from the pamphlet African Opportunity, *by Lord Milverton, a former governor of Nigeria.*

The African has had self-government. Until about fifty years ago he had had it for countless centuries, and all it brought him was blood-stained chaos, a brief, insecure life, haunted by fear, in which evil tradition and custom held him enslaved to superstition, hunger, disease, squalor and ruthless cruelty, even to his family and friends. For countless centuries, while all the pageant of history swept by, the African remained unmoved—in primitive savagery.

The Gold Coast nationalist J. E. Casely Hayford responded to that sort of attack by giving examples of progressive and beneficial government in precolonial Africa.

A people who could, indigenously, and without a literature, evolve the orderly representative government which obtained in Ashanti and the Gold Coast before the advent of the foreign interloper, are a people to be respected and shown consideration when they proceed to discuss questions of self-government.

How do these quotations illustrate the importance of history in an argument about the future?

Source: Quotations from Thomas Hodgkin, *Nationalism in Colonial Africa* (New York: New York University Press, 1957), 172–173.

---

both craft skills and basic literacy, providing access to employment as minor functionaries, teachers, clergy, or shopkeepers. These schools educated a new elite, many of whom learned not only skills and literacy but Western political ideas as well.

Christianity was introduced into Africa by Western missionaries, except in Ethiopia, where it was indigenous. Islam, in contrast, spread through the influence and example of African traders. Islam also emphasized literacy—in Arabic rather than in a European language—and was less disruptive of traditional African customs such as polygamy. Christianity was most successful in the coastal regions of West and South Africa, where the European influence was strongest. Islam tended to spread inland from the East African coast and southward from the Sahel° toward the West African coast.

The contrast between the liberal ideas imparted by Western education and the realities of racial discrimination under colonial rule contributed to the rise of nationalism among educated Africans. In Senegal, **Blaise Diagne°** agitated for African participation in politics and fair treatment in the French army. In the 1920s, J. E. Casely Hayford began organizing a movement for greater autonomy in British West Africa (see Society and

Culture: Self-Government in Africa). In South Africa, Western-educated lawyers and journalists founded the **African National Congress** in 1909 to defend the interests of Africans. These nationalist movements were inspired by the ideas of Pan-Africanists from America such as W. E. B. Du Bois and Marcus Garvey, who advocated the unity of African peoples around the world, as well as by European ideas of liberty and nationhood. Until World War II, however, they were small and had little influence.

The Second World War (1939–1945) had a profound effect on the peoples of Africa, even those far removed from the theaters of war. The war brought hardships, such as increased forced labor, inflation, and requisitions of raw materials. Yet it also brought hope. During the campaign to oust the Italians from Ethiopia, Emperor **Haile Selassie°** (r. 1930–1974) led his own troops into his capital Addis Ababa and reclaimed his title. A million Africans served as soldiers and carriers in Burma, North Africa, and Europe, where many became aware of Africa's role in helping the Allied war effort. They listened to Allied propaganda in favor of European liberation movements and against Nazi racism, and they returned to their countries with new and radical ideas.

Sahel (SAH-hel)   **Diagne** (dee-AHN-yuh)

Haile Selassie (HI-lee seh-LASS-ee)

The early twentieth century was a relatively peaceful period for sub-Saharan Africa. But this peace—enforced by the European occupiers—masked profound changes that were to transform African life after the Second World War. The building of cities, railroads, and other enterprises brought Africa into the global economy, often at great human cost. Colonialism also brought changes to African culture and religion, hastening the spread of Christianity and Islam. And the foreign occupation awakened political ideas that inspired the next generation of Africans to demand independence (see Chapter 33).

THE INDIAN INDEPENDENCE MOVEMENT, 1905–1947

India was a colony of Great Britain from the late eighteenth to the mid-twentieth century. Under British rule, the subcontinent acquired many of the trappings of Western-style economic development, such as railroads, harbors, modern cities, and cotton and steel mills, as well as an active and worldly middle class. The economic transformation of the region awakened in this educated middle class a sense of national dignity that demanded political fulfillment. In response, the British gradually granted India a limited amount of political autonomy while maintaining overall control. Religious and communal tensions among the Indian peoples were carefully papered over under British rule. Violent conflicts tore India apart after the withdrawal of the British in 1947 (see Map 32.1).

The Land and the People

Much of India is fertile land, but it is vulnerable to the vagaries of nature, especially droughts caused by the periodic failure of the monsoons. When the rains failed from 1896 to 1900, 2 million people died of starvation.

Despite periodic famines, the Indian population grew from 250 million in 1900 to 319 million in 1921 and 389 million in 1941. This growth created pressures in many areas. Landless young men converged on the cities, exceeding the number of jobs available in the slowly expanding industries. To produce timber for construction and railroad ties and to clear land for tea and rubber plantations, government foresters cut down most of the tropical hardwood forests that had covered

the subcontinent in the nineteenth century. In spite of deforestation and extensive irrigation, the amount of land available to peasant families shrank with each successive generation. Economic development—what the British called the "moral and material progress of India"—hardly benefited the average Indian.

Indians were divided into many classes. Peasants, always the great majority, paid rents to the landowner, interest to the village moneylender, and taxes to the government and had little left to improve their land or raise their standard of living. The government protected property owners, from village moneylenders all the way up to the princes and maharajahs° who owned huge tracts of land. The cities were crowded with craftsmen, traders, and workers of all sorts, mostly very poor. Although the British had banned *sati*° (the burning of widows on their husbands' funeral pyres), in other respects women's lives changed little under British rule.

The peoples of India spoke many different languages: Hindi in the north, Tamil in the south, Bengali in the east, Gujerati around Bombay, Urdu in the northwest, and dozens of others. As a result of British rule and increasing trade and travel, English became, like Latin in medieval Europe, the common medium of communication of the Western-educated middle class. This new class of English-speaking government bureaucrats, professionals, and merchants were to play a leading role in the independence movement.

The majority of Indians practiced Hinduism and were subdivided into hundreds of castes, each affiliated with a particular occupation. Hinduism discouraged intermarriage and other social interactions among the castes and with people who were not Hindus. Muslims constituted one-quarter of the people of India but formed a majority in the northwest and in eastern Bengal. Muslim rulers had dominated northern and central India until they were displaced by the British in the eighteenth century. More reluctant than Hindus to learn English, Muslims felt discriminated against by both British and Hindus.

British Rule and Indian Nationalism

Colonial India was ruled by a viceroy appointed by the British government; the country was administered by a few thousand members of the Indian Civil Service. These men, imbued with a sense of duty toward their subjects, formed one of the most honest (if not the most efficient)

maharajah (mah-huh-RAH-juh)   *sati* (suh-TEE)

Map 32.1   The Partition of India, 1947   Before the British, India was divided among many states, ethnic groups, and religions. When the British left in 1947, the subcontinent split along religious lines. The predominantly Muslim regions of Sind and Punjab in the northwest and East Bengal in the east formed the new nation of Pakistan. The predominantly Hindu center became the Republic of India. Jammu and Kashmir remained disputed territories and poisoned relations between the two new countries.

bureaucracies of all time. Drawn mostly from the English gentry, they liked to think of India as a land of lords and peasants. They considered it their duty to protect the Indian people from the dangers of industrialization and radical politics.

As Europeans, they admired modern technology but tried to control its introduction into India so as to maximize the benefits to Britain and to themselves. For example, they encouraged railroads, harbors, telegraphs, and other communications technologies, as

Construction Site in Colonial India British civil engineers were active throughout India building roads, railroads, and canals. Here, a British official supervises Indian workers building a bridge. (The Billie Love Collection)

well as irrigation and plantations, because they increased India's foreign trade and strengthened British control. At the same time, they discouraged the cotton and steel industries and limited the training of Indian engineers in order to spare India the social and political upheavals that had accompanied the Industrial Revolution in Europe.

At the turn of the century, the majority of Indians—especially the peasants, landowners, and princes—accepted British rule. But the Europeans' racist attitude toward dark-skinned people increasingly offended those Indians who had learned English and absorbed English ideas of freedom and representative government and then discovered that thinly disguised racial quotas excluded them from the Indian Civil Service, the officer corps, and prestigious country clubs.

In 1885 a small group of English-speaking Hindu professionals founded a political organization called the **Indian National Congress.** For twenty years, its members respectfully petitioned the government for access to the higher administrative positions and for a voice in official decisions, but they had little influence outside intellectual circles. Then, in 1905, Viceroy Lord Curzon divided the province of **Bengal** in two to improve the efficiency of its administration. This decision, made without consulting anyone, angered not only educated Indians, who saw it as a step taken to lessen their influence, but also millions of uneducated Hindu Bengalis, who suddenly found themselves outnumbered by Muslims in East Bengal. Soon Bengal was the scene of demonstrations, boycotts of British goods, and even incidents of violence against the British.

In 1906, while the Hindus of Bengal were protesting the partition of their province, Muslims, fearful of Hindu dominance elsewhere in India, founded the **All-India Muslim League.** Caught in an awkward situation, the government responded by granting Indians a limited franchise based on wealth. Muslims, however, were on average poorer than Hindus, for many poor and low-caste Hindus had converted to Islam to escape caste discrimination. Taking advantage of these religious divisions, the British instituted separate representation and different voting qualifications for Hindus and Muslims. Then, in 1911, the British transferred the capital of India from Calcutta to Delhi°, the former capital of the Mughal° emperors. These changes disturbed Indians of all classes and religions and raised their political consciousness. Politics, once primarily the concern of westernized intellectuals, turned into two mass movements: one by Hindus and one by Muslims.

To maintain their commercial position and prevent social upheavals, the British resisted the idea that India could, or should, industrialize. Their geologists looked for minerals, such as coal or manganese, that British industry required. However, when the only Indian member of the Indian Geological Service, Pramatha Nath Bose, wanted to prospect for iron ore, he had to resign because the government wanted no part of an Indian steel industry that could compete with that of Britain. Bose joined forces with Jamsetji Tata, a Bombay textile magnate who decided to produce steel in spite of British opposition. With the help of German and American engineers and equipment, Tata's son Dorabji opened the first steel mill in India in 1911, in a town called Jamshedpur in honor of his father. Although it produced only a fraction of the steel that India required, Jamshedpur became a powerful symbol of Indian national pride. It prompted Indian nationalists to ask, why did a country that could produce its own steel need foreigners to run its government?

During World War I, Indians supported Britain enthusiastically; 1.2 million men volunteered for the army, and millions more Indians voluntarily contributed money to the government. Many expected that the British would reward such loyalty with political concessions. Others organized to demand such concessions and began demanding a voice in the government. In 1917, in response to the agitation, the British government announced "the gradual development of self-governing institutions with a view to the progressive realization of responsible government in India as an integral part of the British Empire." This sounded like a promise of self-government, but the timetable was left so vague that nationalists denounced it as a devious maneuver to postpone India's independence.

In late 1918 and early 1919, a violent influenza epidemic broke out among soldiers in the war zone of northern France. Within a few months, it spread to every country on earth and killed over 20 million people. India was especially hard hit; of the millions who died, one out of four was Indian. This dreadful toll increased the mounting political tensions. Leaders of the Indian National Congress declared that the British reform proposals were too little too late. On April 13, 1919, in the city of Amritsar in Punjab, General Reginald Dyer ordered his troops to fire into a peaceful crowd of some 10,000 demonstrators, killing at least 379 and wounding 1,200. As waves of angry demonstrations swept over India, the period of gradual accommodation between the British and the Indians came to a close.

Mahatma Gandhi and Militant Nonviolence

For the next twenty years, India teetered on the edge of violent uprisings and harsh repression, possibly even war. That it did not succumb was due to **Mohandas K. Gandhi** (1869–1948), a man known to his followers as "Mahatma," the "great soul."

Gandhi began life with every advantage. His family was wealthy enough to send him to England for his education. After his studies, he lived in South Africa, where he practiced law for the small Indian community living there. During World War I he returned to India and was one of many Western-educated Hindu intellectuals who joined the Indian National Congress.

Gandhi had some unusual political ideas. Unlike many radical political thinkers of his time, he denounced the popular ideals of power and struggle and combat. Instead, inspired by both Hindu and Christian concepts, he preached the saintly virtues of *ahimsa*° (nonviolence) and *satyagraha*° (the search for truth). He refused to countenance violence among his followers, and several times he called off demonstrations when they turned violent.

Gandhi had an affinity for the poor that was unusual even among socialist politicians. In 1921 he gave up the Western-style suits worn by lawyers and the fine raiment of wealthy Indians and henceforth wore simple peasant garb: a length of homespun cloth below his waist and a shawl to cover his torso (see Environment and Technology: Gandhi and Technology). He spoke for the farmers

---

Delhi (DEL-ee)   **Mughal** (MOO-guhl)

ahimsa (uh-HIM-sah)   *satyagraha* (suh-TYAH-gruh-huh)

Gandhi and Technology

Gandhi at the Spinning Wheel Mahatma Gandhi chose the spinning wheel as his symbol because it represented the traditional activity of millions of rural Indians whose livelihoods were threatened by industrialization.   (Margaret Bourke-White, *LIFE Magazine* © Time Warner Inc.)

In the twentieth century, all political leaders but one have embraced modern industrial technology. That one exception is Gandhi.

After deciding to wear only handmade cloth, Gandhi made a bonfire of imported factory-made cloth and began spending half an hour every day spinning yarn on a simple spinning wheel, a task he called a "sacrament." The spinning wheel became the symbol of his movement. Any Indian who wished to come before him had to dress in handwoven cloth.

Gandhi had several reasons for reviving this ancient craft. One was revulsion against the materialism of the West, which he contrasted with the poverty of his own people:

The incessant search for material comforts and their multiplication is such an evil, and I make bold to say that the Europeans themselves will have to remodel their outlook if they are not to perish under the weight of the comforts to which they are becoming slaves.

Gandhi believed that foreign cotton mills had impoverished his people:

A hundred and fifty years ago, we manufactured all our cloth. Our women spun fine yarns in their own cottages, and supplemented the earnings of their husbands. . . . India grows all the cotton she needs. She exports several million bales of cotton to Japan and Lancashire and receives much of it back in manufactured calico, though she is capable of producing all the cloth and all the yarn necessary for supplying her wants by hand-weaving and hand-spinning. . . . The spinning wheel was presented to the nation for giving occupation to the millions who had, at least four months of the year, nothing to do.

But most of all, to Gandhi, the spinning wheel was a political symbol of "national consciousness and a contribution by every individual to a definite constructive national work":

If three hundred million people did the same thing every day . . . because they were inspired by the same ideal, we would have enough unity of purpose to achieve independence.

Nevertheless, Gandhi was a shrewd politician who understood the usefulness of modern devices for mobilizing the masses and organizing his followers. He wore a watch and used the telephone and the printing press to keep in touch with his followers. When he traveled by train, he rode third class—but in a third-class railroad car of his own. His goal was the independence of his country, and he pursued it with every nonviolent means he could find.

Gandhi's ideas challenge us to rethink the purpose of technology. Was he opposed on principle to all modern devices? Was he an opportunist who used those devices that served his political ends and rejected those that did not? Or did he have a higher principle that accounts for his willingness to use the telephone and the railroad but not factory-made cloth?

Source: Quotations from Louis Fischer, *Gandhi: His Life and Message for the World* (New York: New American Library, 1954), 82–83. Copyright 1954, renewed © 1982 by Louis Fischer. Used by permission of Viking Penguin, a division of Penguin Putman Inc.

and the outcasts, whom he called *harijan*°, "children of God." He attracted ever-larger numbers of followers among the poor and the illiterate, who soon began to revere him; and he transformed the cause of Indian independence from an elite movement of the educated into a mass movement with a quasi-religious aura.

Gandhi was a brilliant political tactician and a master of public relations gestures. In 1929, for instance, he led a few followers on an 80-mile (129-kilometer) walk, camped on a beach, and gathered salt from the sea in a blatant and well-publicized act of civil disregard for the government's monopoly of salt. But he discovered that unleashing the power of popular participation was one thing and controlling its direction was quite another. Within days of his "Walk to the Sea," demonstrations of support broke out all over India, in which the police killed 100 demonstrators and arrested over 60,000.

Many times, during the 1930s, Gandhi threatened to fast "unto death," and several times he did come close to death, to protest the violence of both the police and his followers and to demand independence. He was repeatedly arrested and spent a total of six years in jail. But every arrest made him more popular. He became a cult figure not only in his own country but also in the Western media. He never won a battle or an election; instead, in the words of historian Percival Spear, he made the British "uncomfortable in their cherished field of moral rectitude," and he gave Indians the feeling that theirs was the ethically superior cause.

India Moves Toward Independence

In the 1920s, slowly and reluctantly, the British began to give in to the pressure of the Indian National Congress and the Muslim League. They handed over to Indians control of "national" areas such as education, the economy, and public works. They also gradually admitted more Indians into the Civil Service and the officer corps.

India took its first tentative steps toward industrialization in the years before the First and then the Second World Wars. Indian politicians obtained the right to erect high tariff barriers against imports in order to protect India's infant industries from foreign, even British, competition. Behind these barriers, Indian entrepreneurs built plants to manufacture iron and steel, cement, paper, cotton and jute textiles, sugar, and other products. This early industrialization provided jobs, though not enough

to improve the lives of the Indian peasants or urban poor. These manufactures, however, helped create a class of wealthy Indian businessmen. Far from being satisfied by the government's policies, they supported the Indian National Congress and its demands for independence. Though paying homage to Gandhi, they preferred his designated successor as leader of the Indian National Congress, **Jawaharlal Nehru**° (1889–1964). A highly educated nationalist and subtle thinker, Nehru, in contrast to Gandhi, looked forward to creating a modern industrial India.

Congress politicians won regional elections but continued to be excluded from the viceroy's cabinet, the true center of power. When World War II began in September 1939, Viceroy Lord Linlithgow declared war without consulting a single Indian. The Congress-dominated provincial governments resigned in protest and found that boycotting government office increased their popular support. When the British offered to give India its independence once the war ended, Gandhi called the offer a "postdated cheque on a failing bank" and demanded full independence immediately. His "Quit India" campaign aroused popular demonstrations against the British and provoked a wave of arrests, including his own.

As in World War I, Indians contributed heavily to the Allied war effort, supplying 2 million soldiers and enormous amounts of resources, especially timber needed for emergency construction. The Second World War divided the Indian people. Most Indian soldiers felt they were fighting to defend their country rather than to support the British Empire. The Indian National Congress, however, opposed India's participation in the war; as Nehru explained: "I would fight Japan sword in hand, but I can only do so as a free man." A small number of Indians, meanwhile, were so anti-British that they joined the Japanese side.

India's subordination to British interests was vividly demonstrated in the famine of 1943 in Bengal. Unlike previous famines, this one was caused not by drought but by the Japanese conquest of Burma, which cut off supplies of Burmese rice that normally went to Bengal. Although food was available elsewhere in India, the British army had requisitioned the railroads to transport troops and equipment in preparation for a Japanese invasion. As a result, supplies ran short in Bengal and surrounding areas, speculators hoarded what little there was, and some 2 million people starved before the army was ordered to supply food.

harijan (HAH-ree-jahn)

Nehru (NAY-roo)

The Partition of India   When India became independent, Muslims fled from Hindu regions, and Hindus fled from Muslims. Margaret Bourke-White photographed a long line of refugees, with their cows, carts, and belongings, trudging down a country road toward safety.   (Margaret Bourke-White, *LIFE Magazine* © Time Inc.)

Partition and Independence

When the war ended, Britain's new Labour Party government prepared for Indian independence, but deep suspicions between Hindus and Muslims complicated the process. The break between the two communities had started in 1937, when the Indian National Congress won the provincial elections and refused to share power with the Muslim League. In 1940, the leader of the League, **Muhammad Ali Jinnah**° (1876–1948) demanded what many Muslims had been dreaming of for years: a country of their own, to be called Pakistan (from "Punjab-Afghans-Kashmir-Sind" plus the Persian suffix -*stan* meaning "kingdom").

As independence approached, talks between Jinnah and Nehru broke down and battle lines were drawn. Violent rioting between Hindus and Muslims broke out in Bengal and Bihar. Gandhi's appeals for tolerance and cooperation fell on deaf ears; in despair, he retreated to his home near Ahmedabad. The British made frantic

proposals to keep India united, but their authority was waning fast.

By early 1947 the Indian National Congress had accepted the idea of a partition of India into two states, one secular but dominated by Hindus, the other Muslim. In June, Lord Mountbatten, the last viceroy, decided that independence must come immediately. On August 15, British India gave way to a new India and Pakistan. The Indian National Congress, led by Nehru, formed the first government of India; Jinnah and the Muslim League established a government for the provinces that made up Pakistan.

The rejoicing over independence was marred by violent outbreaks between Muslims and Hindus. In protest against the mounting chaos, Gandhi refused to attend the independence day celebration. Throughout the land, Muslim and Hindu neighbors turned on one another, and armed members of one faith hunted down people of the other faith. For centuries Hindus and Muslims had intermingled throughout most of India. Now, leaving all their possessions behind, Hindus fled from predominantly Muslim areas, and Muslims fled from Hindu areas. Trainloads of desperate refugees of one faith were

---

Jinnah (jee-NAH)

attacked and massacred by members of the other or were left stranded in the middle of deserts. Within a few months, some 12 million people had abandoned their ancestral homes and a half-million lay dead. In January 1948, Gandhi died too, gunned down by an angry Hindu refugee.

THE MEXICAN REVOLUTION, 1910–1940

In the nineteenth century, Latin America achieved independence from Spain and Portugal but did not industrialize. Throughout much of the century most Latin American republics suffered from ideological divisions, unstable governments, and violent upheavals. By trading their raw materials and agricultural products for foreign manufactured goods and capital investments, they became economically dependent on the wealthier countries to the north, especially on the United States and Great Britain. Their societies, far from fulfilling the promises of their independence, remained deeply split between wealthy landowners and desperately poor peasants.

In this chapter we focus on three Latin American republics: Mexico, Brazil, and Argentina. They contained well over half of Latin America's land, population, and wealth, and their relations with other countries and their economies were quite similar. Mexico, however, underwent a traumatic social revolution, while Argentina and Brazil evolved more peaceably.

Mexico in 1910

Few countries in Latin America suffered as many foreign invasions and interventions as Mexico. A Mexican saying observed wryly: "Poor Mexico: so far from God, so close to the United States." In Mexico, the chasm between rich and poor was so deep that only a revolution could move the country toward prosperity and democracy.

Mexico was the Latin American country most influenced by the Spanish during three centuries of colonial rule. Mexico gained its independence in 1821. At the beginning of the twentieth century, Mexican society was divided into rich and poor and among persons of Spanish, Indian, and mixed ancestry. A few very wealthy families of Spanish origin, less than 1 percent of the population, owned 85 percent of Mexico's land, mostly in huge *haciendas* (estates). Closely tied to this elite were the handful of American and British companies that controlled most of Mexico's railroads, silver mines, plantations, and other productive enterprises. At the other end of the social scale were Indians and *mestizos°*, people of mixed Indian and European ancestry. Most of them were peasants who worked on the haciendas or farmed small communal plots near their ancestral villages.

The urban middle class was small and had little political influence. Few professional and government positions were open to them, and foreigners owned most businesses. Industrial workers also were few in number; the only significant groups were textile workers in the port of Veracruz on the Gulf of Mexico and railroad workers spread throughout the country.

During the colonial period, the Spanish government had made halfhearted efforts to defend Indians and mestizos from the land-grabbing tactics of the haciendas. After independence in 1821, wealthy Mexican families and American companies used bribery and force to acquire millions of acres of good agricultural land from villages in southern Mexico. Peasants lost not only their fields but also their access to firewood and pasture for their animals. Sugar, cotton, and other commercial crops replaced the cultivation of corn and beans, and peasants had little choice but to work on haciendas. To survive, they had to buy food and other necessities on credit from the landowner's store; eventually, they fell permanently into debt. Sometimes whole communities were forced to relocate.

In the 1880s, American investors purchased from the Mexican government dubious claims to more than 2.5 million acres (1 million hectares) traditionally held by the Yaqui people of Sonora, in northern Mexico. When the Yaqui resisted the expropriation of their lands, they were brutally repressed by the Mexican army.

Northern Mexicans had no peasant tradition of communal ownership, for the northern half of the country was too dry for farming, unlike the tropical and densely populated south. The north was a region of silver mines and cattle ranches, some of them enormous. It was thinly populated by cowboys and miners. The harshness of their lives and vast inequities in the distribution of income made northern Mexicans as resentful as people in the south.

Despite many upheavals in Mexico in the nineteenth century, the government in 1910 seemed in control; no

---

mestizo (mess-TEE-zoh)

one expected a revolution. For thirty-four years, General Porfirio Díaz° (1830–1915) had ruled Mexico under the motto "Liberty, Order, Progress." To Díaz, "liberty" meant freedom for rich hacienda owners and foreign investors to acquire more land. The government imposed "order" through rigged elections and a policy of *pan o palo* (bread or the stick)—that is, bribes for Díaz's supporters and summary justice for those who opposed him. And "progress" meant mainly the importing of foreign capital, machinery, and technicians to take advantage of Mexico's labor, soil, and natural resources.

During the Díaz years (1876–1910), Mexico City—with paved streets, streetcar lines, electric street lighting, and public parks—became a showplace, and new telegraph and railroad lines connected cities and towns throughout Mexico. But this material progress benefited only a handful of well-connected businessmen. The boom in railroads, agriculture, and mining at the turn of the century actually caused a decline in the average Mexican's standard of living.

Though a mestizo himself, Díaz discriminated against the nonwhite majority of Mexicans. He and his supporters tried to eradicate what they saw as Mexico's embarrassingly rustic traditions. On many middle- and upper-class tables, French cuisine replaced traditional Mexican dishes. The wealthy replaced sombreros and ponchos with European garments, and they preferred horse racing and soccer to the traditional bullfighting and cockfighting. To the educated middle class—the only group with a strong sense of Mexican nationhood—this devaluation of Mexican culture became a symbol of the Díaz regime's failure to defend national interests against foreign influences.

Emiliano Zapata   Zapata, the leader of a peasant rebellion in southern Mexico during the Mexican Revolution, stands in full revolutionary regalia: sword, rifles, bandoleers, boots, and sombrero.   (Brown Brothers)

Revolution and Civil War, 1911–1920

Unlike the independence movement in India, the Mexican Revolution was not the work of one party with a well-defined ideology. Instead, it developed haphazardly, led by a series of ambitious but limited leaders, each representing a different segment of Mexican society.

The first was Francisco I. Madero (1873–1913), the son of a wealthy landowning and mining family, educated in the United States. When minor uprisings broke out in 1911, the government collapsed and Díaz fled into exile. In 1913, after two years as president, Madero was overthrown and murdered by one of his former supporters, General Victoriano Huerta. Woodrow Wilson (1856–

1924), president of the United States, showed his displeasure by sending the United States Marines to occupy Veracruz.

The inequities of Mexican society and foreign intervention in Mexico's affairs angered Mexico's middle class and industrial workers. They found leaders in Venustiano Carranza, a landowner, and in Alvaro Obregón°, a schoolteacher. Calling themselves Constitutionalists, Carranza and Obregón organized private armies and in

---

Díaz (DEE-as)

Obregón (oh-bray-GAWN)

Map 32.2   The Mexican Revolution   The Mexican Revolution began in two distinct regions of the country. One was the mountainous and densely populated area south of Mexico City, particularly Morelos, homeland of Emiliano Zapata. The other was the dry and thinly populated ranch country of the north, such as Chihuahua, home of Pancho Villa. The fighting that ensued crisscrossed the country along the main railroad lines, shown on the map.

1914 succeeded in overthrowing Huerta. By then, the revolution had spread to the countryside.

As early as 1911, **Emiliano Zapata** (1879–1919), an Indian farmer, had led a revolt against the haciendas in the mountains of Morelos, south of Mexico City (see Map 32.2). His soldiers were peasants, some of them women, mounted on horseback and armed with pistols and rifles. For several years, they periodically came down from the mountains, burned hacienda buildings, and returned land to the Indian villages to which it had once belonged.

Another leader appeared in Chihuahua, a northern state where seventeen individuals owned two-fifths of the land and 95 percent of the people had no land at all. Starting in 1913, **Francisco "Pancho" Villa** (1877–1923), a former ranch hand, mule driver, and bandit, organized an army of three thousand men, most of them cowboys. They too seized land from the large haciendas, not to

rebuild traditional communities as in southern Mexico but to create family ranches.

Zapata and Villa were part agrarian rebels, part social revolutionaries. They enjoyed tremendous popular support but could never rise above their regional and peasant origins and lead a national revolution. The Constitutionalists had fewer soldiers than Zapata and Villa; but they held the major cities, controlled the country's exports of oil, and used the proceeds of oil sales to buy modern weapons. Fighting continued for years, and gradually the Constitutionalists took over most of Mexico. In 1919 they defeated and killed Zapata; Villa was assassinated four years later. An estimated 2 million people lost their lives in the civil war, and much of Mexico lay in ruins.

During their struggle to win support against Zapata and Villa, the Constitutionalists adopted many of their rivals' agrarian reforms, such as restoring communal

***The Agitator*, a Mural by Diego Rivera**   Diego Rivera (1886–1957) was politically committed to the Mexican Revolution and widely admired as an artist. This mural, painted at the National Agricultural School at Chapingo near Mexico City, shows a political agitator addressing peasants and workers. With one hand, the speaker points to miners laboring in a silver mine; with the other, to a hammer and sickle.   (Universidad Autonoma de Chapingo/CENIDIAP-INBA)

lands to the Indians of Morelos. The Constitutionalists also proposed social programs designed to appeal to workers and the middle class. The Constitution of 1917 promised universal suffrage and a one-term presidency; state-run education to free the poor from the hold of the Catholic Church; the end of debt peonage; restrictions on foreign ownership of property; and laws specifying minimum wages and maximum hours to protect laborers. Although these reforms were too costly to implement right away, they had important symbolic significance, for they enshrined the dignity of Mexicans and the equality of Indians, mestizos, and whites, as well as of peasants and city people.

The Revolution Institutionalized, 1920–1940

In the early 1920s, after a decade of violence that exhausted all classes, the Mexican Revolution lost momentum. Only in Morelos did peasants receive land, and President Obregón and his closest associates made all important decisions. Nevertheless, the Revolution changed the social makeup of the governing class in important ways. For the first time in Mexico's history, representatives of rural communities, unionized workers, and public employees were admitted to the inner circle.

In the arts, the Mexican Revolution sparked a surge of creativity. The political murals of José Clemente Orozco and Diego Rivera and the paintings of Frida Kahlo focused on social themes, showing peasants, workers, and soldiers in scenes from the Revolution.

In 1928 Obregón was assassinated. His successor, Plutarco Elías Calles°, founded the National Revolutionary Party, or PNR (the abbreviation of its name in Spanish). The PNR was a forum where all the pressure groups and vested interests—labor, peasants, businessmen, landowners, the military, and others—worked out compromises. The establishment of the PNR gave the Mexican Revolution a second wind.

Lázaro Cárdenas°, chosen by Calles to be president in 1934, brought peasants' and workers' organizations into the party, renamed it the Mexican Revolutionary Party (PRM), and removed the generals from government positions. Then he set to work implementing the reforms promised in the Constitution of 1917. Cárdenas redistributed 44 million acres (17.6 million hectares) to peasant communes. He closed church-run schools, replacing them with government schools. He nationalized

Calles (KAH-yace)
Lázaro Cárdenas (LAH-sah-roe KAHR-dih-nahs)

the railroads and numerous other businesses. Cárdenas's most dramatic move was the expropriation of foreign-owned oil companies.

In the early 1920s, Mexico was the world's leading producer of oil, but a handful of American and British companies exported almost all of it. In 1938 Cárdenas seized the foreign-owned oil industry, more as a matter of national pride than of economics. The oil companies expected the governments of the United States and Great Britain to come to their rescue, perhaps with military force. But Mexico and the United States chose to resolve the issue through negotiation, and Mexico retained control of its oil industry.

When Cárdenas's term ended in 1940, Mexico, like India, was still a land of poor farmers with a small industrial base. The Revolution had brought great changes, however. The political system was free of both chaos and dictatorships. A small group of wealthy people no longer monopolized land and other resources. The military was tamed, the Catholic Church no longer controlled education, and the nationalization of oil had demonstrated Mexico's independence from foreign corporations and military intervention.

What did the Mexican Revolution accomplish? It did not fulfill the democratic promise of Madero's campaign, but it did allow far more sectors of the population to participate in politics. The Revolution also promised far-reaching social reforms, such as free education, higher wages and more security for workers, and the redistribution of land to the peasants. These long-delayed reforms began to be implemented during the Cárdenas administration. They fell short of the ideals expressed by the revolutionaries, but they laid the foundation for the later industrialization of Mexico.

ARGENTINA AND BRAZIL, 1900–1949

On the surface, Argentina and Brazil seem very different. Argentina is Spanish-speaking, temperate in climate, and populated almost exclusively by Europeans. Brazil is tropical, Portuguese-speaking, and inhabited by people of mixed European and African origin, plus a substantial Indian minority. But in the twentieth century, their economic, political, and technological experiences were remarkably similar.

The Transformation of Argentina

Most of Argentina consists of *pampas*°, flat, fertile land that is easy to till, much like the prairies of the midwestern United States and Canada. Throughout the nineteenth century, Argentina's economy was based on two exports: the hides of longhorn creole cattle and the wool of merino sheep, which roamed the pampas in huge herds. Centuries earlier, Europeans had haphazardly introduced the animals and the grasses they ate. Natural selection had made the animals tough and hardy.

At the end of the nineteenth century, railroads and refrigerator ships, which allowed the safe transportation of meat, changed not only the composition of Argentina's exports but also the way they were produced—in other words, the land itself. European consumers preferred the soft flesh of Lincoln sheep and Hereford cattle to the tough sinewy meat of creole cattle and merino sheep. The valuable Lincolns and Herefords could not be allowed to roam and graze on the pampas. They were carefully bred and received a diet of alfalfa and oats. To safeguard them, the pampas had to be divided, plowed, cultivated, and fenced with barbed wire to keep out predators and other unwelcome animals. Once fenced, the land could be used to produce wheat as well as beef and mutton. Within a few years, grasslands that had stretched to the horizon were transformed into farmland. Like the North American midwest, the pampas became one of the world's great producers of wheat and meat.

Argentina's government represented the interests of the *oligarquía*°, a very small group of wealthy landowners. Members of this elite controlled enormous haciendas where they raised cattle and sheep and grew wheat for export. They also owned fine homes in Buenos Aires°, a city that was built to look like Paris. They traveled frequently to Europe and spent so lavishly that the French coined the superlative "rich as an Argentine." They showed little interest in any business other than farming, however, and were content to let foreign companies, mainly British, build Argentina's railroads, processing plants, the public utilities. In exchange for its agricultural exports, Argentina imported almost all its manufactured goods from Europe and the United States. So important were British interests in the Argentinean economy that the language used on the railroads was not Spanish but English, and the biggest department store in Buenos Aires was a branch of Harrod's of London.

pampas (POM-pus) *oligarquía* (oh-lee gar-KEE-ah)
Buenos Aires (BWAY-nihs AIR-eze)

Brazil and Argentina, to 1929

Before the First World War, Brazil produced most of the world's coffee and cacao, grown on vast estates, and natural rubber, gathered by Indians from rubber trees growing wild in the Amazon rain forest. Brazil's elite was made up of coffee and cacao planters and rubber exporters. Like their Argentinean counterparts, they spent their money lavishly on palaces in Rio de Janeiro° and on the world's most beautiful opera house in Manaus°, deep in the Amazon. They had little interest in other forms of development, let British companies build railroads, harbors, and other infrastructure, and imported all manufactured goods. At the time, this situation seemed to offer a rational division of labor that allowed each country to do what it did best. If the British did not grow coffee, why should Brazil build locomotives?

Both Argentina and Brazil had small but outspoken middle classes that demanded a share in government and looked to Europe as a model. Beneath each middle class were the poor. In Argentina these were mainly Spanish and Italian immigrants who had ended up as landless farm laborers or workers in urban packing plants. In Brazil there was a large class of sharecroppers and plantation workers, many of them descendants of slaves.

Rubber exports collapsed after 1912, replaced by cheaper plantation rubber from Southeast Asia. The outbreak of war in 1914 put an end to imports from Europe as Britain and France focused all their industries on war production and Germany was cut off entirely. To a certain extent, the United States replaced the European countries as suppliers of machinery and as consumers of coffee. European immigrants built factories to manufacture textiles and household goods. Desperate for money to pay for the war, Great Britain sold off many of its railroad, streetcar, and other companies to the governments of Argentina and Brazil.

The disruption of the old trade patterns weakened the landowning class. In Argentina, the urban middle class obtained the secret ballot and universal male suffrage in 1916 and elected a liberal politician, Hipólito Irigoyen°, as president. In Brazil, junior officers rebelled periodically against the government but accomplished little. In neither country did the urban middle class take power away from the wealthy landowners. Instead, the two classes shared power at the expense of both the landless peasants and the urban workers.

The 1920s were a period of peace and prosperity in South America, in contrast to Mexico. Trade with Europe

Rio de Janeiro (REE-oh day zhuh-NAIR-oh)
Manaus (meh-NOWSE)
Hipólito Irigoyen (ee-POH-lee-toe ee-ree-GO-yen)

resumed, prices received for agricultural exports remained high, and both Argentina and Brazil used profits accumulated during the war to industrialize and improve their transportation systems and public utilities. Yet as they were moving forward, new technologies again left them dependent on the advanced industrial countries.

Brazilians are justly proud that the first person to fly an airplane outside the United States was Alberto Santos-Dumont, a Brazilian. He did so in 1906 in France, where he lived most of his life and had access to engine manufacturers and technical assistance. Aviation reached Latin America after World War I, when European and American companies such as Aéropostale and Pan American Airways introduced airmail service between the cities and linked Latin America with the United States and Europe.

Before and during World War I, radio, then called "wireless telegraphy," was used not for broadcasting but for point-to-point communications. Transmitters powerful enough to send messages across oceans or continents were extraordinarily complex and expensive: their antennas covered many acres, they used as much electricity as a small town, and they cost tens of thousands of pounds sterling (millions of year-2000 dollars).

Right after the war, the major powers scrambled to build powerful transmitters on every continent to compete with the telegraph cable companies and to take advantage of the boom in international business and news reporting. At the time, no Latin American country possessed the knowledge or funds to build its own transmitters. In 1919, therefore, President Irigoyen of Argentina granted a radio concession to a German firm. France and Britain protested this decision, and eventually four powerful radio companies—one British, one French, one German, and one American—formed a cartel to control all radio communications in Latin America. This cartel set up a national radio company in each Latin American republic, installing a prominent local politician as its president, but the cartel held all the stock and therefore received all the profits. Thus, even as Brazil and Argentina were taking over their railroads and older industries, the major industrial countries controlled the diffusion of the newer aviation and radio technologies.

The Depression and the Vargas Regime in Brazil

The Depression hit Latin America as hard as it hit Europe and the United States; in many ways, it marks a more important turning point for the region than either of the world wars. As long-term customers cut back their orders, the value of agricultural and mineral exports fell by two-thirds between 1929 and 1932. Argentina and Brazil could no longer afford to import manufactured goods. An imploding economy also undermined their shaky political systems. Like European countries, Argentina and Brazil veered toward authoritarian regimes that promised to solve their economic problems.

In 1930, **Getulio Vargas°**, (1883–1953), governor of the state of Rio Grande do Sul°, staged a coup and proclaimed himself president of Brazil. He proved to be a masterful politician. He wrote a new constitution that broadened the franchise and limited the president to one term. He raised import duties and promoted national firms and state-owned enterprises, culminating in the construction of the Volta Redonda steel mill in the 1930s. By 1936, industrial production had doubled, especially in textiles and small manufactures. Brazil was on its way to becoming an industrial country. Vargas's policy, called **import-substitution industrialization,** became a model for other Latin American countries as they attempted to break away from neocolonial dependency.

The industrialization of Brazil brought all the familiar environmental consequences. Powerful new machines allowed the reopening of old mines and the digging of new ones. Cities grew as poor peasants looking for work arrived from the countryside. Around the older neighborhoods of Rio de Janeiro and São Paulo°, the poor turned steep hillsides and vacant lands into immense *favelas°* (slums) of makeshift shacks.

The countryside also was transformed. Scrubland was turned into pasture, and new acreage was planted in wheat, corn, and sugar cane. Even the Amazon rain forest—half of the land area of Brazil—was affected. In 1930, American industrialist Henry Ford invested $8 million to clear land along the Tapajós River and prepare it to become the site of the world's largest rubber plantation. Ford encountered opposition from Brazilian workers and politicians, the rubber trees proved vulnerable to diseases, and he had to abandon the project—but not before leaving 3 million acres (1.2 million hectares) denuded of trees. The ecological changes of the Vargas era, however, were but a tiny forerunner of the degradation of the Brazilian environment that was to take place later in the century.

Vargas instituted many reforms favorable to urban workers, such as labor unions, pension plans, and disability insurance, but he refused to take any measures that might help the millions of landless peasants or harm the interests of the great landowners. Although the Brazilian economy recovered from the Depression, the benefits of recovery were so unequally distributed that communist and fascist movements demanded even more radical changes.

In 1938, prohibited by his own constitution from being reelected, Vargas staged another coup, abolished the constitution, and instituted the Estado Novo°, or "New State," with himself as supreme leader. He abolished political parties, jailed opposition leaders, and turned Brazil into a fascist state. When the Second World War broke out, however, Vargas aligned Brazil with the United States and contributed troops and ships to the Allied war effort.

Despite his economic achievements, Vargas harmed Brazil. By running roughshod over laws, constitutions, and rights, he infected not only Brazil but all of South America with the temptations of political violence. It is ironic, but not surprising, that Vargas was overthrown in 1945 by a military coup.

Argentina After 1930

Economically, the Depression hurt Argentina almost as badly as it hurt Brazil. Politically, however, the consequences were delayed for many years. In 1930, General José Uriburu° overthrew the popularly elected President Irigoyen. The Uriburu government represented the large landowners and big business interests. For thirteen years the generals and the oligarquía ruled, doing nothing to lessen the poverty of the workers or the frustrations of the middle class. When World War II broke out, Argentina sympathized with the Axis but remained officially neutral.

In 1943 another military revolt flared, this one among junior officers angry at conservative politicians. It was led by Colonel **Juan Perón°** (1895–1974). The intentions of the rebels were clear:

> Civilians will never understand the greatness of our ideal; we shall therefore have to eliminate them from the government and give them the only mission which corresponds to them: work and obedience.[1]

Once in power, the officers took over the highest positions in government and business and began to lavish money on military equipment and their own salaries. Their goal, inspired by Nazi victories, was nothing less than the conquest of South America.

As the war turned against the Nazis, the officers saw their popularity collapse. Perón, however, had other

---

Getulio Vargas (jay-TOO-lee-oh VAR-gus)
Rio Grande do Sul (REE-oh GRAN-dee do SOOL)
São Paulo (sow PAL-oh)   *favela* (feh-VEL-luh)

Estado Novo (esh-TAH-doe NO-vo)
José Uriburu (hoe-SAY oo-ree-BOO-roo)
Juan Perón (hoo-AHN pair-OWN)

Eva and Juan Perón Eva Perón was a formidable political campaigner and the real power behind her husband's rise to power. Here Eva and Juan are addressing a political rally. (Archivo General de la Nacion, Buenos Aires)

plans. Inspired by his charismatic wife **Eva Duarte Perón°** (1919–1952), he appealed to the urban workers. Eva Perón became the champion of the *descamisados°*, or "shirtless ones," and campaigned tirelessly for social benefits and for the cause of women and children. With his wife's help, Perón won the presidency in 1946 and created a populist dictatorship in imitation of the Vargas regime in Brazil.

Like Brazil, Argentina industrialized rapidly under state sponsorship. Perón spent lavishly on social welfare projects as well as on the military, depleting the capital that Argentina had earned during the war. Though a skillful demagogue who played off the army against the navy and both against the labor unions, Perón could not create a stable government out of the chaos of coups and conspiracies. He had to back down from a plan to make Eva his vice president. When she died in 1952, he lost his political skills (or perhaps they were hers), and soon thereafter he was overthrown in yet another military coup.

Eva Duarte Perón (AY-vuh doo-AR-tay pair-OWN)
descamisados (des-cah-mee-SAH-dohs)

Mexico, Argentina, and Brazil: A Comparison

Until 1910, Mexico, Argentina, and Brazil shared a common history and similar cultures. In the first half of the twentieth century, their economies followed parallel trajectories, based on their unequal relations with the industrialized countries of Europe and North America. All three countries—indeed, all of Latin America—struggled with the failure of neocolonial economics to improve the lives of the middle class, let alone the peasants. And when the Depression hit, all three turned to state intervention and import-substitution industrialization. Like all industrializing countries, they did so by mining, farming, ranching, cutting down forests, and irrigating land, all at the expense of the natural environment.

Yet their political histories diverged radically. Mexico underwent a traumatic and profound social revolution. Argentina and Brazil, meanwhile, languished under conservative regimes devoted to the interests of wealthy landowners, sporadically interrupted by military coups and populist demagogues. Mexicans, thanks to their experience of revolution, developed an acute sense of their national identity and civic pride in their history—pride largely missing in South America. Despite shortcomings, Mexico took seriously its commitment to education, land reform, social justice, and political stability as a national goal, not merely as the campaign platform of a populist dictator.

Conclusion

Sub-Saharan Africa, India, and Latin America lay outside the theaters of war that engulfed most of the Northern Hemisphere, but they were deeply affected by global events and by the demands of the industrial powers. Sub-Saharan Africa and India were still under colonial rule, and their political life revolved around the yearnings of their elites for political independence and their masses for social justice. Mexico, Argentina, and Brazil were politically independent, but their economies, like those of Africa and India, were closely tied to the economies of the industrial nations with which they traded. Their deeply polarized societies and the stresses caused by their dependence on the industrial countries clashed with the expectations of ever larger numbers of their peoples.

In Mexico, these stresses brought about a long and violent revolution, out of which Mexicans forged a lasting sense of national identity. Argentina and Brazil moved toward greater economic independence, but at the price of militarism and dictatorship. In India, the conflict between growing expectations and the reality of colonial rule produced both a movement for independence and an ethnic split that tore the nation apart. In sub-Saharan Africa, demands for national self-determination and economic development were only beginning to be voiced by 1949 and were not to come to fruition until the second half of the century.

Nationalism and the yearning for social justice were the two most powerful forces for change in the early twentieth century. These ideas originated in the industrialized countries but resonated in the independent countries of Latin America as well as in colonial regions such as the Indian subcontinent and sub-Saharan Africa. However, they did not always unite people against their colonial rulers or foreign oppressors; instead, they often divided them along social, ethnic, or religious lines. Western-educated elites looked to industrialization as a means of modernizing their country and ensuring their position in it, while peasants and urban workers supported nationalist and revolutionary movements in the hope of improving their lives. Often these goals were not compatible.

■ Key Terms

Blaise Diagne

African National Congress

Haile Selassie

Indian National Congress

Bengal

All-India Muslim League

Mohandas K. (Mahatma) Gandhi

Jawaharlal Nehru

Muhammad Ali Jinnah

Emiliano Zapata

Francisco "Pancho" Villa

Lázaro Cárdenas

Getulio Vargas

import-substitution industrialization

Juan Perón

Eva Duarte Perón

■ Suggested Reading

On Africa under colonial rule the classic overview is Melville Herskovits, *The Human Factor in Changing Africa* (1958). Two excellent general introductions are Roland Oliver and Anthony Atmore, *Africa Since 1800*, 4th ed. (1994), and A. E. Afigbo et al., *The Making of Modern Africa*, vol. 2, *The Twentieth Century* (1986). More detailed and challenging are *UNESCO General History of Africa*, vols. 7 and 8; *The Cambridge History of Africa*, vols. 7 and 8; and Adu Boahen, *African Perspectives on Colonialism* (1987). Outstanding novels about Africa in the colonial era include Chinua Achebe, *Arrow of God* (1964); Buchi Emecheta, *The Joys of Motherhood* (1980); and Peter Abraham, *Mine Boy* (1946).

For a general introduction to Indian history see Sumit Sarkar, *Modern India, 1885–1947* (1983), and Percival Spear, *India: A Modern History*, rev. ed. (1972). On the influenza epidemic of 1918–1919 see Alfred W. Crosby, *America's Forgotten Pandemic: The Influenza of 1918* (1989). The Indian independence movement has received a great deal of attention. Judith M. Brown's most recent book on Gandhi is *Gandhi: Prisoner of Hope* (1989). *Gandhi's Truth: On the Origin of Militant Nonviolence* (1969) by noted psychoanalyst Erik Erikson is also recommended. Two collections of memoirs of the last decades of British rule are worth looking at: Charles Allen, ed., *Plain Tales of the Raj: Image of British India in the Twentieth Century* (1975), and Zareer Masani, ed., *Indian Tales of the Raj* (1988). The transition from colonialism to partition and independence is the subject of the very readable *Freedom at Midnight* (1975) by Larry Collins and Dominique Lapierre. The environment is discussed in M. Gadgil and R. Guha, *This Fissured Land: An Ecological History of India* (1993).

Thomas Skidmore and Peter Smith, *Modern Latin America*, 3d ed. (1992), offers the best brief introduction. Two fine general overviews of modern Mexican history are Enrique Krauze, *Mexico: Biography of a Power* (1997), and Colin MacLachlan and William Beezley, *El Gran Pueblo: A History of Greater Mexico* (1994). On the Mexican Revolution, two recent books are essential: Alan Knight, *The Mexican Revolution*, 2 vols. (1986), and John M. Hart, *Revolutionary Mexico: The Coming and Process of the Mexican Revolution* (1987). But see also two classics by sympathetic Americans: Frank Tannenbaum, *Peace by Revolution: Mexico After 1910* (1933), and Robert E. Quirk, *The Mexican Revolution, 1914–1915* (1960). Mexico's most celebrated revolutionary is the subject of Manuel Machado, *Centaur of the North: Francisco Villa, the Mexican Revolution, and Northern Mexico*

(1988). Mariano Azuela, *The Underdogs* (1988), is an interesting fictional account of this period. The standard work on Brazil is E. Bradford Burns, *A History of Brazil*, 3d ed. (1993). The history of modern Argentina is ably treated in David Rock, *Argentina, 1517–1987: From Spanish Colonization to Alfonsín* (1987). Mark Jefferson, *Peopling the Argentine Pampas* (1971), and Jeremy Adelman, *Frontier Development: Land, Labour and Capital on the Wheatlands of Argentina and Canada, 1890–1914* (1994), describe the transformation of the Argentinean environment.

■ Note

1. George Blanksten, *Perón's Argentina* (Chicago: University of Chicago Press, 1953), 37.

THE PERILS AND PROMISES OF A GLOBAL COMMUNITY,

1945 – 2000

CHAPTER 33
THE COLD WAR AND DECOLONIZATION, 1945–1975

CHAPTER 34
CRISIS, REALIGNMENT, AND THE DAWN OF THE POST–COLD WAR WORLD, 1975–1991

CHAPTER 35
THE END OF A GLOBAL CENTURY, 1991–2000

he notion of a postwar era in which all the world's peoples could rejoice in the defeat of totalitarianism became increasingly hollow as the Cold War set in between the United States and the Soviet Union and more and more peoples engaged in struggles for national independence. From 1945 to 1991, conflicts between communist and noncommunist forces in emerging nations repeatedly involved the superpowers, sometimes as arms suppliers or allies, sometimes as combatants. The Korean War and the Vietnam War engaged American troops; the Soviet Union became bogged down in a war in Afghanistan. Leaders of the Third World, a group of states proclaiming nonalignment in the Cold War, tried to advance their state-building programs by playing off the

United States against the Soviet Union and gaining favors from both sides.

A turning point of sorts arrived around 1975. Escalating oil prices, provoked by conflicts in the Middle East, shook the world's economic foundations. The major nuclear powers began to recognize the futility of the arms race. The countries of East Asia rapidly industrialized. And the attitudes of young people around the world increasingly clashed with those of the parental, World War II, generation.

In the relatively nonindustrialized parts of the world, population grew rapidly. Governments in Latin America, Africa, South Asia, China, and the Middle East faced serious problems in providing the necessities of life. The extension of agriculture and other pressures on resources sped the deterioration of the environment.

The dissemination of new technologies, ranging from "green revolution" agricultural practices to consumer electronics, transformed daily life. Regional cultures, many of them religiously based, felt threatened by the spread of Western consumer society and entertainment. The vision of a global culture excited some people while repelling others.

Formal relations among groups of states—the United Nations, Cold War alliances, and free trade agreements—brought the world's peoples closer together than ever before. With the emergence of a truly global community, peacekeeping, human rights, and gender equality became international issues.

As the Cold War faded rapidly from memory after 1991, the world was seen by many to lack an overarching political or economic structure. Globalization became the watchword of those most deeply committed to economic growth and high technology. Rivalry between the poor South and the rich North struck others as a better reading of world affairs. Still others looked on environmental degradation as the greatest world problem. The postwar era had certainly come to an end, but no one was certain about what was next to come.

	1950	1960	1970
Americas	• **1945** United Nations charter signed in San Francisco • **1946** International Monetary Fund and World Bank founded • **1952** U.S. tests first hydrogen bomb	• **1962** Cuban missile crisis • **1959** Cuban Revolution • **1964** Military takes power in Brazil Neil Armstrong walks on moon **1969** •	
Europe	**1948–1952** Marshall Plan helps rebuild western Europe • **1949** NATO founded • **1955** Warsaw Pact formed Soviet troops crush revolt in Hungary **1956** • • **1957** Common Market founded	• **1961** Berlin Wall built Student uprising in France **1968** •	
Africa	• **1948** Apartheid becomes official in South Africa Ghana first British colony in Africa to win independence **1957** • • **1958** Guinea wins independence from France	• **1960** Nigeria, Congo, Somalia, Togo win independence • **1963** Kenya independent	
Middle East	• **1948** State of Israel founded; first Arab-Israeli War • **1956** Suez crisis **1954–1962** Algerian war for Independence Organization of Petroleum Exporting Countries founded **1960** •		• **1967** Six Day Arab-Israeli War
Asia and Oceania	Communist Revolution in China **1949** **1951–1953** Korean War **1954–1975** Vietnam War • **1949** Indonesia wins independence from Netherlands	Cultural Revolution in China **1966–1969** Japan becomes world economic power **1970s**	

ARCTIC OCEAN

Union of Soviet Socialist Republics
(Russia)

Britain
Poland
Germany
EUROPE
France
Yugoslavia

ASIA

N. Korea
S. Korea
Japan

Israel Iraq Iran Afghanistan
Pakistan
China

Algeria Libya Egypt
MIDDLE EAST
Persian Gulf

Taiwan

AFRICA

Bangladesh
India

Guinea
Togo
Ghana
Nigeria

Thailand
Vietnam

Congo
Kenya

Somalia

Singapore

PACIFIC OCEAN

Indonesia

Angola

Mozambique

INDIAN OCEAN

East
Timor

Rhodesia
(Zimbabwe)

SOUTH
ATLANTIC
OCEAN

South
Africa

AUSTRALIA

0   1000   2000   3000 Km.

0   1000   2000   3000 Mi.

1980	1990	2000

• **1973** Military coup overthrows Allende in Chile

• **1976** Military takes
power in Argentina

1983–1989 Democracy
restored in Brazil, Argentina, Chile

NAFTA agreement among
Canada, U.S., Mexico **1994** •

• **1994** Maya uprising in
southern Mexico

• **1975** Helsinki Accords

Solidarity union founded
in Poland **1980** •

Fall of communist regimes
in eastern Europe **1989** •

End of USSR **1990** •

• **1990** Reunification of Germany

Introduction of euro **1999** •

1992–2000 Disintegration of Yugoslavia

• **1975** Angola and Mozambique win independence from Portugal

1970–1980 White domination of Rhodesia
yields to international pressure

• **1985** Africa equals Europe in population

1994–1999 Nelson Mandela
president of South Africa

• **1973** October Arab-Israeli War leads
to oil embargo, price hikes

• **1979** Islamic Revolution overthrows shah of Iran

1980–1988 Iran-Iraq War

• **1991** Persian Gulf War

Average Japanese income exceeds average U.S. income **1986** •

• **1980s** Taiwan, South Korea, Singapore industrialize

• **1971** Independence of Bangladesh

• **1979** USSR enters war in Afghanistan

• **1989** Chinese troops suppress Tiananmen Square protest

East Timor wins independence from Indonesia **1999** •

Asian financial crisis starts in Thailand **1997** •

33

THE COLD WAR AND DECOLONIZATION,

1945–1975

**The Cold War • Decolonization and Nation Building •
Beyond a Bipolar World**

ENVIRONMENT AND TECHNOLOGY: **The Green Revolution**

SOCIETY AND CULTURE: **Silent Spring**

Soviet Postal Tribute to First Woman Cosmonaut   Valentina Tereshkova became
the first woman in space when she went aloft on the *Vostok-6* mission.

n 1946, in a speech at Fulton, Missouri, Great Britain's wartime leader Winston Churchill said: "From Stettin in the Baltic to Trieste in the Adriatic, an iron curtain has descended across the Continent. . . . I am convinced there is nothing they [the communists] so much admire as strength, and there is nothing for which they have less respect than weakness, especially military weakness." The phrase **"iron curtain"** became a watchword of the **Cold War,** the state of political tension and military rivalry that was then beginning between the United States and its allies ("running dogs of imperialism" in Soviet parlance) and the Soviet Union and its allies ("satellites" in American parlance).

In the Atlantic Charter that Churchill and President Franklin Roosevelt issued four months before the United States entered the war in 1941, and then in the 1942 declaration signed by twenty-six "United Nations" (Roosevelt's term for the alliance against the Axis), they had looked forward to a postwar world of economic cooperation and restoration of sovereignty to peoples suffering Axis occupation and, above all, to a world where war and territorial conquest would not be tolerated. By the time Churchill delivered his "iron curtain" speech, however, Britain's electorate had voted him out of power, Harry S Truman had succeeded to the presidency after Roosevelt's death, and the Soviet Union was dominating eastern Europe and supporting communist movements in China, Iran, Turkey, Greece, and Korea. Although Soviet diplomats sat with their former allies in the newly founded United Nations Organization, confrontation rather than cooperation was the hallmark of relations between East and West.

The intensity of the Cold War, with its accompanying threat of nuclear destruction, sometimes obscured a postwar phenomenon of even greater importance. Western domination of Asia, Africa, and Latin America was largely ended, and the colonial empires of the New Imperialism were gradually dismantled. The new generation of national leaders to head the states in these regions sometimes skillfully played Cold War antagonism to their own advantage. Their real business, however, was nation building, an enterprise charged with almost insurmountable problems and conflicts.

Each land subject to imperialism had its own specific history and conditions and followed its own route to independence. Thus the new nations had a difficult time finding a collective voice in a world increasingly oriented toward two superpowers, the United States and the Soviet Union. Some sided openly with one or the other. Others banded together in a posture of neutrality and spoke with one voice about their need for economic and technical assistance and the obligation of the wealthy nations to satisfy those needs.

The Cold War military rivalry stimulated extraordinary advances in weaponry and associated technologies, but many new nations faced basic problems of educating their citizens, nurturing industry, and escaping the economic constraints imposed by their former imperialist masters. The environment suffered severe pressures, whether from oil exploration and transport to feed the growing economies of the wealthy nations or from deforestation in poor regions challenged by the need for cropland. Neither rich nor poor realized the costs associated with environmental change.

As you read this chapter, ask yourself the following questions:

- What impact did economic philosophy have on both the Cold War and the decolonization movement?

- How was a third world war averted?

- Was world domination by the superpowers good or bad for the rest of the world?

THE COLD WAR

The wartime alliance between the United States, Great Britain, and the Soviet Union had been an uneasy one. Fear of working-class revolution, which the Nazis had played upon in their rise to power, was not confined to Germany. Political and economic leaders committed to free markets and untrammeled capital investment

The Green Revolution

Concern about world food supplies grew directly out of the serious shortages that many nations faced because of the devastation and trade disruptions of World War II. The Food and Agriculture Organization of the United Nations, the Rockefeller Foundation, and the Ford Foundation took leading roles in fostering crop research and educating farmers about agricultural techniques. In 1966 the International Rice Research Institute (established in 1960–1962) began distributing seeds for an improved rice variety known as IR-8. Crop yields from this and other new varieties, along with improved farming techniques, were so impressive that the term *Green Revolution* was coined to describe a new era in agricultural history.

On the heels of the successful new rice strains came new varieties of corn and wheat. Building on twenty years of Rockefeller-funded research in Mexico, the Centro Internacional de Mejoramiento de Maiz y Trigo (International Center for the Improvement of Maize and Wheat) was established in 1966 under Norman Borlaug, who was awarded the Nobel Peace Prize four years later. This organization distributed around the world short, stiff-strawed varieties of wheat that were resistant to disease and responsive to fertilizer.

By 1970 other centers for research on tropical agriculture had been established in Ibadan, Nigeria, and Cali, Colombia. But the success of the Green Revolution and the growing need for its products called for a more comprehensive effort. The Consultative Group on International Agricultural Research brought together World Bank expertise, private foundations, international organizations, and national foreign aid agencies to undertake worldwide support of efforts to increase food productivity and improve natural resource management.

Miracle Rice   New strains of so-called "miracle rice" made many nations in south and southeast Asia self-sufficient in food production after decades of worry about the growth of population outstripping agricultural productivity. (Victor Englebert)

had loathed socialism in its several forms for more than a century. After World War II, the iron curtain in Europe and communist insurgencies in China and elsewhere seemed to confirm the threat of worldwide revolution.

Western leaders quickly came to perceive the Soviet Union as the nerve center of world revolution and as a military power capable of launching a war as destructive and terrible as the one recently ended. But Soviet leaders, particularly after the United States and the countries of western Europe established the **North Atlantic Treaty Organization (NATO)** military alliance in 1949, felt themselves surrounded by hostile forces just when they were trying to recover from the terrible losses sustained in the war against the Axis. The distrust and suspicion between the two sides played out on a worldwide stage. The United Nations provided the venue for face-to-face debate.

CHRONOLOGY

	Cold War	Decolonization
1945		
	1948–1949 Berlin airlift	**1947** Partition of India
	1949 NATO formed	**1949** Dutch withdraw from Indonesia
1950	**1950–1953** Korean War	
	1952 United States detonates first hydrogen bomb	
		1954 CIA intervention in Guatemala; defeat at Dienbienphu ends French hold on Vietnam
	1955 Warsaw Pact concluded	**1955** Bandung Conference
	1956 Soviet Union suppresses Hungarian revolt	
	1957 Soviet Union launches first artificial satellite into earth orbit	**1957** Ghana becomes first British colony in Africa to gain independence
		1959 Fidel Castro leads revolution in Cuba
1960		**1960** Shootings in Sharpeville intensify South African struggle against apartheid; Nigeria becomes independent
	1961 East Germany builds Berlin Wall	
		1962 Algeria wins independence
	1962 Cuban missile crisis	
1970		**1971** Bangladesh secedes from Pakistan
	1975 Helsinki Accords; end of Vietnam War	

The United Nations

In 1944 representatives from the United States, Great Britain, the Soviet Union, and China met and drafted specific charter proposals that finally bore fruit in the treaty called the United Nations Charter, ratified on October 24, 1945. Like the League of Nations, the **United Nations** had two main bodies: the General Assembly, with representatives from all member states; and the Security Council, with five permanent members—China, France, Great Britain, the United States, and the Soviet Union—and seven rotating members. A full-time bureaucracy headed by a Secretary General carried out the day-to-day business of both bodies. Various United Nations agencies focused on specialized international problems—for example, UNICEF (United Nations Children's Emergency Fund), FAO (Food and Agriculture Organization) and UNESCO (United Nations Educational, Scientific and Cultural Organization) (see Environment and Technology: The Green Revolution). Unlike the League of Nations, which required unanimous agreement in both of its deliberative bodies, the United Nations operated by majority vote, except that the five permanent members of the Security Council had veto power in that chamber.

All signatories to the United Nations Charter renounced war and territorial conquest. Nevertheless, peacekeeping, the sole preserve of the Security Council, became a vexing problem. The permanent members exercised their veto when necessary to protect their friends and interests. Throughout the Cold War, the United Nations was seldom able to forestall or quell international conflicts, though from time to time it sent observers or peacekeeping forces to monitor truces or agreements otherwise arrived at.

The decolonization of Africa and Asia greatly swelled the size of the General Assembly but not the Security Council. Many of the new nations looked to the United Nations for material assistance and access to a wider political world. While the vetoes of the Security Council's permanent members often stymied actions touching even indirectly on Cold War concerns, the General Assembly became an arena for expressing opinions on many issues involving decolonization, a movement that the Soviet Union strongly encouraged but the Western colonial powers resisted.

In the early years of the United Nations, General Assembly resolutions carried great weight. An example is a 1947 resolution that sought to divide Palestine into sovereign Jewish and Arab states. Gradually, though, the flood of new members produced a voting majority concerned more with poverty, racial discrimination, and the struggle against imperialism than with the Cold War. As a result, the Western powers increasingly disregarded the General Assembly, allowing the new nations of the world to have their say but not to act collectively.

Capitalism and Communism

In July 1944, with Allied victory a foregone conclusion, economic specialists representing over forty countries met at Bretton Woods, a New Hampshire resort, to devise a new international monetary system. The signatories eventually agreed to fix exchange rates while creating an International Monetary Fund (IMF) and a World Bank (formally the International Bank for Reconstruction and Development). The IMF was to use currency reserves from member nations to finance temporary trade deficits, and the **World Bank** was to provide funds for reconstructing Europe and helping needy countries after the war.

The Soviet Union attended the Bretton Woods Conference and signed the agreements, but by 1946, when they went into effect, suspicion between the Soviet Union and the United States and Britain had deepened. While the rest of the world moved to a monetary system that relied for stability on most countries holding reserves of dollars and the United States holding reserves of gold, the Soviet Union established a closed monetary system for itself and the new communist regimes in eastern Europe. In the Western countries, supply and demand determined prices; in the Soviet command economy, government priorities and agencies allocated goods and set prices, irrespective of market forces.

Many leaders from the newly independent states, having won the struggle against imperialism, preferred the Soviet Union's socialist example to the capitalism of their former colonizers. Thus the relative success of economies patterned on Eastern or Western models became an element in the Cold War rivalry. Each side trumpeted economic successes measured by such things as industrial output, changes in per capita income, and productivity gains as evidence of its superiority.

During World War II, the U.S. economy finally escaped the lingering effects of the Great Depression (see Chapter 31). Increased military spending and the draft brought full employment and high wages. The wartime conversion of factories from the production of consumer goods created pent-up demand for those goods.

With peace, the United States enjoyed prosperity and an international competitive advantage because of the massive destruction in Europe.

The economy of western Europe was heavily damaged during World War II, and in many European countries the early postwar years were bleak. With prosperity, the United States was able to support the reconstruction of western Europe. The **Marshall Plan** provided $12.5 billion to friendly European countries between 1948 and 1952. By 1961 more than $20 billion in economic aid had been disbursed. European determination backed up with American dollars spurred recovery. By 1963, a resurgent European economy had doubled 1940 output.

Western European governments generally increased their role in economic management during this period. In Great Britain, the Labour Party government of the 1950s nationalized coal, steel, railroads, and health care. The French government nationalized public utilities, the auto, banking, and insurance industries, and parts of the mining industry. These steps provided large infusions of capital for rebuilding and for acquiring new technologies.

In 1948 European governments also launched a process of economic cooperation and integration with the creation of the Organization of European Economic Cooperation (OEEC). After cooperative policies on coal and steel proved successful, some OEEC countries were ready to begin lowering tariffs to encourage the movement of goods and capital. In 1957 France, West Germany, Italy, the Netherlands, Belgium, and Luxembourg signed a treaty creating the European Economic Community, also known as the Common Market. By the 1970s the Common Market nations had nearly overtaken the United States in industrial production. The economic alliance expanded after 1970, as Great Britain, Denmark, Greece, Ireland, Spain, Portugal, Finland, Sweden, and Austria joined. The enlarged alliance called itself the **European Community (EC).**

Prosperity brought dramatic changes to European society. Average wages increased, unemployment fell, and social welfare benefits were expanded. Governments increased spending on health care, unemployment benefits, old age pensions, public housing, and grants to poor families with children. The combination of economic growth and income redistribution raised living standards and fueled demand for consumer goods. Automobile ownership, for example, grew approximately ninefold between 1950 and 1970.

The Soviet experience provided a dramatic contrast. The rapid development of a powerful Soviet state after 1917 had challenged traditional Western assumptions about economic development and social policy. From the 1920s, the Soviet state relied on bureaucratic agencies and political processes to determine the production, distribution, and price of goods. Housing, medical services, retail shops, factories, the land—even musical compositions and literary works—were viewed as collective property and were therefore regulated and administered by the state.

The economies of the Soviet Union and its eastern European allies were just as devastated at the end of the Second World War as those of western Europe. However, the Soviet command economy had enormous natural resources, a large population, and abundant energy at its disposal. Moreover, Soviet planners had made large investments in technical and scientific education, and the Soviet state had developed heavy industry in the 1930s and during the war years. As a result, recovery was rapid at first. Then, as the postwar period progressed, bureaucratic control of the economy grew less efficient, and industrial might became increasingly measured by the production of consumer goods such as television sets and automobiles rather than tons of coal and steel. In the 1970s the gap with the West widened. The Soviet economy failed to meet domestic demand for clothing, housing, food, automobiles, and consumer electronics. Agricultural inefficiency forced the Soviet Union to rely on food imports.

The socialist nations of eastern Europe were compelled to follow the Soviet economic model, although some national differences appeared. Poland and Hungary, for example, implemented agricultural collectivization more slowly than did Czechoslovakia. Despite the differences, however, economic planners throughout the region coordinated industrialization and production plans with the Soviet Union. Significant growth occurred among the socialist economies, but the inefficiencies and failures that plagued the Soviet economy troubled them as well.

The United States and the Soviet Union competed in providing loans and grants and in supplying arms (at bargain prices) to countries willing to align with them politically. Thus the relative success or failure of capitalism and communism in Europe and the United States was not necessarily the strongest consideration in other parts of the world when the time came to construct new national economies.

Cold War Confrontation in 1959   U.S. vice president Richard M. Nixon and Soviet premier Nikita Khrushchev had a heated exchange of views during Nixon's visit to a Moscow trade fair. Two years earlier, the Soviet Union had launched the world's first space satellite.   (Seymour Raskin/Magnum Photos, Inc.)

West Versus East in Europe and Korea

For Germany, Austria, and Japan, peace brought foreign military occupation and new governments installed and controlled by the occupiers. For the Soviet Union, war's end meant opportunities for workers' movements struggling for power. Military occupation facilitated the communist victories in eastern Europe. The rapid emergence of communist regimes in Poland, Czechoslovakia, Hungary, Bulgaria, Romania, Yugoslavia, and Albania appalled Western leaders.

For the United States, the shift from viewing the Soviet Union as an ally against Germany to seeing it as a worldwide enemy took two years. In the waning days of World War II, the United States had seemed amenable to the Soviet desire for free access to the Bosphorus and Dardanelles straits that, under Turkish control, restricted naval deployments from the Black Sea to the Mediterranean. But in July 1947 the **Truman Doctrine** offered military aid to help both Turkey and Greece resist Soviet military pressure and subversion. (This initiative quickly grew into the Marshall Plan.) In 1951 Greece and Turkey were admitted to NATO. NATO's Soviet counterpart, the **Warsaw Pact,** emerged in 1955 in response to the Western powers' decision to allow West Germany to rearm within limits set by NATO (see Map 33.1).

The much-feared and long-prepared-for third great war in Europe did not occur. The Soviet Union tested Western resolve in 1948–1949 by blockading the areas of Berlin occupied by British, French, and American forces, which were surrounded by Soviet-controlled East Germany. Airlifts of food and fuel defeated the blockade. In 1961 the East German government accentuated Germany's political division by building the Berlin Wall, as much to prevent its citizens from fleeing to the noncommunist western part of the city as to keep westerners from entering East German territory. The West tested the East, in turn, by encouraging a rift between the Soviet Union and Yugoslavia. Western aid and encouragement resulted in Yugoslavia signing a defensive treaty with Greece and Turkey (but not with NATO) and deciding against joining the Warsaw Pact.

Soviet power set clear limits on how far any eastern European country might stray from Soviet domination. In 1956 Soviet troops crushed an anti-Soviet revolt in Hungary. Czechoslovakia suffered Hungary's fate in 1968. The West, a passive onlooker, had no recourse but to acknowledge that the Soviet Union had the right to intervene in the domestic affairs of any Soviet-bloc nation whenever it wished.

A more explosive crisis erupted in Korea, where the Second World War had left Soviet troops in control north of the thirty-eighth parallel and American troops in control to the south. When no agreement could be reached on holding countrywide elections, communist North Korea and noncommunist South Korea became independent states in 1948. Two years later, North Korea invaded South Korea. The United Nations Security Council, in the absence of the Soviet delegation, voted to condemn the invasion and called on members of the United Nations to come to the defense of South Korea. The ensuing **Korean War** lasted until 1953. The United States was the primary ally of South Korea. The People's Republic of China supported North Korea.

The conflict in Korea remained limited to the Korean peninsula because the United States feared that launching attacks into China might prompt China's ally, the Soviet Union, to retaliate and bring about the dreaded third world war. Americans and South Koreans advanced from a toehold in the south to the North Korean–Chinese border. Then, after China sent troops across the border, the North Koreans and the Chinese pushed the Americans and South Koreans back, and the fighting settled into a static war in the mountains along the thirty-eighth parallel. The two sides eventually agreed to a truce along that line; but the ceasefire lines remained fortified, no peace treaty was concluded, and the possibility of renewed warfare between the two Koreas continued well past the end of the Cold War.

Japan benefited from the Korean War in an unexpected way. Massive purchases of supplies by the United States and spending by American servicemen on leave provided a financial stimulus to the Japanese economy similar to the stimulus that Europe received from the Marshall Plan.

U.S. Defeat in Vietnam

A shooting war also developed in Vietnam. In 1954 United States president Dwight D. Eisenhower (1953–1961) and his foreign policy advisers debated long and hard about whether to aid France in its failing effort to sustain colonial rule in Vietnam. They decided against doing so, perceiving that the days of the European colonial empires were numbered. After winning independence, however, communist North Vietnam supported a communist guerrilla movement—the Viet Cong—against the noncommunist government of South Vietnam. At issue was the ideological and economic orientation of an independent Vietnam.

When John F. Kennedy became president (1961–1963), he and his advisers decided to support the South Vietnamese government of President Ngo Dinh Diem°.

Diem (dee-YEM)

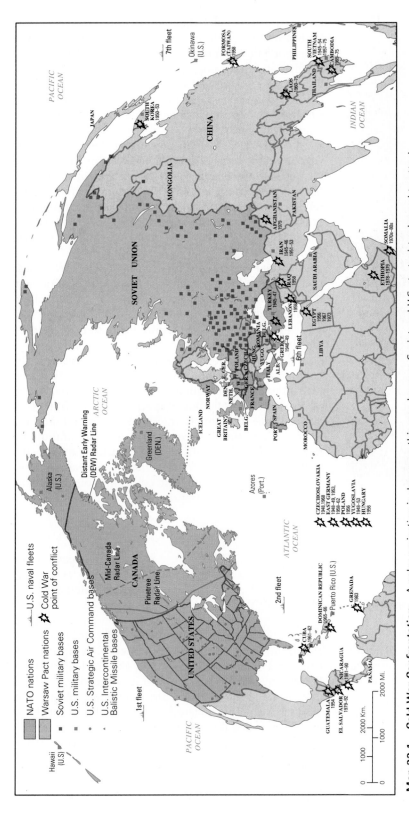

Map 33.1   Cold War Confrontation   A polar projection is shown on this map because Soviet and U.S. strategists planned to attack one another by missile in the polar region, hence the Canadian–American radar lines. Military installations along the southern border of the Soviet Union were directed primarily at China.

The Vietnamese People at War   American and South Vietnamese troops burned many villages to deprive the enemy of civilian refuges. This policy undermined support for the South Vietnamese government in the countryside.   (Dana Stone/ Black Star)

They realized that the Diem government was corrupt and unpopular, but they feared that a communist victory would encourage communist movements throughout Southeast Asia and alter the Cold War balance of power. Kennedy steadily increased the number of American military advisers from 685 to almost 16,000 while secretly encouraging the overthrow and execution of Diem in hopes of seeing a more popular and honest government come to power.

Lyndon Johnson, who became president (1963–1969) after Kennedy was assassinated, gained support from Congress for unlimited expansion of U.S. military deployment after an apparent North Vietnamese attack on two U.S. destroyers in the Gulf of Tonkin. By the end of 1966, 365,000 U.S. troops were engaged in the **Vietnam War.** Nothing the Americans tried, however, succeeded in stopping the Viet Cong guerrillas and their North Vietnamese allies. Diem's successors turned out to be just as corrupt and unpopular as he was, and the heroic nationalist image of North Vietnam's leader Ho Chi Minh° evoked strong sympathies among many South Vietnamese.

In 1973 a treaty between North Vietnam and the United States ended U.S. involvement in the war and promised future elections. Two years later, in violation of the treaty, Viet Cong and North Vietnamese troops overran the South Vietnamese army and captured the southern capital of Saigon, renaming it Ho Chi Minh City. The two parts of Vietnam were reunited in a single state ruled from the north.

The war was bloody and traumatic. The Vietnamese had over a million casualties. The deaths of fifty-eight thousand Americans ensured that the United States would not easily be drawn into another shooting war. The war effort gave rise to serious economic problems in the United States because President Johnson refused to curtail his ambitious program of welfare measures. The conflict also stirred an antiwar movement that was instrumental in convincing the U.S. government that many Americans did not support the war. Nevertheless, at the same time, many members of the military and their civilian supporters were angry about limitations on the conduct of operations. The restrictions were designed to prevent China from entering the war and possibly touching off a nuclear confrontation, but many people saw them as depriving the armed forces of a chance for victory.

The Race for Nuclear Supremacy

Just as fear of nuclear warfare affected strategic decisions in the Korean and Vietnam Wars, the existence of weapons of mass destruction affected all aspects of Cold War confrontation. The devastation of Hiroshima and Nagasaki with atomic weapons (see Chapter 31) had ushered in a new era. Nuclear weapons fed into a logic of total war that was already reaching a peak in Nazi genocide and terror bombing and in massive Allied air raids on large cities. After the Soviet Union exploded its first nuclear device in 1949, fears of a worldwide holocaust grew and then became even greater

Ho Chi Minh (hoe chee min)

when the United States exploded a far more powerful weapon, the hydrogen bomb, in 1952 and the Soviet Union followed suit less than a year later. Fear of the theft of nuclear secrets by Soviet spies fostered a sense of paranoia in the United States. The conviction that the nuclear superpowers were willing to use their terrible weapons if their vital interests were threatened spread despair around the world.

In 1954 President Eisenhower warned Soviet leaders against attacking western Europe. In response to such an attack, he said, the United States would reduce the Soviet Union to "a smoking, radiating ruin at the end of two hours." A few years later, the Soviet leader Nikita Khrushchev° offered an equally stark promise: "We will bury you." His reference was to economic competition, but the image produced in Americans was of literal burial. Rhetoric aside, both men—and their successors—had the capacity to deliver on nuclear threats, and everyone in the world knew that all-out war with nuclear weapons would produce the greatest global devastation in human history.

Everyone's worst fears seemed about to be realized in 1962 when the Soviet Union deployed nuclear-tipped missiles in Cuba in response to the U.S. installation of similar missiles in Turkey. The world held its breath. Confronted by unyielding diplomatic pressure and military threats from President Kennedy, Khrushchev backed down and pulled the missiles from Cuba. Subsequently the United States removed its missiles from Turkey. As frightening as the **Cuban missile crisis** was, the fact that the superpower leaders accepted tactical defeat rather than launch an attack gave reason for hope that nuclear weapons might be contained.

The number, means of delivery, and destructive force of nuclear weapons increased enormously. The bomb dropped on Hiroshima, equal in strength to 12,500 tons of TNT, had destroyed an entire city. By the 1960s, explosive yields were measured in megatons (millions of tons of TNT), and it became possible to load a single missile with several weapons of this scale, each of which could be targeted to a different site. When these missiles were placed on submarines, a major component of U.S. nuclear forces, defending against them seemed impossible.

Arms limitation also saw progress. In 1963, Great Britain, the United States, and the Soviet Union agreed to ban the testing of nuclear weapons in the atmosphere, in space, and under water, thus reducing the environmental danger of radioactive fallout. In 1968, the

United States and the Soviet Union together proposed a world treaty against further proliferation of nuclear weapons. It was signed by 137 countries. Not until 1972, however, did the two superpowers truly recognize the futility of squandering their wealth on ever-larger missile forces. They began the arduous and extremely slow process of negotiating weapons limits, a process made even slower by the vested interests of military officers and arms industries in each country, what President Eisenhower had called the "military-industrial complex."

In Europe, the Soviet-American arms race outran the economic ability of atomic powers France and Britain to keep pace. Instead, the European states sought to relax tensions. Between 1972 and 1975, the Conference on Security and Cooperation in Europe (CSCE) brought delegates from thirty-seven European states, the United States, and Canada to Helsinki. The goal of the Soviet Union was to gain European acceptance of the political boundaries of the Warsaw Pact nations. The Helsinki Final Act—commonly known as the **Helsinki Accords**—affirmed that no boundaries should be changed by military force. It also contained formal (but nonbinding) declarations calling for economic, social, and governmental contacts across the iron curtain, and for cooperation in humanitarian fields, a provision that paved the way for dialogue about human rights.

Space exploration was another offshoot of the nuclear arms race. The contest to build larger and more accurate missiles for delivery of warheads prompted the superpowers to prove their skills in rocketry by launching space satellites. The Soviet Union placed a small Sputnik satellite into orbit around the earth in October 1957. The United States responded with its own satellite three months later. The space race was on, a contest in which accomplishments in space were understood to signify equivalent achievements in the military sphere. Sputnik administered a deep shock to American pride and confidence, but in 1969 two Americans, Neil A. Armstrong and Edwin E. "Buzz" Aldrin, became the first humans to walk on the moon.

Despite rhetorical Cold War saber-rattling by Soviet and American leaders, the threat of nuclear war forced a measure of restraint on the superpower adversaries. Because fighting each other directly would have risked escalation to the level of nuclear exchange, they carefully avoided crises that might provoke such confrontations. Even when arming third parties to do their fighting by proxy, they set limits on how far such fighting could go. Some of these proxy combatants, however, understood the limitations of the superpowers well enough to manipulate them for their own purposes.

Khrushchev (KROOSH-chef)

Map 33.2   Decolonization, 1947–1990   Notice that independence came a decade or so earlier in South and Southeast Asia than in Africa. Numerous countries that gained independence after World War II in the Caribbean, in South and Central America, and in the Pacific are not shown.

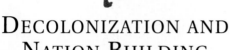

DECOLONIZATION AND NATION BUILDING

Whereas the losing countries in World War I—Germany, Austria-Hungary, and the Ottoman Empire—were stripped of colonies and torn apart to be reborn as new nations in the Balkans and the Middle East, it was primarily countries on the winning side in World War II—Great Britain, France, the Netherlands, Belgium—that ended up losing their colonies (see Map 33.2). However, this time decolonization did not come about through a series of war-ending treaties or through the mechanism of a League of Nations. Instead, each colony raised its demand for freedom and recognition, sometimes making that demand at the point of a bayonet. Although each country followed its own road to independence, all of the countries gaining independence shared feelings of excitement and rebirth.

Circumstances differed profoundly from place to place. In some Asian countries, where colonial rule was of long standing, newly independent states found themselves in possession of viable industries, communications networks, and education systems. In other countries, notably in Africa, decolonization gave birth to nations facing dire economic problems and internal disunity based on language or ethnicity. In Latin America, where political independence already had been achieved, the quest was for freedom from foreign economic domination, particularly by the United States.

Despite their differences, a sense of kinship arose among the new and old nations of Latin America, Africa, and Asia. As the North Americans, Europeans, and Chinese settled into the exhausting deadlock of the Cold War, visions of independence and national growth captivated the rest of the world.

New Nations in South and Southeast Asia

After partition in 1947, the independent states of India and Pakistan were strikingly dissimilar. Muslim Pakistan defined itself according to religion and quickly fell under the control of military leaders. India, a secular republic led by Prime Minister Jawaharlal Nehru, was much larger and inherited most of the considerable industrial and educational resources the British had developed, along with the larger share of trained civil servants and military officers. Ninety percent of its population was Hindu, most of the rest Muslim.

Adding to the tensions of independence (see Chapter 32) was the decision of the Hindu ruler of the northwestern state known as Jammu and Kashmir to join India without consulting his overwhelmingly Muslim subjects. War between India and Pakistan over Kashmir broke out in 1947 and ended with an uneasy truce, only to resume briefly in 1965. Though Kashmir remained a flashpoint of patriotic feeling, the two countries managed to avoid further warfare.

Despite recurrent predictions that multilingual India might break up into a number of linguistically homogeneous states, most Indians recognized that unity benefited everyone; and the country pursued a generally democratic and socialist line of development. Pakistan, in contrast, did break up. In 1971 its Bengali-speaking eastern section seceded to become the independent country of Bangladesh. Their shared political heritage notwithstanding, these South Asian countries grew steadily apart after independence, following markedly different economic, political, religious, and social paths.

As the Japanese had supported anti-British Indian nationalists, so they encouraged the dreams of some anticolonialists in the countries they had occupied in Southeast Asia. Other nationalists, particularly those belonging to communist groups, saw the Japanese as an imperialist enemy; and the harsh character of Japanese occupation eventually alienated the mass of the population in the occupied countries. Nevertheless, the defeats the Japanese inflicted on British, French, and Dutch colonial armies set an example of an Asian people standing up to European colonizers.

In the Dutch East Indies, a man named simply Sukarno (1901–1970) cooperated with the Japanese in hopes that the Dutch, who had dominated the region economically since the seventeenth century, would never return. After a military confrontation, Dutch withdrawal was finally negotiated in 1949, and Sukarno went on to become the dictator of his resource-rich but underdeveloped island nation. He ruled until 1965, when a military coup ousted him and brutally eliminated Indonesia's powerful communist party.

Elsewhere in the region, nationalist movements won independence as well. Britain granted independence to Burma (now Myanmar°) in 1948 and established the Malay Federation that same year. (Singapore, once a member of the federation, became an independent city-state itself in 1965.) In 1946 the United States kept its promise of postwar independence for the Philippine Islands but retained close economic ties and leases on military bases.

Myanmar (myahn-MAH)

In all these cases, communist insurgents plagued the departing colonial powers and the newly formed governments. The most important postwar communist movement arose in the part of Southeast Asia known as French Indochina. There Ho Chi Minh (1890–1969), who had spent several years in France during World War I, played the pivotal role. In France, Ho had joined the communist party. After training in Moscow, he returned to Vietnam to found the Indochina Communist Party in 1930. He and his supporters took refuge in China during World War II.

At war's end, the new French government was determined to keep its prewar colonial possessions. Ho Chi Minh's nationalist coalition, then called the Viet Minh, fought the French with help from the People's Republic of China. After a brutal struggle, the French stronghold of Dienbienphu° fell in 1954, marking the doom of France's colonial enterprise. Ho's Viet Minh government took over in the north, and a noncommunist nationalist government ruled in the south. Fighting between North and South Vietnam eventually became a major Cold War conflict, as we have seen.

The Struggle for Independence in Africa

The postwar French government was as determined to hold on to Algeria as it was to keep Vietnam. Since invading the country in 1830, France had followed policies very different from those of the British in India. French settlement had been strongly encouraged, and Algeria had been declared an actual part of France rather than a colony. By the mid-1950s, 10 percent of the Algerian population was French, and Algeria's economy was strongly oriented toward France. Though Islam, the religion of 90 percent, prohibited the drinking of alcohol, Algerian vineyards produced immense quantities of wine for French tables. Algerian oil and gas fields were the mainstay of the French petroleum industry.

The revolt in 1954 was pursued with great brutality by both sides. The Algerian revolutionary organization, the Front de Libération National (FLN), was supported by Egypt and other Arab countries acting on the principle that all Arab peoples should be able to choose their own governments. French colonists, however, considered the country rightfully theirs and swore to fight to the bitter end. When Algeria finally won independence in 1962, a flood of angry colonists returned to France. Their departure undermined the Algerian economy because very few Arabs had received technical training or acquired management experience. Despite bitter feel-

Dienbienphu (dee-yen-bee-yen-FOO)

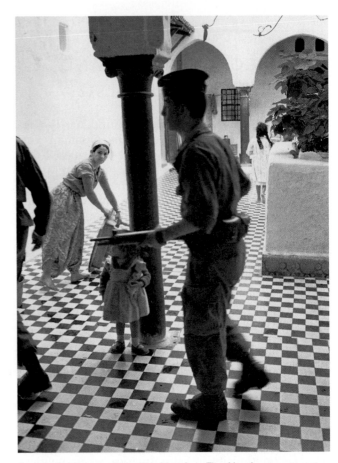

French Soldiers on Patrol in Algeria The Algerian war was one of the most savage struggles for independence in the era of decolonization. The French held out a more secular, Western-style view of life but did not hesitate to intrude into homes and residential areas in search of their enemies. At independence in 1961, most Algerian leaders spoke French more readily than Arabic. (Marc Riboud/Magnum Photos, Inc.)

ings left by the war, Algeria retained close and seemingly indissoluble economic ties to France, and Algerians increasingly fled unemployment at home by emigrating to France and taking low-level jobs.

None of the several wars for independence in sub-Saharan Africa matched the Algerian struggle in scale. But even without war, most of the new states suffered from many problems. Boundaries that the imperial powers had established in the nineteenth century did not coincide with natural geographic or ethnic divisions. Neglect of education under colonial rule left too few educated Africans to run government ministries and to staff newly established schools without European assistance. In some places, overdependence on export crops such as cacao or peanuts held economies hostage to swings in international prices. States lacked national road and railroad networks. And population growth, resulting in part from colonial improvements in medical care and public health, foreshadowed worsening poverty and unemployment as well as population pressures that would jeopardize wildlife by expanding the amount of land used for agriculture. In the 1950s and 1960s, however, enthusiasm for liberation overcame worries about these material problems.

Some of the politicians who led the nationalist movements had devoted their lives to ridding their homelands of foreign occupation. An example is Kwame Nkrumah° (1909–1972), who in 1957 became prime minister of Ghana (formerly the Gold Coast), the first British colony in Africa to achieve independence. Only a few hundred Ghanaian children of Nkrumah's generation had graduated each year from the seven-year elementary schools, and he was one of only a handful who made it through teacher training college. After graduation he spent a decade reading philosophy and theology in the United States and absorbing ideas about black pride and independence then being propounded by W. E. B. Du Bois and Marcus Garvey.

After a brief stay in Britain—where he joined Kenyan nationalist Jomo Kenyatta to found an organization devoted to African freedom—Nkrumah returned in 1947 to the Gold Coast to work for independence. The time was right. Great Britain was exhausted by war and unwilling to squander money and blood to hold restive colonies that were not sources of valuable resources. Independent Ghana thus came into being without war or protracted bloodshed. Nkrumah became president in 1960. He turned out to be more effective internationally as a spokesman for colonized peoples than he was at home as an administrator. In 1966 a group of army officers ousted him.

Jomo Kenyatta (ca. 1894–1978) traveled a more difficult road in Kenya, where a substantial number of European coffee planters strenghtened Britain's desire to retain control. A movement known as the Mau Mau, formed mostly by the Kikuyu° people, became active in 1952. As violence between settlers and Mau Mau fighters escalated, British troops hunted down the Mau Mau leaders and resettled the Kikuyu. The British charged Kenyatta with being a Mau Mau leader and held him in prison and then in internal exile for eight years during a declared state of emergency. They released him in 1961, and negotiations with the British to write a constitution for an independent Kenya followed. In 1964 Kenyatta was elected the first president of the Republic of Kenya.

He proved to be an effective, though autocratic, ruler. Kenya benefited from greater stability and prosperity than Ghana.

In contrast with the African nationalists in the British colonies and their counterparts in Algeria, African leaders in the sub-Saharan French colonies were reluctant to call for independence. They visualized change in terms of promises made in 1944 by the Free French movement of General Charles de Gaulle at a conference in Brazzaville, in French Equatorial Africa. Acknowledging the value of his African territorial base, his many African troops, and the food supplied by African farmers, de Gaulle had promised the colonial leaders who attended the conference—none of them African—more democratic government and broader suffrage, though not representation in the French National Assembly. He also had promised to abolish forced labor and imprisonment of Africans without charge; to expand education, in French only, down to the village level; to improve health services; and to open more administrative positions, though not the top ones, to Africans. The word *independence* was never mentioned at Brazzaville, but the politics of postwar colonial self-government led in that direction.

Most of the new group of African politicians seeking election in the colonies of French West Africa were trained as civil servants. Because of the French policy of job rotation, they had typically served in a number of different colonies and thus had a broad outlook. They realized that some colonies—such as Ivory Coast with its coffee and cacao exports, fishing, and hardwood forests—had good economic prospects and others, such as landlocked, desert Niger, did not. Furthermore, they recognized the importance of French public investment in the region—a billion dollars between 1947 and 1956—and their own dependence on civil service salaries, which in places totaled 60 percent of government expenditures.

As the Malagasy politician Philibert Tsirinana° said at a press conference in 1958: "When I let my heart talk, I am a partisan of total and immediate independence [for Madagascar]; when I make my reason speak, I realize that it is impossible." Charles de Gaulle, returning to power in France in 1958, at the height of the Algerian war, spoke to the issue of rationality when he said: "One cannot conceive of both an independent territory and a France which continues to aid it."

Ultimately, however, the heart prevailed everywhere. Guinea, under the dynamic leadership of Sékou Touré°, led the way in 1958. By the time Nigeria, the most

---

Kwame Nkrumah (KWAH-mee nn-KROO-muh)
Kikuyu (kih-KOO-you)

Tsirinana (tsee-REE-nah-nah)
Sékou Touré (SAY-koo too-RAY)

populous West African state, achieved independence from Great Britain in 1960, the leaders of the former French colonies of Ivory Coast (now Côte d'Ivoire), Niger, Dahomey (now Benin), Senegal, and Upper Volta (now Burkina Faso) could attend the celebrations as independent heads of state.

Decolonization in Africa presented innumerable scenes of people of European descent struggling with indigenous Africans to retain personal privileges, control of resources, and political power. Race conflict became particularly severe in the temperate southern part of the continent. African guerrillas struggled against Portuguese rule in Angola and Mozambique, prompting the Portuguese army to revolt against the home government in 1974. The new Portuguese government granted independence to its African colonies the following year. In 1980, after a ten-year fight, European settlers in the British colony of Southern Rhodesia acceded to majority African rule. The new government changed the country's name, which had honored the memory of the British imperialist Cecil Rhodes, to Zimbabwe, the name of a great stone city built by indigenous Africans long before the arrival of European settlers. This left only South Africa and neighboring Southwest Africa in the hands of ruling European minorities. The change had been swift; Africa had entered the postwar period almost entirely under European control.

After World War II, a succession of South African governments had constructed a state and society based on a policy of racial separation, or *apartheid*°. South Asians and people of mixed parentage, approximately 12 percent of the population, were classified as "nonwhite" along with the 74 percent of the population who were indigenous Africans. These groups were subjected to strict limitations on place of residence, right to travel, and access to jobs and public facilities. "Homelands" somewhat similar to Amerindian reservations in the United States were created in comparatively undesirable parts of the country. The largest and most productive tracts of land were held by the 14 percent of the population descended from Dutch and English settlers.

Rising in opposition was the African National Congress (ANC), formed in 1912. After police fired on demonstrators in the African town of Sharpeville in 1960, a lawyer named Nelson Mandela (b. 1918) organized guerrilla resistance by the ANC. Mandela was sentenced to life in prison in 1964 (see Chapter 35 Society and Culture: Nelson Mandela). The ANC continued to lead a bloody and prolonged struggle against apartheid.

apartheid (uh-PAHRT-ate)

The Quest for Economic Freedom in Latin America

In Latin America, independence from European rule was achieved earlier, but American and European economic domination increased (see Chapters 29 and 32). Chile's copper, Cuba's sugar, Colombia's coffee, and Guatemala's bananas were all controlled from abroad. The largest resort hotel in Havana was owned by American mobster Meyer Lansky. The communications networks of several countries were in the hands of ITT (International Telephone and Telegraph Company), a U.S. corporation.

In Mexico the Institutional Revolutionary Party, or PRI (the abbreviation of its name in Spanish), controlled the government in the postwar years. Despite PRI rhetoric about revolutionary independence and economic development, the yawning gulf between rich and poor, urban and rural, persisted. According to one estimate from the mid-1960s, not more than 300 foreign and 800 Mexican companies dominated the country, and some 2,000 families made up the industrial-financial elite. At the other end of the economic scale were peasants and the 14 percent of the population classified as Indian.

While Mexico's problems derived only partly from foreign influence and investment, Guatemala's situation was more common. Jacobo Arbenz Guzmán, elected in 1951, was typical of Latin American leaders who tried to confront the power of foreign interests. His expropriation of large estates angered large landowners, the United Fruit Company in particular. This U.S. corporation not only dominated banana exports but held vast tracts of land in reserve for possible future use. Reacting to reports that Arbenz was becoming friendly toward communism, the United States Central Intelligence Agency (CIA), in one of its first major overseas operations, prompted a takeover by the Guatemalan military in 1954. CIA intervention removed Arbenz from the scene; it also condemned Guatemala to decades of governmental instability and growing violence between leftist and rightist elements in society.

In Cuba, economic domination by the United States prior to 1960 was overwhelming. U.S. companies owned 40 percent of raw sugar production, 23 percent of nonsugar industry, 90 percent of telephone and electrical services, and 50 percent of public service railways. Many of Cuba's American-owned industries depended on factories in the United States for essential supplies. The needs of the U.S. economy largely determined Cuban foreign trade. A 1934 treaty granted Cuban sugar preferential treatment in the American market in return for American manufacturers gaining access to the Cuban market. As a consequence, by 1956 sugar accounted for

80 percent of Cuba's exports and 25 percent of Cuba's national income. But demand in the United States dictated that only 39 percent of the land owned by the sugar companies be in production. Similarly, immense deposits of nickel in Cuba went untapped because the U.S. government, which owned them, considered them only as a reserve.

Profits went north to the United States or to a small class of wealthy Cubans, many of them, like the owners of the Bacardi rum company, of foreign origin. Between 1951 and 1958 Cuba's economic growth rate was 1.4 percent per year, less than the rate of population increase; and most of the year a quarter of the working population was unemployed. Cuba's ruler during that period, Fulgencio Batista, became a symbol of corruption, repression, and foreign economic domination.

In 1959, a popular rebellion forced Batista to flee the country. Fidel Castro, the lawyer leader of the rebels, his brother Raoul Castro, and Ernesto "Che" Guevara°, who was the main theorist of communist revolution in Latin America, created a new regime. Fidel Castro (b. 1927) gave a number of speeches in the United States in the wake of his victory. Large crowds cheered him as a heroic champion against dictatorship and American economic imperialism. Within a year, his government redistributed land, lowered urban rents, and raised wages, effectively transferring 15 percent of the national income from rich to poor. Within twenty-two months the Castro government seized almost all U.S. property in Cuba and most Cuban corporations. This action resulted in a blockade by the United States, the flight of middle-class and technically trained Cubans, a drop in foreign investment, and the beginning of chronic food shortages.

Little evidence supports the view that Castro undertook his revolution to install a communist government. But at that time the East-West rivalry of the Cold War was increasingly influencing international politics, and Castro soon turned to the Soviet Union for economic aid. In doing so, he unwittingly committed his nation to economic stagnation and to dependence on a foreign power as damaging as the previous relationship with the United States had been.

In April 1961 some fifteen hundred Cuban exiles, whom the CIA had trained for a year in Guatemala, landed at the Bay of Pigs in an effort to overthrow Castro. The Cuban army defeated the attempted invasion in a matter of days, partly because the new U.S. president, John F. Kennedy, decided not to provide all the air support that the plan, which had originated in the Eisen-

Che Guevara (chay guh-VAHR-uh)

Cuban Poster of Charismatic Leader Ernesto 'Che' Guevara A leading theorist of communist revolution in Latin America, Argentine-born Guevara was in Guatemala at the time of the CIA-sponsored coup against Jacobo Arbenz in 1954. He later met and had a strong influence on Fidel Castro. He was killed in 1967 while leading an insurgency in Bolivia.   (Christopher Morris/Black Star)

hower administration, called for. The failure of the Bay of Pigs invasion tarnished the reputation of the United States and the CIA and provoked Castro into declaring that he and his revolution were and always had been Marxist-Leninist.

Challenges of Nation Building

Decolonization occurred on a vast scale. Fifty-one nations signed the United Nations Charter in the closing months of 1945. During the United Nations' first decade, twenty-five new members joined, a third of them upon gaining independence. During the next decade, forty-six more new members were admitted, nearly all of them former colonial territories.

Each of these nations had to organize and institute some form of government. Comparatively few were able to do so without experiencing coups, rewritten constitutions, or regional rebellions. Leaders did not always agree on the form independence should take. In the absence of established constitutional traditions, individual leaders frequently tried to impose their own visions by force. Most of the new nations, while trying to establish political stability, also faced severe economic challenges, including foreign ownership and operation of key resources and the need to build infrastructure. Overdependence on world demand for raw materials and on imported manufactured goods persisted in many places long after independence.

Because the achievement of political and economic goals called for educated and skilled personnel, education was another common concern in the newly emerging nations. Addressing that concern required more than building and staffing schools. In some countries, leaders had to decide which language to teach and how to inculcate a sense of national unity in students from different— and sometimes historically antagonistic—ethnic, religious, and linguistic groups. Another problem was how to provide satisfying jobs for new graduates, many of whom had high expectations because of their education.

Only rarely were the new nations able to surmount these hurdles. Even the most successful economically and educationally, such as South Korea, suffered from tendencies toward authoritarian rule. Similarly, Costa Rica, a country with a remarkably stable parliamentary regime from 1949 onward and a literacy rate of 90 percent, remained heavily dependent on world prices for agricultural commodities and on importation of manufactured goods.

Beyond a Bipolar World

Although no one doubted the dominating role of the East-West superpower rivalry in world affairs, the newly independent states had concerns that were primarily domestic and regional. The challenge they faced was to find a way to pursue their ends within the bipolar structure of the Cold War—and possibly to take advantage of the East-West rivalry. Where nationalist forces sought to assert political or economic independence, Cold War antagonists provided arms and political support even when the nationalist goals were quite different from those of the superpowers. For other nations, the ruinously expensive superpower arms race opened opportunities to expand their industries and export capabilities. In short, the superpowers dominated the world but did not control it. And as time progressed, they dominated it less and less.

The Third World

As one of the most successful leaders of the decolonization movement, Indonesia's President Sukarno was an appropriate figure to host a meeting in 1955 of twenty-nine African and Asian countries at Bandung, Indonesia. The conferees proclaimed solidarity among all peoples fighting against colonial rule. The Bandung Conference marked the beginning of an effort by the many new, poor, mostly non-European nations emerging from colonialism to gain more weight in world affairs by banding together. The terms **nonaligned nations** and **Third World,** which became commonplace in the following years, signaled these countries' collective stance toward the rival sides in the Cold War. If the West, led by the United States, and the East, led by the Soviet Union, represented two worlds locked in mortal struggle, the Third World consisted of everyone else.

Leaders of the so-called Third World countries preferred the label *nonaligned,* which signified freedom from membership on either side. However, many leaders in the West noted that the Soviet Union supported national liberation movements and that the nonaligned movement included communist countries such as China and Yugoslavia. As a result, they decided not to take the term *nonaligned* seriously. In a polarized world, they saw Sukarno, Nehru, Nkrumah, and Egypt's Gamal Abd al-Nasir° as stalking horses for a communist takeover of the world. This may also have been the view of some Soviet leaders, since the Soviet Union was quick to offer some of these countries military and financial aid.

For the movement's leaders, however, nonalignment was primarily a means to extract money and support from one or both superpowers. By flirting with the Soviet Union or its ally the People's Republic of China, a country could get cheap or free weapons and training and barter agreements that offered an alternative to selling agricultural or mineral products on Western-dominated world markets. The same flirtation might also prompt the United States and its allies to proffer grants and loans, cheap or free surplus grain, and investment in industry and infrastructure.

A skillfully played balancing game allowed nonaligned countries to play the two sides against each other and gain from both sides in the process. Egypt under Nasir, who had led a military coup against the Egyptian monarchy in 1952, and, after 1970, under Nasir's successor Anwar al-Sadat°, played the game well. The United States offered to build a dam at Aswan°, on the Nile River, to increase Egypt's electrical generating and irrigation capacity. When Egypt turned to the Soviet

Gamal Abd al-Nasir (gah-MAHL AHB-d al–NAH-suhr)
al-Sadat (al–seh-DAT)   **Aswan** (AS-wahn)

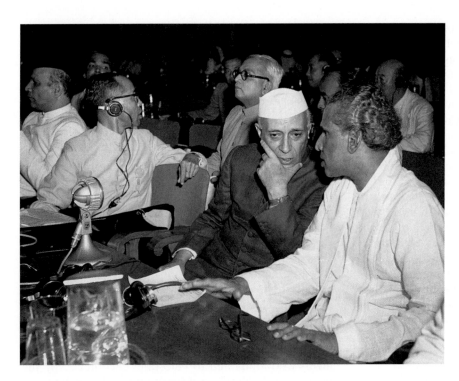

Bandung Conference, 1955   India's Jawaharlal Nehru (reading a document) was a central figure at this conference held in Indonesia to promote solidarity among nonaligned developing nations. The nonalignment movement failed to achieve the influence that Nehru, Egypt's Nasir, and Indonesia's Sukarno sought.   (Wide World Photos)

Union for arms, the United States reneged on the dam project in 1956. The Soviet Union then picked it up and in the 1960s brought it to conclusion. In 1956, Israel, Great Britain, and France conspired to invade Egypt. Their objective was to overthrow Nasir, regain the Suez Canal (he had recently nationalized it), and secure Israel from any Egyptian threat. The invasion succeeded militarily, but the United States and the Soviet Union both pressured the invaders to withdraw, thus saving Nasir's government. In 1972, Sadat evicted his Soviet military advisers but a year later used his Soviet weapons to attack Israel. After he lost that war, he announced his faith in the power of the United States to solve Egypt's political and economic problems.

Numerous other countries adopted similar balancing strategies. In each case, local leaders were trying to develop their nation's economy and assert or preserve their nation's interests. Manipulating the superpowers was simply a means toward those ends and implied very little about true ideological orientation.

Japan and China

No countries took better advantage of the opportunities presented by the superpowers' preoccupation than did Japan and China. Japan signed a peace treaty with most of its former enemies in 1951 and regained independence from American occupation the following year. Renouncing militarism and its imperialist past (see Chapter 28), Japan remained on the sidelines throughout the Korean War. Its new constitution, written under American supervision in 1946, allowed only a limited self-defense force, banned the deployment of Japanese troops abroad, and gave the vote to women.

The Japanese turned their talents and energies to rebuilding their industries and engaging in world commerce. Peace treaties with countries in Southeast Asia specified reparations payable in the form of goods and services, thus reintroducing Japan to that region as a force for economic development rather than as a military occupier. Nevertheless, bitterness over the oppression of the wartime occupying forces remained strong, and Japan had to move slowly in developing new regional markets for its manufactured goods. The Cold War isolated Japan and excluded it from most world political issues. It thus provided an exceptionally favorable environment for Japan to develop its economic strength.

Three industries that took advantage of government aid and the newest technologies paved the way for Japan's emergence as an economic superpower after 1975. Electricity was in short supply in 1950; Tokyo itself suffered evening power outages. Projects producing 60 million kilowatts of electricity were completed between 1951 and 1970, almost a third through dams on Japan's many rivers. Between 1960 and 1970 steel production more than quadrupled, reaching 15.7 percent of the total capacity of countries outside the Soviet bloc. The ship-building industry produced six times as much tonnage in 1970 as in 1960, almost half of the new tonnage produced outside the Soviet bloc.

While Japan benefited from being outside the Cold War, China was deeply involved in Cold War politics. When Mao Zedong° and the communists defeated the nationalists in 1949 and established the People's Republic of China (PRC), their main ally and source of arms was the Soviet Union. By 1956, however, the PRC and the Soviet Union were beginning to diverge politically, partly in reaction to the Soviet rejection of Stalinism and partly because of China's reluctance to be cast forever in the role of student. Mao had his own notions of communism, focusing strongly on the peasantry, whom the Soviets ignored in favor of the industrial working class.

Mao's Great Leap Forward in 1958 was supposed to vault China into the ranks of world industrial powers by maximizing the use of labor in small-scale, village-level industries. The policy failed but demonstrated Mao's willingness to carry out massive economic and social projects of his own devising.

In 1966 Mao instituted another radical nationwide program, the **Cultural Revolution.** He ordered the mass mobilization of Chinese youth into Red Guard units. His goal was to kindle revolutionary fervor in a new generation. He also wished to ward off the stagnation and bureaucratization he saw in the Soviet Union. Red Guard units criticized and purged teachers, party officials, and intellectuals for "bourgeois values," but they themselves suffered from factionalism. Internal party conflict continued until 1971, when Mao admitted that attacks on individuals had gotten out of hand. Meanwhile, small-scale industrialization resulted in record levels of agricultural and industrial production. The last years of the Cultural Revolution were dominated by radicals led by Mao's wife Jiang Qing°, who focused on restrictions on artistic and intellectual activity.

In the meantime, the rift between the PRC and the Soviet Union had opened so wide that United States President Richard Nixon (1969–1974), by reputation a staunch anticommunist, put out secret diplomatic feelers to revive relations with China. In 1971 the United States dropped objections to the PRC joining the United Nations and occupying China's permanent seat on the Security Council. This decision necessitated the expulsion from the United Nations of the Chinese nationalist government based on the island of Taiwan, which had persistently claimed to be the only legal Chinese authority. The following year, Nixon visited Beijing, making dramatically clear the new cooperation between the People's Republic of China and the United States.

The Middle East

The superpowers could not control all dangerous international disputes. Independence had come gradually to the Arab countries of the Middle East. Britain granted Syria and Lebanon independence after World War II. Other Arab countries—Iraq, Egypt, Jordan—enjoyed nominal independence during the interwar period but remained under indirect British control until the 1950s, when military coups overthrew King Faruq° of Egypt in 1952 and King Faysal° II of Iraq in 1958. King Husayn° of Jordan dismissed his British military commander in 1956 in response to the Suez crisis, but his poor desert country remained dependent on British, and later American, financial aid.

Overshadowing all Arab politics, however, was the struggle with Israel. British policy on Palestine between the wars oscillated between sentiment favoring Zionist Jews—who emigrated to Palestine, encouraged by the Balfour Declaration—and sentiment for the indigenous Palestinian Arabs, who felt themselves being pushed aside and suspected that the Zionists were aiming at an independent state. As more and more Jews sought a safe haven from persecution by the Nazis, Arabs felt more and more threatened by mass immigration. The Arabs unleashed a guerrilla uprising against the British in 1936, and Jewish groups turned to militant tactics a few years later. Occasionally, Arabs and Jews confronted each other in riots or killings, making it clear that peaceful coexistence in Palestine would be difficult or impossible to achieve.

After the war, under intense pressure to resettle European Jewish refugees, Britain conceded that it saw no way of resolving the dilemma and turned the Palestine problem over to the United Nations. In November 1947, the General Assembly voted in favor of partitioning Palestine into two states, one Jewish and one Arab. The Jewish community made plans to declare independence while the Palestinians, who felt the proposed land division was unfair, reacted in horror and took up arms. When Israel declared its independence in May 1948, neighboring Arab countries sent armies to help the Palestinians crush the newborn state.

Israel, however, prevailed on all fronts. Some 700,000 Palestinians became refugees. They found shelter in United Nations refugee camps in Jordan, Syria,

---

Mao Zedong (maow dzuh-dong)   **Jiang Qing** (jyahn ching)

Faruq (fuh-ROOK)   **Faysal** (FIE-suhl)   **Husayn** (hoo-SANE)

Oil Crisis at the Gas Station   Dislocations in the oil industry caused by OPEC price rises that began in 1974 produced long lines at the gas pump and local shortages. The crisis brought Middle East politics home to consumers and created a negative stereotype of "oil sheikhs."   (Keza/Liaison)

Lebanon, and the Gaza Strip (a bit of coastal land on the Egyptian-Israeli border). The right of these refugees to return home remains a focal point of Arab politics. In 1967 Israel responded to threatening military moves by Egypt's Nasir by preemptively attacking Egyptian and Syrian air bases. In six days, Israel won a smashing victory. When Jordan entered the war, Israel won control of Jerusalem, which it had previously split with Jordan, and the West Bank. Acquiring all of Jerusalem satisfied Jews' deep longing to return to their holiest city, but Palestinians continued to regard Jerusalem as their destined capital, and Muslims in many countries protested Israeli control of the Dome of the Rock, a revered Islamic shrine located in the city. Israel also occupied the Gaza Strip, the strategic Golan Heights in southern Syria, and the entire Sinai Peninsula (see Map 33.3). These acquisitions resulted in a new wave of Palestinian refugees.

The rival claims to Palestine continued to plague Middle Eastern politics. The Palestine Liberation Organization (PLO), headed by Yasir Arafat°, waged guerrilla war against Israel, frequently engaging in acts of terrorism. The militarized Israelis were able to blunt or absorb these attacks and launch counterstrikes that likewise involved assassinations and bombings. Though the United States proved a firm friend of Israel, and the Soviet Union armed the Arab states, neither superpower saw the

---

Arafat (AR-uh-fat)

struggle between Zionism and Palestinian nationalism as a vital concern—until oil became a political issue.

The phenomenal concentration of oil wealth in the Persian Gulf states—Iran, Iraq, Kuwait, Saudi Arabia, Qatar, Bahrain, and the United Arab Emirates—was not fully realized until after World War II when demand for oil rose sharply as civilian economies recovered. As a world oversupply diminished in the face of rising demand, oil-producing states in 1960 formed the **Organization of Oil Exporting Countries (OPEC)** to promote their collective interest in higher revenues.

Oil politics and the Arab-Israeli conflict intersected in October 1973. A surprise Egyptian attack across the Suez Canal threw the Israelis into temporary disarray. Within days the war turned in Israel's favor, and an Egyptian army was trapped at the canal's southern end. The United States then arranged a ceasefire and the disengagement of forces. But before that could happen, the Arab oil-producing countries voted to embargo oil shipments to the United States and the Netherlands as punishment for their support of Israel.

The implications of oil as an economic weapon profoundly disturbed the worldwide oil industry. Prices rose—along with feelings of insecurity. In 1974 OPEC responded to the turmoil in the oil market by quadrupling prices, setting the stage for massive transfers of wealth to the producing countries and provoking a feeling of crisis throughout the consuming countries.

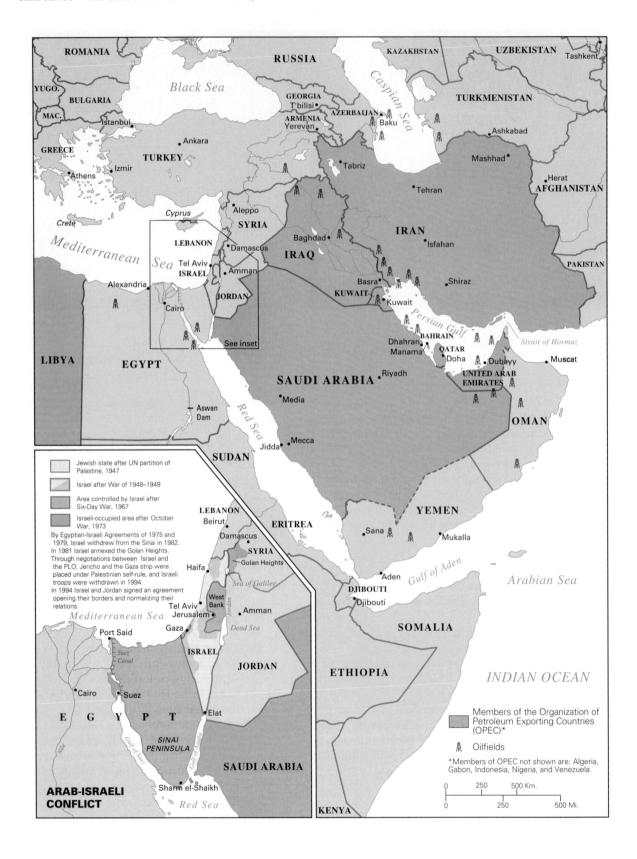

Jewish state after UN partition of Palastine, 1947

Israel after War of 1948–1949

Area controlled by Israel after Six-Day War, 1967

Israeli-occupied area after October War, 1973

By Egyptian-Israeli Agreements of 1975 and 1979, Israel withdrew from the Sinai in 1982. In 1981 Israel annexed the Golan Heights. Through negotiations between Israel and the PLO, Jericho and the Gaza strip were placed under Palestinian self-rule, and Israeli troops were withdrawn in 1994.
In 1994 Israel and Jordan signed an agreement opening their borders and normalizing their relations.

ARAB-ISRAELI CONFLICT

Members of the Organization of Petroleum Exporting Countries (OPEC)*

Oilfields

*Members of OPEC not shown are: Algeria, Gabon, Indonesia, Nigeria, and Venezuela.

0   250   500 Km.

0   250   500 Mi.

Silent Spring

The research laboratories that spawned an arsenal of new weapons during World War II also developed highly effective insecticides and herbicides. The potency of DDT was discovered in 1939, and thousands of soldiers were dusted with DDT powder to control lice. Related compounds like dieldrin and aldrin proved many times stronger. The herbicide Agent Orange was later used by the United States to defoliate jungles in Vietnam and reveal enemy infiltration routes.

In 1962, Rachel Carson, a marine biologist, published Silent Spring, *a book in which she warned about lethal accumulations of insecticides and herbicides in water and soil that were causing die-offs of wildlife. She also warned of a "silent spring" resulting from the extermination of song birds. Carson's work was one of the first to describe the dangers of uncontrolled technological change and focus public attention on environmental issues.*

The new chemicals come from our laboratories in an endless stream; almost five hundred annually find their way into actual use in the United States alone. The figure is staggering and its implications are not easily grasped—500 new chemicals to which the bodies of men and animals are required somehow to adapt each year, chemicals totally outside the limits of biologic experience. . . .

Along with the possibility of the extinction of mankind by nuclear war, the central problem of our age has therefore become the contamination of man's total environment with such substances of incredible potential for harm—substances that accumulate in the tissues of plants and animals and even penetrate the germ cells to shatter or alter the very material of heredity upon which the shape of the future depends.

How did Rachel Carson's warning affect subsequent government policies? What are some other examples of wartime technology affecting later civilian life?

Source: Rachel Carson, *Silent Spring* (Boston: Houghton Mifflin, 1962), 7–8.

The Emergence of Environmental Concerns

The Cold War and the massive investments made in postwar economic recovery had focused public and governmental attention on technological innovations and enormous projects such as hydroelectric dams and nuclear power stations. Only a few people, such as the marine biologist Rachel Carson (see Society and Culture: Silent Spring), warned that untested technologies and all-out drives for industrial productivity were rapidly degrading the environment. The superpowers were particularly negligent of the environmental impact of pesticide and herbicide use, automobile exhaust, industrial waste disposal, and radiation hazards.

In 1968 a wave of student unrest swept many parts of the world. At Columbia University in New York City students protested racism and the war in Vietnam. In Paris and Tokyo they rioted to reform higher education. In Mexico they were outraged at the amount of money the government was spending to host the Olympic Games. The current of youth activism grew rapidly and focused awareness on environmental problems. Earth Day was first celebrated in 1970, the year in which the United States established its Environmental Protection Agency.

The problem of finite natural resources became more broadly recognized when oil prices skyrocketed. Making gasoline engines and home heating systems more efficient and lowering highway speed limits to conserve fuel became matters of national debate in the United States while poorer countries struggled to find the money to import oil. A widely read 1972 study called

Map 33.3   Middle East Oil and the Arab-Israeli Conflict, 1947–1973   Oil resources were long controlled by private European and American companies. In the 1960s most countries, guided by OPEC, negotiated agreements for sharing control, leading eventually to national ownership. This set the stage for the use of oil as a weapon in the Arab-Israeli war of 1973 and for the succeeding oil price increases.

The Limits of Growth forecast a need to cut back on consumption of natural resources in the twenty-first century. Thus as the most dangerous moments of the Cold War seemed to be passing, ecological and environmental problems of worldwide impact vied with the superpower rivalry and Third World nation building for public attention.

CONCLUSION

The impact of the Second World War on the popular mind was so immense that for several decades people commonly referred to the time they were living in as the "postwar era," not needing to specify which war they were referring to. The Cold War and the decolonization movement seemed to arise as logical extensions of World War II. The question of who would control the parts of Europe and Asia liberated from Axis occupation led to Churchill's notion of an iron curtain dividing East and West. The war exhaustion of the European imperialist powers encouraged Asian and African peoples to seek independence and embark on building their own nations.

Intellectuals often framed their understanding of the period in terms of a philosophical struggle between capitalism and socialism dating back to the nineteenth century. But for leaders facing the challenge of governing new nations and creating viable economies, economic philosophy became inextricably intertwined with questions of how to take advantage of the Cold War rivalry between the United States and the Soviet Union.

Historians do not all agree on the year 1975 as the end of the postwar era. The end of the Vietnam War, the beginning of the world oil crisis, and the signing of the Helsinki Accords that brought a measure of agreement among Europeans on both sides of the iron curtain were pivotal events for some countries. But the number of independent countries in the world had grown enormously, and each was in the process of working out its own particular problems. What marks the mid-1970s as the end of an era, therefore, is not a single event so much as the emergence of new concerns. Young people in particular—the new generation that had no memories of World War II—seemed less concerned with the Cold War and the specter of nuclear annihilation than with newly recognized threats to the world environment and personal opportunities for making their way in the world. In the wealthier nations, this meant taking advantage of

economic growth and increasing technological sophistication. In the developing world, it meant seeking the education and employment needed for playing active roles in the drama of nation building.

■ Key Terms

Third World	Warsaw Pact
Cold War	Cultural Revolution (China)
iron curtain	European Community
nonaligned nations	Helsinki Accords
United Nations	Marshall Plan
World Bank	Organization of Petroleum
Korean War	Exporting Countries (OPEC)
Vietnam War	Truman Doctrine
Cuban missile crisis	
North Atlantic Treaty Organization (NATO)	

■ Suggested Reading

The period since 1945 has been particularly rich in memoirs by government leaders. Some that are particularly relevant to the Cold War and decolonization are Dean Acheson (United States secretary of state under Truman), *Present at the Creation* (1969); Nikita Khrushchev, *Khrushchev Remembers* (1970); and Anthony Eden (British prime minister), *Full Circle* (1960).

Geoffrey Barraclough, *An Introduction to Contemporary History* (1964), is a remarkable early effort at understanding the broad sweep of history during this period.

Scholarship on the origins of the Cold War is extensive and includes Akira Iriye, *The Cold War in Asia: A Historical Introduction* (1974); Bruce Kuniholm, *The Origins of the Cold War in the Middle East* (1980); Madelaine Kalb, *The Congo Cables: The Cold War in Africa—From Eisenhower to Kennedy* (1982); and Michael J. Hogan, *A Cross of Iron: Harry S Truman and the Origins of the National Security State* (1998). For a recent reconsideration of earlier historical viewpoints see Melvyn P. Leffler and David S. Painter (eds.), *Origins of the Cold War: An International History* (1994).

Good general histories of the Cold War include Martin Walker, *The Cold War: A History* (1993), and Walter Lafeber, *America, Russia, and the Cold War, 1945–1992* (1993). The latter puts emphasis on how the Cold War eroded American democratic values. For a look at the Cold War from the Soviet perspective see William Taubman, *Stalin's America Policy* (1981); for the American perspective see John Lewis Gaddis, *Strategies of Containment: A Critical Appraisal of Postwar American National Security Policy* (1982). The Cuban missile crisis is well covered in Graham Allison, *Essence of Decision: Explaining the Cuban*

Missile Crisis (1971), and Michael Beschloss, *The Crisis Years: Kennedy and Khrushchev, 1960–1963* (1991).

The nuclear arms race and the associated Soviet–U.S. competition in space are well covered by McGeorge Bundy, *Danger and Survival: Choices About the Bomb in the First Fifty Years* (1988), and Walter MacDougall, *The Heavens and the Earth: A Political History of the Space Age* (1985). Among the many novels illustrating the alarming impact of the arms race on the general public are Philip Wylie, *Tomorrow!* (1954), and Nevil Shute, *On the Beach* (1970). At a technical and philosophical level, Herman Kahn's *On Thermonuclear War* (1961) had a similar effect.

The end of the European empires is broadly treated by D. K. Fieldhouse, *The Colonial Empires* (1982); the British Empire in particular, by Brian Lapping, *End of Empire* (1985). For a critical view of American policies toward the decolonized world see Gabriel Kolko, *Confronting the Third World: United States Foreign Policy, 1945–1980* (1988).

For books on some of the specific episodes of decolonization treated in this chapter see, on Algeria, Alistaire Horne, *A Savage War of Peace: Algeria, 1954–1962* (1987); on Cuba, Hugh Thomas, *Cuba: The Pursuit of Freedom* (1971); on the Suez crisis of 1956, Keith Kyle, *Suez 1956* (1991); on Britain's role in the Middle East over the period of the birth of Israel, William Roger Louis, *The British Empire in the Middle East, 1945–1951* (1984); on Vietnam, George Herring, *America's Longest War: The United States and Vietnam, 1950–1975* (1986), and Stanley Karnow, *Vietnam: A History* (1991); and on Latin America, Eric Wolf, *The Human Condition in Latin America* (1972).

The special cases of Japan and China in this period are covered by Takafusa Nakamura, *A History of Showa Japan, 1926–1989* (1998); Marius B. Jansen, *Japan and China: From War to Peace, 1894–1972* (1975); and Maurice Meisner, *Mao's China and After: A History of the People's Republic* (1986). John Merrill, *Korea: The Peninsular Origins of the War* (1989), presents the Korean War as a civil and revolutionary conflict as well as an episode of the Cold War. Among the hundreds of books on the Arab-Israeli conflict, Charles D. Smith, *Palestine and the Arab-Israel Conflict* (1992), and Trevor N. Dupuy, *Elusive Victory: The Arab-Israeli Wars, 1947–1974* (1978), stand out.

34

CRISIS, REALIGNMENT, AND THE DAWN OF THE POST–COLD WAR WORLD, 1975–1991

Postcolonial Crises and Asian Economic Expansion, 1975–1990 • The End of the Bipolar World, 1989–1991 • The Challenge of Population Growth • Unequal Development and the Movement of Peoples • Technological and Environmental Change

ENVIRONMENT AND TECHNOLOGY: The Personal Computer

SOCIETY AND CULTURE: China's Family-Planning Needs

Dry Docks Owned by Korea's Hyundai Corporation
Korea's rapid industrialization symbolizes Pacific Rim economic growth.

On Thursday, July 22, 1993, police officers in Rio de Janeiro's banking district attempted to arrest a young boy caught sniffing glue. In the resulting scuffle, one police officer was injured by stones thrown by a group of homeless children who lived in nearby streets and parks. Late the following night, hooded vigilantes in two cars fired hundreds of shots at a group of these children sleeping on the steps of a church. The attackers killed five children there and two more in a park. The murderers were later identified as off-duty police officers.

At that time more than 350,000 abandoned children lived in Rio's streets and parks and resorted to begging, selling drugs, stealing, and prostitution to survive. In 1993 alone death squads and drug dealers killed more than four hundred of them. Few people sympathized with the victims. One person living near the scene of the July shootings said, "Those street kids are bandits, and bandits have to die. They are a rotten branch that has to be pruned."

At the end of the twentieth century the brutality of those children's lives was an increasingly common feature of life in the developing world, where rapid population growth was outstripping economic resources.[1] Similar problems of violence, poverty, and social breakdown could be found in most developing nations.

In wealthy industrialized nations as well, politicians and social reformers worried about the effects of unemployment, family breakdown, substance abuse, and homelessness. As had been true during the eighteenth-century Industrial Revolution (see Chapter 24), dramatic economic growth, increased global economic integration, and rapid technological progress in the post–World War II period coincided with growing social dislocation and inequality. Among the most important events of the period were the emergence of new industrial powers in Asia and the precipitous demise of the Soviet Union and its socialist allies.

New challenges also appeared in the form of world population growth and large-scale migrations. Population grew most rapidly in the world's poorest nations, worsening social and economic problems and undermining fragile political institutions. In the industrialized nations the arrival of large numbers of culturally and linguistically distinct immigrants fueled economic growth but also led to the appearance of anti-immigrant political movements and, in some cases, violent ethnic conflict.

As you read this chapter, ask yourself the following questions:

- How did the Cold War affect politics in Latin America and the Middle East in the 1970s and 1980s?
- What forces led to the collapse of the Soviet Union?
- What is the relationship between the rate of population growth and the wealth of nations?
- How did technological change affect the global environment in the recent past?

POSTCOLONIAL CRISES AND ASIAN ECONOMIC EXPANSION, 1975–1989

Between 1975 and 1991, wars and revolutions provoked by a potent mix of ideology, nationalism, ethnic hatred, and religious fervor spread death and destruction through many of the world's least developed regions. These conflicts often had ties to earlier experiences of colonialism and foreign intervention, but the character and objectives of each conflict reflected a specific set of historical experiences. Throughout these decades of conflict the two superpowers sought to avoid direct military confrontation while working to gain strategic advantages. To accomplish these ends, the United States and the Soviet Union each supplied arms and financial assistance to nations or insurgent forces hostile to the other. Once they became linked to the geopolitical rivalry of the superpowers, conflicts provoked by local and regional causes tended to become more deadly and long lasting. Conflicts in which the rival super powers financed and armed competing factions or parties were called **proxy wars.**

In Latin America the rivalry of the superpowers helped to transform conflicts over political rights, social justice, and economic policies into a violent cycle of revolution, military dictatorship, and foreign meddling. In Iran and Afghanistan resentment against foreign intrusion and religiously based hostility to modernization led to revolutionary transformations. Here again superpower ambitions and regional political instability helped provoke war and economic decline. These experiences were not universal. During this same period, a small number of Asian nations experienced rapid transformation. Japan gained a position among the world's leading industrial powers while a small number of other Asian economies quickly entered the ranks of industrial and commercial powers.

The collapse of the Soviet system in eastern Europe at the end of the 1980s ended the Cold War and undermined socialist economies elsewhere. As developing and former socialist nations opened their markets to foreign investment and competition, economic transformation was often accompaniued by wrenching social change. Growing economic interconnectedness across the world coincided with increased inequality. By the early 1990s, it was clear that the world's wealthiest industrial nations were reaping most of the benefits of economic integration.

This period also witnessed a great increase in world population and in international immigration. Population growth and increased levels of industrialization had a dramatic impact on the global environment. Every continent felt the destructive effects of forest depletion, soil erosion, and pollution. Wealthy nations with slow rates of population growth found it easier to respond to these environmental challenges than did poor nations experiencing rapid population growth. These were some of the challenges facing the late twentieth century: growing inequalities among nations and within nations, rapid population expansion, and degradation of the environment.

Revolutions, Repression, and Democratic Reform in Latin America

After the Cuban Revolution Fidel Castro sought to end the domination of the United States and uplift the Cuban masses by changing the economy in fundamental ways. Both objectives led to confrontation with the United States. The Cuban Revolution was the first revolution in the Western Hemisphere to nationalize foreign investment, redistribute the wealth of the elite, and forge an alliance with the Soviet Union. The fact that a communist government could come to power and thwart efforts by the United States to overthrow it energized the revolutionary left throughout Latin America (see Chapter 33). Unable to overthrow Castro and fearful that revolution would spread across Latin America, the United States organized its political and military allies in Latin America, determined to defeat communism at all costs.

Brazil was the first to experience the full effects of the conservative reaction to the Cuban Revolution. Claiming that Brazil's civilian political leaders could not protect the nation from communist subversion, the army overthrew the democratically elected government of President João Goulart° in 1964. The military suspended the constitution, outlawed all existing political parties, and exiled former presidents and opposition leaders. Death squads—illegal paramiliary organizations sanctioned by the government—detained, tortured, and executed thousands of citizens. The dictatorship also undertook an ambitious economic program that promoted industrialization through import substitution, using tax and tariff policies to compel foreign-owned companies to increase investment in manufacturing.

This combination of dictatorship, violent repression, and government promotion of industrialization came to be called the "Brazilian Solution." Elements of this "solution" were imposed across much of Latin America in the 1970s and early 1980s, beginning in Chile. In 1970 Chile's new president, **Salvador Allende°,** undertook an ambitious program of socialist reforms to redistribute wealth from the elite and middle classes to the poor. He also nationalized most of Chile's heavy industry and mines, including the American-owned copper companies that dominated the Chilean economy. From the beginning of Allende's presidency the administration of United States president Richard Nixon (1969–1973) worked in Chile to organize opposition to Allende's reforms and to overturn his election. Afflicted by inflation, mass consumer protests, and declining foreign trade, Allende was overthrown in 1973 by a military uprising led by General Augusto Pinochet° and supported by the United States. President Allende and thousands of Chileans died in this uprising, and thousands of others were illegally seized, tortured, and imprisoned without trial. Once in power Pinochet rolled back Allende's reforms, reduced state participation in the economy, and encouraged foreign investment.

In 1976 Argentina followed Brazil and Chile into dictatorship. Isabel Martínez de Perón° became president after the death of her husband Juan Perón in 1974 (see Chapter 32). Argentina was racked by high inflation, terrorism, and labor protests. Impatient with the policies of

---

João Goulart (juwow go-LARHT)
Salvador Allende (sal-vah-DOR ah-YEHN-day)
Augusto Pinochet (ah-GOOS-toh pin-oh-CHET)
Isabel Martínez de Perón (EES-ah-bell mar-TEEN-ehz deh pair-OWN)

Chronology

	The Americas	Middle East	Asia	Eastern Europe
1970	**1964** Military takeover in Brazil **1970** Salvador Allende elected president of Chile **1973** Allende overthrown **1976** Military takeover in Argentina **1979** Sandinistas overthrow Anastasio Somoza in Nicaragua		**1975** Vietnam war ends **1978** China opens its economy	
1980		**1979** Islamic Revolution overthrows shah of Iran **1980–1988** Iran-Iraq War		**1978** USSR sends troops to Afghanistan
	1983–1990 Democracy returns in Argentina, Brazil, and Chile		**1986** Average Japanese income overtakes income in United States	**1985** Mikhail Gorbachev becomes Soviet head of state
	1989 United States invades Panama		**1989** Tiananmen Square confrontation	**1989** USSR withdraws troops from Afghanistan; Berlin Wall falls **1989–1991** End of communism in eastern Europe
1990	**1990** Sandinistas defeated in elections in Nicaragua	**1990** Iraq invades Kuwait **1991** Persian Gulf War		**1990** Reunification of Germany

the president, the military seized power and suspended the constitution. During the next seven years the military fought what it called the **Dirty War** against terrorism. More than nine thousand Argentines lost their lives, and thousands of others endured arrest, terrible tortures, and the loss of property.

Despite reverses in Brazil, Chile, and Argentina, however, revolutionary movements persisted elsewhere. The high-water mark of the revolutionary movement came in 1979 in Nicaragua with the overthrow of the corrupt dictatorship of Anastasio Somoza. The broad alliance of revolutionaries and reformers that gained this victory called themselves **Sandinistas°.** They took their name from Augusto César Sandino, who had led Nicaraguan opposition to U.S. military intervention between 1927 and 1932. The Sandinistas received significant political

and financial support from Cuba and, once in power, sought to imitate the command economies of Cuba and the Soviet Union. The Nicaraguan Revolution nationalized properties owned by members of the Nicaraguan elite and U.S. citizens.

During his four-year term, United States president Jimmy Carter (1977–1980) championed human rights in the hemisphere and stopped the flow of U.S. arms to regimes with the worst records. Carter sought to placate Latin American resentment for past U.S. interventions by renegotiating the Panama Canal treaty, agreeing to the reestablishment of Panamanian sovereignty in the Canal Zone at the end of 1999. He also tried and failed to find some common ground with the Sandinistas. In 1981, Ronald Reagan became president and abandoned this policy of conciliation.

Reagan was committed to reversing the results of the Nicaraguan Revolution and defeating a revolution-

---

Sandinistas (sahn-din-EES-tahs)

The Nicaraguan Revolution Overturns Somoza
A revolutionary coalition that included Marxists drove the dictator Anastasio Somoza from power in 1979. The Somoza family had ruled Nicaragua since the 1930s and maintained a close relationship with the United States. (Susan Meiselas/Magnum Photos, Inc.)

ary movement in neighboring El Salvador. His options, however, were limited by the U.S. Congress, which feared that Central America might become another Vietnam. Congress resisted any suggestion that U.S. combat forces be used in Nicaragua or El Salvador and put strict limits on military aid. The Reagan administration sought to roll back the Nicaraguan Revolution by the use of punitive economic measures and by the recruitment and arming of anti-Sandinista Nicaraguans. Called Contras (counterrevolutionaries), this military force was financed by both legal and illegal funds provided by the Reagan administration.

The Contras were unable to defeat the Sandinistas, but they did gain a bloody stalemate by the end of the 1980s. Confident that they were supported by the majority of Nicaraguans and assured that the U.S. Congress was close to cutting off aid to the Contras, the Sandinistas called for free elections in 1990. But they had miscalculated and lost the election. Exhausted by more than a decade of violence, a majority of Nicaraguan voters rejected the Sandinistas and elected a middle-of-the-road coalition led by Violeta Chamorro°.

The revolutionaries of El Salvador hoped to imitate the initial success of the Sandinistas of Nicaragua. Taking their name from a martyred leftist leader of the 1930s,

the FMLN (Farabundo Martí° National Liberation Front) organized an effective guerrilla force. The United States responded by providing hundreds of millions of dollars in military assistance annually and by training units of the El Salvadoran army. Despite these investments in military modernization, the Salvadoran military was guilty of widespread human rights abuses, including the assassination of Archbishop Oscar Romero and other members of the Catholic clergy. Responding to these human rights abuses, the U.S. Congress placed strict limits on the number of U.S. military advisers that could be sent to El Salvador and tried to force political reforms. External events finally brought peace to El Salvador. With the electoral defeat of the Sandinistas in Nicaragua and the collapse of the Soviet Union (see below), popular support for the rebels' vision of a socialist El Salvador waned, and the FMLN rebels negotiated an end to the war, transforming themselves into a civilian political party.

The military dictatorships established in Brazil, Chile, and Argentina all came to an end between 1983 and 1990. In each case reports of kidnappings, tortures, and corruption by military governments undermined public support. In Argentina, the military junta's foolish decision to seize the Falkland Islands—the Argentines

Violeta Chamorro (vee-oh-LET-ah cha-MOR-roe)

Farabundo Martí (fah-rah-BOON-doh mar-TEE)

called them the "Malvinas"—in 1982 from Great Britain ended in an embarrassing military defeat and precipitated the return to civilian rule. The Argentine junta had helped President Reagan support the Contras in Nicaragua and believed he would keep Britain's Prime Minister Margaret Thatcher from taking military action. When the Argentine garrison in the Falklands surrendered, military rule in Argentina itself collapsed.

In Chile and Brazil the military dictatorships ended without the drama of foreign war. Despite significant economic growth under Pinochet, Chileans resented the violence and corruption of the military. In 1988 Pinochet called a plebiscite to extend his authority, but the majority vote went against him. A year later Chile elected its first civilian president in eighteen years. Brazil's military initiated a gradual transition to civilian rule in 1985 and four years later had its first popular presidential election. By 1991 nearly 95 percent of Latin America's population lived under civilian rule.

By the end of the 1980s, both oil-importing and oil-exporting nations in Latin America were in economic trouble. Brazil and other oil importers had borrowed heavily to cover budget deficits caused by high oil prices engineered by OPEC. Oil exporters such as Mexico and Venezuela at first enjoyed a windfall as prices rose. Expecting prices to remain high, they borrowed to increase production and develop refining capacity. When oil prices fell in the 1980s, they were hard-pressed to repay debts. In 1982 Mexico was forced to declare that it could not make debt payments, triggering a world financial crisis. By 1988, Latin American nations owed more than $400 billion to external lenders, and Brazil alone owed $113 billion. Debt remained an impediment to economic development in Latin America into the 1990s.

In 1991 Latin America was more dominated by the United States than it had been in 1975. In the 1980s the United States used military force to achieve its objectives on a number of occasions. In 1983, for example, President Reagan authorized a military invasion of the tiny Caribbean nation of Grenada, justifying his action by the need to protect a small number of American students from the actions of a pro-Cuban government. Six years later United States President George Bush sent a large military force into Panama to overthrow and arrest the dictator General Manuel Noriega°, who was associated with both drug smuggling and attacks on U.S. military personnel. These actions were powerful reminders to Latin Americans of prior experience with foreign intervention and occupation (see Chapter 25).

Manuel Noriega (MAN-wel no-ree-EGG-ah)

Islamic Revolutions in Iran and Afghanistan

Although the Arab-Israel conflict and the oil crisis (see Chapter 33) concerned both superpowers, the prospect of their direct military involvement remained remote. When unexpected crises developed in Iran and Afghanistan, however, significant strategic issues came to the foreground because both countries adjoined Soviet territory, thus making Soviet military intervention more likely. Exercising post–Vietnam War caution, the United States reacted to the crises with restraint. The Soviet Union chose a bolder and ultimately disastrous course.

The Iranian Revolution of 1979 proved enormously frustrating to the United States. In 1941 Muhammad Reza Pahlavi° succeeded his father as shah of Iran. In 1953, covert intervention by the United States Central Intelligence Agency (CIA) helped the shah retain his throne in the face of a movement to usurp royal power. Even when he finally nationalized the foreign-owned oil industry, the shah continued to enjoy special American support. As oil revenues increased following the price increases of the 1970s, the United States encouraged the shah to spend his nation's growing wealth on equipping the Iranian army with advanced American weaponry.

Resentment in Iran against the Pahlavi family's autocracy dated from the 1925 seizure of power by the shah's father. The shah's dependence on the United States stimulated further opposition. By the 1970s, popular resentment against the ballooning wealth of the elite families that supported the shah and the inefficiency, malfeasance, and corruption of his government led to mass opposition.

Ayatollah Ruhollah Khomeini°, a Shi'ite° philosopher-cleric who had spent most of his eighty-plus years in religious and academic pursuits, became the voice and symbolic leader of the opposition. Massive street demonstrations and crippling strikes forced the shah to flee Iran and ended the monarchy in 1979. In the Islamic Republic of Iran, which replaced the monarchy, Ayatollah Khomeini was supreme arbiter of disputes and guarantor of religious legitimacy. He oversaw a parliamentary regime that was based on European models, but he imposed religious control of legislation and public behavior. Elections were held, but the electoral process was not open to all: monarchists, communists, and other groups opposed to the idea of an Islamic Republic were barred from running for office. Shi'ite clerics

Reza Pahlavi (REH-zah PAH-lah-vee)
Ayatollah Ruhollah Khomeini (A-yat-ol-LAH ROOH-ol-LAH ko-MAY-nee)   Shi'ite (SHE-ite)

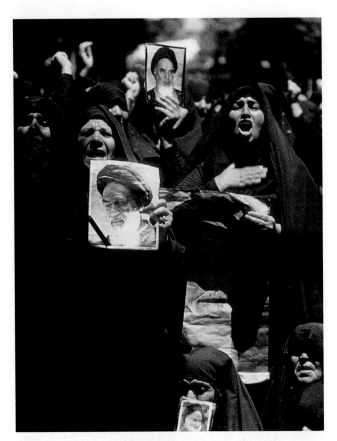

Muslim Women Mourning the Death of Ayatollah Khomeini in 1989   An Islamic revolution overthrew the shah of Iran in 1979. Ayatollah Khomeini sought to lead Iran away from the influences of Western culture and challenged the power of the United States in the Persian Gulf.   (Alexandra Avakian/Woodfin Camp & Associates)

threatened the interests of both the United States and Israel. In November 1979 Iranian radicals seized the U.S. embassy in Tehran and then held fifty-two diplomats hostage for 444 days. Americans felt humiliated by their inability to do anything, particularly after the failure of a military rescue attempt.

In the fall of 1980, shortly after negotiations for the release of the hostages began, **Saddam Husain°,** the ruler of neighboring Iraq, invaded Iran to topple the Islamic Republic. His own dictatorial rule rested on a secular, Arab nationalist philosophy and long-standing friendship with the Soviet Union, which had provided him with advanced weaponry. He feared that the fervor of Iran's revolutionary Shi'ite leaders would infect his own country's Shi'ite majority and threaten his power. The war pitted American weapons in the hands of the Iranians against Soviet weapons in the hands of the Iraqis, but the superpowers avoided overt involvement during eight years of bloodshed. Covertly, however, the United States sent arms to Iran, hoping to gain the release of other American hostages held by radical Islamic groups in Lebanon and to help finance the Contra war against the Sandinista government of Nicaragua. When this deal came to light in 1986, the resulting political scandal intensified American hostility toward Iran. Openly tilting toward Iraq, President Reagan sent the United States Navy to the Persian Gulf, ostensibly to protect nonbelligerent shipping. The move helped force Iran to accept a cease-fire in 1988.

While the United States faced anguish and frustration in Iran, the Soviet Union found itself facing even more serious problems in neighboring Afghanistan. Since World War II, the Soviet Union had succeeded in staying out of shooting wars by using proxies to challenge the United States. But in 1978, the Soviet Union sent its army to Afghanistan to support a fledgling communist regime against a hodgepodge of local, religiously inspired guerrilla bands that had taken control of much of the countryside.

With the United States, Saudi Arabia, and Pakistan paying, equipping, and training the Afghan rebels, the Soviet Union found itself in the same kind of unwinnable war the United States had stumbled into in Vietnam. Unable to justify the continuing drain on manpower, morale, and economic resources and facing widespread domestic discontent over the war, Soviet leaders finally withdrew their troops in 1989. The Afghan communists held on for another three years. But once rebel groups took control of the entire country they began to fight among themselves over who should rule.

with little training for government service emerged in many of the highest posts, and stringent measures were taken to combat Western styles and culture. Universities were temporarily closed, and their faculties were purged of secularists and monarchists. Women were compelled to wear modest Islamic garments outside the house, and semi-official vigilante committees policed public morals and cast a pall over entertainment and social life.

The United States under President Carter had criticized the shah's repressive regime, but the overthrow of a long-standing ally and the creation of the Islamic Republic were blows to American prestige. The new Iranian regime was religiously doctrinaire. It also was anti-Israeli and anti-American. Khomeini saw the United States as a "Great Satan" opposed to Islam, and he helped to foster Islamic revolutionary movements elsewhere, which

Saddam Husain (sah-DAHM who-SANE)

Asian Transformation

Japan has few mineral resources and is dependent on oil imports, but the Japanese economy weathered the oil price shocks of the 1970s better than did the economies of Europe and the United States. In fact, Japan experienced a faster rate of economic growth in the 1970s and 1980s than did any other major developed economy, growing at about 10 percent a year. Average income also increased rapidly, overtaking that of the United States in 1986 and surpassing it in the 1990s.

There are some major differences between the Japanese industrial model and that of the United States. During the American occupation, Japanese industrial conglomerates, zaibatsu, (see Chapter 30) were broken up. Although ownership of major industries became less concentrated as a result, new industrial alliances appeared. There are now six major *keiretsu*° that each include firms in industry, commerce, construction, and a major bank tied together in an interlocking ownership structure. There are also minor keiretsu dominated by a major corporation, like Toyota, and including its major suppliers. These combinations of companies have close relationships with government. Government assistance in the form of tariffs and import regulations inhibiting foreign competition was crucial in the early stages of development of Japan's automobile and semiconductor industries, among others.

Through the 1970s and 1980s Japanese success at exporting manufactured goods produced huge trade surpluses with other nations, prompting the United States and the European Community to try to force an opening of the Japanese market through tough negotiating. These efforts had only limited success. In 1990 Japan enjoyed a trade surplus with the rest of the world that was twice as large as in 1985. Many experts assumed that the competitive advantages that Japan enjoyed in the 1980s would propel Japan past the United States as the world's preeminent industrial economy. But problems appeared at the end of the decade. Japanese housing and stock markets had become highly overvalued, in part because the large trade imbalances increased the monetary supply. Also, the close relationship of government, banks, and industries had led to speculation and corruption that undermined the nation's confidence.

The Japanese model of close cooperation between government and industry was imitated by a small number of Asian states. The most important of them was South Korea, which had a number of assets that helped to promote economic development. The combination of inexpensive labor, strong technical education, and substantial domestic capital reserves allowed South Korea to overcome the devastation of the Korean War in little more than a decade. Despite large defense expenditures, South Korea developed heavy industries such as steel and shipbuilding as well as consumer industries such as automobiles and consumer electronics. Japanese investment and technology transfers accelerated this process. Led by four giant corporations, which accounted for nearly half of South Korea's gross domestic product (GDP) and produced a broad mix of goods, the Korean economy began to match Japanese economic growth rates by the 1980s. Hyundai, one of the four giant corporations, manufactured products ranging from supertankers and cars to electronics and housing.

Taiwan, Hong Kong, and Singapore also developed modern industrial and commercial economies. As a result of their rapid economic growth, these three nations and South Korea were often referred to as the **Asian Tigers.** Taiwan suffered a number of political reverses, including the loss of its United Nations seat to the People's Republic of China in 1971 and the withdrawal of diplomatic recognition by the United States. Nevertheless, it achieved remarkable economic progress. In contrast with South Korea, smaller, more specialized companies led development in Taiwan. Also, Taiwan was able to gain a foothold in the economy of the People's Republic of China while maintaining its traditional markets in the United States and South Asia. Between 1955 and 1990, Taiwan's per capita GDP (gross domestic product) increased from 10 percent of the U.S. levels to 50 percent.

Hong Kong and Singapore—both small societies with extremely limited resources—also enjoyed rapid economic development. Singapore's initial economic takeoff was based on its busy port and on banking and commercial services. As capital accumulated in these profitable sectors, this society of around 3 million people diversified by building textile and electronics industries. Singapore's rate of growth in GDP was double that of Japan from 1970 to 1980. Hong Kong's economic prosperity too was tied to its port and to the development of banking and commercial services, which were increasingly tied to the growing economy of China. Hong Kong also developed a highly competitive industrial sector dominated by textile and consumer electronics production. Worried about Hong Kong's reintegration into the People's Republic of China in 1997, local capitalists moved significant amounts of capital to the United States, Canada, and elsewhere, slowing economic growth in Hong Kong.

All of these **newly industrialized economies (NIEs)** shared many characteristics that helped explain their

---

keiretsu (kay-REHT-soo)

rapid industrialization. All had disciplined and hard-working labor forces, and all invested heavily in education. For example, as early as 1980, Korea had as many engineering graduates as Germany, Britain, and Sweden combined. All had high rates of personal saving that allowed them to generously fund investment in new technology. In 1987, the saving rates in Taiwan and South Korea were three times higher than in the United States. All emphasized outward-looking export strategies. And, like Japan, all these dynamic Pacific Rim economies benefited from government sponsorship and protection. All were beneficiaries of the extraordinary expansion in world trade and international communication that permitted technology to be disseminated more rapidly than at any time in the past. As a result, newly industrializing nations began with current technologies.

In China after Mao Zedong's death in 1976, the communist leadership introduced a comprehensive economic reform that allowed more individual initiative and permitted individuals to accumulate wealth. Beginning in 1978, the Communist Party in Sichuan province freed more than six thousand firms to compete for business outside the state planning process. The results were remarkable. Under China's leader **Deng Xiaoping°** these reforms were expanded across the nation. China also began to permit foreign investment for the first time since the communists came to power in 1949. Between 1978 and the end of the 1990s foreign investors committed more than $180 billion to the Chinese economy, and McDonald's, Coca-Cola, Airbus, and other foreign companies opened for business. But more than 100 million workers were still employed in state-owned enterprises, and most foreign-owned companies were segregated in special economic zones. The result was a dual industrial sector—one modern and efficient and connected to international markets, the other dominated by government and directed by political decisions.

When Mao came to power in 1949, the meaning of the Chinese Revolution was made clear in the countryside, where collective ownership and organization were imposed. Deng Xiaoping did not privatize land, but he did permit the contracting of land to individuals and families, who were free to consume or sell whatever they produced. By 1984, 93 percent of China's agricultural land was in effect in private hands and producing for the market, tripling agricultural output.

Perhaps the best measure of the success of Deng's reforms is that between 1980 and 1993 China's per capita output more than doubled, averaging more than 8 percent growth per year in comparison with the world average of slightly more than 1 percent and Japan's average of 3.3 percent. This growth was overwhelmingly the result of exports to the developed nations of the West, especially the United States. Nevertheless, per capita measures of wealth indicated that China remained a poor nation. China's per capita GDP was roughly the same as Mexico's, about $3,600 per year. By comparison, Taiwan had a per capita GDP of $14,700.

Much of China's command economy remained in place, and the leadership of the Chinese Communist Party resisted serious political reform. Deng Xiaoping's strategy of balancing change and continuity, however, helped China avoid some of the social costs and political consequences experienced by Russia and other European socialist countries that abruptly plunged into capitalism and democracy. As Chinese officials put it, "[China was] changing a big earthquake into a thousand tremors." The nation's leadership faced a major challenge in 1989. Responding to mass movements in favor of democracy across the globe and to inflation, Chinese students and intellectuals, many of whom had studied outside China, led a series of protests demanding more democracy and an end to inflation and corruption. This movement culminated in **Tiananmen Square°,** in the heart of Beijing. Hundreds of thousands of protesters gathered, refusing to leave. The government decided on the use of force. After weeks of standoff, tanks pushed into the square, killing hundreds, perhaps thousands. Many more were arrested. Although the Communist party survived this challenge, it was not clear whether rapid economic growth, increasing inequality, high levels of unemployment, and massive migration from the countryside to the cities could occur without triggering a political transformation.

THE END OF THE BIPOLAR WORLD, 1989–1991

After the end of World War II, competition between the United States and the Soviet Union and their respective allies created a bipolar world. Every conflict, no matter how local its origins, held the potential of engaging the attention of one or both of the superpowers. The Korean War, decolonization in Africa, the Vietnam War, the Cuban Revolution, hostilities between Israel and its neighbors, and numerous other events increased tension

---

Deng Xiaoping (dung shee-yao-ping)

Tiananmen (tee-yehn-ahn-men)

between the superpowers, each armed with nuclear weapons. Given this succession of provocations, budgets within both blocs were dominated by defense expenditures, and political culture everywhere was dominated by arguments over the relative merits of the two competing economic and political systems.

Few in 1980 predicted the startling collapse of the Soviet Union and the socialist nations of the Warsaw Pact. Western observers tended to see communist nations as both more uniform in character and more subservient to the Soviet Union than was true. Long before the 1980s deep divisions had appeared among communist states. Yugoslavia broke with the Soviet Union in the 1940s; China actually fought a brief border war with the Soviet Union in the 1960s; and the government of newly unified communist Vietnam invaded communist Cambodia in the 1970s. But in general, the once-independent nations and ethnic groups that had been brought within the Soviet Union and the eastern European nations seemed securely transformed by the experiences and institutions of communism. By 1990, however, nationalism was resurgent and communism was nearly finished.

Crisis in the Soviet Union

Under United States President Ronald Reagan and the Soviet Union's General Secretary Leonid Brezhnev°, the rhetoric of the Cold War remained intense. Massive new U.S. investments in armaments, including a space-based missile protection system that never became operational, placed heavy burdens on the Soviet economy, which was unable to absorb the cost of developing similar weapons. Soviet economic problems were systemic; shortages of food, consumer goods, and housing were an ongoing part of Soviet life. Obsolete industrial plants and centralized planning that stifled initiative and responsiveness to market demand led to a declining standard of living relative to the West. Government bureaucrats and Communist Party favorites received special privileges, including permission to shop in stores that stocked Western goods, but the average citizen faced long lines and waiting lists for goods. Soviet citizens contrasted their lot with the free and prosperous life of the West—depicted in the increasingly accessible Western media. The arbitrariness of the bureaucracy, the cynical manipulation of information, and deprivations created a generalized crisis in morale.

Despite the unpopularity of the war in Afghanistan and growing discontent, Brezhnev refused to modify his

rigid and unsuccessful policies. But he was unable to contain an underground current of protest. In a series of powerful books, the writer Alexander Solzhenitzyn° castigated the Soviet system and particularly the Stalinist prison camps. He won a Nobel Prize in literature but was charged with treason and expelled from the country in 1974. Self-published underground writings (*samizdat°*) by critics of the regime circulated widely despite government efforts to suppress them. The physicist Andrei Sakharov and his wife Yelena Bonner protested the nuclear arms race and human rights violations and were condemned to banishment within the country. Some Jewish dissidents spoke out against anti-Semitism, but many more left for Israel or the United States.

By the time **Mikhail Gorbachev°** took up the reins of the Soviet government in 1985, war weariness, economic decay, and vocal protest had reached critical levels. Casting aside Brezhnev's hard line, Gorbachev authorized major reforms in an attempt to stave off total collapse. His policy of political openness (*glasnost*) permitted criticism of the government and Communist Party. His policy of *perestroika°* "restructuring" was an attempt to address long-suppressed economic problems by moving away from central state planning and toward a more open economic system. In 1989 he ended the war in Afghanistan, which had cost many lives and much money.

The Collapse of the Socialist Bloc

Events in eastern Europe were very important in forcing change on the Soviet Union. In 1980 protests by Polish shipyard workers in the city of Gdansk led to the formation of **Solidarity,** a labor union that soon enrolled 9 million members. The Roman Catholic Church in Poland, strengthened by the elevation of a Pole, Karol Wojtyla°, to the papacy as John Paul II in 1978, gave strong moral support to the protest movement.

The Polish government imposed martial law in 1980 in response to the growing power of Solidarity and its allies, giving the army effective political control. Seeing Solidarity under tight controls and many of its leaders in prison, the Soviet Union decided not to intervene. But Solidarity remained a potent force with a strong institutional structure and nationally recognized leaders. As Gorbachev loosened political controls in the Soviet Union after 1985, communist leaders elsewhere lost confidence in Soviet resolve and critics and reformers in Poland and

---

Leonid Brezhnev (leh-oh-NEED BREZ-nef)

Solzhenitzen (sol-zhuh-NEET-sin)　*samizdat* (sah-meez-DAHT)
Gorbachev (GORE-beh-CHOF)　*perestroika* (per-ih-STROY-kuh)
Karol Wojtyla (KAH-rol voy-TIL-ah)

Map 34.1   The End of Soviet Domination in Eastern Europe   The creation of new countries out of Yugoslavia and Czechoslovakia and the reunification of Germany marked the most complicated changes of national borders since World War I. The Czech Republic and Slovakia separated peacefully, but Slovenia, Croatia, Macedonia, and Bosnia and Herzegovina achieved independence only after bitter fighting.

throughout eastern Europe were emboldened (see Map 34.1).

Beleaguered Warsaw Pact governments vacillated between relaxation of control and the suppression of dissent. As the Catholic clergy in Poland had supported Solidarity, Protestant and Orthodox religious leaders aided the rise of opposition groups elsewhere. This combination of nationalism and religion provided a powerful base for opponents of the communist regimes. Threatened by these forces, communist governments sought to quiet the opposition by seeking solutions to their severe economic problems. They turned to the West for trade and financial assistance. They also opened their nations to travelers, ideas, styles, and money from Western countries, all of which accelerated the demand for change.

By the end of 1989, communist governments across eastern Europe had fallen. The dismantling of the Berlin Wall, the symbol of a divided Europe and the bipolar world, vividly represented this transformation. In Poland, Hungary, Czechoslovakia, and Bulgaria communist leaders decided that change was inevitable and initiated political reforms. In Romania the dictator Nicolae Ceausescu° refused to surrender power, thus provoking a rebellion that ended with his arrest and execution. The comprehensiveness of these changes became clear in 1990, when Solidarity leader Lech Walesa° was elected president of Poland and dissident playwright Vaclav Havel° was elected president of Czechoslovakia.

Nicolae Ceausescu (neh-koh-LIE chow-SHES-koo)
Lech Walesa (leck wah-LESS-ah)   **Vaclav Havel** (vah-SLAV hah-VEL)

Worker Unrest in Eastern Europe After the collapse of the Soviet Union, workers such as these angry women surrounding plant managers in Minsk, capital of Belarus, demanded improvements in their working conditions. (Yuri Ivanoff/*LIFE Magazine* © Time Inc.)

Following the fall of the Berlin Wall, a tidal wave of patriotic enthusiasm swept aside the once-formidable communist government of East Germany. In the chaotic months that followed, East Germans crossed to West Germany in large numbers, and governmental services in the eastern sector nearly disappeared. Some Europeans recalled German militarism earlier in the century and worried about reunification. But there was little concrete opposition, and in 1990 Germany was reunified. Numerous problems followed reunification, including high levels of unemployment and budget deficits, but nearly fifty years of confrontation and tension across the heart of Europe seemed to end over night.

Soviet leaders looked on with dismay at the collapse of communism in the Warsaw Pact countries. They knew that similarly powerful nationalist sentiments existed within the Soviet Union as well. The year 1990 brought declarations of independence by Lithuania, Estonia, and Latvia, three small states on the Baltic Sea that the Soviet Union had annexed in 1939. And soon, violent ethnic strife erupted in the Caucasus region. Gorbachev tried to accommodate the rising pressures for change, but the tide was running too fast.

The end of the Soviet Union came suddenly in 1991 (see Map 34.2). After Communist hardliners botched a poorly conceived coup against Gorbachev, disgust with communism boiled over. Boris Yeltsin, the president of the Russian Republic and long-time member of the Communist Party, led popular resistance to the coup in Moscow and emerged as the most powerful leader in the country. Russia, the largest republic in the Soviet Union, was effectively taking the place of the disintegrating USSR. With the central government of the Soviet Union scarcely functioning, nationalism, long repressed by Soviet authorities, reappeared throughout the Soviet Union. In September 1991 the Congress of People's Deputies—the central legislature of the USSR, long subservient to the Communist Party—voted to dissolve the union. Mikhail Gorbachev went into retirement.

The ethnic and religious passions that fueled the breakup of the Soviet Union soon challenged the survival of Yugoslavia and Czechoslovakia. The dismemberment of Yugoslavia began with declarations of independence in Slovenia and Croatia in 1991. A year later, Czechoslovakia peacefully divided into the Czech Republic and Slovakia. Across eastern Europe ethnic and religious conflict was soon to turn violent.

Map 34.2   The End of the Soviet Union   When Communist hardliners failed to overthrow Gorbachev in 1991, popular anti-Communist sentiment swept the Soviet Union. Following Boris Yeltsin's lead in Russia, the republics that constituted the Soviet Union declared their independence.

The Persian Gulf War, 1990–1991

The first significant conflict to occur after the breakup of the Soviet Union and the end of the Cold War was the Persian Gulf War. The immediate causes were local and bilateral. Iraq's ruler, Saddam Husain, had borrowed a great deal of money from neighboring Kuwait and sought unsuccessfully to get Kuwait's royal family to reduce the size of this debt. He was also eager to gain control of Kuwait's oil fields. Husain believed that the smaller and militarily weaker nation could be quickly defeated and suspected, as a result of a conversation with an American diplomat, that the United States would not react. The invasion came in August 1990.

Saudi Arabia, a key regional ally of the United States and a major oil producer, felt threatened by Iraq's action and helped draw the United States into the conflict. Soon the United States and its allies had concentrated an imposing military force of 500,000 in the region. With his

intention to use force endorsed by the United Nations and with many Islamic nations supporting military action, President George Bush ordered an attack in early 1991. Iraq proved incapable of countering the sophisticated weaponry of the coalition. The missiles and bombs of the United States destroyed not only military targets but also "relegated [Iraq] to a pre-industrial age," reported the United Nations after the war. Although Iraq's military defeat was comprehensive, Husain remained in power and the country was not occupied. Husain, in fact, crushed an uprising in the months following this defeat. In the wake of this event the United States and its key allies imposed "no fly" zones that denied Iraq's military aircraft access to the northern and southern regions of the country. As a result, military tensions and periodic armed confrontations continued.

In the United States the results of the war were interpreted to mean that the U.S. military defeat in the Vietnam War could be forgotten and that U.S. military capability was unrivaled. Unable to deter military action by the U.S.-led coalition or to meaningfully influence the diplomacy that surrounded the war, Russia had been of little use to its former ally Iraq and its impotence was clear.

THE CHALLENGE OF POPULATION GROWTH

For most of human history population growth was viewed as beneficial, and human beings were seen as a source of wealth. Since the late eighteenth century, however, population growth has been viewed with increasing alarm. At first it was feared that food supplies could not keep up with population growth. Then social critics expressed concern that growing population would lead to class and ethnic struggle as numbers overwhelmed resources. By the second half of the twentieth century, population growth was increasingly seen as a threat to the environment. Are urban sprawl, pollution, and soil erosion inevitable results of population growth? These questions and debates remain today, but clearly population is both a cause and a result of increased global interdependency.

Demographic Transition

The population of Europe almost doubled between 1850 and 1914, putting enormous pressure on rural land and urban housing and overwhelming fragile public assistance institutions that provided some crisis assistance (see Chapter 28). This dramatic growth forced a large wave of immigration across the Atlantic, helping to develop North and South America and invigorating the Atlantic economy. Population growth also contributed to Europe's industrial revolution by lowering labor costs and increasing consumer demand.

Educated Europeans of the nineteenth century were ambivalent about the rapid increase in human population. Some saw it as a blessing that would promote economic well-being. Others warned that the seemingly relentless increase would bring disaster. Best known of these pessimists was the English cleric **Thomas Malthus,** who in 1798 argued convincingly that unchecked population growth would outstrip food production. When Malthus looked at Europe's future, he used a prejudiced image of China to terrify his European readers. A visitor to China, he claimed, "will not be surprised that mothers destroy or expose many of their children; that parents sell their daughters for a trifle; . . . and that there should be such a number of robbers. The surprise is that nothing still more dreadful should happen."[2]

The generation that came of age in the years immediately following World War II inherited a world in which the views of Malthus were casually dismissed. Industrial and agricultural productivity had multiplied supplies of food and other necessities. Cultural changes associated with expanded female employment, older age at marriage, and more effective family planning had combined to slow the rate of population increase. And by the late 1960s, Europe and other industrial societies had made what was called the **demographic transition** to lower fertility rates (average number of births per woman) and reduced mortality. The number of births in the developed nations was just adequate for the maintenance of current population levels. Thus many experts argued that the population growth then occurring in developing nations was a short-term phenomenon that would be ended by the combination of economic and social changes that had altered European patterns.

By the late 1970s, however, the demographic transition had not occurred in the Third World, and the issue of population growth had become politicized. The leaders of some developing nations actively promoted large families, arguing that larger populations would increase national power. These arguments remained a persistent part of the debate between developed and developing nations. Industrialized, mostly white, nations raised concerns about rapid population growth in Asia, Africa, and Latin America. Populist political leaders in those regions asked whether these concerns were not fundamentally racist.

The question exposed the influence of racism in the population debate and temporarily disarmed Western advocates of birth control. However, once the economic shocks of the 1970s and 1980s revealed the vulnerability of developing economies, governments in the developing world jettisoned pronatalist policy. In the 1970s Mexico's government had encouraged high fertility, and population growth in Mexico rose to 3 percent per year. By the 1980s Mexico started to promote birth control, and the annual population growth rate fell to 2.3 percent.

World population exploded in the twentieth century (see Table 34.1). At current rates of growth, world population increases by a number equal to the total population of the United States every three years. Unlike population growth in the eighteenth and nineteenth centuries, when much of the increase occurred in the

Table 34.1   Population for World and Major Areas, 1750–2050

Population Size (Millions)							
Major Area	1750	1800	1850	1900	1950	1998	2050
World	791	978	1,262	1,650	2,521	5,901	8,909
Africa	106	107	111	133	221	749	1,766
Asia	502	635	809	947	1,402	3,585	5,268
Europe	163	203	276	408	547	729	628
Latin America and the Caribbean	16	24	38	74	167	504	809
North America	2	7	26	82	172	305	392
Oceania	2	2	2	6	13	30	46
Percentage Distribution							
Major Area	1750	1800	1850	1900	1950	1998	2050
World	100	100	100	100	100	100	100
Africa	13.4	10.9	8.8	8.1	8.8	12.7	19.8
Asia	63.5	64.9	64.1	57.4	55.6	60.8	59.1
Europe	20.6	20.8	21.9	24.7	21.7	12.4	7.0
Latin America and the Caribbean	2.0	2.5	3.0	4.5	6.6	8.5	9.1
North America	0.3	0.7	2.1	5.0	6.8	5.2	4.4
Oceania	0.3	0.2	0.2	0.4	0.5	0.5	0.5

Source: J. D. Durand, "Historical Estimates of World Population: An Evaluation" (Philadelphia: University of Pennsylvania, Population Studies Center, 1974, mimeographed); United Nations, *The Determinants and Consequences of Population Trends,* vol. 1 (New York: United Nations, 1973); United Nations, *World Population Prospects as Assessed in 1963* (New York: United Nations, 1966); United Nations, *World Population Prospects: The 1998 Revision* (New York: United Nations, forthcoming); United Nations Population Division, Department of Economic and Social Affairs, http://www.popin.org/pop1998/4.htm.

wealthiest nations, population growth at the end of the twentieth century was overwhelmingly in the poorest nations. Fertility rates had dropped in most developing nations but remained much higher than rates in the industrialized nations. At the same time, improvements in hygiene and medical treatment caused mortality rates to fall. The result has been rapid population growth.

The Industrialized Nations

In the developed industrial nations of western Europe and in Japan at the beginning of the twenty-first century, fertility levels are so low that population will fall unless immigration increases. In Japan women have an average of 1.39 children; in Italy the number is 1.2. Sweden provides cash payments, tax incentives, and job leaves to families with children, but the average number of births there fell to 1.4 in recent years. The low fertility found in mature industrial nations is tied to higher levels of female education and employment, the material values of consumer culture, and access to contraception and abortion. Educated women now defer marriage and child rearing until they are established in careers. An Italian woman in Bologna, the city with the lowest fertility in the world, put it this way: "I'm an only child and if I could, I'd have more than one child. But most couples I know wait until their 30's to have children. People want to have their own life, they want to have a successful career. When you see life in these terms, children are an impediment."[3]

In industrialized nations life expectancy has improved as fertility has declined. The combination of abundant food, improved hygiene, more effective medicines, and medical care has lengthened human lives. About 12.5 percent of the population was age sixty-five or over in wealthy nations in 1990. In western Europe this percentage ranged from 13 in France to 18 in Sweden. Italy soon will have more than 20 adults fifty years old or over for each five-year-old child.

The combination of falling fertility and rising life expectancy in the industrialized nations presents a challenge very different from the one foreseen by Malthus. These nations generally offer a broad array of social services, including retirement income, medical services, and housing supplements for the elderly. As the number of retirees increases relative to the number of people who are employed, the costs of these services may become unsustainable. Clearly Japan, the United States, and the nations of western Europe will have to reexamine programs that encourage early retirement.

In Russia and other former socialist nations, current birthrates are now actually lower than death rates—levels inadequate to sustain the current population size. Birthrates were already low before the collapse of the socialist system and have contracted further with recent economic problems. Since 1975 fertility rates have fallen between 20 and 40 percent across the former Soviet bloc. By the early 1980s, abortions were as common as births in much of eastern Europe.

At the same time life expectancy has also fallen. Life expectancy for Russian men is now only fifty-seven years, down almost ten years since 1980. In the Czech Republic, Hungary, and Poland, life expectancy is improving in response to improved economic conditions, but in most of the rest of eastern Europe the Russian pattern of declining life expectancy is found. High unemployment, low incomes, food shortages, and the dismantling of the social welfare system of the communist era have all contributed to this decline.

The Developing Nations

Even if the industrialized nations decided to promote an increase in family size in the twenty-first century, they would continue to fall behind the developing nations as a percentage of world population. At current rates, 95 percent of all future population growth will be in developing nations (see Map 34.3 and Table 34.1). A comparison between Europe and Africa illustrates these changes. In 1950, Europe had twice the population of Africa. By 1985, Africa had drawn even. According to projections, by 2025 Africa's population will be three times larger than Europe's. Given the performance of African economies, future generations of Africans will likely face increased levels of famine, epidemics, and social breakdown.

As the 1990s ended, other developing regions had rapid population growth as well. While all developing nations had an average birthrate of 33.6 per thousand inhabitants, Muslim countries had a rate of 42.1. This rate is more than 300 percent higher than the rate for the developed nations of the West (13.1 births per thousand). The populations of Latin America and Asia also were expanding dramatically, but at rates slower than those in sub-Saharan Africa or the Muslim nations.

Chinese Family–Planning Campaign   Hoping to slow population growth, the Chinese government has sought to limit parents to a single child. Billboards and other forms of mass advertising have been an essential part of the campaign to gain compliance with national family-planning directives.   (Picard/Sipa Press)

Map 34.3 **World Population Growth** At current rates of growth, every three years, the world's population will increase by the equivalent of a nation the size of the United States. Most of this population increase will be in some of the world's poorest nations. By 2050, for example, Pakistan, a nation of only 40 million in 1950, will surpass the United States and become the country with the world's third largest population. (National Geographic Maps 1998/10 Map Supplement Population Growth. Used by permission of National Geographic Society.)

SOCIETY & CULTURE

China's Family-Planning Needs

China has the world's largest population—over a billion people. Although China enjoyed rapid economic growth in the closing years of the twentieth century, population pressures continued to present severe problems. In 1993 the Chinese economy became the world's tenth largest. Nevertheless, China's per capita GDP (gross domestic product) of $370 remained at Third World levels. Heavy pressure on families to have only one child resulted in the killing of female infants and the abandonment of children with disabilities. Peng Yu, vice minister of the State Family Planning Commission, explained the need for efforts at population control.

China is a developing country with a huge population but limited cultivated land, inadequate per capita resources and a weak economic foundation. . . . Despite continuous efforts in family planning, the huge base has created an annual net increase of around 14 million in recent years, equal to the total population of a medium-sized country. At present, per capita cultivated land in China has declined to less

than 0.1 hectare, equivalent to only one-fourth the world average as are [its] per capita freshwater resources. . . . Although national income has been climbing by 25 percent annually, the increase has been eaten up by new population growth, resulting in reduced fund accumulation and also holding up the speed of economic construction. A fast-growing population has also created great difficulties in employment, education, housing, transportation, and health care. Confronted by such grim realities, to guarantee basic living conditions and constantly improve standards of living, China cannot follow the Western mode under which natural falling birth rates coincide with gradual economic growth.

The Chinese government's family-planning practices have been harshly criticized. Why has the Chinese government sought to control population growth? What effect has population growth had on the environment and economic development? What ethical questions are raised by the effort of any government to limit population growth?

Latin America's population increased from 165 million in 1950 to 405 million in 1985 and is projected to reach 778 million in 2025, despite declining birthrates.

In Asia, the populations of India and China continued to grow despite government efforts to reduce family size (see Society and Culture: China's Family-Planning Needs). In China, efforts to enforce a limit of one child per family led to large-scale female infanticide as rural families sought to produce male heirs. India's policies of forced sterilization created widespread outrage and led to the electoral defeat of the ruling Congress Party. Yet both countries achieved some successes. Between 1960 and 1982, India's birthrate fell from 48 to 34 per thousand, while China's rate declined even more sharply—from 39 to 19. Still, by 2025 both China, which today has 1.13 billion people, and India, today with 853 million, will both reach 1.5 billion.

It is unclear whether the nations of Asia, Africa, and Latin America will undergo the lowered fertility and mortality rates experienced in the West during the Industrial Revolution. Yet real progress has occurred, and

fertility rates have fallen in the developing world where women have had access to education and employment outside the home.

Old and Young Populations

Population pyramids generated by demographers clearly illustrate the profound transformation in human reproductive patterns and life expectancy in the years since World War II. Figure 34.1 shows the 1985 age distributions in Pakistan, South Korea, and Sweden—nations at three different stages of economic development. Sweden is a mature industrial nation. South Korea is a rapidly industrializing nation that has surpassed many European nations in both industrial output and per capita wealth. Pakistan is a poor, traditional Muslim nation with rudimentary industrialization, low educational levels, and little effective family planning.

In 1985 nearly 50 percent of Pakistan's population was under age sixteen. The resulting pressures on the

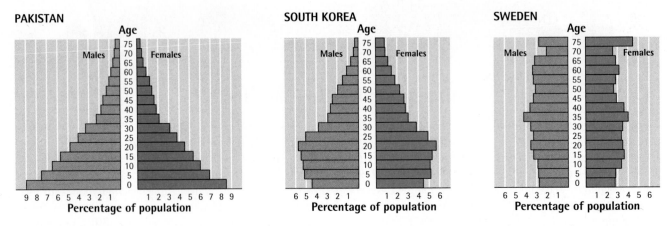

Figure 34.1   Age Structure Comparison: Islamic Nation (Pakistan), Non-Islamic Developing Nation (South Korea), and Developed Nation (Sweden), 1985   *Source:* Data from the World Bank.

economy were extraordinary. Every year 150,000 men reached age sixty-five—and another 1.2 million turned sixteen. Pakistan, therefore, had to create more than a million new jobs a year or face steadily growing unemployment and steadily declining wages. Sweden confronted a different problem. Sweden's aging population, growing demand for social welfare benefits, and declining labor pool meant that Sweden's industries faced the possibility of becoming less competitive and its citizens confronted the likelihood of declining living standards. In South Korea, a decline in fertility dramatically altered the ratio of children to adults, so that South Korea faced neither Pakistan's pressure to create jobs nor Sweden's growing demands for welfare benefits for the aged.

The demographic challenges faced by Sweden and other developed nations are less daunting than those confronting the developing nations. Poor nations must overcome problems such as shortages of investment capital, poor transportation and communication networks, and low educational levels, while they struggle to create jobs. Wealthy, well-educated, and politically stable nations can invest in robots and other new technologies to reduce labor needs and increase industrial and agricultural efficiency as their populations age.

The demographic problem and potential technological adjustments are most clearly visible in Japan. Unless current demographic patterns are reversed, Japan will have the oldest population among industrial nations by 2025. In Canada, Germany, the United States, and most other industrialized nations, young immigrants from poorer nations are entering the work force in large numbers. Japan has resisted immigration, instead investing heavily in technological solutions to the problems cre-

ated by its aging labor force. As of 1994, Japan had 75 percent of the world's industrial robots. Although Japanese industries are able to produce more goods with fewer workers, Japan will still face long-term increases in social welfare payments.

UNEQUAL DEVELOPMENT AND THE MOVEMENT OF PEOPLES

Two characteristics of the postwar world should now be clear. First, despite decades of experimentation with state-directed economic development, most nations that were poor in 1960 were as poor or poorer at the end of the 1990s. The only exceptions were a few rapidly developing Asian industrial nations and an equally small number of oil-exporting nations. Second, world population increased to startlingly high levels, and most of the increase was in the poorest nations.

The combination of intractable poverty and growing population generated a surge in international immigration. Few issues stirred more controversy. Even moderate voices sometimes framed the discussion of immigration as a competition among peoples. One commentator summarized his analysis this way: "As the better-off families of the northern hemisphere individually decide that having only one or at the most two children is sufficient, they may not recognize that they are in a small way vacating future

Table 34.2   Urban Residents as a Percentage of the Total Population in Selected Developing Nations

Nation	1960	1995
Nigeria	18	39
Tanzania	4	25
Morocco	29	48
Tunisia	40	57
India	18	28
Brazil	46	78
Mexico	51	75

Source: World Tables 1976 (Baltimore: Johns Hopkins University Press, 1976); *The Economist Book of Vital World Statistics* (Times Book: London, 1990); and *World Tables 1995* (Baltimore: Johns Hopkins University Press, 1995).

space (that is, jobs, parts of inner cities, shares of population, shares of market preferences) to faster-growing ethnic groups both inside and outside their boundaries. But that, in fact, is what they are doing."[4]

Large numbers of legal and illegal immigrants from poor nations with growing populations are entering the developed industrial nations, with the exception of Japan. Large-scale migrations within developing countries are a related phenomenon. The movement of impoverished rural residents to the cities of Asia, Africa, and Latin America (see Map 34.3 and Table 34.2) has increased steadily since the 1970s. This internal migration often serves as the first step toward migration abroad.

The Problem of Growing Inequality

Since 1945 global economic productivity has expanded more rapidly than at any other time in the past. Faster, cheaper communications and transportation have combined with improvements in industrial and agricultural technologies to create levels of material abundance that would have amazed those who experienced the first Industrial Revolution (see Chapter 24). Despite this remarkable economic expansion and growing market integration, the majority of the world's population remains in poverty. The industrialized nations of the Northern Hemisphere now enjoy a larger share of the world's wealth than they did a century ago. The thousands of homeless street children who live among the gleaming glass and steel towers of Rio's banking district can be seen as a metaphor for the social consequences of postwar economic development.

The gap between rich and poor nations has grown much wider since 1945. In 1993, Switzerland and Japan had the highest per capita GNPs (gross national products)—$35,760 and $31,490, respectively; the U.S. figure was $24,740; and Greece, the poorest nation in the European Union, had a per capita GNP of $7,220. The nations of the former Soviet Union and eastern Europe have per capita GNPs similar to those in the better-off nations of the Third World. Russia's per capita GNP in 1993 was $2,340, similar to Brazil's $2,930. Among developing economies in 1993, Algeria and Thailand had per capita GNPs of approximately $2,000, and in Nigeria, India, and China the figure was below $1,000. One billion of the world's people, approximately 20 percent, lived on less than $500 a year in 1993. This poverty was concentrated in Africa, Latin America, and Asia.

Wealth inequality within nations also grew. Regions tied to new technologies that provided competitive advantages became wealthier while other regions lost ground. In the United States, for example, the south and southwest grew richer in the last three decades relative to the older industrial regions of the midwest. Regional inequalities also appeared in developing nations. Generally, capital cities such Buenos Aires, in Argentina, and Lagos, in Nigeria, attracted large numbers of migrants from rural areas because they offered more opportunities, even if those opportunities could not compare to the ones available in developed nations.

Even in the industrialized world, people were divided into haves and have-nots. During the presidency of Ronald Reagan (1981–1989), wealth inequality in the United States reached its highest level since the 1929 stock market crash. Some scholars estimated that the wealthiest 1 percent of households in the United States controlled more than 30 percent of the nation's total wealth. In 1992, households receiving Aid to Families with Dependent Children (AFDC) in the United States

Garbage Dump in Manila, Philippines Garbage pickers are a common feature of Third World urban development. Thousands of poor families in nearly every Third World city sort and sell bottles, aluminum cans, plastic, and newspapers to provide household income. (Geoff Tompkinson/Aspect Picture Library Ltd.)

had an average income of $4,680. In the same year the average income of the 1,059 partners in New York City's largest law firms was $957,000.[5] Even in Europe, where tax and inheritance laws redistributed wealth, unemployment, homelessness, and substandard housing were increasingly common.

Internal Migration: The Growth of Cities

Migration from rural areas to urban centers in developing nations increased threefold from 1925 to 1950. After that, the pace accelerated. Shantytowns sprawling around major cities in developing nations are commonly seen as signs of social breakdown and economic failure. Nevertheless, city life was generally better than life in the countryside. A World Bank study estimated that three out of four migrants to cities made economic gains. Residents of cities in sub-Saharan Africa, for example, were six times more likely than rural residents to have safe water. An unskilled migrant from the depressed northeast of Brazil could triple his or her income by moving to Rio de Janeiro.

As the scale of rural-to-urban migration grew, these benefits proved more elusive, however. In many West African cities, basic services were crumbling under the pressure of rapid population growth. In 1990 in Mexico City, one of the world's largest cities, more than thirty thousand people lived in garbage dumps, where they scavenged for food and clothing. Worsening conditions and the threat of crime and political instability led many governments to try to slow migration to cities and, in some cases, to return people to the countryside. Indonesia, for example, has relocated more than half a million urban residents since 1969. Despite some successes with slowing the rate of internal migration, nearly every poor nation still faces the challenge of rapidly growing cities.

Global Migration

Each year hundreds of thousands of men and women leave the developing world to emigrate to industrialized nations. After 1960 this movement increased in scale, and ethnic and racial tensions in the host nations worsened. Political refugees and immigrants faced murderous violence in Germany; growing anti-immigrant sentiment led to a new right-wing political movement in France; and an expanded Border Patrol attempted to more effectively seal the U.S. border with Mexico. By the 1990s, levels of immigration posed daunting social and cultural challenges for both host nations and immigrants.

Immigrants from the developing nations brought to host nations many of the same benefits that the great migration of Europeans to the Americas provided a century ago (see Chapter 25). Many European nations actively promoted guest worker programs and other inducements to immigration in the 1960s when an expanding European economy first confronted labor shortages. However, attitudes toward immigrants changed as the size of the immigrant population grew and as European economies slowed in the 1980s. Facing higher levels of unemployment, native-born workers saw immigrants as competitors willing to work for lower wages and less likely to support unions. However, because cultural and ethnic characteristics have traditionally formed the basis of national identity in many European countries (see Chapter 28), worsening relations between immigrants and the native-born may have been inevitable. Put simply, many Germans are unable to think of the German-born son or daughter of Turkish immigrants as a German.

Because immigrants generally are young adults and commonly retain the positive attitudes toward early marriage and large families dominant in their native cultures, immigrant communities in Europe and the United States tended to have fertility rates higher than the rates of the host populations. In Germany in 1975, for example, immigrants made up about 7 percent of the population but accounted for nearly 15 percent of all births. Although immigrant fertility rates decline with prolonged residence in industrialized societies, the family size of second-generation immigrants is still larger than that of the host population. Therefore, even without additional immigration, immigrant groups grow faster than the longer-established population. Although the fertility of the Hispanic population in the United States is lower than the rates in Mexico and other Latin American nations, Hispanic groups will contribute well over 20 percent of all population growth in the United States during the next twenty-five years.

As the Muslim population in Europe and the Asian and Latin American populations in the United States expand in the twenty-first century, cultural conflicts will test definitions of citizenship and nationality. The United States will have some advantages in meeting these challenges because of long experience with immi-gration and relatively open access to citizenship. Yet in the 1990s the United States was moving slowly in the direction of European efforts to restrict immigration and defend a culturally conservative definition of nationality.

Technological and Environmental Change

Technological innovation powered the economic expansion that began after World War II. New technologies increased productivity and disseminated human creativity. They also altered the way people lived, worked, and played. Because most of the economic benefits were concentrated in the advanced industrialized nations, technology increased the power of those nations relative to the developing world. Even within developed nations, postwar technological innovations did not benefit all classes, industries, and regions equally. There were losers as well as winners.

Population growth and increased levels of migration and urbanization led to the global expansion of agricultural and industrial production. This multiplication of farms and factories intensified environmental threats. At the end of the twentieth century, loss of rain forest, soil erosion, global warming, pollution of air and water, and extinction of species threatened the quality of life and the survival of human societies. Here again, differences between nations were apparent. Environmental protection, like the acquisition of new technology, had progressed furthest in societies with the most economic resources.

New Technologies and the World Economy

Nuclear energy, jet engines, radar, and tape recording were among the many World War II developments that later had an impact on consumers' lives. When applied to industry, new technology increased productivity, reduced labor requirements, and improved the flow of information. Pent-up demand for consumer goods also spurred new research and the development of new technologies. As the Western economies recovered from the war and incomes rose, consumers wanted new products that reduced their workloads or provided entertainment. The consumer electronics industry rapidly developed new products.

The Personal Computer

From Mainframe to Laptop
During the last forty years the computer revolution has changed the way we work. (left: Courtesy, IBM Corporation; bottom: Dagmar Fabricius/Liaison)

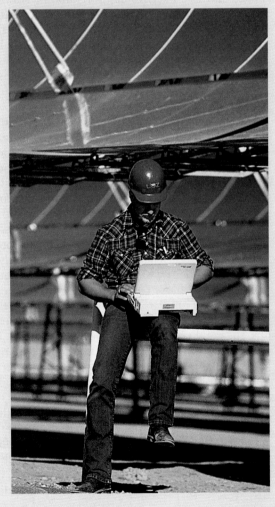

The period since World War II witnessed wave after wave of technological innovations. Few of them have had a greater impact on the way people work, learn, and live than the personal computer. In the 1970s computing was done on large mainframe computers owned by institutions and businesses, and IBM (International Business Machines) dominated the computer industry. By the mid-1990s desktop and laptop computers had marginalized the mainframe and dispersed the economic and political power associated with the computer. The computer industry experienced a rapid succession of revolutions made possible by the microchip and miniaturization.

Improvements in existing technologies accounted for much of the developed world's productivity increases during the 1950s and 1960s. Larger and faster trucks, trains, and airplanes cut transportation costs. Both capitalist and socialist governments made these changes possible by building highway systems, improving railroad track, and constructing airports. Governments also bore much of the cost for developing and constructing nuclear power plants.

No technology had greater significance in this period than the computer. The first computers were expensive, large, and slow. Only large corporations, governments, and universities could afford them. But by the mid-1980s desktop computers had replaced typewriters in most of the developed world's offices, and technological advances continued. Each new generation of computers was smaller, faster, and more powerful than the one before (see Environmental and Technology: The Personal Computer).

Computers also altered manufacturing. Small dedicated computers were used to control and monitor machinery in some industries. In the developed world, companies forced by competition to improve efficiency and product quality brought robots into the factory. Europe followed Japan's initiative in this field, especially in automobile production and mining. The United States introduced robots more slowly because it enjoys lower labor costs.

The transnational corporation became the primary agent of these technological changes. From the eighteenth century, powerful commercial companies have conducted business across national borders. By the twentieth century, the growing economic power of corporations in the industrialized nations allowed them to invest directly in the mines, plantations, and public utilities of less developed regions. In the post–World War II years, many of these companies became truly transnational, having multinational ownership and management. International trade agreements and open markets furthered the process. Ford Motor Company not only produced and sold cars internationally, but its shareholders, workers, and managers also had an international character. The Japanese automaker Honda imported into Japan cars it manufactured in Ohio. Similarly, German Volkswagen made cars in Mexico for sale in the United States.

As transnational manufacturers, agricultural conglomerates, and financial giants became wealthier and more powerful, they increasingly escaped the controls imposed by national governments. If labor costs were too high in Japan, antipollution measures too intrusive in the United States, or taxes too high in Great Britain, transnational companies relocated—or threatened to do so. Governments in the developing world were often hard-pressed to control the actions of these powerful enterprises. As a result, the worst abuses of labor or of the environment usually occurred in poor nations.

Conserving and Sharing Resources

In the 1960s, environmental activists and political leaders began warning about the devastating environmental consequences of population growth, industrialization, and the expansion of agriculture onto marginal lands. Assaults on rain forests and redwoods, the disappearance of species, and the poisoning of streams and rivers raised public consciousness. Environmental damage occurred in the advanced industrial economies and in the poorest of the developing nations. Perhaps the worst environmental record was achieved in the former Soviet Union, where industrial and nuclear wastes were often dumped with little concern for environmental consequences. The accumulated effect of scientific studies and public debate led to national and international efforts to slow, if not undo, damage to the environment.

The expanding global population required increasing quantities of food, housing, energy, and other resources as the twentieth century ended. In the developed world, industrial activity increased much more rapidly than population grew, and the consumption of energy (coal, electricity, and petroleum) rose proportionally. Indeed, the consumer-driven economic expansion of the post–World War II years became an obstacle to addressing environmental problems. Modern economies depend for their well-being on the profligate consumption of goods and resources. Stock markets closely follow measures of consumer confidence—the willingness of people to buy. When consumption slows, industrial nations enter a recession. How could the United States, Germany, or Japan change consumption patterns to protect the environment without endangering corporate profits, wages, and employment levels?

Population growth since 1945 has been most dramatic in the developing countries where environmental pressures were also extreme. In Brazil, India, and China, for example, the need to expand food production led to rapid deforestation and the extension of farming and grazing onto marginal lands. The results were predictable: erosion and water pollution. Population growth in Indonesia forced the government to permit the cutting of nearly 20 percent of the total forest area. These and many other poor nations also attempted to force industrialization because they feared that their rapidly growing populations could not be provided for unless the transition from agriculture to manufacturing was completed. The argument for this policy was compelling. Why should Indians or Brazilians remain poor while Americans, Europeans, and Japanese remained rich?

Responding to Environmental Threats

Despite the gravity of environmental threats, there were many successful efforts to preserve and protect the environment. The Clean Air Act, the Clean Water Act, and the Endangered Species Act were passed in the United States in the 1970s as part of an environmental effort that included the nations of the European Community and Japan. Environmental awareness spread by means of the media and grassroots political movements, and most nations in the developed world enforced strict antipollution laws and sponsored massive recycling efforts. Many also encouraged resource conservation by rewarding energy-efficient factories and the manufacturers of fuel-efficient cars and by promoting the use of alternative energy sources such as solar and wind power.

These efforts produced significant results. In western Europe and the United States, air quality improved dramatically. In the United States, smog levels were down nearly a third from 1970 to 2000 even though the number of automobiles increased more than 80 percent. Emissions of lead and sulfur dioxide were down as well. The Great Lakes, Long Island Sound, and Chesapeake Bay were all much cleaner at the end of the century than they had been in 1970. The rivers of North America and Europe also improved. Still, more than thirty thousand deaths each year in the United States are attributed to exposure to pesticides and other chemicals.

New technologies made much of this improvement possible. Pollution controls on automobiles, planes, and factory smokestacks reduced harmful emissions. Similar progress was made in the chemical industry. Scientists identified the chemicals that threaten the ozone layer, and the phase-out of their use in new appliances and cars began.

Clearly the desire to preserve the natural environment was growing around the world. In the developed nations, continued political organization and enhanced awareness of environmental issues seemed likely to lead to step-by-step improvements in environmental policy. In the developing world and most of the former Soviet bloc, however, population pressures and weak governments were major obstacles to effective environmental policies. In China, for example, respiratory disease caused by pollution was the leading cause of death. Thus it was likely that the industrialized nations would have to fund global improvements, and the cost was likely to be high. Achieving this global redistribution of wealth and political power will be the most difficult task facing the environmental movement in the coming years.

CONCLUSION

The world was profoundly altered between 1975 and 1991. The Cold War dominated international relations to the end of the 1980s. Every conflict threatened to provoke a confrontation between the nuclear-armed superpowers, for both the United States and the Soviet Union feared that every conflict and every regime change represented a potential threat to their strategic interests. As a result, the superpowers were drawn into a succession of civil wars and revolutions. The costs in lives and property were terrible, the gains small. As defense costs escalated, the Soviet system crumbled. By 1991 the Soviet Union and the socialist Warsaw Pact had disappeared, transforming the international stage.

Latin America was pulled into the violence of the late Cold War period and paid a terrible price. The 1970s and 1980s witnessed a frontal assault on democratic institutions, a denial of human rights, and economic decline. This was the period of death squads and Dirty War. With the end of the Cold War, peace returned there and democracy began to replace dictatorship.

In the Persian Gulf, the end of the Cold War did not lead to peace. Iran and Iraq have experienced deep cycles of political turmoil, war, and foreign threats since the late 1970s.

The world also was altered by economic growth and integration, by population growth and movement, and by technological and environmental change. Led by the postwar recovery of the industrial powers and the remarkable economic expansion of Japan and the Asian Tigers, the world economy grew dramatically. The development and application of new technology contributed significantly to this process. International markets were more open and integrated than at any other time. The new wealth and exciting technologies of the postwar era were not shared equally, however. The capitalist West and a few Pacific Rim nations grew richer and more powerful while most of the world's nations remained poor.

Population growth in the developing world was one reason for this divided experience. Unable to find adequate employment or, in many cases, bare subsistence, people in developing nations migrated across borders hoping to improve their lives. These movements often provided valuable labor in the factories and farms of the developed world, but they also provoked cultural, racial, and ethnic tension. Problems of inequality, population growth, and international migration would continue to challenge the global community in the coming decades.

Technology seemed to offer some hope for meeting these challenges. Engineering, financial services, education, and other professions developed an international character thanks to the communications revolution. Ambitious and talented people in the developing world could now fully participate in global intellectual and economic life. However, most people working in the developing world remained disconnected from this liberating technology by poverty. Technology also bolstered efforts to protect the environment, providing the means to clean auto and factory emissions—even while it helped produce much of the world's pollution. Technology has been intertwined with human culture since the beginning of human history. Our ability to control and direct its use will determine the future.

◼ Key Terms

proxy wars	newly industrialized
Salvador Allende	economies (NIEs)
Dirty War	Deng Xiaoping
Sandinistas	Tiananmen Square
Ayatollah Ruhollah	Mikhail Gorbachev
Khomeini	*perestroika*
Saddam Husain	Solidarity
keiretsu	Thomas Malthus
Asian Tigers	demographic transition

◼ Suggested Reading

Among the works devoted to postwar economic performance are W. L. M. Adriaasen and J. G. Waardensburg, eds., *A Dual World Economy: Forty Years of Development Experience* (1989); P. Krugman, *The Age of Diminished Expectations: U.S. Economic Policy in the 1990s* (1990); B. J. McCormick, *The World Economy: Patterns of Growth and Change* (1988); and H. van der Wee, *Prosperity and Upheaval: The World Economy, 1945–1980* (1986).

For Latin America, Thomas E. Skidmore and Peter H. Smith, *Modern Latin America*, 4th ed. (1996), provides an excellent general introduction to the period 1975 to 1991. The literature on the era of repression is large. *Nunca Mas* (1986), the official report of the Argentine government, provides a moving introduction. Also see news stories in 1999 and 2000 about the arrest of Augusto Pinochet in London and the resulting legal proceedings. The movie *Official Story* (available with subtitles or dubbed) offers an effective look at the legacy of the Dirty War in Argentina. For Central America see Walter La Feber, *Inevitable Revolutions: The United States in Central America* (1983).

For the Pacific Rim see Jonathan Spence, *The Search for Modern China* (1990); Edwin O. Reischauer, *The Japanese* (1988); H. Patrick and H. Rosovsky, *Asia's New Giant: How the Japanese Economy Works* (1976); and Staffan B. Linder, *Pacific Century: Economic and Political Consequences of Asian-Pacific Dynamism* (1986).

There are many fine studies of Europe and the Soviet system. See, for example, C. Kindleberger, *Europe's Postwar Growth* (1976). More focused examinations of the Soviet bloc are provided in K. Dawisha, *Eastern Europe, Gorbachev and Reform: The Great Challenge* (1988); Barbara Engel and Christine Worobec, eds., *Russia's Women: Accommodation, Resistance, Transformation* (1990); David Remnick, *Lenin's Tomb: The Last Days of the Soviet Empire* (1993); and Charles Maier, *Dissolution: The Crisis of Communism and the End of East Germany* (1997).

The story of the Iranian Revolution and the early days of the Islamic Republic of Iran is well told by Shaul Bakhash, *The Reign of the Ayatollahs: Iran and the Iranian Revolution* (1990). Barnet Rubin, *The Fragmentation of Afghanistan* (1995), provides excellent coverage of the struggle between Soviet forces and the Muslim resistance in that country.

A number of studies examine the special problems faced by women in the postwar period. See, for example, Elisabeth Croll, *Feminism and Socialism in China* (1978); J. Ginat, *Women in Muslim Rural Society: Status and Role in Family and Community* (1982); June Hahner, *Women in Latin America* (1976); P. Hudson, *Third World Women Speak Out* (1979); A. de Souza, *Women in Contemporary India and South Asia* (1980); and M. Wolf, *Revolution Postponed: Women in Contemporary China* (1985).

For general discussions of economic, demographic, and environmental problems facing the world see R. N. Gwynne, *New Horizons? Third World Industrialization in an International Framework* (1990); W. Alonso, ed., *Population in an Interacting World* (1987); P. R. Ehrlich and A. E. Ehrlich, *The Population Explosion* (1990); James Fallows, *More like Us: Making America Great Again* (1989); Paul M. Kennedy, *Preparing for the Twenty-first Century* (1993); and J. L. Simon, *Population Matters: People, Resources, Environment and Immigration* (1990).

For issues associated with technological and environmental change see M. Feshbach and A. Friendly, *Ecocide in the U.S.S.R.* (1992); John Bellamy Foster, *Economic History of the Environment* (1994); S. Hecht and A. Cockburn, *The Fate of the Forest: Developers, Destroyers, and Defenders of the Amazon* (1989); K. Marton, *Multinationals, Technology, and Industrialization: Implications and Impact in Third World Countries* (1986); S. P. Huntington, *The Third Wave: Demoralization in the Late Twentieth Century* (1993); L. Solomon, *Multinational Corporations and the Emerging World Order* (1978); and B. L. Turner II et al., eds., *The Earth as Transformed by Human Action: Global and Regional Changes in the Biosphere over the Past 300 Years* (1990).

■ Notes

1. *New York Times,* July 24, 1993, 1.
2. Quoted in Antony Flew, "Introduction," in Thomas Robert Malthus, *An Essay on the Principle of Population and a Summary View of the Principle of Population* (New York: Penguin Books, 1970), 30.
3. "Population Implosion Worries a Graying Europe," *New York Times,* July 10, 1998.
4. Paul Kennedy, *Preparing for the Twenty-first Century* (New York: Random House, 1993), 45.
5. Andrew Hacker, "Unjust Desserts?" *New York Review of Books,* March 3, 1994, 20.

35

THE END OF
A GLOBAL CENTURY,
1991–2000

A Fragmented World • The Struggle for Rights •
Elements of a Global Culture
ENVIRONMENT AND TECHNOLOGY: Global Warming
SOCIETY AND CULTURE: Nelson Mandela

Orly Airport in Paris   The growing pace of transportation and communications
was a distinctive feature of late twentieth-century life.

As the year 1999 ended, *Time* magazine, in keeping with its long-standing tradition of choosing a "Person of the Year," decided to name the "Person of the Century." Instead of simply consulting among themselves or hiring a polling company to conduct a statistically sound survey, the editors conducted a poll over the Internet. Individuals with access to the Internet—well under half of the U.S. population—could vote for whomever they liked as many times as they wished. After deleting the names they considered frivolous, the editors came up with several lists of winners, ranging from revolutionaries to sports heroes. At the very top of the list was Albert Einstein; Franklin D. Roosevelt and Mahatma Gandhi were the first and second runners-up.

Time's contribution to the end-of-the-century passion for recapitulations encapsulated how many people viewed the world around them. Albert Einstein opened the door to the scientific wonders of the Atomic Age and inadvertently made possible the Cold War's "balance of terror." Franklin D. Roosevelt led the military alliance that crushed fascism in World War II, leaving the United States the world's most powerful nation. Mahatma Gandhi pioneered nonviolence in the face of injustice as a technique for winning rights and in the process helped set in motion the wave of decolonization of the post–World War II decades. And the Internet, *Time*'s technological collaborator, symbolized a revolution in communication that promised to bring the peoples of the world into ever closer contact.

Despite these emblems of the twentieth century's achievements, however, the twenty-first century dawned on a world deeply concerned about ethnic conflicts, human rights violations, environmental problems, and economic uncertainties. While powerful economic and cultural forces pushed for greater globalization, peoples in many lands sought ways to preserve or achieve autonomy and identity and safeguard human rights. While affluent individuals in the most developed countries enjoyed unprecedented prosperity, growing disparities between rich and poor, both within and among countries, cast a shadow on the future.

As you read this chapter, ask yourself the following questions:

- How did technology contribute to the process of globalization in the late twentieth century?
- What are the main sources of conflict in the post–Cold War world?
- What role does the struggle for human rights play in the contemporary world?

A FRAGMENTED WORLD

Religion, ethnicity, and race had played supporting roles during the era of empire and ideological struggle, but they took stage center with the fading of the Cold War. From the onset of the New Imperialism in the mid-nineteenth century (see Chapter 29) down to the peace settlements at the close of World War I (see Chapter 30), the European powers had readily—often arbitrarily—drawn and redrawn lines on maps. In the era of decolonization, these arbitrary boundaries became accepted borders for new nations. During the Cold War, the West tended to see local efforts to change political boundaries as communist plots; and most governments in the newly independent states were too preoccupied with the problems of governance and economic development to put much effort into attempts to redraw boundaries. To dispel fears of territorial aggression, regional groups such as the Organization of African Unity affirmed the colonial borders as national boundaries despite their lack of relationship to ethnic and linguistic realities. This generally conservative attitude toward change was reinforced by a number of violent episodes that aroused fears that the world order somehow might dissolve.

Challenges to the Nation-State

The modern state system that conceives of the world as a community of sovereign nation-states wielding absolute authority within recognized borders began with the Peace of Westphalia in 1648. Exhausted by the Thirty Years War, the Catholic and Protestant rulers of Europe signed treaties designed to bring Europe's Wars of Religion to an end. But although international commitment

CHRONOLOGY

	Politics	Economics and Society
1991		**1991** CNN covers Persian Gulf War live from Baghdad
	1992 Yugoslavia disintegrates—Croatia and Slovenia become independent states	
	1992–1995 Bosnia crisis	
	1994 Maya uprising in southern Mexico	**1993** Nobel Peace Prize to Nelson Mandela
1995	**1995** Nerve gas released in Tokyo subway	**1995** World Trade Organization founded
		1997 Asian financial crisis
	1998 Terrorist bombings of U.S. embassies in Kenya and Tanzania; India and Pakistan test atomic bombs	
	1999 Kosovo crisis; East Timor secedes from Indonesia	**1999** Nobel Peace Prize to Doctors Without Borders

to the concept of the sovereign nation-state reduced violence between states, it did not erase the passions of groups within states who felt alienated from their rulers or their rulers' religion.

Europeans subsequently worked hard to make religious toleration a reality at home. But in the parts of the world they colonized, they tended to see the local populations as divided into two opposed groups analogous to Protestants and Catholics. Divisions between Sunni and Shi'ite Muslims in the Middle East, between Hindus and Muslims in India, and between Arabs and Berbers in Algeria were all viewed through the distorting lens of European religious conflict. Instead of analyzing the specific nature of each ethnic or religious system they encountered, the United States and Europe tried in vain to establish Western-style democracy and secularism as a general formula for ensuring peace and tolerance.

The conflicts were many, extending even to countries with only small religious minorities (see Map 35.1). The Tamil-speaking Hindu population in Sri Lanka fought a prolonged and merciless guerrilla struggle throughout the 1980s and 1990s against the dominant Singhalese-speaking Buddhists. Dissidents in mostly Catholic East Timor fought for separation from Muslim Indonesia from the moment Portuguese rule ended in 1975 down to 1999, when their goal was finally achieved by popular referendum. In East Africa, Eritrea fought for and won independence from religiously and linguistically different Ethiopia in 1993. The ethnic hatreds between the Hutu people and the Tutsi people that repeatedly wracked Rwanda and Burundi spilled over into Congo (then Zaire) in 1998, overturning the long-standing dictatorship of President Joseph Mobutu. Even constitutionally secular

India saw instances of violence against Muslims and Christians in the name of Hindu nationalism.

In some instances, large-scale violence was avoided. Czechs and Slovaks agreed to divide postcommunist Czechoslovakia into the Czech Republic and the Republic of Slovakia in 1993. A brief uprising among the Maya population of southern Mexico in 1994 drew needed government attention and aid to that part of the country. And Malay-Chinese animosities in Malaysia and Indonesia were largely submerged in prosperity until economic calamity struck those countries in 1997.

In Yugoslavia, a population that had seemed harmonious until 1991 dissolved into a morass of separatist and warring groups. This conflict drew particular attention because of the complexity of the situation and its location on the border of an eastern Europe and a western Europe trying to restore connections after four decades of Iron Curtain separation. Industrial and urban Slovenia and agricultural Croatia, the most northerly parts of Yugoslavia, were predominantly Roman Catholic and had strong historic links to Austria and Hungary, respectively. Both were recognized as independent states in 1992 after brief struggles with federal Yugoslav forces.

The Yugoslavian province of Bosnia and Herzegovina faced greater difficulties. The people living there spoke Serbo-Croatian, but 40 percent were Muslims, 30 percent Eastern Orthodox Serbs, and 18 percent Croatian Catholics. The religious division dated back to Ottoman times, when this part of Yugoslavia was a border zone between Islam and Christian Europe. The murderous three-sided fighting that broke out with the declaration of Bosnian national independence in 1992 gave rise to the term **ethnic cleansing.** Originally journalists used

Map 35.1 World Religions Believers in Islam, Christianity, and Buddhism make up large percentages of the population in many countries. Differing forms of these religions seldom coincide with national boundaries. As religion revives as a source of social identity or a rationale for political assertion or mass mobilization, the possibility of religious activism spreading across broad geographic regions becomes greater, as does the likelihood of domestic discord in multireligious states.

Majority religion

- Christian
- Muslim
- Atheist/Nonreligious
- Hindu
- Buddhist
- Local religions

60% Minority religion

Notes: 1. Israel: the majority of the population is Jewish

2. Tibet: the majority of the population is Buddhist

3. Chinese province of Xinjiang: the majority of the population is Muslim

4. Indonesian island of Bali: the majority of the population is Hindu

Albanian Refugees from Kosovo   Lines of familiar-looking refugees from the complex Yugoslavia crisis reminded Europeans of the grim days following World War II. Parallel refugee situations in Afghanistan, Iraq, Rwanda, or Somalia had less immediacy and generated less pressure for international intervention.   (Peter Turnley/Black Star)

the term to refer to the efforts of Bosnian Serbs to evict Bosnian Muslims from their homes and destroy all vestiges of Muslim presence, from manuscripts in the national library to mosques and historic Ottoman buildings. Today the term means any effort by one racial, ethnic, or religious group to eliminate the people and culture of a different group.

The Bosnia crisis challenged the international community to consider whether one country could rightly intervene in another nation's civil war when the intervening power had no national interests at stake. Since the territories that retained the name Yugoslavia—the southern regions centered on the heavily populated province of Serbia—were helping the Bosnian Serbs, and independent Croatia was helping the Croatians of Bosnia, the question was whether anyone was going to come to the aid of the Muslims, Bosnia's largest ethnic group. No Muslim state had the capability to intervene in a major way. Iran and other Muslim states sent some

aid and charged that religious prejudice was the reason for European unwillingness to help the Muslims. Finally, after much indecision—and extensive television coverage of atrocities and wanton destruction—the United States made a cautious intervention and eventually brokered a tentative settlement in 1995.

The shooting had hardly stopped in Bosnia when tension began to heighten in Kosovo, a southern province of Yugoslavia, populated mostly by Albanian-speaking Muslims. In 1389 the Ottoman Empire defeated the kingdom of Serbia in the Battle of Kosovo, and Kosovo became an enduring and powerful symbol of Serbian national aspirations. By the 1990s, however, Serbs constituted only a minority of Kosovo's population. The NATO alliance repeatedly urged Serbia to stop mistreating the Kosovars (that is, the Albanian-speaking Muslims of Kosovo) and to permit them to participate in Yugoslavia's federal government as they had done before 1989, when Kosovo was an autonomous province within Yugoslavia. When

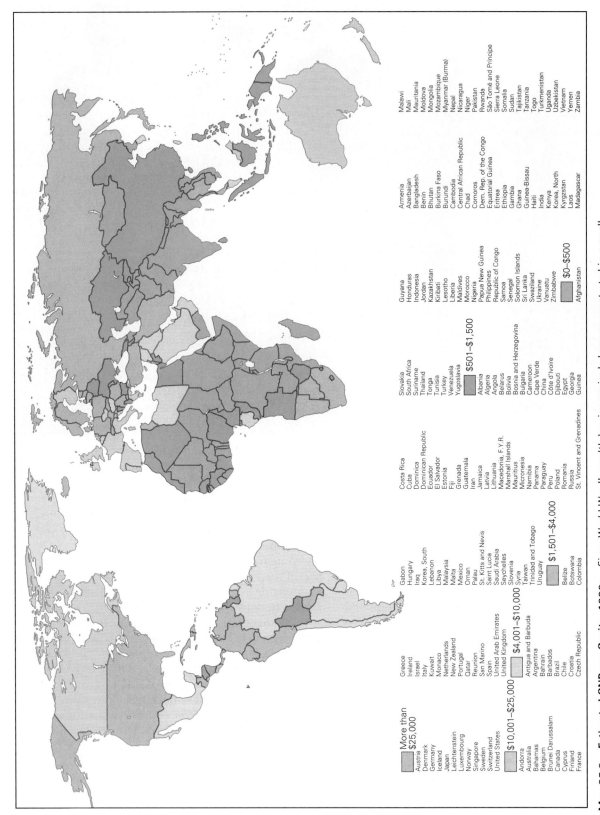

Map 35.2   Estimated GNP per Capita, 1990s   Since World War II, wealth has increasingly been concentrated in a small number of industrialized nations in the Northern Hemisphere. The cost of developing and acquiring new technologies has widened the gap between rich and poor nations.

NATO's warnings went unheeded, the United States, Britain, and France—acting under the NATO umbrella—launched an aerial war against Serbia in 1999. Suffering few casualties themselves, the NATO allies—but mainly the United States—damaged military and infrastructural targets in Serbia and forced the withdrawal of Serbian forces from Kosovo.

In the aftermath of the air attacks, no one was certain whether new principles of international action had been established. Having nearly single-handedly won the Kosovo war without losing any American lives to enemy fire, the United States had again proven its might. But it was unclear whether such things as violations of human rights, ethnic cleansing, and atrocities, on the one hand, or the military weakness of the force perpetrating the abuses, on the other, would determine when and where future U.S. or NATO interventions might occur. Chronic internal conflicts in Turkey against Kurdish-speaking peoples, and in Sudan against Christian and animist groups were cited as instances in which human rights concerns might call for international intervention. However, these trouble spots were also places where a long-standing alliance (Turkey) or geographical remoteness (Sudan) weighed heavily against intervention. Also in the aftermath of the events of Yugoslavia, the European Union took steps to organize a collective military force outside of NATO so as to have a basis for independent action in any future crisis.

Problems of the Global Economy

Issues of foreign intervention and national sovereignty also surfaced in the economic realm. In the nineteenth century the imperialist nations exported raw materials from their overseas colonies and shipped in manufactured goods, destroying local handicraft industries and making the colonies dependent on international commodity prices. If a slump occurred in the market for cotton cloth, colonial economies that depended heavily on the export of raw cotton suffered more than the economies of the imperialist nations that wove the cloth. When industrial profits were high, the imperialists invested surplus capital in industrializing nations with populations of European ancestry, such as the United States, or in building railroads, ports, and other facilities to increase commodity exports from the colonies to the industrial nations.

World economic development after World War II at first followed this pattern—that is, favoring industry in Europe and commodity production elsewhere. Marshall Plan aid by the United States to rebuild industrial western Europe was paralleled by investments by the USSR to favor industry in Russia and eastern Europe. The Caspian and Central Asian republics of the Soviet Union were left dependent on exchanging cotton, wheat, petroleum, and other basic commodities for industrial products.

The pattern gradually changed, however, partly because of Cold War conflicts. American purchases of supplies during the Korean War stimulated economic growth in Japan in the 1950s. In the 1960s and 1970s, American involvement in Vietnam entailed similar expenditures, which helped Singapore, Hong Kong, and Taiwan develop vigorous industrial economies. At the same time, Japan concluded a series of treaties formally ending World War II. Its 1965 peace treaty with South Korea, for example, a country it had exploited harshly during the decades of annexation from 1910 to 1940, was accompanied by economic agreements that fueled a strong Korean economic resurgence. These unprecedented new avenues for the international flow of money helped these East Asian countries reach levels of industrial prosperity previously enjoyed only in Europe and North America.

Other factors similarly altered the world pattern of wealth distribution (see Map 35.2). During the decade of high oil prices starting in 1974, the oil-producing states became rich, but foreign debt became a major problem for some of the world's biggest countries, including Mexico and Brazil (see Chapter 34). After the collapse of the Soviet Union in 1991, the newly independent republics in eastern Europe required enormous investment to adapt their inefficient command economies to the global marketplace. By century's end it was still unclear whether Russia's faltering economy would make a successful transition to capitalism.

At the same time, Southeast Asia boomed. Benefiting from investment and technical expertise from Japan and other industrial nations, Thailand, Malaysia, and Indonesia experienced rapid economic growth. As the world's tallest skyscraper rose in Kuala Lumpur, industry mushroomed. Deforestation proceeded with equal rapidity as hardwood trees in Indonesia and other tropical countries, including Brazil, were cut down and sold on the world market. Groups concerned with protecting animal habitats and saving species from extinction protested these assaults, but quick profits and a national interest in economic development proved of greater weight (see Environmental and Technology: Global Warming).

The fevered pace of economic growth in Asia exploded in 1997 in a financial crisis that sent currency and stock values plummeting first in Thailand and then in neighboring countries, eventually triggering serious recession in Japan and having effects as far away as Brazil. Though the damage to the industrial economies of Europe and North America was limited, slackened demand for oil in Asia caused petroleum prices to fall to historic

Global Warming

Until the 1980s, environmental alarms focused mainly on localized episodes of air and water pollution, exposure to toxic substances, waste management, and the disappearance of wilderness. The development of increasingly powerful computers and complex models of ecological interactions in the 1990s, however, made people aware of the global scope of certain environmental problems.

Many scientists and policymakers came to perceive global warming, the slow increase of the temperature of earth's lower atmosphere, as an environmental threat requiring preventive action on an international scale. The warming was caused by a layer of atmospheric gases—called *greenhouse gases* (carbon dioxide, methane, nitrous oxide, and ozone)—that allowed solar radiation to reach the earth and warm it but kept infrared energy (heat) from radiating from the earth's surface into space. Called the *greenhouse effect*, this process normally keeps the earth's temperature at a level suitable for life. However, twentieth century increases in greenhouse-gas emissions from industry, agriculture, and transportation added to this insulating atmospheric layer. Though scientists disagree about which computer model of climatic change is most reliable, many have warned that

global temperature increases might melt glaciers and icecaps and raise sea levels by many feet. They also have cautioned that warming might be more intense in the polar regions and that changes in oceanic currents and wind patterns could trigger disastrous weather changes.

Though 1998 was the warmest year of modern times and 1995 the second warmest, scientists continued to disagree over the exact extent and cause of global warming. International agreements to limit greenhouse-gas production signed in 1992 and 1997 were controversial because of the effect they could have on curtailing industry in North America, Europe, and Japan—regions that contribute disproportionately high levels of greenhouse gases to the atmosphere. Leaders of developing countries fear that limits on gas emissions could cripple their plans for industrial and economic expansion. Nevertheless, if the most alarming predictions—that sea-level rises could inundate coastal regions and some of the world's largest cities—come to pass, further agreements will be needed. It is unclear whether nations are prepared to cooperate on world environmental programs that might seem to limit their sovereignty or run against their national economic interests.

Flooding in Bangladesh
Typhoon-driven floods submerge the low-lying farmlands of Bangladesh with tragic regularity. Any significant rise in the sea level will make parts of the country nearly uninhabitable. (D. Aubert/Sygma)

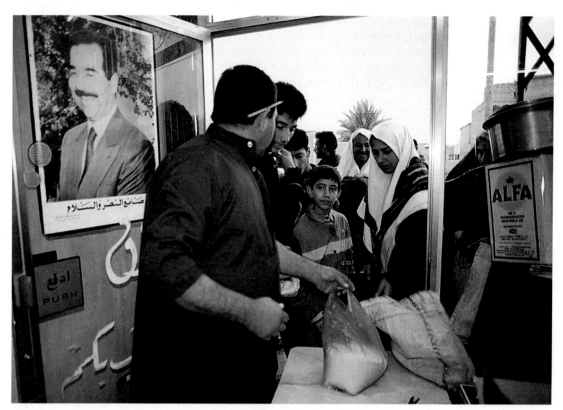

Postwar Food Distribution in Iraq   Economic sanctions placed on Iraq by the United Nations after the 1991 Gulf War required international monitoring of food distribution made possible by the sale of limited amounts of Iraqi oil. Though sanctions were intended to weaken Saddam Husain, shown in the photo to the left of food distributors, hardship experienced by the general population strengthened his control and focused resentment on the United Nations.   (Samara Boustani/Sygma)

lows in 1999. This decline threatened the economies of the oil-producing states sufficiently to prod them into agreeing to production limits to bring prices back up.

The financial crises in Asia and Russia exemplified the tight interconnections within the global economy and raised the question of whether prosperous nations were obliged to rescue failing economies. A financial bailout for Mexico became a heated political issue in the United States in 1995, the year after the North American Free Trade Agreement (NAFTA), eliminating tariffs among the United States, Canada, and Mexico, went into effect. Arguing that Mexican prosperity was in the U.S. national interest, President Bill Clinton (1993–2001) pushed through a rescue plan that turned out to be successful. Other countries went to the International Monetary Fund and World Bank for assistance. These bodies made their assistance conditional on internal economic reforms that were often politically difficult, such as terminating government subsidies for basic foodstuffs and liberalizing investment.

Economic sanctions—embargoes, boycotts, freezing of assets, and restrictions on investment, all intended to harm another country's economy—became popular as a weapon, though one that only rich nations could wield. The United States, sometimes with the collaboration of its European allies, imposed severe sanctions on Iraq, Libya, Iran, Yugoslavia, and a number of other countries it had disputes with. Though the ultimate goal of such sanctions was normally to change a target government's policies, oil boycotts (Libya, Iraq) and bans on American investment (Iran) generally fell short of this objective, though they were often successful in inflicting economic damage.

In 1995, in an effort to foster and bring order to international trade, the world's major trading powers established the **World Trade Organization (WTO)** as the climax of a final round of negotiations under the rubric General Agreement on Tariffs and Trade (GATT). Charged with enforcing GATT agreements hammered out during periodic negotiating sessions over forty-seven years, the WTO seeks to reduce barriers to world trade. Despite a membership of 110 nations, however, the WTO is not without enemies, as became evident in Seattle in 1999, when street demonstrations, partly organized by American labor unions fearful of foreign competition, forced the organization to suspend a meeting.

Old Threat, New Dangers

As new military technologies gave the United States and a few other states the ability to wage war with minimal casualties to themselves, other ways of deploying violence for political ends became popular. One technique was to launch violent terrorist attacks. **Terrorism** rested on the belief that horrendous acts of violence could provoke harsh reprisals or, if repeated frequently, demonstrate such government incompetence that existing regimes would lose legitimacy and the people would look to the terrorists as a strong, organized, determined replacement. By no means a new force in world affairs, terrorism thrived in the late twentieth century because it was hard to combat and well adapted to television news coverage. Global broadcasting gave terrorist acts publicity, thus generating fear among the public and increasing the likelihood of governments losing control.

Palestinian groups dedicated to destroying Israel set the tone for later media-centered terrorism with airplane hijackings in 1968 and the capture and eventual murder of eleven Israeli athletes during the Munich Olympic Games of 1972. Both of these outrages became media events that galvanized sympathy for Israel, but they also led fearful television viewers to believe that Palestinian groups were much stronger than they actually were. Fear of Palestinian violence unquestionably contributed to the on-again, off-again peace process that Israel agreed to during secret discussions in Oslo, Norway, in 1991.

Political groups around the world staged innumerable terrorist acts, from bombings in the British Isles by the Irish Republican Army, to the assassinations in India of prime ministers Indira Gandhi (1984) and Rajiv Gandhi (1991), to the release of nerve gas in the Tokyo subway system by an apocalyptic Buddhist sect in 1995. The simultaneous bombing of U.S. embassies in Kenya and Tanzania in 1998 demonstrated the frustration and vulnerability of even the most powerful governments. Usamah bin Ladin°, a Saudi veteran of the Afghan war

---

Usamah bin Ladin (oo-SAH-mah bin LAH-din)

against the USSR, was named by the United States as the mastermind of the bombings. Yet despite a token retaliatory air attack on his base in Afghanistan, a country with which the United States had no diplomatic relations, he remained untouchable and seemingly continued his terrorist plotting against the United States.

Nuclear proliferation offered a far more plausible threat to world peace, and fear that nuclear devices would fall into the wrong hands was especially strong in government circles. During the Cold War, the world had lived with a sense of impending nuclear doom. This feeling quickly evaporated after communism collapsed in Europe in 1991. Yet thousands of nuclear weapons remained. Despite safeguards to keep them from being sold or stolen, the possibility of nuclear weapons falling into the hands of terrorists or states interested in blackmailing their neighbors could not be discounted. Nor was there adequate assurance that radioactive materials could be disposed of safely without environmental contamination.

In addition, a number of countries undertook to construct their own nuclear devices, usually in secret. Oddly, the balance of nuclear forces between the United States and the Soviet Union throughout the Cold War had increasingly come to be seen as an element of stability. Because neither side could have started a nuclear war without facing total annihilation, both sides were bound never to use their ghastly arsenals. Without the threat of mutual destruction, however, it seemed possible that one or two nuclear weapons could be used in a restricted regional context. Thus a new form of nuclear anxiety arose. The problem for the world community was **nuclear nonproliferation:** how to prevent a country like North Korea or Iraq from deploying nuclear weapons. The United States sought commitments from North Korea to refrain from developing nuclear weapons, and the United Nations used intrusive inspections of suspected nuclear facilities to disarm Iraq. But there was no assurance that either form of deterrence would prove effective in the long run. Anxiety over nuclear proliferation increased when India and Pakistan openly tested nuclear bombs and missile delivery systems in 1998.

Chemical and biological weapons, which could kill massively and indiscriminately and be delivered in missile warheads, posed a similar threat. But preventing their manufacture was more difficult. Nuclear weapons required advanced technology and large investments in factories and equipment, but lethal chemicals and biological agents could be produced by seemingly ordinary chemical and pharmaceutical plants using standard equipment. United Nations inspections of Iraqi war-

Nelson Mandela

The drama of decolonization in Africa climaxed in 1994 when Nelson Rolihlahla Mandela was elected president of South Africa in the first election open to citizens of all races. Born in 1918, Mandela became an active protester for civil rights as a college student in 1940. While working for a law degree, he helped found the Youth League of the African National Congress (ANC) in 1944.

After violent racial clashes in 1960 prompted the banning of the ANC, Mandela became its underground leader, challenging the apartheid regime (see Chapter 33) and calling for a new constitution based on democratic principles. Facing the full military mobilization of the apartheid state, he organized armed resistance and was arrested in 1962. While serving a life sentence, he refused several offers of freedom that would have required recognition of government racial policies.

In 1990, when it became evident that apartheid could not be maintained, Mandela was released and the next year elected President of the ANC. In 1993 he was awarded the Nobel Peace Prize, and in the following year he was elected president of South Africa. The following excerpt comes from his inauguration address.

Our daily deeds as ordinary South Africans must produce an actual South Africa that will reinforce humanity's belief in justice, strengthen its confidence in the nobility of the human soul and sustain all our hopes for a glorious life for all. . . .

To my compatriots, I have no hesitation in saying that each one of us is as intimately attached to the soil of this beautiful country as are the jacaranda trees of Pretoria and the mimosa trees of the bushveld. . . .

That spiritual and physical oneness we all share with this common homeland explains the depth of the pain we all carried in our hearts as we saw our country tear itself apart in a terrible conflict, and as we saw it spurned, outlawed and isolated by the peoples of the world, precisely because it had become the universal base of the pernicious ideology and practice of racism and racial oppression.

We, the people of South Africa, feel fulfilled that humanity has taken us back into its bosom, that we, who were outlaws not so long ago, have today been given the rare privilege to be host to the nations of the world on our own soil. . . .

The time for the healing of wounds has come.

The moment to bridge the chasms that divide us has come.

Why was Mandela's election considered a great victory for human rights? What is the significance of Mandela's use of the word compatriot?

Source: Inauguration Address of Nelson Mandela as State President of South Africa, May 10, 1994.

making potential (carried out as part of the settlement of the 1991 Persian Gulf War) uncovered and destroyed extensive stocks of chemical munitions and plants for producing nerve gas and lethal germs. However, no means of preventing Iraq or any other country from developing these weapons was devised. In 1998 Iraqi resistance to inspections provoked a military confrontation with the United States and effectively terminated the inspection program. Thus the most concerted international effort to limit a country's military capability suffered a severe setback, and the issue returned to the United Nations Security Council for reconsideration.

THE STRUGGLE FOR RIGHTS

Some critics chastised U.S. president Jimmy Carter in 1979 for pressing the shah of Iran to improve Iran's human rights record. His pressure, they felt, hastened the shah's downfall (see Chapter 34). However, the question of rights played an increasingly important role in international affairs in the 1990s (see Society and Culture: Nelson Mandela). While environmental and animal liberation groups pressed for extensions of the concept of rights, some religious communities deemed rights agitation an attack on their traditions. When governments were criticized on rights issues, they commonly protested that the matters were purely internal and that any interference from abroad was an attack on state sovereignty.

Human Rights

In addition to maintaining peaceful relations between states, the United Nations also aimed to protect the rights of individuals. A General Assembly resolution passed on December 10, 1948—called the **Universal Declaration of Human Rights**—contained thirty articles that it proclaimed to be "a common standard of achievement for all peoples and nations."[1] It condemned slavery, torture, cruel and inhuman punishment, and arbitrary arrest, detention, or exile. It called for freedom of movement, assembly, and thought. It asserted rights to life, liberty, and security of person; to impartial public trials; and to education, employment, and leisure. The declaration ringingly asserted the principle of equality, most fully set forth in Article 2:

> Everyone is entitled to all the rights and freedoms set forth in this Declaration, without distinction of any kind, such as race, color, sex, language, religion, or political or other opinion, national or social origin, property, birth or other status.[2]

The roots of the declaration lay mostly in European and American history. Religious tolerance emerged from Europe's bloody religious wars of the sixteenth and seventeenth centuries. The idea of inalienable rights came from the U.S. Constitution (1788) and Bill of Rights (1791) and the French Declaration of the Rights of Man (1789). The struggle against slavery and the woman suffrage movement in the nineteenth and twentieth centuries extended the concept of tolerance to all races and both sexes (see Chapters 25 and 28). The concept of social justice steadily advanced in Europe and America with the legalization of labor unions, the spread of universal education, and the establishment of government programs to care for the needy and ensure adequate standards of living for all citizens.

Not all the countries that voted for the declaration in 1948 shared this European heritage, but its principles dovetailed with humanitarian concerns in a variety of non-European cultures and nations. Most countries later joining the United Nations willingly signed the declaration because it implicitly condemned the persistence of discriminatory European colonial regimes. Despite this apparent agreement, however, some people had philosophical reservations about the declaration's formulation of human rights. They asked whether such a set of principles could be called universal when so many of the world's religious and cultural traditions had not been consulted in its drafting.

Did the declaration's assertion of total equality, for example, mean that the traditional social distinctions represented by the Hindu castes were unacceptable? Was the declaration breached by nations that used religion, language, skin color, or membership in a particular ethnic group to distinguish more privileged from less privileged citizens—a group of nations that included Israel, the United States, South Africa, and Saudi Arabia, among many others? Did the section declaring that "everyone has a right to a nationality" implicitly condemn suppressing ethnic minorities—as Turkey, Iraq, and Iran did with their Kurdish populations; China did with Tibetans; and France did with immigrant Muslims from North Africa?

Lacking mechanisms for addressing issues on this scale, human rights activists, often working through international philanthropic bodies known as **nongovernmental organizations (NGOs),** focused their efforts on easily agreed-upon violations of human decency: torture, imprisonment without trial, summary execution by government death squads, and famine relief, and refugee assistance. NGOs devoted to relieving hunger and oppression and bringing human rights abuses to world attention proliferated in the 1970s. Amnesty International, founded in 1961 and numbering a million members in 162 countries by the 1990s, concentrated on gaining freedom for people illegally imprisoned. Médecins Sans Frontières (Doctors Without Borders), founded in 1971, was awarded the Nobel Peace Prize in 1999 for the medical assistance it offered in scores of crisis situations. Even entertainers became involved in relieving suffering through Live Aid, a 1985 rock concert in London and Philadelphia that raised millions of dollars for famine assistance.

Such efforts raised the prominence of human rights as a global concern and put pressure on governments to consider human rights when making foreign policy decisions. Skeptics observed, however, that a Western country could prod a non-Western country to improve its human rights performance—for example, by barring the government from cutting off a thief's hand as stipulated by Islamic law—but reverse criticism of a Western country—for example, condemnation of persistent racial discrimination in the United States—often fell on deaf ears. Thus the human rights movement was sometimes seen not as an effort to make the world as a whole more humane but as another form of Western cultural imperialism, a club with which to beat former colonial societies into submission.

Women's Rights

No issue exemplified this dichotomy of views so clearly as women's rights. The feminist movement that peaked in the early twentieth century had concentrated on acquiring voting rights (see Chapters 28 and 30). Inspired by parallel efforts to combat racial discrimination and end the war in Vietnam, feminist activism revived in the United States in the 1960s and spread around the world. The movement focused on equal access to education and jobs and on quality-of-life matters such as ending sexual exploitation, gaining control of reproduction, and abandoning confining clothing styles. Ironically, the decades in which the feminist movement (followed by movements for gay and lesbian rights in North America and Europe) became a major force also saw sexuality become a more explicit and prominent aspect of commercial, artistic, and social life.

Feminists in the West decried the oppression of women in other parts of the world. At the same time, some non-Western women complained about the deterioration of morality and family life in the West and what they considered to be the feminists' misplaced concern with matters such as clothing. As with human rights, non-Western peoples disputed the West's definition of priorities. Western women and many secularized Muslim women protested Islam's requirement that a woman cover her head and wear loose-fitting garments to conceal the shape of her body, practices enforced by law in countries such as Iran and Saudi Arabia. Nevertheless, many outspoken Muslim women voluntarily donned concealing garments as expressions of personal belief, statements of resistance to secular dictatorship, or defenses against coarse male behavior. Some African women saw their real problems as deteriorating economic conditions, AIDS, and the customary practice of circumcising girls, a form of genital mutilation that could cause chronic infections or permanently impair sexual enjoyment.

Efforts to coordinate the struggle for women's rights internationally gained momentum in the 1970s with a series of highly publicized international conferences. But the search for a universally accepted women's rights agenda proved elusive, because of local concerns and strong disagreement on abortion and other issues. Nevertheless, a rising global tide of women's education, access to employment, political participation, and control of fertility augured well for the eventual achievement of gender equality.

Beijing Women's Conference in 1995   This gathering of women, under United Nations auspices, from every part of the world illustrated the challenges posed by women's search for equality. The Chinese government, consistent with its policies of suppressing dissent and closely regulating social life, tried to limit press access to the conference. As in many other instances, these efforts to silence or control women's voices on issues like abortion and family planning proved ineffective.   (Alesandra Boulat/Sipa Press)

Still, culturally shaped disagreement on women's rights and other philosophical and social issues persisted at the end of the twentieth century. The greatest likelihood was that the diverse peoples of the world would seldom be able to do more than agree to disagree. World developmental patterns pointed to worsening social and economic problems in Africa and growing economic power in Asia. Thus the continuing appeal of standards too closely identified with European and American values seemed to be in doubt.

ELEMENTS OF A GLOBAL CULTURE

With the disintegration of the Soviet Union into fifteen separate republics in 1990–1991, overt political imperialism seemed an increasingly distant memory (see Chapter 34). Yet concerns grew in many quarters about **cultural imperialism.** Critics complained that entertainment conglomerates were flooding the world's movie theaters and television screens with Western tastes and styles and that Western manufacturers were flooding world markets with Western goods—both relying on sophisticated advertising techniques that vigorously promoted worldwide consumption and cultural conformity. In this view, global marketing was an especially insidious effort not only to overwhelm the world with a single Western outlook shaped by capitalist ideology, but also to suppress or devalue traditional cultures and alternative ideologies; the United States was the primary culprit.

But in truth, technology, not ideology, played the central role in spreading Western culture. The idea that the West engaged in cultural imperialism rested in part on the fact that Americans invented and developed so much of the technology that formed and spread popular culture in the twentieth century. A close analysis of cultural trends reveals a diversity of voices that the case for cultural imperialism overlooks.

The Medium and the Message

After World War II, much of Europe's and Japan's industry lay in ruins, and the United States became the world's main exporter of movies. Hollywood exported an image of the United States as a land of gangsters and cowboys, pratfalls and musical romance. By the 1960s, depictions of American life broadened. Still, emphasis on crime, luxurious living, and—from the 1970s on—explicit sexuality presented a skewed but influential and fairly consistent image of America.

European and Japanese cinema recovered slowly from the war. European and Japanese filmmakers earned high marks for artistic accomplishment, but their work generally appealed to relatively small international markets. Hollywood's main international competition in the field of popular cinema came from Bombay, whose joyous musicals had wide appeal; Egypt, famed for musicals and comedies; and Hong Kong, which specialized in martial arts films. Films of high artistic merit made in the USSR, Brazil, China, India, and, after the 1979 revolution, Iran, won international prizes but did not attract mass international audiences.

Television, made possible by the invention of an electron scanning gun by the American Vladimir Zworykin° in 1928, became widely available to consumers only after World War II and did not spread to most non-Western countries until the 1960s. Hollywood's dominance in the world movie industry was not replicated in television. By the time videotape technology (invented in 1956) and satellite broadcasting (begun in 1962) became generally available, the newly independent governments resulting from decolonization were already using radio and television broadcasting for nation building and were disinclined to rely on foreign programs.

Moviemaking tended to be privately organized even in countries that imposed government censorship. In contrast, television outside the United States usually became a government monopoly, following the pattern of telegraph and postal service and radio broadcasting. Government control of news reports and approval of other programming was intended to disseminate a unified national viewpoint. Many state broadcasters eventually turned to American sources to meet the demand for shows because broadcasting American soap operas, adventure series, and situation comedies was cheaper than producing them locally. The United States, however, was not the only external source of programming. Many nations purchased shows from Brazil, Mexico, and Great Britain.

When American producers realized that satellite transmission provided an opening to an international market, MTV (Music Television) and CNN (Cable News Network) came into being. Specializing in rock music videos aimed at a youth audience, MTV became an international enterprise offering special editions in different parts of the world. Music videos shown in Uzbekistan°, for example, often featured Russian bands, and Chinese groups appeared in MTV programs shown in Singapore. CNN developed its international potential after becoming the most-viewed and informative news source during the 1991 Persian Gulf War, when it broadcast live from Baghdad. Providing news around the clock, CNN began to supplant other commercial and government news programming as the best source of information about rapidly developing events. However, CNN's fundamentally American view of the news, even

---

Vladimir Zworykin (VLAD-ih-meer ZWOR-ih-kin)
Uzbekistan (uzz-BEK-ih-stan)

Rock Concert for African Famine Relief
The Live-Aid concerts like this one in London's Wembley Stadium were organized in the late 1980s by Bob Geldof. Popular music had been used for centuries to mobilize public concern and engage the feelings of young people. Modern electronics and satellite technology amplified its impact and carried it throughout the world.   (Redferns Music Picture Library)

in its international editions, prompted some governments to limit its reception.

Zworykin's electron scanning gun also made possible the computer screen. At first, the computer industry, which mushroomed for defense and business purposes in the post–World War II decades, had little connection with television or movies. The three technologies were quite different. Movies recorded light and shadow on film. Television used electromagnetic waves. Computers were based on a digital system in which every bit of information was expressed as a combination of zeros and ones and millions of bits were required for even a simple screen display. But with adequate electronic storage capacity and enough speed in recovering stored information, every point on a photographic image or electron wave could be expressed digitally and transmitted to the computer screen as a moving picture. In the 1990s Japan introduced the first digital television broadcasting at about the time that disks containing digitized movies and computer programs with movielike action became increasingly available.

More widespread was communication over the Internet, a linkage of academic, government, and business computer networks. Developed originally for U.S. defense research in the 1960s, the Internet became a major cultural phenomenon with the proliferation of personal computers in the 1980s. With the establishment of the World Wide Web as an easy-to-use graphic interface in the 1990s, the number of Internet users skyrocketed (see Map 35.3). Myriad new companies formed to explore "e-commerce," the commercial dimension of the Internet. By century's end, many American college students were spending less time studying conventional books and scholarly resources than they were spending to explore the Web for entertainment and to accomplish class assignments.

As had happened so often throughout history, technological developments had unanticipated consequences. The new telecommunications and entertainment technologies derived disproportionately from American invention, industry, and cultural creativity (Japan became a powerful secondary factor on the industrial side in the

Map 35.3   Per Capita Access to the Internet   Internet servers, computers through which users can connect their personal computers with the Internet, are most numerous in industrialized countries. As the Internet expands into more countries, questions of language difference will become more pronounced.   *Source:* Data from July 1999. Used with permission of Matrix Information and Directory Services, Inc. Visit our website at www.mids.org.

Number of hosts on the Internet, July 1999

10,000,000
1,000,000
100,000

10,000
1,000
100
10
1

1970s). Thus they could be seen as portents of Western, especially American, cultural domination. But the American input was rather uneven, and the more widespread the new technologies became, the greater the opportunities they afforded to people around the world to adapt them to their own purposes.

The Spread of Popular Culture

The new technologies changed perceptions of culture. At the end of the nineteenth century, sophisticated Europeans and Americans, like earlier elite groups from imperial Rome to Ming China, valued most what they considered **high culture**—paintings, literature, and other works created to satisfy their tastes. They sneered at **popular culture** as localized entertainment for villagers and common folk—vigorous, picturesque, and quaint, but essentially vulgar. Influenced by the preferences of the European imperialist powers, modernizing elite groups around the world turned their backs on their own artistic traditions. Fascinated with everything Western, they built opera houses, established symphony orchestras, and experimented with European literary forms. Thus European notions of high culture—masterworks created exclusively by composers, artists, and thinkers of European descent—took root in many parts of the world, and non-Western cultural forms lost prestige in their own locales.

By the beginning of the twentieth century, popular culture began to become more and more visible. Illustrious European composers and choreographers had been turning to folk tunes and dances for inspiration since the eighteenth century. And the search for fresh sounds and images intensified with the advent of modernism in Europe in the mid-nineteenth century. Modernist writers, composers, and artists valued novelty and individuality of expression over classical structures and traditional formal narratives. These artists explored the workings of the subconscious rather than attempting to portray an objective reality. Since experimental or unconventional modernist works often outraged and offended patrons of the arts, the capacity to create a sensation and provoke outrage became a hallmark of modernism. Artists and composers strove to explore ever broader frontiers of feeling and experience. Some were captivated by the sounds and images of Europe's new industrial society; others drew inspiration from popular culture. Spanish artist Pablo Picasso (1881–1973), for example, borrowed the imagery of African masks in some of his paintings, circuses and carnivals in others, and newspaper typography in still others.

This mining of popular cultures by elite artists did little to inspire a wide interest in those cultures, however.

The invention of the phonograph by Thomas Edison in 1878 was the key that opened popular culture to global audiences. After three decades of further technological development, inexpensive recordings on disks became a reality. Phonograph records spread American popular music around the world. Jazz and blues had originated in the black culture of the American south at the end of the nineteenth century and moved north with black musicians in the twentieth century. The newborn recording industry made the works of pianist Jelly Roll Morton, guitar player Robert Johnson, singer Bessie Smith, and other musicians widely available.

Though blues remained primarily a black American taste, jazz recordings and jazz musicians became popular in Europe in the 1920s. The driving force behind jazz was the creative skill of black musicians such as Duke Ellington, Louis Armstrong, Ella Fitzgerald, and Billie Holiday. Orchestral composers such as the Russian Igor Stravinsky and the Frenchman Maurice Ravel utilized jazz rhythms and themes just as Picasso borrowed ideas from African masks. However, jazz remained the music of nightclubs and dance parties instead of concert halls. By World War II, black jazz musicians had become so much a part of the international image of the United States that Nazi propaganda frequently incorporated vile racial caricatures of them. Ironically, while jazz was widely perceived abroad as quintessential American popular culture, it remained largely the preserve of the African-American minority at home. Millions of white Americans preferred the more sedate tunes published by New York's commercial music houses, which employed some of the musical language of jazz but seldom displayed the black intensity of feeling and capacity for innovation.

The international popularity of jazz derived from the appeal of its rhythms and naturalness—that is, from the music itself—not from its approval by a colonial ruling class, as with the nineteenth-century vogue for grand opera. The same was true of rock 'n' roll, a dynamic, sensual, and audacious popular music that arose in the 1950s and became even more widespread than jazz. Rock grew out of black rhythm-and-blues and derived initially from innovative black American performers like Chuck Berry. The rise to international stardom in the early 1960s of Britain's Beatles helped make rock 'n' roll a worldwide phenomenon. The core of rock remained American and British, but popular musicians from all over the world recorded in rock-influenced styles. Some achieved broad acclaim, as did Jamaica's Bob Marley with his Caribbean reggae style. Others gained strong local followings by blending rock with traditional forms, as happened with Malagasy music in Madagascar and Rai music in Algeria.

Japanese Adult Male Comic Book Comic magazines emerged after World War II as a major form of publication in Japan and a distinctive product of Japanese culture. Different series are directed to different age and gender groups. Issued weekly and running to some 300 pages in black and white, the most popular magazines sell as many copies as major news magazines do in the United States. (Private Collection)

The rhythms and feelings of former black slaves in the American south could never have evolved into a core element of global culture without the recording industry. However, the preponderant role of the United States in the post–World War II world was also important. The equally African-inspired rhythms of the Brazilian samba and Cuban rumba, for example, never gained a significant international following comparable to that of jazz and rock 'n' roll.

In the post–World War II decades, mass production and advertising (both developed largely in the United States) opened another door to the worldwide spread of popular culture. American consumer products began to find international markets, and European, Japanese, and transnational companies soon became as aggressive as American companies in international marketing. Home-grown industries in small or poorer countries found it harder and harder to hold their own without government protection. In marketplaces around the world, imports displaced domestically produced consumer goods, from children's toys to copper cooking pots.

In the 1970s and 1980s, critics around the world identified the United States as the chief propagator of a worldwide consumer culture. This judgment seemed to be confirmed by the international cachet of American brand names like Levi's, Coca-Cola, Marlboro, Gillette, McDonald's, and Kentucky Fried Chicken. But names blazoned in neon atop the skyscrapers of Tokyo—Hitachi, Sony, Sanyo, and Mitsubishi—also commanded instant recognition, as did such European names as Nestlé, Mercedes, Pirelli, and Benetton. The concept of a globe-girdling American consumer culture had been overtaken by internationalization.

A sidewalk stand in Amman, Jordan, in 1986 featured inexpensive yellow sweatshirts bearing the legend "Oklahoma" with a large number beneath it. The shirts were made in Hong Kong; the buyers were Arabs; and the reference was to American football, then rarely played outside North America. At the same time, sidewalk stands in New York's Greenwich Village were stocked with checked Arab kaffiyas (headscarves). The internationalization of styles, as of music, had become two-way. Yet, on balance, the overall direction of change in popular culture and consumer taste during the decades following World War II was indeed toward the United States. Two years after the breakup of the Soviet Union, a shopper in Bishkek, the capital of Kyrgyzstan° in the heart of Central Asia, could buy women's underpants stenciled with a picture of a Marlboro cigarette pack, and a diner in Moscow could go to Pizza Hut for an exotic, if fairly expensive, treat.

When Marxism was challenging capitalism for world domination, Marxist theories argued that the tendency of capitalist economies to produce too many goods compelled industrialized nations to seek ever-larger markets and thereby exploit the entire world for the benefit of corporate shareholders. They interpreted the spread of American products as simply another form of imperialism, inevitably destroying local crafts, styles, and cultural traditions. But most young Turks, Nigerians, Taiwanese and others who liked to wear Levis's jeans,

Kyrgyzstan (KIR-gih-stan)

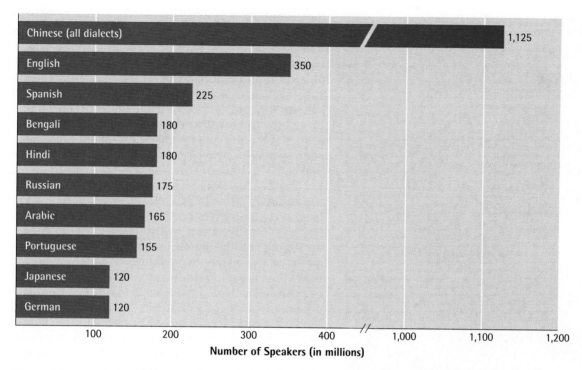

Figure 35.1   The Top Ten Languages   Numbers include all dialects of the language. For example, Chinese includes Mandarin, Wu, and less common dialects. *Source:* Andrew Dalby, *Dictionary of Languages* (New York: Columbia University Press, 1998). Published with permission of Columbia University Press, from Andrew Dalby, *Dictionary of Languages.* ©1998 as conveyed through the Copyright Clearance Center, Inc.

drink Coke, smoke Camels, and listen to rock 'n' roll had little sense of being under the thumb of the imperialists. Although their nations' economies may have been in thrall to transnational business concerns, they themselves generally felt free to condemn American foreign policy and considered their personal style preferences simply a result of living within an increasingly global culture. Thus the reality of cultural imperialism remained far more ambiguous than European imperialism had been in the days of colonial viceroys and gunboat diplomacy.

Global Connections and Elite Culture

While the globalization of popular culture became a subject of dispute, cultural links across national and ethnic boundaries at a more elite level generated less controversy. The end of the Cold War reopened intellectual and cultural contacts between former adversaries, making possible such things as Russian-American collaboration on space missions and extensive business contacts among former rivals. European and American scientific laboratories benefited as well from the intellectual gifts of an increasing number of graduate students and researchers from China, India, Pakistan, Turkey, and elsewhere. Given the scarcity of high-level research laboratories outside Europe, America, and Japan, many of these students chose to remain in their countries of training after graduation, contributing to a "brain drain" that primarily benefited the West.

In this way, technical training helped contribute to the rising importance of English as a global second language. British imperialism had planted English on every continent by the beginning of the twentieth century. Spurred by American economic and political eminence in the second half of the century, as well as by American movies and television, the language spread even as the British Empire faded away. French, by contrast, faded with the French Empire (see Figure 35.1). English became the most commonly taught second language in the world, and a number of technology-intensive industries, including air transportation and computers, used it extensively. In newly independent countries, universities

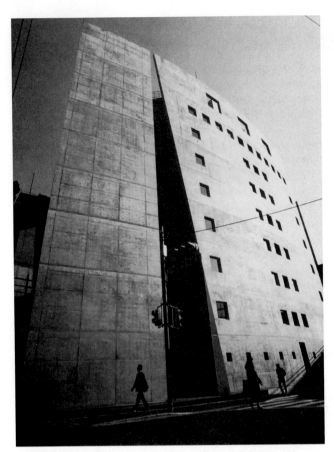

Postmodern Japanese Architecture Kiyoshi Sey Takeyama, born in 1954, designed the D-Hotel in Osaka in 1985. "Relations can often be clarified by interrupting things. . . . I built massive, incomplete walls, simultaneously expressing desire for and renunciation of communication with others. This ambivalence sums up our life in the contemporary city." Takeyama and other young Japanese architects pursue an architecture that responds more to modern Japanese culture than to the earlier modernism of the international style. (Courtesy, AMORPHE Takeyama and Associates)

those capitals along highways that followed limited-access designs pioneered by the German autobahns and American thruways. The causeway linking the island-nation of Bahrain with mainland Saudi Arabia, for example, was indistinguishable in design from an American superhighway. The designs of new underground rail systems in Cairo, Mexico City, and Calcutta similarly reflected the internationalization of engineering and design. It became commonplace for a project in one country to be designed by an architectural firm in a second and built by a construction firm from a third.

The International Style was criticized, however, for neglecting local architectural traditions. Critics either blasted the designs for heedlessly indulging the creative fancies of the architects or complained that architects turned out boringly similar designs that imparted an unattractive uniformity to previously distinctive cities. In the United States, this criticism formed the foundation of **postmodernism,** a movement that called for abandoning the rigid rules of architectural modernism and showing greater sensitivity to history and local context, and for allowing diverse voices, such as those of minorities, to be heard. Some architects, including a growing number from non-Western countries, responded to the postmodern critique. Conventional glass and steel skyscrapers continued to be built, but liberation from the International Style permitted architects in different countries to follow their own inclinations and experiment with a broad array of forms, surface decoration, and references to earlier architectural traditions.

Postmodernism was not confined to architecture. Dance, music, literature, and cultural theory were all affected by postmodernist impulses, though the forms they took differed from one area to another. Common to much postmodernist thought was a sense that the modernist styles that composed the artistic avant-garde between 1850 and 1950 reflected the limited perspective of an elite, white, male Euro-American intelligentsia preoccupied with individualism and innovation. Against this background, postmodernism championed an aesthetic based on multicutluralism, social inclusion, historical continuity, and styles and forms from everyday life.

By fostering local diversity within the context of global change, architectural postmodernism had a substantial international impact. But it was not the only indicator of cultural change on a global scale. Among the ten winners of the Nobel Prize for Literature between 1982 and 1991 were writers from Colombia, Nigeria, Egypt, Mexico, and the West Indies. By contrast, the previous decade's winners had included only one non-European. The prize committee thus helped the world recognize the growing strength of its cultural diversity.

that took pride in teaching in the national language often had science faculties that operated in English. The emergence of this potential global language made travel for business and pleasure increasingly easy and greatly facilitated the operations of multinational corporations.

Architectural design and engineering afford another example of globalization at the higher cultural level. The International Style pioneered by European architects in the 1920s (see Chapter 30) was the guiding aesthetic for the austere, ornament-free skyscrapers sheathed in glass that began to rise in world capitals in the 1960s. At the same time, people were traveling to

The West, for good or ill, dominated the early postimperialist era because the web of international contact made possible by advanced technologies had yet to reach its full extent or become accessible to most people. According to one estimate, at the end of the century, half of the world's people had never spoken on a telephone. The cultural changes spurred by technology were only in midcourse, and technology seemed likely to offer a means of releasing profound creative energies in unexpected locales.

The Endurance of Cultural Diversity

Diverse cultural traditions persisted at the twentieth century's end despite the globalization of industrial society and the integration of economic markets. Japan demonstrated that a country with a non-Western culture could perform at a high economic level. The Western concern for the individual was less valued in Japan than the ability of each individual to fit into a group, whether as a corporation employee, a member of an athletic team, or a student in a class. Moreover, the Japanese considered it unmannerly to directly contradict, correct, or refuse the request of another person.

From a Western point of view, these Japanese customs seemed to discourage individual initiative and personality development and to preserve traditional hierarchies. Japanese women, for example, even though they often worked outside the home, responded only slowly to the American and European feminist advocacy of equality in economic and social relations. However, the Japanese approach to social relations was well suited to an industrial economy. The efficiency, pride in workmanship, and group solidarity of Japanese workers, supported by closely coordinated government and corporate policies, played a major role in transforming Japan from a defeated nation with a demolished industrial base in 1945 to an economic power by the 1980s.

Japan's success in the modern industrial world called into question an assumption common in the immediate postwar era. Since industrialization was pioneered by Europeans and Americans, many Westerners thought that the spread of industrialization to different parts of the world would require the adoption of Western culture in every area of life. As awareness of the economic impact of Japanese culture and society began to spread, however, it became apparent that Taiwan and South Korea, along with Singapore and Hong Kong (a British colony before being reunited with China in 1997), were developing dynamic industrial economies of their own. Until the Asian financial crisis of 1997, Muslim Malaysia and Buddhist Thailand had appeared to be embarking on the same road to development. Had Japan been unique, or would cultural variety prove fully compatible with industrial growth and prosperity worldwide?

Clearly, the long-standing Western assumption of European and American exceptionalism—the belief that all of world history culminated in the exceptional convergence of political freedom, secularism, and industrialization in the West—needed to be abandoned. So, too, did the corollary that the twenty-first century would be as thoroughly dominated by Western culture and economic and political power as the previous two centuries had been.

Also coming into question was whether industrialization offered the only viable route to prosperity. As computer technology continued to change almost all aspects of life, perhaps in the twenty-first century countries could achieve prosperity primarily through their control of information and telecommunications.

The lesson to be drawn from the success of Japan and the other rising economic powers of Asia was not that Western technology pointed the way to universal well-being, but rather that human ingenuity and adaptability are endlessly fertile and creative. Human cultural achievement has historically followed unpredictable paths, reaching one sort of climax in one time and place and a different sort in another. In the same spirit, the future locus of spiritual and cultural achievement remained essentially unpredictable at the start of a new millennium.

CONCLUSION

The final decade of the twentieth century witnessed a burgeoning of computer and telecommunications technology that fostered the worldwide spread of popular culture while at the same time enabling businesses and financial markets to operate on a truly global scale. It also witnessed an intensification of world concerns for human rights as fears of international conflicts between great powers faded into the past. But in some respects it was more strongly marked by things that came to an end than by things that had their start.

For nearly eight decades, from the outbreak of World War I to the dissolution of the Soviet Union, a world whose economic and political destiny had seemed firmly in the grip of European imperialism witnessed an

Millennium Celebration in Sydney, Australia   Uncertainties about what lay ahead for the world in the twenty-first century took a backseat to exuberant festivities as the millennium ended. The sleek modern silhouette of Sidney's opera house and the neon signs of major corporations epitomized the hopes of many.   (Sydney Morning Herald/Sipa Press)

increasingly lethal struggle between competing European ideologies. The outcome of the struggle, in which all the peoples of the world eventually became principals or pawns, was often in doubt. Each camp accused the other of leading humanity down the road to slavery—slavery to fascist or communist dictators according to one side, slavery to the insatiable greed of capitalist profiteers according to the other. Each camp similarly had a vision of how it would organize the world in the event of victory. Adolf Hitler visualized a "thousand year Reich [empire]" serving the desires of an Aryan superrace. Communists spoke of a "workers' paradise" of equality and brotherhood. Responding to these oppressive visions, Western leaders extolled the virtues of "freedom," a world order that would permit all peoples to elect their own governments and allow every individual to pursue his or her individual destiny in an open and competitive market environment.

Victory, when it came, proved far more complicated and puzzling than Western ideologues had anticipated. Though "democratization" and "economic liberalization" became watchwords of Western, and particularly American, foreign policy, many of the world's peoples proved less concerned with liberal ideology than with ethnic, linguistic, and religious quarrels, or with simply maintaining life and hope in circumstances of increasing poverty and overpopulation. Developing countries and postcommunist countries alike looked to the United States, Europe, and Japan for financial salvation, introducing democratic institutions and open markets only to the degree necessary to gain Western support.

The United States and the other major industrial countries recognized that they could not meet all of the world's demands, but they were reluctant to put too much trust in international bodies such as the United Nations, which had no financial resources beyond the dues paid by its member states. Thus the end of the global contest among European ideologies did not produce a workable model of a world community. To the contrary, local conflicts and atrocities proliferated in the 1990s, and more and more countries debated whether to seek nuclear weapons or other weapons of mass destruction in anticipation of future confrontations.

Yet while world order seemed as unattainable as ever, economic, technological, and cultural forces drew the world's peoples ever closer together. Since the victors in the world struggle had been the capitalists rather than the fascists or communists, private business and consumer economics expanded aggressively into every region of the globe, checked only by market conditions and rearguard efforts by authoritarian governments, such as that of China, to control the pace and direction of change.

For most of the world's population, the 1990s brought greater desire for and access to consumer goods, and a globalized culture became more and more a reality. But the logic of global economic growth, with its immense demands on clean water, clear air, and nonrenewable resources, made it clear that some of the world's greatest problems, including how to preserve the shared global environment for future generations of humanity, had no obvious solutions and had only begun to be addressed.

■ Key Terms

ethnic cleansing

economic sanctions

World Trade Organization (WTO)

terrorism

nuclear nonproliferation

Universal Declaration
  of Human Rights

nongovernmental
  organizations (NGOs)

cultural imperialism

high culture

popular culture

postmodernism

■ Suggested Reading

Many of the subjects in this chapter are covered by thematic essays in Richard W. Bulliet, ed., *The Columbia History of the Twentieth Century* (1998).

The Bosnian crisis is well covered in Susan L. Woodward, *Balkan Tragedy: Chaos and Dissolution After the Cold War* (1995). Other world crises involving international intervention are treated in William J. Durch, ed., *UN Peacekeeping, American Policy, and the Uncivil Wars of the* 1990s (1996). Terrorism is well covered by Bruce Hoffman, *Inside Terrorism* (1998). Gilles Kepel, *The Revenge of God: The Resurgence of Islam, Christianity, and Judaism in the Modern World* (1994), deals with recent religio-political movements. Human rights are well surveyed by Jack Donnelly, *International Human Rights,* 2d ed. (1998).

A seminal book in the awakening of the feminist movement in the 1970s is Betty Friedan, *The Feminine Mystique* (1974). For the revival of feminism in Europe see Gisela Kaplan, *Contemporary Western European Feminism* (1992). For non-Western perspectives see Phyllis Andors, *The Unfinished Liberation of Chinese Women, 1949–1980* (1983), and Chandra Talpade Mohanty, Ann Russo, and Lourdes Torres, eds., *Third World Women and the Politics of Feminism* (1991).

The interrelationships between high culture and popular culture during the twentieth century are treated from very different perspectives by Greil Marcus, *Lipstick Traces: A Secret History of the Twentieth Century* (1989), and Kurt Varnedoe, *High and Low: Modern Art and Popular Culture* (1991). The former concentrates on the avant-garde from Dada to Punk Rock, the latter on images from popular culture used in art. Two very readable books by James B. Twitchell, *Carnival Culture: The Trashing of Taste in America* (1992) and *Adcult USA: The Triumph of Advertising in American Culture* (1996), detail the rise of popular culture in the United States and present various reactions to this phenomenon.

Many interpretations of and approaches to postmodernism are sampled in Thomas Docherty, ed., *Postmodernism: A Reader* (1993). These may be compared with a classic early statement of modernism, Amédée Ozenfant, *Foundations of Modern Art* (1931).

Thomas P. Hughes, *American Genesis: A Century of Invention and Technological Enthusiasm, 1870–1970* (1989), offers a far-ranging account of the American role in twentieth-century technological change by an outstanding historian of technology. Books on films and the film industry around the world are legion. A good place to start is Gerald Mast, *A Short History of the Movies* (1986). A similar survey of jazz music is available from Marshall W. Stearns, *The Story of Jazz* (1970). For the rock video phenomenon see E. Ann Kaplan, *Rocking Around the Clock: Music Television, Postmodernism, and Consumer Culture* (1987).

Some noteworthy novels that have attempted to visualize the near future on the basis of current perceptions of technological change, environmental deterioration, and growth of transnational corporations are David Brin, *Earth* (1990), and Bruce Sterling, *Islands in the Net* (1988). See too William Gibson's "Sprawl" trilogy *Neuromancer* (1984), *Count Zero* (1987), and *Mona Lisa Overdrive* (1988).

■ Notes

1. "Universal Declaration of Human Rights," in *Twenty-five Human Rights Documents* (New York: Center for the Study of Human Rights, Columbia University, 1994), 6.
2. Ibid.

GLOSSARY

The glossary for *The Earth and Its Peoples,* 2/e is for the complete text, Chapters 1 through 35.

Abbas the Great (1571–1629) Shah of Iran (r. 1587–1629). The most illustrious ruler of the **Safavid Empire,** he moved the imperial capital to Isfahan in 1598, where he erected many palaces, mosques, and public buildings. (*p. 533*)

Abbasid Caliphate Descendants of the Prophet Muhammad's uncle, al-Abbas, the Abbasids overthrew the **Umayyad Caliphate** and ruled an Islamic empire from their capital in Baghdad (founded 762) from 750 to 1258. (*p. 234*)

abolitionists Men and women who agitated for a complete end to slavery. British abolitionists pressed for the abolition of the transatlantic slave trade in 1808 and slavery in 1834. In the United States the activities of abolitionists were one factor leading to the Civil War (1861–1865). (*p. 636*)

absolutism The theory popular in France and other early modern European monarchies that royal power should be free of constitutional checks. (*p. 452*)

Acheh Sultanate Muslim kingdom in northern Sumatra. Main center of Islamic expansion in Southeast Asia in the early seventeenth century, it declined after the Dutch seized **Malacca** from Portugal in 1641. (*p. 541*)

acculturation The adoption of the language, customs, values, and behaviors of host nations by immigrants. (*p. 640*)

acllas Women selected by Inca authorities to serve in religious centers as weavers and ritual participants. (*p. 318*)

Aden Port city in the modern south Arabian country of Yemen. It has been a major trading center in the Indian Ocean since ancient times. (*p. 385*)

African National Congress An organization dedicated to obtaining equal voting and civil rights for black inhabitants of South Africa. Founded in 1912 as the South African Native National Congress, it changed its name in 1923. Though it was banned and its leaders were jailed for many years, it eventually helped bring majority rule to South Africa. (*p. 809*)

Afrikaners South Africans descended from Dutch and French settlers of the seventeenth century. Their Great Trek founded new settler colonies in the nineteenth century. Though a minority among South Africans, they held political power after 1910, imposing a system of racial segregation called apartheid after 1949. (*pp. 665, 735*)

Agricultural Revolution(s) (ancient) The change from food gathering to food production that occurred between ca. 8000 and 2000 B.C.E. Also known as the Neolithic Revolution. (*p. 17*)

Agricultural Revolution (eighteenth century) The transformation of farming that resulted in the eighteenth century from the spread of new crops, improvements in cultivation techniques and livestock breeding, and the consolidation of small holdings into large farms from which tenants and sharecroppers were forcibly expelled. (*p. 600*)

Aguinaldo, Emilio (1869–1964) Leader of the Filipino independence movement against Spain (1895–1898). He proclaimed the independence of the Philippines in 1899, but his movement was crushed and he was captured by the United States Army in 1901. (*p. 743*)

Akbar I (1542–1605) Most illustrious sultan of the Mughal Empire in India (r. 1556–1605). He expanded the empire and pursued a policy of conciliation with Hindus. (*p. 536*)

Akhenaten Egyptian pharaoh (r. 1353–1335 B.C.E.). He built a new capital at Amarna, fostered a new style of naturalistic art, and created a religious revolution by imposing worship of the sun-disk. The Amarna letters, largely from his reign, preserve official correspondence with subjects and neighbors. (*p. 66*)

Alexander (356–323 B.C.E.) King of Macedonia in northern Greece. Between 334 and 323 B.C.E. he conquered the Persian Empire, reached the Indus Valley, founded many Greek-style cities, and spread Greek culture across the Middle East. Later known as Alexander the Great. (*p. 136*)

Alexandria City on the Mediterranean coast of Egypt founded by Alexander. It became the capital of the Hellenistic kingdom of the **Ptolemies.** It contained the famous Library and the Museum—a center for leading scientific and literary figures. Its merchants engaged in trade with areas bordering the Mediterranean and the Indian Ocean. (*p. 138*)

Allende, Salvador (1908–1973) Socialist politician elected president of Chile in 1970 and overthrown by the military in 1973. He died during the military attack. (*p. 856*)

All-India Muslim League Political organization founded in India in 1906 to defend the interests of India's Muslim minority. Led by Muhammad Ali Jinnah, it attempted to negotiate with the **Indian National Congress.** In 1940, the League began demanding a separate state for Muslims, to be called Pakistan. (See also **Jinnah, Muhammad Ali.**) (*p. 813*)

amulet Small charm meant to protect the bearer from evil. Found frequently in archaeological excavations in Mesopotamia and Egypt, amulets reflect the religious practices of the common people. (*p. 37*)

Anasazi Important culture of what is now the southwest of the United States (1000–1300 C.E.). Centered on Chaco Canyon in New Mexico and Mesa Verde in Colorado, the Anasazi culture built multistory residences and worshiped in subterranean buildings called kivas. (*p. 308*)

aqueduct A conduit, either elevated or under ground, using gravity to carry water from a source to a location—usually a city—that needed it. The Romans built many aqueducts in a period of substantial urbanization. (*p. 156*)

Arawak Amerindian peoples who inhabited the Greater Antilles of the Caribbean at the time of Columbus. (*p. 423*)

Arkwright, Richard (1732–1792) English inventor and entrepreneur who became the wealthiest and most successful textile manufacturer of the early **Industrial Revolution.** He invented the water frame, a machine that, with minimal human supervision, could spin many strong cotton threads at once. (*p. 604*)

Armenia One of the earliest Christian kingdoms, situated in eastern Anatolia and the western Caucasus and occupied by speakers of the Armenian language. (*p. 221*)

Asante African kingdom on the **Gold Coast** that expanded rapidly after 1680. Asante participated in the Atlantic economy, trading gold, slaves, and ivory. It resisted British imperial ambitions for a quarter century before being absorbed into Britain's Gold Coast colony in 1902. (*p. 736*)

Ashikaga Shogunate (1336–1573) The second of Japan's military governments headed by a shogun (a military ruler). Sometimes called the Muromachi Shogunate. (*p. 365*)

Ashoka Third ruler of the **Mauryan Empire** in India (r. 270–232 B.C.E.). He converted to Buddhism and broadcast his precepts on inscribed stones and pillars, the earliest surviving Indian writing. (*p. 184*)

Ashur Chief deity of the Assyrians, he stood behind the king and brought victory in war. Also the name of an important Assyrian religious and political center. (*p. 94*)

Asian Tigers Collective name for South Korea, Taiwan, Hong Kong, and Singapore—nations that became economic powers in the 1970s and 1980s. (*p. 861*)

Atahualpa (1502?–1533) Last ruling Inca emperor of Peru. He was executed by the Spanish. (*p. 438*)

Atlantic system The network of trading links after 1500 that moved goods, wealth, people, and cultures around the Atlantic Ocean basin. (*p. 497*)

Augustus (63 B.C.E.–14 c.e.) Honorific name of Octavian, founder of the **Roman Principate,** the military dictatorship that replaced the failing rule of the **Roman Senate.** After defeating all rivals, between 31 B.C.E. and 14 C.E. he laid the groundwork for several centuries of stability and prosperity in the Roman Empire. (*p. 151*)

Auschwitz Nazi extermination camp in Poland, the largest center of mass murder during the **Holocaust.** Close to a million Jews, Gypsies, Communists, and others were killed there. (*p. 800*)

australopithecines The several extinct species of humanlike primates that existed during the Pleistocene era (genus *Australopithecus*). (*p. 9*)

autocracy The theory justifying strong, centralized rule, such as by the **tsar** in Russia or **Haile Selassie** in Ethiopia. The autocrat did not rely on the aristocracy or the clergy for his or her legitimacy. (*p. 553*)

ayllu Andean lineage group or kin-based community. (*p. 312*)

Aztecs Also known as Mexica, the Aztecs created a powerful empire in central Mexico (1325–1521 C.E.). They forced defeated peoples to provide goods and labor as a tax. (*p. 305*)

Babylon The largest and most important city in Mesopotamia. It achieved particular eminence as the capital of the Amorite king **Hammurabi** in the eighteenth century B.C.E. and the Neo-Babylonian king Nebuchadnezzar in the sixth century B.C.E. (*p. 29*)

balance of power The policy in international relations by which, beginning in the eighteenth century, the major European states acted together to prevent any one of them from becoming too powerful. (*p. 455*)

Balfour Declaration Statement issued by Britain's Foreign Secretary Arthur Balfour in 1917 favoring the establishment of a Jewish national homeland in Palestine. (*p. 761*)

Bannermen Hereditary military servants of the **Qing Empire,** in large part descendants of peoples of various origins who had fought for the founders of the empire. (*p. 684*)

Bantu Collective name of a large group of sub-Saharan African languages and of the peoples speaking these languages. (*p. 219*)

Batavia Fort established ca.1619 as headquarters of Dutch East India Company operations in Indonesia; today the city of Jakarta. (*p. 543*)

Battle of Midway U.S. naval victory over the Japanese fleet in June 1942, in which the Japanese lost four of their best aircraft carriers. It marked a turning point in World War II. (*p. 795*)

Battle of Omdurman British victory over the Mahdi in the Sudan in 1898. General Kitchener led a mixed force of British and Egyptian troops armed with rapid-firing rifles and machine guns. (*p. 730*)

Beijing China's northern capital, first used as an imperial capital in 906 and now the capital of the People's Republic of China. (*p. 351*)

Bengal Region of northeastern India. It was the first part of India to be conquered by the British in the eighteenth century and remained the political and economic center of British India throughout the nineteenth century. The 1905 split of the province into predominantly Hindu West Bengal and predominantly Muslim East Bengal (now Bangladesh) sparked anti-British riots. (*p. 812*)

Berlin Conference (1884–1885) Conference that German chancellor Otto von Bismarck called to set rules for the partition of Africa. It led to the creation of the Congo Free State under King **Leopold II** of Belgium. (See also **Bismarck, Otto von.**) (*p. 732*)

Bhagavad-Gita The most important work of Indian sacred literature, a dialogue between the great warrior Arjuna and the god Krishna on duty and the fate of the spirit. (*p. 185*)

bipedalism The ability to walk upright on two legs, characteristic of hominids. (*p. 9*)

Bismarck, Otto von (1815–1898) Chancellor (prime minister) of Prussia from 1862 until 1871, when he became chancellor of Germany. A conservative nationalist, he led Prussia to victory against Austria (1866) and France (1870) and was responsible for the creation of the German Empire in 1871. (*p. 714*)

Black Death An outbreak of **bubonic plague** that spread across Asia, North Africa, and Europe in the mid-fourteenth century, carrying off vast numbers of persons. (*p. 397*)

Bolívar, Simón (1783–1830) The most important military leader in the struggle for independence in South America. Born in Venezuela, he led military forces there and in Colombia, Ecuador, Peru, and Bolivia. (*p. 623*)

Bolsheviks Radical Marxist political party founded by Vladimir Lenin in 1903. Under Lenin's leadership, the Bolsheviks seized power in November 1917 during the Russian Revolution. (See also **Lenin, Vladimir.**) (*p. 761*)

Bonaparte, Napoleon. See **Napoleon I.**

Borobodur A massive stone monument on the Indonesian island of Java, erected by the Sailendra kings around 800 C.E. The winding ascent through ten levels, decorated with rich relief carving, is a Buddhist allegory for the progressive stages of enlightenment. (*p. 193*)

bourgeoisie In early modern Europe, the class of well-off town dwellers whose wealth came from manufacturing, finance, commerce, and allied professions. (*p. 459*)

Brant, Joseph (1742–1807) Mohawk leader who supported the British during the American Revolution. (*p. 581*)

breech-loading rifle Gun into which the projectiles had to be individually inserted. Later guns had magazines, a compartment holding multiple projectiles that could be fed rapidly into the firing chamber. (*p. 681*)

British raj The rule over much of South Asia between 1765 and 1947 by the East India Company and then by a British government. (*p. 659*)

bubonic plague A bacterial disease of fleas that can be transmitted by flea bites to rodents and humans; humans in late stages of the illness can spread the bacteria by coughing. Because of its very high mortality rate and the difficulty of preventing its spread, major outbreaks have created crises in many parts of the world in many countries. (See also **Black Death.**) (*pp. 280, 332*)

Buddha (563–483 B.C.E.) An Indian prince named Siddhartha Gautama, who renounced his wealth and social position. After becoming "enlightened" (the meaning of *Buddha*) he enunciated the principles of Buddhism. This doctrine evolved and spread throughout India and to Southeast, East, and Central Asia. (See also **Mahayana Buddhism; Theravada Buddhism.**) (*p. 180*)

business cycles Recurrent swings from economic hard times to recovery and growth, then back to hard times and a repetition of the sequence. (*p. 615*)

Byzantine Empire Historians' name for the eastern portion of the Roman Empire from the fourth century onward, taken from "Byzantion," an early name for Constantinople, the Byzantine capital city. The empire fell to the Ottomans in 1453. (See also **Ottoman Empire.**) (*p. 250*)

caliphate Office established in succession to the Prophet Muhammad, to rule the Islamic empire; also the name of that empire. (See also **Abbasid Caliphate; Sokoto Caliphate; Umayyad Caliphate.**) (*p. 232*)

capitalism The economic system of large financial institutions—banks, stock exchanges, investment companies—that first developed in early modern Europe. *Commercial capitalism,* the trading system of the early modern economy, is often distinguished from *industrial capitalism,* the system based on machine production. (*p. 506*)

caravel A small, highly maneuverable three-masted ship used by the Portuguese and Spanish in the exploration of the Atlantic. (*p. 427*)

Cárdenas, Lázaro (1895–1970) President of Mexico (1934–1940). He brought major changes to Mexican life by distributing millions of acres of land to the peasants, bringing representatives of workers and farmers into the inner circles of politics, and nationalizing the oil industry. (*p. 820*)

Carthage City located in present-day Tunisia, founded by **Phoenicians** ca. 800 B.C.E. It became a major commercial center and naval power in the western Mediterranean until defeated by Rome in the third century B.C.E. (*p. 107*)

Caste War A rebellion of the Maya people against the government of Mexico in 1847. It nearly returned the Yucatán to Maya rule. Some Maya rebels retreated to unoccupied territories where they held out until 1901. (*p. 636*)

Catholic Reformation Religious reform movement within the Latin Christian Church, begun in response to the **Protestant Reformation.** It clarified Catholic theology and reformed clerical training and discipline. (*p. 447*)

Celts Peoples sharing a common language and culture that originated in Central Europe in the first half of the first millennium B.C.E.. After 500 B.C.E. they spread as far as Anatolia in the east, Spain and the British Isles in the west, and later were overtaken by Roman conquest and Germanic invasions. Their descendants survive on the western fringe of Europe (Brittany, Wales, Scotland, Ireland). (*p. 90*)

Champa A state formerly located in what is now southern Vietnam. It was hostile to Annam and was annexed by Annam and destroyed as an independent entity in 1500. (*p. 366*)

Champa rice Quick-maturing rice that can allow two harvests in one growing season. Originally introduced into Champa from India, it was later sent to China as a tribute gift by the Champa state. (See also **tributary system.**) (*p. 295*)

Chang'an City in the Wei Valley in eastern China. It became the capital of the Zhou kingdom and the Qin and early Han Empires. Its main features were imitated in the cities and towns that sprang up throughout the Han Empire. (*p. 164*)

Charlemagne (742–814) King of the Franks (r. 768–814); emperor (r. 800–814). Through a series of military conquests he established the Carolingian Empire, which encompassed all of Gaul and parts of Germany and Italy. Though illiterate himself, he sponsored a brief intellectual revival. (*p. 250*)

chartered companies Groups of private investors who paid an annual fee to France and England in exchange for a monopoly over trade to the West Indies colonies. (*p. 498*)

Chavín The first major urban civilization in South America (900–250 B.C.E.). Its capital, Chavín de Huántar, was located high in the Andes Mountains of Peru. Chavín became politically and economically dominant in a densely populated region that included two distinct ecological zones, the Peruvian coastal plain and the Andean foothills. (*p. 89*)

Chiang Kai-shek (Jiang Jieshi; 1887–1975) General and leader of Nationalist China after 1925. Although he succeeded **Sun Yat-sen** as head of the **Guomindang,** he became a military dictator whose major goal was to crush the communist movement led by **Mao Zedong.** (*p. 788*)

chiefdom Form of political organization with rule by a hereditary leader who held power over a collection of villages and towns. Less powerful than kingdoms and empires, chiefdoms were based on gift giving and commercial links. (*p. 311*)

Chimú Powerful Peruvian civilization based on conquest. Located in the region earlier dominated by **Moche.** Conquered by **Inca** in 1465. (*p. 314*)

chinampas Raised fields constructed along lake shores in Mesoamerica to increase agricultural yields. (*p. 301*)

city-state A small independent state consisting of an urban center and the surrounding agricultural territory. A characteristic political form in early Mesopotamia, Archaic and Classical Greece, Phoenicia, and early Italy. (See also **polis.**) (*p. 32*)

civilization An ambiguous term often used to denote more complex societies but sometimes used by anthropologists to describe any group of people sharing a set of cultural traits. (*p. 28*)

Cixi, Empress Dowager (1835–1908) Empress of China and mother of Emperor Guangxi. She put her son under house arrest, supported antiforeign movements, and resisted reforms of the Chinese government and armed forces. (*p. 721*)

clipper ship Large, fast, streamlined sailing vessel, often American built, of the mid-to-late nineteenth century rigged with vast canvas sails hung from tall masts. (*p. 666*)

Cold War (1945–1991) The ideological struggle between communism (Soviet Union) and capitalism (United States) for world influence. The Soviet Union and the United States came to the brink of actual war during the **Cuban missile crisis** but never attacked one another. The Cold War came to an end when the Soviet Union dissolved in 1991. (See also **North Atlantic Treaty Organization; Warsaw Pact.**) (*p. 831*)

colonialism Policy by which a nation administers a foreign territory and develops its resources for the benefit of the colonial power. (*p. 731*)

Columbian Exchange The exchange of plants, animals, diseases, and technologies between the Americas and the rest of the world following Columbus's voyages. (*p. 472*)

Columbus, Christopher (1451–1506) Genoese mariner who in the service of Spain led expeditions across the Atlantic, reestablishing contact between the peoples of the Americas and the Old World and opening the way to Spanish conquest and colonization. (*p. 430*)

Confederation of 1867 Negotiated union of the formerly separate colonial governments of Ontario, Quebec, New Brunswick, and Nova Scotia. This new Dominion of Canada with a central government in Ottawa is seen as the beginning of the Canadian nation. (*p. 627*)

Confucius Western name for the Chinese philosopher Kongzi (551–479 B.C.E.). His doctrine of duty and public service had a great influence on subsequent Chinese thought and served as a code of conduct for government officials. (*p. 62*)

Congress of Vienna (1814–1815) Meeting of representatives of European monarchs called to reestablish the old order after the defeat of **Napoleon I.** (*p. 594*)

conquistadors Early-sixteenth-century Spanish adventurers who conquered Mexico, Central America, and Peru. (See **Cortés, Hernán; Pizarro, Francisco.**) (*p. 436*)

Constantine (285–337 C.E.) Roman emperor (r. 312–337). After reuniting the Roman Empire, he moved the capital to Con-stantinople and made Christianity a favored religion. (*p.159*)

Constitutional Convention Meeting in 1787 of the elected representatives of the thirteen original states to write the Constitution of the United States. (*p. 583*)

constitutionalism The theory developed in early modern England and spread elsewhere that royal power should be subject to legal and legislative checks. (*p. 452*)

contract of indenture A voluntary agreement binding a person to work for a specified period of years in return for free passage to an overseas destination. Before 1800 most **indentured servants** were Europeans; after 1800 most indentured laborers were Asians. (*p. 670*)

Cortés, Hernán (1485–1547) Spanish explorer and conquistador who led the conquest of Aztec Mexico in 1519–1521 for Spain. (*p. 437*)

Cossacks Peoples of the Russian Empire who lived outside the farming villages, often as herders, mercenaries, or outlaws. Cossacks led the conquest of Siberia in the sixteenth and seventeenth centuries. (*p. 552*)

cottage industries Weaving, sewing, carving, and other small-scale industries that can be done in the home. The laborers, frequently women, are usually independent. (*p. 353*)

cotton The plant that produces fibers from which cotton textiles are woven. Native to India, cotton spread throughout Asia and then to the New World. It has been a major cash crop in various places, including early Islamic Iran, Yi Korea, and nineteenth-century Egypt and the United States. A related species was exploited for fiber in pre-Columbia America. (*p. 363*)

Council of the Indies The institution responsible for supervising Spain's colonies in the Americas from 1524 to the early eighteenth century, when it lost all but judicial responsibilities. (*p. 476*)

***coureurs des bois* (runners of the woods)** French fur traders, many of mixed Amerindian heritage, who lived among and often married with Amerindian peoples of North America. (*p. 489*)

creoles In colonial Spanish America, term used to describe someone of European descent born in the New World. Elsewhere in the Americas, the term is used to describe all nonnative peoples. (*p. 482*)

Crimean War (1853–1856) Conflict between the Russian and Ottoman Empires fought primarily in the Crimean Peninsula. To prevent Russian expansion, Britain and France sent troops to support the Ottomans. (*p. 679*)

Crusades (1096–1291) Armed pilgrimages to the Holy Land by Christians determined to recover Jerusalem from Muslim rule. The Crusades brought an end to western Europe's centuries of intellectual and cultural isolation. (*p. 270*)

Crystal Palace Building erected in Hyde Park, London, for the Great Exhibition of 1851. Made of iron and glass, like a gigantic greenhouse, it was a symbol of the industrial age. (*p. 606*)

Cuban missile crisis (1962) Brink-of-war confrontation between the United States and the Soviet Union over the latter's placement of nuclear-armed missiles in Cuba. (*p. 839*)

cultural imperialism Domination of one culture over another by a deliberate policy or by economic or technological superiority. (*p. 894*)

Cultural Revolution (China) (1966–1969) Campaign in China ordered by **Mao Zedong** to purge the Communist Party of his opponents and instill revolutionary values in the younger generation.(*p. 848*)

culture Socially transmitted patterns of action and expression. *Material culture* refers to physical objects, such as dwellings, clothing, tools, and crafts. Culture also includes arts, beliefs, knowledge, and technology. (*p. 11*)

cuneiform A system of writing in which wedge-shaped symbols represented words or syllables. It originated in Mesopotamia and was used initially for Sumerian and Akkadian but later was adapted to represent other languages of western Asia. Because so many symbols had to be learned, literacy was confined to a relatively small group of administrators and **scribes**. (*p. 39*)

Cyrus (600–530 B.C.E.) Founder of the Achaemenid Persian Empire. Between 550 and 530 B.C.E. he conquered Media, Lydia, and Babylon. Revered in the traditions of both Iran and the subject peoples, he employed Persians and Medes in his administration and respected the institutions and beliefs of subject peoples. (*p. 117*)

czar See **tsar.**

Dalai Lama Originally, a title meaning "universal priest" that the Mongol khans invented and bestowed on a Tibetan lama (priest) in the late 1500s to legitimate their power in Tibet. Subsequently, the title of the religious and political leader of Tibet. (*p. 556*)

Daoism Chinese school of thought, originating in the Warring States Period with Laozi (604–531 B.C.E.). Daoism offered an alternative to the Confucian emphasis on hierarchy and duty. Daoists believe that the world is always changing and is devoid of absolute morality or meaning. They accept the world as they find it, avoid futile struggles, and deviate as little as possible from the *Dao*, or "path" of nature. (See also **Confucius.**) (*p. 63*)

Darius I (ca. 558–486 B.C.E.) Third ruler of the Persian Empire (r. 521–486 B.C.E.). He crushed the widespread initial resistance to his rule and gave all major government posts to Persians rather than to Medes. He established a system of provinces and tribute, began construction of Persepolis, and expanded Persian control in the east (Pakistan) and west (northern Greece). (*p. 118*)

Darwin, Charles (1809–1882) English naturalist. He studied the plants and animals of South America and the Pacific islands, and in his book *On the Origin of Species by Means of Natural Selection* (1859) set forth his theory of **evolution.** (*p. 715*)

Declaration of the Rights of Man (1789) Statement of fundamental political rights adopted by the French **National Assembly** at the beginning of the French Revolution. (*p. 586*)

deforestation The removal of trees faster than forests can replace themselves. (*p. 462*)

Delhi Sultanate (1206–1526) Centralized Indian empire of varying extent, created by Muslim invaders. (*p. 374*)

democracy A system of government in which all "citizens" (however defined) have equal political and legal rights, privileges, and protections, as in the Greek city-state of Athens in the fifth and fourth centuries B.C.E. (*p. 127*)

demographic transition A change in the rates of population growth. Before the transition, both birth and death rates are high, resulting in a slowly growing population; then the death rate drops but the birth rate remains high, causing a population explosion; finally the birth rate drops and the population growth slows down. This transition took place in Europe in the late nineteenth and early twentieth centuries, in North America and East Asia in the mid-twentieth, and, most recently, in Latin America and South Asia. (*p. 867*)

Deng Xiaoping (1904–1997) Communist Party leader who forced Chinese economic reforms after the death of **Mao Zedong.** (*p. 862*)

development In the nineteenth and twentieth centuries, the economic process that led to industrialization, urbanization, the rise of a large and prosperous middle class, and heavy investment in education. (*p. 642*)

devshirme "Selection" in Turkish. The system by which boys from Christian communities were taken by the Ottoman state to serve as **Janissaries.** (*p. 526*)

dhow Ship of small to moderate size used in the western Indian Ocean, traditionally with a triangular sail and a sewn timber hull. (*p. 382*)

Diagne, Blaise (1872–1934) Senegalese political leader. He was the first African elected to the French National Assembly. During World War I, in exchange for promises to give French citizenship to Senegalese, he helped recruit Africans to serve in the French army. After the war, he led a movement to abolish forced labor in Africa. (*p. 809*)

Dias, Bartolomeu (1450?–1500) Portuguese explorer who in 1488 led the first expedition to sail around the southern tip of Africa from the Atlantic and sight the Indian Ocean. (*p. 428*)

diaspora A Greek word meaning "dispersal," used to describe the communities of a given ethnic group living outside their homeland. Jews, for example, spread from Israel to western Asia and Mediterranean lands in antiquity and today can be found throughout the world. (*p. 103*)

Dirty War War waged by the Argentine military (1976–1982) against leftist groups. Characterized by the use of illegal imprisonment, torture, and executions by the military. (*p. 857*)

divination Techniques for ascertaining the future or the will of the gods by interpreting natural phenomena such as, in early China, the cracks on oracle bones or, in ancient Greece, the flight of birds through sectors of the sky. (*p. 59*)

division of labor A manufacturing technique that breaks down a craft into many simple and repetitive tasks that can be performed by unskilled workers. Pioneered in the pottery works of Josiah Wedgwood and in other eighteenth-century factories, it greatly increased the productivity of labor and lowered the cost of manufactured goods. (See also **Wedgwood, Josiah.**) (*p. 603*)

driver A privileged male slave whose job was to ensure that a slave gang did its work on a plantation. (*p. 503*)

Druids The class of religious experts who conducted rituals and preserved sacred lore among some ancient Celtic peoples. They provided education, mediated disputes between kinship groups, and were suppressed by the Romans as a potential focus of opposition to Roman rule. (See also **Celts.**) (*p. 92*)

durbar An elaborate display of political power and wealth in British India in the nineteenth century, ostensibly in imitation of the pageantry of the **Mughal Empire.** (*p. 661*)

Dutch West India Company (1621–1794) Trading company chartered by the Dutch government to conduct its merchants' trade in the Americas and Africa. (*p. 498*)

economic sanctions Boycotts, embargoes, and other economic measures that one country uses to pressure another country into changing its policies. (*p. 889*)

Edison, Thomas (1847–1931) American inventor best known for inventing the electric light bulb, acoustic recording on wax cylinders, and motion pictures. (*p. 703*)

Einstein, Albert (1879–1955) German physicist who developed the theory of relativity, which states that time, space, and mass are relative to each other and not fixed. (*p. 774*)

El Alamein Town in Egypt, site of the victory by Britain's Field Marshal Bernard Montgomery over German forces led by General Erwin Rommel (the "Desert Fox") in 1942–1943. (*p. 793*)

electricity A form of energy used in telegraphy from the 1840s on and for lighting, industrial motors, and railroads beginning in the 1880s. (*p. 702*)

electric telegraph A device for rapid, long-distance transmission of information over an electric wire. It was introduced in England and North America in the 1830s and 1840s and replaced telegraph systems that utilized visual signals such as semaphores. (See also **submarine telegraph cables.**) (*p. 609*)

encomienda A grant of authority over a population of Amerindians in the Spanish colonies. It provided the grant holder with a supply of cheap labor and periodic payments of goods by the Amerindians. It obliged the grant holder to Christianize the Amerindians. (*p. 479*)

Enlightenment A philosophical movement in eighteenth-century Europe that fostered the belief that one could reform society by discovering rational laws that governed social behavior and were just as scientific as the laws of physics. (*pp. 468, 574*)

equites In ancient Italy, prosperous landowners second in wealth and status to the senatorial aristocracy. The Roman emperors allied with this group to counterbalance the influence of the old aristocracy and used the *equites* to staff the imperial civil service. (*p. 152*)

Estates General France's traditional national assembly with representatives of the three estates, or classes, in French society: the clergy, nobility, and commoners. The calling of the Estates General in 1789 led to the French Revolution. (*p. 585*)

Ethiopia East African highland nation lying east of the Nile River. (See also **Menelik II; Selassie, Haile.**) (*p. 221*)

ethnic cleansing Effort to eradicate a people and its culture by means of mass killing and the destruction of historical buildings and cultural materials. Ethnic cleansing was used by both sides in the conflicts that accompanied the disintegration of Yugoslavia in the 1990s. (*p. 883*)

European Community (EC) An organization promoting economic unity in Europe formed in 1967 by consolidation of earlier, more limited, agreements. Replaced by the European Union (EU) in 1993. (*p. 834*)

evolution The biological theory that, over time, changes occurring in plants and animals, mainly as a result of **natural selection** and genetic mutation, result in new species. (*p. 6*)

extraterritoriality The right of foreign residents in a country to live under the laws of their native country and disregard the laws of the host country. In the nineteenth and early twentieth centuries, European and American nationals living in certain areas of Chinese and Ottoman cities were granted this right. (*p. 682*)

Faisal I (1885–1933) Arab prince, leader of the Arab Revolt in World War I. The British made him king of Iraq in 1921, and he reigned under British protection until 1933. (*p. 760*)

Fascist Party Italian political party created by Benito Mussolini during World War I. It emphasized aggressive nationalism and was Mussolini's instrument for the creation of a dictatorship in Italy from 1922 to 1943. (See also **Mussolini, Benito.**) (*p. 786*)

fief In medieval Europe, land granted in return for a sworn oath to provide specified military service. (*p. 256*)

First Temple A monumental sanctuary built in Jerusalem by King Solomon in the tenth century B.C.E. to be the religious center for the Israelite god Yahweh. The Temple priesthood conducted sacrifices, received a tithe or percentage of agricultural revenues, and became economically and politically powerful. The First Temple was destroyed by the Babylonians in 587 B.C.E., rebuilt on a modest scale in the late sixth century B.C.E., and replaced by King Herod's Second Temple in the late first century B.C.E. (destroyed by the Romans in 70 C.E.) (*p. 102*)

Five-Year Plans Plans that Joseph Stalin introduced to industrialize the Soviet Union rapidly, beginning in 1928. They set goals for the output of steel, electricity, machinery, and most other products and were enforced by the police powers of the state. They succeeded in making the Soviet Union a major industrial power before World War II. (See also **Stalin, Joseph.**) (*p. 781*)

foragers People who support themselves by hunting wild animals and gathering wild edible plants and insects. (*p. 13*)

Forbidden City The walled section of Beijing where emperors lived between 1121 and 1924. A portion is now a residence for leaders of the People's Republic of China. (*p. 355*)

Franklin, Benjamin (1706–1790) American intellectual, inventor, and politician He helped to negotiate French support for the American Revolution. (*p. 577*)

free-trade imperialism Economic dominance of a weaker country by a more powerful one, while maintaining the legal independence of the weaker state. In the late nineteenth century, free-trade imperialism characterized the relations between the Latin American republics, on the one hand, and Great Britain and the United States, on the other. (*p. 744*)

fresco A technique of painting on walls covered with moist plaster. It was used to decorate Minoan and Mycenaean palaces and Roman villas, and became an important medium during the Italian Renaissance. (*p. 73*)

Funan An early complex society in Southeast Asia between the first and sixth centuries C.E. It was centered in the rich rice-growing region of southern Vietnam, and it controlled the passage of trade across the Malaysian isthmus. (*p. 191*)

Gama, Vasco da (1460?–1524) Portuguese explorer. In 1497–1498 he led the first naval expedition from Europe to sail to India, opening an important commercial sea route. (*p. 428*)

Gandhi, Mohandas K. (Mahatma) (1869–1948) Leader of the Indian independence movement and advocate of nonviolent resistance. After being educated as a lawyer in England, he returned to India and became leader of the **Indian National Congress** in 1920. He appealed to the poor, led nonviolent demonstrations against British colonial rule, and was jailed many times. Soon after independence he was assassinated for attempting to stop Hindu-Muslim rioting. (*p. 813*)

Genghis Khan (ca. 1167–1227) The title of Temüjin when he ruled the Mongols (1206–1227). It means the "oceanic" or "universal" leader. Genghis Khan was the founder of the Mongol Empire. (*p. 325*)

gens de couleur Free men and women of color in Haiti. They sought greater political rights and later supported the Haitian Revolution. (See also **L'Ouverture, François Dominique Toussaint.**) (*p. 593*)

gentry In China, the class of prosperous families, next in wealth below the rural aristocrats, from which the emperors drew their administrative personnel. Respected for their education and expertise, these officials became a privileged group and made the government more efficient and responsive than in the past. The term *gentry* also denotes the class of landholding families in England below the aristocracy. (*p. 166*)

Ghana First known kingdom in sub-Saharan West Africa between the sixth and thirteenth centuries C.E. Also the modern West African country once known as the Gold Coast. (*p. 215*)

Gold Coast (Africa) Region of the Atlantic coast of West Africa occupied by modern Ghana; named for its gold exports to Europe from the 1470s onward. (*p. 428*)

Golden Horde Mongol khanate founded by Genghis Khan's grandson Batu. It was based in southern Russia and quickly adopted both the Turkic language and Islam. Also known as the Kipchak Horde. (*p. 333*)

Gorbachev, Mikhail (b. 1931) Head of the Soviet Union from 1985 to 1991. His liberalization effort improved relations with the West, but he lost power after his reforms led to the collapse of Communist governments in eastern Europe. (*p. 863*)

Gothic cathedrals Large churches originating in twelfth-century France; built in an architectural style featuring pointed arches, tall vaults and spires, flying buttresses, and large stained-glass windows. (*p. 405*)

Grand Canal The 1,100-mile (1,700-kilometer) waterway linking the Yellow and the Yangzi Rivers. It was begun in the **Han** period and completed during the Sui Empire. (*p. 277*)

Great Circuit The network of Atlantic Ocean trade routes between Europe, Africa, and the Americas that underlay the **Atlantic system.** (*p. 508*)

Great Ice Age Geological era that occurred between ca. 2 million and 11,000 years ago. As a result of climate shifts, large numbers of new species evolved during this period, also called the Pleistocene epoch. (See also **Holocene.**) (*p. 9*)

"great tradition" Historians' term for a literate, well-institutionalized complex of religious and social beliefs and practices adhered to by diverse societies over a broad geographical area. (See also **"small tradition."**) (*p. 217*)

Great Western Schism A division in the Latin (Western) Christian Church between 1378 and 1417, when rival claimants to the papacy existed in Rome and Avignon. (*p. 411*)

Great Zimbabwe City, now in ruins (in the modern African country of Zimbabwe), whose many stone structures were built between about 1250 and 1450, when it was a trading center and the capital of a large state. (*p. 385*)

guild In medieval Europe, an association of men (rarely women), such as merchants, artisans, or professors, who worked in a particular trade and banded together to promote their economic and political interests. Guilds were also important in other societies, such as the Ottoman and Safavid empires. (*p. 403*)

Gujarat Region of western India famous for trade and manufacturing; the inhabitants are called Gujarati. (*p. 380*)

gunpowder A mixture of saltpeter, sulfur, and charcoal, in various proportions. The formula, brought to China in the 400s or 500s, was first used to make fumigators to keep away insect pests and evil spirits. In later centuries it was used to make explosives and grenades and to propel cannonballs, shot, and bullets. (*p. 289*)

Guomindang Nationalist political party founded on democratic principles by **Sun Yat-sen** in 1912. After 1925, the party was headed by **Chiang Kai-shek,** who turned it into an increasingly authoritarian movement. (*p. 769*)

Gupta Empire (320–550 C.E.) A powerful Indian state based, like its Mauryan predecessor, on a capital at Pataliputra in the Ganges Valley. It controlled most of the Indian subcontinent through a combination of military force and its prestige as a center of sophisticated culture. (See also **theater-state.**) (*p. 186*)

Habsburg A powerful European family that provided many Holy Roman Emperors, founded the Austrian (later Austro-Hungarian) Empire, and ruled sixteenth- and seventeenth-century Spain. (*p. 449*)

hadith A tradition relating the words or deeds of the Prophet Muhammad; next to the **Quran,** the most important basis for Islamic law. (*p. 241*)

Hammurabi Amorite ruler of **Babylon** (r. 1792–1750 B.C.E.). He conquered many city-states in southern and northern Mesopotamia and is best known for a code of laws, inscribed on a black stone pillar, illustrating the principles to be used in legal cases. (*p. 34*)

Han A term used to designate (1) the ethnic Chinese people who originated in the Yellow River Valley and spread throughout regions of China suitable for agriculture and (2) the dynasty of emperors who ruled from 206 B.C.E. to 220 C.E. (*p. 164*)

Hanseatic League An economic and defensive alliance of the free towns in northern Germany, founded about 1241 and most powerful in the fourteenth century. (*p. 401*)

Harappa Site of one of the great cities of the Indus Valley civilization of the third millennium B.C.E. It was located on the northwest frontier of the zone of cultivation (in modern Pakistan), and may have been a center for the acquisition of raw materials, such as metals and precious stones, from Afghanistan and Iran. (*p. 48*)

Hatshepsut Queen of Egypt (r. 1473–1458 B.C.E.). She dispatched a naval expedition down the Red Sea to Punt (possibly Somalia), the faraway source of myrrh. There is evidence of opposition to a woman as ruler, and after her death her name and image were frequently defaced. (*p. 66*)

Hebrew Bible A collection of sacred books containing diverse materials concerning the origins, experiences, beliefs, and practices of the Israelites. Most of the extant text was compiled by members of the priestly class in the fifth century B.C.E. and reflects the concerns and views of this group. (*p. 99*)

Hellenistic Age Historians' term for the era, usually dated 323–30 B.C.E., in which Greek culture spread across western Asia and northeastern Africa after the conquests of **Alexander** the Great. The period ended with the fall of the last major Hellenistic kingdom to Rome, but Greek cultural influence persisted until the spread of Islam in the seventh century C.E. (*p. 137*)

Helsinki Accords (1975) Political and human rights agreement signed in Helsinki, Finland, by the Soviet Union and western European countries. (*p. 839*)

Henry the Navigator (1394–1460) Portuguese prince who promoted the study of navigation and directed voyages of exploration down the western coast of Africa. (*p. 425*)

Herodotus (ca. 485–425 B.C.E.) Heir to the technique of *historia*—"investigation"—developed by Greeks in the late Archaic period. He came from a Greek community in Anatolia and traveled extensively, collecting information in western Asia and the Mediterranean lands. He traced the antecedents of and chronicled the **Persian Wars** between the Greek city-states and the Persian Empire, thus originating the Western tradition of historical writing. (*p. 128*)

Herzl, Theodore (1860–1904) Austrian journalist and founder of the Zionist movement urging the creation of a Jewish national homeland in Palestine. (*p. 760*)

Hidalgo y Costilla, Miguel (1753–1811) Mexican priest who led the first stage of the Mexican independence war in 1810. He was captured and executed in 1811. (*p. 625*)

Hidden Imam Last in a series of twelve descendants of Muhammad's son-in-law Ali, whom **Shi'ites** consider divinely appointed leaders of the Muslim community. In occlusion since ca. 873, he is expected to return as a messiah at the end of time. (*p. 532*)

hieroglyphics A system of writing in which pictorial symbols represented sounds, syllables, or concepts. It was used for official and monumental inscriptions in ancient Egypt. Because of the long period of study required to master this system, literacy in hieroglyphics was confined to a relatively small group of **scribes** and administrators. Cursive symbol-forms were developed for rapid composition on other media, such as **papyrus.** (*p. 44*)

high culture Canons of artistic and literary masterworks recognized by dominant economic classes. (*p. 897*)

Hinduism A general term for a wide variety of beliefs and ritual practices that have developed in the Indian subcontinent since antiquity. Hinduism has roots in ancient Vedic, Buddhist, and south Indian religious concepts and practices. It spread along the trade routes to Southeast Asia. (*p. 181*)

Hiroshima City in Japan, the first to be destroyed by an atomic bomb, on August 6, 1945. The bombing hastened the end of World War II. (*p. 797*)

history The study of past events and changes in the development, transmission, and transformation of cultural practices. (*p. 11*)

Hitler, Adolf (1889–1945) Born in Austria, Hitler became a radical German nationalist during World War I. He led the National Socialist German Workers' Party—the **Nazi Party**—in the 1920s and became dictator of Germany in 1933. He led Europe into World War II. (*p. 786*)

Hittites A people from central Anatolia who established an empire in Anatolia and Syria in the Late Bronze Age. With wealth from the trade in metals and military power based on chariot forces, the Hittites vied with New Kingdom Egypt for control of Syria-Palestine before falling to unidentified attackers ca. 1200 B.C.E. (See also **Ramesses II.**) (*p. 64*)

Holocaust Nazis' program during World War II to kill people they considered undesirable. Some 6 million Jews perished during the Holocaust, along with millions of Poles, Gypsies, Communists, Socialists, and others. (*p. 800*)

Holocene The geological era since the end of the **Great Ice Age** about 11,000 years ago. (*p. 21*)

Holy Roman Empire Loose federation of mostly German states and principalities, headed by an emperor elected by the princes. It lasted from 962 to 1806. (*pp. 260, 449*)

hominid The biological family that includes humans and humanlike primates. (*p. 9*)

Homo erectus An extinct human species. It evolved in Africa about 2 million years ago. (*p. 10*)

Homo habilis The first human species (now extinct). It evolved in Africa about 2.5 million years ago. (*p. 9*)

Homo sapiens The current human species. It evolved in Africa about 200,000 years ago. It includes archaic forms such as Neanderthals (now extinct) and all modern humans. (*p. 10*)

hoplite A heavily armored Greek infantryman of the Archaic and Classical periods who fought in the close-packed phalanx formation. Hoplite armies—militias composed of middle- and upper-class citizens supplying their own equipment—were for centuries superior to all other military forces. (*p. 126*)

horse collar Harnessing method that increased the efficiency of horses by shifting the point of traction from the animal's neck to the shoulders; its adoption favors the spread of horse-drawn plows and vehicles. (*p. 269*)

House of Burgesses Elected assembly in colonial Virginia, created in 1618. (*p. 486*)

humanists (Renaissance) European scholars, writers, and teachers associated with the study of the humanities (grammar, rhetoric, poetry, history, languages, and moral philosophy), influential in the fifteenth century and later. (*p. 408*)

Hundred Years War (1337–1453) Series of campaigns over control of the throne of France, involving English and French royal families and French noble families. (*p. 413*)

Husain, Saddam (b. 1937) President of Iraq since 1979. Waged war on Iran in 1980–1988. In 1990 he ordered an invasion of Kuwait but was defeated by United States and its allies in the Gulf War (1991). (*p. 860*)

Ibn Battuta (1304–1369) Moroccan Muslim scholar, the most widely traveled individual of his time. He wrote a detailed account of his visits to Islamic lands from China to Spain and the western Sudan. (*p. 373*)

Ibn Khaldun (1332–1406) Arab historian. He developed an influential theory on the rise and fall of states. Born in Tunis, he spent his later years in Cairo as a teacher and judge. In 1400 he was sent to Damascus to negotiate the surrender of the city, where he met and exchanged views with **Timur.** (*p. 336*)

Il-khan A "secondary" or "peripheral" khan based in Persia. The Il-khans' khanate was founded by Hülegü, a grandson of **Genghis Khan,** was based at Tabriz in modern Azerbaijan. It controlled much of Iran and Iraq. (*p. 333*)

import-substitution industrialization An economic system aimed at building a country's industry by restricting foreign trade. It was especially popular in Latin American countries such as Mexico, Argentina, and Brazil in the mid-twentieth century. It proved successful for a time but could not keep up with technological advances in Europe and North America. (*p. 823*)

Inca Largest and most powerful Andean empire. Controlled the Pacific coast of South America from Ecuador to Chile from its capital of Cuzco. (*p. 316*)

indentured servant A migrant to British colonies in the Americas who paid for passage by agreeing to work for a set term ranging from four to seven years. (*p. 486*)

Indian Civil Service The elite professional class of officials who administered the government of British India. Originally composed exclusively of well-educated British men, it gradually added qualified Indians. (*p. 661*)

Indian National Congress A movement and political party founded in 1885 to demand greater Indian participation in government. Its membership was middle class, and its demands were modest until World War I. Led after 1920 by Mohandas K. Gandhi, it appealed increasingly to the poor, and it organized mass protests demanding self-government and independence. (See also **Gandhi, Mohandas K.**) (*pp. 663, 812*)

Indian Ocean maritime system In premodern times, a network of seaports, trade routes, and maritime culture linking countries on the rim of the Indian Ocean from Africa to Indonesia. (*p. 207*)

indulgence The forgiveness of the punishment due for past sins, granted by the Catholic Church authorities as a reward for a pious act. Martin Luther's protest against the sale of indulgences is often seen as touching off the **Protestant Reformation.** (*p. 446*)

Industrial Revolution The transformation of the economy, the environment, and living conditions, occurring first in England in the eighteenth century, that resulted from the use of steam engines, the mechanization of manufacturing in factories, and innovations in transportation and communication. (*p. 599*)

investiture controversy Dispute between the popes and the Holy Roman Emperors over who held ultimate authority over bishops in imperial lands. (*p. 261*)

Iron Age Historians' term for the period during which iron was the primary metal for tools and weapons. The advent of iron technology began at different times in different parts of the world. (*p. 85*)

iron curtain Winston Churchill's term for the Cold War division between the Soviet-dominated East and the U.S.-dominated West. (*p. 831*)

Iroquois Confederacy An alliance of five northeastern Amerindian peoples (after 1722 six) that made decisions on military and diplomatic issues through a council of representatives. Allied first with the Dutch and later with the English, the Confederacy dominated the area from western New England to the Great Lakes. (*p. 488*)

Islam Religion expounded by the Prophet Muhammad (570–632 C.E.) on the basis of his reception of divine revelations, which were collected after his death into the **Quran.** In the tradition of Judaism and Christianity, and sharing much of their lore, Islam calls on all people to recognize one creator god—Allah—who rewards or punishes believers after death according to how they led their lives. (See also **hadith.**) (*p. 231*)

Israel In antiquity, the land between the eastern shore of the Mediterranean and the Jordan River, occupied by the Israelites from the early second millennium B.C.E. The modern state of Israel was founded in 1948. (*p. 98*)

Jackson, Andrew (1767–1845) First president of the United States born in humble circumstances. He was popular among frontier residents, urban workers, and small farmers. He had a successful political career as judge, general, congressman, senator, and president. After being denied the presidency in 1824 in a controversial election, he won in 1828 and was reelected in 1832. (*p. 629*)

Jacobins Radical republicans during the French Revolution. They were led by Maximilien Robespierre from 1793 to 1794. (See also **Robespierre, Maximilien.**) (*p. 588*)

Janissaries Infantry, originally of slave origin, armed with firearms and constituting the elite of the Ottoman army from the fifteenth century until the corps was abolished in 1826. See also **devshirme.** (*p. 526, 675*)

Jesuits Members of the Society of Jesus, a Roman Catholic order founded by Ignatius Loyola in 1534. They played an important part in the **Catholic Reformation** and helped create conduits of trade and knowledge between Asia and Europe. (*p. 548*)

Jesus (ca. 5 B.C.E.–34 C.E.) A Jew from Galilee in northern Israel who sought to reform Jewish beliefs and practices. He was executed as a revolutionary by the Romans. Hailed as the Messiah and son of God by his followers, he became the central figure in Christianity, a belief system that developed in the centuries after his death. (*p. 155*)

Jinnah, Muhammad Ali (1876–1948) Indian Muslim politician who founded the state of Pakistan. A lawyer by training, he joined the **All-India Muslim League** in 1913. As leader of the League from the 1920s on, he negotiated with the British and the **Indian National Congress** for Muslim participation in Indian politics. From 1940 on, he led the movement for the independence of India's Muslims in a separate state of Pakistan, founded in 1947. (*p. 816*)

joint-stock company A business, often backed by a government charter, that sold shares to individuals to raise money for its trading enterprises and to spread the risks (and profits) among many investors. (*p. 460*)

Juárez, Benito (1806–1872) President of Mexico (1858–1872). Born in poverty in Mexico, he was educated as a lawyer and rose to become chief justice of the Mexican supreme court and then president. He led Mexico's resistance to a French invasion in 1863 and the installation of Maximilian as emperor. (*p. 633*)

junk A very large flatbottom sailing ship produced in the **Tang** and **Song Empires,** specially designed for long-distance commercial travel. (*p. 288*)

Kamakura Shogunate The first of Japan's decentralized military governments. (1185–1333). (*p. 294*)

kamikaze The "divine wind," which the Japanese credited with blowing Mongol invaders away from their shores in 1281. (*p. 365*)

Kangxi (1654–1722) Qing emperor (r. 1662–1722). He oversaw the greatest expansion of the **Qing Empire.**

karma In Indian tradition, the residue of deeds performed in past and present lives that adheres to a "spirit" and determines what form it will assume in its next life cycle. The doctrines of karma and reincarnation were used by the elite in ancient India to encourage people to accept their social position and do their duty. (*p. 177*)

keiretsu Alliances of corporations and banks that dominate the Japanese economy. (*p. 861*)

khipu System of knotted colored cords used by preliterate Andean peoples to transmit information. (*p. 312*)

Khomeini, Ayatollah Ruhollah (1900?–1989) Shi'ite philosopher and cleric who led the overthrow of the shah of Iran in 1979 and created an Islamic republic. (*p. 859*)

Khubilai Khan (1215–1294) Last of the Mongol Great Khans (r. 1260–1294) and founder of the **Yuan Empire.** (*p. 351*)

Kievan Russia State established at Kiev in Ukraine ca. 879 by Scandinavian adventurers asserting authority over a mostly Slavic farming population. (*p. 267*)

Korean War (1950–1953) Conflict that began with North Korea's invasion of South Korea and came to involve the United Nations (primarily the United States) allying with South Korea and the People's Republic of China allying with North Korea. (*p. 836*)

Koryo Korean kingdom founded in 918 and destroyed by a Mongol invasion in 1259. (*p. 292*)

Kush An Egyptian name for Nubia, the region alongside the Nile River south of Egypt, where an indigenous kingdom with its own distinctive institutions and cultural traditions arose beginning in the early second millennium B.C.E. It was deeply influenced by Egyptian culture and at times under the control of Egypt, which coveted its rich deposits of gold and luxury products from sub-Saharan Africa carried up the Nile corridor. (*p. 70*)

labor union An organization of workers in a particular industry or trade, created to defend the interests of members through strikes or negotiations with employers. (*p. 709*)

laissez faire The idea that government should refrain from interfering in economic affairs. The classic exposition of laissez-faire principles is Adam Smith's *Wealth of Nations* (1776). (*p. 615*)

lama In Tibetan Buddhism, a teacher. (*p. 351*)

Las Casas, Bartolomé de (1474–1566) First bishop of Chiapas, in southern Mexico. He devoted most of his life to protecting Amerindian peoples from exploitation. His major achievement was the New Laws of 1542, which limited the ability of Spanish settlers to compel Amerindians to labor for them. (See also **encomienda.**) (*p. 476*)

Latin West Historians' name for the territories of Europe that adhered to the Latin rite of Christianity and used the Latin language for intellectual exchange in the period ca. 1000–1500. (*p. 394*)

League of Nations International organization founded in 1919 to promote world peace and cooperation but greatly weakened by the refusal of the United States to join. It proved ineffectual in stopping aggression by Italy, Japan, and Germany in the 1930s, and it was superseded by the **United Nations** in 1945. (*p. 763*)

Legalism In China, a political philosophy that emphasized the unruliness of human nature and justified state coercion and control. The **Qin** ruling class invoked it to validate the authoritarian nature of their regime and its profligate expenditure of subjects' lives and labor. It was superseded in the **Han** era by a more benevolent Confucian doctrine of governmental moderation. (*p. 62*)

"legitimate" trade Exports from Africa in the nineteenth century that did not include the newly outlawed slave trade. (*p. 654*)

Lenin, Vladimir (1870–1924) Leader of the Bolshevik (later Communist) Party. He lived in exile in Switzerland until 1917, then returned to Russia to lead the Bolsheviks to victory during the Russian Revolution and the civil war that followed. (*p. 761*)

Leopold II (1835–1909) King of Belgium (r. 1865–1909). He was active in encouraging the exploration of Central Africa and became the ruler of the Congo Free State (to 1908). (*p. 732*)

Li Shimin (599–649) One of the founders of the **Tang Empire** and its second emperor (r. 626–649). He led the expansion of the empire into Central Asia. (*p. 277*)

liberalism A political ideology that emphasizes the civil rights of citizens, representative government, and the protection of private property. This ideology, derived from the **Enlightenment,** was especially popular among the property-owning middle classes of Europe and North America. (*p. 713*)

Library of Ashurbanipal A large collection of writings drawn from the ancient literary, religious, and scientific traditions of Mesopotamia. It was assembled by the sixth century B.C.E. Assyrian ruler Ashurbanipal. The many tablets unearthed by archaeologists constitute one of the most important sources of present-day knowledge of the long literary tradition of Mesopotamia. (*p. 98*)

Linear B A set of syllabic symbols, derived from the writing system of **Minoan** Crete, used in the Mycenaean palaces of the Late Bronze Age to write an early form of Greek. It was used primarily for palace records, and the surviving Linear B tablets provide substantial information about the economic organization of Mycenaean society and tantalizing clues about political, social, and religious institutions. (*p. 75*)

Little Ice Age A century-long period of cool climate that began in the 1590s. Its ill effects on agriculture in northern Europe were notable. (*p. 462*)

llama A hoofed animal indigenous to the Andes Mountains in South America. It was the only domesticated beast of burden in the Americas before the arrival of Europeans. It provided meat and wool. The use of llamas to transport goods made possible specialized production and trade among people living in different ecological zones and fostered the integration of these zones by **Chavín** and later Andean states. (*p. 90*)

loess A fine, light silt deposited by wind and water. It constitutes the fertile soil of the Yellow River Valley in northern China. Because loess soil is not compacted, it can be worked with a simple digging stick, but it leaves the region vulnerable to devastating earthquakes. (*p. 58*)

Long March (1934–1935) The 6,000-mile (9,600-kilometer) flight of Chinese Communists from southeastern to northwestern China. The Communists, led by **Mao Zedong,** were pursued by the Chinese army under orders from **Chiang Kai-shek.** The four thousand survivors of the march formed the nucleus of a revived Communist movement that defeated the **Guomindang** after World War II. (*p. 789*)

L'Ouverture, François Dominique Toussaint (1743–1803) Leader of the Haitian Revolution. He freed the slaves and gained effective independence for Haiti despite military interventions by the British and French. (*p. 593*)

ma'at Egyptian term for the concept of divinely created and maintained order in the universe. Reflecting the ancient Egyptians' belief in an essentially beneficent world, the divine ruler was the earthly guarantor of this order. (See also **pyramid.**) (*p. 42*)

Macartney mission (1792–1793) The unsuccessful attempt by the British Empire to establish diplomatic relations with the **Qing Empire.** (*p. 560*)

Magellan, Ferdinand (1480?–1521) Portuguese navigator who led the Spanish expedition of 1519–1522 that was the first to sail around the world. (*p. 431*)

Mahabharata A vast epic chronicling the events leading up to a cataclysmic battle between related kinship groups in early India. It includes the Bhagavad-Gita, the most important work of Indian sacred literature. (*p. 185*)

Mahayana Buddhism "Great Vehicle" branch of Buddhism followed in China, Japan, and Central Asia. The focus is on reverence for **Buddha** and for bodhisattvas, enlightened persons who have postponed nirvana to help others attain enlightenment. (*p. 181*)

Malacca Port city in the modern Southeast Asian country of Malaysia, founded about 1400 as a trading center on the Strait of Malacca. Also spelled Melaka. (*p. 387*)

Malay peoples A designation for peoples originating in south China and Southeast Asia who settled the Malay Peninsula, Indonesia, and the Philippines, then spread eastward across the islands of the Pacific Ocean and west to Madagascar. (*p. 190*)

Mali Empire created by indigenous Muslims in western Sudan of West Africa from the thirteenth to fifteenth century. It was famous for its role in the trans-Saharan gold trade. (See also **Timbuktu.**) (*p. 375*)

Malthus, Thomas (1766–1834) Eighteenth-century English intellectual who warned that population growth threatened future generations because, in his view, population growth would always outstrip increases in agricultural production. (*p. 867*)

Mamluks Under the Islamic system of military slavery, Turkic military slaves who formed an important part of the armed forces of the **Abbasid Caliphate** of the ninth and tenth centuries. Mamluks eventually founded their own state, ruling Egypt and Syria (1250–1517). (*pp. 236, 344*)

Manchuria Region of Northeast Asia bounded by the Yalu River on the south and the Amur River on the east and north. (*p. 354*)

Manchus Federation of Northeast Asian peoples who founded the **Qing Empire.** (*p. 556*)

Mandate of Heaven Chinese religious and political ideology developed by the **Zhou,** according to which it was the prerogative of Heaven, the chief deity, to grant power to the ruler of China and to take away that power if the ruler failed to conduct himself justly and in the best interests of his subjects. (*p. 61*)

mandate system Allocation of former German colonies and Ottoman possessions to the victorious powers after World War I, to be administered under League of Nations supervision. (*p. 770*)

manor In medieval Europe, a large, self-sufficient landholding consisting of the lord's residence (manor house), outbuildings, peasant village, and surrounding land. (*p. 254*)

mansabs In India, grants of land given in return for service by rulers of the **Mughal Empire.** (*p. 536*)

Mansa Kankan Musa Ruler of Mali (r. 1312–1337). His pilgrimage through Egypt to **Mecca** in 1324–1325 established the empire's reputation for wealth in the Mediterranean world. (*p. 376*)

manumission A grant of legal freedom to an individual slave. (*p. 505*)

Mao Zedong (1893–1976) Leader of the Chinese Communist Party (1927–1976). He led the Communists on the **Long March** (1934–1935) and rebuilt the Communist Party and Red Army during the Japanese occupation of China (1937–1945). After World War II, he led the Communists to victory over the **Guomindang.** He ordered the **Cultural Revolution** in 1966. (*p. 789*)

maroon A slave who ran away from his or her master. Often a member of a community of runaway slaves in the West Indies and South America. (*p. 505*)

Marshall Plan U. S. program to support the reconstruction of western Europe after World War II. By 1961 more than $20 billion in economic aid had been dispersed. (*p. 834*)

Marx, Karl (1818–1883) German journalist and philosopher, founder of the Marxist branch of **socialism.** He is known for two books: *The Communist Manifesto* (1848) and *Das Kapital* (Vols. I–III, 1867–1894). (*p.* 709)

mass deportation The forcible removal and relocation of large numbers of people or entire populations. The mass deportations practiced by the Assyrian and Persian Empires were meant as a terrifying warning of the consequences of rebellion. They also brought skilled and unskilled labor to the imperial center. (*p.* 95)

mass production The manufacture of many identical products by the division of labor into many small repetitive tasks. This method was introduced into the manufacture of pottery by Josiah Wedgwood and into the spinning of cotton thread by Richard Arkwright. (See also **Arkwright, Richard; Industrial Revolution; Wedgwood, Josiah.**) (*p.* 602)

Mauryan Empire The first state to unify most of the Indian subcontinent. It was founded by Chandragupta Maurya in 324 B.C.E. and survived until 184 B.C.E. From its capital at Pataliputra in the Ganges Valley it grew wealthy from taxes on agriculture, iron mining, and control of trade routes. (See also **Ashoka.**) (*p.* 184)

Maya Mesoamerican civilization concentrated in Mexico's Yucatán Peninsula and in Guatemala and Honduras but never unified into a single empire. Major contributions were in mathematics, astronomy, and development of the calendar. (*p.* 302)

Mecca City in western Arabia; birthplace of the Prophet **Muhammad,** and ritual center of the Islamic religion. (*p.* 230)

mechanization The application of machinery to manufacturing and other activities. Among the first processes to be mechanized were the spinning of cotton thread and the weaving of cloth in late-eighteenth- and early-nineteenth-century England. (*p.* 603)

medieval Literally "middle age," a term that historians of Europe use for the period ca. 500 to ca. 1500, signifying its intermediate point between Greco-Roman antiquity and the Renaissance. (*p.* 250)

Medina City in western Arabia to which the Prophet Muhammad and his followers emigrated in 622 to escape persecution in Mecca. (*p.* 231)

megaliths Structures and complexes of very large stones constructed for ceremonial and religious purposes in **Neolithic** times. (*p.* 23)

Meiji Restoration The political program that followed the destruction of the **Tokugawa Shogunate** in 1868, in which a collection of young leaders set Japan on the path of centralization, industrialization, and imperialism. (See also **Yamagata Aritomo.**) (*p.* 694)

Memphis The capital of Old Kingdom Egypt, near the head of the Nile Delta. Early rulers were interred in the nearby **pyramids.** (*p.* 43)

Menelik II (1844–1911). Emperor of Ethiopia (r. 1889–1911). He enlarged Ethiopia to its present dimensions and defeated an Italian invasion at Adowa (1896). (*p.* 737)

mercantilism European government policies of the sixteenth, seventeenth, and eighteenth centuries designed to promote overseas trade between a country and its colonies and accumulate precious metals by requiring colonies to trade only with their motherland country. The British system was defined by the Navigation Acts, the French system by laws known as the *Exclusif.* (*p.* 506)

Meroë Capital of a flourishing kingdom in southern Nubia from the fourth century B.C.E. to the fourth century C.E. In this period Nubian culture shows more independence from Egypt and the influence of sub-Saharan Africa. (*p.* 71)

mestizo The term used by Spanish authorities to describe someone of mixed Amerindian and European descent. (*p.* 484)

Middle Passage The part of the **Great Circuit** involving the transportation of enslaved Africans across the Atlantic to the Americas. (*p.* 508)

Ming Empire (1368–1644) Empire based in China that Zhu Yuanzhang established after the overthrow of the **Yuan Empire.** The Ming emperor **Yongle** sponsored the building of the **Forbidden City** and the voyages of **Zheng He.** The later years of the Ming saw a slowdown in technological development and economic decline. (*pp.* 355, 554)

Minoan Prosperous civilization on the Aegean island of Crete in the second millennium B.C.E. The Minoans engaged in far-flung commerce around the Mediterranean and exerted powerful cultural influences on the early Greeks. (*p.* 73)

mit'a Andean labor system based on shared obligations to help kinsmen and work on behalf of the ruler and religious organizations. (*p.* 312)

Moche Civilization of north coast of Peru (200–700 C.E.). An important Andean civilization that built extensive irrigation networks as well as impressive urban centers dominated by brick temples. (*p.* 313)

Moctezuma II (1466?–1520) Last Aztec emperor, overthrown by the Spanish conquistador Hernán Cortés. (*p.* 437)

modernization The process of reforming political, military, economic, social, and cultural traditions in imitation of the early success of Western societies, often with regard for accommodating local traditions in non-Western societies. (*p.* 652)

Mohenjo-Daro Largest of the cities of the Indus Valley civilization. It was centrally located in the extensive floodplain of the Indus River in contemporary Pakistan. Little is known about the political institutions of Indus Valley communities, but the large-scale of construction at Mohenjo-Daro, the orderly grid of streets, and the standardization of building materials are evidence of central planning. (*p.* 48)

moksha The Hindu concept of the spirit's "liberation" from the endless cycle of rebirths. There are various avenues—such as physical discipline, meditation, and acts of devotion to the gods—by which the spirit can distance itself from desire for the things of this world and be merged with the divine force that animates the universe. (*p.* 179)

monasticism Living in a religious community apart from secular society and adhering to a rule stipulating chastity, obedience, and poverty. It was a prominent element of medieval Christianity and Buddhism. Monasteries were the primary centers of learning and literacy in medieval Europe. (*p.* 261)

Mongols A people of this name is mentioned as early as the records of the **Tang Empire,** living as nomads in northern

Eurasia. After 1206 they established an enormous empire under **Genghis Khan,** linking western and eastern Eurasia. (*p. 325*)

monotheism Belief in the existence of a single divine entity. Some scholars cite the devotion of the Egyptian pharaoh **Akhenaten** to the Aten (sun-disk) and his suppression of traditional goals as the earliest instance. The Israelite worship of Yahweh developed into an exclusive belief in one god, and this concept passed into Christianity and Islam. (*p. 102*)

monsoon Seasonal winds in the Indian Ocean caused by the differences in temperature between the rapidly heating and cooling landmasses of Africa and Asia and the slowly changing ocean waters. These strong and predictable winds have long been ridden across the open sea by sailors, and the large amounts of rainfall that they deposit on parts of India, Southeast Asia, and China allow for the cultivation of several crops a year. (*pp. 174, 371*)

Morelos, José María (1765–1814) Mexican priest and former student of Miguel Hidalgo y Costilla, he led the forces fighting for Mexican independence until he was captured and executed in 1814. (See also **Hidalgo y Costilla, Miguel.**) (*p. 626*)

most-favored-nation status A clause in a commercial treaty that awards to any later signatories all the privileges previously granted to the original signatories. (*p. 686*)

movable type Type in which each individual character is cast on a separate piece of metal. It replaced woodblock printing, allowing for the arrangement of individual letters and other characters on a page, rather than requiring the carving of entire pages at a time. It may have been invented in Korea in the thirteenth century. (See also **printing press.**) (*p. 293*)

Mughal Empire Muslim state (1526–1857) exercising dominion over most of India in the sixteenth and seventeenth centuries. (*p. 536*)

Muhammad (570–632 C.E.) Arab prophet; founder of religion of Islam. (*p. 230*)

Muhammad Ali (1769–1849) Leader of Egyptian modernization in the early nineteenth century. He ruled Egypt as an Ottoman governor, but had imperial ambitions. His descendants ruled Egypt until overthrown in 1952. (*p. 652*)

mulatto The term used in Spanish and Portuguese colonies to describe someone of mixed African and European descent. (*p. 484*)

mummy A body preserved by chemical processes or special natural circumstances, often in the belief that the deceased will need it again in the afterlife. In ancient Egypt the bodies of people who could afford mummification underwent a complex process of removing organs, filling body cavities, dehydrating the corpse with natron, and then wrapping the body with linen bandages and enclosing it in a wooden sarcophagus. (*p. 46*)

Muscovy Russian principality that emerged gradually during the era of Mongol domination. The Muscovite dynasty ruled without interruption from 1276 to 1598. (*p. 551*)

Muslim An adherent of the Islamic religion; a person who "submits" (in Arabic, *Islam* means "submission") to the will of God. (*p. 231*)

Mussolini, Benito (1883–1945) Fascist dictator of Italy (1922–1943). He led Italy to conquer Ethiopia (1935), joined Germany in the Axis pact (1936), and allied Italy with Germany in World War II. He was overthrown in 1943 when the Allies invaded Italy. (*p. 786*)

Mycenae Site of a fortified palace complex in southern Greece that controlled a Late Bronze Age kingdom. In Homer's epic poems Mycenae was the base of King Agamemnon, who commanded the Greeks besieging Troy. Contemporary archaeologists call the complex Greek society of the second millennium B.C.E. "Mycenaean." (*p. 74*)

Napoleon I (1769–1832). Overthrew French Directory in 1799 and became emperor of the French in 1804. Failed to defeat Great Britain and abdicated in 1814. Returned to power briefly in 1815 but was defeated and died in exile. (*p. 591*)

Nasir al-Din Tusi (1201–1274) Persian mathematician and cosmologist whose academy near Tabriz provided the model for the movement of the planets that helped to inspire the Copernican model of the solar system. (*p. 337*)

National Assembly French Revolutionary assembly (1789–1791). Called first as the Estates General, the three estates came together and demanded radical change. It passed the **Declaration of the Rights of Man** in 1789. (*p. 585*)

nationalism A political ideology that stresses people's membership in a nation—a community defined by a common culture and history as well as by territory. In the late eighteenth and early nineteenth centuries, nationalism was a force for unity in western Europe. In the late nineteenth century it hastened the disintegration of the Austro-Hungarian and Ottoman Empires. In the twentieth century it provided the ideological foundation for scores of independent countries emerging from **colonialism.** (*p. 713*)

natural selection The biological process by which variations that enhance a population's ability to survive in a particular environment become dominant in a species over very long periods and lead to the **evolution** of a new species. (*p. 6*)

nawab A Muslim prince allied to British India; technically, a semi-autonomous deputy of the Mughal emperor. (*p. 657*)

Nazi Party German political party joined by Adolf Hitler, emphasizing nationalism, racism, and war. When Hitler became chancellor of Germany in 1933, the Nazi Party became the only legal party and an instrument of Hitler's absolute rule. Its formal name was National Socialist German Workers' Party. (See also **Hitler, Adolf.**) (*p. 786*)

Nehru, Jawaharlal (1889–1964) Indian statesman. He succeeded Mohandas K. Gandhi as leader of the **Indian National Congress.** He negotiated the end of British colonial rule in India and became India's first prime minister (1947–1964). (*p. 815*)

Neo-Assyrian Empire An empire extending from western Iran to Syria-Palestine, conquered by the Assyrians of northern Mesopotamia between the tenth and seventh centuries B.C.E. They used force and terror and exploited the wealth and labor of their subjects. They also preserved and continued the cultural and scientific developments of Mesopotamian civilization. (*p. 93*)

Neo-Babylonian kingdom Under the Chaldaeans (nomadic kinship groups that settled in southern Mesopotamia in the early first millennium B.C.E.), **Babylon** again became a major political and cultural center in the seventh and sixth centuries B.C.E. After participating in the destruction of Assyrian power, the monarchs Nabopolassar and Nebuchadnezzar took over the southern portion of the Assyrian domains. By destroying the **First Temple** in Jerusalem and deporting part of the population, they initiated the **diaspora** of the Jews. (*p. 110*)

Neolithic The period of the Stone Age associated with the ancient **Agricultural Revolution(s).** It follows the **Paleolithic** period. (*p. 11*)

Nevskii, Alexander (1220–1263) Prince of Novgorod (r. 1236–1263). He submitted to the invading Mongols in 1240 and received recognition as the leader of the Russian princes under the Golden Horde. (*p. 339*)

New Economic Policy Policy proclaimed by Vladimir Lenin in 1924 to encourage the revival of the Soviet economy by allowing small private enterprises. Joseph Stalin ended the N.E.P. in 1928 and replaced it with a series of **Five-Year Plans.** (See also **Lenin, Vladimir.**) (*p. 766*)

New France French colony in North America, with a capital in Quebec, founded 1608. New France fell to the British in 1763. (*p. 489*)

New Imperialism Historians' term for the late-nineteenth- and early-twentieth-century wave of conquests by European powers, the United States, and Japan, which were followed by the development and exploitation of the newly conquered territories for the benefit of the colonial powers. (*p. 726*)

Newly Industrialized Economies (NIEs) Rapidly growing, new industrial nations of the late twentieth century, including the **Asian Tigers.** (*p. 861*)

new monarchies Historians' term for the monarchies in France, England, and Spain from 1450 to 1600. The centralization of royal power was increasing within more or less fixed territorial limits. (*p. 414*)

nomadism A way of life, forced by a scarcity of resources, in which groups of people continually migrate to find pastures and water. (*p. 326*)

nonaligned nations Developing countries that announced their neutrality in the **Cold War.** (*p. 846*)

nongovernmental organizations (NGOs) Nonprofit international organizations devoted to investigating human rights abuses and providing humanitarian relief. Two NGOs won the Nobel Peace Prize in the 1990s: International Campaign to Ban Landmines (1997) and Doctors Without Borders (1999). (*p. 892*)

North Atlantic Treaty Organization (NATO) Organization formed in 1949 as a military alliance of western European and North American states against the Soviet Union and its east European allies. (See also **Warsaw Pact.**) (*p. 832*)

nuclear nonproliferation Goal of international efforts to prevent countries other than the five declared nuclear powers (United States, Russia, Britain, France, and China) from obtaining nuclear weapons. The first Nuclear Non-Proliferation Treaty was signed in 1968. (*p. 890*)

Olmec The first Mesoamerican civilization. Between ca. 1200 and 400 B.C.E., the Olmec people of central Mexico created a vibrant civilization that included intensive agriculture, wide-ranging trade, ceremonial centers, and monumental construction. The Olmec had great cultural influence on later Mesoamerican societies, passing on artistic styles, religious imagery, sophisticated astronomical observation for the construction of calendars, and a ritual ball game. (*p. 86*)

Oman Arab state based in Musqat, the main port in the southwest region of the Arabian peninsula. Oman succeeded Portugal as a power in the western Indian Ocean in the eighteenth century. (*p. 542*)

Opium War (1839–1842) War between Britain and the **Qing Empire** that was, in the British view, occasioned by the Qing government's refusal to permit the importation of opium into its territories. The victorious British imposed the one-sided **Treaty of Nanking** on China. (*p. 684*)

Organization of Petroleum Exporting Countries (OPEC) Organization formed in 1960 by oil-producing states to promote their collective interest in generating revenue from oil. (*p. 849*)

Ottoman Empire Islamic state founded by Osman in northwestern Anatolia ca. 1300. After the fall of the **Byzantine Empire,** the Ottoman Empire was based at Istanbul (formerly Constantinople) from 1453 to 1922. It encompassed lands in the Middle East, North Africa, the Caucasus, and eastern Europe. (*p. 522*)

Páez, José Antonio (1790–1873) Venezulean soldier who led Simón Bolívar's cavalry force. He became a successful general in the war and built a powerful political base. He was unwilling to accept the constitutional authority of Bolívar's government in distant Bogotá and declared Venezuela's independence from Gran Colombia in 1829. (*p. 629*)

Paleolithic The period of the Stone Age associated with the **evolution** of humans. It predates the **Neolithic** period. (*p. 11*)

Panama Canal Ship canal cut across the isthmus of Panama by United States Army engineers; it opened in 1915. It greatly shortened the sea voyage between the east and west coasts of North America. The United States turned the canal over to Panama on January 1, 2000. (*p. 746*)

papacy The central administration of the Roman Catholic Church, of which the pope is the head. (*pp. 258, 445*)

papyrus A reed that grows along the banks of the Nile River in Egypt. From it was produced a coarse, paperlike writing medium used by the Egyptians and many other peoples in the ancient Mediterranean and Middle East. (*p. 44*)

Parthians Iranian ruling dynasty between ca. 250 B.C.E. and 226 C.E. (*p. 204*)

patron/client relationship In ancient Rome, a fundamental social relationship in which the patron—a wealthy and powerful individual—provided legal and economic protection and assistance to clients, men of lesser status and means, and in return the clients supported the political careers and economic interests of their patron. (*p. 149*)

Paul (ca. 5–65 C.E.) A Jew from the Greek city of Tarsus in Anatolia, he initially persecuted the followers of Jesus but, after receiving a revelation on the road to Syrian Damascus, became a Christian. Taking advantage of his Hellenized background and Roman citizenship, he traveled throughout Syria-Palestine, Anatolia, and Greece, preaching the new religion and establishing churches. Finding his greatest success among pagans ("gentiles"), he began the process by which Christianity separated from Judaism. (*p. 156*)

pax romana Literally, "Roman peace," it connoted the stability and prosperity that Roman rule brought to the lands of the Roman Empire in the first two centuries C.E. The movement of people and trade goods along Roman roads and safe seas allowed for the spread of cultural practices, technologies, and religious ideas. (*p. 154*)

Pearl Harbor Naval base in Hawaii attacked by Japanese aircraft on December 7, 1941. The sinking of much of the U.S. Pacific Fleet brought the United States into World War II. (*p. 793*)

Peloponnesian War A protracted (431–404 B.C.E.) and costly conflict between the Athenian and Spartan alliance systems that convulsed most of the Greek world. The war was largely a consequence of Athenian imperialism. Possession of a naval empire allowed Athens to fight a war of attrition. Ultimately, Sparta prevailed because of Athenian errors and Persian financial support. (*p. 135*)

percussion caps Gunpowder-filled capsules that, when struck by the hammer of a gun, ignite the explosive charge in a gun. Their use meant that guns no longer needed to be ignited by hand. (*p. 681*)

perestroika Policy of "openness" that was the centerpiece of Mikhail Gorbachev's efforts to liberalize communism in the Soviet Union. (See also **Gorbachev, Mikhail.**) (*p. 863*)

Pericles (ca. 495–429 B.C.E.) Aristocratic leader who guided the Athenian state through the transformation to full participatory democracy for all male citizens, supervised construction of the Acropolis, and pursued a policy of imperial expansion that led to the **Peloponnesian War.** He formulated a strategy of attrition but died from the plague early in the war. (*p. 130*)

Perón, Eva Duarte (1919–1952) Wife of **Juan Perón** and champion of the poor in Argentina. She was a gifted speaker and popular political leader who campaigned to improve the life of the urban poor by founding schools and hospitals and providing other social benefits. (*p. 824*)

Perón, Juan (1895–1974) President of Argentina (1946–1955, 1973–1974). As a military officer, he championed the rights of labor. Aided by his wife **Eva Duarte Perón**, he was elected president in 1946. He built up Argentinean industry, became very popular among the urban poor, but harmed the economy. (*p. 823*)

Persepolis A complex of palaces, reception halls, and treasury buildings erected by the Persian kings **Darius I** and Xerxes in the Persian homeland. It is believed that the New Year's festival was celebrated here, as well as the coronations, weddings, and funerals of the Persian kings, who were buried in cliff-tombs nearby. (*p. 119*)

Persian Wars Conflicts between Greek city-states and the Persian Empire, ranging from the Ionian Revolt (499–494 B.C.E.) through Darius's punitive expedition that failed at Marathon (490 B.C.E.) and the defeat of Xerxes' massive invasion of Greece by the Spartan-led Hellenic League (480–479 B.C.E.). This first major setback for Persian arms launched the Greeks into their period of greatest cultural productivity. **Herodotus** chronicled these events in the first "history" in the Western tradition. (*p. 131*)

personalist leaders Political leaders who rely on charisma and their ability to mobilize and direct the masses of citizens outside the authority of constitutions and laws. Nineteenth-century examples include José Antonio Páez of Venezuela and Andrew Jackson of the United States. Twentieth-century examples include Getulio Vargas of Brazil and Juan Perón of Argentina. (See also **Jackson, Andrew; Paez, José Antonio; Perón, Juan; Vargas, Getulio.**) (*p. 628*)

Peter the Great (1672–1725) Russian tsar (r. 1689–1725). He enthusiastically introduced Western languages and technologies to the Russian elite, moving the capital from Moscow to the new city of St. Petersburg. (*p. 552*)

pharaoh The central figure in the ancient Egyptian state. Believed to be an earthly manifestation of the gods, he used his absolute power to maintain the safety and prosperity of Egypt. (*p. 42*)

Phoenicians Semitic-speaking Canaanites living on the coast of modern Lebanon and Syria in the first millennium B.C.E. From major cities such as Tyre and Sidon, Phoenician merchants and sailors explored the Mediterranean, engaged in widespread commerce, and founded **Carthage** and other colonies in the western Mediterranean. (*p. 103*)

pilgrimage Journey to a sacred shrine by Christians seeking to show their piety, fulfill vows, or gain absolution for sins. Other religions also have pilgrimage traditions, such as the Muslim pilgrimage to **Mecca** and the pilgrimages made by early Chinese Buddhists to India in search of sacred Buddhist writings. (*p. 270*)

Pilgrims Group of English Protestant dissenters who established Plymouth Colony in Massachusetts in 1620 to seek religious freedom after having lived briefly in the Netherlands. (*p. 487*)

Pizarro, Francisco (1475?–1541) Spanish explorer who led the conquest of the **Inca** Empire of Peru in 1531–1533. (*p. 438*)

Planck, Max (1858–1947) German physicist who developed quantum theory and was awarded the Nobel Prize for physics in 1918. (*p. 774*)

plantocracy In the West Indian colonies, the rich men who owned most of the slaves and most of the land, especially in the eighteenth century. (*p. 502*)

polis The Greek term for a **city-state,** an urban center and the agricultural territory under its control. It was the characteristic form of political organization in southern and central Greece in the Archaic and Classical periods. Of the hundreds of city-states in the Mediterranean and Black Sea regions settled by Greeks, some were oligarchic, others democratic, depending on the powers delegated to the Council and the Assembly. (*p. 125*)

popular culture Entertainment spread by mass communications and enjoying wide appeal. (*p. 897*)

positivism A philosophy developed by the French count of Saint-Simon. Positivists believed that social and economic problems could be solved by the application of the scientific method, leading to continuous progress. Their ideas became popular in France and Latin America in the nine-teenth century. (*p. 616*)

postmodernism Post-World War II intellectual movement and cultural attitude focusing on cultural pluralism and release from the confines and ideology of Western high culture. (*p. 900*)

Potosí Located in Bolivia, one of the richest silver mining centers and most populous cities in colonial Spanish America. (*p. 479*)

printing press A mechanical device for transferring text or graphics from a woodblock or type to paper using ink. Presses using movable type first appeared in Europe in about 1450. See also **movable type.** (*p. 409*)

Protestant Reformation Religious reform movement within the Latin Christian Church beginning in 1519. It resulted in the "protesters" forming several new Christian denominations, including the Lutheran and Reformed Churches and the Church of England. (*p. 446*)

proxy wars During the **Cold War,** local or regional wars in which the superpowers armed, trained, and financed the combatants. (*p. 855*)

Ptolemies The Macedonian dynasty, descended from one of Alexander the Great's officers, that ruled Egypt for three centuries (323–30 B.C.E.). From their magnificent capital at Alexandria on the Mediterranean coast, the Ptolemies largely took over the system created by Egyptian pharaohs to extract the wealth of the land, rewarding Greeks and Hellenized non-Greeks serving in the military and administration. (*p. 138*)

Puritans English Protestant dissenters who believed that God predestined souls to heaven or hell before birth. They founded Massachusetts Bay Colony in 1629. (*p. 487*)

pyramid A large, triangular stone monument, used in Egypt and Nubia as a burial place for the king. The largest pyramids, erected during the Old Kingdom near Memphis with stone tools and compulsory labor, reflect the Egyptian belief that the proper and spectacular burial of the divine ruler would guarantee the continued prosperity of the land. (See also **ma'at.**) (*p. 42*)

Qin A people and state in the Wei Valley of eastern China that conquered rival states and created the first Chinese empire (221–206 B.C.E.). The Qin ruler, **Shi Huangdi,** standardized many features of Chinese society and ruthlessly marshalled subjects for military and construction projects, engendering hostility that led to the fall of his dynasty shortly after his death. The Qin framework was largely taken over by the succeeding **Han** Empire. (*p. 163*)

Qing Empire Empire established in China by Manchus who overthrew the **Ming Empire** in 1644. At various times the Qing also controlled Manchuria, Mongolia, Turkestan, and Tibet. The last Qing emperor was overthrown in 1911. (*p. 556*)

Quran Book composed of divine revelations made to the Prophet Muhammad between ca. 610 and his death in 632; the sacred text of the religion of **Islam.** (*p. 232*)

railroads Networks of iron (later steel) rails on which steam (later electric or diesel) locomotives pulled long trains at high speeds. The first railroads were built in England in the 1830s. Their success caused a railroad-building boom throughout the world that lasted well into the twentieth century. (*p. 704*)

Rajputs Members of a mainly Hindu warrior caste from northwest India. The Mughal emperors drew most of their Hindu officials from this caste, and **Akbar I** married a Rajput princess. (*p. 537*)

Ramesses II A long-lived ruler of New Kingdom Egypt (r. 1290–1224 B.C.E.). He reached an accommodation with the **Hittites** of Anatolia after a standoff in battle at Kadesh in Syria. He built on a grand scale throughout Egypt. (*p. 68*)

Rashid al-Din (d.1318) Adviser to the **Il-khan** ruler Ghazan, who converted to Islam on Rashid's advice. (*p. 334*)

recaptives Africans rescued by Britain's Royal Navy from the illegal slave trade of the nineteenth century and restored to free status. (*p. 655*)

reconquest of Iberia Beginning in the eleventh century, military campaigns by various Iberian Christian states to recapture territory taken by Muslims. In 1492 the last Muslim ruler was defeated, and Spain and Portugal emerged as united kingdoms. (*p. 414*)

Renaissance (European) A period of intense artistic and intellectual activity, said to be a "rebirth" of Greco-Roman culture. Usually divided into an Italian Renaissance, from roughly the mid-fourteenth to mid-fifteenth century, and a Northern (trans-Alpine) Renaissance, from roughly the early fifteenth to early seventeenth century. (*pp. 407, 445*)

Revolutions of 1848 Democratic and nationalist revolutions that swept across Europe. The monarchy in France was overthrown. In Germany, Austria, Italy, and Hungary the revolutions failed. (*p. 595*)

Rhodes, Cecil (1853–1902) British entrepreneur and politician involved in the expansion of the British Empire from South Africa into Central Africa. The colonies of Southern Rhodesia (now Zimbabwe) and Northern Rhodesia (now Zambia) were named after him. (*p. 736*)

Robespierre, Maximilien (1758–1794) Young provincial lawyer who led the most radical phases of the French Revolution. His execution ended the Reign of Terror. See **Jacobins.** (*p. 589*)

Roman Principate A term used to characterize Roman government in the first three centuries C.E., based on the ambiguous title *princeps* ("first citizen") adopted by Augustus to conceal his military dictatorship. (*p. 151*)

Roman Republic The period from 507 to 31 B.C.E., during which Rome was largely governed by the aristocratic **Roman Senate.** (*p. 148*)

Roman Senate A council whose members were the heads of wealthy, landowning families. Originally an advisory body to the early kings, in the era of the **Roman Republic** the Senate effectively governed the Roman state and the growing empire. Under Senate leadership, Rome conquered an empire of unprecedented extent in the lands surrounding the Mediterranean Sea. In the first century B.C.E. quarrels among powerful and ambitious senators and failure to address social and economic problems led to civil wars and the emergence of the rule of the emperors. (*p. 148*)

Romanization The process by which the Latin language and Roman culture became dominant in the western provinces of the Roman Empire. The Roman government did not actively seek to Romanize the subject peoples, but indigenous peoples in the provinces often chose to Romanize because of the political and economic advantages that it brought, as well as the allure of Roman success. (*p. 155*)

Romanov, Mikhail (1596–1645) Russian tsar (r. 1613–1645) A member of the Russian aristocracy, he became tsar after the old line of Muscovite rulers was deposed. (*p. 551*)

Royal African Company A trading company chartered by the English government in 1672 to conduct its merchants' trade on the Atlantic coast of Africa. (*p. 507*)

sacrifice A gift given to a deity, often with the aim of creating a relationship, gaining favor, and obligating the god to provide some benefit to the sacrificer, sometimes in order to sustain the deity and thereby guarantee the continuing vitality of the natural world. The object devoted to the deity could be as simple as a cup of wine poured on the ground, a live animal slain on the altar, or, in the most extreme case, the ritual killing of a human being. (*p. 127*)

Safavid Empire Iranian kingdom (1502–1722) established by Ismail Safavi, who declared Iran a Shi'ite state. (*p. 531*)

Sahel Savanna Belt south of the Sahara; literally "coastland" in Arabic. (*p. 215*)

samurai Literally "those who serve," the hereditary military elite of the **Tokugawa Shogunate.** (*p. 563*)

Sandinistas Members of a leftist coalition that overthrew the Nicaraguan dictatorship of Anastasia Somoza in 1979 and attempted to install a socialist economy. The United States financed armed opposition by the Contras. The Sandinistas lost national elections in 1990. (*p. 857*)

Sasanid Empire Iranian empire, established ca. 226, with a capital in Ctesiphon, Mesopotamia. The Sasanid emperors established **Zoroastrianism** as the state religion. Islamic Arab armies overthrew the empire ca. 640. (*p. 225*)

satrap The governor of a province in the Achaemenid Persian Empire, often a relative of the king. He was responsible for protection of the province and for forwarding tribute to the central administration. Satraps in outlying provinces enjoyed considerable autonomy. (*p. 118*)

savanna Tropical or subtropical grassland, either treeless or with occasional clumps of trees. Most extensive in **sub-Saharan Africa** but also present in South America. (*p. 217*)

schism A formal split within a religious community. See **Great Western Schism.** (*p. 260*)

scholasticism A philosophical and theological system, associated with Thomas Aquinas, devised to reconcile Aristotelian philosophy and Roman Catholic theology in the thirteenth century. (*p. 408*)

Scientific Revolution The intellectual movement in Europe, initially associated with planetary motion and other aspects of physics, that by the seventeenth century had laid the groundwork for modern science. (*p. 466*)

"scramble" for Africa Sudden wave of conquests in Africa by European powers in the 1880s and 1890s. Britain obtained most of eastern Africa, France most of northwestern Africa. Other countries (Germany, Belgium, Portugal, Italy, and Spain) acquired lesser amounts. (*p. 731*)

scribe In the governments of many ancient societies, a professional position reserved for men who had undergone the lengthy training required to be able to read and write using **cuneiforms, hieroglyphics,** or other early, cumbersome writing systems. (*p. 35*)

seasoning An often difficult period of adjustment to new climates, disease environments, and work routines, such as that experienced by slaves newly arrived in the Americas. (*p. 504*)

Selassie, Haile (1892–1975) Emperor of Ethiopia (r. 1930–1974) and symbol of African independence. He fought the Italian invasion of his country in 1935 and regained his throne during World War II, when British forces expelled the Italians. He ruled **Ethiopia** as a traditional **autocracy** until he was overthrown in 1974. (*p. 809*)

Semitic Family of related languages long spoken across parts of western Asia and northern Africa. In antiquity these languages included Hebrew, Aramaic, and Phoenician. The most widespread modern member of the Semitic family is Arabic. (*p. 32*)

"separate spheres" Nineteenth-century idea in Western societies that men and women, especially of the middle class, should have clearly differentiated roles in society: women as wives, mothers, and homemakers; men as breadwinners and participants in business and politics. (*p. 711*)

sepoy A soldier in South Asia, especially in the service of the British. (*p. 658*)

Sepoy Rebellion The revolt of Indian soldiers in 1857 against certain practices that violated religious customs; also known as the Sepoy Mutiny. (*p. 661*)

Serbia The Ottoman province in the Balkans that rose up against **Janissary** control in the early 1800s. After World War II the central province of Yugoslavia. Serb leaders struggled to maintain dominance as the Yugoslav federation dissolved in the 1990s. (*p. 676*)

serf In medieval Europe, an agricultural laborer legally bound to a lord's property and obligated to perform set services for the lord. In Russia some serfs worked as artisans and in factories; serfdom was not abolished there until 1861. (*pp. 254, 553*)

shaft graves A term used for the burial sites of elite members of Mycenaean Greek society in the mid-second millennium B.C.E. At the bottom of deep shafts lined with stone slabs, the bodies were laid out along with gold and bronze jewelry, implements, weapons, and masks. (*p. 75*)

shamanism The practice of identifying special individuals (shamans) who will interact with spirits for the benefit of the community. Characteristic of the Korean kingdoms of the early medieval period and of early societies of Central Asia. (*p. 292*)

Shang The dominant people in the earliest Chinese dynasty for which we have written records (ca. 1750–1027 B.C.E.). Ancestor worship, divination by means of oracle bones, and the use of bronze vessels for ritual purposes were major elements of Shang culture. (*p. 59*)

Shi Huangdi Founder of the short-lived **Qin** dynasty and creator of the Chinese Empire (r. 221–210 B.C.E.). He is remembered for his ruthless conquests of rival states, standardization of practices, and forcible organization of labor for military and engineering tasks. His tomb, with its army of life-size terracotta soldiers, has been partially excavated. (*p. 163*)

Shi'ites Muslims belonging to the branch of Islam believing that God vests leadership of the community in a descendant of Muhammad's son-in-law Ali. Shi'ism is the state religion of Iran. (See also **Sunnis.**) (*pp. 225, 531*)

Siberia The extreme northeastern sector of Asia, including the Kamchatka Peninsula and the present Russian coast of the Arctic Ocean, the Bering Strait, and the Sea of Okhotsk. (*p. 551*)

Sikhism Indian religion founded by the guru Nanak (1469–1539) in the Punjab region of northwest India. After the Mughal emperor ordered the beheading of the ninth guru in 1675, Sikh warriors mounted armed resistance to Mughal rule. (*p. 538*)

Silk Road Caravan routes connecting China and the Middle East across Central Asia and Iran. (*p. 203*)

"small tradition" Historians' term for a localized, usually non-literate, set of customs and beliefs adhered to by a single society, often in conjunction with a **"great tradition."** (*p. 217*)

socialism A political ideology that originated in Europe in the 1830s. Socialists advocated government protection of workers from exploitation by property owners and government ownership of industries. This ideology led to the founding of socialist or labor parties throughout Europe in the second half of the nineteenth century. (See also **Marx, Karl.**) (*p. 709*)

Socrates Athenian philosopher (ca. 470–399 B.C.E.) who shifted the emphasis of philosophical investigation from questions of natural science to ethics and human behavior. He attracted young disciples from elite families but made enemies by revealing the ignorance and pretensions of others, culminating in his trial and execution by the Athenian state. (*p. 133*)

Sokoto Caliphate A large Muslim state founded in 1809 in what is now northern Nigeria. (*p. 651*)

Solidarity Polish trade union created in 1980 to protest working conditions and political repression. It began the nationalist opposition to communist rule that led in 1989 to the fall of communism in eastern Europe. (*p. 863*)

Song Empire Empire in central and southern China (960–1126) while the Liao people controlled the north. Empire in southern China (1127–1279; the "Southern Song") while the Jin people controlled the north. Distinguished for its advances in technology, medicine, astronomy, and mathematics. (*p. 285*)

Srivijaya A state based on the Indonesian island of Sumatra, between the seventh and eleventh centuries C.E. It amassed wealth and power by a combination of selective adaptation of Indian technologies and concepts, control of the lucrative trade routes between India and China, and skillful showmanship and diplomacy in holding together a disparate realm of inland and coastal territories. (See also **theater-state.**) (*p. 192*)

Stalin, Joseph (1879–1953) Bolshevik revolutionary, head of the Soviet Communist Party after 1924, and dictator of the Soviet Union from 1928 to 1953. He led the Soviet Union with an iron fist, using **Five-Year Plans** to increase industrial production and terror to crush all opposition. (*p. 780*)

Stalingrad City in Russia, site of a Red Army victory over the Germany army in 1942–1943. The Battle of Stalingrad was the turning point in the war between Germany and the Soviet Union. Today Volgograd. (*p. 793*)

Stanley, Henry Morton (1841–1904) British-American explorer of Africa, famous for his expeditions in search of Dr. David Livingstone. Stanley helped King **Leopold II** establish the Congo Free State. (*p. 732*)

steam engine A machine that turns the energy released by burning fuel into motion. Thomas Newcomen built the first crude but workable steam engine in 1712. **James Watt** vastly improved his device in the 1760s and 1770s. Steam power was later applied to moving machinery in factories and to powering ships and locomotives. (*p. 607*)

steel A form of iron that is both durable and flexible. It was first mass-produced in the 1860s and quickly became the most widely used metal in construction, machinery, and railroad equipment. (*p. 701*)

steppes Treeless plains, especially the high, flat expanses of northern Eurasia, which usually have little rain and are covered with coarse grass. They are good lands for nomads and their herds. Living on the steppes promoted the breeding of horses and the development of military skills that were essential to the rise of the Mongol Empire. (*pp. 217, 326*)

stirrup Device for securing a horseman's feet, enabling him to wield weapons more effectively. First evidence of the use of stirrups was among the Kushan people of northern Afghanistan in approximately the first century C.E. (*p. 206*)

stock exchange A place where shares in a company or business enterprise are bought and sold. (*p. 460*)

Stone Age The historical period characterized by the production of tools from stone and other nonmetallic substances. It was followed in some places by the Bronze Age and more generally by the Iron Age. (*p. 11*)

submarine telegraph cables Insulated copper cables laid along the bottom of a sea or ocean for telegraphic communication. The first short cable was laid across the English Channel in 1851; the first successful transatlantic cable was laid in 1866. (See also **electric telegraph.**) (*p. 704*)

sub-Saharan Africa Portion of the African continent lying south of the Sahara. (*p. 216*)

Suez Canal Ship canal dug across the isthmus of Suez in Egypt, designed by Ferdinand de Lesseps. It opened to shipping in 1869 and shortened the sea voyage between Europe and Asia. Its strategic importance led to the British conquest of Egypt in 1882. (*p. 726*)

Suleiman the Magnificent (1494–1566) The most illustrious sultan of the **Ottoman Empire** (r. 1520–1566); also known as Suleiman Kanuni, "The Lawgiver." He significantly expanded the empire in the Balkans and eastern Mediterranean. (*p. 526*)

Sumerians The people who dominated southern Mesopotamia through the end of the third millennium B.C.E. They were responsible for the creation of many fundamental elements of Mesopotamian culture—such as irrigation technology, **cuneiform,** and religious conceptions—taken over by their **Semitic** successors. (*p. 32*)

Sunnis Muslims belonging to branch of Islam believing that the community should select its own leadership. The majority religion in most Islamic countries. (See also **Shi'ites.**) (*p. 225*)

Sun Yat-sen (1867–1925) Chinese nationalist revolutionary, founder and leader of the **Guomindang** until his death. He attempted to create a liberal democratic political movement in China but was thwarted by military leaders. (*p. 768*)

Swahili Bantu language with Arabic loanwords spoken in coastal regions of East Africa. (*p. 542*)

Swahili Coast East African shores of the Indian Ocean between the Horn of Africa and the Zambezi River; from the Arabic *sawahil,* meaning "shores." (*p. 383*)

Taiping Rebellion (1853–1864) The most destructive civil war before the twentieth century. A Christian-inspired rural rebellion threatened to topple the **Qing Empire.** (*p. 687*)

Tamil kingdoms The kingdoms of southern India, inhabited primarily by speakers of Dravidian languages, which developed in partial isolation, and somewhat differently, from the Aryan north. They produced epics, poetry, and performance arts. Elements of Tamil religious beliefs were merged into the Hindu synthesis. (*p. 185*)

Tang Empire Empire unifying China and part of Central Asia, founded 618 and ended 907. The Tang emperors presided over a magnificent court at their capital, Chang'an. (*p. 277*)

Tanzimat "Restructuring" reforms by the nineteenth-century Ottoman rulers, intended to move civil law away from the control of religious elites and make the military and the bureaucracy more efficient. (*p. 678*)

tax farming A government's use of private collectors to collect taxes. Individuals or corporations contract with the government to collect a fixed amount for the government and are permitted to keep as profit everything they collect over that amount. (*p. 334*)

technology transfer The communication of specific plans, designs, or educational programs necessary for the use of new technologies from one society or class to another. (*p. 358*)

Tecumseh (1768–1813) Shawnee leader who attempted to organize an Amerindian confederacy to prevent the loss of additional territory to American settlers. He became an ally of the British in War of 1812 and died in battle. (*p. 634*)

Tenochtitlan Capital of the Aztec Empire, located on an island in Lake Texcoco. Its population was about 150,000 on the eve of Spanish conquest. Mexico City was constructed on its ruins. (*p. 305*)

Teotihuacan A powerful **city-state** in central Mexico (100–75 C.E.). Its population was about 150,000 at its peak in 600. (*p. 300*)

Terrorism Political belief that extreme and seemingly random violence will destabilize a government and permit the terrorists to gain political advantage. Though an old technique, terrorism gained prominence in the late twentieth century with the growth of worldwide mass media that, through their news coverage, amplified public fears of terrorist acts. (*p. 890*)

theater-state Historians' term for a state that acquires prestige and power by developing attractive cultural forms and staging elaborate public ceremonies (as well as redistributing valuable resources) to attract and bind subjects to the center. Examples include the **Gupta Empire** in India and **Srivijaya** in Southeast Asia. (*p. 186*)

Thebes Capital city of Egypt and home of the ruling dynasties during the Middle and New Kingdoms. Amon, patron deity of Thebes, became one of the chief gods of Egypt. Monarchs were buried across the river in the Valley of the Kings. (*p. 43*)

Theravada Buddhism "Way of the Elders" branch of Buddhism followed in Sri Lanka and much of Southeast Asia. Therevada remains close to the original principles set forth by the **Buddha;** it downplays the importance of gods and emphasizes austerity and the individual's search for enlightenment. (*p. 181*)

third-century crisis Historians' term for the political, military, and economic turmoil that beset the Roman Empire during much of the third century C.E.: frequent changes of ruler, civil wars, barbarian invasions, decline of urban centers, and near-destruction of long-distance commerce and the monetary economy. After 284 C.E. Diocletian restored order by making fundamental changes. (*p. 157*)

Third World Term applied to a group of developing countries who professed nonalignment during the **Cold War.** (*p. 846*)

three-field system A rotational system for agriculture in which one field grows grain, one grows legumes, and one lies fallow. It gradually replaced two-field system in medieval Europe. (*p. 396*)

Tiananmen Square Site in Beijing where Chinese students and workers gathered to demand greater political openness in 1989. The demonstration was crushed by Chinese military with great loss of life. (*p. 862*)

Timbuktu City on the Niger River in the modern country of Mali. It was founded by the Tuareg as a seasonal camp sometime after 1000. As part of the **Mali** empire, Timbuktu became a major major terminus of the trans-Saharan trade and a center of Islamic learning. (*p. 388*)

Timur (1336–1405) Member of a prominent family of the Mongols' Jagadai Khanate, Timur through conquest gained control over much of Central Asia and Iran. He consolidated the status of Sunni Islam as orthodox, and his descendants, the Timurids, maintained his empire for nearly a century and founded the **Mughal Empire** in India. (*p. 336*)

Tiwanaku Name of capital city and empire centered on the region near Lake Titicaca in modern Bolivia (375–1000 C.E.). (*p. 315*)

Tokugawa Shogunate (1600–1868) The last of the three shogunates of Japan. (*p. 563*)

Toltecs Powerful postclassic empire in central Mexico (900–1168 C.E.). It influenced much of Mesoamerica. Aztecs claimed ties to this earlier civilization. (*p. 305*)

tophet A cemetery containing burials of young children, possibly sacrificed to the gods in times of crisis, found at **Carthage** and other **Phoenician** settlements in the western Mediterranean. (*p. 108*)

trans-Saharan caravan routes Trading network linking North Africa with **sub-Saharan Africa** across the Sahara. (*p. 210*)

Treaty of Nanking (1842) The treaty that concluded the **Opium War.** It awarded Britain a large indemnity from the **Qing Empire,** denied the Qing government tariff control over some of its own borders, opened additional ports of residence to Britons, and ceded the island of Hong Kong to Britain. (*p. 685*)

Treaty of Versailles (1919) The treaty imposed on Germany by France, Great Britain, the United States, and other Allied Powers after World War I. It demanded that Germany dismantle its military and give up some lands to Poland. It was resented by many Germans. (*p. 763*)

treaty ports Cities opened to foreign residents as a result of the forced treaties between the **Qing Empire** and foreign signatories. In the treaty ports, foreigners enjoyed **extraterritoriality.** (*p. 685*)

tributary system A system in which, from the time of the **Han** Empire, countries in East and Southeast Asia not under the direct control of empires based in China nevertheless enrolled as tributary states, acknowledging the superiority of the emperors in China in exchange for trading rights or strategic alliances. (*p. 279*)

tribute system A system in which defeated peoples were forced to pay a tax in the form of goods and labor. This forced transfer of food, cloth, and other goods subsidized the development of large cities. An important component of the Aztec and Inca economies. (*p. 307*)

trireme Greek and Phoenician warship of the fifth and fourth centuries B.C.E. It was sleek and light, powered by 170 oars arranged in three vertical tiers. Manned by skilled sailors, it was capable of short bursts of speed and complex maneuvers. (*p. 132*)

tropical rain forest High-precipitation forest zones of the Americas, Africa, and Asia lying between the Tropic of Cancer and the Tropic of Capricorn. (*p. 217*)

tropics Equatorial region between the Tropic of Cancer and the Tropic of Capricorn. It is characterized by generally warm or hot temperatures year-round, though much variation exists due to altitude and other factors. Temperate zones north and south of the tropics generally have a winter season. (*p. 370*)

Troy Site in northwest Anatolia, overlooking the Hellespont strait, where archaeologists have excavated a series of Bronze Age cities. One of these may have been destroyed by Greeks ca. 1200 B.C.E., as reported in Homer's epic poems. (*p. 76*)

Truman Doctrine Foreign policy initiated by U.S. president Harry Truman in 1947. It offered military aid to help Turkey and Greece resist Soviet military pressure and subversion. (*p. 836*)

tsar (czar) From Latin *caesar,* this Russian title for a monarch was first used in reference to a Russian ruler by Ivan III (r. 1462–1505). (*pp. 340, 551*)

Tulip Period (1718–1730) Last years of the reign of Ottoman sultan Ahmed III, during which European styles and attitudes became briefly popular in Istanbul. (*p. 530*)

Tupac Amaru II Member of Inca aristocracy who led a rebellion against Spanish authorities in Peru in 1780–1781. He was captured and executed with his wife and other members of his family. (*p. 493*)

tyrant The term the Greeks used to describe someone who seized and held power in violation of the normal procedures and traditions of the community. Tyrants appeared in many Greek **city-states** in the seventh and sixth centuries B.C.E., often taking advantage of the disaffection of the emerging middle class and, by weakening the old elite, unwittingly contributing to the evolution of **democracy.** (*p. 127*)

Uigurs A group of Turkic-speakers who controlled their own centralized empire from 744 to 840 in Mongolia and Central Asia. (*p. 284*)

ulama Muslim religious scholars. From the ninth century onward, the primary interpreters of Islamic law and the social core of Muslim urban societies. (*p. 238*)

Umayyad Caliphate First hereditary dynasty of Muslim caliphs (661 to 750). From their capital at Damascus, the Umayyads ruled an empire that extended from Spain to India. Overthrown by the **Abbasid Caliphate.** (*p. 232*)

umma The community of all Muslims. A major innovation against the background of seventh-century Arabia, where traditionally kinship rather than faith had determined membership in a community. (*p. 231*)

underdevelopment The condition experienced by economies that depend on colonial forms of production such as the export of raw materials and plantation crops with low wages and low investment in education. (*p. 642*)

United Nations International organization founded in 1945 to promote world peace and cooperation. It replaced the **League of Nations.** (*p. 833*)

Universal Declaration of Human Rights A 1946 United Nations covenant binding signatory nations to the observance of specified rights. (*p. 892*)

universities Degree-granting institutions of higher learning. Those that appeared in Latin West from about 1200 onward became the model of all modern universities. (*p. 407*)

Urdu A Persian-influenced literary form of Hindi written in Arabic characters and used as a literary language since the 1300s. (*p. 388*)

utopian socialism A philosophy introduced by the Frenchman Charles Fourier in the early nineteenth century. Utopian socialists hoped to create humane alternatives to industrial capitalism by building self-sustaining communities whose inhabitants would work cooperatively. (See also **socialism.**) (*p. 616*)

Vargas, Getulio (1883–1954) Dictator of Brazil from 1930 to 1945 and from 1951 to 1954. Defeated in the presidential election of 1930, he overthrew the government and created Estado Novo ("New State"), a dictatorship that emphasized industrialization and helped the urban poor but did little to alleviate the problems of the peasants. (*p. 823*)

variolation The technique of enhancing immunity by exposing patients to dried mucous taken from those already infected. (*p. 559*)

varna/jati Two categories of social identity of great importance in Indian history. *Varna* are the four major social divisions: the *Brahmin* priest class, the *Kshatriya* warrior/administrator class, the *Vaishya* merchant/farmer class, and the *Shudra* laborer class. Within the system of *varna* are many *jati,* regional groups of people who have a common occupational sphere, and who marry, eat, and generally interact with other members of their group. (*p. 177*)

vassal In medieval Europe, a sworn supporter of a king or lord committed to rendering specified military service to that king or lord. (*p. 256*)

Vedas Early Indian sacred "knowledge"—the literal meaning of the term—long preserved and communicated orally by

Brahmin priests and eventually written down. These religious texts, including the thousand poetic hymns to various deities contained in the Rig Veda, are our main source of information about the Vedic period (ca. 1500–500 B.C.E.). (*p. 175*)

Victorian Age The reign of Queen Victoria of Great Britain (r. 1837–1901). The term is also used to describe late-nineteenth-century society, with its rigid moral standards and sharply differentiated roles for men and women and for middle-class and working-class people. (See also **"separate spheres."**) (*p. 711*)

Vietnam War (1954–1975) Conflict pitting North Vietnam and South Vietnamese communist guerrillas against the South Vietnamese government, aided after 1961 by the United States. (*p. 838*)

Villa, Francisco "Pancho" (1878–1923) A popular leader during the Mexican Revolution. An outlaw in his youth, when the revolution started, he formed a cavalry army in the north of Mexico and fought for the rights of the landless in collaboration with **Emiliano Zapata.** He was assassinated in 1923. (See also **Zapata, Emiliano.**) (*p. 819*)

Wari Andean civilization culturally linked to **Tiwanaku,** perhaps beginning as colony of Tiwanaku. (*p. 314*)

Warsaw Pact The 1955 treaty binding the Soviet Union and countries of eastern Europe in an alliance against the **North Atlantic Treaty Organization.** (*p. 836*)

Washington, George (1732–1799) Military commander of the American Revolution. He was the first elected president of the United States (1789–1799). (*p. 581*)

water wheel A mechanism that harnesses the energy in flowing water to grind grain or to power machinery. It was used in many parts of the world but was especially common in Europe from 1200 to 1900. (*p. 398*)

Watt, James (1736–1819) Scot who invented the condenser and other improvements that made the **steam engine** a practical source of power for industry and transportation. The watt, an electrical measurement, is named after him. (*p. 607*)

Wedgwood, Josiah (1730–1795) English industrialist whose pottery works were the first to produce fine-quality pottery by industrial methods. (*p. 603*)

Western Front A line of trenches and fortifications in World War I that stretched without a break from Switzerland to the North Sea. Scene of most of the fighting between Germany, on the one hand, and France and Britain, on the other. (*p. 757*)

Wilson, Woodrow (1856–1924) President of the United States (1913–1921) and the leading figure at the Paris Peace Conference of 1919. He was unable to persuade the U.S. Congress to ratify the **Treaty of Versailles** or join the **League of Nations.** (*p. 762*)

witch-hunt The pursuit of people suspected of witchcraft, especially in northern Europe in the late sixteenth and seventeenth centuries. (*p. 464*)

Women's Rights Convention An 1848 gathering of women angered by their exclusion from an international antislavery meeting. They met at Seneca Falls, New York to discuss women's rights. (*p. 640*)

World Bank A specialized agency of the United Nations that makes loans to countries for economic development, trade promotion, and debt consolidation. Its formal name is the International Bank for Reconstruction and Development. (*p. 834*)

World Trade Organization (WTO) An international body established in 1995 to foster and bring order to international trade. (*p. 889*)

Xiongnu A confederation of nomadic peoples living beyond the northwest frontier of ancient China. Chinese rulers tried a variety of defenses and stratagems to ward off these "barbarians," as they called them, and finally succeeded in dispersing the Xiongnu in the first century C.E. (*p. 168*)

Yamagata Aritomo (1838–1922) One of the leaders of the **Meiji Restoration.** (*p. 722*)

Yi kingdom (1392–1910) The Yi dynasty ruled Korea from the fall of the **Koryo** kingdom to the colonization of Korea by Japan. (*p. 362*)

yin/yang In Chinese belief, complementary factors that help to maintain the equilibrium of the world. Yin is associated with masculine, light, and active qualities; yang with feminine, dark, and passive qualities. (*p. 63*)

Yongle Reign period of Zhu Di (1360–1424), the third emperor of the **Ming Empire** (r. 1403–1424). He sponsored the building of the **Forbidden City,** a huge encyclopedia project, the expeditions of **Zheng He,** and the reopening of China's borders to trade and travel. (*p. 355*)

Yuan Empire (1271–1368) Empire created in China and Siberia by **Khubilai Khan.** (*p. 349*)

Yuan Shikai (1859–1916) Chinese general and first president of the Chinese Republic (1912–1916). He stood in the way of the democratic movement led by **Sun Yat-sen.** (*p. 768*)

Zapata, Emiliano (1879–1919) Revolutionary and leader of peasants in the Mexican Revolution. He mobilized landless peasants in south-central Mexico in an attempt to seize and divide the lands of the wealthy landowners. Though successful for a time, he was ultimately defeated and assassinated. (*p. 819*)

Zen The Japanese word for a branch of **Mahayana Buddhism** based on highly disciplined meditation. It is known in Sanskrit as *dhyana*, in Chinese as *chan*, and in Korean as *son*. (*p. 289*)

Zheng He (1371–1433) An imperial eunuch and Muslim, entrusted by the Ming emperor **Yongle** with a series of state voyages that took his gigantic ships through the Indian Ocean, from Southeast Asia to Africa. (*pp. 355, 422*)

Zhou The people and dynasty that took over the dominant position in north China from the **Shang** and created the concept of the **Mandate of Heaven** to justify their rule. The Zhou era, particularly the vigorous early period (1027–771 B.C.E.), was remembered in Chinese tradition as a time of prosperity and benevolent rule. In the later Zhou period (771–221 B.C.E.), centralized control broke down, and warfare among many small states became frequent. (*p. 61*)

ziggurat A massive pyramidal stepped tower made of mud-bricks. It is associated with religious complexes in ancient Mesopotamian cities, but its function is unknown. (*p. 37*)

Zoroastrianism A religion originating in ancient Iran with the prophet Zoroaster. It centered on a single benevolent deity—Ahuramazda—who engaged in a twelve-thousand-year struggle with demonic forces before prevailing and restoring a pristine world. Emphasizing truth-telling, purity, and reverence for nature, the religion demanded that humans choose sides in the struggle between good and evil. Those whose good conduct indicated their support for Ahuramazda would be rewarded in the afterlife. Others would be punished. The religion of the Achaemenid and Sasanid Persians, Zoroastrianism may have spread within their realms and influenced Judaism, Christianity, and other faiths. (*p. 120*)

Zulu A people of modern South Africa whom King Shaka united beginning in 1818. (*p. 649*)

INDEX

Germany and, 755, 758 *(map)*, 760
  home front, 760
    Russia and, 761, 762
    stalemate, 756–757, 759
  the Holocaust in, 800
  home front in, 801–802
  mobility of armed forces in, 792
  in North Africa, 793, 794 *(map)*
  Soviet Union and, 792–793, 796–797, 800
    home front, 801–802
  technology and, 798–800
Wright, Frank Lloyd, 776
Wright, Wilbur and Orville, 775
Writing (written language)
  Arabic script, 532
  in the East Indies, 541
WTO (World Trade Organization), 889–890

Xavier, Francis, 548
Xhosa people, 735

Yamagata Aritomo, 693, 722, 722 *(illus.)*
Yamamoto, 795
Yamamoto, Isoroku, 793
Yaqui people, 817
Yellow fever, 474
Yellow River (Huang He), 767
Yeltsin, Boris, 865
Yemen, coffee in, 530
Yermak Timofeyovich, 553
Yi kingdom (Korea), 556
Yi Sonsin, 556
Yohannes IV, Emperor (Ethiopia), 652
Yorktown, Battle of (Virginia), 582
Young Turks, 683, 753
Yuan Shikai, 768, 769
Yucatán, Maya in, 635–636
Yugoslavia, 764, 863
  disintegration of, 865, 883
  Kosovo crisis and, 885, 887

Zaibatsu (Japanese conglomerates), 722, 768, 861
Zambezi River, 654
Zanzibar, 656
Zapata, Emiliano, 806, 818 *(illus.)*, 819
Zeng Guofan, 688, 690
Zetkin, Clara, 710
Zheng He, 420 *(map)*, 422–423
Zimbabwe, 844
Zionism, 760–761, 772
Zollverein, 616
Zulu kingdom, 649, 651
Zulu people, 651 *(illus.)*, 665
  British war against, 735–736
Zworykin, Vladimir, 894